THE THANATOPHIDIA OF INDIA

BEING A DESCRIPTION OF THE

VENOMOUS SNAKES

OF THE

INDIAN PENINSULA

THE THANATOPHIDIA OF INDIA

BEING A DESCRIPTION OF THE

VENOMOUS SNAKES

OF THE

INDIAN PENINSULA,

WITH AN ACCOUNT OF

THE INFLUENCE OF THEIR POISON ON LIFE;
AND A SERIES OF EXPERIMENTS.

BY

J. FAYRER, M.D., C.S.I., F.R.S.E.

GYAN

Published by

Gyan Publishing House
5, Ansari Road
Daryaganj, New Delhi-110002
Phone: 011-47034999, 9811692060
E-mail: books@gyanbooks.com

Distribution Network
gyanbooks.com
India, USA, Canada, UK, Australia, France

ISBN: 978-81-212-7769-3 (PB)
First Published, 1872

2nd Impression 2023

Printed at: Gyan Press, Delhi.

THE THANATOPHIDIA OF INDIA BEING A DESCRIPTION OF THE VENOMOUS SNAKES OF THE INDIAN PENINSULA

Author: J. FAYRER

THE THANATOPHIDIA OF INDIA

BEING A DESCRIPTION OF THE

VENOMOUS SNAKES

OF THE

INDIAN PENINSULA

THE THANATOPHIDIA OF INDIA

BEING A DESCRIPTION OF THE

VENOMOUS SNAKES

OF THE

INDIAN PENINSULA,

WITH AN ACCOUNT OF

THE INFLUENCE OF THEIR POISON ON LIFE;

AND A SERIES OF EXPERIMENTS.

BY

J. FAYRER, M.D., C.S.I., F.R.S.E.

HONORARY PHYSICIAN TO THE QUEEN, SURGEON-MAJOR H.M. BENGAL ARMY, PROFESSOR OF SURGERY AND SENIOR SURGEON IN THE CALCUTTA MEDICAL COLLEGE AND ITS HOSPITAL, FELLOW OF THE UNIVERSITY OF CALCUTTA, AND LATE PRESIDENT OF THE ASIATIC SOCIETY OF BENGAL.

LONDON:

J. AND A. CHURCHILL, NEW BURLINGTON STREET.

1872.

Hast thou the pretty worm of Nilus there,
That kills and pains not?

Truly, I have him: but I would not be the party that should desire you to touch him, for his biting is immortal: . . . . . . but he that will believe all that they say, shall never be saved by half that they do. . . . . . . You must think this, look you, that the worm will do his kind.

Antony and Cleopatra.

It is too late; the life of all his blood
Is touch'd corruptibly; . . . . .
. . . . and there the poison
Is, as a fiend, confined to tyrannize,
On unreprievable condemnéd blood.

King John.

The leperous distilment; whose effect
Holds such an enmity with blood of man,
That, swift as quicksilver, it courses through
The natural gates and alleys of the body;
And, with a sudden vigour, it doth posset and curd,
Like aigre droppings into milk,
The thin and wholesome blood.

Hamlet.

No medicine in the world can do thee good,
In thee there is not half an hour's life.

Ibid.

LONDON:
SAVILL, EDWARDS AND CO., PRINTERS, CHANDOS STREET,
COVENT GARDEN.

TO HIS EXCELLENCY

THE RIGHT HON. THE EARL OF MAYO, K.P., G.M.S.I., &c. &c.

VICEROY AND GOVERNOR-GENERAL OF INDIA,

THIS WORK,

WHICH IS INTENDED FOR THE BENEFIT OF THE VAST POPULATION OF THE INDIAN EMPIRE,

Is Dedicated,

BY HIS EXCELLENCY'S FAITHFUL SERVANT,

THE AUTHOR.

PREFACE.

THE object of this work is to supply a want I have often heard expressed—that of reliable information on the Venomous Snakes of India.

Beyond the pale of science but little is known on the subject of Ophiology, and though the information contained in the great works of Günther, Jan, and others is very ample, it is not generally available.

The most vague ideas prevail as to the properties of the Ophidia; the most innocent are confounded with the most deadly, and this ignorance is not confined to the nature of the snakes themselves, but extends to the effects of their poison and those of the reputed antidotes. India has a large share of Ophidia; about twenty families with numerous genera and species being known to naturalists. Of these only four families are poisonous, but among them are some of the most deadly snakes. I have endeavoured to illustrate all the principal forms, and to give a description of each, including an account of the action of its poison on Man and the lower animals. The annual mortality from snake-bite in India is very great, and if a more extended knowledge of these reptiles and their habits should tend in any way to its diminution, my principal aim in producing the work would be accomplished.

There is no pretension to novelty in the description of the characters of the snakes.

The classifications and definitions are chiefly taken from, or based on, Günther, or other authors of repute, the anatomical descriptions from Owen and Huxley, and to these authorities I make my acknowledgments for much valuable information, remarking at the same time that I have carefully verified their descriptions by comparison with, and by careful dissections of the snakes themselves. Close observation of the principal Indian forms of poisonous snakes during life, for a period of more than three years, enables me to confirm their accuracy, and occasionally to supplement with additional facts.

In that part of the work where the experiments are described, I believe I have added something to our previous knowledge both of the action of the poison and of the effects of remedies; on the whole, I trust I have gathered together an amount of information on the subject of the poisonous snakes of India that may be generally useful.

In collecting materials I have been much indebted to the several Governments; to Dr. Murray, the head of the Medical Department, and to the officers by whose permission, and through whose aid, I have obtained the return of deaths during the year 1869, as well as details of cases of snake-bite, and other information.

I would express my thanks to those gentlemen who have assisted me in my investigations and been present at the experiments. To Dr. J. Anderson, Curator of the Indian Museum, and Dr. F. Stoliczka, of the Geological Survey, I am under great obligation for much valuable information, and for aid in arranging, collecting, and describing the genera and species; and also to Mr. Sceva, late Osteologist of the Indian Museum, for his constant and unwearying aid in conducting the various experiments. For permission to examine and figure several rare specimens, I am indebted to the Trustees of the Indian Museum. Mr. Richards, Civil Surgeon, of Bancoorah; Mr. Stewart, Civil Surgeon, of Pooree; Major MacMahon, Deputy Commissioner of Delhi; the Rev. Mr. Winton, of Rangoon; Mr. Galiffe, of Calcutta; Dr. Shortt, of Madras; Dr. W. B. Beatson, of Nagpore, and others, have procured for me living or dead specimens of the rarer forms of the poisonous snakes, favoured me with the results of their experiments, and spared themselves no trouble in sending me contributions which have been most valuable, and for which I return them my best thanks.

I have also to express my acknowledgments to Professors Chevers, Partridge, Ewart, Palmer, Cutcliffe, for the devotion of much of their valuable time to witnessing and attesting the experiments; and to Professor C. Macnamara and Messrs. Lewis and Cunningham, of H.M.S., for their microscopic examinations of the blood of the poisoned animals.

To Mr. A. Grote I am also deeply indebted for much valuable counsel in all matters connected with the production of this work; to Babu Rajendralala Mitra, of Calcutta, for supervising the Sanscrit, Bengalli, or other Indian terms; and to Dr. F. C. Webb, of London, for his cordial assistance in conducting the work through the Press.

The illustrations were executed at the School of Art in Calcutta. They are all from nature, most from life itself. To Mr. Locke, the Principal of the Institution, and to his talented pupils, I am indebted for a series of drawings which are as faithful to the originals as they are creditable to the artists and the Institution.

Whilst I believe I have omitted no Indian venomous snake of any importance in my description, I am sensible that there must still be many omissions. But should the result of my investigations prove of service to science and to the Indian public generally, I shall feel satisfied that neither the observation and work of three years, nor the sacrifice of much animal life has been thrown away.

This work had been completed, and was about to issue from the Press, when the great calamity occurred which deprived India of its Viceroy and its people of their ruler and friend. I dedicate it to his memory.

TABLE OF CONTENTS.

SECTION I.

Zoological and Anatomical Characters and Distribution.

SECTION II.

SECTION III.

SECTION IV.

SECTION V.

APPENDIX.

LIST OF PLATES.

* The native artists in transcribing these names have in some instances spelt them differently from the way in which they are spelt in the body of the work. The orthography is uncertain.

NAJA TRIPUDIANS

Plate I

Khorah Gokurrah.

Length including tail	5
Tail	9
Circum	5½

From life

Drawn by Annoda Prasad Bagchee Student.

Gov. Sch. of Art. Calcutta

NAJA TRIPUDIANS.

Dudia Keautiah.

From Life.

Plate 2.

Drawn by Annoda Prosad Bagchee Student.

Govt. Sch. of Art. Calcutta.

M. & N. HANHART CHROMO-LITH

NAJA TRIPUDIANS.

Plate 3

Banshunniah Keautiah.

From Life

Length 4.3 circum 4"

Drawn by Annoda Prasad Bagchee Student

Gov. Sch. of Art Calcutta

Plate 1.

NAJA TRIPUDIANS.

Keautiah.
From Life.

Tenduha Keautiah.

Drawn by Annada Prasad Bagchee Student.

Govt. Sch. of Art Calcutta.

M & N HANHART CHROMO LITH

NAJA TRIPUDIANS

Keautiah

From Life

Plate 5

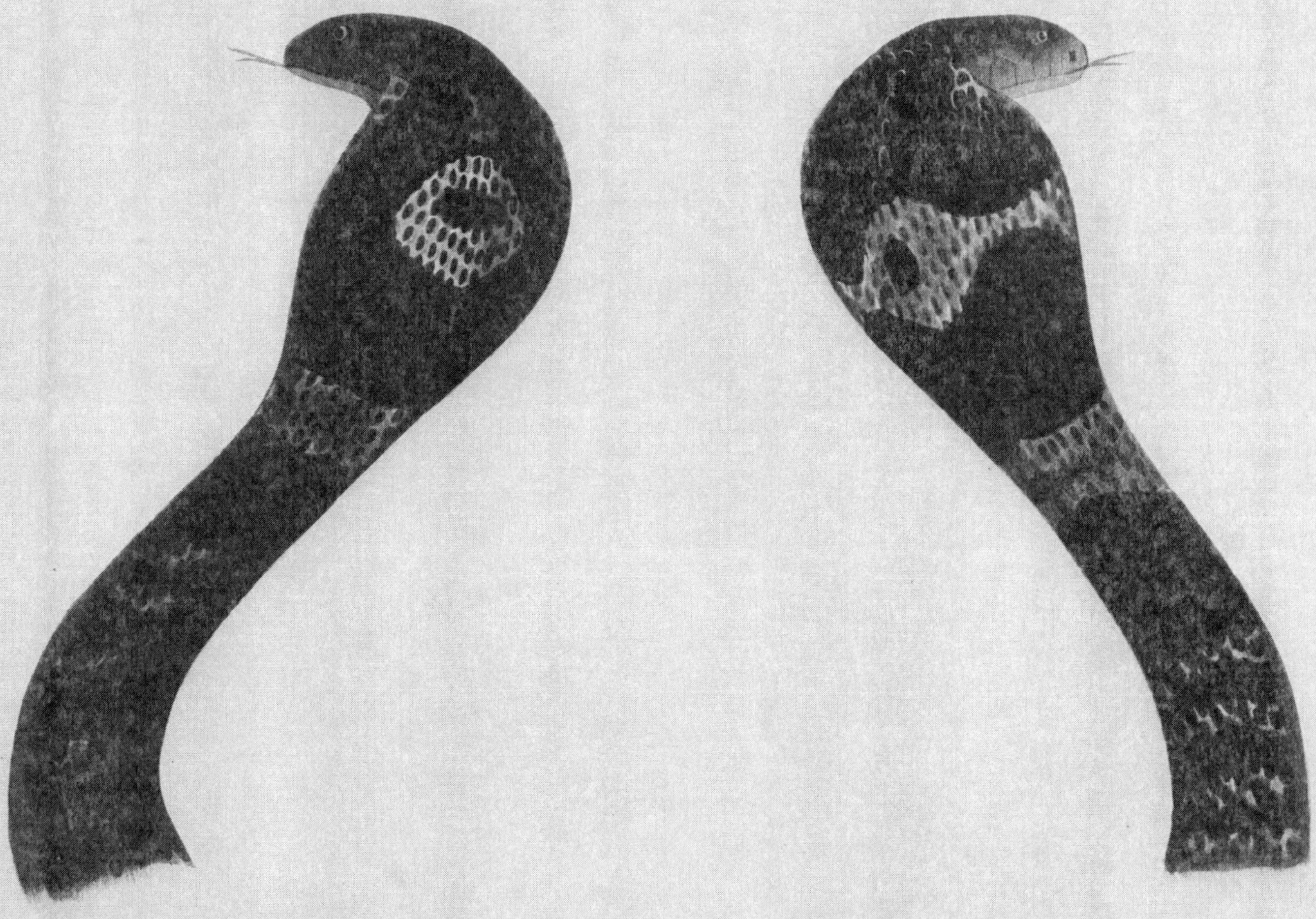

Gerribhanga Keautiah

Tentulia Kurrees Keautiah

Drawn by Annada Prosad Bagchee, Student

Gov! School of Art, Calcutta

M. & N. Hanhart Chromo Lith.

NAJA TRIPUDIANS

Plate 6

Kurrees Gokurrah from Nagpore C.P.

Length including tail 5 10

Tail

Girth

From Life

Khoyah Gokurrah from Delhi

From Life

Dudea Kurrees Gokurrah from Calcutta

From Life

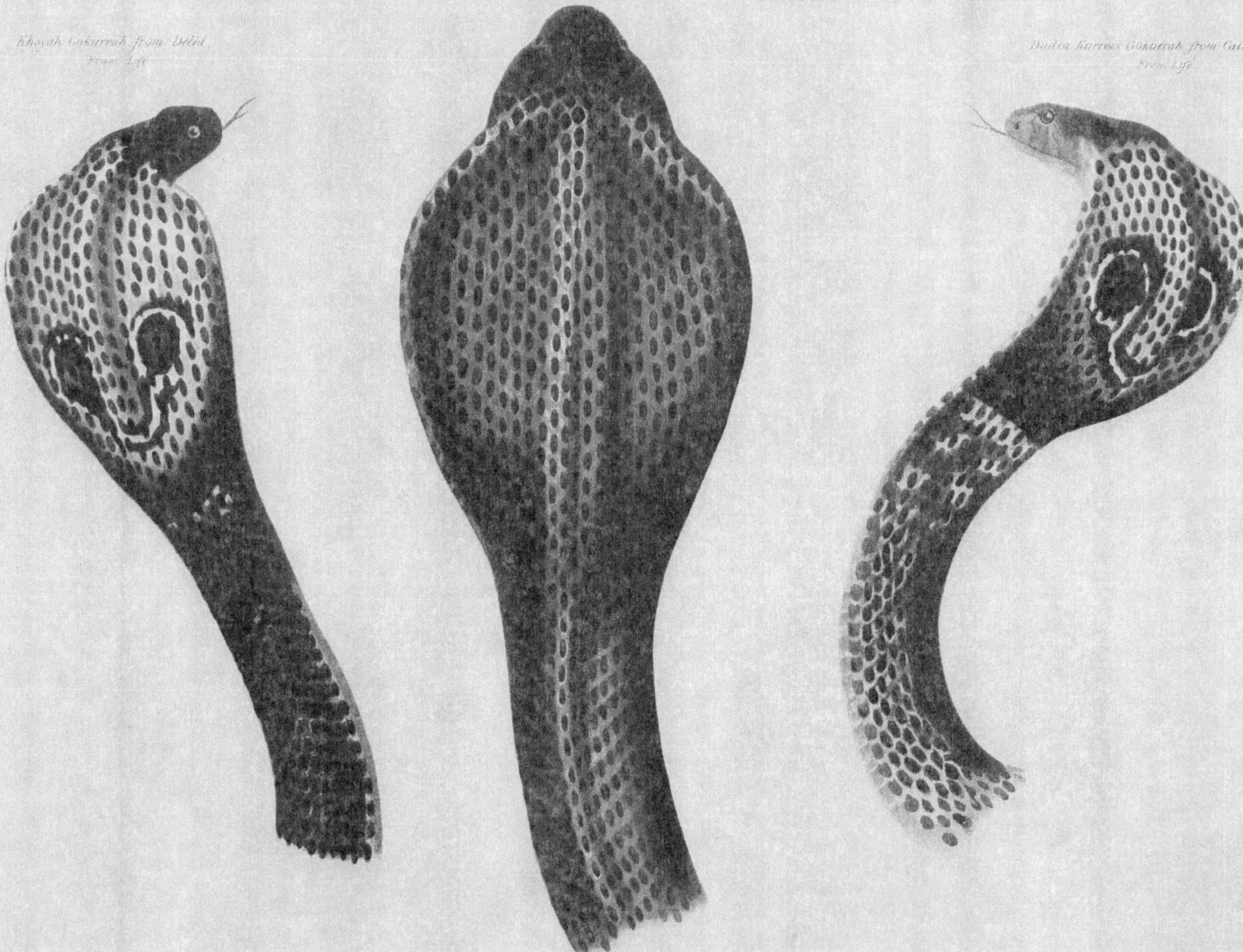

Drawn by Annoda Prosaud Bagchee, Student

Gov^t Sch. of Art Calcutta

OPHIOPHAGUS ELAPS

Plate 7

OPHIOPHAGUS ELAPS (HAMADRYAS) DUSKY VARIETY.

Plate 9.

BUNGARUS FASCIATUS

From Life

Length 3.10 Circum 3.

Drawn by Annoda Prosad Bagchee Student.

Gov. Sch. of Art Calcutta.

M. & N. HANHART CHROMO LITH

FROM NATURE

GALLOPHIS MACLELLANDII.

IND. MUS.

Length 1' 2¼

Circum "¼

Drawn by Hurrish Chunder Khan Student

BUNGARUS CŒRULEUS.

From Life.

Length 2. 6 Circum 1½

Drawn by Annoda Prosad Bagchee Student

Govt Sch of Art Calcutta

HANHART CHROMO LITH.

DABOIA RUSSELLII.

From Life

Length 3.8. Circum. 5

Plate II.

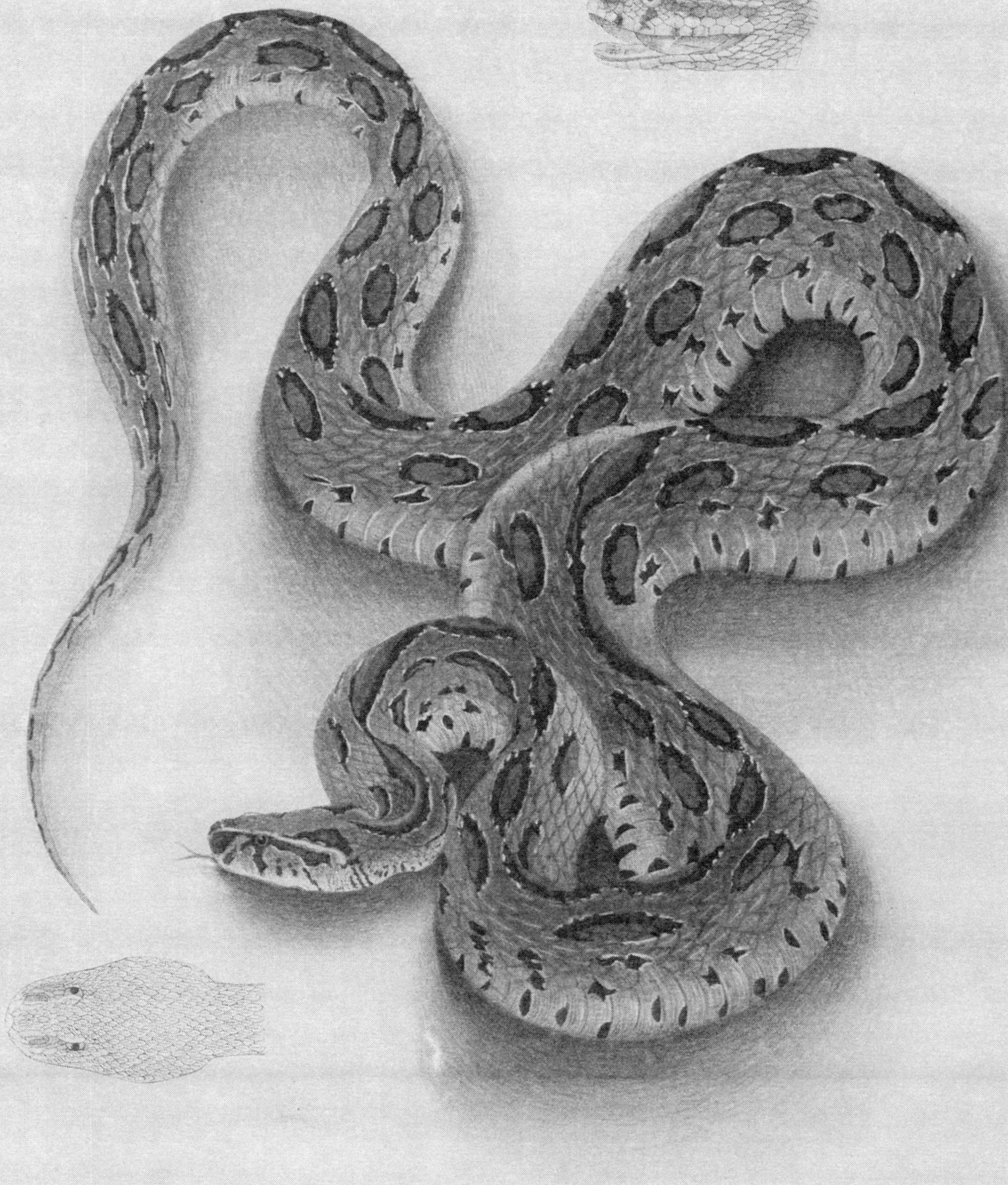

Drawn by Annada Prosad Bagchee, Student

Govt. Sch. of Art Calcutta

M & N HANHART LITH

ECHIS CARINATA.

From Life

Life Size

Plate 12

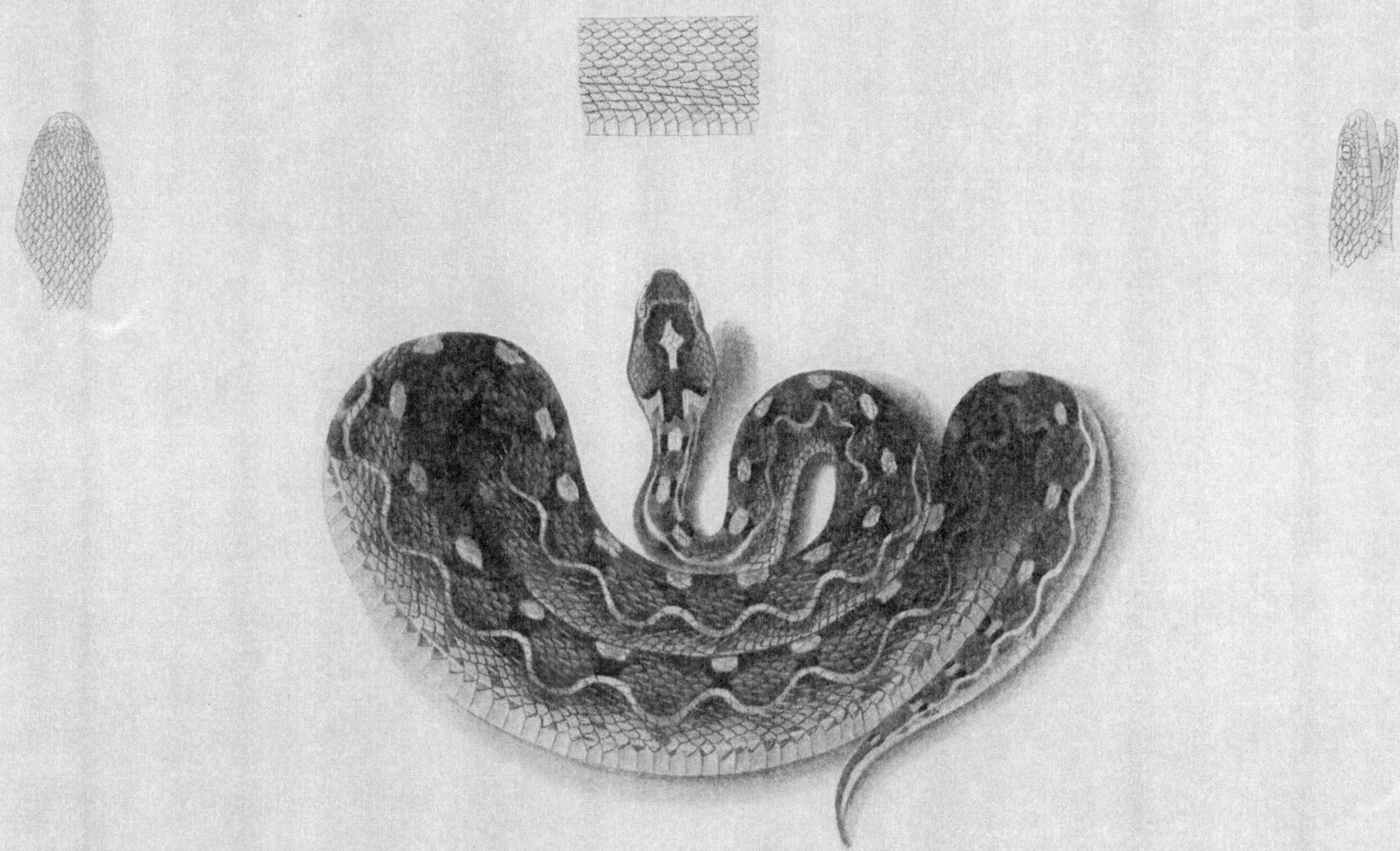

Drawn by Annoda Prosad Bagchee, Student.

Govt School of Art, Calcutta.

M & N HANHART CHROMO LITH.

TRIMERESURUS CARINATUS.

Specimen in Indian Museum

Length 3' Circum 4"

Plate 13

Drawn by Hurrish Chunder Khan, Student

Govt. Sch. of Art Calcutta

M & N HANHART CHROMO LITH

TRIMERESURUS ANAMALLENSIS.

from Nature

Length 1 5 *Circum* 1¼

TRIMERESURUS ERYTHRURUS

from Nature

	ft. in.	
Length including Tail	2	2
Tail		3½
Girth of body		2
D° *of neck*		¾

Drawn by Annoda Prosad Bagchee Stud[t]

Drawn by Nilyanunda Dey Stud[t]

M & N HANHART CHROMO LITH.

Gov. Sch[l] *of Art, Calcutta*

Plate 15.

TRIMERESURUS MONTICOLA.

From Life

Length 29
Girth 3½
Tail 3

TRIMERESURUS ANDERSONII.

From Nature *Ind. Mus.*

Length 19
Girth 2
Tail 2⅝

Drawn by Hurrish Chunder Khan Student

Govt. School of Art Calcutta

TRIMERESURUS STRICATUS.

Specimen in Indian Museum

Length 1 2½ circum 1½

Plate 16.

HALYS HIMALAYANUS

Specimen in Indian Museum

Length 1 11 circum 2½

Drawn by Hurrish Chunder Khan, Student.

Govt. Sch. of Art Calcutta

M & N HANHART CHROMO LITH.

Plate 17

HYPNALE NEPA (CARAWALA)

From a drawing of Dr Shortts

Madras

PELAMIS BICOLOR.

From Poorie

Length 1 ⅝, Circum ⅞.

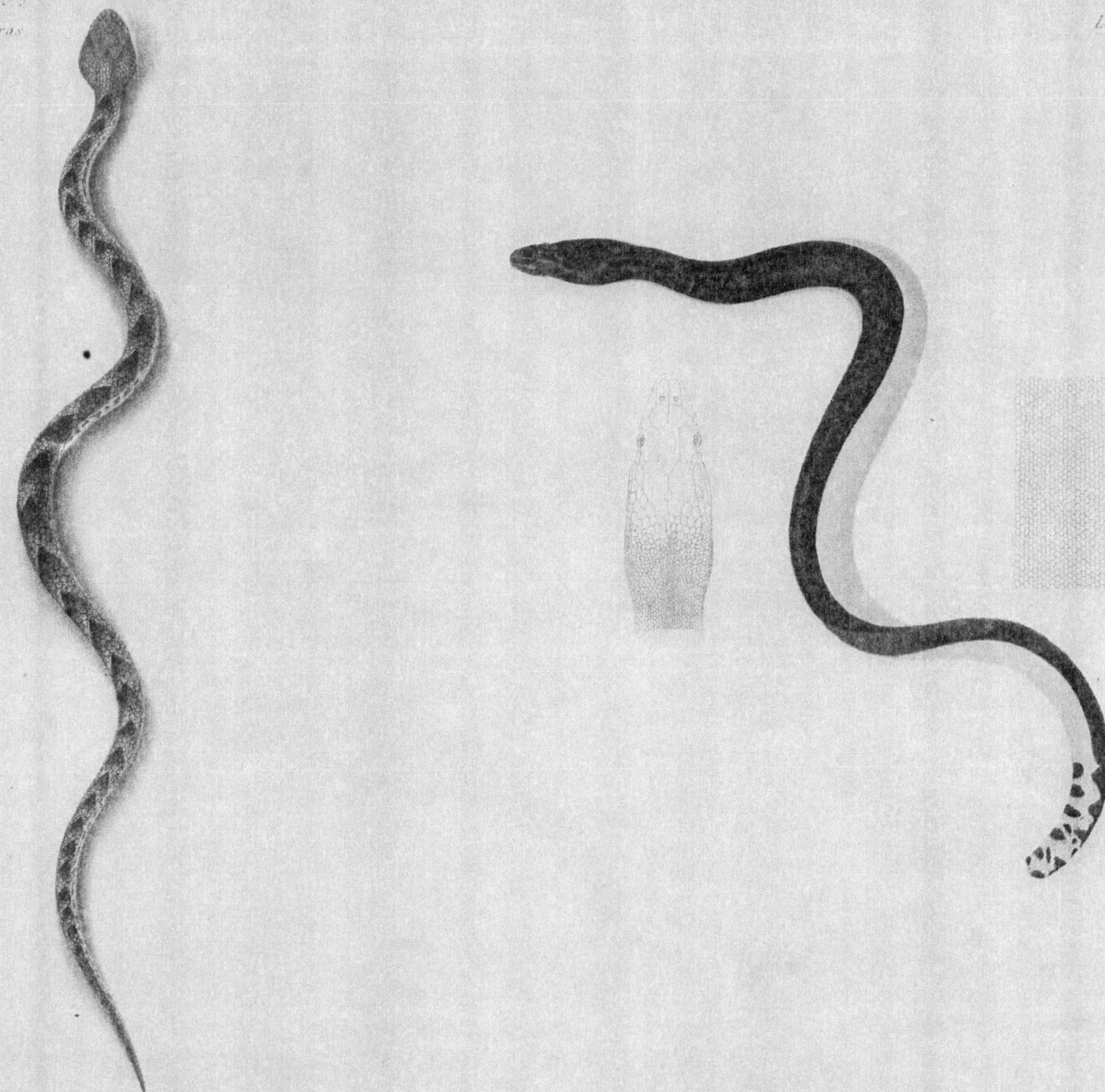

Copied by Hurrish Chunder Khan from an original drawing by C. Abbey Madras

Drawn by Hurrish Chunder Khan Student Gov. Sch. of Art Calcutta

VALAKADYEN

ENHYDRINA BENGALENSIS

Plate 18

Ind. Mus

Length 3-1 Circum 4

From Life

Drawn by Hurrish Khan, Student

Govt School of Art Calcutta

PLATURUS FISCHERI.

Plate 19.

From Nature (Ind. Mus.)

Drawn by Behary Lall Das Student

Govt. Sch. of Art Calcutta

M.&N. HANHART CHROMO LITH

HYDROPHIS JERDONII.

Plate 20

Length including tail
Tail
Girth of body

Drawn by Nityananda Dey Student

HYDROPHIS ROBUSTA.

Plate 21

HYDROPHIS CRASSICOLLIS

FROM NATURE

Plate 22

Length including tail	4	3
Tail		4
Girth of body		3
Girth of neck		2

Drawn by Vileunendra Dar. Student

HYDROPHIS CYANOCINTA.

FROM NATURE

	Ind. Mts.	
Length including tail	5	9
Tail		6
Girth of body		4½

Drawn by Belnari 1st Class Student

Govt. Sch. of Art. Calcutta

HYDROPHIS STUARTII (ANDERSON.)

Plate 24

HYDROPHIS CURTA

SPECIMEN IN INDIAN MUSEUM

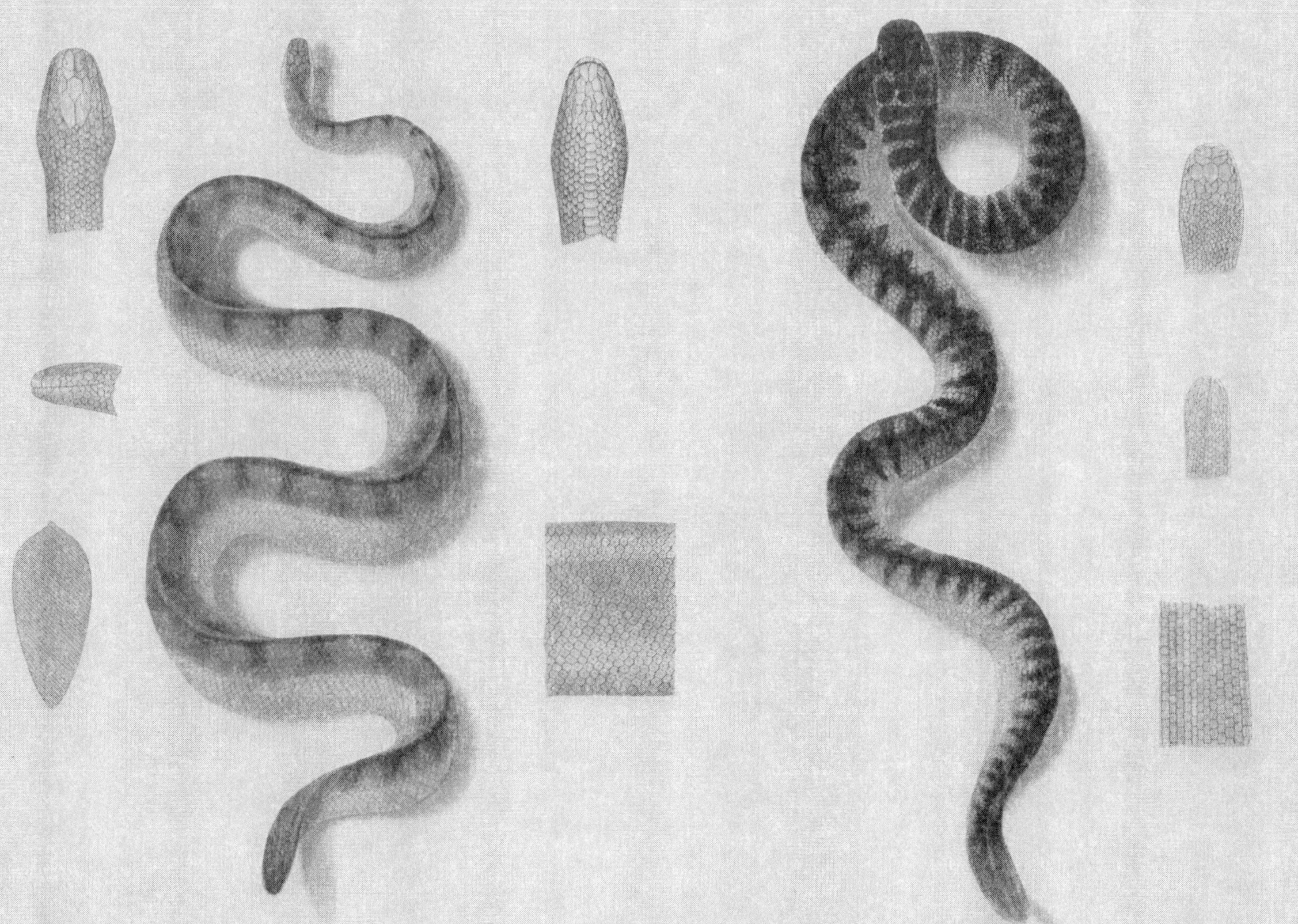

Plate 25

HYDROPHIS NIGRA (ANDERSON)

DRAWN FROM NATURE POOREE ORISSA

Length including Tail 1.6½
Girth of Body 1½
Length of Tail 2"

HYDROPHIS NIGROCINCTA.

FROM NATURE IND. MUS

Length including Tail 1.11
Tail 2¾
Girth of Body 2½
Girth of Neck 1½

Annoda Prasad Bagchee Student

Govt. School of Art, Calcutta

Plate 26

HYDROPHIS CORONATA

Length 3' 2½ Circum 3"

From Life

Drawn by
Hurrish Chunder Khan Student

M & N HANHART, CHROMOLITH.

Govt. Sch. of Art
Calcutta.

HYDROPHIS CHLORIS.

Plate 27.

FROM NATURE. IND. MUS.

Length including tail	33½
Tail	2½
Girth of body	2½
Girth of neck	¾

Drawn by Hurrish Chunder Khan Student. *Gov. School of Art, Calcutta.*

M. & N. HANHART CHROMOLITH.

HYDROPHIS STRICTICOLLIS.

Plate 28

Length including tail	3
tail	3½
Girth of neck	¾
" " body	3

Drawn by Annoda Prosad Bagchee Student. *Govt. Sch. of Art Calcutta.*

Figs. 1.2.3 shew how the Cobra is held by the Snake-men
4.5 are from dissections by J. Fayrer M.D.

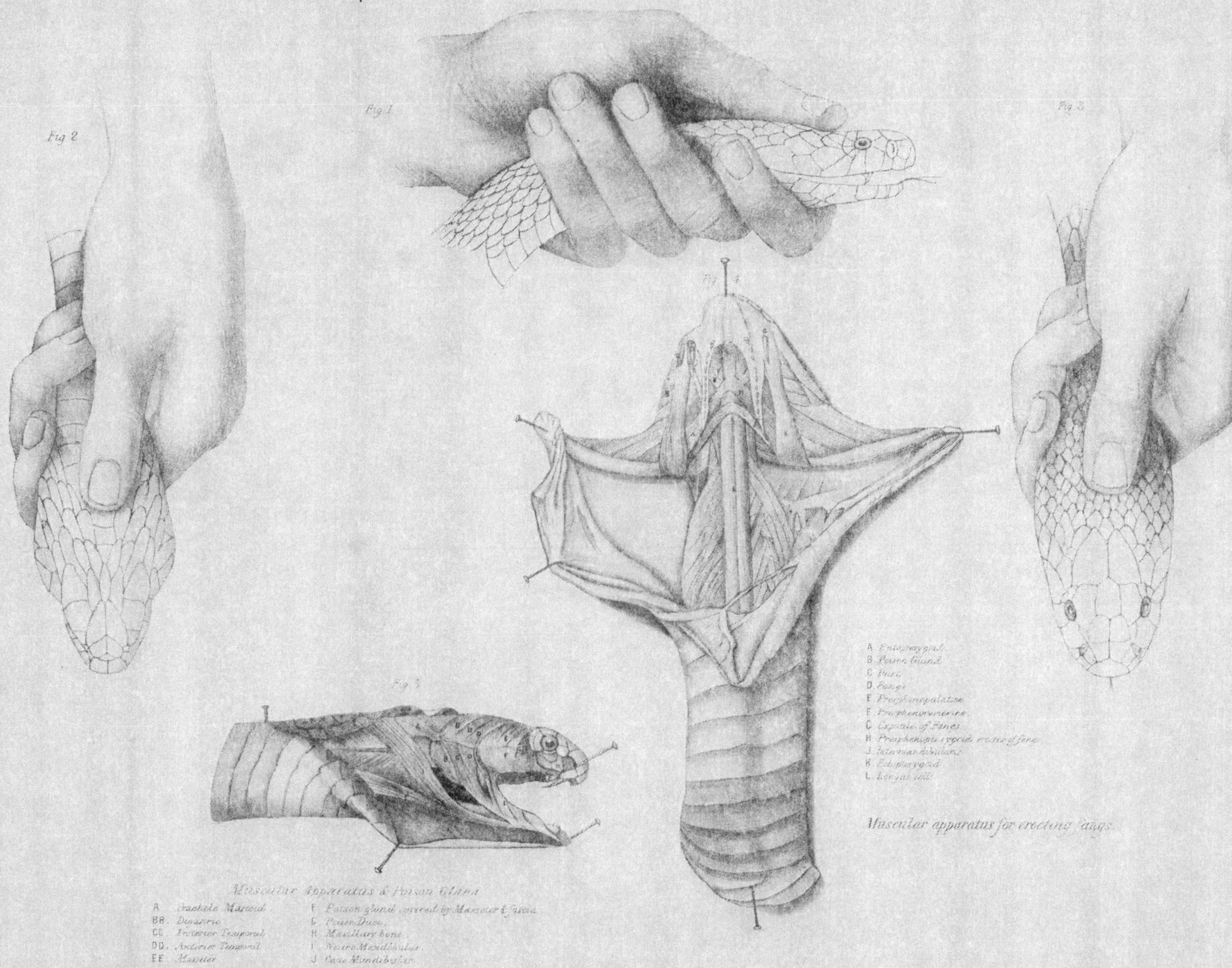

Drawn by Annoda Prosad Bagchee, & Hurrish Chunder Khan Students

Govt. School of Art Calcutta.

M. & N. HANHART LITH.

DABOIA RUSSELLII.

Muscular Apparatus for erecting fangs

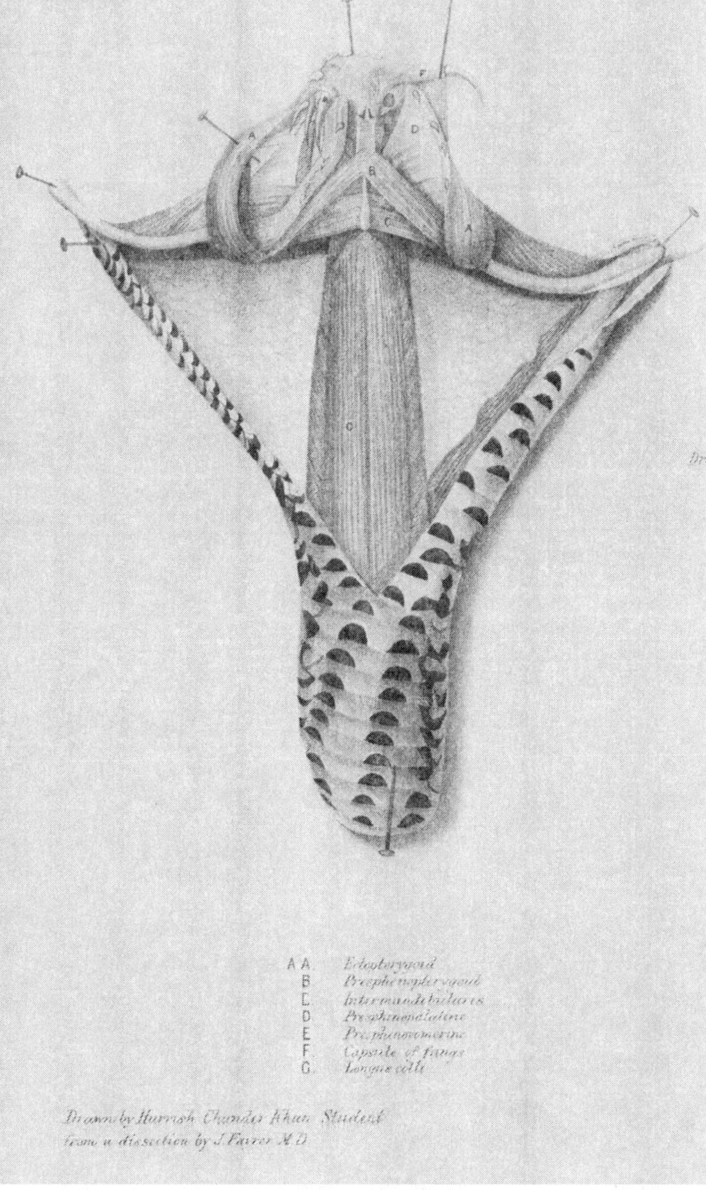

AA. *Ectopterygoid*
B. *Presphenopterygoid*
C. *Intermandibularis*
D. *Presphenopalatine*
E. *Presphenovomerine*
F. *Capsule of fangs*
G. *Longus colli*

Drawn by Hurrish Chunder Khan Student
from a dissection by J. Fayrer M.D.

Diagrams of the Shields on the head of a Colubrine Snake

From Life

Ptyas mucosus

A. *Rostral.*
B. *Anterior frontal.*
B. *Posterior frontal.*
C. *Vertical.*
D. *Occipital.*
E. *Superciliary.*
F. *Temporal.*

L.M. *Nasals.*
N. *Loreal.*
O. *Anterior Ocular or Orbital.*
P. *Posterior Ocular or Orbital.*
Q. *Upper labials.*

G. *Median or lower labials.*
H.H. *Lower labials.*
I.K. *Chin shields.*

Drawn by Anoda Prosad Bagchee Stu^t.

Gov^t. Sch. of Art Calcutta

DABOIA RUSSELLII.

Muscles of head and poison gland

AA. *Fascia covering temporal muscles anterior and posterior*
B. *Small gland*
C. *Tendinous insertion of fascia*
D. *Poison duct*
E. *Fang*
F. *Reserve fangs*
G. *Mandible*
H. *Ectopterygoid muscle and a portion of its fascia*
J. *Poison gland covered by fascia and masseter muscle*
K. *Masseter inserted into mandible*
L. *Temporal insertion.*
M. *Digastric*

Gov^t. Sch. of Art Calcutta

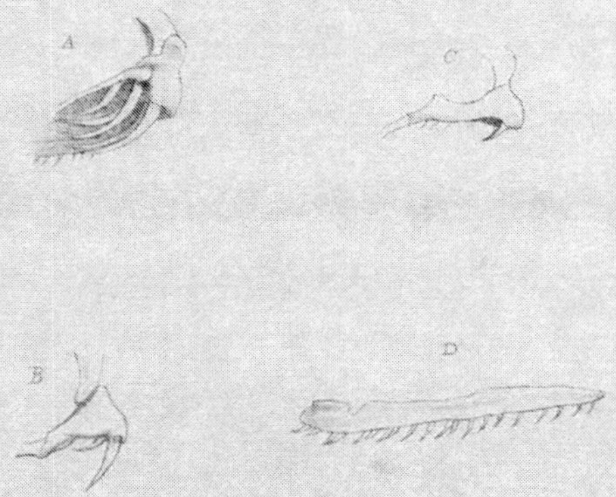

A Maxillary bone & Fangs of Daboia russellii
B — — — — Naja tripudians
C — — — — Bungarus fasciatus
D — — — teeth — Ptyas mucosus

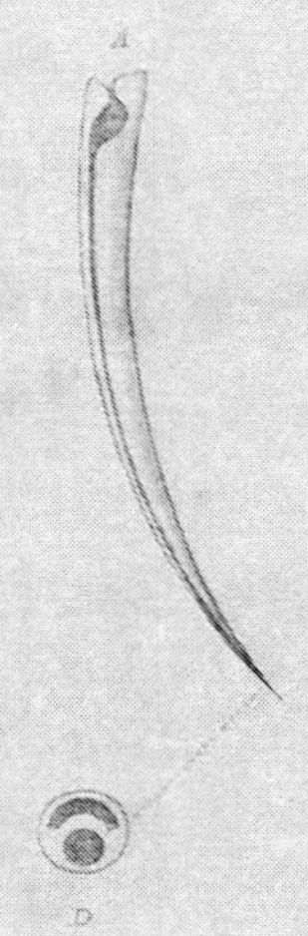

A. Fang of Daboia
D. Transverse section

B. Fang of Naja tripudians
E. Transverse section

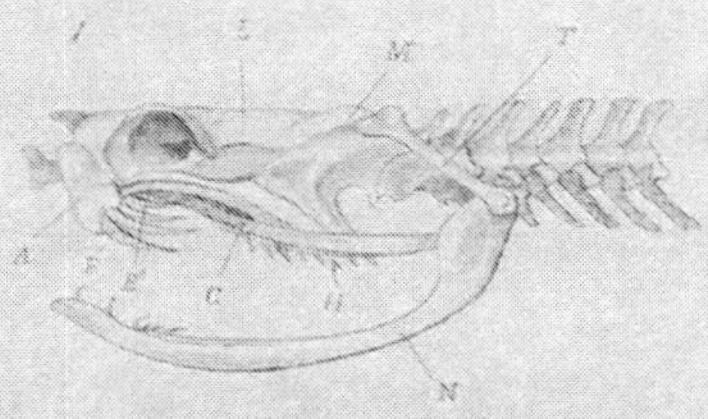

C Fang of Hydrophis
F Transverse section

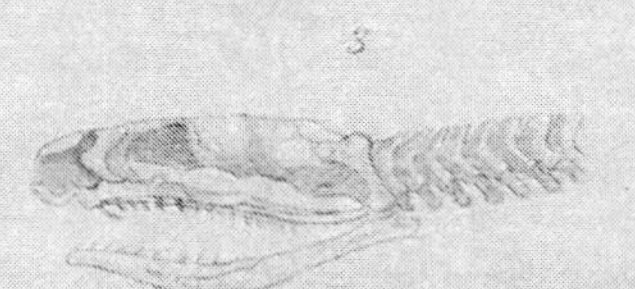

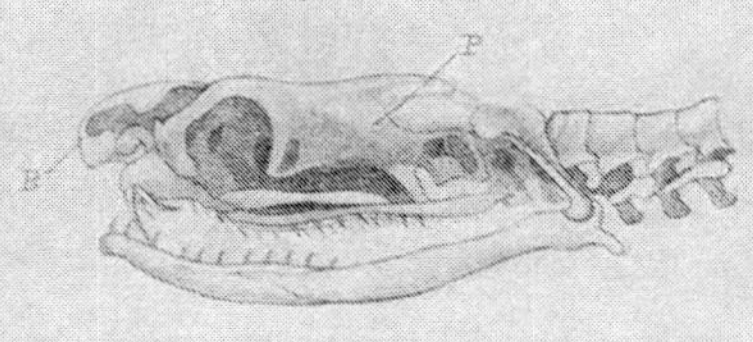

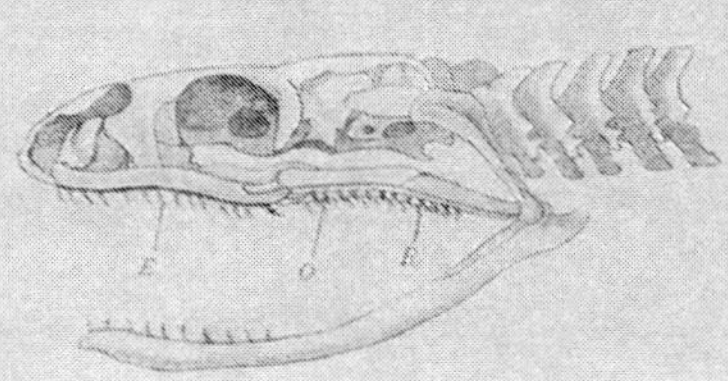

1 Daboia russellii
2 Naja tripudians

3 Bungarus fasciatus
4 Ptyas mucosus

A. Maxillary bone
E. Maxillary teeth
F. Poison fang
G. Palatine bone
H. Pterygoid bone
N. Mandible
T. Tympanic bone

M. Mastoid bone
E'. Ecto-pterygoid bone
O. Palatine teeth
R. Pterygoid teeth
B. Intermaxillary bone
P. Parietal bone
L. Frontal bone

M & N HANHART LITH.

THE THANATOPHIDIA OF INDIA.

SECTION I.

ZOOLOGICAL AND ANATOMICAL CHARACTERS, HABITS, AND DISTRIBUTION.

The Inspector-General of Hospitals, having at my request sanctioned the distribution among Medical Officers in the Bengal Presidency of a circular letter* and printed form, with the object of obtaining information on the subject of snake-poisoning in the Presidency, I think it may be well to supplement that circular with a short description of the list of poisonous snakes thereunto appended, and with a few remarks on some important anatomical and zoological peculiarities of these reptiles, as it may be useful to those who have not paid particular attention to this branch of Natural History.

The list, in giving merely the names of the varieties, species, and genera of the Thanatophidia, or poisonous snakes, indicates generally the localities where they may be looked for, and the relative frequency or rarity in which they may be expected to occur. A more detailed account may, perhaps, aid those who are disposed to assist in collecting and recording reliable information on a subject interesting alike to science and humanity.

The order Ophidia, of the sub-class Reptilia proper, is divided into three sub-divisions :—

1. Ophidii Colubriformes, innocuous snakes.
2. Ophidii Colubriformes Venenosi, or poisonous colubrine snakes.
3. Ophidii Viperiformes, or viperine snakes—poisonous.

The two last sub-orders, under the designation of Thanatophidia, a name peculiarly applicable to them, as they occur in India and in the Bengal Presidency especially, I propose to describe.

I will premise the description of individual genera and species by a few remarks on the general characteristics of the three sub-orders, and especially on those which distinguish the innocuous from the venomous snakes; and of the latter, the differences which mark the viperine from the colubrine forms.

The characters possessed in common by the three sub-orders are the elongate form; the absence of any exo-skeleton, sternum, pectoral arch, sacrum or limbs, with the exception in a few of the Colubrines, of rudimentary pelves, or hinder extremities. The mandibles are united by an extensible ligament, and are articulated with tympanic bones, which allow of the extensive gape through which the snake swallows its prey. Snakes have neither external ears nor eyelids, but the eye is covered by a transparent glassy capsule, which exfoliates with the epidermis, when that is shed. The body is naked, but it has this epidermis, which is frequently exfoliated, laid in scale-like folds and shields on the head and ventral surface. The number and arrangement of these non-imbricated shields on the head is of value in the classification of the genera and species. They are named as follows :—

Rostral.	Ocular anterior, or præ-orbital.
Anterior frontal.	,, posterior, or post-orbital.
Posterior frontal.	Upper labials.
Vertical.	Temporals.
Supra-ciliary.	Mental.
Occipital.	Lower labials.
Nasals.	Chin shields.
Loreal.	

Snakes are provided with sharp, recurved teeth which are anchylosed to the maxillary, palatine, and pterygoid bones, and it is by the form and arrangement of these teeth that the poisonous are most easily distinguished from the innocuous species. Certain Ophidia approaching nearly to the Saurian forms, such as the *Typhlopidæ*, *Tortricidæ*, *Uropeltidæ*, have rudimentary pelves and a narrow mouth, without the enormous gape; but in these it is only a matter of less development. The lungs are unsymmetrical, one being much larger than the other. The heart has three cavities, one ventricle and two auricles; the urinary bladder is wanting.

The organs of locomotion are the ribs, which articulate with rudimentary transverse processes of the vertebræ, and correspond nearly to the number of dorsal vertebræ, and the ventral plates or scales.

Snakes are all carnivorous, existing on living animals or eggs; the prey is swallowed entire, as they have no organs of mastication. They are oviparous, ovo-viviparous, or viviparous. They are "hæmatocrya," or cold-blooded. Their blood is rich in solid constituents, and has red corpuscles of an elliptical shape, which are flattened and bi-convex, and smaller than in other reptilia.

These are some of the most marked characteristics of the order Ophidia, that are common to the three sub-orders into which it is sub-divided. Before describing those which differentiate one sub-order from the other, I would make a few remarks on the osteology of the cranium, the dentition, and on the glandular apparatus, to which the venomous snakes owe their deadly properties. The Ophidia are distributed generally over the surface of the globe, wherever climate and other circumstances are favourable to their existence; India has perhaps a larger share than any other country, and the poisonous forms constitute a considerable proportion of the whole number of families.

Of twenty-one families well known to naturalists, in this country, four are poisonous. The most deadly of the poisonous colubrine snakes—such as the *Ophiophagus elaps*, and *Naja tripudians*—are Indian, whilst of the viperine forms, the *Viperidæ* are represented by the formidable *Daboia russellii*, than which there is probably no more deadly Viper, and the *Crotalidæ* by the *Trimeresuri*. All the members of this family are much less formidable than their African and

* Vide Appendix, No. 1.

American congeners, such as the *Crotalus horridus*, or Rattlesnake, the Jararacca, or *Craspedocephalus brazilensis*, which are much more deadly than any of the Crotalidæ of this country.

The four poisonous families are :—

Elapidæ. Hydrophidæ.	Colubrine.
Viperidæ. Crotalidæ.	Viperine.

The seventeen innocuous families are :

1. Typhlopidæ.	10. Dendrophidæ.
2. Tortricidæ.	11. Dryiophidæ.
3. Xenopeltidæ.	12. Dipsadidæ.
4. Uropeltidæ.	13. Lycodontidæ.
5. Calamaridæ.	14. Amblycephalidæ.
6. Oligodontidæ.	15. Pythonidæ.
7. Colubridæ.	16. Erycidæ.
8. Homalopsidæ.	17. Acrochordidæ.
9. Psammophidæ.	

The four poisonous families contain :—

	Genera.
Elapidæ	5
Hydrophidæ	4
Viperidæ	2
Crotalidæ	4
	15

The cranium of a snake is built up of a number of bones which have their homologues in the Mammalian skull, but are more complex, and modified in accordance with the structure and habits of the reptile. It is unnecessary to describe, in detail, the bones which enter into the formation of the cranial cavity, which is very small, being in proportion to the imperfectly developed encephalon it protects. But as those which enter into the structure of the maxillary and mandibular arches are of importance in distinguishing the venomous from the non-venomous snakes, it is well that a short description of them should be given. It is the peculiar structure of the jaws, indeed, that forms one of the chief characteristics of the Ophidians. The bones which compose the upper jaw and palate, as well as the mandibles, are freely moveable, the latter being loosely hung from the tympanic bones, and are united in front by ligament. The mastoid bones with which the tympanic bones articulate are also moveable, so that the distensibility of the mouth is very great, as it often needs to be, to enable the snake to swallow prey larger in diameter than itself.

The mechanism of deglutition in the Ophidia is very remarkable; the mouth can not only be opened vertically, but transversely, and further, each lateral half has the power of separate and independent motion which is called into action when the prey is swallowed. By the continual action of the jaws and teeth, the animal brought within the grasp of the mouth, is slowly drawn in and engulfed; it is first held firmly by the sharp recurved teeth, one side of the jaw is then protruded, the teeth being withdrawn to be again implanted further on; the same process is repeated alternately on either side, until the prey is finally drawn within the grasp of the gullet. This is the mode of deglutition in the Python and other non-venomous snakes. A similar process, with certain modifications in the dental arrangement, obtains in the poisonous snakes; the chief structural distinction being found in the maxillary teeth, which in them are long, sharp, recurved, and perforated fangs, through which the secretion of the poison gland is hypodermically injected into the bitten animal. Before describing the maxillary arch, it may be well to say a few words about the dentition of serpents generally. The non-venomous forms have two rows of teeth in the upper jaw: the outer or maxillary, the inner or palatine. In the majority, the outer row has from twenty to twenty-five teeth, though in some genera, as *Tortrix*, *Homalopsis*, they are less numerous; in the typical venomous snakes the maxillary bone is very short, and the outer row is represented by a single long tubular fang, which is firmly anchylosed into the moveable maxillary bone, with loose reserve fangs in the mucous fold surrounding it. In other genera, *Dryiophis*, *Dipsas*, the maxillary teeth increase in size towards the posterior part of the bone, and the terminal teeth are even grooved on their convex surface; these teeth may enable the snake to retain a firm hold on its prey, or they may give entry to acrid saliva, but they are not connected by a duct with any poison gland.

The grooved or perforated poison fangs are firmly fixed in the maxillary bone, and are covered by a fold or capsule of mucous membrane, in which they are ensheathed, and in which several reserve poison teeth, in different stages of growth, lie loose until one of them is called for by the loss of the actual fang. Its successor then becomes anchylosed to the maxillary bone, and communicates with the duct of the poison gland.

The teeth of the Ophidia generally are conical, sharp pointed, and recurved weapons, firmly fixed in the bones with which they are connected. In some snakes the pre-maxillary, or intermaxillary bone is without teeth; in others it is furnished with them. The maxillary bones, in the poisonous snakes, have one or two grooved fangs, one only of which on either side is effective; and in some of the poisonous colubrine snakes, as Cobra or *Bungarus*, there may be one or more smaller teeth of the ordinary kind immediately behind the poison fangs. In the non-venomous colubrine snakes the maxillary bone has a whole row of equal sized recurved teeth. This rule, though general, is not absolute, for some snakes have fangs although they are not venomous.

Günther says of the *Psammodynastes pulverulentus*:—"This snake has a very repulsive aspect: its dark, undefined colours, short and thick head, and swollen lips, caused by large hidden fangs, give it the appearance of a venomous snake; it remains small, the largest specimen I have seen being only 21 inches long, the tail measuring 4½ inches. It has a wide geographical range, occurring in Khasya, Sikkim, Assam, Pegu, Mergui, Cochinchina, Sumatra, Java, and the Philippine Islands."

There are some good specimens in the Indian Museum lately presented by Major Godwin Austen from the Khasya hills. The long fangs are distinctly marked, and the snake looks very like a venomous one. The palatine teeth are of about the same size as the maxillary in non-venomous snakes. The pterygoid teeth are somewhat smaller. A diagram of the dentition of the *Ptyas* or Dhamin would be as in Figure 1; of the Cobra or *Bungarus* as in Figure 2; of the *Daboia* or Viper as in Figure 3.

Dhamin (Ptyas Mucosus). Innocent Snake. Figure 1. — *Naja tripudians. Cobra.* Figure 2. — *Daboia russellii. Viper.* Figure 3.

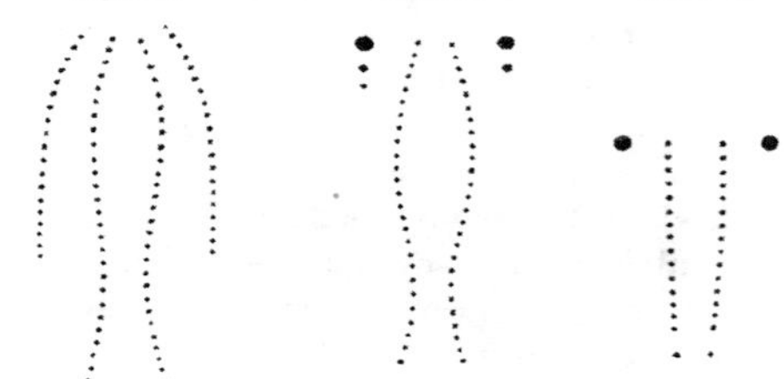

The dotted lines show the directions of the marks that would be made by the bites of—

1. DHAMIN. 2. COBRA. 3. DABOIA RUSSELLII.

The actual number of maxillary, palatine, and pterygoid teeth is not indicated by the marks, but merely the direction they take.

In the Viper they are not much above 8 or 10 palatine or pterygoid, only one maxillary.

In the Cobra 25 or 26 pterygoid or palatine, and one, or perhaps a second, small (though not a poison fang) maxillary.

In the Ptyas (Dhamin) or harmless snake, from 35 to 40 pterygoid or palatine teeth, and 20 to 22 maxillary teeth.

The examination of the wound inflicted by a snake might thus, to a very great extent, enable one to judge whether it were poisonous or not. On the other hand, the bite of the *Hydrophidæ* might present much the appearance of the non-venomous terrestrial snakes; the anterior maxillary tooth or fang is so small and so little different from the other maxillary teeth, that the distinct marks of two fangs would probably not be present, and yet the bite might be a most dangerous one; for, as Günther says, "There cannot be the slightest doubt that the sea-snakes belong to the most poisonous species of the whole order. Russell and Cantor have ascertained it by direct observation: tortoises, other snakes, and fish died from their bite in less than an hour, and a man succumbed after four hours." It is necessary that this should be borne in mind, although with reference to the land snakes, exceptions to this rule are rare.

In the typical poisonous snakes, the maxillary bone is reduced to a mere wedge of bone, giving support only to the poison fangs. The ecto-pterygoid bone is elongated in proportion, and it is mainly through the medium of the articulation of the maxillary bone with this bone that its hinge-like motion enables the snake to depress or erect the fang at will. The tooth, it is to be observed, has no independent motion, it moves only with the bone with which it is united, that bone being moved during muscular action by the pressure on it of the ecto-pterygoid. In the viperine snakes, in which the poison fangs are very large, the degree of mobility is remarkably great, and the snake, when irritated and about to strike, gives them a peculiar and independent vibratile movement which is very striking. In them the natural position of the fang is the recumbent one. When the snake strikes, and as it opens its mouth, the maxillary bone is pushed forward, and the fang is erected. The poison fangs are described as grooved or perforated teeth, but, strictly speaking, they are not so. Like other teeth, they are solid, composed of dentine and cement, but they are folded over so as to form a cylinder in some cases; in others an open groove. It is as though you took a leaf and folded it longitudinally until its edges overlapped to form a tube, or approached each other so as to form a groove. The various degrees of involution are represented permanently in the fangs of different poisonous snakes. For example, in the *Hydrophidæ*, the fang is only so folded as to form an open groove; in the *Elapidæ* the canal is a tube; in the *Viperidæ* it is even more so, all appearance of this involution having disappeared. The groove or canal communicates at the base by a triangular opening with the poison duct; and the apex is open near the point. It will be seen from this, that the groove or perforation is external to the pulp cavity. The dentine of the fang is arranged so as to radiate vertically round the canal, and it is covered externally with a coat of cement, which gives its polish and hardness. The fangs vary much in size in different families of poisonous snakes. In the Viper they are very long and sharp pointed, and most formidable weapons from their size, having the power to inflict a deep wound. They are perforated from the base to the apex by the poison canal which runs along the anterior convex side of the tooth; they are firmly anchylosed to the maxillary bone, which is exceedingly mobile.

In the *Elapidæ* the structure of the fang is similar, but it is relatively much smaller, and there is little or no movement in the maxillary bone, which is longer than in the *Viperidæ*, and has sometimes one or two ordinary teeth behind the poison fang. It is also a most formidable weapon, independently of its connexion with the poison gland, but only half the size of the viperine fang. In the *Hydrophidæ* the fang is still smaller, and the canal remains as an open groove along which the poison is injected into the wound inflicted.

The amount of involution I believe varies in the *Hydrophidæ*; for example, in the fangs of a large *Enhydrina*, four feet long by six inches in girth, I found the fangs partially grooved and partially closed. Excepting on close examination, the groove appears nearly as much closed as the Cobra's fang. It is, after all, merely a question of degree, not of kind.

The *Hydrophidæ* or salt-water snakes are a very poisonous family. The bite is very dangerous notwithstanding the small size of the fang.

A few words now on the formation of the Ophidian skull. It has three pairs of frontal bones; the two anterior form the anterior part of the orbit, the two median lie between them and the two posterior, which form the posterior boundary of the orbit. The nasal bones lie immediately in front of the middle frontal, and the inter-maxillary bone between them forms the muzzle of the snake. The parietals lie behind the post-frontals, and at their posterior angles are the two mastoid bones, which overlap as they articulate with them. The mastoid bones, which are moveable, articulate with the long and slender tympanic or inter-articular bones; they articulate at the opposite extremity with the mandibles, each of which consists of three segments—the articular, the coronary, and the dentary. These are united in front to form the lower jaw by an elastic ligament; the result of this loose and ligamentous union of the mastoids, the tympanic and the mandibles, is to give great extensibility to the aperture through which the prey is introduced into the gullet. The upper jaw is composed of the pterygoids, the palatines, the ecto-pterygoids, the maxillaries, and the pre-maxillary. The maxillary arch is thus made up of the maxillary bones, which, in the *Viperidæ*, the typical poisonous snakes, are short, moveable, and furnished with one long tubular fang each. The non-venomous colubrine snakes, on the other hand, have a long fixed maxillary bone set with a number of non-perforated teeth, as before described. The maxillary bones of the poisonous colubrine snakes are a modification of the latter. They are longer than in the viperine family, and less moveable. They have a tubular poison fang, but it is smaller; and they have in some cases one or more fixed and non-perforated teeth immediately behind the poison fang. Such may be seen in the *Naja* and *Bungarus*. The maxillary bones articulate with the palatine, the ecto-pterygoid with the anterior frontal, and in the non-venomous snakes with the pre-maxillary. This bone varies much in form in different genera.

The pterygoid articulates with the palatine, ecto-pterygoid, and basi-sphenoid; and in the Viper it abuts against the tympanic pedicle, and thus influences the movement by which, through the ecto-pterygoid, the maxillary bone is pushed forward and the fang erected. The ecto-pterygoid overlaps the posterior portion of the maxillary at one end, and at the other it joins the pterygoid. The mandibular arch is composed of the tympanic bones which articulate with the mastoid at one end, and with the condyles of the lower jaw or mandibles at the other; this mandible on either side being, as I have said, composed of three segments, and the posterior part of the pterygoid, which —in the Viper—abuts against the end of the tympanic pedicle.

The bones which enter into the formation of the cranial cavity are—parietals, basi-occipital, occipital, ex-occipital, sphenoid, ali-sphenoid, basi-sphenoid, pre-sphenoid, and orbito-sphenoid; the lachrymal and turbinal bones, and vomer. These are connected with the maxillary arch. In the Vipers especially there is a prominent bony spine on the base of the skull, to which the longus colli muscles have a firm attachment. This gives these snakes the great power of striking that they possess.

The muscular apparatus connected with the bones I have just briefly described, is next to be shortly considered, especially that portion of it which is concerned in the act of grasping the prey and inflicting the poisoned wound.

The following are the muscles concerned in these processes :— The masseter, which arises from the ecto-pterygoid and passes backwards, winding round the tympano-mandibular joint, to be inserted into the mandible as far forward as the dentary. The membranous origin of this muscle extends over the poison gland.

The temporal muscle arises from the parietal bone, and is inserted into the coronary process of the mandible. It is partly covered by the masseter. The posterior temporal takes its origin from the anterior part of the mastoid and parietal, and is inserted into the coronoid ridge near the joint.

The tympano-mandibular, or digastric, arises from the posterior part of the tympanic bone, and is inserted into that of the angular process of the mandible.

From the fascia of the anterior vertebræ, a muscle, called the neuro-mandibular, and another smaller slip, called the costo-mandibular, extend downwards and forwards, to be inserted into the lower border of the mandible. The action of these muscles is to retract and depress the lower jaw.

The ecto-pterygoid passes forwards and expands into a fascia, which, in the poisonous snakes, covers the sac in which the fangs are enveloped. It is inserted also into the lower part of the posterior extremity of the maxillary bone. It helps to fix the maxillary when the fang is used, and it also retracts the fang when the erectile force is relaxed. The ento-pterygoid arises from the pterygoid bone, and passes outwards and backwards, to be inserted into the posterior part of the lower jaw—*i.e.*, the inner surface of the angular and sur-angular elements covered by the ecto-pterygoid. Its action is to draw together the mandibles, whilst it separates and draws backwards the palato-pterygoid bones. The anterior parts of the mandibles, which are relaxed in the stretching of the ligament during deglutition, are drawn together again, and corrugated by a transverse band of muscular fibres called the inter-mandibular. This muscle also sends off a slip on either side, which expands on the inter-mandibular integument, the action being to corrugate it after the stretching it has undergone, and it is aided in producing this effect by an additional thin layer of muscle.

The pre-spheno-pterygoid arises from the pre-sphenoid, and extends backwards and outwards to the pterygoid and ecto-pterygoid, where they unite. In contracting, it draws or rather pushes forwards the pterygoid, ecto-pterygoid, and maxillary bones, rotating the latter and erecting the fang.

The pre-spheno-palatine takes its origin from the side of the fore-part of the pre sphenoid, and passes outwards to its insertion along the inner surface of the palatine. From the side of the pre-sphenoid the pre-spheno-vomerine muscle arises; it sends a slender tendon to the vomer, the action of which is to depress and retract the pre-maxillary, restoring it to its natural position with other bones which have been displaced in swallowing the prey.

Such are the muscular arrangements by which the mouth is opened vertically, and laterally; the poison gland compressed and the venom injected through the poison fang, which, by a simultaneous combined action of muscles and consequent movement of bone, has become erect, and is fixed in that position during the infliction of the deadly blow by which the fangs are imbedded in the flesh of the snake's prey.

A few words now on the poison gland, and its duct.

The poison glands are situated behind the eye, and in front of the tympanic bones. They are oval bodies about the size of an almond in the Cobra; the secreting structure consists of a series of elongated lobes diverging from the principal duct. The lobes are sub-divided into lobules, which are sub-divided into cæca. These, having secreted the poison, convey it through the poison duct to the base of the poison fangs in the capsule of mucous membrane surrounding them. These glands are of different form and size in different families of snakes, but they are all modifications of the structure I have de-

Diagram of the Poison Gland of a Poisonous Snake.

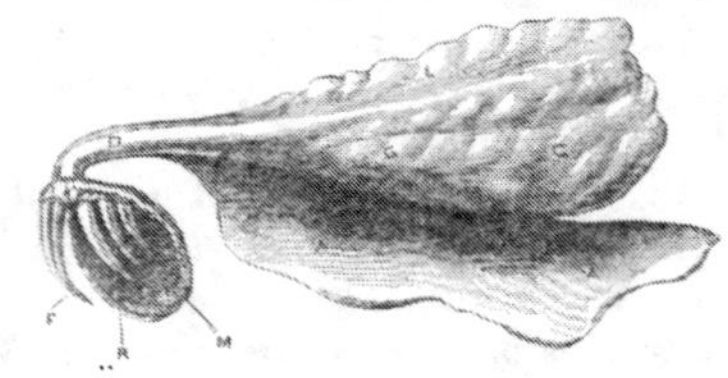

L. Lobe of Gland.
D. Duct.
F. Fang.
G G. Gland.
M. Mucous Capsule of Fang.
R. Reserved Fangs.
A A. Fascia covering Gland.

scribed. The gland is encased in a capsule, and is partially covered by fibres of muscle (the masseter), whose action in closing the jaw at the same time compresses the gland, and squeezes the poison through the duct into the perforated tooth.

The secretion of the gland varies much in colour and viscosity in different snakes, but its general appearance is that of a clear, lightly viscid fluid, soluble in water, and slightly acid in reaction. It manifests its deadly effects most powerfully if inoculated into the blood when the snake is fresh and vigorous in the warm weather, and when it has not bitten for some time. It seems to act through the circulation, paralysing the nerve centres, and thus destroying the vital force. But there is no doubt, I believe, that, notwithstanding all that has been said to the contrary, it is capable of absorption through the mucous membranes with which it is brought into contact, though with much less dangerous effects than when it is introduced into the blood. In certain experiments in which the poison of the Cobra was placed on the conjunctiva of dogs, the symptoms of poisoning were rapidly and strongly, though not in all cases fatally, developed. I shall have more to say on the subject of snake poison subsequently, but meanwhile I would remark that there are certain differences in the action of venom derived from different families of snakes.

Thus, the poison of the *Naja* kills without destroying the coagulability of the blood; whilst that of the Viper—the *Daboia*—produces perfect and permanent fluidity. This is the case with the lower animals. Apparently it is not always so in Man.

The poison may be diluted with water, or even ammonia or alcohol, without destroying its deadly properties. It may be kept for months or years, dried between slips of glass, and still retain its virulence. It is capable of absorption through delicate membranes, and therefore it cannot safely be applied to any mucous surfaces, though no doubt its virulence is much diminished in the endosmosis. It kills when introduced into the stomach, when put into the eye, or when applied to the peritoneum. The Prince of Canino, L. Bonaparte, gave in 1843 an analysis of the venom of the Viper (*Pelias berus*), and he pointed out the presence of a principle representing the ptyaline of saliva. This he called viperine. He also found albumen and mucous fatty matter, substances soluble in alcohol, yellow colouring matter, and saline matters.

The elementary analysis of viperine has yet to be made; it appears to act by a catalytic force—that is, it kills by some occult influence on the nerve centres; viperine is a neutral substance, and very unstable.

The terms echidnine, crotaline, have been given to a similar principle derived from other snakes. They are no doubt identically the same.

The poison acts most rapidly on birds and mammals. Less so on the cold-blooded animals, but fishes, frogs, molluscs, and non-venomous snakes are destroyed by it, and often die very rapidly.

I have not been able to satisfy myself positively, after many experiments made on purpose, that the poisonous snakes are absolutely insensible to their own, or to the venom of others, but to a great extent they certainly are so.

I have repeatedly made Cobras and Daboias bite themselves, and each other, and they never seemed the worse for it. But I believe that the poison does take effect on snakes of a less deadly character; and though I have generally seen the *Bungarus* escape, I have seen an occasional death of this snake after a bite by a Cobra, that, I think, might with some reason be attributed to the poison. The non-venomous snakes die rapidly—the *Ptyas*, a large, vigorous, and fierce snake, though non-venomous, succumbs within an hour or so to the bite of a Cobra.

The flesh of an animal dead from snake-poison does not seem to be affected; animals and men eat it with impunity. The sweepers and Dhomes who attended my experiments always took away the poisoned fowls and ate them.

The blood of an animal killed by snake-poison is itself poisonous; and if injected into an animal rapidly manifests its poisonous effects. I have transmitted the venom through a series of three animals, with fatal result. I have had little or no opportunity of studying the local effects of the poison, death has always occurred so rapidly that there has been no time for secondary or local changes.

The Ophidia are oviparous and viviparous.

The colubrine snakes generally are oviparous; but there are exceptions, such as the *Hydrophidæ* and *Homalopsidæ*, which are viviparous, producing from four to sixteen or more young ones.

Mr. Stewart, Civil Surgeon of Poorie, tells me that he took sixteen eggs, with well-formed embryos, out of *Hydrophis cyanocincta*. The eggs were as large as hen's eggs, and the young embryos were six inches in length.

The viperine snakes, as their name implies, are all viviparous.

The distinction is not one of such great importance, as might at first appear. In the oviparous snakes the young are produced from eggs of an oblong obovate form with a soft leathery white shell. These, from ten to forty or fifty in number, are deposited in some place where the natural heat is sufficient to hatch them.

Of all the Ophidia the Python only, according to some authorities, incubates; it coils itself over the eggs, and sits on them till they are hatched.

The viviparous, or rather ovo-viviparous snakes produce their young alive. The eggs are hatched in the oviduct, development having proceeded in them to the point at which the delicate covering of the egg bursts before or during parturition, and the young ones come into the world alive, and immediately show all the activity of their race. A higher temperature than that which is natural to the Viper, in its ordinary condition, is necessary to effect this. The temperature of the reptile increases at these times, and the gravid female is said to expose herself to the heat by basking in the sun's rays, at which time she is more sluggish and inert than on ordinary occasions. The female of all snakes is said to be larger than the male; there are certain differences in colour also which may distinguish the sexes. In the *Hydrophidæ* the male is known from the female by a distinct swelling on each side of the tail extending from the root to or beyond the middle of its length. But in other snakes there is no certain external anatomical character to distinguish the sex; dissection of course reveals it. The tail in males is thicker than in females. Pressure on the ventral surface of the tail, forwards towards the vent, causes in males the protrusion of two vascular bodies.

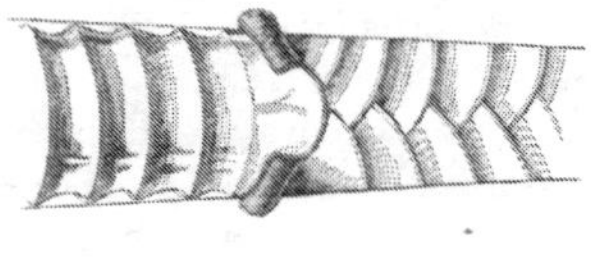

In cold and temperate climates, snakes hybernate or remain in a state of lethargy or torpidity. Active life is suspended until returning warmth rouses the vital energies into a state of activity. They differ much in their modes of life, habitation, food, &c., although they are all carnivorous, feeding on molluscs, insects, reptiles, birds, mammals, eggs, and milk. Vegetable matters have been found in the stomach, but snakes are essentially carnivorous, and most, if not all, take their food only whilst it is alive.

Irrespective of the ordinary natural classification, snakes are arranged under the following heads :—

Tree snakes: those that live for the most part in trees or bushes, and are characterized by their brilliant colours, generally green, their slender and whip-like form, and great activity. Both non-venomous colubrine and viperine snakes are found in this section.

Water snakes, are the salt-water and the fresh-water snakes; —the first are all venomous, the second are all innocent.

The salt-water snakes have a peculiar form adapted to their mode of life—a compressed tail, and nostrils above the snout; they are all poisonous, and many, if not all, are viviparous.

The fresh-water snakes have the nostrils like those of the salt-water snakes. They live in the fresh, though they may be found, like the others, in brackish water; they have not the compressed tail; they are viviparous, and all belong to the sub-order of non-venomous Colubrines.

Ground snakes.—Representatives are found in all the three sub-orders. They live generally above ground. They are more or less cylindrical in shape and very flexible in body. The greater number of snakes are found in this section.

Burrowing snakes, live much under ground; have a rigid cylindrical body, short tail, narrow mouth, and small teeth. No ventral shields; they are all innocuous.

The Thanatophidia, as already stated, comprise the two sub-orders, Ophidii Colubriformes Venenosi, and Ophidii Viperiformes, which are represented in India, the former by the *Elapidæ* and *Hydrophidæ*; the latter by the *Crotalidæ* and *Viperidæ*. In these families the most deadly snakes are found.

A few words on the characteristics of each of the sub-orders and their sub-divisions as found in Bengal.

The members of the poisonous colubrine sub-order are distinguished by their form, which is like that of the innocuous snakes, and by the formation of the maxillary bone, which, though shorter than that of the harmless snakes, is much longer and less moveable than that of the Vipers. The poison fang is shorter, and less moveable than that of the Viper owing to the comparative immobility of the maxillary bone, with which it is anchylosed. The canal through which the poison flows is less developed in the poisonous Colubrines than in the Vipers, and in the *Hydrophidæ* it is actually an open groove. The maxillary bone also in some cases bears other teeth besides the poison fang.

The snakes of the sub-order *Viperidæ* are distinguished by their broad head, as well as by the small, very mobile maxillary bone, to which is anchylosed a long perforated poison fang.

There are other less important distinctions, which will be noticed in describing genera and species. It may be briefly noticed that the general characters of a viperine or a colubrine snake are easily recognised. The formation of the maxillary bone and the dentition are certain guides in distinguishing one from the other.

ELAPIDÆ.

This family has several genera in British India. It is subdivided into the *Najidæ*, or snakes with hoods or dilatable necks, and the *Elapidæ*, which have no hoods.

In the first section, *Najidæ*, there are two genera—*Naja* and *Ophiophagus*.

In the second, *Elapidæ*, there are three Indian genera—viz., *Bungarus*, *Xenurelaps*, and *Callophis*.

The family of *Elapidæ* is characterized by a cylindrical body; a rather short and tapering tail; nostril lateral. The head has the normal number of shields above, but the loreal is always absent; eye rather small, with a round pupil. The poison fang has a mark on its convexity, indicating the groove, which is quite open in the *Hydrophidæ*.

NAJA.

Naja tripudians.

Günther gives the following description of the genus *Naja*:—

"Body and tail of moderate length; belly flat; head rather high and short, not very distinct from neck, which is very dilatable, the anterior ribs being elongate. The shields of the head normal, but the loreal is absent. Nostril wide, lateral, between two shields; eye of moderate size, with round pupil. One præ-, three, sometimes two or four post-oculars. Six upper labials, the third and fourth entering the orbit; the third forms the lower half of the anterior margin of the orbit. Scales smooth, much imbricate, in numerous series round the hood. Anal entire; sub-caudals two-rowed. The fang is grooved, with foramen at its extremity; one or two small ordinary teeth at a short distance behind it."

There is only one species, and that is *Naja tripudians*, or the Cobra di Capello, or Naga.

Coluber naja, *L. Sys. Nat.*
Naja lutescens, *Cantor*.
,, tripudians, *Günther; Gray*.
,, larvata, *Cantor*.
,, atra, *Cantor*.
,, kaouthia, *Cantor*.

But there are several varieties, each having a distinct name given to it by the natives. They are all most deadly, and though the snake-charmers consider some more poisonous than others, it is probable that any difference that may exist is more due to the vigour of the individual snake than to any thing attributable to the particular variety. They all have the hood, and they never attack without distending it. They raise the anterior third of the body from the ground, slide slowly along on the posterior two-thirds, and with the hood dilated remain on the alert, darting the head forward to the attack when anything hostile approaches. This attitude is very striking, and few objects are more calculated to inspire awe than a large Cobra, when with his hood erect, hissing loudly, and his eyes glaring, he prepares to strike. Nevertheless, they are not, I believe, aggressive; and unless interfered with or irritated, they crawl along the ground with the neck undilated, looking not unlike the innocent snakes, but the moment they are disturbed, they assume the menacing attitude I have described.

The *Naja tripudians*, or Cobra, grows to the length of five feet and a half, or even more; I have recently received a living female Cobra from Nagpore, C.P. sent by Dr. W. B. Beatson. It is of the variety called "Kurrees Gokurrah," of a light chocolate colour, without any mark on the hood. It is five feet eight inches long, including the tail, which measures eleven and a quarter inches. In girth it is six and a quarter inches. It is very powerful and fierce, and Dr. Beatson tells me that it killed a fowl in one minute.

This is the largest Cobra I have seen, but I believe they attain even a greater size than this. The Cobra is found all over Hindustan up to 8000 feet high in the Himalaya; but Mr. Hodgson says he has never seen it in the Nepal valley.* It is equally dreaded and fatal everywhere. The varieties are numerous, and they are distinguished by the markings on the hood, and by various shades of colour, from the darkest olive or black with a purple iridescence, to a pale chocolate, fawn, or yellow colour. They are all, notwithstanding their differences of colour or marking, considered by naturalists to be but varieties of one species. They have various names in different parts of India, and are regarded by the snake-catchers as different species, and as having different powers of destruction. Such differences most likely depend on age, vigour, or other circumstances, as naturally the intensity of the poison of the different varieties is probably almost equal.

The Cobra is a nocturnal snake, that is, it is most active in the night, but it is often seen moving about in the day. It is oviparous; the eggs, from eighteen to twenty-five in number, are obovate, and about the size of those of a pigeon, the shell is white, but tough and leathery. The Cobras feed on small animals, birds' eggs, frogs, fish, or insects; they rob hen roosts and swallow the eggs whole; they prefer taking their food at dusk or in the night. They are said to drink a great deal of water; but it is certain that they will live weeks, even months, in captivity without touching food or water. They go into water readily, and swim well, but are essentially terrestrial snakes. They can climb, and occasionally ascend trees in search of food. Cobras are not unfrequently found in the roofs of huts, holes in walls, fowl houses, old ruins, under logs of wood, in cellars, old brick kilns, and old masonry of stone, brickwork, or mud. Such are the common dwelling-places of these reptiles, and where they are frequently disturbed by men, who stepping on or inadvertently disturbing and touching them, receive their death-wound.

The Cobra is most deadly, and its poison, when thoroughly inoculated by a fresh and vigorous snake, is quickly fatal. Paralysis of the nerve centres takes place, and death occurs with great rapidity, sometimes in a few minutes, especially when the fangs, having penetrated a vein, inoculate the poison immediately into the venous circulation. The number of deaths caused yearly in India by these snakes is perfectly appalling. The cases in which recovery occurs are, it is to be feared, very few; treatment appears to be of little avail unless it be almost immediate, and then in the case of a genuine bite there is but little hope of saving life. As to the mode of treatment, and other matters connected with the bite of the Cobra, and the great mortality caused by it in India, they will be described subsequently.

* I believe *it is* to be found in the Nepal valley. I have seen it in the Oude Terai.

The Cobras are the favourites of the snake-catchers, and it is astonishing with what ease and freedom they are seized and handled by these men even when in possession of their fangs. The snake-catchers render them temporarily harmless by cutting out the poison fangs, but these are quickly reproduced, unless, as most generally happens, with the fang all the reserve fangs and germs are removed, in which case the snake is harmless for life. Their graceful movements in the erect attitude they assume with the hood distended as they follow the movements of the snake-charmer's hands, make them an object of wonder as well as fear to all, and the superstitions of the natives about them are endless. The muntra or spell is far more potent in their idea than any drug, and to such they generally trust when bitten. How frequently these fail the records of any Civil station in India will prove, and it is to be feared that the more material remedies of the physician are scarcely more potent for good.

The snake-catchers in Bengal describe a great variety of Cobras. The following list was furnished by a very intelligent Mahommedan, who has had much experience, and who, though not a snake-catcher originally by profession, has been one for several years, and is exceedingly expert in catching and handling these reptiles. The first great distinction made by these people, is between the Cobras with spectacles on the hood, or "Gokurrahs," and those with one ocellus or other mark on the hood, named "Keautiahs." They maintain that these are distinct species, and that they vary considerably not only in appearance, but in habits and properties. Some Gokurrahs, however, have no mark at all on the hood.

The Gokurrah has the following varieties :—

1, Kála—black ; 2, Koyah—black and white ; 3, Gomunah—wheat coloured ; 4, Puddah—yellow coloured ; 5, Dudiah—whitish coloured ; 6, Tentuliah—tamarind-seed coloured ; 7, Kurrees—earthy coloured ; 8, Tameshur—coppery coloured ; 9, Puddun nag—golden coloured.

The 2nd, 3rd, and 7th are the most common varieties about Calcutta.

The Keautiah has the following :—

1, Kála—black ; 2, Tentuliah—tamarind-seed coloured ; 3, Kurrees—earthy coloured ; 4, Sonera—gold coloured ; 5, Dudiah—whitish coloured ; 6, Bans-buniah—mottled white and black ; 7, Giribungha—brownish coloured ; 8, Koyah—black and white coloured ; 9, Sankha-mookhi— like the Sankni or *Bungarus fasciatus*—black and yellow. The Cobra is called in many parts of Hindostan "Kála sámp," "Nág sámp."

1st, 2nd, and 6th are most common about Calcutta, and no doubt in different parts of Bengal many other varieties are described, and different names are given to those above-mentioned, for the natives are fond of refining on points of this kind.

I append a note, kindly furnished by Mr. Westmacott of the Civil Service, of the names of certain varieties described in Puruliah, and no doubt many others might be collected, the nomenclature being different in different parts of the country.

"*Notes on Varieties of Cobras, taken at Puruliah, Maunbhoom*, 1866.

"*Airá Gahman.*—Average length 51½ inches. Top of head purple brown, shading into bright orange in the lower half of the hood. Back two shades of vinaceous brown in faint stripes. Spectacles, white bordered, dark brown. Throat band and spectacles underneath ashy brown. Belly pinky white.

"*Manilág.*—Average length 36½ inches. Not very common. A remarkably slender neck and broad jaw. Top of head light brown, shading into yellow in the hood, and back and belly yellowish white.

"(Memo.—I cannot recollect whether this was a spectacled *Gahman*).

"*Bichá Jarmá Gahman.*—Average 47 inches. Above ruddy brown and yellow. Hood reddish-brown. Spectacles yellow, bordered ruddy brown.

"*Kaliy.*—Average length 51 inches. The common black Cobra, whole body black. Ring on hood, two throat bands, and a collar below the hood ranging in individuals from a creamy white to a dirty grey.

"*Kánta Káris Gahman.*—Average length 48 inches, a light made snake. Above vinaceous brown, with yellow tinge in the hood. Spectacles red. Throat bands purple brown.

"*Dudhiya Gahman.*—Average length 44 inches. Top of head vinaceous brown, darker on the hood and lighter along the back. Below ashy white. Spectacles white, with a dark brown well-defined border.

"*Párula.*—A beautiful snake of which I never procured but one specimen, which I failed in preserving. Length 41 inches. All above a light shade of purple brown. No spectacles. Hood bright red.

"*Sarsa Gahman.*—The common yellow Cobra, largest variety of all.

"*Charara Gahman.*—A large yellow Cobra. I have not noted the differences between these two varieties.

"*Basta Karicha Gahman.*—Average length 50 inches. A very dark vinaceous brown, white spectacles, bordered light red."

The chief difference however insisted on, is that between the Gokurrah and the Keautiah, and these they regard as distinct from each other as is a Sankni (*Bungarus fasciatus*) from a Krait (*Bungarus cæruleus*). The Gokurrah, they say, is essentially a snake of the town or city. The Keautiah is of the fields and jungle. The Gokurrah is slower to kill, as its poison is thicker though most deadly. The Keautiah's poison is thinner, and takes effect sooner, though it is not more fatal than that of the Gokurrah.

Both, they say, incubate, and the snake-man informs me that over and over again he has dug them out of holes sitting on their eggs.

The Gokurrah takes to the water reluctantly ; the Keautiah freely, and will remain for a considerable period under water.

The hood of the Keautiah is smaller relatively than that of the Gokurrah, and the body is more attenuated ; it is more slender and active than the Gokurrah.

The varieties of both eat about every sixth day ; they deposit their eggs once in the year, and that in the rainy season.

The Keautiah is often found during the rainy season in the huts of the villages, where it has been driven to take shelter by inundation. It is as unusual to find a Keautiah, though, in the ruins or débris of an old building, as it is to find a Gokurrah in the open country. The snake-catchers here say that they believe that whereas the Gokurrah is found all over Hindostan, the Keautiah is, if not confined to Bengal, rare in the N.W., and other parts of India. This, however, is by no means certain, and requires confirmation.

Some of the snake-catchers have a curious notion concerning the sex of the Cobra. They say that the hooded snakes are all females, and poisonous ; and that the males are all hoodless and innocent. The male, in fact, of the *Ophiophagus* or Sunkerchor, as well as of the *Naja*, Gokurrah, or Keautiah, is the Dhamin or *Ptyas mucosus*. They assert that there can be no doubt of this, and that they have irrefragable evidence of it, and that the Dhamin is proof also against the Cobra's poison if bitten.

It is needless to say, notwithstanding all this, that the story is a fable. The *Ptyas* is an innocent snake belonging to a different family, and succumbs rapidly to the poison when bitten by a Cobra, as I have proved over and over again by experiment.

The Cobra is an object of superstitious veneration and awe to the Hindoos, in whose mythological histories it takes a prominent place.

In a religion that deprecates the wrath of a cruel and

destructive power, by worshipping and propitiating the Deity in whom that power is vested, it is natural that the type of destruction and the incarnation of evil, as represented in this reptile, should be regarded with peculiar deference.

Many Hindoos object, I am told, to destroy the Cobra, and if they find it in their houses, as sometimes is the case, when one has taken up its abode in a hole or crevice in the wall for years, it is propitiated and conciliated, fed and protected, as though to injure it were to invoke misfortune on the house and family.

Should fear, and perhaps the death of some inmate bitten by accident, prove stronger than superstition, it may be caught, tenderly handled, and deported to some field, where it is released and allowed to depart in peace, not killed. This feeling happily is not universal, and the Cobra has many enemies to limit his increase. Besides the natural enemies, such as the *Herpestes* (Ichneumon) and other creatures, numbers are destroyed by the low caste people, who follow the vocation of snake-catchers or charmers, and others also search out the snakes and kill them for the sake of reward. But still the loss of human life from their bites is very great, and seems to call loudly for some plan by which it may be mitigated. An idea of the loss of life caused throughout India yearly by the bite of the Cobra and other venomous snakes, but especially by the Cobra, as it is by far the most common, may be formed from the following information extracted from a recent report of the Commissioner of Burdwan to the Bengal Government.

He says, "The number of deaths from snake-bite during the last nine years is shown in the annual printed police returns to have been as follows:—

1860 ...	878	1863 ...	1048	1866 ...	929
1861 ...	989	1864 ...	1035	1867 ...	984
1862 ...	1041	1865 ...	1184	1868 ...	1144

Total 9232 persons killed in nine years out of a population of 5,701,072.

"There may be a little inaccuracy in the above figures, but they have been compiled over a series of nine years, and it cannot be questioned that they show that there is a mortality of above 1000 persons every year, in a population of nearly 6,000,000 people."

In the district of Midnapore—which the commissioner considers the worst—in the year 1865 there were 530 deaths from snake-bite recorded, out of a population of 1,200,000 persons.

In the district of Beerbhoom, on the other hand, there were in one year sixty cases of death from snake-poisoning, out of a population of 743,685 persons. It appears from the report that women suffer more than men.

In 1858 a reward of four annas was given by Government for each venomous snake destroyed in the division, and the Magistrate reported in December that Rs. 1961-8 had been paid for 1845 snakes destroyed during the year. The reward was reduced to two annas for every poisonous snake brought in, but this was not sufficient inducement, and the numbers rapidly diminished.

		Snakes.		Rs.	As.
In 1859	...	957	...	124	4
„ 1860	...	217	...	27	0
„ 1861	...	8	...	1	0

The Magistrate remarked "that there are few persons who would risk their lives to bring in a live snake for two annas."

In Bancoorah, another district of the Burdwan division, the Magistrate proposed that the reward of two annas should be given for all poisonous snakes brought in dead or alive. This was sanctioned with a proviso that the Magistrate himself should see the snake's head cut off. The reward was raised to four annas for each snake in 1862. On the 14th July following, the Magistrate reported that the increased reward had produced its effect—47 snakes had been brought in on one day, and 70 on another day; Rs. 89 had been spent in less than a month.

On the 21st July of the same year, the Magistrate proposed to reduce the reward to two annas; he says, "97 snakes were brought in on Saturday, and 118 to-day." The duty of personally supervising the decapitation of the snakes became so irksome, that the Magistrate applied to higher authority for permission to depute some one to see this done; but the request was refused.

On the 20th October, the Commissioner reported, that from the 29th May to 14th October, 1862, 18,423 snakes had been killed, giving an average of 110 snakes a day; and he applied for a grant of Rs. 10,000 to provide for the rewards, at the same time proposing to reduce the reward to two annas.

On the 6th January, 1863, the Government of Bengal remarked that whereas from 29th May to 14th October, 18,423 snakes had been killed, and from 15th October to 7th December the number had increased to 26,029, giving an average of 463½ per diem, the Lieutenant-Governor expressed his surprise that the average number of snakes killed daily should have increased during the cold weather, and the Magistrate was requested to submit an explanation on this point. The Magistrate explained it by ascribing it to the increased expertness of the snake-catchers, and the large number of persons who had abandoned their occupation and taken to this comparatively lucrative mode of obtaining a livelihood. It was considered probable that many of these snakes might not have been poisonous, but the Magistrate rejoined that he had exercised great care in discriminating, and that 40,000 rupees would not have paid the rewards had they been given for all kinds of snakes. From this one would conclude that the advantages of Bancoorah as a residence must be doubtful. It gives a sad proof of the fatal character of the bites of the Indian Thanatophidia, and there is reason to believe that the greater share of the mortality is due to the Cobra.

OPHIOPHAGUS.

Ophiophagus elaps.

There is only one species of the genus *Ophiophagus*—viz., *Ophiophagus elaps*; Hamadryad; Native name, "Sunkerchor;" "Ai ráj," in Orissa.

Naja bungarus, *Schlegel.*
„ elaps, *Schlegel.*
„ vittata, *Elliott.*
Hamadryas ophiophagus, *Cantor.*
Trimeresurus ophiophagus, *Dum. and Bibr.*
Hamadryas elaps, *Günther.*

This is probably the largest and most formidable venomous snake known.* It grows to the length of twelve or fourteen feet, and is not only very powerful, but also active and aggressive. It is hooded like the Cobra, and resembles it in its general configuration and characters.

Günther's definition of it is as follows:—"Body rather elongate; tail of proportionate length; head rather short, depressed, scarcely distinct from neck, which is dilatable. Occipitals surrounded by three pairs of large shields, the two anterior of which are temporals. Nostril between two nasals. Loreal none; one or two præ-, three post-oculars. Scales smooth, much imbricate, in transverse rows, in fifteen series round the body, but in many more round the neck; those of the vertebral series are rather larger than the others. Ventrals more than 200; anal entire; anterior sub-caudals simple, posterior two rowed,

* Waterton, in his "Wanderings," mentions a viperine snake (*Crotalidæ*) named *Lachesis mutus*, found in British Guiana, and called by the Dutch the Bushmaster or Curucucu. It inhabits trees, is sometimes fourteen feet in length; is very poisonous, and is perhaps the largest poisonous snake yet discovered. Its coloration is said to be very beautiful.

sometimes all bifid. Maxillary with a large fang in front, which is perforated at the end, showing a longitudinal groove in front; a second, small, simple tooth at some distance behind the fang."

The colour of this snake varies according to age and locality. The adult is some shade of olive green or brown. According to Günther it is:—

"α. Olive green above; the shields of the head, the scales of the neck, hinder part of the body and of the tail edged with black; trunk with numerous oblique, alternate black and white bands converging towards the head; lower parts marbled with blackish, or uniform pale greenish." This variety is found in Bengal, Assam, the Malayan Peninsula, and Southern India.

"β. Brownish olive, uniform anteriorly, with the scales black edged posteriorly; each scale of the tail with a very distinct white, black-edged ocellus, as in *Ptyas mucosus*." This variety is not found in Bengal; Günther says it is found in the Philippine Islands, and perhaps in Burmah.

"γ. Uniform brownish black, scales of the hinder part of the body and of the tail somewhat lighter in the centre; all the lower parts black, except the chin and throat, which are yellow." This variety is found in Borneo.

"Young specimens have a much more varied coloration: they are black, with numerous white, equidistant, narrow cross bands descending obliquely backwards; head with four white cross bands: one occupies the extremity of the snout, the second across the posterior frontals, the third across the crown of the head, behind the orbit; the fourth across the occiput to the angle of the mouth; the two latter bands are composed of oval spots. In a specimen from the Anamallay Mountains the belly is black, and the white bands extend across, being wider than on the back; in a second specimen, of which the locality is unknown, the belly is white, each ventral having a blackish margin."

The young *Ophiophagus* might well be mistaken for a snake of another genus.

Major Beddome says the young *Ophiophagus* is very like the *Dipsas dendrophila*, an innocent snake. The shields surrounding the occipitals are large, and give a distinctive character to the snake. "There is one præ-orbital, 7 upper labials, the third and fourth entering into the orbit, the third the largest, the sixth and seventh very low; temporals large, 2+2; ventrals 215–262; sub-caudals 80–100; the number of entire anterior sub-caudals varies much."

The *Ophiophagus* is probably the largest and most deadly of the Thanatophidia; fortunately, though widely distributed, it is not very common. According to Günther it is found in almost every part of the Indian continent; in the Andaman and Philippine Islands, in Java, Sumatra, Borneo, and according to Duméril, in New Guinea. Major Beddome of Madras says he has killed one nearly fourteen feet in length near Cuttack in Bengal, where it is common. I had a living specimen of the dusky variety from Rangoon, nearly twelve feet in length. It does not appear to be much, if at all, known in the North-West or in Central India; it is most common in the damp climates of Assam, Bengal, Orissa, and Southern India. It has been caught in the Botanical Gardens, near Calcutta, and it is said by the snake-catchers to be not uncommon in the Soonderbunds.

I have heard of an officer being attacked by one in Assam, and being in considerable danger. Dr. Anderson, curator of the Indian Museum, has the dried skin of an individual sent from Assam, that measures 11 feet 9¼ inches in length; a specimen in the Indian Museum, killed in the Botanical Gardens, Calcutta, measures 8 feet 3¾ inches in length and 5⅜ inches in girth. For these measurements I am indebted to Dr. J. Anderson.

The *Ophiophagus*, like many other snakes, takes to the water at times. A friend informs me that he recently shot one in the river near Teryah Ghat, at the foot of the Khasya Hills. He was going slowly up a narrow stream in his boat when he met it coming towards him, with its head raised several inches out of the water. A charge of shot disabled it, and it was captured near the river bank, where it sought refuge. My informant had not the means of preserving the snake, so he cut off its head and made a drawing, which is evidently that of an *Ophiophagus*. It was above nine feet in length.

The Rev. Dr. Mason, in his work on Burmah, gives the following account of the Hamadryad, which is, if not identically the same, merely a variety of the Bengal species:—

"The natives describe a venomous serpent that grows ten or twelve feet long, with a short, blunt head, a dilatable neck, thick trunk, and short tail. It is of a darker colour than the common Cobra, nearly black.

"I have never seen it, but the description given me accords so well with the generic characters of *Hamadryas*, that it must be a species of that genus. 'The *Hamadryas*,' says Dr. Cantor, 'is very fierce, and is always ready not only to attack, but to pursue, when opposed;' this too is a conspicuous trait in our Tenasserim serpent.

"An intelligent Burman told me that a friend of his one day stumbled upon a nest of these serpents, and immediately retreated, but the old female gave chase. The man fled with all speed over hill and dale, dingle and glade, and terror seemed to add wings to his flight, till reaching a small river he plunged in, hoping he had then escaped his fiery enemy; but lo! on reaching the opposite bank up reared the furious Hamadryad, its dilated eyes glistening with rage, ready to bury its fangs in his trembling body. In utter despair he bethought himself of his turban, and in a moment dashed it upon the serpent, which darted upon it like lightning, and for some moments wreaked its vengeance in furious bites; after which it returned quietly to its former haunts. Karens from Pegu describe a species of Hamadryad (the belted Hamadryad) with black and whitish transverse bands. It is often seen twelve feet long by a foot in circumference; and one of my informants tells me he has seen them nearly three fathoms long, and proportionately large. It does not appear to be known in these Provinces, but the Burmese and Karens have well established names for the species; and it must be, I think, Cantor's."

The Bengali name is Sunkerchor, breaker of shells. It is found in the forest and grass jungle; it is said to live in hollow trees, and to climb them readily, being frequently found resting on the branches.

As its name implies, it feeds upon other snakes, though probably when its usual food is not forthcoming, it is contented with birds, mammals, fish, frogs, &c.

It resembles the Cobra, except that it is longer in proportion to its size, and its hood is relatively smaller; it is, however, more graceful in its movements, and turns more rapidly. It is occasionally seen with the snake-charmers, who prize it highly as a show; but they say it is exceedingly dangerous to catch, and difficult to handle before its fangs are removed.

In September, 1868, a living specimen of about eight or nine feet long was brought to me by some snake-men, but its fangs had long been extracted, cicatrices indicating their former presence. It was of a light olive green, with arrow-head shaped transverse bars. It was very much under the control of the snake-man who exhibited it, and sat up, erecting its hood and following the motions of his hand exactly like a Cobra. On two different occasions it ate snakes in my presence, two specimens of *Passerita mycterizans*, that had been killed by a Cobra. The snake man put the head of the *Passerita* into the Hamadryad's mouth, and in about a quarter of an hour it gradually swallowed it; during the process it moved slowly about with the head, neck, and hood dilated, and it looked very odd with the smaller snake hanging out of its mouth. The fangs had been, as I have said, extracted, but on pressing the poison gland, a deep yellow-coloured viscid fluid exuded. I collected a few drops of this and inoculated a drop of it into the thigh of a fowl. The bird sickened and died in about three hours; with much the same symptoms as in poisoning by the Cobra; the blood of the fowl coagulated firmly after death. It would appear from this, that although the snake be deprived of its fangs, the glands still retain the power of secreting poison, but that it was altered in appearance and properties I think very probable.

I have just received a living *Ophiophagus* from Rangoon, nine feet six inches in length.* It is of a light olive colour in front, but dark towards the tail, with the bands as above described. It seems sluggish and indisposed to attack; when roused it hisses, and slightly expands the hood, raising its head some inches from the ground. A living *Passerita mycterizans* was put in the cage, but it has not touched it; a dog was also placed in the cage with it, but it could not be made to strike. In short, it seemed disinclined to be troubled, and as though it wished to be let alone. It is very powerful, and the snake-man seemed disinclined to handle it without other professional aid, as he was alone.†

The dilatable neck is not altogether peculiar to the *Najidæ*. I have recently observed that, in *Compsosoma radiatum*, an innocent snake, the neck and much of the whole body dilates vertically when it is excited and about to strike, presenting a very remarkable appearance, but the power of dilating the neck is better marked in the *Najidæ* than in any other snake. The *Tropidonotus macrophthalmus*, an innocuous colubrine snake, which attains a length of 39 inches according to Günther, and is found in Khasya and Sikkim up to 4000 feet, has this anatomical peculiarity. It is known by its large eye and dilatable neck; the scales, Günther says, "show an arrangement very similar to that of a Cobra, for which it is frequently taken. All the specimens I have seen show unmistakeable signs that their captors considered it best to kill them from a distance, and to inflict a death-wound as near to the head as possible."

T. macrophthalmus is "brown or blackish-brown above, uniform or with a dorsal series of reddish-brown spots; neck with an indistinct arrow-shaped mark. Anterior part of the belly with large quadrangular blackish-brown spots, posterior part and lower side of the tail more or less clouded with brown.

"Young specimens have indistinct square, dark spots on the back, arranged in quincunx, and a bright yellow collar broadly edged with black."

The natives say almost every snake is poisonous, and they give this character to the Lizards as well. The fabulous Biscopra, *Varanus*, is believed to be as deadly as Cleopatra's asp; whilst the Tookai, *Platydactylus*, Gecko of Burmah, has got an equally evil repute among the Burmese, and with as little reason. The fact is, that though some of the Saurians may be able to bite hard, they are all perfectly innocent as to venom. There is no such thing as a Lizard of any kind with a poison gland connected with a fang, and however positively it may be affirmed, it may be as positively denied that any Lizard is venomous.

BUNGARUS.

In this genus there are only two Indian species to be described. They are both common, and one of them, the *Bungarus cæruleus* or "Krait," is probably next to the Cobra the most destructive snake to human life in India, though not actually so venomous as some others. The name is of vernacular origin, "Bungarum Pamah" being the native term for the typical species, *B. fasciatus* on the Coromandel coast.

* I subsequently received another of the dusky variety nearly twelve feet long, and later, one caught near Calcutta, of more than ten feet in length; it was of a lighter colour.

† He did so subsequently without difficulty, making a man hold the tail, whilst he managed the head.

Günther says of this genus, that "All the species occur on the continent of India; they are extremely closely allied to one another, so that it is sometimes difficult to distinguish species from varieties." I only know of two species that occur in the Peninsula of Hindostan, the *B. fasciatus* and *B. cæruleus*, and these are so extremely unlike, that it is impossible to conceive how they could ever be mistaken for each other.

Günther certainly describes two other species: *B. ceylonicus*, which somewhat resembles *B. fasciatus*, and *B. semifasciatus*, which somewhat resembles *B. cæruleus;* but as they are not found in India, the first being Cingalese and the second Chinese, I do not include them in my description. The large black or deep blue and yellow-banded *Bungarus* or Sankni, is to an ordinary observer totally different from the smaller and dark-coloured one, or Krait, however much they may be alike in more essential characters. Another species of some naturalists, "*Bungarus flaviceps*," is placed by Günther in another genus, of which it is the only representative, *Megærophis*. This is placed by some authorities among the Bungarums, and is very nearly allied to them. It is not found in India, but in Borneo, Java, Sumatra, and Penang, where it attains the length of six feet or more.

Günther gives the following general description of the genus *Bungarus:*—

Body rather elongate; tail comparatively short; head more or less dilated, depressed, with broad, rounded muzzle, scarcely distinct from neck, which is not dilatable. Eye small, with round pupil. Rostral shield broader than high, reaching to upper surface of snout; anterior frontals half the size of posterior; vertical five-sided; occipitals tapering behind. Nostril rather wide between two nasals. Loreal none; one præ-, two post-oculars. Seven upper labials, the third and fourth entering the orbit. Scales smooth, moderately imbricate, disposed in oblique rows, forming fifteen longitudinal series round the body; those of the vertebral series are very broad, hexagonal. Ventrals between 200 and 250; anal and sub-caudals entire. Scales without apical groove. Maxillary bone with a fang in front; a second small simple tooth at some distance behind the fang.

The Bungarums are diurnal terrestrial snakes, but like others, they generally prefer the shade to the sunshine. They are found in the open country, in grass and low jungle, and in fields. They live in holes in the ground, sometimes down among the roots of trees at a considerable depth. They are not frequently seen in inhabited places, though they do at times find their way into native huts and houses. I killed a very large one in Rangoon many years ago, that got into a hut full of dhoolie-bearers at the field hospital during the last Burmese war. They feed on small animals, snakes, frogs, toads, lizards, and they are very poisonous; but owing to the shortness of the fang, which is much smaller than that of the Cobra, their bite is less dangerous, and excision being more practicable, treatment may be useful and recoveries more numerous. Bites from the *B. fasciatus* are comparatively rare; those of the Krait, *B. cæruleus*, are very common, and the police returns show a large mortality among the rural population therefrom.

The *Bungarus* is not particularly aggressive, and tries to escape when discovered, but if attacked it retaliates fiercely, and its bite is very dangerous. The *B. fasciatus* lies coiled in curves, and when disturbed jerks itself out like a spring, but without extending its whole length of body.

Bungarus fasciatus.

The first species to be described is the *Bungarus fasciatus*, or "Sankni," "Bungarum Pamah" according to Russell of the Cormandel coast, "Rajsamp" of some natives.

Bungarus annularis, *Schleg.; Daud.*
„ fasciatus, *Cantor*.
Pseudoboa fasciata, *Schneid.*

This *Bungarus* grows to a great size. Günther says four feet, but it has been found over six feet. I killed one in Rangoon many years ago over five feet in length. Mason says it grows to six or eight feet. A specimen now in the Indian Museum is 58$\frac{3}{8}$ inches long, 4$\frac{3}{8}$ inches in circumference. It is very remarkable in its coloration, being composed of a series of black or steel blue and bright gamboge yellow rings. There is a peculiar metallic lustre on the skin which is very beautiful. Its tongue is flesh coloured; lips and throat gamboge coloured.

The *Bungarus fasciatus* is tolerably common in Bengal and in Southern India, as well as Burmah, and it is also known in the north-west, where it is sometimes called "Koclia Krait." Its bite is very dangerous, but the police returns do not show that it causes many deaths; probably because it is not so much in the way of being met with as the Cobra or Krait. Its fangs are relatively to those of the Cobra very small, and its bite in dogs causes death much slower than the Cobra's bite. It is much less valued by the snake-men than the Cobra, as it does not erect its head, nor is it amenable to their tuition. Dogs bitten by *B. fasciatus* died at various periods from four hours twenty-eight minutes to ten days.

Dr. P. Russell has figured this snake in his great work on Indian serpents, and in describing it he notices what is very striking, the trigonal shape of its body, the sharp dorsal ridge and declining sides. Günther's definition of it is as follows:—"The first temporal shield is scarcely longer than high. Ventrals 200–233; sub-caudals 32–36. Body with alternate broad black and yellowish rings, extending across the belly; there are from twenty-five to thirty-three of these black rings round the trunk; the first is the broadest, and produced into a triangular process, the point of which rests on the vertical shield. Head black anteriorly and on the sides, separated from the triangular process by a yellow V-like mark. Lower parts and throat uniform yellow." The hexagonal vertebral shields and the hard blunt and almost bony end of the tail, with which some natives think the snake can sting, are very characteristic.

Bungarus cæruleus.

This is the Krait* of India, and next to the Cobra is the snake most destructive to human life. It is figured by Russell in his great work, and is called by him "Gedi Paragoodoo." It is called "Dhomun Chiti" in some parts of Bengal. It has a variety of synonyms:—

Pseudoboa cærulea, *Schneider*.
Boa Krait, *Williams*.
Boa lineata, *Shaw*.
Bungarus cæruleus, *Daud*.
,, lividus, *Cantor*.
,, candidus, *Cantor*
,, arcuatus, *Dum. and Bib*.
,, lineatus, *Günther*.

This snake is described by Günther as follows:—"The first temporal shield is considerably longer than high. Ventrals 201–221; sub-caudals 38–56. Lower parts uniform white; upper parts bluish or brownish-black, uniform, or with more or less numerous, very narrow white cross streaks, not quite as broad as a scale, and generally radiating from a white vertebral spot. No collar." I would add that the lower part, the ventral surface, is sometimes, as in a specimen from the Indian Museum, Calcutta, now before me, of a dark livid colour, or of a yellow tinge, and that the light-coloured bands are broader than a scale uniting with the general light colour of the ventral surface.

Günther describes three varieties:—

"*α*. Upper parts uniform blackish-brown: *B. lividus*, Cantor, from Assam. In young specimens the head is white, with a black line between the occipitals.

"*β*. A vertebral series of equidistant small white spots, from which narrow transverse streaks proceed."

"*γ*. Upper parts with narrow white streaks arranged in pairs: *B. arcuatus, Dum. and Bib.*"

The coloration of the dark parts varies from a deep, almost steel blue black to a chocolate brown. Tongue white. Iris black. This species of *Bungarus* is common all over India; it seems to be more destructive to life in the Upper Provinces than in Lower Bengal. The fangs are much smaller than those of the Cobra, and its poison is not so rapid in its action, which circumstance, with the comparative smallness of the wound, gives greater hope of cure, but it is, as I have said, very dangerous and destructive, as shown by the police returns.

It grows to a considerable size: the one before me from the Indian Museum, measures 47$\frac{3}{8}$ inches in length, and 2$\frac{5}{8}$ in circumference.* Dr. P. Russell gives 29 inches as the length, but it certainly attains a much larger size than this. Günther says 54 inches. The trunk is of nearly equal thickness from the neck to within four or five inches of the tail. The scales in the dorsal ridge are large and hexagonal. Dr. Russell says that this snake was sent to him from Masulipatam, under the name of "Cobra Monil." Günther says that Europeans in the peninsula of India give the same name Cobra Monil to the *Daboia russellii* or "Tic-polonga."

The Krait seems to be common all over India. I am not aware if it be found in the Himalaya. It is found in the fields, grassy plains, rice khets, low scrubby jungle, and among débris of wood or buildings. It sometimes insinuates itself into houses in the verandah, bath-rooms, on the ledges of doors or jhilmils, into bookcases, cupboards, &c., and in such situations it is not unfrequently the cause of fatal accident. I know of an instance where, after a night's dâk in a palanquin, a lady, in taking out her things on arriving at her destination, found a Krait coiled up under her pillow; it had been her travelling companion all night.

The Krait may be mistaken for *Lycodon aulicus*,† an innocent snake, the colouring and general appearance being in many cases very similar. The least examination of the mouth would detect the difference, but at first sight they are much alike, and are often mistaken, the *Lycodon* suffering for its resemblance to its poisonous fac-simile.

XENURELAPS.

Xenurelaps bungaroides.

There is only one species as yet known of the genus *Xenurelaps*, and Günther says there is only one specimen of it preserved, and that is in the Museum of the University of Oxford. It is 15$\frac{7}{8}$ inches long, the tail measuring 1$\frac{7}{8}$ of an inch. This specimen came from Chirra Punji in the Khasya Hills: the only habitat given by Günther.

It is very closely allied to and resembles a *Bungarus*. Günther gives the following definitions of the genus:—

"Body sub-cylindrical, long and slender; belly rounded; head short, sub-triangular, with rounded snout, not distinct from neck, which is not dilatable; tail short. The shields of the head normal, but the loreal is absent. Nostril lateral, between two shields; eye small, with round pupil; one præ-, two post-oculars. Scales smooth, not much imbricate, in fifteen rows; those of the vertebral series enlarged, hexagonal. Anal entire; sub-caudals bifid. Maxillary with a grooved fang in front, and with a small smooth tooth behind."

---

* *Note by Major MacMahon, Deputy Commissioner of Delhi, on the origin of the name Karait or Krait.*—"Kálgundait is the proper Urdu name for the *Bungarus cæruleus*. Krait is, I presume, merely an English corruption of the Urdu word Kálgundait. If not it must be a Bengali corruption of it, as no native of Delhi would understand you if you spoke of the Karait or Krait. I presume Kál means death, or perhaps Kála, black. However, it is the common word used in a figurative sense for famine.

"Kála gundedar, a black snake spotted."

* I have since received a living specimen from Delhi, 49 inches in length.

† The *Lycodon aulicus* is not so dark coloured as the Krait.

The single known species is—

Xenurelaps bungaroides, *Günther*.

Elaps bungaroides, *Cantor*.

Günther's definition of the species is "very similar in general habit to a *Bungarus*. Shields of the upper surface of the head normal, the occipitals somewhat tapering behind. Rostral as broad as high. Nostril open, round. Loreal none, the præorbital being in immediate contact with the post-nasal. Two post-oculars; seven upper labials, the third and fourth entering the orbit. Temporals 1 + 2 + 3, the anterior in contact with both post-oculars. Six lower labials; two pairs of short chin-shields, the anterior in contact with three lower labials. Scales in fifteen series, those of the vertebral series enlarged, hexagonal. Ventrals 237; and entire; sub-caudals 46. Upper parts black, with narrow white, angular, transverse lines, the angle of which is pointed forwards; these lines are more distinct in front than behind; there are about forty-eight on the trunk. The lower part of the rostral shield white; a white line across the snout, before the eyes; two interrupted, divergent white lines commence on the vertical shield, each descending to the side of the neck; another band descends from behind the eye to the fifth and sixth labial. Lower parts whitish, with irregular blackish cross bands."

In the Proceedings of the Asiatic Society of Bengal, No. iii., March, 1870, page 82, Mr. Jerdon says, he has obtained "a single specimen of the very rare *Xenurelaps bungaroides*, of which only one specimen is known, the type specimen in the Museum at Oxford." Jerdon describes his specimen thus:—"It is 15 inches long, of which the tail is 2½. It has 224 ventral scutæ, and 44 sub-caudals, and 13 to 15 rows of scales on the body. It only differs from Günther's description by having one white intercepted line commencing on the vertical, and extending to the throat on each side. When alive the colour of the body was a deep rich madder-brown, and the bands were yellow, paling posteriorly. The chin and throat are whitish, which passes into red, gradually deepening on the posterior part of the body and tail, and there are numerous oblong black marks on the abdominal and sub-caudal centres."

I have been unable to collect any information about this snake; it is not in the Indian Museum.

Dr. Cantor describes it as "black blue above, with white arrow-shaped stripes; beneath alternately white and black blue."

It is called *Elaps bungaroides* from its resemblance to *B. cæruleus* or the Krait.

In habits and properties, as in appearance, it most probably resembles the *B. cæruleus*. Information being much needed about the snake; it is to be hoped that naturalists on the frontiers will endeavour to procure specimens and such information as to its habits, as will throw light on the subject.

CALLOPHIS.

This genus has several species in India; they are all venomous, though from the shortness of the fangs, and as they are generally of small size, it is probable that a fatal result would not be produced by their bite in man. The poison is virulent, nevertheless, and fowls bitten by some of the species succumbed in from one to three hours. The known Indian species are:—

Callophis intestinalis.	Callophis trimaculatus.
,, macclellandii.	,, nigrescens.
,, annularis.	,, cerasinus.

They are all more or less distinguished by the presence of a bright colour on the more sombre hue of the general surface of the body.

They are sluggish, apparently defective both in sight and hearing, for they allow themselves to be approached with little sign of fear. They are not aggressive, and bite reluctantly, but if irritated, they can be made to bite, and, as I have said, the poison proves fatal to fowls.

They are ground snakes, and are slow in their movements. They seem to prefer hilly to level country, and they live chiefly on snakes. Günther says, the *Calamariæ*, an innocent family, which they much resemble in appearance, are their principal food.

Günther's description of them is as follows:—"Body subcylindrical, very long and slender; belly rounded; head short, obtuse, with broad snout, not distinct from neck, which is not dilatable; tail, short. The shields of the head normal, but the loreal is absent. Nostril wide, lateral, between two shields; eye small, with round pupil; one præ-, two post-oculars; temporals in a single longitudinal series. Six, seven, or eight upper labials, the third and fourth entering the orbit. Scales smooth, not much imbricate, in thirteen rows, those of the vertebral series not enlarged. Sub-caudals bifid. Maxillary with a grooved fang in front, without other teeth behind.

"The *Callophides* are very similar to one another: their body is cylindrical, of nearly the same width throughout, and much elongate, the number of ventral shields almost always exceeding 200. The head is of moderate length, slightly depressed, not distinct from neck, with broad rounded snout. The nostril is lateral, rather narrow, situated between two shields; eye small, with round pupil. Cleft of the mouth of moderate width, not much extensible. The shields on the upper side of the head normal, the occipitals generally somewhat elongate. Loreal absent; the single præ-ocular forms a short suture with the hinder nasal; it extends on to the upper surface of the head, but does not reach the vertical, which is comparatively narrow. Two post-oculars, in contact with the single anterior temporal. The number of upper labials does not exceed eight, generally there are less than eight, the third and fourth entering the orbit. Scales invariably in thirteen rows, smooth, polished, not much imbricate. Tail short, tapering, with bifid sub-caudals."

CALLOPHIS INTESTINALIS.

This species is found in Central India (Malwah) according to Günther. The only specimen in the Indian Museum in Calcutta is one marked from Singapore, under the synonym of *Elaps fasciata*, Cantor. The Proceedings of the Zoological Society, part 7, 1839, p. 34, gives the following description of it:—"Pale reddish-brown above, with a bright yellow dorsal line, with black serrated margins; in the tail three black bands; the abdominal surface whitish yellow, enclosed on each side by a black line." Habitat, Singapore. Its synonyms are:—

Elaps furcatus, *Schlegel; Schneider*.

Aspis intestinalis, *Laur. Syn. Amphib.*

Maticora lineata, *Gray*.

Elaps intestinalis, *Cantor*.

Callophis intestinalis, *Günther*.

Günther describes the Malwah variety as follows, the description somewhat differs from that given by Cantor:—

"Head light brown above, yellowish below, spotted with black on the sides; a vermilion, black-edged band runs from the occiput to the tip of the tail; a buff-coloured band, with an upper and lower black border, runs along the joining edges of the two outer series of scales; the upper black border is as broad as the stripe of reddish-grey ground-colour on the side of the back. Belly with alternate pale citrine and black cross bands, the latter colour occupying three or four ventral shields together, whilst the former rarely occupies more than two; tail with three black rings, which, however, are sometimes absent.

"Upper labials 6; ventral shields 223–271; sub-caudals 24–26."

"It attains to a length of 2 feet, the tail measuring 1½ inch."

"At a meeting of the Asiatic Society on the 6th April, 1870, Dr. Stoliczka exhibited a specimen of the rare *Callophis intestinalis* obtained from Upper Burmah. The species has the poison glands extending from the head to about one-third of the total length of the body, lying free in the cavity of the anterior part, and causing the heart to be much further removed backward than is generally the case in other species of snakes.—*Pro. Asiatic Soc.*, April, 1870.

Callophis macclellandii.

Elaps macclellandii, *Reinh. Cal. Journal Nat. Hist.*, 1844.
" personatus, *Blyth, Journ. Asiat. Soc. Beng.*, 1855.
" univirgatus, *Günther's Colubrine Snakes.*
Callophis univirgata, *Günther, Proc. Zool. Soc.*, 1859.
" macclellandii, *Günther, Proc. Zool. Soc.*, 1861.

Günther's description of the species generally is as follows :—

"Upper labials seven ; temporals small, 1+1+1 ; anal bifid.

"Head and neck black above, with a yellow cross band behind the eyes. Body and tail reddish-brown, generally with a black vertebral line from the nape to the tip of the tail. Belly yellowish, with black cross bands or quadrangular black spots."

Günther describes three varieties of this snake :—

"α. Belly with uninterrupted black cross bands, alternately limited to the belly, or extending up the sides of the body, so as to cover scales of the four outer rows and give the appearance of a lateral series of large black spots. The three last cross bands of the trunk form complete rings crossing the vertebral line ; tail with three other black rings. This specimen is 26¼ inches long, tail 2½ inches. Ventrals 218 ; sub-caudals 28.

"β. Belly with quadrangular black spots rather irregularly disposed, and not extending up the sides. Tail without black rings. This specimen is 18 inches long, tail 1½ inch. Ventrals 224 ; sub-caudals 25.

"γ. The cross bands reach entirely across the back, forming rings, from twenty-two to twenty-eight in number ; no black vertebral line, which, however, is indicated by isolated small spots. Ventrals 196–218 ; sub-caudals 27–34. Varieties α and β are from Nepal and Darjeeling ; γ from Assam."

There is a good specimen of this snake in the Indian Museum, but it has been bleached by the action of the spirit ; it is from Assam. Museum No. 123.

Callophis annularis.

Günther says of it :—"Head and neck black above, with a broad yellow cross band behind the eyes. Body and tail reddish-brown, without longitudinal band, but with forty narrow, equidistant, black, white-edged rings ; each of them is about as broad as a scale on the back (those round the tail being broader), and occupies one ventral shield on the belly. Belly yellowish, with a black cross band in the middle between the rings ; each of these cross bands occupies a ventral shield, so that about every third ventral is black.

"Upper labials six ; temporals small, 1+1+1 : the first very narrow, the third the largest. Ventrals 208 ; anal bifid ; sub-caudals 33."

Günther adds :—"I have examined only one specimen of this species, remarkable on account of its singular coloration. It is marked 'India,' and is 19 inches long, the tail measuring 2 inches."

Callophis trimaculatus.

Vipera trimaculata, *Daud. Rept.*
Elaps trimaculatus, *Merr. Tent.*
Coluber melanurus, *Shaw, Zool.*
Callophis trimaculatus, *Günther, Proc. Zool. Soc.*, 1859.

Günther thus describes this species :—

"Light bay above : an indistinct line formed by minute brown dots, along each series of scales. The upper side of the head, the neck, and a spot below the eye black ; snout with some irregular small yellow spots ; a yellow spot on each temporal shield ; a sub-triangular yellow spot on the middle of the neck ; the black of the neck edged with yellow behind. Tail marbled with black below, and with two black rings, each of which is variegated with yellow. Belly uniform white (red during life).

"Upper labials six; temporals elongate, 1+1, equal in size. Ventrals 258–274 ; anal bifid ; sub-caudals 35."

Russell has figured this snake in his Indian Serpents, figure viii. vol. i. Günther says he has received one from Bengal agreeing with Russell's typical specimen. The snake is very small, being only 12 inches long, tail measuring ⅞ inch.

There are specimens in the Indian Museum described as *Elaps melanurus*, Cantor, from Rangoon. These were presented by Dr. Fayrer in the year 1853. They are bleached and altered in colour by the action of the spirit. Museum No. 124.

Callophis nigrescens.

Callophis nigrescens, *Günther.*
" concinnus, *Beddome.*
" malabaricus, *Jerdon ; Beddome.*

Günther's description is as follows :—

"Upper parts dark blackish ash, or black, the lower uniform red. Upper part of the head symmetrically marbled with black ; a black spot below the eye ; another descends from the occipital to the angle of the mouth ; a black horseshoe-like collar, with the convexity directed forwards ; a narrow black vertebral line slightly edged with yellowish runs from the collar to the tip of the tail ; a series of small ovate black spots, indistinctly edged with whitish, along each side of the trunk, disappearing posteriorly ; tail coloured like body, without black rings. In old examples the black dorsal stripe and the black lateral spots disappear, and only the whitish edges of the latter remain, forming indistinct longitudinal lines.

"Vertical shield elongate. Upper labials seven ; temporals 1+1, the anterior twice the size of the posterior. Ventrals 232–247 ; anal entire, in one specimen bifid ; sub-caudals 33–42.

"I have examined three specimens of this species, one of which was sent by Captain R. H. Beddome from the Nilgherries ; the largest is 4 feet long, the tail measuring 5 inches."

Callophis cerasinus.

Major Beddome describes a species obtained from the Wynaad, Malabar forests, at an elevation of 3000 feet.

"Rostral slightly produced back between the anterior frontals ; anterior frontals only half the size of the posterior, the latter touch the orbit ; no loreal and no ante-ocular ; nostril between two nasals ; seven upper labials, third, fourth, and fifth very high ; third and fourth enter the orbit ; one small post-ocular ; vertical six-sided elongated, pointed behind ; supraciliary small ; occipitals large, elongated, pointed behind, with a pair of large temporals on each side ; anal entire ; back purplish-brown, with a shining nacreous lustre, with transverse broad irregular-shaped black bands extending to the top of the tail (about 40) at nearly equal distances, and which are continued (though not broad) underneath the belly and tail, but do not quite meet; sides (2 or 2½ of lowest row of scales) and belly of a bright cherry colour ; head black in front, neck with the fifth, sixth, and seventh labials, and a portion of the occipitals cherry-coloured; length 21½ inches, of which the tail is 2 inches ; circumference 1⅓ inch ; sub-caudals 13 ; abdominals 228."

OPHIDII VIPERIFORMES.

This sub-order has two families: the *Viperidæ* or Vipers, the *Crotalidæ* or Pit-Vipers.

I shall pass on to the description of the Indian forms of this sub-order, to complete that of the terrestrial poisonous snakes, leaving the *Hydrophidæ* or pelagic Thanatophidia for subsequent consideration. The *Ophidii Viperiformes* or viperine, differ essentially from the colubrine snakes. The maxillary bone is very short, and bears only one tooth, the long scimitar-like poison fang. A description of it has already been given.

The head is generally broad, triangular, and covered with small scales instead of shields (there are exceptions, as *Peltopelor macrolepis*.) The body is short and robust, and the tail is sharp. The scales are frequently carinated. Some of the Indian forms are arboreal, and all are venomous. The broad triangular head generally without shields, the long moveable fang, and the comparatively short and robust body distinguish the viperine from the colubrine snakes. A deep pit in the loreal region between the eye and the nostril is characteristic of the *Crotalidæ*.

The family of *Viperidæ* is represented in India by one of its most formidable genera, *Daboia*.

The family of *Crotalidæ* is represented by *Trimeresurus, Hypnale*, and others; but they fall far short of their congeners in the New World, where the *Crotalus horridus* and *Craspedocephalus braziliensis* are almost, if not quite, as deadly as the *Ophiopagus, Naja*, and *Daboia* of India.

The *Calloselasma*, the single species of a genus of the *Crotalidæ* of the same name, is represented as attaining to the length of three feet, and being very deadly. Günther says, "Kuhl was eye-witness of a case where two men, bitten by one and the same snake, expired five minutes after." But this snake is an inhabitant of Java and Siam, and is not, that I am aware of, found in India. I allude to it merely to show that there is at least one deadly form of Asiatic *Crotalus*. The Indian species are mostly arboreal, and though venomous, are much less dangerous and fatal than the venomous colubrine or viperine snakes, but deaths from their bite have been recorded.

The *Crotalidæ* of America are remarkable by a peculiar series of horny scales or rings at the tip of the tail, which make a rustling or rattling sound when the snake is agitated, and hence the name "rattlesnake." The only rudiment of this rattle in the Indian *Crotalidæ* is found in the genus *Halys*, where the tail terminates in a horny point or scale. The viperine snakes are as a rule viviparous. Dr. Anderson, of the Indian Museum, informs me that he has taken as many as forty young ones out of a *Daboia russellii*.

I have heard it stated that the *Trimeresuri* are oviparous, perhaps ovo-viviparous, but I have no personal knowledge that such is the case.

VIPERIDÆ.

I describe the *Viperidæ* or Vipers first, for although represented by only two species, yet one, the *Daboia*, so far surpasses any of the Indian *Crotalidæ* in death-dealing power, that, as Thanatophidia, they are entitled to precedence.

Günther gives the following general description of the family:—

"Body robust; tail rather short, not prehensile; head broad or thick, generally scaly above, or incompletely shielded; no pit in the loreal region; eye of moderate size, with vertical pupil.* Viviparous."

* *Daboia russellii* has a round pupil.—Cope, Philadelphia. I have myself recently examined the *Daboia's* pupil in different lights. It is not round, but oval, and when exposed to a strong light, it contracts to a vertical slit. The iris is yellow, but across it there is a dark brown streak which aids in giving the appearance of roundness to the pupil when dilated.

A Pupil dilated in shade.

A

B ,, in moderate light.

B

C ,, in strong light.

C

The Vipers are terrestrial snakes. British India produces only two forms, the *Daboia* and *Echis*, whilst the *Crotalidæ* are represented by a variety of *Trimeresuri, Peltopelor, Halys*, and *Hypnale*. Other formidable representatives of the *Viperidæ* are found in Africa and Australia.

DABOIA.

Daboia russellii.

There is only one species of the genus *Daboia*:—

Daboia russellii or Tic-polonga, *Günther*.
Tic-polonga, *Davy*.
Coluber russellii, *Shaw*.
Vipera elegans, *Daud*.
,, daboia, *Daud*.
Daboia elegans, *Gray*.
,, pulchella, *Gray*.
,, russellii, *Gray*.

Günther gives the following description of the *Daboia*, which corresponds with those I have examined and experimented with:

"Greyish" (light chocolate colour) "brown, with three series of large black, white-edged rings, those of the middle series ovate, those of the outer circular; sometimes very small black, white-edged ocelli are scattered between the rings. A yellow line on each side of the upper surface of the head, the two lines convergent on the snout. Rostral and labial shields yellow with brown margins; a sub-triangular brown, black-edged spot below the eye. Belly uniform yellowish or marbled with brownish; generally more or less numerous semicircular brown spots on the hinder margins of the ventral shields. Ventrals 163–170; sub-caudals 45–60."

I would remark on this, that the specimens I have examined vary a good deal in the form and arrangement of the rings and spots and of the coloured patches on the head, but the description well denotes their general appearance. The *Daboia* or Russell's Viper, is called by the natives about Calcutta "Uloo Bora," from the uloo grass in which it is often found. In Bengal it is called "Jessur," "Siah-chunder Amaiter." It is common in Bengal, and is frequently caught in the Botanic Gardens near Calcutta. It is common in the south of India, Ceylon, and Burmah. Günther says it is known to Europeans in India as the "Cobra monil," Beaded snake, or Chain Viper. I do not know whether it is found in Central India,* the North-Western, Central Provinces, and Punjab; if so, it is less common than in the south.

It is the "Tic-polonga" of Ceylon, and is justly dreaded there as a very deadly snake. Dr. Russell describes it in his work on Indian snakes, under the name of "Katuka Rekula Poda." He says it is doubtful whether it is not as venomous as the Cobra. My experiments incline me to agree with Dr. Russell, and to give it, at all events, a place next to the Cobra. Fowls bitten by this snake expired in from thirty-five seconds to several minutes; dogs, in from seven minutes to several hours; a cat in fifty-seven minutes; a horse in eleven and a half hours. Death was not in any case so rapid as after the Cobra bite, but though slower in its action, the poison seemed just as deadly. The blood remains fluid after death from the poison of the *Daboia,* whereas after Cobra poisoning it coagulates firmly on being removed from the heart and great vessels. The *Daboia* is nocturnal in its habits; in confinement it is sluggish, and does not readily strike, unless roused and irritated, when it bites with great force and determination. When disturbed it hisses fiercely, and when it strikes, does so with great vigour. Its long moveable fangs are very prominent objects, and with them it is capable of inflicting a very deep as well as poisoned wound. The markings on its body are very beautiful, and justify the synonym *V. elegans*. It lives on small animals, such as rats, mice, and frogs. My snake-man says it will go into water. It is, however, terrestrial in its habits;† its loud hissing when disturbed is calculated to warn those who come within its dangerous proximity. Though so deadly, it does not appear by the returns to cause many deaths, but this may be owing to the fact that the natives seldom know, often do not see, the snake that has inflicted the fatal wound. It is much less known, and its misdeeds are therefore doubtless often ascribed to the Cobra. In the official returns of deaths from snake bites, a large number are attributed to snakes unknown. If the real offender could be detected, it is probable that the *Daboia* would have a more prominent place than it occupies at present.

It is apparently a hardy reptile. I had one about forty-four inches in length, which lived for a whole year without food or water; it obstinately refused either, and was vigorous and venomous to the last. It died suddenly at the School of Art, where it had been sent to be figured.

I have heard, I know not how far it may be true, that it often kills cattle, biting them when grazing. It attains to the length of 50 inches, probably more, but I have seen none of greater length. A specimen now before me is 44 inches long and 4½ in circumference. The hill specimens are smaller.

* Mr. W. T. Blanford says it is found in Central India.—*Proc. As. Soc. Bengal,* August, 1870, p. 257. It is probably found all over the plains of India, as well as in the hills. It has been found in the Himalaya, as high as 5000 feet in Kulu, in Cashmir up to 6000 feet; but it is more common at from 2000 to 4000 feet. Stoliczka says it is found in sunny places.

† Tennent says that it climbs trees in Ceylon.—*Nat. History of Ceylon,* p. 305.

ECHIS.

ECHIS CARINATA.

The genus *Echis* contains only one Indian species, *Echis carinata*. The native name is "Afäe" in Delhi; it is unknown to the natives in the neighbourhood of Calcutta.

Pseudoboa carinata, *Schneid.*
Echis carinata, *Merr. Tent.*

Dr. Russell has described and figured this Viper in his great work on Serpents as "Horatta Pam," vol. i. pl. 2.

It is much smaller than the *Daboia;* it is venomous, but Günther says its bite is not known to have proved fatal. This I think is very doubtful; one in my possession killed a fowl in four minutes, another in two minutes, and a dog in about four hours.* I have received some very fine living specimens from Delhi 20 to 23 inches long. The *Echis* is a terrestrial

* Extracts from the Report of Dr. Imlach, Civil Surgeon at Shikarpore, dated 14th February, 1855, addressed to the Superintending Surgeon, Sind, on the snake season of 1854.—*Transactions of Medical and Physical Society of Bombay,* No. III., new series, 1855-56, p. 80.

"Six months may be regarded on the average as the period during which snakes wander about, commencing from about the earlier part of May, and continuing until towards the latter part of October, or according as the cold season may set in, sooner or later.

The number of cases reported have amounted to 306; the mortality among this number to 63; giving a percentage of fatal cases of 20·58: not a very great proportion after all, considering the next to nothing remedial measures usually adopted by the gentle Sindians.

From among the 306 cases of snake-bite, 262 occurred in males, the remainder 44 having been in the instance of females: and the comparative mortality of males and females being respectively 53 and 10: giving the relative percentage mortality among males as 20·21, whilst on the part of females there is a slight increase, the proportion amounting to 22·72.

The small number of cases occurring amongst females (and of these only 10 fatal cases for the season) shows that the natives of this Collectorate [Upper Sind] have not resorted to 'mortality from snake-bite,' as a means of accounting for any murderous deeds: a practice which might have been supposed to exist among a class of people who, till within the past few years, had a sort of acknowledged claim to the lives of their female relations when caught in the act of, or suspected of fleshly weakness, and when of course it would have been their aim, as a matter of attempted self-protection, to have given forth as fair a reason for death as possible.

The Kuppur, which I take to be the *Scytab bysonata,* and which to me appears simply to differ from the West Indian snake of that name in regard to colour, is without exception the most deadly poisonous snake in Sind; and a reference to the police returns shows that in by far the greatest majority of cases, serious injury and death have been caused from the bite of this species.

It frequently is 23 inches long. Fifteen inches may be regarded as about the average length of the Kuppur; the larger, and I imagine older specimens, have but little exceeded in this, but their diameter has by about double exceeded that of the ordinary size of the reptile, which measures somewhere from about 2 to 2¼ inches round the largest part of the body.

The head, covered with very small scales, is of a flat irregular hexagonal shape, the greatest length of side being from the point where the mouth ends backward. I much regret that it is not in my power to send a painting of the reptile. The extreme ferocity of expression, if one may use the term, is, I think, peculiar to the Kuppur. Compared with the head and body, the neck is comparatively small, the actual tail portion fines off somewhat abruptly, and barely exceeds an inch and a half in length, and is remarkably small compared to the circumference of the actual body. The marks on the head probably aid towards adding to an evil expression, but still, noting the general habits, you cannot help seeing that the brilliant eye indicates a vicious inclination, and even, however long you may leave the Kuppur unmolested, still you always find his crest erect and his head fixedly in the direction of the party who may be watching him, ready for the defensive. Opportunity having been frequent, I have over and over again watched his remaining for long in one position, and even when the Kuppur thinks fit to avoid his opponent, still the change of position is caused by a peculiar sliding movement backwards, the head invariably being directed towards his enemy.

The marks on the head, or rather what may be termed the forehead of the Kuppur, exhibit in white and brown, somewhat the appearance of a cross; the ground mark of the body is of a dull muddy grey colour, the sides of the body being marked along with crescentic double marks of black and white, the concavity of each being towards the abdomen.

In several specimens of this snake I have observed double or rather two fangs on each side of the jaw, but I omitted to make special note as to whether this is of common or unusual occurrence.

The poison of this snake introduced into the system of the fowl induces death in about three quarters of a minute.

Death in a fowl occurs much in the same way as in the human subject; the mucous membrane is powerfully acted on, the head gradually droops, the legs give way, and the creature rolls on its side in the last agony of passing life."

The "Kuppur" I think must be the *Echis carinata,* as the description corresponds with that of this Viper; and this would show that it is more dangerous than Günther supposes, and corresponds with the opinion expressed by Major MacMahon, Deputy Commissioner of Delhi, who says it has the repute of being a deadly snake.

snake, and is viviparous; it lives, according to Günther, on *Scolopendræ*, for he says he has found only these in its stomach.

The *Echis* is very fierce and aggressive—it is always on the defensive—ready to attack; it throws itself into a double coil, the folds of which are in perpetual motion, and as they rub against each other, they make a loud rustling sound very like hissing. This sound is produced by the three or four outer rows of carinated scales, which are very prominent and point downwards at a different angle to the rest; their friction against each other causes the sound. This little Viper does not, I think, hiss at all. Its fangs are very long and mobile, like those of *Daboia*. Its eye has a peculiarly vicious appearance.

I have never seen it in Bengal, nor am I certain that it is found there; but it is common in the North-West Provinces, Central Provinces, and Punjab, and generally in the South of India. Günther says, "it is common in many parts of the Peninsula of India—in the Anamallay Mountains, in the Carnatic, and the vicinity of Madras."

It is a small Viper; a specimen from the Indian Museum is 22½ inches in length, and about 3 in circumference, though no doubt it has somewhat shrunk by the action of the spirit.

The generic description, according to Günther, is as follows:—

"Head covered with keeled scales: a pair of very small frontals behind the rostral shield. Nostril small, round, directed upwards, situated in a large nasal shield, which is subdivided behind the nostril. Sides of the head covered with keeled scales, two series of which are between the eye and the low upper labials. Scales much imbricate, strongly keeled, in from twenty-five to twenty-nine series, those in the lateral series have their tips directed obliquely downwards." With these they make the rustling sound. "Sub-caudals one-rowed."

It is very active, and can dart a considerable distance—a foot or more—to strike its prey: it is by far the most active and aggressive poisonous snake I have seen. It is called about Delhi, "Afäe" or "Afäi," an Arabic word, and vulgarly pronounced "Hafaé" by the uneducated natives.

The specific description of *Echis carinata* given by Günther is as follows:—"Brown or brownish-grey, with a series of sub-quadrangular or ovate whitish spots, edged with blackish-brown; a sub-semicircular whitish band on each side of each of the dorsal spots, enclosing a round dark-brown lateral spot. A pair of oblong brown, black-edged spots on the crown of the head, convergent anteriorly; a brown spot below, and an oblique broad streak behind the eye. Belly whitish, with more or less numerous round brown specks. Ventrals 149–154; sub-caudals 21–26."

This definition accurately describes the individuals before me, a specimen from the Indian Museum, and also living specimens from Delhi, for which I am indebted to Major MacMahon, the Deputy Commissioner of that district.

CROTALIDÆ.

THE family of *Crotalidæ* or Pit-Vipers has several genera in British India. I have before observed that they are not so dangerous as their American congeners, though all are venomous.* They are distinguished, as has been already stated, by the pit or depression between the eye and the nostrils in the loreal region; the triangular broad head and the short thick body. The *Halys* is the only Indian genus or species that has any vestige of the caudal appendage which has given to some of the American *Crotalidæ* the name Rattlesnake; and in this species it is reduced to a simple horny spine at the end of the tail.

Many of the Indian *Crotalidæ* are arboreal snakes, and in colour resemble the foliage or branches of the trees in which they live.

The *Crotalidæ* are considered by naturalists generally, I believe, to be viviparous, but I have recently been informed that Mr. Nicholson of Rangoon says that the *Trimeresuri* are oviparous, and that eggs have been removed by him from the body containing no appearance of an embryo; which would imply that the eggs would be laid, and the young developed like those of the colubrine snakes.

It is probable that they are ovo-viviparous, and the question of the liberation of the young from the egg before or after its extrusion from the oviduct, is not one of great physiological importance, though interesting enough as a fact in the natural history of the individual genus or species. The generic distinctions of the *Crotalidæ* are described by Günther as follows:—

"Body robust; tail of moderate length or rather short, sometimes prehensile; head broad, sub-triangular, frequently scaly above or imperfectly shielded; a deep pit" (the use of which is not known), "on the side of the snout, between the eye and nostril; eye of moderate size, with vertical pupil. Viviparous."

There are several Indian genera:—

Trimeresurus	T. gramineus.
	T. erythrurus.
	T. carinatus.
	T. anamallensis.
	T. monticola.
	T. strigatus.
	T. mucrosquamatus.
	T. andersonii.
Peltopelor	P. macrolepis.
Halys	H. himalayanus.
	H. or Trigonocephalus elliotti.
Hypnale	H. nepa.

TRIMERESURUS.

Günther's definition of this genus is the following:—

"Head triangular, covered above with small scales, except the foremost part of the snout and the supraciliary region, which generally are shielded; body with more or less distinctly keeled scales, in from seventeen to twenty-seven series. Body and tail of moderate length, prehensile. Sub-caudals two-rowed."

These snakes are fierce and venomous, but very few deaths are ascribed to their bites. Some of the *Trimeresuri* attain to a considerable size: a *T. carinatus* from the Indian Museum, captured at Port Canning near Calcutta, is 36 inches in length and nearly 4 inches in circumference, and is a much more powerful snake than a *Bungarus cæruleus* for example, now in my possession, 31 inches in length and 2½ in girth, which killed a dog in less than three hours, and a fowl in three or four minutes.

The fangs of the *Trimeresuri* are long, and capable of inflicting a deep puncture; it cannot therefore be the small size of the snake or of its poison fangs that makes it less deadly: this is doubtless due to a less virulent venom.

I am compelled to differ from Dr. Günther when he says, "The degree of danger depends but little on the species which has inflicted the wound, but rather on the bulk of the individual, on the quantity of its poison, on the temperature, and on the place of the wound;" for though there can be no doubt that all the conditions he enumerates—size, quantity of poison, state of the snake at the time of inflicting the wound, temperature—have much influence on the action of the poison, yet, quantity for quantity, the poisons of different genera, even species, vary considerably in intensity. My experiments, as far as they go, seem to show that in equal quantities the poison of the Cobra is more active than that of the Hamadryad, which is three times its size.* That of the *Bungarus cæruleus* is more deadly than that of the *Bungarus fasciatus*, which is much larger. That of the *Daboia* is perhaps equal or little inferior to that of the Cobra, and is far more deadly than the venom of the *Bungarus fasciatus*, perhaps of the *Bungarus cæruleus*, and *Echis*, and if we may depend on what is recorded, than of the *Trimeresuri*. My impression is, that of all the Indian terrestrial Thanatophidia, the Cobras stand first in the scale of destructiveness; the *Daboia* next; then the Hamadryad; next the *Bungarus cæruleus;* then the *Bungarus fasciatus* and *Echis*, the *Crotalidæ* and *Callophides.* My own experience is at present confined to the Cobra, Hamadryad, *Bungarus fasciatus*, *Bungarus cæruleus*, *Daboia*, *Echis*, and certain *Hydrophidæ*, but from what I have read and heard from others, I gather that the *Callophides* and the *Crotalidæ* of British India come last in the scale. I exclude the *Hydrophidæ* for the present; these remarks applying chiefly to the terrestrial poison snakes. I am aware that it is stated on high authority that the *Calloselasma rhodostoma*, a comparatively small species, attaining to three feet in length, of a genus of the *Crotalidæ*, and found in Siam and Java, is very deadly; but so far as I know there is not so deadly a member of the family of *Crotalidæ* in Hindostan. Further experiments will, however, I hope, enable me to speak more positively on this important point in the natural history of the Thanatophidia. Cantor,† Jerdon, Russell, and others

* The *Calloselasma rhodostoma*, found in Java and Siam, is said to be very deadly. Kuhl, as has been before mentioned, saw two men bitten by the same snake die in five minutes.

* The Rev. Mr. Vinton, Karen Missionary in Rangoon, who has experimented frequently with the poisonous snakes of Burmah, says that he is convinced that the venom of the *Ophiophagus* is less deadly in equal quantities than that of the Cobra. The *Ophiophagus* is more dangerous on account of the greater quantity of venom. and the pertinacity with which, when disturbed, it maintains its hold, apparently with the view of injecting as much of the poison as possible.

† Cantor says of the *Trimeresuri:* "Although the genus has venomous organs as highly developed as *Crotalus* or *Vipera*, the effect produced by wounds of two species at least appears to be less dangerous than might be *à priori* supposed."—*Journal As. Soc. Bengal*, vol. xvi. p. 1045.

According to Russell's experiments with the venom of *T. gramineus*, chickens expired within eight to thirty-three minutes, pigeons in fourteen to eighteen minutes; a pig recovered in six to seven hours; a dog in two to three hours, after being wounded (Russell, vol. i. p. 60). Mr. Hodgson has seen a man who was who have experimented with the *Trimeresuri*, say that the effects of their poison are less dangerous than those of other venomous snakes. The symptoms are severe pain and swelling of the bitten part or of the whole limb, with nausea, sickness, depression, fever, and then sloughing of the bitten part, after which recovery is rapid. In weak or sickly individuals fatal results might occur, but such cases are exceptional.

In the long list of deaths from snake-bite in India in 1869, a few cases are recorded from *Trimeresuri* bites.

The *Trimeresuri* are said to be naturally sluggish, and are apt to lie quietly hidden by the leaves or branches they resemble in colour until disturbed, when they are sometimes fierce and aggressive, bite savagely, and make a hissing sound as they prepare to strike, which they do by first drawing back the head and anterior part of the body, and then darting it forward with great rapidity. They, like the *Daboia*, are said to vibrate the tail at the same time; this is, I imagine, when the tail is not employed in clasping a branch of the tree, in which, as many of them are arboreal, they are most frequently found. Their food is said to consist of small birds, mammals, and tree and other frogs; in search of the latter the arboreal species are said to descend to the earth.

According to some naturalists, Günther and others, they are viviparous; but I am told that Mr. Nicholson of the Royal Artillery at Rangoon, who has had opportunities of studying their habits, states positively that they are strictly oviparous. Of this I have no personal knowledge.

I am indebted to Dr. F. Stoliczka, of the Geological Survey of India, for the following valuable notes on the habits and distribution of the *Trimeresuri* and other poison snakes :—

" *T. gramineus* I only saw once going up to Nynee Tâl, a little beyond Kalidunga, in the low hills. The specimen was on a bush, between thick foliage.

" *T. erythrurus* I found very common about the limestone hills near Moulmein. They are exactly of the same green colour as the foliage amongst which they hide themselves. I saw small specimens very often on low plants. It was on some umbelliferous plant, growing about two feet, with a spreading crown of leaves above. The *Trimeresurus* had his prehensile tail wound below the top round the stalk, and was lying above on the leaf crown in a simple or double coil. They were very sluggish, and did not make the least attempt at moving off when I came near, and even took them off the plant; neither did they offer to bite, unless pressed with a stick to the ground. But when they once got excited they turned round furiously. One had broken both his fangs in striking them into the stick with which I pressed him to the ground.

" In Penang I got also *T. erythrurus* in a similar position as at Moulmein, on the large ferns that grow there. In the Wellesley Province I caught one on a low bush near the mangrove swamp.

" *T. carinatus* I got on the north side of the road going up to Simla, and another specimen I found in the valley below Subathoo; both were on low bushes on the road, and appeared equally sluggish and lazy as the Moulmein *T. erythrurus*.

" I believe the *Trimeresuri* chiefly live on insects. I never found any vertebrate food in their stomach, though I daresay they do not despise it when they get hold of it without great difficulty. Whether they are more active at night, or, in fact, whether their habits are at all nocturnal, I cannot say. I should doubt it, though from the nature of their pupil they would appear to be so, but I think their habits are only crepuscular.

" I did not observe *Callophis* alive, but from their external character of body they cannot be tree-snakes. I suppose their habits are similar to those of *Bungarus*, but their more vivid and variegated colouring would, I think, indicate a more diurnal than nocturnal habit. The peculiarly elongated poison glands have only been observed in *C. intestinalis* and *bivirgatus*, both of which have very small heads. I am not aware that any of the other species have been examined.

" As far as general distribution of all the *Crotalidæ* is concerned, they must be considered as characteristic of the Malay fauna; which is that of the Malay Peninsula, Burmah, Cachar, and Assam (here towards the east becoming Indo-Chinese), Eastern Bengal, almost as far west as the Hooghly, the base of the Eastern and Central Himalaya, with the last remnants probably as far west as the Sutlej; though the Malayan character is strongly diminished west of Nepal. In South India, the Malabar coast, with a few patches of higher hills, and the greater part of Ceylon, must have had originally a Malay fauna. As far as I know from the records of localities, *Trimeresuri* are found only in these localities of Malay fauna.

" *Halys* I should be inclined to consider as the representative of the Vipers of the Old World; the genus characterizes the temperate climates of the hills; but when Günther says that they are only found on the northern side of the Himalaya, he is incorrect. Of course he has no notion of the climatal conditions, and strangely also, not of the geographical situation of the hills. What we call northern side of the Himalayan slopes is Thibet, that is, north of the central highest chain, and in Thibet there are no snakes until we come down into the lower Indus and into the less elevated country of Central Asia.

" One thing is decidedly noticeable in the colour of these snakes; that they adapt themselves to the locality in which they live. The species of *Halys* are dark-coloured, like *Vipera berus* of Europe, and are found on the ground. The dark-coloured *Trimeresuri*, as for instance, *T. monticola*, I met once only going up to Nynee Tâl on an old stump of a tree. The *T. convictus* of Penang is also met on the ground, and so also did I see the Nicobar *T. mutabilis*, only near the ground between shrubs. The green *Trimeresuri* are generally found higher upon trees or plants, and also possess as a rule a longer and more compressed body.

" *Daboia* I should call a characteristic Indian Viper, and the same applies to *Echis*, though this latter is clearly of African type.

" The *Callophides* belong to the Malay fauna, like the *Trimeresuri;* their head-quarters are the Malay Peninsula; the same is the case with *Ophiophagus*.

" I think as most of the Viperine snakes are viviparous, it seems not improbable that the *Trimeresuri* are also viviparous: but of course without direct observation we can form no certain opinion on such a point.

" I do not know any external characters for distinguishing the sex, and have not heard that any records exist on that point. In my paper on *Tropidonotus platyceps*, I have noted that the males have stronger keeled scales than the females, but whether that will be confirmed in other species further observations must show.

" *Trimeresurus erythrurus* I got from Moulmein, Wellesley Province, Penang, and Java.

" *T. purpureus*.—Steindachner says it also occurs in the Nicobars. I did not get it there.

" *T. mutabilis* and *cantoris* are from the Nicobars and Andamans; they are not known from other localities.

" *T. convictus* is as yet a unique specimen from Penang hills.

" I believe *T. erythrurus* has been got from Assam; *T. gramineus* and *T. carinatus* occur in Burmah, Assam, Cachar, Bengal, and the North-west Himalaya as far as the Sutlej (along the Hills), but I do not know of any recorded specimen from further westward. Perhaps Anderson may have got some for the Museum. *T. monticola* is a true hill form of the Central and Eastern

wounded by this species suffer fearfully from pain and swelling, but he never heard of a fatal case.—*Transact. Zool. Soc. Lond.*, vol. ii. p. 307.

Blyth says, in *Journal of Asiatic Society of Bengal*, 1851, p. 524: "A small *T. gramineus* from Sylhet had bitten a labouring man, but the wound merely caused a painful swelling of the arm, which however did not prevent the patient from returning to his work after a few hours—*i.e.*, in the afternoon of the same day."

Himalaya, and the Khasya and Cachar Hills, and Anderson got it from Yunan.* It evidently goes into the Indo-Chinese fauna."

TRIMERESURUS GRAMINEUS.

Vipera viridis, *Daud. Rept.*
„ gramineus, *Cantor.*
Trimesurus viridis, *Gray.*
„ elegans, *Gray.*
Coluber gramineus, *Shaw.*
Trimeresurus gramineus, *Günther.*

There are several specimens in the Indian Museum, and one before me, 18½ inches in length and 1½ in girth, of which the tail measures 2⅝ inches, came from Assam.

In this snake the upper labial shield forms the front part of the loreal pit. There is an azygos shield between the supra-nasals, sometimes two small shields take its place.

It has from nineteen to twenty-one series of carinated scales. Ventrals 158–170; sub-caudals 58–71. The scales on the head are small and smooth, or indistinctly keeled. The colour is like that of *T. carinatus*, lighter on the sides and belly; the tail is sometimes red; a yellowish or brick-red line runs along the outer series of scales.

It is common in Assam and the Khasya Hills. Dr. Stoliczka says he has never observed it in the interior of the N. W. Himalaya, though he has often found *T. carinatus* in those localities. Dr. Stoliczka is doubtful of its being found in Ladak Proper, where, according to Günther, it is met with, as the climate is too cold and the height too great.

He says (*Journal Asiatic Society*, part ii., No. 3 of 1870, page 216):—"It would be interesting to know which part of the country is alluded to (by Günther), for Ladak Proper has scarcely any arboreal vegetation, except a few poplars and willows in the Indus Valley. I passed three times through Ladak (I mean the Upper Indus Valley about Leh, and the elevated country on both sides of it), but I never saw a single snake; and the existence of a *Trimeresurus* is of all the most improbable in a country situated above 10,000 feet, and subject to the most rigidly cold climate, so that hardly any arboreal vegetation can thrive."

T. gramineus is smaller than *T. carinatus*. Günther says it attains to 32 inches, whilst he gives *T. carinatus* 37. The specimen of *T. gramineus* in the Indian Museum, from Assam, is a small one.

This snake is described and figured by Dr. Russell, in his great work on Indian Serpents, as "Bodroo Pam," plate 9, vol. i.

TRIMERESURUS ERYTHRURUS.

Trigonocephalus erythrurus, *Cantor.*
Trimesurus albolabris, *Gray.*
Trigonocephalus viridis, *Schleg.*

Günther says that Russell describes it (vol. ii. plate 20) also as "Bodroo Pam," a variety of that described in vol. i. plate 9. It is very like the two preceding. Dr. Stoliczka says that its head is elongately oval, and more depressed than either *T. carinatus* or *T. gramineus*. The lips and chin are white, the lateral line is white bordered with purple or greenish below. Colour grass green, lighter on the sides and belly. Günther says that old females do not show either the white lips or line. In this species there is not generally an azygos shield between the supra-nasals, but Dr. Stoliczka says that there is sometimes a small azygos shield. The scales on the body are strongly carinated, in twenty-one to twenty-three series. It is said (by Günther) to grow to the length of 33 inches, and to be found in the Delta of the Ganges. Dr. Stoliczka found it common in the limestone hills about Moulmein, in Penang, and Java. The specimen now before me from the Indian Museum, measures 25 inches in length and 2¼ in girth; the tail is 2⅝ inches in length. The Rev. J. G. Haensel, Missionary, in a letter to the Rev. C. L. Latrobe, writing about the Nicobar Islands, says:—"Serpents are numerous in some places, but they are far less abundant and numerous than on the coast of Coromandel. The chief cause of this difference I am apt to ascribe to a custom prevalent among the natives, of setting the long grass on the mountains on fire two or three times a year: as these reptiles like to lay their eggs in the grass, great quantities of them are thus destroyed.* One kind of serpent struck me here as a singular species; it is of a green colour, has a broad head and mouth like a frog, very red eyes, and its bite is so venomous that I saw a woman die within half an hour after receiving the wound. She had climbed a high tree in search of fruit, and not observing the animal among the branches, was suddenly bitten in the arm. Being well aware of the danger, she immediately descended, but on reaching the ground, rolled to and fro, like one in a state of intoxication. The people brought her immediately to me; and while I was applying blisters and other means for extracting the poison, she died in my hands."

Mr. V. Ball of the Geological Survey, who kindly furnished me with the above extract, also refers in his interesting account of the Nicobar Islands, published in the selections from the records of the Government of India, No. lxxvii., to a remark by Dr. Rink in his geographical sketch of those Islands, published in 1847, to the effect:—"Snakes of smaller size are to be met with in every excursion into the forest, but only two species are said to be poisonous (*Trigonocephalus*). I have only once seen a native with a swollen leg resulting from the bite of a snake; and cases of death from it are said to be very rare."

The snakes alluded to in both these accounts are evidently *Trimeresuri*, and Dr. Rink confirms the opinion that they are less deadly than other poisonous snakes; on the other hand, the Rev. Mr. Haensel's account would make it appear that his specimen was very deadly, and from the description of the colours, shape of the head, and habitat, he is probably referring to *Trimeresurus carinatus* or *T. erythrurus*. The snake may have been an unusually vigorous one, and the woman may have been small and weak. Other instances of deaths from their bites have been recorded, but on the whole the weight of evidence shows them to be less venomous than the Vipers.

TRIMERESURUS CARINATUS.

Trimesurus carinatus, *Gray.*
„ bicolor, *Gray.*
„ porphyraceus, *Blyth.*

A fine specimen from the Indian Museum, caught at Port Canning, near Calcutta, now before me, measures 36 inches in length and nearly 5 in girth. It is of a dark grass green above throughout, darker on the head and tail, and of a lighter green below, approaching white on the ventral surface. There is no light coloured line running along the outer series of scales, as in some specimens. The head is broad and triangular, covered with small carinated scales. The second upper labials form the anterior margin of the loreal pit. There is one well developed azygos shield between the supra-nasals. The scales on the body are in 25 rows, and are prominently carinated.

This corresponds very closely with Günther's description, which is as follows:—

"The second upper labial shield forms the front part of the facial pit. Scales in from twenty-three to twenty-five rows;

* In October, 1870, Dr. Stoliczka brought me a very fine living specimen of *T. monticola* from a height of 5000 feet, near Darjeeling.

* This can hardly apply to *Trimeresuri*, which are said to be viviparous.

those on the crown of the head and on the temples small, strongly carinated. Ventrals 164–169; sub-caudals 54–60. Grass green above, tail yellowish green; a more or less distinct yellowish line runs along the outer series of scales, and is sometimes absent. Lower parts greenish-white."

This species is found in Bengal, Sikkim, probably the Himalaya generally, and in Burmah. It resembles *T. gramineus* very closely. Dr. Stoliczka says (*Journal Asiatic Society*, part ii., No. 3 of 1870, page 218), the distinction is chiefly in the head, which is short and rather broad and stout, and in the large size of the supraciliaries. He says also that "there are usually one or two azygos shields; very rarely there is no azygos shield, but in such a case the supra-nasals just touch each other, not forming a broad suture as in *T. erythrurus*.

"The general colour is usually green, sometimes there are large blackish spots on the sides; the lateral line is either well developed, white margined with coral red below, or it is absent. Tail pale, ruddy above, usually equal to one-sixth the total length." Dr. Stoliczka speaks of a young specimen from the hills, at a height of about 6000 feet, north-east of Simla.

The *Trimeresurus carinatus*, *T. gramineus*, and *T. erythrurus* resemble each other very closely; apparently there is no certainty in either the number of scales, or the presence of the side line, or the rufous tint of the tail. I follow the order of authorities on Ophiology in describing them as different species.

I have had no opportunity as yet of testing the poisonous power of this snake.

Trimeresurus anamallensis.

I have had no opportunity of studying the characters of this snake, or of comparing it with Günther's description, which is as follows:—"The second upper labial shield forms the front part of the facial pit; generally a small shield between the supra-nasals. Scales on the head and on the body more or less distinctly keeled, in twenty-one series. Ventrals 148–158; sub-caudals 51–55. Ground-colour generally yellowish-green, with a dorsal series of large rhombic black spots, each spot subdivided by, or variegated with yellow. Upper side of the head marbled with black in adult specimens, uniform greenish in young ones; a black or brown band runs from the back edge of the eye to the angle of the mouth; supraciliary with one or two black cross streaks. Belly yellowish green, with numerous yellow and black spots along its side. Tail black, with yellow and green spots. *Young* specimens may be recognised by the dark temple-streak; but nearly all the other markings are very indistinct, and the ground colour is a reddish olive; tail with white extremity.

"A specimen received with others from the same locality has a brownish-purple ground colour, with a dorsal series of brown spots; belly marbled with purple; tail black, with irregular greenish rings and with some indistinct small yellowish spots. This specimen also has the supraciliary divided into two, but, nevertheless, we consider it merely a variety. Of about a dozen specimens from the Anamallay Mountains the largest is 24 inches long, tail measuring 3½ inches."

Günther adds:—"I have for some time considered this species as possibly identical with *Trigonocephalus* (*Cophias*) *malabaricus*, n. s.? Jerdon, *Journ. As. Soc. Beng.*, 1854, xxii. p. 523, which is characterized thus:—'Very closely allied to *T. nigromarginatus*. Has twenty-one rows of smooth scales. Ventrals 145–149; sub-caudals 48–53. Green above, with brown transverse and zigzag markings. Up to 2 feet long nearly. Not uncommon in all the forests of the west coast.'

"It is almost impossible to recognise a species from such a diagnosis. Moreover, Mr. Jerdon describes the scales as smooth, whilst they are keeled in our species, as in all the *Trimeresuri*. Mr. Elliot possesses a drawing of a young specimen, named *T. malabaricus*, Jerd. It resembles our species in coloration, but has a white, black-edged temple-streak instead of a black one. Mr. Jerdon does not mention either a black or a white temple-streak."

I have since received three specimens of *T. anamallensis* from Dr. Shortt of Madras.

A is 19 inches long, of which the tail is 2¾, and 1¾ inch in girth. It is of a light greenish colour, with irregularly rhomboidal black or dark brown marks along the back.

The head is beautifully marked, marbled with the same colours, and there is a distinct dark line leading from the eye to the commissure of the mouth.

It has on the neck 22–26 rows of shields, middle of the body 23, further on 21, and posteriorly 16 rows. This is noteworthy, as Günther says "simply in 21 series." 155 ventral shields, 57 sub-caudals, very closely the number given by Günther.

B, a much larger specimen, 27 inches long, of which the tail is 3½. It is 2¾ inches in girth. The body colour is much the same as in A, but the dark markings are comparatively indistinct. The head in each specimen is very broad and triangular. B has 28 series of scales on the neck, and in the middle of the body only the regular number, 21. There is nothing else peculiar about it.

C is a large specimen, about the same size as B, but much decomposed. Its coloration is darker than that of A and B, but otherwise all the same.

All three have the supraciliary divided into two shields, as noticed by Günther.

Trimeresurus monticola.

Parias maculata, *Gray.*

There are two fine specimens from the Indian Museum before me, both from Darjeeling. One is 23 inches in length and 3 inches in girth. The tail is 3½ inches in length.

The other is 27 inches in length and 2 in girth.

The second upper labial forms the front of the pit. There are two small shields behind the nostril, sometimes a small azygos shield below this. The scales on the head are smooth, those on the body slightly carinated. There are 23 series. Ventrals 137–141; sub-caudals 41. The supraciliaries are very large.

The coloration varies, in one specimen it is pale brown, with a vertebral row of large, square, dark brown blotches. Along the sides a row of small dark spots; a pale temple-streak. Belly dark mottled.

The larger male specimen, which is also from Darjeeling, is of a dark brown or almost blackish-ash colour with the rhomboid patches along the vertebræ.

There is a peculiar mark in the middle of the neck like a U, which is of a yellowish or whitish colour.

This is a Himalayan species; both the Museum specimens referred to came from Darjeeling, but it is found also in Nepal, Sikkim, and probably in Khasya and other parts of the Eastern Himalayan range.

I have also received a very fine living female specimen of *T. monticola* from Dr. Stoliczka, who brought it with him from Darjeeling; it was captured in October near a house in Rungby, 5000 feet above the sea, and about twelve miles S.E. of Darjeeling. It is 29 inches long, of which the tail measures 3 inches, and at the thickest part of the body 3½ inches in girth. It is of a cinnamon-grey colour, beautifully marked with square dark spots; the head is dark brown, with a metallic lustre, and the U-shaped mark on the neck very distinct. There are 22 series of slightly carinated scales on the neck. The fangs are moderately large. The eye small, with vertical pupil.

The supra-nasals are separated by two small shields.

Trimeresurus strigatus.

Trimesurus strigatus, *Gray*.
Trigonocephalus neelgherriensis, *Jerdon*.

This species is found on the Nilgherries and Deccan, and is common about Ootacamund.

A specimen in the Indian Museum measures 14½ inches, girth 1¼ inch; it is brown, with a line of darker coloured irregular vertebral spots. It has a horseshoe-shaped whitish mark on the neck. There is a triangular dark spot below the eye and loreal pit, and a dark brown band leading from the eye to the neck. The lower jaw and belly marked with black spots. The end of the tail terminates in a scale; in young specimens it is white.

Günther describes it:—"The shield forming the front part of the facial pit is separate from the second upper labial. Supraciliary shield narrow; no large shields behind the rostral. The whole upper surface of the head is covered with small nearly smooth scales. Nine or ten upper labials, becoming smaller in size behind. Scales distinctly keeled, in twenty-one series. Ventrals 136–142; sub-caudals 31–40. Tail but slightly prehensile, terminating in a short conical scale."

It is a small snake, the largest specimen Dr. Günther has examined being nineteen inches in length.

Major Beddome describes *T. neelgherriensis* (Jerdon):—"Dark brown with black markings; 23 rows of carinated scales; scutæ 142; scutellæ 46."

It is the same species.

Trimeresurus mucrosquamatus.

Trigonocephalus mucrosquamatus, *Cantor*.

The Indian Museum has at present no individual of this species, nor have I been able to obtain it. Günther says it is found in the Naga Hills and Assam. Cantor describes it thus:—"Brownish-grey above, with black, white-edged rings, covered with oval, half-keeled, pointed, imbricate scales; whitish beneath, dotted with black. Ventrals 218; sub-caudals 91."

Günther says:—"This species has not been recognised by later herpetologists," and that the typical specimen is lost. Only the drawing of it made by Cantor is preserved in the library of the Oxford Museum.

Trimeresurus andersonii.

Mr. Theobald has named what he considers a new species after Dr. Anderson, the Curator of the Indian Museum. It is described in his Catalogue of the Asiatic Society's (now Indian) Museum, pp. 75 to 76. It has 25 rows of carinated scales, 182 ventrals, and 56 sub-caudals in one specimen, and 71 in the other; girth 1⅝ inch, length 20 inches, length of tail 2½ inches. The second upper labial forms the anterior margin of the præ-orbital pit; supra-nasals separated by an azygos shield. The colour above and below is a uniform rich brown. Belly and sides marked conspicuously with white spots. Found in Assam. A second individual, named by Mr. Theobald in the same catalogue as *T. obscurus*, has the "back of a uniform brown, sides green, spotted and mottled. Belly greenish-white, brown barred and spotted, supraciliaries well defined." But it is very doubtful if this be distinct from *T. andersonii*. The length of the Museum specimen is 20 inches, of which the tail is 2¾ inches. The girth is 1⅝ inch.

Trimeresurus wardii, *Jerdon*.

Günther says of this:—"Quite indeterminable is another of Mr. Jerdon's species, for which he has proposed the name of *T. wardii*."

Major Beddome, in the *Madras Quarterly Journal of Medical Science*, No. ix., July, 1862, p. 2, describes it as follows:—"Greenish with purplish-brown diamond spots on back and sides, 12–14 inches long. *Hab.* Nilgherries."

PELTOPELOR, *Günther*.

Peltopelor macrolepis.

Trimesurus macrolepis, *Beddome*.

There is only one species of the genus *Peltopelor* known: it was discovered by Major Beddome of Madras, and is now called the *Peltopelor macrolepis*. It is arboreal, and nearly allied to the *Trimeresurus*; it comes from the Anamallay Mountains, where, Major Beddome says, it is common in the grass at 6000 feet elevation. He also procured a specimen from the Pulney Hills, in the moist forests at 4000 feet elevation.

Major Beddome's description is "dark green, lighter below, the lowermost row of scales on each side white, forming a white line on each side of the abdomen (Günther calls it a yellow line); scales in twelve to fourteen rows, the lowest row the smallest, all pointed and very prominently carinated; head covered with very large plate-like scales. Ventral scutæ 133–138; sub-caudals 53–56 pairs; rostral triangular, erect." The largest specimen examined by Günther was 21 inches, of which the tail measured 4¾ inches.

HALYS, *Gray*.

This genus has two species in Hindostan. It is characterized by its broad obtuse head, covered with shields. There are twenty-three to twenty-seven series of carinated scales; sub-caudals two-rowed; tail short, not prehensile, terminates in a spine.

Halys elliotti.

The first species is one found in the Nilgherries, and described by Mr. Jerdon, who named it *Trigonocephalus elliotti*. (*Journal Asiatic Society, Bengal*, xxii., 1854, page 523.) "Form massive; scales in 23 rows; ventral shields 151; sub-caudals 43. Olive green above; pearl white beneath; two feet long and upwards."

Found in the lower slopes of the Nilgherries.

There is no specimen of this snake in the Indian Museum. I depend on Günther, Jerdon, and Beddome for the account of it.

Halys himalayanus.

Trigonocephalus affinis, *Günther*.

A specimen from the Indian Museum before me measures 23 inches in length, 2¼ in girth. Günther's description of it is:—"Snout of moderate length, broader than long, with the nose rather protruding. Rostral shield oblique, higher than broad; frontals well developed, not broken up into smaller shields. The anterior frontals short, transversely produced, and tapering on the sides; both taken together form a sort of crescent. Posterior frontals large, somewhat pointed in front, and rounded behind. Vertical and supraciliaries as usual in this genus; occipitals rather small, rounded. Five upper labials, a sixth and seventh being confluent with the temporals; the second is small, not entering the margin of the facial pit; the third enters the orbit. There is a series of three large temporal shields, the two hinder of which form a portion of the lip; the space between these temporals and the occipital is covered with small scales.

Body of moderate length, rounded; its middle is covered with twenty-three series of strongly keeled scales. Ventrals 162–166; anal entire; sub-caudals 43–51. The tail terminates in a long spine. Dark brown, with large band-like spots across the back; these spots are very indistinct, scarcely differing from the ground-colour, and becoming visible only by their black edges; belly almost entirely black, marbled with yellowish. A broad blackish-brown band runs from the eye along the series of temporal shields to the angle of the mouth; it has a narrow black and white edge above and below, and is better defined in the young individual than in the old one Lower labials marbled with yellowish and blackish."

This species is very common all over the north-west Himalayas. Dr. Stoliczka says, "Especially between 5 and 8000 feet, but on the Hatu Mountain near Kotegurh, and about Serahan, I observed it as high as 10,000 feet. It feeds principally on mice." The largest specimen he saw was 34 inches in length. In describing the character of *H. himalayanus* Dr. Stoliczka says: — "The upper ground colour of this snake varies from brownish-green to almost brownish-black, but generally with some lighter spots, bands, or marblings, and that of the lower part is of a greenish-yellow purple tinge, the purplish colour sometimes predominating, especially on the sub-caudals; the whole of the lower side is more or less strongly marbled with greenish-black, rarely is the under side nearly all black, but the chin is always yellowish. The upper labials are yellowish-white, and in continuation of this colour, there is in younger specimens a very conspicuous whitish lateral band occupying the base of the ventrals and the adjoining row of scales. In old specimens this lateral band is only indicated on the throat, becoming obsolete on the body."

He also says:—"All the specimens which I examined had only twenty-one series of scales. One nearly full grown, from the neighbourhood of Kotegurh (north-east of Simla) measures 25¼ inches, of which the tail is 3¼, terminating with a very small single sub-caudal scale. Ventrals 160; sub-caudals 42."

"It is met with on the paths generally after rains and in shady places between overhanging forest trees."

I have no information as to the degree of venomous power it possesses.

HYPNALE, *Fitz.*

Hypnale nepa.

The genus *Hypnale* has only one species, *Hypnale nepa*, or the "Carawilla" of Southern India.

Coluber nepa, *Laur.*
Carawala, *Davy.*
Cophias hypnale, *Merr. Tent.*
Trigonocephalus hypnale, *Wagl.*
Trimesurus? ceylonensis, *Gray.*
Trigonocephalus zara, *Gray.*

I have had no opportunity of studying this snake from nature, but Günther gives the following description of it:—

"Head broad, triangular; snout covered with numerous small shields above, the crown of the head being normally shielded. Body of moderate length, with keeled scales in seventeen rows. Tail rather short, not prehensile, terminating in a short conical scale. Sub-caudals two-rowed." "Ventrals 140–152, sub-caudals 31–45." "Brown or grey or reddish olive, with a double dorsal series of brown or black spots; the spots of both sides sometimes confluent into cross bands. Sides and belly finely marbled and dotted with brown or black. Upper lip brown or black, well marked by a darker line running from behind the eye to the angle of the mouth; a more or less distinct white or whitish temporal streak above the dark line, sometimes continued along the side of the neck, with an interrupted brown band above and below it. Chin and throat blackish or brownish, variegated with yellow or grey. Sometimes specimens occur of a more uniform coloration: the dorsal spots, the dark temporal line, and a pair of whitish spots on each side of the throat are the most constant markings. Other specimens are flesh-coloured, with small black markings as described. All these varieties may be seen in fœtus taken out of the same female."

It is found in Southern India, Malabar, and the Anamallay Mountains; also in Ceylon. The largest specimen Günther has seen is 19 inches long, the tail measuring 2½ inches. It is viviparous. Günther says he has found in one female five perfectly developed fœtus, 5 inches long, and in another seven eggs, which did not show any development of embryo.

"The *Carawala* is much dreaded, although its bite is but exceptionally fatal to man, and in such cases death does not occur before the lapse of some days."

I have had no opportunity of testing by experiment the properties of this snake.

Russell describes it in his Indian Serpents, vol. ii. plate 22.

HYDROPHIDÆ.

The members of this family may be recognised at once by the peculiarities of their conformation, which is adapted to an aquatic mode of life.

They are all venomous, and inhabit the salt-water estuaries and tidal streams; they have a very wide range of distribution, being found in the Indian and Pacific Oceans, from Madagascar to the Isthmus of Panama. They are most numerous, Günther says, in the Eastern Archipelago and in the seas between Southern China and North Australia, "being represented on the outskirts of the geographical range mentioned by only one species, and that the most common—*Pelamis bicolor*."

I propose to describe some of those only that are found on the Indian coasts. They are very numerous, and many of them closely resemble each other, so that I shall figure and describe only the most remarkable.

The sea snakes have great varieties of form, but the transitions from one to another are very gradual. Some of them attain a considerable size; Günther speaks of some species attaining to the length of twelve feet. The longest I have seen is under five feet; there is no reason to believe that they attain to so great a size as certain fabulous stories would suggest.

They are very poisonous. The case related of a sailor of H.M.'s ship *Algerine*, who was bitten by one recently caught at Madras, proves them to be so. I am informed by Mr. Galiffe that a fisherman bitten by a salt-water snake somewhere near the salt lakes, died in one hour and a quarter. And my own experiments and those of Mr. Stewart at Pooree prove, that not only when able to bite voluntarily, but even when weak and unable to bite, when the jaws were compressed on the animal, death resulted. The fishermen on the coast know their dangerous properties and carefully avoid them.

They have smaller jaws and much smaller fangs than the land snakes generally, with open grooves, though not always completely open, as supposed by some naturalists; but the virus is very active, and appears to act as speedily and certainly as that of the terrestrial poisonous colubrine snakes. They have an elongated body like the land snakes; in some instances it is short and thick, whilst in others it is very thick towards the tail and most disproportionately elongated and attenuated in the neck; the head is very minute. The hinder part of the body and tail is flattened and compressed vertically, almost like the fin or tail of a fish, and it answers the same purpose, for with it they swim with grace and rapidity. They swim like fish, and live, with some exceptions, continually in the sea or tidal water. When thrown on the land by the surf, as they constantly are at Pooree and other places along the coast, they are helpless and almost blind. Their food consists of fish and other aquatic animals, which they pursue and overtake in the salt water. There are certain parts of the Bay of Bengal in which they are often seen in great numbers, and their movements in the clear blue water are very agile, graceful, and beautiful.

The *Platurus* seem to be a transitional stage between the sea and land snakes; its general formation and large ventral scutæ indicate its power of going on land and probably seeking its food there as well as in the sea. The *Hydrophidæ* generally have no ventral plates well marked. The abdominal scales differ little from those of the rest of the body, which are generally hexagonal laid side by side, occasionally slightly imbricate and in some tubercular, a small tubercle being found in the centre of each scale. *Platurus* has abdominal scutæ like the land snakes, and is sometimes found in marshy ground near the sea.

The nostrils, eyes, and head shields of the sea snakes are peculiar. The eyes are small with circular pupils, which contract so much when the snake is taken out of water that it is said to be almost blind. The nostrils are on the surface, so that they can breathe when only the surface of the snout is above water. The openings are protected by a valvular apparatus internally.

The head shields are peculiar and differ in their arrangement from the head shields of the land snakes.

The nasals are large and replace the anterior frontals, which are absent.

There is a single pair of frontals, a vertical, a pair of supraciliaries, and a pair of occipitals; one ocular and one or two postoculars: no loreal. The labials are irregularly arranged and subdivided.

"There is a triangular mental shield in front of the lower jaw, behind which the first pair of lower labials form a suture together; one or two pairs of chin shields follow." *Enhydrina* has a peculiar notch in the lower jaw, by which the gape can be much increased. This notch is filled by a lobular process of the rostral shield, which fits into it when the mouth is closed; on each side of this notch there is an opening for the points of the tongue to protrude. This again is shorter in *Hydrophidæ* than in terrestrial snakes; it is used as a feeler in the usual way.

They are said to be very delicate and to die rapidly in captivity, even when preserved in tanks of salt water. Mr. Stewart of Pooree found that he could keep them alive for a short time by placing them in holes in the ground into which the sea-water percolated. A very fine specimen of *Hydrophis coronata* caught near Calcutta, and sent to me by Mr. Galiffe, lived about ten days in a cage, occasionally being put into a jar of fresh water, although many experiments were made to make it bite, in which its very small head must have been considerably bruised.

There are seven genera of this family:—

Platurus.	Acalyptus.
Aipysurus.	Hydrophis.
Disteira.	Enhydrina.
Pelamis.	

But of these only four, I believe, are represented in the Indian Ocean, viz.:—

Platurus.	Enhydrina.
Hydrophis.	Pelamis.

Of these, Platurus has two species: Hydrophis, about twenty-seven; Enhydrina one, or according to some naturalists, two; Pelamis one species.

PLATURUS.

Günther gives two species of this genus, *Platurus scutatus* and *Platurus fischeri*. A very fine specimen from the Indian Museum, caught in one of the tidal streams near Port Canning, is 49 inches in length, of which the tail measures 3¾ inches, 4 in girth of body, and 2¼ in girth of neck. The first appearance of the snake is not unlike that of *Bungarus fasciatus*, from its black and yellow ringed markings.

Platurus has several characters like those of the land snakes. The tail is not prehensile. The ventral shields are like those of the land snakes. Body is subcylindrical, and not compressed like the *Hydrophidæ*. The scales of the body are imbricate, smooth, 19–25 series. There are two series of subcaudals. The shields of the head are regularly disposed; two pairs of frontals, with an azygos shield between the hind pair. The eye is small. The nostrils are lateral in a single nasal shield; no loreal; one præ- and two post-oculars; seven upper labials, the third and fourth of which enter the orbit; temporals scale-like. The throat has two pairs of chin shields anteriorly, and scales posteriorly. The tail is longer and thicker in males than in females. The anal is bifid. The poison fang is short, a single small tooth is sometimes found behind the fang.

Platurus scutatus.

Coluber laticaudatus, *L. Mus. Ad. Fried.*
Laticauda scutata, *Laur. Syn. Rept.; Cantor Mal. Rept.*
Hydrus colubrinus, *Schneider.*
Platurus fasciatus, *Latr. Rept.*
Hydrophis colubrinus, *Schleg.*

Günther's description of this species is:—

"Generally an azygos shield between the posterior frontals; scales of the front part of the trunk in twenty-one or twenty-three longitudinal series; ventral shields from 213–241. Body surrounded by from twenty-five to fifty black rings. Crown of the head black; the first and second black mark of the head and neck are joined below by a black longitudinal band, commencing from the chin; snout and side of the head yellow, with a black band running through the eye"

It is common in the Bay of Bengal, and grows to five feet or more.

Platurus fischeri, *Jan.*

Günther's description is as follows:—

"No azygos shield between the posterior frontals; scales of the front part of the trunk in nineteen longitudinal series; ventral shields 232–241. Trunk surrounded by from thirty-three to thirty-six black rings, which are broader than the interspaces. A black band crosses the occiput and extends forward over the vertical plate and over the lower jaw, but, generally, it is not confluent with the next following ring. Upper part of the snout yellow; upper labials black."

Of eight specimens examined by Günther, the largest was only 30 inches long.

I am indebted to Dr. J. Anderson, Curator of the Indian Museum, for the following description of the fine specimen in that Museum previously alluded to, which he considers to be *P. fischeri*, with some slight difference from Günther's description.

"The specimen which I provisionally refer to this species has nineteen rows of smooth scales round the fore part of the trunk, in longitudinal series, and 235 ventrals. There is no azygos shield between the posterior frontals, and in all of these characters it agrees with this species. But on comparing the head with Günther's drawing, I find that the anterior frontals in my specimen differ from it, in being long and pointed anteriorly, and considerably larger than the posterior pair, and in the vertical being proportionally larger than in *P. fischeri*, and the occipitals larger and more pointed. It has one præ- and two post-oculars, and the third and fourth labials are below the eye. Two pairs of large chin shields, the posterior shields with a large scale between their posterior extremities. It also differs from *P. fischeri* in having fifty-six black rings round the trunk instead of thirty-six, but I do not attach much importance to this, as *P. scutatus* shows about an equal variation; but at the same time, Günther's statement that his eight specimens show the same assemblage of characters as laid down in his description, and the occurrence of fifty-six rings in my specimen, suggest that their multiplicity is either due to greater age (it measures forty-nine inches in length) or to variation. The head too is wholly black, with the exception of a yellow band from the posterior margin of one eye to the other. The upper surface is olive green, and the sides and belly rich dark gamboge yellow, and the fifty-six rings are intensely bluish-black, and the scales generally have a very bright shining lustre."

From Tolly's nullah, a tidal stream, Calcutta.

If this form should prove to be new, I would indicate it as *P. affinis*. New species, Anderson.

ENHYDRINA, *Gray.*

Günther says there is only one species in this genus, which differs only from *Hydrophis* in the deep cleft in the lower jaw, where the mandibles do not unite, and the fold of integument connecting them forms a deep notch.

Dr. Stoliczka (*Journal Asiatic Society*, No. iii., 1870, p. 213), says that there are two species of Enhydrina—*E. bengalensis*, Gray, or *E. valakadyen*, Boie, and *E. schistosa*, Daud.

Russell, in his Indian Serpents, describes two species: "Valakadyen" and "Hooghly Pattee," as called by the natives. Dr. Stoliczka considers that these are really distinct species, the latter being very much less common than the former—no specimen at that time existing in the Indian Museum. In coloration they resemble each other, but Dr. Stoliczka says, "The *H. schistosa* is more slender, and its tail proportionally less in length; the head more ovately prolonged, and the gape wider; the shields of the head are consequently more elongated. The body is more compressed; the scales on it are along the back much elongated, imbricated, and carinated on the sides," more oval or hexagonal and less distinctly keeled round the middle: they vary in from sixty-six to seventy longitudinal series.

Other naturalists, I believe, consider that there is only one species, and that *E. schistosa* is merely a variety.

Günther's description is as follows:—

Enhydrina bengalensis.

Valakadyen, *Russell.*
Hydrus valakadyn, *Boie.*
Hydrophis schistosa (not *Daud.*) *Schleg.; Fischer; Dum. & Bib.*
Hydrus schistosus, *Cantor.*
Hydrophis bengalensis; H. subfasciata, *Gray.*
Enhydrina bengalensis; E. valakadyen, *Gray.*
Thalassophis werneri, *Schmidt.*

"Head rather short, of moderate width; neck and body moderately elongate. Rostral shield very small, lobuliform, its projecting point fitting into a corresponding cavity of the lower jaw; the fourth upper labial shield below the eye; mental shield very narrow and long, situated in a groove; anterior lower labials much elongate; throat covered with scales, without shields. One post-ocular, sometimes divided into two. Neck surrounded by forty-eight series of scales. Scales scarcely imbricate, hexagonal, each provided with a short keel; ventral shields not, or but little, different from the scales of the adjoining series; they are 284–314 in number. Terminal scale of the tail rather large. The young has broad black rhombic bands across the back, which become fainter with age, and finally disappear entirely."

The fang of *Enhydrina* is short, but well marked; the groove is open part of its length but not throughout. The body is somewhat compressed; the belly carinate; the tail flat and compressed, almost like a fish's fin; the nostrils vertical; the eyes small.

I have received fine specimens from the neighbourhood of Calcutta, from the tidal streams near Mutlah. One lived twenty-four hours after it reached me; it was made to close its jaws on a fowl, and killed it in seven minutes. Some hours after its death its jaws were forcibly closed on a fowl's thigh, and the bird died in four hours. The poison is evidently very virulent. The colour of the specimen, which is 36 inches in length and 3½ inches in girth, is bluish-grey, with dark grey bands across the back; belly whitish. It is figured and described in Russell's Indian Serpents, vol. ii. table xi. as "Valakadyen;" vol. ii. table x. as "Hooghly Pattee."

Russell says the Valakadyen has no fangs, but this is clearly a mistake, the fangs are well marked, and it is very poisonous. It is common in the Bay of Bengal, and is found in the tidal streams of the Soonderbuns. Fine specimens have been sent to me from the tidal streams near Calcutta. The largest specimen is 48 inches long, of which the tail is 5¼ inches; the largest part of body in girth is 5¾ inches; neck 2½ inches. Colour bluish-grey, with darker bands of deeper shade of same colour. Belly whitish; tail compressed like the fin or tail of a fish. The specimen is a female.

PELAMIS.

This genus has only a single species, one of the most common of the sea-snakes, and has the widest range of distribution. It is common in the Bay of Bengal and in all the eastern seas.

Günther's description is:—"Head flat, with very long, spatulate snout; neck rather stout; body of moderate length. Nasal shields contiguous, longer than broad, pierced by the nostril posteriorly; only one pair of frontals. Scales not imbricate, not polished, tubercular or concave. Ventral shields none or very narrow. Lower jaw without notch in front."

Pelamis platurus.

Pelamis platurus, *Linn.*
,, bicolor, *Daud.*; *Günther.*
Hydrus bicolor, *Schneider.*
Hydrophis variegata, *Schleg.*
,, pelamis, *Schleg.*
Pelamis ornata, *Gray.*

"Two or three post-orbitals. Neck surrounded by from forty-five to fifty-one longitudinal series of scales. From 378 to 440 scales in a lateral longitudinal series between the angle of the mouth and the vent. Coloration variable."

A specimen sent by Mr. Stewart from Pooree, is 12½ inches long, and is uniform black above, the sides and the belly being of a bright gamboge yellow, tail with black spots, separated by a well-defined line. It is described as being very poisonous, and killed a fowl rapidly.

It is called "Kullundur" by the native fishermen on that coast, and is deemed by them to be very poisonous.

Günther describes four varieties:—

α. Colour black above; sides and belly uniform brownish olive; tail with black spots.

β. Back black; belly and sides brown, separated by a black and a yellow band. Large spots posteriorly.

γ. Black of back narrow, becomes sinuous behind middle of the body; posteriorly a dorsal series of rhombic confluent spots. Sides and belly with an irregular series of rounded, black or brown spots. This variety has been named *sinuata.*

δ. "Yellow, with about fifty brown, black-edged cross bands, extending nearly to the belly, which is crossed by narrow vertical brownish-black streaks, alternating with the dorsal bands. Some of the dorsal bands are confluent, forming a zigzag band. Head yellow, variegated with black. *H. variegata,* Schleg.; *P. ornata,* Gray; *varietas alternans,* Fischer."

The individual from Pooree is the young of Variety α.

HYDROPHIS, *Daud.*

This genus has many species, and furnishes the greater proportion of sea-snakes found on these coasts. Günther gives about twenty-seven species as occurring in the Indian Seas, and Dr. Anderson of the Indian Museum informs me that he has described several additional new species. It is very probable that others have not yet been described. They present considerable variety of form and coloration; some have elongated necks and small heads, the posterior part of the body being much larger than the anterior. Others have not this characteristic; but they have all a strong family likeness, and may be recognised at once by their compressed bodies, fin-like tails, and the general absence of well-marked ventral scutæ. They are all poisonous, and both of the few with which I have experimented, and of those with which experiments have been made, and the particulars sent to me, the virus seemed very deadly. The fangs are small and grooved, the involution not being so complete as in the land snakes. They are entirely pelagic, though they may be found in tidal rivers, and when thrown on shore by the surf, or caught and placed on land, are helpless. They seem to be delicate, and seldom live long in captivity—a *H. coronata* sent to me from one of the tidal streams near Calcutta lived some days, being occasionally placed in fresh water, and it proved its venomous properties by destroying a small chicken on whose thigh its very small jaws were forcibly closed.

Günther's description of the genus is as follows:—"Posterior part of the body strongly compressed. Head short or of moderate length, shielded above; only one pair of frontals; nostrils superior, in a single nasal shield, both nasals being contiguous to each other. Scales imbricate, or not imbricate, not polished, generally with a tubercle or with a keel. Ventral shields very narrow, or quite rudimentary or entirely absent. Lower jaw without notch in front."

He divides them into two classes. Those in which the scales are more or less distinctly imbricate; and those in which they are placed side by side and not imbricate, and these again are variously subdivided.

The following are the species said to be found in the Indian Seas. Besides descriptions of new species by Dr. Anderson, I have given the characters in detail, from Günther, of those only that I have figured. The others are to be found in his great work on Indian reptiles. I have selected characteristic species, and the figures are all from recent specimens, from the Bay of Bengal or tidal streams near Calcutta or from such as are preserved in the Indian Museum. It would protract this work to too great a length to describe or figure more than are sufficient fairly to illustrate the most characteristic species of the genus.

Hydrophis jerdonii. Indian Coast and Penang.
,, stokesii. Doubtful.
,, major. Indian Ocean generally.
,, robusta. Indian Coast, Indian Ocean generally.
,, cærulescens. Bay of Bengal, Penang.
,, aspera. Said to be found at Singapore.
,, spiralis. Indian Ocean.
,, cyanocincta. Bay of Bengal, Ceylon, Indian Ocean.
,, subcincta. Said to be from the Indian Ocean.
,, nigrocincta. Bay of Bengal.
,, torquata. Penang, Soonderbuns, Bay of Bengal, Indian Ocean.

Hydrophis chloris. Soonderbuns, Bay of Bengal.
,, lindsayi. Indian Coast.
,, latifasciata. Mergui.
,, coronata. Bay of Bengal, Soonderbuns.
,, diadema. Probably Indian.
,, gracilis. Indian Coast, Bay of Bengal.
,, fasciata. Indian Coast, Bay of Bengal.
,, cantoris. Penang.
,, lapemoides. Indian Coast, Ceylon.
,, longiceps. Indian Ocean.
,, stricticollis. Doubtful.
,, ornata. Indian Ocean.
,, elliotti. Indian Coast, Ceylon.
,, pachycercus. Indian Ocean.
,, viperina. Indian Coast.
,, curta. Indian Coast (near Pooree).
,, hardwickii. Penang.
,, fayreriana, n. s. *Anderson.* Indian Coast, Bay of Bengal, Pooree.
,, tuberculata, n. s. *Anderson.* Tidal streams, Calcutta.
,, crassicollis, n. s. *Anderson.* Bay of Bengal.

The following descriptions of *H. jerdonii, H. robusta, H. cyanocincta, H. nigrocincta, H. chloris, H. coronata, H. stricticollis, H. curta,* are all from Günther.

The descriptions of the new species, *H. crassicollis, H. tuberculata, H. fayreriana* are by Dr. Anderson, Curator of the Indian Museum.

I have recently received from Dr. Stewart, B.M.S., Civil Surgeon, Pooree, the following valuable collection of *Hydrophidæ,* among which are two other new species, named by Dr. Anderson, to whom I am also indebted for their description, *Hydrophis stewartii,* after Dr. Stewart, and *Hydrophis nigra.*

	Lengths.
Hydrophis viperina, *Schmidt*	30″
*H. crassicollis, *Anderson* (?)	56″ 5‴
H. gracilis, *Shaw*	34″
H. chloris, *Daudin*	38″
H. lindsayi, *Gray*	27″ 3‴
H. cantoris, *Gray*	20″ 3‴
H. jerdonii, *Gray*	36″
† { H. spiralis, *Shaw,* var.: / H. spiralis, *Shaw* (22″) } Dr. Anderson is doubtful about this species.	
H. stewartii (n. s.), *Anderson*	38″ 3‴
H. nigra (n. s.), *Anderson*	19″
Enhydrina valakadyen, *Boie.*	

The above, with a fine specimen of *Chersydrus granulatus,* Schneider, an innocent aquatic snake, were all caught or picked up, or thrown on the beach, on the coast near Pooree, Cuttack, Bay of Bengal.

Hydrophis jerdonii.

Hydrus nigrocinctus, var., *Cantor.*
Kerilia jerdonii, *Gray.*

"Head short, with the snout declivous and rather pointed; body of moderate length. Frontal shields small, not much larger than præ-ocular; one post-ocular; five upper labial shields, the third and fourth of which enter the orbit, the last below the post-ocular; two or three large temporals on the side of each occipital, the anterior of which enters the labial margin behind the fifth labial shield. Two pairs of chin-shields, in contact with one another. Scales imbricate, large, higher than long, with the apex slightly truncated; each scale with a strong keel; they are disposed in fifteen or seventeen series round the neck, and in nineteen or twenty-one in the middle of the body. Ventral shields distinct, but not twice as large as the scales of the adjoining series, bituberculate 235–238 in number. Anal shields small; terminal scale of the tail large. A series of seven simple teeth behind the grooved fang in front. Trunk with from thirty-four to thirty-eight black cross bands, broadest on the back and extending to the belly in young and half-grown specimens."

Hydrophis robusta.

Hydrophis nigrocincta, *Schleg.; Fischer.*

"Head of moderate size and width; neck and body not elongate. Two or three upper labials below the orbit; one post-ocular; anterior temporal shield large; two pairs of chin-shields, which are in contact with one another. Thirty-one series of scales round the neck. Scales slightly imbricate, each with a subcentral tubercle; those on the highest part of the body are rounded or subtruncated behind, as high as long. Ventrals twice or thrice as broad as the scales of the adjoining series, smooth, 310 in number. Terminal scale of the tail rather large. Trunk with thirty-five narrow, distant, black rings, extending round the belly, sometimes interrupted on the side and dilated on the back; head without markings in the adult; throat and belly whitish.

"This snake, of which we have examined two adult examples, 6 feet long, is found on the coasts of the mainland of India as well as in the Archipelago. It has been confounded with other species by all the previous herpetologists. The figure given by Fischer is very recognisable."

Hydrophis cyanocincta. The Chittul

Hydrophis cyanocinctus, *Daud.*
Léiosélasme striée, *Lacép.*
Hydrophis striata, *Schleg.*
,, sublævis, *Gray.*
,, subannulata, *Gray.*
Hydrus striatus, *Cantor.*

"Head of moderate size and width; neck and body rather elongate; generally two labial shields below the eye; two post-oculars (exceptionally confluent into one); two or more temporal shields on the side of each occipital. Two pairs of chin-shields, the anterior of which are in contact with each other. Twenty-nine to thirty-three series of scales round the neck. Scales slightly imbricate, rhombic, faintly keeled, those on the highest part of the body rather longer than high. Ventrals 320–360—406–426, twice or thrice as large as the scales of the adjoining series; almost all are entire, not longitudinally divided, and bitubercular; four anal shields, the outer of which are larger than the inner; terminal scale of the tail rather small, or of moderate size. Greenish olive on the back, yellowish on the sides and belly; trunk with from fifty to seventy-five black cross bands, which are broadest on the back, and broader than the interspaces of the ground colour; they are narrower on the sides, sometimes disappearing altogether with age on the sides and belly, or visible only as irregular spots on the ventral shields. In young and half-grown specimens they surround the body entirely, and are sometimes joined by a black band running along the whole line of the ventral shields. The head is greenish olive above and yellowish on the sides; in the young black, variegated with yellow, the yellow colour sometimes forming a frontal and temporal band.

"This is one of the commonest sea-snakes, occurring on the coasts of Ceylon, Madras, in the Bay of Bengal, in the East Indian Archipelago, and in the seas of China and Japan. It attains to a length of more than 6 feet. Old males have a remarkably thick and rounded tail."

* This appears to be a variety, as the first large temporal shield takes the place of the seventh labial, which is distinct in the type and large.

† This is a characteristic specimen.

Hydrophis nigrocincta.

Hydrophis nigrocinctus, *Daud.*
Enhydris nigrocinctus, *Merr.*

"Head small; neck slender, its length being about one-fourth of the total; body moderately elongate. Rostral shield rather broader than long; only the fourth upper labial forms the lower part of the orbit; two post-oculars; three temporal shields on the side of each occipital. Two pairs of chin-shields, the anterior of which are in contact with each other. Twenty-seven to twenty-nine series of scales round the neck. Scales imbricate, rhombic, keeled, those on the highest part of the body as broad as long. Ventrals distinct, not quite twice as broad as the scales of the adjoining series, smooth, 320–331 in number. Four large anal shields. The tail terminates in a large scale. The trunk is encircled by 43–(53–)61 complete rings of black colour. The width of these rings is equal on the sides and on the belly; on the vertebral line only they are a little broader; they are narrower than the interspaces, which occupy from four to five transverse series of scales, whilst a black ring occupies only three. The interspaces are greenish-olive on the back, yellowish on the sides and on the belly. The crown of the head and the upper lip are blackish, a yellow band running along the whole upper margin of the head; lower jaw whitish. Tail with from nine to eleven black cross bars."

Hydrophis chloris.

Hydrophis chloris, *Daud.*
,, obscura, *Gray.*
? ,, gracilis, *Cantor.*

"Head very small, of moderate width; neck very slender, the length of the thin part of the body being more than one-third of the total. Rostral shield very small, much broader than long; one post-ocular; the third upper labial is not in contact with the nasal. Two pairs of chin-shields, in contact with each other. Thirty-one to thirty-three series of scales round the neck; scales on the back with a faint keel, and with a small tubercle near the apex. Ventral shields distinct, especially on the thin portion of the body, but not much larger than the scales of the adjoining series, 473–500 in number. Four anal shields, the outer of which are very large. Trunk greenish-olive above, yellowish on the side and below: from fifty-nine to sixty-seven rhombic blackish bands across the back, which are much narrower and fainter on the sides, and extend round the belly; their angles on the vertebral line are sometimes confluent, especially on the anterior part of the body, where the yellowish ground-colour between the cross bands is sometimes reduced to round spots disposed in pairs. Head and anterior part of the belly entirely black. *Young* specimens have the markings of a deep black."

Hydrophis coronata.

Hydrophis hardwickii, *Gray.*
,, fasciata, *Gray.*

"Head very small, twice as long as broad; neck very slender, its length being more than one-third of the total. Rostral shield small, broader than long; one post-ocular; the third upper labial is not in contact with the nasal. Two pairs of chin-shields, which are in contact with each other. Nineteen to twenty-three series of scales round the neck. Scales imbricate: those on the highest part of the body higher than long, those on the sides with a small tubercle, those on the back with a keel. Ventral shields very distinct, nearly twice as large as the scales of the adjoining series, 321–337 in number, each with two small tubercles. Four anal shields, the outer of which are rather larger than the others. Trunk with from fifty-three to fifty-nine complete blackish rings, which are broader than the interspaces of the yellowish-olive ground-colour. Head and ventral side of the thin neck-like portion of the body black; the former with a yellow horseshoe-shaped mark across the frontals and nasals, and extending backwards over the superciliary edge to the temple. Tail with ten or eleven blackish cross bars."

Hydrophis stricticollis.

"Head narrow, elongate, not quite twice as long as broad; body slender, especially in its anterior portion. Two pairs of chin-shields, both of which are in contact with each other. Only one anterior temporal, which is as high as long. One post-ocular. Thirty-four series of scales round the neck. Ventral shields distinct, but only the anterior are twice as broad as the scales of the adjoining series; they are 398 in number. Six small præ-anal shields. Scales smooth in young specimens. Body with fifty-five blackish rings, not quite as broad as the yellowish ground-colour between them; they are rather broader and darker on the back than on the belly, and sometimes sub-interrupted in the vertebral and ventral line. Head yellow above, with irregular blackish confluent spots; whitish below. Tail with eleven blackish vertical bars."

Hydrophis curta.

Hydrus curtus, *Shaw.*
Lapemis curtus, *Gray.*
Hydrophis propinquus, *Jan.*

"Head short, thick, obtuse; anterior part of the body stout; body not elongate. The occipital shields are always divided into two or more pieces, or entirely broken up into small shields. Two pairs of chin-shields, separated in the middle by small gular scales. Only one post-ocular. Thirty to thirty-four series of scales round the neck; 209–252 scales in a lateral series between the angle of the mouth and the vent. Ventral shields nearly twice as broad as the scales of the adjoining series, 156–160 in number. Four small præ-anal shields. Fifty to fifty-three black bands across the back; they are broadest in the middle, nearly touching each other, and tapering on the sides; the yellowish ground-colour between them does not occupy more space than the bands. Generally the bands do not extend downwards to the belly, but sometimes they are continued as faint traces to the ventral shields, which are white, or, in the specimens with longer cross bands, blackish. A more or less distinct yellowish streak on the temple. Tail black, with only two yellow transverse spots at its root."

Hydrophis crassicollis (n. s.), *Anderson.*

"Head hardly distinct from the neck. Neck and body of nearly equal girth throughout. Round neck 2″ 2‴; round middle of body 2″ 9‴. Body elongated; 34 series of scales round the neck; 40 round the middle of body. Scales almost smooth on the neck and anterior third of the body, two feeble keel-like tubercles, one before the other, very obscure, but more strongly developed on the two posterior thirds. Ventrals twice the size of the adjoining scales, quite smooth, broken up here and there, on the posterior five-eighths of the body. Two pairs of anal shields, the central pair of moderate size, elongated, the external pair very large. The vertical is pointedly linguate. One præ-, and two post-oculars. The third, fourth, and fifth labials enter the orbit, on one side, but only the third and the fourth on the opposite side, the fifth being transversely divided into two shields which do not reach quite as high as the orbital margin. Two pairs of large chin-shields, the anterior pair quadrangular and the posterior pair rather elongated. Olive yellow above, yellowish on the scales and under surface, 62 broad black bands on the back contracting to a point on the sides, but prolonged very indistinctly on to them, and the ventral aspect, where they expand as a large blackish spot. Near the tail the dorsal bands become connected together, and their continuations on the ventral aspect follow a similar arrangement. Six black rings on the tail, confluent below; the latter third entirely black.

"Hooghly below Calcutta. Length (total) 4 feet 5″ 6‴, tail 4″ 3‴.

"The peculiarity of this species is its elongated body, the uniform breadth which it preserves throughout its length, and the enlarged and smooth ventrals." It is found in the tidal streams near Calcutta.

Hydrophis tuberculata (n. s.), *Anderson.*

"Head slightly broader than the neck and of moderate length. Neck not very slender. Rostral broader than high. Fourth and fifth labials below the eye; one præ-ocular, and two post-oculars. Three to four temporals along the side of each occipital, the anterior one the largest, and almost entering the labial margin. The nasals are large and quadrangular, and much larger than the frontals, which are rounded behind. The vertical is emarginate and much smaller than the elongated occipitals. All the shields of the head, including the lower labials and the scales in the immediate vicinity of the head, are thickly studded over with minute granules. Thirty-eight rows of slightly imbricate scales round the neck, each scale with two prominent tubercles, one before the other. Ventrals 321, small, about twice the size of the adjoining scales, irregular, sometimes dividing, those on the fore part of the body largest. Each ventral with several minute tubercles on either side. Four anal shields, the external the largest. Terminal scale of tail moderately large, tuberculated at its base. Trunk encircled by 59 black bands, 8 black bars on the tail. The bands are broadest and blackest on the back, contracting on the sides into narrow indistinct lines, continued on to the ventral surface. Ground-colour olive-yellow above, bright gamboge-yellow below. A dark olive patch on the crown of the head, with a pale yellowish band from orbit to orbit, and passing backwards through the temporals to the neck. An obscure dark line through the upper labials, which are yellowish. Length, 49 inches.

"*Hab.* Tidal streams, Calcutta.

"This species is very closely allied to *H. granosa*, from which it is separated by the small number of scales round the neck, by its two post-oculars and two pairs of large chin-shields, and by differences in the form of the shields of the head."

Hydrophis fayreriana (n. s.), *Anderson.*

"Head short and thick; snout broad and rounded. Body moderately long and stout, of nearly equal breadth throughout, narrower on the anterior fifth. Frontal shields large, tapering, about the same size as the nasals. One præ-ocular, small, its broadest end pointing forwards; one post-ocular. Seven upper labials, the fifth the largest, the sixth and seventh labials with a shield above them, suggesting that they are only detached portions of a large sixth labial. Third and fourth labials entering the orbit, oblong, higher than broad, the first pair of lower labials meeting behind the chin shield, with a number of scale-like shields behind them. Thirty-four rows of smooth, non-imbricated and non-tuberculated scales round the neck. Those on the ventral surface larger than those on the back sides, but no distinct row of enlarged ventrals; the median rows, however, are slightly imbricate, and number 193 from the throat to the anus. Five pairs of small præ-anal shields. Thirty-nine series of broad, olive-brown, cross bands on the back, extending to the sides, but not into the belly, and rounded below, separated by narrow pale lines, about half a scale's breadth. Tail olive-brown above, black on its lower third. Length 30½ inches, tail 3½ inches, gape ¾ inch.

"*Hab.* Pooree, Cuttack coast."

This species appears to be closely allied to *H. hardwickii*, from which it is distinguished by the absence of tubercles, in the adult, by the partial imbrication of the middle rows of ventral scales, and by their greater number.

Hydrophis nigra (n. s.), *Anderson.*

"Neck but moderately slender, less than two-thirds the length of body. Head broader than neck, long with nearly straight sides, the præ-orbital equalling the temporal breadth. Snout moderately long, broad, rounded, and rather spatulate. Rostral much broader than high, its posterior extremity being on a line with the rostro-labial suture: feebly notched on its inferior margin. Nasals broader posteriorly than they are long. The third labial not in contact with the nasal, and it is almost excluded from the orbit by the fourth labial and præ-ocular. One post-ocular. The fifth and sixth labials transversely divided. Two temporals, of which the anterior is the larger. Two pairs of chin-shields, the anterior in contact, the shields of the posterior pair separated by an azygos scale. Thirty-two rows of scales round the body, slightly imbricate and smooth. Ventrals forty-eight; the first twenty-five or so six times as large as the adjoining scales, which are rather small: the remainder diminish in size, but nearly all are distinct and undivided. Three pairs of anal-shields, of which the outer are the largest.

"Uniform intense black, without any trace of markings. Length 19″ (inches), of which the tail is 2″. Length of snout to occiput 0″ 7‴. Breadth across angle of mouth 0″ 4‴. Breadth before eyes 0″ 4‴. Breadth on a line with nasal suture 0″ 3‴. Snout to eye 0″ 3‴. Eye to angle of mouth two and a half lines. Angle of jaw to tip of snout 0″ 8‴.

"*Loc.* Pooree, Cuttack."

Hydrophis stewartii (n. s.), *Anderson.*

"The neck moderately long and slender, and the head rather short and not much broader than the neck. The remainder of the body very much compressed. Rostral considerably broader than high. The nasals as broad posteriorly as they are long. The third and fourth labials enter the orbit, the former not being in contact with the nasal. Three temporals, the anterior the largest. Two post-oculars. Vertical much pointed behind. Occipitals long and narrow. Two almost quadrangular chin-shields in contact with each other. Thirty-three rows of scales round the neck. The scales hexagonal, not imbricate, with a feeble central tubercle. Ventrals 387, smooth. The first forty on the neck about four times as large as the adjoining scales, those behind them being small and narrow as they are traced backwards, and hardly discernible on the last six inches of the trunk. Two pairs of small scale-like anals. Tail broad, markedly dilating from its root. Lips yellowish. Upper surface of head and upper surface of neck and trunk greenish-olive. Under surface of head and sides and under surface of neck and trunk salmon-coloured. Fifty-seven very obscure darker olive, almost black bars on the dorsal area of the neck and compressed portion, but not extending on to the light-coloured sides. The tail greenish-olive, mottled, and tipped with black.

"Length 38″ 3‴, of which the tail constitutes 2″ 8‴. Girth round neck, two inches behind head, 2″ 5‴. Greatest depth of body (five inches before tail) 1″ 8‴. Greatest thickness at that point 0″ 6‴. Thickness at upper margin of lower third in same locality 0″ 3‴. Thickness at ventral margin at same situation 0″ 2‴. Snout to occiput 0″ 11‴. Breadth across angle of mouth 0″ 7‴.

"*Loc.* Pooree, Cuttack."

The following species are also briefly described in Günther's Synopsis. They are found in the Indian Seas or on the coast:—

I. "*With Scales more or less Distinctly Imbricate.*

*(B.) "*Scales much imbricate, rather small, in forty-three to forty-seven series round the neck; ventral shields split into two.* Hydrus. (*Shaw.*) *Gray.*"

HYDROPHIS STOKESII.

"Body stout."

(C.) "*Scales in twenty-three to thirty-eight series round the neck; head not very small; anterior part of the body* (*neck*) *not, or moderately slender.* Hydrophis. (*Daud.*) *Günther.*"

HYDROPHIS MAJOR.

"Head rather short and broad; neck and body of moderate length. One post-ocular. Belly with only a few ventral shields."

H. CÆRULESCENS.

"Head rather small; neck and body somewhat elongate. One post-ocular; scales strongly keeled. Ventrals not much larger than the adjoining scales."

H. ASPERA.

"Head of moderate size and width; neck and body somewhat elongate. Two post-oculars; scales strongly keeled, the keel of each scale with two tubercular prominences."

H. SPIRALIS.

"Head of moderate size and width; neck and body somewhat elongate. One post-ocular. Back with a series of round black spots, alternating with black cross bands."

H. SUBCINCTA.

"Head rather small and narrow; neck slender. Two post-oculars; twenty-three series of scales round the neck. Ventrals not twice as large as the adjoining scales. Trunk with forty-one cross bands."

H. TORQUATA.

"Head rather small; neck slender. One post-ocular; thirty-three to thirty-five series of scales round the neck; vertical short.

(D.) "*Head very small; neck exceedingly slender.* Liopala. (*Gray*). *Günther.*"

H. LINDSAYI.

"The length of the thin part of the body is one-third of the total. One post-ocular; thirty-one to thirty-three series of scales round the neck. Trunk, with from forty-eight to fifty-eight blackish cross bands extending to the middle of the side."

H. LATIFASCIATA.

"One post-ocular; twenty-three series of scales round the neck. Trunk with thirty-eight broad black cross bands, confluent on the back and belly."

H. DIADEMA.

"Two post-oculars; thirty-three series of scales round the neck. Trunk with sixty-two blackish rings."

* Group (A) contains one species, *H. jerdonii*, already described, p. 26.

II. "*With Scales not imbricate, placed Side by Side.*

(A.) "*Head very small; neck exceedingly slender.* Microcephalophis. (*Less.*) *Gray.*"

H. GRACILIS.

"One post-ocular. Ventral shields 228–294, those on the hinder half of the body split into two."

H. FASCIATA.

"Two post-oculars. Ventral shields 316, all undivided."

H. CANTORIS.

"One post-ocular. Ventral shields 412–440, those on the hinder half of the body split into two.

(B.) "*Head of moderate size; anterior part of the body not, or moderately elongate.* Thalassophis. (*Schmidt*). *Günther.*"

H. LAPEMOIDES.

"Head narrow, elongate; body rather slender. Two post-oculars. Ventral shields twice as broad as the adjoining scales, 350 in number."

H. LONGICEPS.

"Head narrow, elongate; body rather slender. Two post-oculars. Ventral shields twice as broad as the adjoining scales, 271 in number. Scales keeled."

H. ORNATA.

"Head rather narrow, and produced; body somewhat elongate. Two post-oculars. Ventral shields twice as broad as the adjoining scales, 252–260 in number. Scales with a central tubercle. The first upper temporal shield much longer than high."

H. ELLIOTTI.

"Head rather thick and short; body of moderate length. Two post-oculars. Ventral shields nearly twice as broad as the adjoining scales, 253–258 in number. The first upper temporal shield is not much longer than high; thirty-five or thirty-seven series of scales round the neck."

H. PACHYCERCUS.

"Head and body of moderate width and length. Two post-oculars; nasal shields longer than broad. Ventrals more than twice as broad as the scales, 258 in number. The first upper temporal shield longer than high; twenty-eight series of scales round the neck."

H. VIPERINA.

"Head of moderate size and width; body of moderate length. Two post-oculars; nasal shields as broad posteriorly as they are long; anterior ventral shields broad."

H. HARDWICKII.

"Head short and thick; body stout. One post-ocular. No distinct ventral shields. Trunk with from forty-one to forty-three blackish cross bands, not extending downwards to the belly."

SECTION II.

DEATHS BY SNAKE-BITE IN THE BENGAL PRESIDENCY DURING 1869.

On the 3rd of January, 1870, I addressed a letter to the Secretaries or Political Agents of the following Governments :*

Bengal	Central Provinces
North-west Provinces	Central India
Punjab	Rajpootana
Oude	British Burmah

soliciting information on the subject of loss of life from snake-poisoning in their territories.

To it I have received prompt and ample replies from a number of officers; and the following abstracts show not only the great mortality, but attest the interest evinced by these gentlemen, and the care and trouble with which, in many instances, they have prepared these returns. I feel much indebted to all who have so fully complied with my request, and take this opportunity of tendering my thanks for the valuable information that has thus been placed by Government at my disposal.

The records represent, it is true, only a portion of India; as the Madras and Bombay Presidencies, as well as other parts of India, are not included. Had similar information been obtained from these Provinces, the list of mortality would doubtless have been much larger; as it is, the number of deaths is perfectly appalling, and the subject well merits close consideration, with the view of discovering, if possible, some remedy.

I have roughly classified the deaths under the head of the snakes that inflicted the fatal wound, but the records are rather vague on this point, and the information not always available. Still they are sufficiently explicit to make it clear, that in order of destructiveness, the Cobra occupies the first place on the list; the Krait (*Bungarus cæruleus*) occupies the second place, whilst under the headings of "Other snakes, and unknown," must be included many deaths due to Cobra, *Bungarus cæruleus*, Hamadryad, *Daboia*, *Bungarus fasciatus*, *Hydrophiacæ*, and some perhaps to *Echis carinata* and the *Trimeresuri*; though as to the last there is reason to believe that deaths from their bites are comparatively very rare.

It has been suggested by those well qualified to form an opinion, that not a few of the deaths, especially of women, ascribed to snake-bites, might, if they could be traced to their real cause, be referred to a totally different heading. It may be so; but still the indisputably fatal cases of snake-bite are terribly numerous, and it is very probable that not all that have occurred are recorded. Sir H. Bartle Frere, E.C.S.I., K.C.B., informs me that when he was Commissioner of Sind he instituted inquiry into the subject of death from snake-bite in that province, and it was no doubt owing to the police returns which were thus sent in to Government that attention was first directed to the subject in Rutnagherry, the Punjab, and elsewhere.

The records of the Commissioner of Sind's office no doubt contain interesting information on the subject, but speaking from memory Sir H. B. Frere says that one of the facts established by the returns was the enormous increase in the mortality from snake-bites during the hot weather. This was partly due to the people sleeping more out of doors at that season, but still more to the great quantity of inundated land which drove the snakes into the grass on the higher land, the mortality rising from an average of two or three per week in the cold weather to as many as ten or twelve per week in the hot weather, in a population of about a million and a quarter. The Rutnagherry as well as the Sind returns showed a very high mortality.

No doubt the explanation given by Sir H. B. Frere of what occurred in Sind applies to the rest of India, and the mortality is greater at certain seasons, not only because the snakes are then concentrated in greater numbers in certain places for the reason assigned, but because during these seasons, with the higher temperature, the activity and vigour of the snakes is increased.

The deadly nature of the bite of the Cobra, Hamadryad, Krait, and Viper, is shown in the numerous experiments that I have made on the lower animals; it is equally demonstrated, with reference to the human race, by the returns of the year 1869, and I fear the inefficacy of all the so-called antidotes is made equally certain.

My own impression, and it is derived from many experiments is, that in case of a real bite, by which I mean when a healthy and vigorous Cobra, Hamadryad, *Bungarus*, or *Daboia* has imbedded its fangs and inoculated the poison, there is very little chance, if any, of saving life, unless the most immediate and vigorous aid be given, and even then, at the best, there is but poor chance of safety. No doubt many bites do not prove fatal, for the reason that the snake has been altogether or comparatively innocent, or that its poison has been weak or defective in quantity, or that the bite has been only partially inflicted.

It is quite possible too that the most vigorous snake may inflict a wound, even draw blood, without fatal poisoning, or indeed sometimes without poisoning at all. This is the case when it strikes without seizing, as snakes often do, or when they have expended their poison by previous biting, or in feeding, or have bitten through clothes or leather. The real bite, when the fatal hypodermic injection of the poison takes place, is when the snake seizes, retains its hold, and thoroughly imbeds its fangs in the part. That bites may be inflicted without poisoning was well shown in an experiment with a Mongoose, which was shut up in a cage with a fresh and vicious Cobra. They fought for some time, and when removed from the cage they both bore marks of the fray, in bleeding wounds about the head. The Mongoose had suffered almost as much as the Cobra, but there were no symptoms of poisoning. It was certain that he had been bitten, and yet that he was not poisoned. Shut up in a cage, no antidote was available; it appeared either that he had some special immunity, or that—most improbable—the Cobra was harmless. The reason was soon explained. The Cobra was made to close its jaws on the Mongoose's thigh; it succumbed to the poison and died in a short time. The fact was, the wounds in the head had been given, as I have said they may be, without injection of poison; they were scratches, and not the punctures through which the poison finds rapid and fatal entry into the circulation.

From such injuries, even when a certain amount of poison has entered, recovery is no doubt quite possible and probable, and much may be done to aid it by medical treatment and the use of stimulants. In cases where poisoning has been

---

* *Vide* Appendix, No. 2.

caused, but in a minor degree, recovery takes place partly from the inherent vigour of the individual, partly by the aid of treatment; but that any creature fairly bitten and poisoned by a vigorous Cobra, Hamadryad, Krait, or *Daboia*, and who would otherwise have died, has been saved from such death by what is popularly called an antidote, I confess that I fear there are not sufficient grounds for belief. I have shown by experiment that if the bitten part can be instantaneously and completely separated from the rest of the body by ligature or excision, poisoning may be averted by preventing entry of the venom into the circulation; whilst every other measure tried, whether local or constitutional, has entirely failed to do any good. The impossibility of applying this treatment in a great proportion of cases is obvious, and it must be remembered that even it has only succeeded occasionally. I propose to give an account of what may be done in snake-bite in all its forms, describing whatever may hold out any prospect of relief or recovery. Meanwhile, there exists the obvious necessity of endeavouring to prevent these numerous fatal accidents by making generally known the appearance and habits of the Thanatophidia, and by instituting rewards for their destruction. With a plain description, and a faithful representation of each species in colours, every district medical, or police officer, would be able at once to distinguish the venomous from the innocent snakes; and thus knowledge enough, at least for all practical purposes, might be imparted to intelligent native subordinates to enable them to recognise the poisonous snakes also. By offering a larger reward for these only, their numbers would soon diminish, and the people would be made acquainted with the characters that distinguish the venomous from the harmless snakes, and would learn to avoid them. Thus only, I believe, can the evil be remedied, so long at all events as the mode of life among the lower and agricultural classes, those who mainly suffer, remains what it now is. I would suggest that Magistrates, District and Police Officers, and Civil Surgeons be authorized to give the following rewards for poisonous snakes:—

	R.	A.
Cobras	0	8
Bungarus cæruleus	0	6
Bungarus fasciatus	0	4
Ophiophagus	0	8
Russell's viper	0	8
Echis	0	4
Trimeresurus	0	2

The sum disbursed would no doubt be large, but the results in saving of human life and destruction of snakes would compensate for the expenditure.

The following are abstracts of the returns above alluded to. Probably many of them are imperfect, for want of accurate records; in some, I believe, the mortality is underrated, as in the Calcutta return, which gives only six cases for 1869. Still they are sufficient to show how great an evil exists in what, one would fain hope, may be regarded, to a certain extent, as a preventible cause of death.

I have received returns from the nine Divisions, including forty-eight Districts in Bengal, showing an aggregate of 6219 deaths from snake-bite in the year 1869.

Of these 2374 were of males over twelve years of age; 2576 were of females over twelve years of age; 663 of male children under twelve, and 606 of female children under twelve years of age; making a total of 3037 males of all ages, and 3182 females of all ages.

Thus of the 6219 persons killed by snakes in one year in Bengal, there was an excess of 145 females over the males; the adult females appear to have been the greatest sufferers, by 2576 against 2374; whilst, on the other hand, female children were fewer, being 606 against 663 male children.

The ages of the sufferers vary from a hundred years to three months.

Although the returns are for the most part vague as to the snake that caused death, it is sufficiently evident that the several varieties of Cobra caused the greatest mortality. 959 deaths are assigned to this snake, 160 to the Krait or *Bungarus cæruleus*, and 348 to other snakes not recognisable under their local vernacular names, 4752 to snakes altogether unknown, most frequently, probably, not having been seen. Doubtless, as the Cobra is in excess in the recorded cases, so it is in those of "other snakes," and "unknown," whilst the remainder must be assigned to the Hamadryad, the *Bungarus cæruleus*, *Bungarus fasciatus*, *Daboia russellii*, and probably a few to the *Trimeresuri* and *Hydrophidæ*. It is worthy of note, that of all the Divisions the Presidency Division — although the Soonderbun District furnished no return, and Calcutta gives only six deaths—shows the largest mortality, being 1341 deaths; whilst the lowest is in Cooch Behar, 79 deaths, the Garrow Hills District, of that Division, furnishing no return at all.

It is tolerably evident, notwithstanding the great mortality, that the figures represent only an approximation to that which really occurs, for some districts have sent no returns at all, whilst others have probably not recorded all that occurred.

From Orissa I have received returns of three Districts, showing that in 1869, 350 deaths occurred. Of these 137 were of adult males, 138 of adult females, 44 of boys and 31 of girls under twelve years of age. Here also, although the difference is expressed only by 1, the adult female mortality exceeds that of the adult males; whereas among children the male exceed the female deaths by 13.

It appears that 128 deaths were due to Cobras, 2 only to the Krait, 52 to "other snakes," and 168 to "snakes unknown;" but a large proportion of these no doubt were also due to Cobras, some to the Krait, *Daboia*, Hamadryad; and it is possible that in this Division, which has a considerable tract of seaboard, some deaths may be ascribed to the salt-water snakes, or *Hydrophidæ*.

From Assam I have received the returns of seven Districts, in three of which no reports are made. The other four give an aggregate of 76 deaths. Of these 50 were of adult males, 14 of adult females, 9 of boys, 3 of girls; the male in this case much exceeding the female deaths.

Twelve deaths are ascribed to other snakes than the Cobra or Krait; 64 were caused by snakes unknown. I think it is more than probable that these returns only represent part of the mortality from snake-bite in Assam.

From Oude I have received the returns of twelve Districts; by which it appears that 1205 persons died of snake-bite in that province in 1869. Of these 364 were adult males, 558 adult females, 137 boys, and 146 girls under twelve years of age.

The adult females were thus 194 in excess of the males, and the young girls 9 in excess of the boys. 607 deaths were caused by Cobras, 105 by Kraits, 20 by "other snakes," and 473 by "snakes unknown." Several infants of tender age perished, and the ages of the sufferers range from a hundred years to one month.

The District of Gondah appears to have been most fatal, giving 206 deaths.

From Central India I have received from fourteen Districts reports of only 90 deaths. Of these 38 were of adult males, 36 of adult females, 8 of boys, and 8 of girls. The number of males and females is thus as nearly as possible equal, there being a slight excess of males. Twenty-one deaths are ascribed to the Cobra, 37 to "other snakes," and 32 to "snakes unknown." Western Malwah, of all the Districts, furnishes the largest number of deaths by 42.

From the Central Provinces I have received no returns, but

am informed officially by the Secretary to the Chief Commissioner, that 606 persons died of snake-bite in the year 1869 in those provinces; no details are given.

From Rajpootana no returns have been received, as I am informed by Colonel Keatinge, in an official communication, that "the Native Governments never receive detailed reports of this nature."

From the North-west Provinces I have received reports from eight Divisions, including thirty-eight Districts, giving a total of 1995 deaths, of which 654 were of adult men, 952 of adult women, 199 of boys, and 190 of girls under twelve years of age. The women were therefore 298 in excess of the men; whilst the boys exceeded the girls by 9.

The Cobra is accountable for 854 deaths, the Krait for 92, "other snakes" for 63, whilst to "snakes unknown" the large number of 986 is assigned; no doubt the majority of the "other snakes" and "snakes unknown" were Cobra and Krait.

From British Burmah I have received returns from Arracan, Pegu, Tenasserim, and Shewé Gyen, giving a total of 120 deaths from snake-bite in the year 1869. Of these 95 were of men, or of boys over twelve years of age, 22 of women over twelve years, 3 of boys under twelve, and no girls under that age. In this case the male preponderate largely over the female deaths of all ages, 98 males and 22 females having suffered.

Forty-five deaths are attributed to the Cobra, and all the rest, with a few exceptions, to the Viper (*Daboia*), the remainder being ascribed to Hamadryads and *Hydrophidæ*. In one case a master of a ship died at Moulmein from a bite inflicted when bathing—no doubt by some form of *Hydrophis*.

From the Punjab I have received returns from the ten Divisions into which that province is divided, from thirty-two Districts, giving the number of deaths from snake-bite as 755. Of these 434 were of males, 184 of females above twelve years of age, 77 of boys and 32 of girls under twelve, making 727. The remaining 28 to make up 755, was the total number of deaths in the District of Umritsur, in which return the ages and sex are not distinguished. The males in this part of India appear to have suffered more than the females, in the proportion of 511 males to 216 females. The earliest age recorded was that of an infant one day old. Only 76 deaths are ascribed to the Cobra, none to the Krait, 242 to other snakes, 437 unknown. Among these no doubt many were due to the *Bungarus*, Cobra, and probably to the *Echis carinata*.

The total number of deaths recorded therefore stands thus:—

Bengal, including Assam and Orissa . . .	6645
North-west Provinces	1995
Punjab	755
Oude	1205
Central Provinces	606
Central India	90
British Burmah	120
Total	11,416

This total, large as it is, I fear cannot be regarded as the real mortality in these Provinces, nor may the numbers be accepted as an absolutely true indication of the relative frequency of deaths in each. The information from which these records were framed was probably only partial and imperfect. I believe that if systematic returns could be kept by the police in every district, subdivision, and municipality, the number of deaths recorded would be much larger. I believe also that were such information available and collected from the whole of Hindostan, it would be found that more than 20,000 persons die annually from snake-bite alone.

If the suggestions that I propose to make, together with the description of the poisonous snakes to which this mortality is due, contribute towards its diminution, I shall feel satisfied that the investigations of the past three years have not been without results.

The area represented by these returns is, I should think, rather less than half that of the Peninsula of Hindostan; but from a return, for which I am indebted to W. W. Hunter, Esq., LL.D., C.S., I find it represents a population of 120,972,263.

Return showing the Number of Deaths from Snake-bites, in the year 1869, in the Province of Bengal. Population, including Orissa and Assam, 48,358,134.

Divisions.	Districts.	Males over 12.	Females over 12.	Males under 12.	Females under 12.	Total Deaths in Districts.	Total Deaths in Divisions.	Names of Snakes.				Remarks.
								Cobra (Kála Gokurrah, Gomunah.)	Krait.	Other Snakes.	Unknown.	
Bhaugulpore and Sonthal Pergunnahs.	Bhaugulpore	87	78	28	11	204	...	17	5	2	180	
	Monghyr	62	64	13	14	153	...	...	6	13	134	One man said to be 140 years old.
	Purneah	34	24	13	6	77	...	1	...	37	39	
	Deoghur	18	14	8	4	44	...	21	9	7	7	One was from a Scorpion bite.
	Godda	14	9	8	1	32	...	4	4	...	24	
	Nya Doomka	8	8	8	1	25	...	...	...	...	25	
	Rajmehal	30	24	9	5	68	...	68	...	...	...	
	Total Deaths in Bhaugulpore, &c.	253	221	87	42	603	603	111	24	59	409	
Burdwan.	Bancoorah	47	48	2	6	103	...	2	...	4	97	
	Beerbhoom	26	24	...	7	57	...	9	5	2	41	
	Burdwan	29	48	2	9	88	...	45	...	2	41	
	Hooghly	97	93	21	13	224	...	12	...	1	211	
	Howrah	73	88	18	24	203	...	17	...	2	184	
	Midnapore	196	217	46	70	529	...	43	...	32	454	
	Total Deaths in Burdwan ...	468	518	89	129	1204	1204	128	5	43	1028	
Chittagong.	Chittagong	5	8	2	...	15	...	...	...	...	15	
	Tipperah	42	19	3	7	71	...	...	...	3	68	
	Noakhally	36	41	8	13	98	...	...	...	...	98	
	Total Deaths in Chittagong ...	83	68	13	20	184	184	...	...	3	181	
Chota Nagpore.	Hazareebaugh	10	19	6	3	38	...	7	7	...	24	
	Lohardugga	74	33	7	8	122	...	23	36	12	51	
	Maunbhoom	57	29	4	1	91	...	44	47	...	...	
	Singbhoom	11	10	...	...	21	...	...	...	2	19	
	Total Deaths in Chota Nagpore...	152	91	17	12	272	272	74	90	14	94	
Cooch Behar.	Garrow Hills	...	...	...	...	...	...	...	...	...	...	No report sent.
	Darjeeling	1	...	1	...	2	...	2	...	...	...	
	Gowalpara	13	15	7	2	37	...	...	...	2	35	
	Julpigoree	19	19	2	...	40	...	7	...	21	12	
	Total Deaths in Cooch Behar ...	33	34	10	2	79	79	9	...	23	47	
Dacca.	Backergunge	89	77	32	27	225	...	5	...	1	219	A boy 1 year old.
	Cachar	5	...	1	...	6	...	...	...	...	6	No name of snake recorded.
	Dacca	70	80	22	35	207	...	2	...	27	178	A girl 7 months old.
	Furreedpore	37	37	19	10	103	...	1	...	...	102	A boy 3 months old.
	Mymensing	83	87	33	29	232	...	...	...	6	226	
	Sylhet	37	20	17	11	85	...	...	...	22	63	
	Total Deaths in Dacca	321	301	124	112	858	858	8	...	56	794	
Patna.	Chumparun	6	9	3	6	24	...	9	6	1	8	
	Gya	27	21	7	5	60	...	6	1	...	53	
	Patna	67	76	21	18	182	...	55	16	3	108	Includes two from Centipedes.
	Sarun	36	39	8	6	89	...	36	10	...	43	
	Shahabad...	4	8	...	3	15	...	9	1	...	5	
	Tirhoot	40	35	13	6	94	...	18	7	1	68	
	Total Deaths in Patna	180	188	52	44	464	464	133	41	5	285	
Presidency.	Calcutta	2	3	...	1	6	...	1	...	...	5	
	Jessore	134	153	59	49	395	...	17	...	41	337	
	Nuddea	129	242	44	53	468	...	217	...	7	244	
	Soonderbuns	...	...	...	...	...	...	...	...	...	...	No report sent.
	24 Pergunnahs	163	196	64	49	472	...	51	...	82	339	
	Total Deaths in the Presidency...	428	594	167	152	1341	1341	286	...	130	925	
Rajshahye.	Bograh	54	66	11	15	146	...	...	...	...	146	
	Dinagepore	65	92	22	19	198	...	43	...	6	149	
	Maldah	34	35	12	7	88	...	13	...	9	66	
	Moorshedabad	65	116	23	17	221	...	4	...	...	217	
	Pubna	82	76	28	27	213	...	...	...	...	213	
	Rajshahye	118	150	...	...	268	...	150	...	...	118	
	Rungpore	38	26	8	8	80	...	...	...	...	80	
	Total Deaths in Rajshahye ...	456	561	104	93	1214	1214	210	...	15	989	
	Grand Total of Deaths in Bengal	2374	2576	663	606	6219	6219	959	160	348	4752	

Return showing the Number of Deaths from Snake-bites, in the Year 1869, *in the Province of Assam.—Population* 1,537,981.

Division.	Districts.	Males over 12.	Females over 12.	Males under 12.	Females under 12.	Total Deaths in Districts.	Total Deaths in Division.	Names of Snakes.				Remarks.
								Cobra (Kála Gokurrah, Gomunah.)	Krait.	Other Snakes.	Unknown.	
Assam.	Khasya and Jynteah Hills ...	...	...	...	...	...	...	...	...	...	...	No deaths reported.
	Durrung	7	3	3	1	14	...	...	...	1	13	
	Kamroop	35	8	5	1	49	...	...	...	8	41	
	Lukhimpore	...	...	...	...	...	...	...	...	...	...	No deaths reported.
	Nowgong	8	2	1	1	12	...	...	...	3	9	
	Seebsaugor	...	1	...	...	1	...	...	...	...	1	
	Naga Hills	...	...	...	...	...	...	...	...	...	...	No deaths reported.
	Total Deaths in Assam ...	50	14	9	3	76	76	...	...	12	64	

Return showing the Number of Deaths from Snake-bites, in the Year 1869, *in the North-West Provinces.—Population* 30,086,098.

Divisions.	Districts.	Males over 12.	Females over 12.	Males under 12.	Females under 12.	Total Deaths in Districts.	Total Deaths in Divisions.	Names of Snakes.				Remarks.
								Cobra (Kála Gokurrah, Gomunah.)	Krait.	Other Snakes.	Unknown.	
Meerut.	Dehra Dhoon	...	...	...	...	...	...	...	...	...	...	No report sent.
	Saharunpore	23	19	4	3	49	...	15	...	3	31	
	Mozuffernugger	9	6	1	2	18	...	...	...	...	18	
	Meerut	10	11	3	1	25	...	25	...	...	...	
	Boolundshuhur	8	15	3	1	27	...	...	...	5	22	
	Allyghur	14	16	1	2	33	...	...	...	2	31	
	Total Deaths in Meerut ...	64	67	12	9	152	152	40	...	10	102	
Agra.	Muttra	8	11	1	1	21	...	...	...	2	19	
	Agra	9	14	3	2	28	...	...	...	2	26	
	Furruckabad	9	16	2	1	28	...	1	...	...	27	
	Mynpoorie	...	...	...	...	...	...	...	...	...	...	No report sent.
	Etawah	11	20	...	3	34	...	...	...	...	34	
	Etah	9	14	...	2	25	...	...	...	...	25	
	Total Deaths in Agra ...	46	75	6	9	136	136	1	...	4	131	
Rohilcund.	Bijnour	32	76	8	10	126	...	...	...	...	126	
	Moradabad	28	71	17	21	137	...	45	...	6	86	
	Budaon	21	56	7	13	97	...	92	...	3	2	
	Bareilly	97	145	40	45	327	...	325	...	1	1	
	Shajehanpore	36	55	13	7	111	...	15	...	...	96	
	Terai Pergunnahs	...	...	...	...	...	...	...	...	...	...	No report sent.
	Total Deaths in Rohilcund...	214	403	85	96	798	798	477	...	10	311	
Allahabad.	Cawnpore	18	23	8	5	54	...	...	...	...	54	
	Futtepore	27	46	9	2	84	...	5	...	...	79	
	Bandah	51	98	10	13	172	...	117	38	5	12	
	Humeerpore	31	24	7	7	69	...	...	...	...	69	
	Allahabad	...	...	...	...	...	...	...	...	...	...	No report sent.
	Jounpore	14	11	4	3	32	...	...	2	2	28	
	Total Deaths in Allahabad...	141	202	38	30	411	411	122	40	7	242	
Benares.	Azimgurh	13	12	3	1	29	...	9	6	4	10	
	Mirzapore	30	47	7	4	88	...	...	7	6	75	
	Benares	31	24	5	15	75	...	17	4	...	54	
	Ghazeepore	27	12	6	6	51	...	37	...	6	8	
	Gorruckpore	52	58	21	8	139	...	85	33	1	20	
	Bustee	4	12	4	1	21	...	18	...	3	...	
	Total Deaths in Benares ...	157	165	46	35	403	403	166	50	20	167	
Jhansie.	Jhansie	16	18	3	1	38	...	24	...	1	13	
	Jalaon	...	...	...	...	...	...	...	...	...	...	No report sent.
	Lullutpore	1	1	...	...	2	...	...	2	...	...	
	Total Deaths in Jhansie ...	17	19	3	1	40	40	24	2	1	13	
Ajmere.	Mahairwara	...	...	1	...	1	...	...	...	...	1	
	Ajmere	...	...	...	...	...	...	...	...	...	...	No report sent.
	Total Deaths in Ajmere ...	...	...	1	...	1	1	...	...	...	1	
Kurnaul.	Kumaon...	8	9	2	5	24	...	24	...	...	...	
	Ghurwal	3	10	2	3	18	...	...	...	11	7	
	Total Deaths in Kumaon ...	11	19	4	8	42	42	24	...	11	7	
	Total Deaths in N.-W. Provinces	650	950	195	188	1983	1983	854	92	63	974	
	One District added, name not known	4	2	4	2	12	12	...	...	...	12	
	Grand Total of Deaths in N.-W. Provinces ...	654	952	199	190	1995	1995	854	92	63	986	

Return showing the Number of Deaths from Snake-bites, in the year 1869, *in the Punjab.—Population* 17,611,498.

Divisions.	Districts.	Males over 12.	Females over 12.	Males under 12.	Females under 12.	Total Deaths in Districts.	Total Deaths in Divisions.	Names of Snakes.				Remarks.
								Cobra.	Krait.	Other Snakes.	Unknown.	
Delhi.	Delhi	8	6	1	1	16	...	5	...	...	11	
	Goorgaon	6	13	4	1	24	...	10	...	1	13	
	Kurnaul	26	7	3	...	36	...	12	...	2	22	
	Total Deaths in Delhi	40	26	8	2	76	76	27	...	3	46	
Derajat.	Dera Ismael Khan	15	4	2	2	23	...	3	...	10	10	
	Ghazee Khan	...	...	...	...	...	...	...	...	...	...	
	Bunnoo	4	1	1	1	7	...	...	...	5	2	
	Total Deaths in Derajat	19	5	3	3	30	30	3	...	15	12	
Hissar.	Hissar	11	8	2	2	23	...	8	...	10	5	
	Rhotuck	13	11	5	2	31	...	...	...	16	15	
	Sirsa	7	1	1	...	9	...	4	...	2	3	
	Total Deaths in Hissar	31	20	8	4	63	63	12	...	28	23	
Jullundur.	Jullundur	5	8	2	...	15	...	...	...	10	5	
	Hooshyarpore	15	9	5	2	31	...	...	...	28	3	
	Kangra	22	17	1	5	45	...	...	...	25	20	
	Total Deaths in Jullundur	42	34	8	7	91	91	...	...	63	28	
Lahore.	Lahore	38	9	8	2	57	...	...	...	31	26	A boy 1 year old.
	Goojranwalla	23	1	2	...	26	...	...	...	10	16	
	Ferozepore	7	7	4	1	19	...	6	...	3	10	
	Total Deaths in Lahore	68	17	14	3	102	102	6	...	44	52	
Mooltan.	Mooltan	22	5	2	...	29	...	...	...	28	1	
	Jhung	30	7	3	1	41	...	6	...	9	26	
	Montgomery	6	3	1	...	10	...	1	...	...	9	
	Mozuffergurh	27	7	3	2	39	...	4	...	4	31	
	Total Deaths in Mooltan	85	22	9	3	119	119	11	...	41	67	
Peshawur.	Peshawur	1	...	1	...	2	...	...	...	1	1	
	Hazara	2	...	1	1	4	...	2	...	2	...	
	Kohat	...	...	...	...	...	...	...	...	...	...	
	Total Deaths in Peshawur	3	...	2	1	6	6	2	...	3	1	
Rawul Pindee.	Rawul Pindee	31	15	6	...	52	...	1	...	10	41	
	Jhelum	14	5	4	2	25	...	...	...	3	22	
	Goojrat	...	...	...	...	...	...	...	...	...	...	
	Shahpore	22	7	4	1	34	...	10	...	5	19	
	Total Deaths in Rawul Pindee	67	27	14	3	111	111	11	...	18	82	
Umballa.	Umballa	29	21	3	1	54	...	...	...	...	54	
	Loodianah	1	...	...	...	1	...	...	...	...	1	
	Simla	...	...	...	...	...	...	...	...	...	...	
	Total Deaths in Umballa	30	21	3	1	55	55	...	...	...	55	
Umritsur.	Umritsur	...	...	...	...	28*	...	...	...	16	12	* Sex not given.
	Goordaspore	14	10	3	3	30	...	4	...	9	17	A boy 1 day old.
	Sealkote	35	2	5	2	44	...	...	...	2	42	
	Total Deaths in Umritsur	49	12	8	5	102	102	4	...	27	71	
	Grand Total of Deaths in the Punjab	434†	184†	77†	32†	755	755	76	...	242	437	† The addition of 28 to the grand totals marked † will give the Grand Total 755.

Deaths from Snake-bites in the Province of Oude, in the year 1869.—*Population* 11,232,368.

Districts.	Males over 12.	Females over 12.	Males under 12.	Females under 12.	Total Deaths.	Names of Snakes.				Remarks.
						Cobra (Kála Gokurrah, Gomunah.)	Krait.	Other Snakes.	Unknown.	
City of Lucknow	1	2	...	1	4	...	4	...	...	
District of Lucknow	7	16	2	4	29	28	1	...	...	
Oonao	14	19	6	...	39	34	5	...	...	
Roy Bareilly	15	22	3	4	44	...	21	3	20	A boy 1 month old amongst these.
Gondah	54	103	22	27	206	...	...	...	206	No name of snake recorded.
Kherie	57	52	19	20	148	139	2	7	...	A boy 1 year old, and an old woman 100 years old, amongst these.
Pertabgurh	4	9	5	3	21	12	6	...	3	
Sultanpore	27	36	9	8	80	55	9	2	14	
Fyzabad	22	74	5	10	111	22	18	8	63	A girl 4 months and a half old amongst these.
Hurdui	46	48	21	16	131	90	3	...	38	A girl 10 months old amongst these.
Seetapore	35	55	8	12	110	88	16	...	6	
Baraitch	45	58	21	23	147	48	20	...	79	A boy 1 year old amongst these.
Barabankie	37	64	16	18	135	91	...	...	44	A boy 1 year old amongst these.
Total	364	558	137	146	1205	607	105	20	473	

Return showing the Number of Deaths from Snake-bites, in the Year 1869, *in the Province of Orissa.—Population* 3,151,476.

Division.	Districts.	Males over 12.	Females over 12.	Males under 12.	Females under 12.	Total Deaths in Districts.	Total Deaths in Division.	Names of Snakes. Cobra (Kála Gokurrah, Gomunah.)	Krait.	Other Snakes.	Unknown.	Remarks.
Orissa.	Balasore...	36	41	6	5	88	...	27	...	2	59	
	Pooree	41	25	17	6	89	...	41	...	5	43	Girl 18 months old.
	Cuttack	60	72	21	20	173	...	60	2	45	66	Woman 100 years old.
	Total Deaths in Orissa ...	137	138	44	31	350	350	128	2	52	168	

Return showing the Number of Deaths from Snake-bites, in the Central Provinces, for the Year 1869.—*Population* 9,668,103. *Population of Berars,* 2,220,074.

Remarks.—No details given from these Provinces; the total of 606 only being returned.

Return showing the Number of Deaths from Snake-bites, in the Year 1869, *in the Province of Central India. Population not given.*

Districts.	Males over 12.	Females over 12.	Males under 12.	Females under 12.	Total Deaths in Districts.	Total Deaths in Divisions.	Names of Snakes. Cobra (Kála Gokurrah, Gomunah.)	Krait.	Other Snakes.	Unknown.	Remarks.
Indore Presidency...	...	...	...	...	...	...	...	...	...	...	No report.
Gwalior Agency	...	...	...	...	...	...	...	...	...	...	No report.
Bhopal Agency	1	1	...	1	3	...	...	...	...	3	
Bundlekund Agency	...	...	...	...	...	...	...	...	...	...	No report.
Nagode Agency { Rewah	3	1	2	1	7	...	7	...	...	...	
Nagode Agency { Nagode...	2	5	...	2	9	...	1	...	...	8	
Nagode Agency { Myhere...	...	5	...	...	5	...	4	...	...	1	
Goonah Agency	...	...	...	...	...	...	...	...	...	...	No report.
Bheel Agency	2	4	3	1	10	...	3	...	3	4	
District Bheel Agency	1	1	2	...	4	...	3	...	...	1	
Mhow Cantonments	2	...	...	...	2	...	...	...	...	2	
Neemuch Cantonments	...	...	...	...	...	...	...	...	...	...	No report.
Rutlam	3	4	...	1	8	...	2	...	3	3	
Western Malwah	24	15	1	2	42	...	1	...	31	10	
Total Deaths in Central India	38	36	8	8	90	90	21	...	37	32	

Return showing the Number of Deaths from Snake-bites, in the Year 1869, *in the Province of Burmah.—Population* 2,395,988.

Division.	Districts.	Males over 12.	Females over 12.	Males under 12.	Females under 12.	Total Deaths.	Names of Snakes. Cobra.	Krait.	Other Snakes.	Unknown.	Remarks.
Burmah.	Arracan	2	...	...	...	2	2	...	...	...	
	Pegu	72	19	1	...	92	28	...	58	6	
	Tenasserim	12	3	1	...	16	5	...	7	4	
	Shewé Gyen	9	...	1	...	10	10	...	...	...	
	Total Deaths in Burmah ...	95	22	3	...	120	45	...	65	10	

Grand Total of Deaths from Snake-bites in 1869.—*Population, excluding that of Central India,* 120,972,263.

Provinces.	Males over 12.	Females over 12.	Males under 12.	Females under 12.	Total Deaths.	Names of Snakes. Cobra.	Krait.	Other Snakes.	Unknown.	Remarks.
Bengal	2,374	2,576	663	606	6,219	959	160	348	4,752	
Orissa	137	138	44	31	350	128	2	52	168	
Assam	50	14	9	3	76	...	...	12	64	
N. W. Provinces	654	952	199	190	1,995	854	92	63	986	
Punjab	* 434	* 184	* 77	* 32	755	76	...	242	437	* The addition of 28 to the grand totals marked * will give the Grand Total 755.
Oude	364	558	137	146	1,205	607	105	20	473	
Central Provinces	...	...	...	...	606	...	...	...	...	No details furnished.
Central India	38	36	8	8	90	21	...	37	32	
Burmah	95	22	3	...	120	45	...	65	10	
Grand Totals	† 4,146	† 4,480	† 1,140	† 1,016	11,416	‡ 2,690	‡ 359	‡ 839	‡ 6,922	† The addition of 606 to the grand totals marked † will give the Grand Total 11,416. ‡ The addition of 634 (*i. e.*, 606 and 28) to the grand totals marked ‡ will give the Grand Total 11,416 :—

Or about 1 in every 10,000. The returns from which these abstracts were made were furnished by Government.

SECTION III.

ON THE TREATMENT OF SNAKE-BITE.

Snake-poison produces fatal or deleterious effects, either by completely paralysing the nerve centres, and thus causing rapid dissolution, or by partially paralysing them, and poisoning the blood, thereby inducing pathological conditions of a secondary nature, which may, according to circumstances, cause the slightest or the most dangerous symptoms.

The effect produced depends on two sets of conditions : first, the species of the snake; its actual state at the time, the quantity and quality of its poison, and the circumstances under which it inflicts the bite ; second, the species, size, and vigour of the living creature, and the circumstances under which it is bitten.

Snake-poison is essentially a neurotic, and when it takes full effect, it kills by annihilating, in some unknown way, the source of nerve force.

It is also an irritant, for, if applied to a mucous membrane, or to the conjunctiva, it causes violent inflammation, absorption at the same time takes place, and symptoms of poisoning are produced.

It is also, to a certain extent, a septic, for if the bitten creature survive, the wound and the parts about it are apt to slough and to induce septicæmia. The poison acts by absorption, that is, by entering the circulation, and so reaching the nerve centres, it produces, according to the quantity or intensity of the venom, either death, or severe local and constitutional symptoms. If it find entry by a large vein, such as the femoral or jugular, life may be destroyed in a few seconds.

The blood itself is affected by the poison. I have not been able to detect any corpuscular changes, such as those described by Professor Halford, nor have I any exact information on the chemical changes it undergoes or may have undergone; but that it is altered there can be no doubt; and in poisoning of the lower animals, at all events by the *Viperidæ*, its coagulability after death is generally destroyed, whilst after death by poisoning by the colubrine snakes the blood generally coagulates.

As the blood is the channel through which the poison acts, it is obvious that the first object should be to arrest, destroy, or prevent its entry into the circulation, or, if it have already entered, to neutralize or counteract its action, or to procure its elimination by the agency of the natural depurating organs and their secretions, and to treat local, consecutive, and constitutional symptoms by such remedial measures as may be required by the patient's condition. Absorption takes place with extreme rapidity ; so fast, indeed, that it was formerly supposed, in the case of some of the more active poisons, that they acted by transmission of a shock through the nervous system ; and so far as we know at present, it is not improbable that such in some instances may be the case. But rapid as the effect of snake-bite sometimes is, there is no reason to believe that generally it operates on the nerve centres through any other channel than that of the vascular system.

The experiments of Blake, Hering, and later of Claude Bernard, show that absorption takes place with such rapidity as to explain the most rapid deaths from such cause. Blake (*vide* Guy's "Forensic Medicine," 3rd edition, p. 388) found that a poison passed from the jugular vein to the lungs of a dog in from four to six seconds, from the jugular vein to the coronary arteries of the heart in seven seconds; a poison injected into the jugular vein was distributed throughout the circulation in nine seconds. Claude Bernard found that a saturated solution of sulphuretted hydrogen introduced into the jugular vein of a dog began to be eliminated from the lungs in three seconds, and when injected into the femoral vein of the same dog in six seconds.

I have neither seen nor heard of any case of snake-poisoning, in man or the lower animals, so rapid—though in some I have observed the first symptoms in a few seconds—as to justify the conclusion that poisoning had occurred otherwise than through the medium of the circulation.

Such being the rapidity of the absorption and action of the poison, it is obvious that if the means, whatever they may be, of destroying or arresting its entry, be not applied immediately, but little benefit can be expected from them. If more than a few seconds have elapsed, we can only hope by these measures to prevent the entry of so much of the poison as may be diffused in the areolar tissue surrounding the bitten spot.

As the chief hope of safety lies in preventing the entry of any poison at all into the circulation, the earlier appropriate measures are resorted to the better is their chance of success. These I will now describe.

The Ligature.—This, if applied immediately at a little distance above the bitten part, may not only arrest the entry of the poison into the circulation, but may also prevent its diffusion in the areolar tissue in a centric direction. The efficacy of this method of treatment has long been recognised by the natives of India, who apply it, not just above the bite only, but at several places on the limb at intervals of some inches. There is reason to believe that if this be done without delay, the course of the poison may sometimes be stayed and life saved. Not long ago I saw a professional snake-charmer in the employ of the King of Oude, who said that he had been bitten in the finger by a fresh Cobra. A ligature was immediately tied in three or four places above the bite, and though he suffered constitutionally to some extent, he had escaped with life. His finger, however, was shrunk and anchylosed, owing to excessive burning, the result of fire which was applied in the form of live-coal, until the tendon shrivelled and was destroyed.

The danger and difficulty lie in not applying the ligature quickly enough. The confusion and alarm caused by the bite, the brief time that must elapse before the simplest ligature can be improvised, are certain to cause dangerous delay; and with every second of time lost the danger increases. There is also the probability that the ligature may not be sufficiently tightened; no mercy therefore can be shown : it must be tightened to the utmost, or it will not effect its purpose, and the poison will enter and do its fatal work. A piece of the dress twisted, a bit of string, a strap, anything that can be made to enclose the limb or part, should be immediately applied, and should be strained to the uttermost by twisting with a piece of stick ; nor should the tension cease until the circulation is entirely arrested, and the part is livid with the retained blood.

The experiments I have made on the lower animals show not only how rapidly the poison enters, if the circulation be not immediately arrested, but also how difficult it is so thoroughly to compress the limb as to completely stop the circulation.

I have found it all but impossible, with the strength of a pair of hands, so to tighten the ligature as to effect complete strangulation of a dog's hind leg.

The method most likely to succeed would be to tie the ligature tightly round the part, including a piece of stick, or some such lever, and then, by twisting the stick, so completely to strangulate the part that circulation ceases—at whatever cost this should be done. If the bite be in a finger, thumb, or toe, the first ligature should be applied a short distance above the bite, a second on the forearm or leg, and even a third higher up ; it is the best, perhaps the only chance of saving life ; and however great the pain it must be endured. No time should then be lost ; the punctures must be scarified so as to allow the blood to flow freely ; and then fire, a live-coal, a red-hot iron, or some caustic, mineral or carbolic acid, must be applied to the wound, so as to destroy the poison which is contained in the strangulated part ; the disorganization must be very complete, or even then it will fail, as enough of the poison may remain to be subsequently absorbed when the ligature is removed, and after all destroy life. In the case of a finger or toe, I believe that immediate amputation would be justifiable, if the sufferer or his companions, an instrument being at hand, had the moral courage to lop off the part at once.

The natives are in the habit of placing a live-coal, or of exploding gunpowder, on the bitten part, and no doubt they are right in doing so.

The place and circumstances under which snake-bites occur, are frequently such as not to leave much choice of means ; but it would generally be possible to extemporize a ligature and a hot coal, or among sportsmen a little gunpowder might be forthcoming. Should the bite be inflicted on a part of the body where a ligature could not be applied, the only expedient remaining is to excise the part to the depth of the punctures, let it bleed freely, and then apply fire or caustic. There is no time for reflection or consideration ; it must be done at once, and thoroughly, or there is no hope of avoiding the influence of the poison. If the snake has been seen and recognised as venomous, no doubt remains as to its necessity. But if it have not been seen, and the marks indicate a poisonous snake-bite, the patient must have the benefit of the doubt, or his chance of life may be lost.

Suction either by the mouth or cupping-glasses is useful ; for the latter purpose any small vessel might suffice ; a little spirit or a piece of burnt paper alone would serve to exhaust the air ; that by the mouth is efficacious, but it must be borne in mind that there is danger in applying the poison to the lips, for it may be absorbed, and evil results follow to the operator. But suction, however practised, should be applied after the ligature in those cases where that application is practicable ; where it is not, after excision, and before the application of caustic or cautery. Fire may be applied, as I have said, either by the live-coal, the hot iron, or by exploding gunpowder on the part, or by the moxa.

The mineral acids, chloride of zinc, carbolic acid, or strong acetic acid, may be applied with a piece of old linen or cotton attached to the end of a piece of stick or other convenient vehicle.

The liquor ammoniæ or liquor potassæ are among the local applications recommended, but I have ascertained, by experiment, that they do not destroy the poisonous properties of the venom, although *mixed with it* in even more than equal quantities, and therefore they are not to be trusted. Ipecacuanha, iodine, and other specifics are recommended as local applications. They are, I fear, useless.

Such are the local measures to be resorted to. At the same time, as there is great and rapidly increasing depression both from mental as well as physical causes, stimulants should be given at once frequently and freely. Hot brandy, or whisky, or rum and water, equal parts of each, are the best. Ammonia is also useful as a stimulant, and may be given in any of its officinal forms, the carbonate, the liquor ammoniæ, or the eau-de-luce. But it is to be given simply as a stimulant, it has no specific or antidotal action beyond this. At the same time, warmth and sinapisms to the præcordial and epigastric regions, in some cases cold douches, and all measures that may tend to rouse and stimulate the failing nervous energy should be resorted to. So far popular notions are supported by science. But another popular mode of treatment of the so-called lethargy induced by the poison, that by walking the person violently about, and keeping him awake by flogging, pinching, and other such violent measures, is, in my opinion, of very doubtful efficacy, if not altogether wrong. The man who is dying from snake-bite is perishing from rapid exhaustion of nerve force. To make him take violent exercise and deprive him of rest seems to me more likely to do harm than good. It would be almost as reasonable to give a man a blow on the head to recover him from concussion of the brain, or to give him antimony to cure him of sea-sickness. Let him lie down ; leave him to rest, to sleep, if he can. Many of the cases of so-called poisoning are not poisoning at all ; the snake has not been seen, and it may have been innocent ; or it may have been a poisonous snake, but exhausted. The punctures are there, and the appearances are all those of snake-bite. But the depression is due to mental shock from the dread of impending death. I have seen such a case.

Rousing, in the fashion I have alluded to, might do good here, but I believe that in real poisoning it can only do harm by exhausting the already sinking powers of life. It may be said it has often succeeded ; people have been so treated and have recovered. Who can say they would not have recovered as soon, perhaps sooner, without it? "*Post hoc*" does not always mean "*Propter hoc.*"

With reference to the snake-stones which, when applied to the bites, are said to absorb and suck out the poison and obviate its evil effects, I have only to say that I believe they are perfectly powerless to produce any such effect. Of this more subsequently.

As unfortunately, in a large number of cases, persons who have been bitten by venomous snakes are not so promptly and vigorously treated, and the poison has found entry and manifested its presence by dangerous symptoms, it is too late to hope for any benefit from the application of the ligature or other local measures having for their object neutralization or destruction of the poison. The only course of treatment now to be adopted, is that of endeavouring to neutralize or counteract the action of the poison which has already affected the nerve centres and poisoned the blood, and to support the strength during the continuance of the depressing influence.

This brings me to speak of the so-called antidotes, many of which have been and are so much vaunted. To name them all would be impossible, but I may say that most reliance has been placed on a few, such as ammonia, arsenic, iodine, bromine, the poison and the bile of other snakes, the guaco plant, ipecacuanha, aristolochia, senega. Indeed nearly every drug in or out of the Pharmacopœia has been recommended ; to say nothing of many other things that have been in vogue among the ignorant, vulgar, or superstitious, and that have nothing whatever but credulity to suggest their utility. I have made repeated experiments with many of them on the lower animals, and have seen nothing to induce me to believe that they have any good effect whatever.

I have no hesitation in saying that I believe them to be useless, and that, excepting for their stimulant action, when they have any, they are inert. When the symptoms of poisoning have set in, either when the ligature and excision, or caustic or cautery have failed, or when they have not been used, I believe that the only rational treatment is to endeavour to rouse the sinking energies, and arrest the tendency to fatal paralysis of the nerve force, by the aid of alcohol or other stimulants, such as ammonia or ether, judiciously administered, avoiding anything that can depress, such as over-exertion or fatigue, especially that produced by the popular practice of making the sufferer walk when his force is almost expended. Brandy or whisky, indeed any form of alcohol, should be given freely and frequently, though not in the large quantities sometimes recommended. Galvanism may also be of service along the spine, to the solar plexus or to the heart; in certain cases cold douches may be useful. Hot bottles and sinapisms may be applied, and every encouragement should be given to the sufferer, for much of the depression depends on mental causes. I have seen a strong man who appeared almost at the point of death (from fright) recover in a very short time when I told him that the snake that had bitten him was innocent, and let it take hold of my finger to prove it so. So that, whatever can be done to remove this element of depression, should be done by encouragement and assurance of safety (when the snake is found to have been innocent or weak), and in other cases, by holding out hopes of recovery, which not unfrequently takes place, not because antidotes have been given, but because the bite has been imperfect or the snake incompetent; and no doubt the recovery may be aided and expedited by treatment such as I have described.

It will be inferred from what I have said that I put little faith in any of the so-called antidotes. My views of the treatment of snake-bite are, that if the early endeavours to prevent the entry of the poison into the system are unsuccessful, as unfortunately is too frequently the case, our reliance must be placed on supporting the strength with alcoholic, ammoniacal, or ethereal stimulants, and by treating consecutive mischief of constitutional or local character by such combination of remedial measures as the peculiar symptoms may suggest. My belief is that if a certain quantity of the poison have entered the circulation we can expect but little benefit from treatment of any kind; where less has entered, yet enough to cause dangerous present and consecutive symptoms, we may do much to support the strength and save life by ordinary rational measures. But that we possess any drug or substance, solid or fluid, that either swallowed or inoculated, can counteract or neutralize the poison once absorbed, and acting on the nerve centres, I do not believe, and I think the notion that we do is a dangerous one, and liable to do harm by inspiring confidence in ways and means in which none should be placed. I have already explained how snake-bites may occur, and yet the bitten person may not be poisoned at all, or so slightly as to leave it quite possible that recovery may take place. In such cases, recovery is due mainly to the inherent vigour of the individual, and in part no doubt to treatment. It is also my belief that a large proportion of such cases would recover without any treatment at all, though in some the judicious use of remedies may turn the balance in the patient's favour. I neither wish to discourage treatment nor to throw cold water on investigation, but merely to state the facts as I think they exist.

It is well that the truth should be known, even though it be not what we could wish; and it is better that we should study preventive measures, and ascertain exactly how much we can do in those cases where our aid may be of avail, than that we should trust to measures which common sense and science alike should make us distrust.

With reference to the subsequent effects, constitutional or local, they should be treated on ordinary surgical principles. The strength should be supported by nutrients and wine, with such mineral or vegetable tonics as may seem appropriate. Collections of pus should be evacuated; the separation of sloughs aided by poultices and antiseptics, and the healing wounds dressed as other wounds of a similar form or character from other causes would be dressed and tended.

Should symptoms of a pyæmic or septicæmic nature arise, we must treat them as we would do similar conditions arising under other circumstances. The result will depend on the extent of blood-poisoning and the vigour of the person.

Although, from what I have said, it will be evident that in cases of real bites from the deadly forms of snake, our reliance is chiefly on early and preventive measures, and not on the so-called antidotes, I hope it will not be inferred that I mean we are altogether powerless; far from it! I believe that in a number of cases—and I have described them—we may be of use, and we can at all events alleviate suffering, give hope and confidence where we are justified in doing so, and do all that science and common sense suggest as likely to be of service. The plan suggested by Dr. Halford, of Melbourne, of injecting ammonia into the veins, does certainly seem more rational than most suggestions that have been made, and I regret exceedingly that in my own experiments it has proved of no avail. The reason may, indeed, be in the greater virulence of the Indian Thanatophidia, and this may be the explanation of my failure, where Dr. Halford has found success. But, after all, the more venomous snake is the most crucial test. I would say the same in reference to the similar use of the liquor potassæ by Dr. Shortt, in Madras. He, I believe, does not attach the same amount of importance to it as Dr. Halford does to the ammonia. In my researches both have been equally powerless, and I confess that I have felt much disappointed that experience has not confirmed the benefit of what certainly were rational suggestions by authorities to whom science is deeply indebted for much valuable information, and most earnest investigation into an important subject.

I would summarize the treatment of snake-bite as follows:—Apply, at once, a ligature, or ligatures, at intervals of a few inches, as tight as you can possibly tie them; and tighten the one nearest to the wound, by twisting it with a stick or other such agent. Scarify the wound, and let it bleed freely. Apply either a hot iron or live-coal, or explode some gunpowder on the part; or apply either carbolic or some mineral acid, or caustic. Let the patient suck the wound whilst you are getting the cautery ready, or if any one else will run the risk, let him do it.

If the bite be on a toe or finger, especially if the snake have been recognised as a deadly one, either completely excise, or immediately amputate at the next joint. If the bite be on another part, where a ligature cannot be applied, or indeed if it be on the limbs above the toes or fingers, cut the part out at once completely.

Let the patient be quiet. Do not fatigue him by exertion. When, or even before symptoms of poisoning make their appearance, give eau-de-luce, or liquor ammoniæ, or carbonate of ammonia, or even better than these, hot spirits and water. There is no occasion to intoxicate the person, but give it freely, and at frequent intervals.

If he become low, apply sinapisms and hot bottles, galvanism or electro-magnetism over the heart and diaphragm. Cold douches may also be useful.

The antidotes, in addition, may be used by those who have faith in them; but as I have said, I fear there is no reason to believe that they are of any use. Encourage and cheer the patient as much as possible. As to local effects, if there be great pain, anodynes may be applied or administered, and antiseptic poultices to remove sloughs; collections of matter must be opened.

Other symptoms are to be treated on general surgical principles.

This, I believe, is the sum and substance of what we can do

in snake-bite. If the person be not thoroughly poisoned, we may help him to recover. If he be badly bitten by one of the more deadly snakes, we can do no more.

I take the following account of the snake-stone from Sir E. Tennent's work on Ceylon :—

They are of the size and appearance of small black almonds, highly polished and of an extremely light substance. They are said to attach themselves closely when applied to the bitten part, the blood that oozes from the bite being rapidly imbibed by the porous substance of the so-called stone. They adhere tenaciously for three or four minutes. Meanwhile the bitten limb is well rubbed downwards from the shoulder towards the fingers. At length they drop off, and the bitten person is said to be free from danger. Instances are narrated where happy results occurred. A bit of root is at the same time passed over the stone. One bit of root so used proved to be an aristolochia stem.

The snake-stone was examined by Professor Faraday, who expressed his belief that "it is 'a piece of charred bone, which has been filled with blood, perhaps, several times, and then carefully charred again. Evidence of this is afforded, as well by the apertures of cells or tubes on its surface, as by the fact that it yields and breaks under pressure, and exhibits an organic structure within. When heated slightly, water rises from it, and also a little ammonia; and if heated still more highly in the air, carbon burns away, and a bulky white ash is left, retaining the shape and size of the stone.' This ash, as is evident from inspection, cannot have belonged to any vegetable substance, for it is almost entirely composed of phosphate of lime. Mr. Faraday adds, that 'if the piece of matter has ever been employed as a spongy absorbent, it seems hardly fit for that purpose in its present state; but who can say to what treatment it has been subjected since it was fit for use, or to what treatment the natives may submit it when expecting to have occasion to use it?'"

Tennent goes on to say: "The probability is that the animal charcoal, when instantaneously applied, may be sufficiently porous and absorbent to extract the venom from the recent wound, together with a portion of the blood, before it has had time to be carried into the system; and that the blood which Mr. Faraday detected in the specimen submitted to him was that of the Indian on whose person the effect was exhibited. The snake-charmers from the coast, who visit Ceylon, profess to prepare the snake-stones for themselves, and preserve the composition a secret. Dr. Davy, on the authority of Sir A. Johnston, says the manufacture of them is a lucrative trade carried on by the monks of Manilla, who supply the merchants of India; and his analysis confirms that of Mr. Faraday. Of the three different kinds which he examined, one being of partially burnt bone and another of chalk, the third consisting chiefly of vegetable matter resembling bezoar, all of them (except the first, which possessed a slight absorbent power) were quite inert, and incapable of having any effect except in the imagination of the patient. Thunberg was shown the snake-stone used by the boors at the Cape in 1772, which was imported for them from the Indies, especially from Malabar, at so high a price that few of the farmers could afford to possess themselves of it. He describes it as convex on one side, black, and so porous that when thrown into water it caused bubbles to arise, and hence by its absorbent qualities it served, if speedily applied, to extract the poison from the wound."

In a foot-note Tennent gives the following further particulars since the foregoing account was published: "I have received a note from Mr. Hardy, relative to the *piedra ponsona*, the snake-stone of Mexico, in which he gives the following account of the method of preparing and applying it:—'Take a piece of hart's horn of any convenient size and shape, cover it well round with grass or hay, enclose both in a thin piece of sheet copper well wrapped round them, and place the parcel in a charcoal fire till the bone is sufficiently charred. When cold, remove the calcined horn from its envelope, when it will be ready for immediate use. In this state it will resemble a solid black fibrous substance of the same shape and size as before it was submitted to this treatment. *Use.*—The wound being slightly punctured, apply the bone to the opening, to which it will adhere firmly for the space of two minutes, and when it falls, it should be received into a basin of water; it should then be dried in a cloth, and again applied to the wound. But it will not adhere longer than about one minute. In like manner it may be applied a third time; but now it will fall almost immediately, and nothing will cause it to adhere any more.'

"These effects I witnessed in the case of a bite of a rattlesnake at Oposura, a town in the province of Souora, in Mexico, from whence I obtained my recipe; and I have given other particulars respecting it in my Travels in the interior of Mexico, published in 1830-31.—*R. W. Hardy, Bath, 30th January, 1860.*"

There is a germ of possible truth in the idea that these stones can be of use, for, if they absorb as they are said to do, no doubt some blood and poison mixed are taken up by their pores.

But when we reflect on the quantity of poison and the force and depth with and to which it is injected through the fang of either Cobra or Viper, and the extreme rapidity with which it is hurried along in the vascular system to the nerve centres, I think it is obvious that the application of one of these stones can be of little use in a *real bite* of a deadly snake, and that a belief in their efficacy is a dangerous delusion, as it may be the cause of the loss of the first two or three seconds, which are so precious to the sufferer, for on what is done in them his life may depend. I may add that I have found the snake-stone as powerless for good as any of the so-called antidotes.

SUGGESTIONS FOR THE IMMEDIATE TREATMENT OF PERSONS BITTEN BY VENOMOUS SNAKES.

(*Intended for the Guidance of Police Officers and others.*)

It is, I believe, usual to supply the police thannahs with liquor ammoniæ to administer to those who are bitten, and who come under the notice of the police before they can be brought under any medical treatment.

The practice is a good one, and I would advocate its continuance and extension. Ammonia is a powerful stimulant, and may do good—it cannot do any harm; administered in doses of ten or fifteen drops with half a wineglass (chittack) of water every quarter of an hour, or even more frequently, it may be of benefit; and as in the police-stations and elsewhere in England tables giving general instructions for the treatment of the drowned or suffocated are hung up by the Humane Society, so in the Indian police-stations, and other public places where such might be useful, I would hang up tables giving brief and clear instructions how to act in the case of snake-bite.

As soon as possible after a person is bitten by a snake apply a ligature, made of a piece of cord, round the limb or part at about 2 or 3 inches above the bite.

Introduce a piece of stick or other lever between the cord and the part, and by twisting tighten the ligature to the utmost.

Apply other two or three ligatures above the first one at intervals of 4 or 6 inches, and tighten them also. After the ligature has been applied scarify, by cutting across the punctures to the depth of ¼ of an inch with a penknife or other similar cutting instrument; let the wounds bleed freely; or better still, excise the punctured part.

Apply either a hot iron or a live coal to the bottom of these wounds as quickly as possible, or some carbolic or nitric acid.

If the bite be not on a finger, toe, or part where a ligature can be applied, raise up the integument with the finger and thumb, and with a sharp penknife cut out a circular piece as big as a finger nail round each puncture—*i.e.*, round the points of the finger and thumb—to the depth of ¼ or ½ an inch. Then apply the hot coal or hot iron to the very bottom of the wounds.

Give fifteen drops of liquor ammoniæ diluted with an ounce of water immediately, and repeat it every quarter of an hour, for three or four doses, or longer, if symptoms of poisoning appear.

Or give hot brandy or rum or whisky or other spirit, with an equal quantity of water, about an ounce of each (for an adult) at the same intervals. Send at once for medical aid; or take the person to the nearest medical man without delay; if none be near, in half an hour, should no symptoms of poisoning have appeared, the ligatures should be relaxed, or the part will perish from gangrene.

If symptoms of poisoning do appear, do not relax the ligatures until the person be recovering from the poison, or until the ligatured part be cold and livid.

Suction of the wounds is likely to be beneficial, but as it may be dangerous to the operator, it cannot be recommended as a duty.

If, notwithstanding, symptoms of poisoning set in and increase, if the patient become faint or depressed, unconscious, nauseated or sick, apply mustard poultices, or liquor ammoniæ on a cloth, over the stomach and heart; continue the stimulants and keep the patient warm, but do not shut him up in a hot stifling room or a small native hut—rather leave him in the fresh air than do this.

Do not make him walk about if weary and depressed; rouse with stimulants, mustard poultices or ammonia, but let him rest.

If the person be brought, as he or she probably will be, some time after the bite has been inflicted, and symptoms of poisoning are present, the same measures are to be resorted to. They are less likely to be successful, but nothing else can be done.

In many cases the prostration is due to fear, the bite may have been that of a harmless or exhausted snake, and persons thus bitten will rapidly recover if treated as I have recommended, and encouraged. If poisoned, but, as frequently is the case, not fatally, these measures are the most expedient; if severely poisoned, no others are likely to be more efficacious.

It will frequently happen that the bitten person is seen by an educated person (though not a medical man) who may have the opportunity of applying the magnetic or electric current to the heart and diaphragm, or of making other additions to the measures already described. By such the so-called antidotes may be given, though I fear they can add but little if any benefit. The snake should always, if possible, be produced.

The measures suggested are no doubt severe, and not such as under any other circumstances should be entrusted to non-professional persons. But the alternative is so dreadful, that even at the risk of unskilful treatment, it is better that the patient should have this chance of recovery.

In addition to a supply of liquor ammoniæ at all police thannahs or other public localities away from the dispensaries and stations, where the ryots might apply for aid in case of bites, I would suggest that a small supply of strong whipcord, an actual cautery iron, and a small knife for the purposes I have described, and a bottle of carbolic or nitric acid should be provided.

A plain summary or translation of these suggestions might be hung up in every police thannah and other public place. The people should be warned against incantations, popular antidotes, and loss of time in seeking for aid.

Every police inspector, of whatever grade, might be taught the application of the simple measures I have described, and should be enjoined to make them known as widely as possible among the police and the people.

SECTION IV.

CASES OF SNAKE-BITE.

I HAVE selected the following cases of snake-bite from returns that have been sent in by medical officers of the Bengal Presidency. They give a fair idea of the symptoms, of the duration of life after the reception of the bite, and of the pathological appearances and condition after death. The details in many are meagre, for the cases are often not seen until after death, and the description and name of the snake are not in every instance reliable, for the reason that it was not seen by the medical officer. Still the cases sufficiently illustrate the subject, and show the fatality of the bite of the Indian poisonous snakes. They also show that little reliance is to be placed on the accounts given by ordinary persons, as to the description of snake that inflicted the wound; and that some were no doubt cases of bites of innocent snakes—the symptoms that followed the bite being the results of terror and anxiety. The natives believe nearly all snakes to be poisonous, and as the accident so often occurs in the night, it is only natural that though the snake is innocuous, the greatest fear should be excited when a person has been bitten; the dread of impending death in some instances well-nigh producing a fatal result.

It will be observed, that in nearly every case where the body was examined the blood is stated to have been fluid. This I am unable to explain, for repeated experiments on the lower animals showed that after death from the colubrine snake poison, the blood coagulated firmly, whilst after death from the viperine poison, the blood always remained permanently fluid. I would venture to suggest that further investigation should be made by those who have the opportunity of doing so, with the view of testing the accuracy of these results, so different in man from the lower animals.

The following cases are reported by Mr. Shircore, Civil Surgeon of the twenty-four Pergunnahs:—

Radhee Bewa, a Mahomedan woman, aged thirty-six years, was bitten by a snake (not seen) on the night of Feb. 27th, 1870, while near a tank at the village of Bistopore. She complained of a great burning pain at the bitten part, and thirst, and was very restless. She was treated by incantations, charms, and native drugs, but died during the night of Feb. 28th, twenty-eight hours after being bitten. The body was examined, and the following appearances noted. The lungs were rather pale, but congested posteriorly. The heart and great vessels contained fluid blood. The abdominal viscera were normal. The blood was fluid. The brain, &c., normal. Cadaveric rigidity was not present when the post-mortem examination was made.

Bassee, a Mahomedan labourer, aged fifty-eight years, was bitten by a snake (probably a Cobra) while crossing the field of Fort William, at daybreak of March 20th, 1870. He complained of pain at the bitten part. He did not receive any treatment, and died one hour and a half after being bitten. The body was examined. The lungs were highly congested. The heart and great vessels contained a great quantity of fluid blood. The abdominal viscera were normal. The blood was fluid. The vessels of the brain were distended with blood. Cadaveric rigidity occurred eight hours after death.

Gunesh Ghose, a Gowallah, aged thirty-two years, was bitten by a snake (not seen) on the night of March 26th, 1870, at Tollygunge, near Calcutta. He is said to have complained of very severe pain at the bitten part. He was treated by incantations and native drugs, but died forty-two hours after receiving the bite. The body was examined. The lungs were natural and healthy. The heart contained thick blood. The abdominal viscera were normal. The blood was semi-fluid, and contained clots. The brain was normal. Cadaveric rigidity was not present when the body was examined.

Alahee, a Mahomedan boy, aged twelve years, was bitten by a snake (name unknown) on the afternoon of April 25th, 1870. He is said to have complained of pain. He was treated by Kobirajes, but died eighteen hours after receiving the bite. The body was examined. The lungs were normal. The heart and great vessels contained a small quantity of fluid blood. The abdominal viscera were normal. The blood was fluid. The brain and nervous system were normal. Cadaveric rigidity was not present when the post-mortem examination was made.

Kouree Latu, a Mahomedan, aged forty-six years, was bitten by a snake (unknown, but probably the *Bungarus cæruleus*, or Krait) on the night of May 5th, 1870, at the village of Acheepore. He is said to have complained of pain, and was treated by incantations and charms, but died ten hours after being bitten. At the post-mortem examination the lungs were found congested. The heart contained fluid blood. The abdominal viscera were normal, excepting the kidneys, which were highly congested. The blood was fluid. The brain, &c., was normal. Cadaveric rigidity occurred six hours after death.

Benee Madhub Khan, a Bengalee boy, aged eight years, was bitten by a snake (name unknown) on the afternoon of May 8th, 1870, at the village of Acheepore. He did not come under the observation of Mr. Shircore, but is said to have complained of pain, and to have quickly become insensible. He was treated by charms, incantations, and the administration of some leaves, but died twenty-four hours after being bitten. The body was sent in for examination. The lungs were healthy. The heart was empty. The abdominal viscera were normal, except the kidneys, which were very much congested. The blood was fluid. The brain was normal. Cadaveric rigidity was not present when the body was examined.

Soondree Podeeni, a Bengalee, aged fifty years, was bitten by a Keautiah (*Naja tripudians*) on the night of July 5th, 1870, at the village of Bistopore. She is said to have complained of a burning pain in the bitten part, and to have been treated by incantations and charms, but she died two hours after receiving the bite. The body was examined. The lungs were normal. The heart and great vessels contained fluid blood. The kidneys were highly congested. The blood was fluid. The brain was normal. Cadaveric rigidity was not present when the body was examined.

Poorno Bewa, a Bengalee woman, aged thirty years, was bitten by a snake (not seen) on the night of July 5th, 1870, at the village of Bistopore. She was treated by incantations and charms, and died ten hours after receiving the bite. The body was examined. The lungs were congested. The heart contained fluid blood. The kidneys were congested. The blood was fluid. The brain was normal. Cadaveric rigidity is said not to have been present when the post-mortem examination was made.

Kader Goallah, a Bengalee, aged twelve years, was bitten by a Keautiah (*N. tripudians*) at noon of July 22nd, 1870, at the village of Ooriapara. He was treated as usual by incantations and charms, and died half an hour after receiving the bite. The body was examined. The lungs were normal. The heart contained fluid blood. The abdominal viscera were normal. The blood was fluid. The brain was normal. Cadaveric rigidity was not present.

Debuarain Mundle, a male Hindoo, aged thirty years, was bitten by a snake (unknown) on July 26th, 1870, at the village of Bistopore. The only symptom noted is, that he complained of a burning pain. He was treated by liquor ammoniæ, but died *six days* after having been bitten. The body was examined. The lungs were normal. The heart and great vessels contained fluid blood. The abdominal viscera, with the exception of the kidneys, which were highly congested, were healthy and normal. The blood was fluid. The brain and nervous system normal. Cadaveric rigidity was not present when the examination was made.

Ram Churn Bose, a male Hindoo, aged twenty-two years, was bitten by a snake (name not given, but probably a Krait), on the night of Oct. 13th, 1870, at Ekhulpore, in the suburbs of Calcutta. He is said to have complained of a burning pain in the bitten part. He was treated by incantations and charms, and died on Oct. 14th, eight hours after the bite. The body was examined. The lungs were normal. The heart and great vessels contained fluid blood. The kidneys were congested. The blood was fluid. The brain was normal. Cadaveric rigidity was not present when the post-mortem examination was made.

I am also indebted to Mr. Shircore for the following account of snake-poisoning affecting the infant through the mother's milk :—

"Case of snake-poisoning in which the mother died, and her infant, who was at the breast after the mother was bitten, died also from the poison.

"On July 16th, 1871, a woman named Gurra Dassee, residing in the village of Rughoohath, near Dum-Dum, in the district of twenty-four Pergunnahs, was aroused from a sound sleep at about 1 A.M. by a smarting sensation in the forefinger of her right hand, and thought that something had bitten her. She had at the time her infant—seven months old—by her side, and her husband, with her other children, was sleeping in the same room a little distance from her. She called out to her husband and told him what had happened; but feeling very drowsy, and receiving no answer from the husband, who is excessively deaf, she fell into a slumber, and while in that state allowed her infant to take her breast. Soon after this she began to experience a painful sensation along her right arm, and a general restlessness of the whole body, and at the same time she observed that her child had likewise become very restless and was foaming at the mouth. Alarmed at this, she got up and called her neighbours, who came immediately to her assistance. Nothing, however, was done in the way of treatment beyond repeating "muntros" (chanting charms) to expel the poison from the body, which is the usual mode of treating cases of snake-bite in India. The consequence was that both mother and child became rapidly worse and died—the mother about four hours after she was bitten, and the child about two hours after she had taken the mother's breast. The snake was not seen by any one, and no attempt was made by a search inside the room to ascertain what kind of snake had bitten the woman. Both the bodies were sent to me by the police, and were examined on the morning of July 17th. The face in both cases was livid and swollen, and there was an issue of bloody froth from the mouth and nostrils. In the forefinger of the right hand of the mother was a distinct mark of a snake-bite. The finger and the hand were considerably swollen, with discoloration of the soft parts. This was very marked in the finger, which, when dissected, appeared as though it had been severely bruised. The blood was quite fluid in both cases, and the organs were all more or less congested. The body of the child was carefully inspected, but not the slightest trace of a bite or any kind of injury could be detected in any part of it. The conclusion drawn from the above facts is, that the mother died from the effects of the snake-bite, and the child was poisoned through her milk."

The following case, reported by native doctor Bisseshur Das, of the Jainser Dispensary, is forwarded by Mr. Cutcliffe, Officiating Civil Surgeon of Dacca :—

Shantomonee, a Brahmin, aged thirty-six years, was bitten by a large snake (name not known) on the foot, on the night of Sept. 7th, 1869. When she was admitted into the Jainser Dispensary, on Sept. 13th, the bitten part was sloughing and fetid, and erysipelatous inflammation is said to have existed as far as the thigh. The native doctor states that he applied strong caustic lotion and charcoal poultices to the injured part, and administered some tonic medicine. She was discharged on Sept. 29th, twenty-two days after receiving the bite.

The following cases are recorded by Mr. Briscoe, Civil Medical Officer of Goalparah :—

Bhanoo, an Assamese, aged eighteen years, was bitten on the foot during the afternoon of April 25th, by a snake, known to the natives as the "Chokoriah Borah" (specific name not ascertained) while on his way to work in the fields near the village of Brijase. He is said to have become insensible, vomited a blackish fluid, and to have died twenty-six hours after having been bitten. The body was not sent in for examination. The "Chokoriah Borah" is possibly one of the *Crotalidæ*.

Jhaman, an Assamese boy, aged ten years, was bitten on the ankle at 10 A.M. on March 19th, at the village of Sachopanee, by a snake, the name of which could not be ascertained. His skin is said to have become bluish in colour. He was treated by the native Jharonah Ozahs (snake-charmers), but died on March 20th, at 8 A.M., twenty-four hours after having been bitten. The body was not sent in for examination.

Bhoog Chand, a Bengalee boy, aged eight years, while walking through a rice-field, was bitten on the foot by a snake known to the natives as the "Chokoriah Borah" (specific name unknown), on May 28th, 1870, at 9 A.M. His skin is said to have become bluish in colour. He was treated by the native Ozahs (snake-charmers), but died on May 29th, at 3 P.M., thirty-one hours after he was bitten. The body was not sent in for examination.

Toopoli Ram, aged thirty-five, a Cachar labourer, was bitten on June 18th, at 4 P.M., in a jungle near the village Kachopatiah, by a green snake. The bite was in the right ankle, and there were two wounds over that joint. When observed the part was of a black colour, it is said, but no other details are given. He appears to have been ill for one day after the bite, but no details are given, as the case did not come under the observation of the medical officer. The snake was probably *Trimeresurus*, either *T. carinatus*, *T. gramineus*, or *T. erythrurus*, as the man seems to have suffered, though not fatally.

Bhanoo, an Assamese, aged eighteen years, was bitten on the afternoon of April 25th, 1870, while going to work in a field, by a snake called the "Chokoriah Borah." He is said to have become insensible, and to have vomited matter of a black colour. He was treated by the native Ozahs (snake-charmers), but died twenty-six hours after the bite. The body was not sent in for examination.

The following case is recorded by Mr. O'Connor, Civil Surgeon of Nowgong, Assam :—

Namal, a Cacharee cultivator, aged sixteen years, was bitten at 9 P.M., January 20th, 1870, by a snake which was not killed, but is described thus :—"A short thick snake, three feet long, three inches in circumference, colour dark brown, with two white stripes, one on each side. Head variegated, from green through blue to yellow." Making allowance for the inaccuracy of native description, this may have been the *Daboia russellii*. The friends say that, "he got suddenly more and more sleepy, and at last died." He was treated—it is not said how—by a Kobiraj, but his death is said not to have occurred until Jan. 22nd. No post-mortem examination of the body was allowed by the friends; but from the general appearance of the body, Mr. O'Connor thinks "there was much venous congestion of the internal organs, and that the blood had turned very dark and thick. The face was swollen slightly, also the body, and the right leg particularly so; above the ankle were four cicatrices of a black colour. There was also an oozing of dark-coloured bloody matter from the mouth. The father and brothers brought in the boy's body, and gave the description of the case."

The following case is recorded by the civil surgeon of Gowhatty, in Assam:—

Khan Poonee, a Cacharee labourer, female, seven years of age, was bitten at a village named Ballaharie, near Rungea, at 5 P.M., on March 12th, 1870. The description of the snake by the friends shows that it was a Cobra (Gokurrah). The girl cried and seemed to suffer much pain. The bitten part on the left ankle bled slightly. The part became dark, and the discoloration spread up the limb. No further details are given. She died at 8.30 A.M., March 13th, in about fifteen and a half hours. The body was too much decomposed for examination when brought to the civil surgeon. There was the mark of a wound, similar to that which might be produced by a snake, on the left ankle, and inflammation had evidently spread from that point.

The following very interesting account of a fatal case of snake-poisoning has been forwarded to me by Dr. Thomson, Staff Surgeon, H.M.S., from Thayetmeyo, in Burmah. From the description, the snake was evidently *Daboia russelli*, or Russell's Viper, the "Ticpolonga" of Ceylon. The subject was a gunner of the Royal Artillery. By kind permission of Dr. Croker, R.A., at present in medical charge of A-23, R.A., I am enabled to furnish the particulars, extracted from the Case Book. The case was recorded by Dr. Murray, Staff Assistant Surgeon, who was in medical charge of the Battery at the time the accident occurred.

R. W., age twenty-three years. Service, nine years. A strong powerfully built man, of good muscular development, was admitted into hospital this morning (May 22nd, 1868). States that soon after daybreak, as he was entering the "fowl-house," which is in close proximity to the barracks, he observed a dark thick-set snake of about two feet and a half in length (species unknown, but not a Cobra), and that he took up a piece of bamboo and began teasing it, whereupon the reptile turned and bit him on the finger. The snake held on for a short time, and it was with some little difficulty the man shook it off. The "fowl-house," where the accident occurred, is distant from the hospital about 600 or 700 yards. The man came at once to hospital, being advised by one of his comrades to do so; when on the way he became very weak. The apothecary saw the patient on his arrival at hospital. It is supposed that a lapse of twenty minutes must have occurred from the time he received the bite until he reached the hospital, and nothing had been done meantime in the way of remedies. The apothecary immediately scarified the wounded finger freely, made the patient suck the wound, and administered ammonia. I was then sent for, and proceeded without delay. On examination I found two small punctured wounds on first phalanx of index finger of the left hand. The finger itself was swollen and livid. The patient complained of very little pain, but seemed naturally anxious, although it was considered by many that the snake was non-venomous. I ordered hot fomentations, with a view to encourage as much as possible the bleeding from the part where it had been freely scarified. I also ordered constant fomentations all over the arm. An aperient was given. It was directed that the patient be carefully watched.

Vespere, 6 P.M.—The bowels were moved during the day, but the patient has been restless, turning on one side then on another. The finger and hand are considerably swollen and discoloured, and the forearm is partially so. The pain is not severe, although he complains of it extending up the arm; no swelling from elbow upwards. Is slightly feverish. Pulse good and not hurried, complains of thirst; ordered lemonade to drink. To have an opiate at bedtime. The hand and arm to be constantly stuped with poppy-heads, and the patient to be carefully watched during the night.

May 23rd—On my visit this morning I found the man most dangerously ill. At times excited, tossing about his arms and legs in every direction, and rolling his head from one side to another. The pulse almost imperceptible. Breathing hurried, forty per minute. Surface covered with cold clammy sweat. Conscious when roused, and then immediately falling back into a stupor. Face suffused. Ordered brandy and water, stimulating draughts of ammonia, and turpentine stupes to extremities. The left hand and arm greatly swollen. Bluish tint over the hand. Surface from elbow to shoulder much reddened. The inflammation extended to the left side of chest, which was also red and swollen. He rallied a little for upwards of an hour between 7 and 8 A.M., and then began to sink. Pupils became contracted, and insensible to the stimulus of light. From 8 A.M. he became rapidly unconscious. Now and again he tossed himself about with such violence that the attendants had some difficulty in keeping him in bed. The treatment mentioned above was persevered in, and in addition, galvanism was applied along the spine and over the chest. At 8.30 A.M. he was moribund. Respirations forty. Restless and unconscious. Heart's action fluttering. Spasmodic twitchings observed over course of diaphragm. Pulse at wrist not detected. Died at 9 A.M.

Post-mortem appearances seven hours after death.—External appearance of the body was that of a person who had been well nourished and healthy, and of great muscular development. The left hand and arm were considerably swollen; there was also swelling of left axilla. Two small punctured wounds were observed on first phalanx of index finger of left hand.*

Head.—On removing calvarium considerable congestion was observed of the vessels on the surface of the brain. There was a general softened state of the brain substance throughout. In right lateral ventricle a small quantity of serous fluid was found.

Thorax.—Lungs collapsed; when cut into were found gorged with blood, the latter being remarkable for its fluidity. The apices of lungs were emphysematous.

Heart.—Size normal, structure healthy. A large clot of blood in left ventricle, extending into ascending portion of aorta, and having appearance and consistence of black currant-jelly; clots were also found in right ventricle and auricle, and in pulmonary arteries. That in the latter was semi-fluid.

Liver.—Normal, and appearance when cut into healthy. Gall-bladder distended with bile.

Bowels.—Appearance healthy. Spleen of natural size: soft and easily broken up by the fingers. Kidneys healthy in structure and normal in size. Bladder empty.

Remarks.—The above case was highly interesting. I saw the man about one hour and a half before death, when his symptoms were exactly as described by Dr. Murray. I did not see the snake, as unfortunately it had been destroyed, and thrown away the day before. The following description, however, was given to me by Assistant Apothecary Roberts, A-23, R.A.:—"It was a snake about two and a half feet in length, with a flat oval head. The thickest part of the body measured about three inches in circumference. The tail was five inches long. The colour of the head and back of a French grey; the belly white. In the middle of the back ran a row of lozenge-shaped spots (white). It had two large curved fangs." I am inclined to believe from the description that the snake was a species of viper.

The following case is reported by Honorary Assistant-Surgeon C. J. Cooper, in Civil Medical Charge of Shoaghyeen, dated Jan. 1st, 1870:—

Ngayoh, a Burman, aged nineteen years, was bitten by a snake on Nov. 7th, 1869, at 8.30 P.M. When returning home from the telegraph office he felt the instep pricked by something, and on raising his foot to the lantern he carried, he found the snake hanging on to the foot; he shook the snake off, and found that the places where the fangs had penetrated were marked with blood. The snake was green, *Vipera viridis*, probably *Trimeresurus erythrurus*, or *T. carinatus*. On admission he was suffering from all the symptoms of severe shock. The neighbourhood of the bite was red and swollen. A ligature was immediately tied round the leg. Spt. amm. aromat. ʒj; tinct. opii, ʒss were given immediately. The track of the snake-bite was covered with ipecacuanha and ammonia. When the ill effects had passed off, the ligature round the leg was removed. Five minims of liquor arsenicalis was ordered to be given every six hours. He recovered, and was apparently well in three hours, but he attended as an out-patient for thirty-three hours after.

* Dr. Murray notes that when the left hand was cut into, the muscles were found disintegrated and of a dark colour. In the upper arm the muscles were found to be soft and infiltrated with serous effusion.

The following case is recorded by Dr. Paul, Civil Surgeon of Tavoy, Burmah, dated Jan. 15th, 1870:—

Maha Lutchmee, a Hindoo female, aged thirty-seven years, was bitten at about 8 P.M. on the night of Nov. 7th, 1869, in the town of Tavoy, by a *Bungarus fasciatus*. She complained of a tingling sensation at the seat of the punctures, which were on the dorsum of the right foot, with some swelling of the part. There was pain in the leg and thigh of that side. The general expression of countenance was anxious. She said that it being dark, she trod on the snake, which bit her on the foot. It was destroyed, and identified by Dr. Paul. She was treated by the administration of liquor ammoniæ internally, and by ipecacuanha, chloroform, and liquor ammoniæ applied externally. The woman recovered, and was discharged well on the following day.

Particulars regarding the death by snake-bite of Captain S., by Assistant Apothecary Wells, Moulmein:—

The late Captain S. had been bathing in the tidal river at the dockhead (his ship being then under repair), at about 8 P.M. on May 23rd, 1869. When in the water he felt as if a crab had got hold of his leg, which he shook off, and feeling no inconvenience from it took no further notice of the circumstance. After the bath Captain S. called at the house of a friend, adjoining the dockyard, where he stayed for about an hour amusing the children of the house by singing and playing on the concertina. He seemed in high spirits, and expressed himself as feeling a sort of glow all over him, which was rather agreeable than otherwise, and his friend remarked that he never saw him (Captain S.) look so well before. On reaching his vessel, about ten o'clock, he complained of a sensation of thickening of the tongue, which rendered articulation difficult and indistinct; and gradually a feeling of stiffness all over the body came on. At about 11 P.M., on attempting to lie down, he felt as if suffocated. Rigidity of the muscles of the neck, arms, and legs increasing, he took some brandy (which was retained only for a short time) and a doctor was sent for, who, when he arrived, prescribed the following mixture:—

℞ Æther. sulphurici, ʒiss.
Tinct. hyoscyami, ʒj.
Mist. camphoræ, ℥iij. M. ft. mist.

A third part for a dose every three hours.

At about 4 A.M. of the 24th, the symptoms above mentioned, with sickness of stomach continuing, the following was prescribed:—

℞ Pulv. jalapæ comp., ʒj.
Calomel., gr. v.

To be taken at once.

℞ Tinct. cannabis ind., ʒj.
Spt. chloroformi, ʒiij.
Spt. ammon. arom., ʒiij.
Mist. camphoræ, ℥xij. M. ft. m.

Half a wineglassful every four hours

At about 8 A.M. the same morning, it was remarked by a Burman, who had just then seen Captain S., that the symptoms were those of a bite from a "gyat" (poisonous water-snake). Captain S. then recalled to mind the fact of his having felt a bite when bathing in the river the previous night, and on examination the marks of the bite were discovered, two on either side of the tendo Achillis, near the ankle. The bites did not seem at all inflamed, nor did they give rise to any feeling of discomfort; in appearance they looked just like mosquito bites, but a little bigger. The following made into a paste was then applied to the wounds :—

Pulv. ipecac., ʒij.
Liq. ammon., ʒj. M.

Slight rigidity and occasional spasms continued all day, with irritability of the stomach. Brandy was freely administered with the cannabis ind. mixture, and the following draught was ordered to be taken at 9 P.M. :—

℞ Morphiæ hydr., gr. ½.
Aquæ, ℥j.

May 25*th*.—Had a tolerable night ; a remission of all the symptoms ; on the whole seemed better ; slight spasms on moving or attempting to sit up in bed. Mixture continued, and the draught ordered to be repeated at bedtime. At about 6 P.M. was seized with violent spasms, which continued with occasional slight remissions for an hour, when the patient expired. Death ensued seventy-one hours after the bites. Cadaveric rigidity set in about three hours after death. No post-mortem was made. The natives believe that the use of brandy in Captain S.'s case prolonged his life so long. Death usually ensues, they say, in from two to twenty-four hours.

The following case is referred to in a paper by Dr. T. Cantor in the "Transactions of the Zoological Society of London," vol. ii. p. 303. It is taken from the statistical report on the health of the navy in the East Indian stations for 1837 and the six following years :—

"The other death in this vessel (H.M.S. *Algerine*) requires a more lengthened notice. On Oct. 9th, while the ship lay at anchor in the Madras Roads, a water-snake was caught, measuring seven feet six inches long, and six inches and a half in girth at the thickest part. After the patient had handled the reptile for some time, it suddenly bit him on the inside of the index finger of the right hand, inflicting a wound resembling that caused by the point of a pin. He declined having the wound fomented, having been bitten by reptiles of the same kind, as he supposed, in the Straits of Malacca, without any bad consequences. At 8 A.M., half an hour after the infliction of the wound, he made a good breakfast, dressed, and about ten o'clock went on deck. After taking a few turns he was suddenly seized with vomiting, the matter ejected being of a dark brown colour, resembling coffee grounds and of a very offensive odour. After a short time his pulse became small, variable, and intermitting, and the pupils were dilated, but contracted steadily by the stimulus of light. The left side of the face was slightly paralysed. There was subsultus tendinum, and the skin was covered with a cold clammy perspiration, the countenance was anxious and indicative of much distress. In consequence of the spasmodic actions of the muscles of the glottis, he breathed with great difficulty ; the integuments from the wound to the wrist were slightly swollen, and on the right side of the neck and face they presented a mottled appearance of dark purple and livid colour. A ligature having been placed above the wrist, and fomentations applied to the hand, a liniment composed of turpentine, liquor ammoniæ, and olive oil was rubbed on the throat and neck. He made frequent attempts to swallow a mixture containing liquor ammoniæ and tinct. opii, but failed. At 10.20, in consequence of the spasmodic action of the muscles of the glottis, he was put into a warm bath, which apparently relieved the symptoms and enabled him to take a dose of the mixture, which caused him to vomit a dark ropy fluid. About twenty minutes after coming out of the bath (in which he remained ten minutes) the spasmodic action of the muscles of the neck and throat became more severe and the whole body assumed a purple colour. The breathing became very difficult from the obstruction caused by a dark brown substance which came away in a stringy form from the air passages. By eleven o'clock he was in a state of coma ; the pupils were contracted, and the pulse imperceptible at the wrist. At 11.20, not quite four hours from the time he was bitten, he died. It does not appear that any post-mortem examination of the body took place. It will be remarked that the symptoms in this case very much resembled those produced by the bite of a rabid animal, although they were much more violent and more speedily fatal."

The following cases are noted by the Civil Surgeon of Chyebassa, Singbhoom :—

Dooroo, a Dhome female, aged twenty-two years, basket-maker, was bitten about 4 A.M. on June 4th, 1870. She was sleeping under a tree near a tank, and was awoke by the snake coiling itself round her leg. She shook it off, but was bitten in the upper part of the calf of the leg, near the ham. The snake was described as the *Bungarus cœruleus*, or Krait, of the length of the arm, called there "Cheeta." The symptoms are not noted, but she died in three and a half hours. The body was examined. Lungs natural. Right cavities of heart filled with fluid and soft coagulated dark blood. Left cavities contained fluid blood. Vessels full of fluid blood. The abdominal viscera were natural. The stomach contained a little frothy fluid. Small intestines of a light reddish tint. Brain and membranes highly congested. Cadaveric rigidity uncertain.

Thugnee Bhooga, female, aged fifty, was bitten at 6 A.M. on June 20th, 1870, in Chyebassa, by a snake which was not recognised. She was asleep when she felt the bite on the foot ; awoke, and saw the snake glide away. There was a single puncture on the dorsum of one foot, but there were no other symptoms nor any evil consequences. A dose of liquor ammoniæ was given at the thannah. It is of course very doubtful whether the snake was venomous.

I am indebted to Assistant-Surgeon Kali Padu Guptu, 24th Regt. P.N.I., Umritsur, for the two following interesting cases of snake-bite (probably the snakes were *Bungarus cœruleus*) in which recovery after hæmaturia and hæmoptysis occurred :—

"On the evening of Sept. 10th Sepoy Jumetha Sing was bitten by a snake in the inner border of the right foot, while he was returning from the latrines. He immediately ran to the regimental hospital which was close by, and said that a black snake about three feet long had bitten him. The native doctor examined the foot and found three small punctures from which there was a slight oozing of blood. He first applied a tight ligature above the ankle, and then touched the punctures with argenti nitras. He watched the man for upwards of two hours, during which no symptoms of drowsiness or stupor were developed. He was perfectly conscious and made no complaint, except of the pain caused by the tight ligature. He was then left alone to sleep, which he could not, perhaps through fear. The next morning the whole foot and the leg as far as the calf became swollen, hot, and very painful, so much so that he could not bear the slightest touch. He complained of pain over the region of the kidneys, and said he was passing *red* urine, which to the naked eye appeared black—being as it were a solution of black venous blood. (The specific gravity and other clinical characters could not be noted for want of the requisite apparatus.) He further complained of great prostration and weakness. I prescribed some diuretics with ten drops of the tinctura ferri muriatis, which did not seem to have the slightest influence on the character of the urine, which continued black as before. The swelling gradually subsided, and disappeared in four or five days. The hæmaturia lasted ten days, and then stopped of itself. After the swelling had gone down and the hæmaturia had ceased, he began to feel better and to regain his usual health. He was discharged quite well on Sept. 23rd."

"The second case was that of E. P., an East Indian clerk, who was bitten by a snake in the right foot at the inner ankle. He had tied two ligatures, one of cloth, and another of cord, before I was called to see him. When I arrived, I saw him surrounded by a number of people, one of whom was muttering some incantations and moving a bunch of some leaves from above downwards; another was putting a piece of stone, said to have been taken out of the head of a very venomous snake, to the wound, and expecting thereby to extract the poison. I began to ask him a few questions about the snake, the time and place where he had been bitten, how he was then feeling, and so on. In the meantime the muttering of incantations had ceased, and the piece of stone dropped off, showing, according to the charmer's own admission, that it had taken no effect. I then incised the part where I had found three small punctures slightly bleeding, and touched it with argenti nitras. As the person had not by this time felt drowsy or sleepy, or in any way queer, I undid one of the ligatures altogether, and loosened the other. This was done after more than an hour had elapsed since the bite. I remained with him half an hour more, and having found no symptoms of poisoning, left him. Before leaving I told him to take a glass of brandy or some kind of spirit and go to bed. As might have been expected, he could not sleep during the night. I saw him the next morning; the foot and leg had become swollen and painful, as in the other case. He told me he had been spitting black blood, and showed me handkerchiefs and cloths all stained. He asked me to prescribe some medicine to arrest the hæmorrhage; I refused, and explained to him my reasons, saying that his blood had been poisoned, and nature was expelling it through one of the outlets. I suppose he was not well pleased, so he sent for the Civil Surgeon, who prescribed, I believe, some kind of gargle. I watched the case, however, with great interest. On the fifth day there was a good deal of hæmorrhage from the wound itself, which opened and poured forth black venous blood. It stopped of itself. The swelling had by that time gone down, and the spitting of blood decreased. He suffered for about ten days, after which he felt all right. He killed the very snake which bit him, and which he believes was the last snake in the compound of his house, and showed it me. I asked him to send it to Dr. Taylor, who told me he would send it down to Calcutta for inspection.

"Now the question arises, was the snake or snakes (though from the similarity of the symptoms in the two cases I am inclined to believe it was the same kind of snake) poisonous? The profuse hæmorrhage and great prostration of strength seem to point to the existence of poison. If this fact be established by the examination of the snake, the following observations may be made:—1. As both the persons were grown-up adults, they did not succumb to the poison, either because the bite was not so effectual as to kill, or the amount of poison in this particular snake was not powerful enough to destroy adult life. 2. And if the latter view be correct, then it will be interesting to ascertain by observation the effect of the bite of the snake on children, or on some of the lower animals, as fowls, dogs, cats, &c. 3. That in partially successful bite or bites by slightly venomous snakes, hæmorrhage of black venous blood seems to be nature's method of cure."

I am indebted to Major C. A. McMahon, Officiating Commissioner of Hissar, for the following very interesting account of a case of death from the bite of *Bungarus cæruleus*, in which hæmaturia was a prominent symptom, and where life seems to have been prolonged by the internal administration of stimulants. Major McMahon writes:—

"Hissar, Oct. 17th.

"MY DEAR DR. FAYRER,—

"I enclose an interesting account of a death from snake bite. Mr. D——, a Customs' patrol, was bitten on Aug. 31st (evening) and did not die until 11 A.M. on Sept. 3rd, having been kept up by ammonia and brandy all that time. The case is interesting because Mr. D—— had skilful treatment from the first, and the most approved remedies appear to have been applied. Mr. D—— became perfectly insensible almost immediately after he was bitten, showing that the poison was powerful and active, and yet he was restored not only to consciousness by the internal administration of ammonia and brandy, but he became sufficiently well to do some work and sign some official papers (the latter fact is not mentioned in the accounts I send you). The influence of the poison having been checked for so long, one would hardly have anticipated a fatal termination about sixty-three hours after the poison was received into the system. It almost seems as if when a man is fairly bitten by a full-grown Cobra or Krait stimulants only postpone the fatal hour. The case is an interesting one, and I shall be glad to have your opinion on it. The snake was evidently a Krait. How ignorant men are of what snakes are deadly and what are not! Mr. D—— surely did not know.

"Yours, &c.,

"C. A. MCMAHON.

"P.S.—The two accounts I enclose are by Mr. Edwardes, District Superintendent of Police, Rohtuk, and the Sub-Assistant-Surgeon of Hansi. I think they give, taken together, a very full, complete, and accurate account of the case.

"*Account of the Case of Mr. D—— by Mr. F. O. Edwardes.*

"'On Aug. 31st, 1871, I was on my tour of inspection at Police Station Mahim, in this District, and on the Customs' Line. A Mr. D——, an assistant patrol, went out patrolling on foot in slippers in the evening, and returned at 8.30 P.M. As he entered the gate of the compound he was bitten on the instep by a small snake, a Korite, or Karite, or Kerite. He had time to kill the snake with his slipper; it was about two feet long, of a yellowish colour, with blackish stripes across its back. On Mr. D—— being bitten he called out to the guard at the thuk, or weighing-house, to bring a lattice, and by the time the man reached a distance of not one hundred yards Mr. D—— was insensible; they brought him to me at 8.30 P.M., or a few minutes after he was bitten, with the part bitten bleeding and a string tied under his knee, which I fancy he himself tied. I gave him ammonia and brandy in a wineglass, cut the part where he was bitten with a penknife and rubbed ammonia into it. On my giving him the second or third dose and rubbing his foot with ammonia and having him walked about, he came round, and at 9 P.M. was all right and perfectly sensible. I still kept walking him about and giving him small doses of ammonia at short intervals, first with brandy and afterwards without, as he did not like the brandy. About 10 P.M. I allowed him to sit down in a chair; he then became a little sick, but came round again. I left him at 11 P.M. perfectly sensible, and the only thing he complained of was a pain in his leg. I was obliged to come into Rohtuk, and was myself unwell. Shortly after Mr. D—— was brought in, and after he came round, I thought it as well to send for the Customs Native Doctor at Hansi, and wrote him a purwanah ordering him to come to Mahim at once; and on my reaching Rohtuk I wrote to Mr. D——'s brother, telling him of the case and advising him to go out. He went out on Sept. 1st, and tells me found his brother very well, but complaining of the leg being tied up and wishing to open it. He remained perfectly sensible and well that day, that night, the next day, Sept. 2nd, but about 1 A.M. of Sept. 3rd began vomiting. At first Mr. D——'s brother thought it was nothing, but on his vomiting a second time he got up and attended to him. On his asking his brother how he felt, he said that he found his chest paining him a great deal, and complained of suffocation. After this Mr. D—— tried to vomit again by putting his finger down his throat, but failed. The native doctor was present, and continued giving ammonia with brandy. He after this once fainted, and began to get weaker and weaker; and after about 3 A.M. he did not speak, and died about 11.30 A.M. on Sept. 3rd. Mr. D——'s brother states that after Mr. D—— fainted he had convulsions three times—that on Sept. 2nd, about 3 or 4 P.M., he noticed that his brother was passing blood in the urine, stools, and vomit, also from the part bitten. He also states that he remarked the blood getting blacker and blacker as death approached.' "

"*Account of the case of Mr. D—— by Sub-Assistant-Surgeon K. R. Paul, Hansi.*

"On Aug. 31st, 1871, Mr. D——, after taking his dinner at 8 P.M. with Mr. Edwardes, Assistant Superintendent of Police, Rohtuk (who had come to Mahim on his tour of inspection), went out patrolling on foot towards the Hansi Lines, and on his return, not very far from his Bungalow, just near the Naka (the high thick thorn hedge carried across the country by the Customs Department to prevent smuggling—neither man nor beast can get over or through it), he saw a small thin black and white snake lying on the road, which he attempted to kill with his foot, but the slipper he had on being loose, unfortunately came off, and the snake bit him on the right foot just above the great toe; he however killed the snake and walked a few steps when he fell and became quite insensible, and was carried by some of the peons to the Bungalow.

"Mr. Edwardes immediately administered some strong doses of brandy and liquor ammoniæ, which made him vomit and brought him to his senses. He was kept awake all night, and brandy and ammonia were administered frequently.

"On the morning of Sept. 1st, at 9 A.M. I received the notice, and immediately started with a proper supply of medicines to Mahim, and found Mr. D—— though quite sensible yet very uneasy; his right foot and leg up to the thigh were very much swollen, and in several places had become blue, especially at the bitten part, from which blood was oozing in drops, owing to its having been previously incised by the knife; and a kind of stone called 'zahr mohra' was applied for the purpose of absorbing the snake poison. The pulse was slow, respiration not difficult, pupils slightly contracted, urine frequent and consisted of pure blood; sputa also frequent and consisted of pure blood. He complained of great thirst and feeling of uneasiness throughout the whole body, stabbing pains now and then at the bitten parts. Stomach very irritable, and would not retain anything.

"*Treatment.*—Stimulating mixture with liquor ammoniæ was exhibited every half hour, which was retained; the swollen parts were fomented with decoction of neem, which greatly relieved the pain and reduced the swelling, and the patient was not allowed to sleep.

"On the morning of the 2nd he said he felt better, sat down for half an hour on an easy-chair, and took a little sago, which was retained. Pulse a little improved, but the urine and sputa were still bloody, though less frequent. Stimulating mixture was continued every second hour instead of half hour; fomentation continued. At 2 P.M. he complained of severe pain in the abdomen, which was relieved by hot fomentation, but he made several unsuccessful attempts to evacuate his bowels.

"At 5 P.M. he asked to have some chicken broth, and wanted to have an undisturbed sleep, which was allowed, as now it was more than forty-eight hours since he had been bitten.

"At 10 P.M. a relapse took place. He vomited the broth mixed with a large quantity of blood, and felt very uneasy and prostrated. Stimulating mixture with liquor ammoniæ was given frequently, every quarter of an hour. At 12 in the night he again felt worse; suffocation and headache ensued. His bed was taken out into the verandah and the medicine was continued. At 2 A.M. (Sept. 3rd) the patient got much weaker, and insensible. Pulse very low; breathing very difficult; convulsions commenced; he could only be roused by loud calling, and with difficulty could swallow the medicine which was given. At 4 A.M. he became convulsed (deeply insensible); he could not be roused at all, neither could he swallow medicine nor water. Cold perspiration broke out over the face; the eyes were depressed; the extremities became cold; the pulse scarcely perceptible; the breathing prolonged and stertorous. Convulsions more frequent; twitching of the right hand and beating of the right foot; the left side of the body became paralysed; eyes insensible to light and congested; involuntary discharge of bloody urine and stools, and at 11 A.M. he breathed his last."

The following cases are recorded by Dr. Woodford, Police Surgeon of Calcutta:—

"Nadar Chunder, a Bengalee Hindoo, aged nine years, was bitten at 2 A.M. of July 29th, 1870. The boy was sleeping on the floor by the side of his father, in a hut in Simla Street, Calcutta: he woke his father, calling out 'I am bitten.' The father states that the child screamed; was convulsed and foamed at the mouth. There was no treatment; he died in fifteen minutes. The body was examined at about 9 A.M. of the 29th, or about seven hours after death. Rigor mortis was complete within an hour after death. The lungs were engorged with blood. Heart firm, both sides filled with liquid blood; great vessels natural. The abdominal viscera generally were congested. The blood remained fluid, it did not coagulate. The brain substance was firm and natural."

Note by Dr. Fayrer: The blood of this boy did not coagulate when set aside after death, under microscope the red globules were crenated, and did not adhere to each other. There were no new cell forms. Forty drops of the blood were injected hypodermically into a fowl's thigh. The bird was perhaps somewhat sluggish after it, but no evil result followed; it recovered.

"Gungadhur Mookerjee, Brahmin, aged forty-five years, was bitten by a Cobra at 9.45 P.M. Aug. 7th, 1870. He had gone out of his house in Sham Pookoor, Calcutta, to pass water, and returned immediately, saying he had been bitten by a large snake. He became insensible in about ten minutes. He said he felt heated, but refused water before he became unconscious. No treatment was adopted; he was dead in fifteen minutes. The body was examined sixteen hours after death. The lungs were engorged with blood. The right side of the heart was distended with fluid blood. Left side full of fluid blood. Great vessels natural. The abdominal viscera were congested, and the stomach contained a quantity of milk. The blood was quite fluid, not coagulable. Brain vessels full of blood. Serum effused between convolutions. Rigor mortis occurred in an hour after death."

The following cases are recorded by Dr. Verchere, Station Staff Surgeon, Barrackpoor. The snakes were most probably Cobras:—

"Achloo, Coolie, aged thirty-two, was sleeping in the hut of a sweetmeat-maker in the Sudder Bazaar, Barrackpoor; there were two other men asleep in the hut, the owner on a charpoy, the deceased and another man on the ground. At 4 A.M., July 27th, 1870, deceased called out that a snake had bitten him. It was quite dark, and nobody saw the snake. The two other men ran out for assistance; they, however, did not give notice to the police or come to the Station Staff Hospital (not five minutes' walk off) for aid, but brought in a Bheestie (water-carrier)—who gave the patient some leaves to smell—and a man of the 13th N.I., who appears to have a reputation as a snake-bite curer; nothing, however, was really done except blowing on the man's face, giving him some leaves to smell, and reciting certain prayers. Soon after he had been bitten the patient was foaming at the mouth. He did not get up, but remained where he had been sleeping, groaning, complaining of slight pain in the arm bitten, but altogether unnaturally quiet. By 6 A.M. he was unable to speak; he was unconscious and could give no answer. He died a little after 7 A.M., about three hours after the bite. No search was made for the snake. The body was brought to hospital at 10 A.M. Post-mortem examination took place at 1.15 P.M., five and a half hours after death. Average temperature of the day 87°, damp heat. Rigor mortis slight; well marked in legs, hardly marked in the upper extremities. Considerable tympanites, sanious dark fluid dropping from mouth. Catarrhal mucosities oozing out of nose. There were four small punctures on the outside of the arm (right) just below the elbow. One of the punctures is a mere slit, as if done with a penknife. Three-quarters of an inch from it are two punctures straight down into the cellular tissue; one bled a few drops of blood, and there is a little dry blood around it. Cutting through the skin a small, soft, half-formed clot, dark red, with a good deal of watery reddish serum all around it, is seen. But there is no swelling or puffiness near the punctures; there is no tumefaction of the limb, the punctures look externally such as the thorns of a bramble would inflict. *Chest.*—On opening the cavity air escaped, as on puncturing a bladder. The lungs were healthy and well distended by air, the left was slightly congested, the right a little more so. A little red fluid oozed out of incisions in both lungs, but both lungs were healthy. No fluid in pleural cavities. The auricles of the heart were quite empty. Left ventricle empty, contained only a little dark red blood amongst the pillars, but no clot. Right ventricle empty also, with only a little dark fluid bathing the sides of it. No appearance of fibrinized clots in heart or large vessels. No formed clots seen in either. A considerable quantity of dark red fluid in the large vessels. No appearance of previous disease in chest. *Abdomen.*—Liver of natural size, consistence, and colour; not congested; the peritoneal covering peels off very easily. Spleen natural in size and colour. Kidneys slightly congested, but otherwise normal; oozing of watery reddish fluid, greater than normal. Stomach half filled with digested rice, but distended. The gastric mucous membrane coated with a gelatinous grey substance, like catarrhal mucosity. Some considerable congestion near the cardiac orifice. Lesser intestine distended with gas, a little congested in places but otherwise normal. Larger intestines normal, empty, not distended. Peritoneum distended by gas. Other organs, not specially mentioned, apparently quite normal. *Head.*—Membranes of brain perfectly normal. No fluid. Brain of ordinary consistence and appearance, but on section showing a great many spots of congestion, almost as much as in concussion of brain. But the ventricles are empty of fluid. There are about two drachms of pale fluid at the base of the brain. Cerebellum healthy, with spots of congestion as in brain.

"*Remarks.*—The arm with the bites not being swollen or puffy, and not showing much less marked rigor mortis than the other arm, the nails not being blue, the brain not being soft, and some discrepancy occurring in the statements made by the men who lived in the same hut about what the man had eaten at night, the stomach and its contents were sent to the Chemical Examiner to Government. The report of the additional Examiner was that no trace of any poisonous substance could be found. July 27th was the heaviest rainfall this year as yet. It rained 2.46 inches from 6 P.M. 26th to 6 P.M. on July 27th. It seems therefore probable that the snake entered the hut to get away from the rain, and went to nestle for shelter and warmth near the deceased who was sleeping on the ground. The deceased happening to move his arm, or rolling half over in his sleep, frightened or hurt the snake, which at once bit him.

"This was my first case of snake-bite in Bengal. I have seen three other cases on the extreme north-western frontier, but there the cases were very different, being those in which a hæmorrhagic or purpuric oozing of blood from the skin and mucous membrane is the most marked symptom. Looking at the case now, after seeing the bodies of other victims, I cannot doubt for a moment that the cause of death was the bite of a snake, almost certainly of a Cobra."

"Hurrie Doss, aged fifteen, a fine, strong, well-fed lad, of the village of Khurdah, four and a half miles from Barrackpoor, is said to have been bitten by a snake at 10 P.M. on July 27th, 1870. The deceased's mother states that Hurrie and another boy, younger, were asleep in a hut on the ground close to her. He awoke up, shouting that a snake was spitting at him, put out his right hand to push off the animal, and was bitten on the wrist. The old woman says that she saw the snake, and described graphically enough the striking of a Cobra. She is quite certain that the snake stood up to strike her half-asleep boy. The deceased did not apparently realize at once that he had been bitten; he took up the younger boy and handed him to his mother, but he did not leave his place. He told his mother that the snake had some dirty white spots on its body. She says that the snake was dark-coloured, and that she did not notice the spots mentioned by her son. The snake made off, and was not seen by anybody else. Deceased complained of burning pain in wrist; hung down his arm, from which a few drops of blood fell. He kept very quiet staring at his drooping hand. Within half an hour he lost his voice and became partially unconscious. He foamed at the mouth a little, and in an hour was quite unconscious. A Brahmin came in, breathed on the patient, sprinkled water over him and recited prayers; he remained nearly two hours in attendance, but the patient never gave sign of consciousness. Koneyhi, a Fakir, went through similar performances. Petumber, a cultivator, also tried some incantations. Finally, a Bengali Kobiraj (native doctor) took up the case. He put some leaves in cold water and sprinkled the water on the head of the patient. No internal remedy was given. The Kobiraj felt the pulse and said the case was hopeless. The boy died at 8 A.M., July 28th, ten hours after he had been bitten.* The body was brought to Barrackpoor in the middle of the day, July 28th. Post-mortem examination 5.30 P.M., nine and a half hours after death, average temperature 86°, very damp. Face puffy; a good deal of tympanites; right arm swollen; nails blue on both hands. Rigor mortis well marked in legs and left arm, but altogether absent from the right arm. Two deep punctures on right wrist surrounded by swelling, the whole wrist, hand, and arm puffy up to the elbow. A little dark fluid oozing from the mouth; catarrhal mucosities bubbling from nose. Half-formed, imperfect, dark clots in cellular tissue under the punctures. The body was not opened, the case being quite plain, and the mother anxious that the body should not be cut.

"*Remarks.*—This was another case on the night of July 27th, when 2·46 inches of rain fell. It is therefore probable that the

* The patient had one natural stool about an hour after the bite. He was then sufficiently conscious to attempt to sit on a pan, and he was supported by two men during defecation.

snake entered the house for protection from wet, and nestled near the boy for warmth, and that on being disturbed by the sleeper moving in his sleep, he began to hiss. The boy, attempting to brush him off as he would a mosquito, was bitten on the right wrist.

"Gya Ram, a Jalliah by caste and fisherman by trade, of the village Bowroh, near Khurdah, was reported to have been bitten by a snake at 9 P.M. on Aug. 2nd, 1870. Age twenty, a wonderfully fine man, largely developed, very tall and well formed, in perfect health, certainly an uncommonly muscular, strong man for a Bengali. Deceased had just married; he was sleeping on the ground in his hut, his wife and sister were sleeping outside the door. The informant is a caste friend of deceased, and lives over the way opposite the deceased's hut; he (that is, Kinoo, the friend) was asleep in his hut when Gya Ram called out 'Kinoo, look here, a snake has bitten me and run away.' Kinoo and some other neighbours went to deceased's hut, and found him sitting on the ground holding up his drooping hand, from which a few drops of blood were falling. Patient complained of a burning pain in hand. Samboo, a Jalliah, first tried breathing on patient and prayers. Then a Brahmin, and finally a Bagdie by caste did the same. No medicine was given internally. In about an hour the patient began to foam at the mouth, and became speechless. He was not purged; his bowels were never moved from time of bite to time of death. He passed no urine either. He kept very quiet, in a state of half unconsciousness. He never spoke after the first hour after the bite, but he groaned a little at times. He died at 10 P.M. There is some discrepancy in the length of time he lived after the bite; most witnesses say that he lived no more than an hour, but from the details gathered it seems that he lived at least one hour and a half. Nobody saw the snake. The village is half a koss from Khurdah, where Hurrie Doss was killed by a snake on July 27th. There are no snake catchers in the village or neighbourhood. The whole population does poojah to snakes. Nobody would kill a snake; they believe snakes to be the sons of a tree,* called in Bengali 'Munsa Mahai (goddess of serpents);' they worship both the Munsa and her son the snake. The body was not brought to Barrackpoor till the afternoon of Aug. 3rd. Post-mortem examination at 5.30 P.M. Aug. 3rd, 1870, nineteen and a half hours after death. Thermometer 88°, very damp heat; calm. Body in excellent state of nutrition, and well preserved. Rigor mortis well marked in legs; not so well marked, but yet well marked in left arm, especially in the fingers. No rigor mortis at all in the right arm—the bitten limb. The bite is on the ring finger of the right hand. The punctures are very minute, with a little dry blood on them; there are two punctures, one larger than the other, and a few scratches further down the finger. The hand is puffy; the dorsum of the hand is raised up into a soft doughy puffiness. The wrist is much swollen. The arm is swollen and hardened up to the elbow. The whole forearm is about one quarter larger than on the other side. The excessive limpness of the right arm, compared to the cadaverous stiffness of the remainder of the body, is very striking. A cut made across the punctures shows a small half formed soft clot, rather dark; it is bathed in reddish serum; the whole hand appears to be infiltrated with a darkish sanious fluid; there is no formed coagulum anywhere under the skin. Nails very blue. A good deal of tympanites; some dark sanious fluid dropping from mouth; a little catarrhal mucosity oozing from nose. *Chest.*—No adhesion. Upper lobe of right lung slightly congested; lower lobe deeply congested, looking like the port-wine coloured infiltration of lung apoplexy. Left lung intensely congested in its upper half; the lower half normal. The whole lungs are wonderfully congested, and remind one of apoplexy of the lungs. *Heart.*—Both auricles empty. The aorta full of dark fluid blood; no fibrinous clots seen anywhere. Right ventricle empty; left ventricle empty; both ventricles look almost as if they had been washed. *Abdomen.*—Every organ appeared sound in abdomen. The intestines were distended by gases. *Head.*—No fluid under membranes of brain. The ventricles quite dry, no fluid at base of brain. The brain substance is very soft, and tears very easily. There are no abnormal points of vascularity; everything looks quite normal except the excessive softness of the tissue of the cerebrum and cerebellum. This may be due to the length of time between death and examination of body.

"*Remarks.*—There was a good deal of rain on the morning of Aug. 2nd; but the sky was clear on the night of Aug. 2nd. It seems, however, that the snake came close to the deceased, who, in attempting to brush him off while in a half sleepy state, was bitten on the right hand. From the similarity of appearances in this and Hurrie Doss's case, it seems that there is some probability that the snake was a Cobra.

"*Note.*—In these three cases, the Bengali test of death by snake-bite was tried. It consists in ascertaining whether the hair of the head comes off easily on being gently pulled. It answered in the first case, that of Achloo, the least otherwise marked case, but it did not prove true in the other two cases."

"Puddoomonee Dassee, wife of Muttondass, carpenter, aged thirty, living at Agarpara, a small village on the banks of the Hooghly, three miles from Khurdah, seven miles from Barrackpoor. Her husband was away on some work up country. She was asleep with a child in a cot near the window of the hut,—at least, two neighbours who live in the next hut state that such was her place when they last saw her on the evening of Aug. 3rd. At about 5 A.M., Aug. 4th, her neighbours heard her shouting and went into the house. Nobody saw the snake; the woman said she had been bitten by a snake, and complained of burning pain in the right foot. She appeared faint and foamed a little at the mouth. In less than half an hour she was speechless, but breathed slowly with much gurgling in the throat. She was quite insensible, and died within two or three hours after she first called out to her neighbours. No treatment. It appears probable that the woman got up, and put her foot on a snake which had taken refuge inside the hut, owing to the swampy state of the country around. Post-mortem examination at 1.30 P.M. Aug. 5th, 1870, about twenty-seven and a half hours after death; thermometer 85°, stormy. Body well nourished; in good state of preservation (it had been rubbed all over with McDougall's powder and water over night, and all orifices closed with pieces of rag soaked in the same lotion); face puffy. No rigor mortis. Punctures of fangs on dorsum of great toe, right foot. Foot and leg much swollen and puffy, leg about one-third larger than the other; no clot under the puncture, only a little pale reddish serum. *Chest.*—Much gas in chest. Lungs intensely congested and the colour of damson; on section the lung tissue appears precisely as in cases of lung apoplexy. Both lungs equally infiltrated with the dark fluid blood. Heart of natural size and quite healthy; all four cavities are perfectly empty, and the inside of the ventricles looks as if it had been washed under a stream of water. Aorta, when cut across, was found partially full of dark liquid blood which ran out; no fibrinous clots; no dark clots. *Abdomen.*—Tympanites. Stomach half-filled with digested rice and vegetables; quite normal. Small and large intestines much distended by gases, but apparently quite healthy. The peritoneal covering of the liver peels very easily, but not quite so much so as in previous cases. Liver tissue slightly congested. Spleen of a dark port-wine colour, on section oozing a great deal of dark sanious fluid; kidneys normal. *Head.*—Pia mater very congested, or rather its vessels distended with dark blood, as in

* The *Euphorbia ligularia.* It resembles in appearance a cactus.

poisoning by opium. No fluid under dura mater. Brain tissue soft; no points of vascularity; the vascularity appears to be confined to the engorged pia mater. Ventricles empty and apparently quite normal. Cerebellum very soft. Pons Varolii almost creamy in consistence. The whole cerebellum is so soft that the striæ of grey and white matter cannot be recognised.

"*Remarks.*—Hair not easily pulled off. Nails of fingers blue; nails of toes not blue, not even on the bitten toe."

The following brief notes of a case of snake-bite are recorded by Sub-Assistant Surgeon Woomesh Chunder Roy of Monghyr:—

"On July 17th, 1869, a Hindoo woman named Jitnee was bitten by a snake, called in the description an adder. It was seen to spring at her arm. She tore it off; it again sprang at her breast; she again tore it off, and it escaped. No further particulars are given. Nothing is said of the symptoms, nor of the duration of life after the bite, except that she died the same day, and that the body on examination was found to present the following appearances. Lungs congested; right lung adherent to the wall of the chest. *Heart.*—Right ventricle full of blackish-red frothy blood. Left ventricle also contained a small quantity of black frothy blood. Liver and spleen, stomach and intestines, healthy. Kidneys congested. Brain congested. One can only conjecture that the snake may have been the *Daboia russellii* or the *Echis carinata*, though I am not aware that the *Echis* has been found in this part of India."

The following cases are reported by Mr. Picachy, Civil Surgeon at Purneah:—

"Nirmull, a Hindoo, aged thirty, was bitten by a snake at noon on May 1st, at a village named Durgapore, in Purneah. He was fishing in a pool of water when bitten. The snake was not seen. No details are given, but it is reported that he died in twelve hours. The body was thrown into a river and unfortunately could not be recovered for post-mortem examination. The case is curious, as the bite is said to have occurred in a pool of water. It may have been either the Cobra or Krait, as there is no venomous freshwater snake. But in the absence of further information the case is not free from the suspicion that death may have been due to other causes."

"Jontee, a Bengali weaver, aged thirty years, was bitten at about 4 P.M. of Sept. 9th, 1870. When watering paddy in a field he came upon a rat-hole full of grain, put his hand in to examine it, and was bitten by the snake which was in the hole. It was seen and described by the natives to be a 'Baira Bora.' Mr. Picachy believes it to have been the *Daboia russellii.* This occurred in a paddy field in a village in Purneah. The only symptom noted by the police who reported the case was swelling of the hand. He was treated by the natives with incantations and charms. Death occurred in about fourteen hours. The body was examined, and the lungs were found to be slightly engorged. The heart and great vessels contained fluid dark-coloured blood. The blood remained fluid and dark after death. The brain was healthy. There was no cadaveric rigidity, it is stated, when the body was examined.

"Notes of post-mortem examination of the body of Mundo Bouri, aged about twenty-seven years, July 14th, 1870. 1. *External appearances.*—Autopsy twenty-one hours after death. Fang marks only just visible above the right elbow. Rigor mortis present. 2. *Head.*—Brain highly congested, and when cut exhibited a great number of bleeding points. 3. *Chest.*—Embolism of heart, as also of the great vessels; otherwise these organs normal. There was a small quantity of fluid in the pericardium. Lungs very much congested, and when cut into, a red, frothy mucus escaped. 4. *Abdomen.*—All organs normal.

"*Remarks.*—This man was bitten by a Krait (*Bungarus cæruleus*), and died in nine hours. Out of fourteen cases examined by me, this is the only instance in which I found coagulated blood in the body.

"Notes of post-mortem examination of the body of Bolai Bouri, about forty-five years, Aug. 10th, 1870. 1. *External appearances.*—Autopsy eighteen hours after death. Rigor mortis present, especially of the lower extremities. The right ear and parts below it were swollen, but no fang marks were observable. 2. *Head.*—Sinuses full of dark fluid blood. Brain congested, and when cut into, numerous bleeding points were observed; a small quantity of fluid in the lateral ventricles. 3. *Chest.*—Heart healthy, and contained fluid blood. Lungs very much congested, and when cut a dark frothy fluid exuded. 4. *Abdomen.*—Liver much congested. Stomach slightly congested. Spleen rather large. Kidneys highly congested. Other organs normal."

The following cases of death from snake-bite were also investigated by Mr. Picachy. The Report is condensed from the Sessions Report of the trial:—

Poonai Fatmah and Joomun Fatmah are brought to trial for having, "on or about Oct. 11th, 1868, at Hurdah, Zillah Purneah, committed culpable homicide not amounting to murder, by causing the deaths of Titroo, Menghon, and Jikree."

1. "Itwarree Mussahar, son of Dhunpat, aged twenty years, Moosahar of Bacha, Pergunnah Soorujgurrah, Zillah Monghyr, labourer. 'I cannot recollect day or month. I came to Chitrapore, Zillah Purneah, being engaged to make bricks for the Darjeeling and Caragola road, and was learning how to charm snakes from the two prisoners, Poonai and Joomun. At length, on a Sunday, the prisoners wanted to make the snake bite me. I did not wish the snake to bite me on any part of the body. They then pulled my ears in a tyrannical manner, and said, Why are you afraid? If the snake does bite, we will charm you, and recover you. Then they brought three snakes, two Kraits and one Keautiah; the latter a young snake, but all were poisonous. The two smaller snakes they put aside, and one large Krait two *haths* long, they placed in front of us, and made Titroo place his right hand on the ground, and made the snake crawl on to his hand; but at first the snake did not bite him, then Poonai struck the snake with a cane, and the snake immediately bit Titroo on his right fore-finger. After this, in the same manner the snake was made to bite Menghon on the right hand, and then in the same manner the right hand of Jikree. After this, in the same manner the snake was made to bite me on the right wrist: the snake then appeared to be dead. After this, the prisoners having made incantations over the snake brought it to life again, and having placed some vermilion on its head, let it go free in a paddy field. After the snake had bitten Titroo he was attacked with great thirst, and began to foam at the mouth: he became senseless. At one *pahur* of the night remaining, Titroo was bitten, and he died half an hour before daybreak. Menghon and Jikree appeared well after Titroo's death; the poison did not seem to have affected them. The prisoners then ran away; Menghon and Jikree returned to their houses, and I heard they died there at mid-day. I was then senseless after I was bitten, my body and head began to turn round, and great perspiration commenced, with severe pain in the stomach, and my eyesight became dim, then I became senseless. I was brought from Bahadurpore to the Hospital, and remained

there five or six days, when I became sensible again. All this took place at Bahadurpore in the courtyard of Moosum: he is not related to the prisoners, neither did he assist them. Some five or six other men besides we four were made to sit down by the prisoners in order that the snake might be made to bite them; but owing to the snake becoming weak, they were not bitten. Seeing all the above, they ran away.'"

2. "Bechoo Sirdar, son of Dookhun, aged twenty-two years, Moosahar of Manikpore, Pergunnah Secundra, Zillah Monghyr, labourer. 'The prisoners Poonai and Joomun were in Assin teaching Titroo, Menghon, Jikree, Itwarree, Laloo, &c., some ten men, snake incantations, and I was also being taught by them. At length, on a Sunday night, the prisoners produced from an earthen pot two Kraits and a Keautiah, snakes, and began to teach us the incantations, and began to make the snakes move about in front of us all. We became afraid, whereupon the prisoners said, Why do you fear? If the snakes bite you, we are *gooroos*, and will soon restore you. After this they made us place our right hands on the ground, and began to make the big Krait snake move towards our heads, we immediately from fear raised our hands. Upon this the prisoners struck us with rattans, and when the snake moved to a distance we again placed our hands on the ground. Then the prisoners took the snakes near to Titroo, Menghon, Jikree, and Itwarree, and made the snake, by striking it with a rattan, bite Titroo on the forefinger of the right hand; the throat of Titroo immediately became dry, and he became senseless; then the snake was made to bite Menghon on the forefinger of the right hand, but Menghon did not suffer or become senseless. After this the snake was made to bite Jikree on the right hand; he did not either become senseless, but remained talking. Then the snake was made to bite Itwarree on the right wrist; he did not appear to suffer. Then Titroo died two hours before dawn, and the prisoners then ran away. We went in search of them, and at 10 A.M. we found them and seized them in a rice-field at Gurnabaree, west of the road, and took them to Bahadurpore. We told them to restore Titroo to life again, but they could not do it, but went and sat down at a distance. Then the police came, and we made the prisoners over to them.

"'I heard Menghon and Jikree died on the day following; Itwarree was placed on a cart and brought to hospital. When Titroo became senseless the prisoners tried to recover the snake, which became torpid after biting Itwarree. The prisoners took the snakes with them when they went off. I did not see them let go by the prisoners. We were to pay one or two rupees for being taught; we were told that if we were bitten by a snake, in repeating the incantations, and fanning the snake, we should recover.'

"Two other witnesses are examined, but they give similar evidence to the preceding.

"The information and deposition of Mr. David Picachy, Civil Surgeon of Purneah, taken before me, J. R. Muspratt, Sessions Judge of Purneah, at Purneah, on this twelfth day of January, 1869, who being put on his oath, saith as follows:

Ques.—"Did you examine the bodies of Titroo, Menghon, and Jikree?

Ans.—"Yes, I did, and found that they had died from the effects of snake-poison. There was nothing abnormal about their internal organs, which could be said to be the result of disease.

Ques.—"In what way did the three bodies exhibit the effects of snake-poison?

Ans.—"Externally there were the marks of snake-bites on their hands and arms, and internally the blood was in a fluid state, and the brain-vessels deeply congested; the former state—viz., the fluid state of the blood—being particularly indicative of snake-poison.

Ques.—"Did you examine the wound of Itwarree?

Ans.—"Yes, and found a scratch on the fore-arm; he was partially senseless when received into Hospital, but could reply to questions I put to him. His wound or scratch looked like that which would be inflicted by a snake. I treated him with ammonia for three days, when he recovered.

Ques.—"How do you account for the escape of Itwarree, the other three having died?

Ans.—"He was the last person bitten, and must have received less poison than the others.

Ques.—"Was he in your opinion suffering from the bite of a poisonous snake?

Ans.—"Yes, he was lethargic and depressed; there was very slight swelling about the scratch. The wounds on the three dead bodies presented a livid appearance, and the corpses were swollen and in a semi-decomposed state, resulting from rapid chemical change after death by animal poison."

These men were sentenced to five years' imprisonment by the Sessions Judge of Purneah, which sentence was confirmed on appeal by the High Court of Calcutta.

The snakes, as described by the witnesses, were two Kraits, (*Bungarus cæruleus*) and one Keautiah (*Cobra di Capella*), the variety with one ocellus on the hood. The larger snake, said to be a *Bungarus*, bit four men; three died, one appears to have narrowly escaped.

The following cases are reported by the Civil Medical Officer of Bancoorah, Bengal:—

Jeebun Paul, a Hindoo, aged fourteen years, was bitten while asleep on the night of June 13th, 1870, at his house in the village of Bishenpore by a snake (either a *Naja tripudians* or *Bungarus cæruleus* most probably). He did not come under observation, and died on the 14th (number of hours after the bite could not be ascertained). The body was examined twenty-nine hours after death, and the following morbid appearances noted. The lungs were very much congested, especially the posterior lobes. The heart and great vessels were filled with fluid blood. The abdominal viscera were more or less congested. The blood was fluid and non-coagulable. The brain was highly congested, and the lateral ventricles contained fluid. Cadaveric rigidity present, especially of the lower extremities, when the body was examined.

Duary Ghose, a male Hindoo, aged eighteen years, was bitten on the night of June 24th, 1870, by a snake (most probably a Cobra), at the village of Oudab. No symptoms were noted, and he was treated by some native Kobirajes, but died three hours after receiving the bite. The body was examined thirty hours after death. The lungs were somewhat congested. The heart contained a small quantity of fluid blood. The abdominal viscera were congested slightly. The blood was fluid and non-coagulable. The brain was congested. Cadaveric rigidity was present, although decomposition had commenced.

I am also indebted to Mr. Richards of Bancoorah for the following case of Cobra bite:—

"Had I been less of a sceptic in regard to antidotes to snake-poison, I might have been induced to expatiate on the infallibility of the treatment adopted in this case. But I am inclined to believe notwithstanding the wound, the bleeding, and the intense swelling, that the bite was an imperfect one, and that any other treatment, and indeed no treatment, would have been equally successful. The case, however, is extremely interesting, more particularly on account of its demonstrating how 'infallible remedies' gain a reputation entirely undeserved. I may state that I have noticed throughout my experiments that *much bleeding* is a favourable circumstance, probably owing to the consequent dilution and expulsion of some of the poison.

"On June 7th, at about noon, I was informed by one of my servants that there was a large Cobra curled up on the kutcha wall inside his house. I went, accompanied by my snake-man, to the servant's house, and saw lodged on the wall, between it and the thatching, a Cobra. All that was visible was about three inches of its centre looped over a piece of wood. The snake-man gently probed it with a small twig, when it began to glide slowly over the piece of wood. I cautioned him on no account to touch it until we were certain in which direction the head was, but he disregarded my advice, and making sure that the snake was progressing head foremost, seized it and dragged it partly out. He was mistaken, the brute was moving backwards in order to extricate his head, and the poor fellow had caught it about four inches from the head. It instantly bit him, but he dragged his hand away quickly, leaving the snake hanging halfway over the wall, hissing and striking in a most furious manner. I immediately seized the man's hand, which was bleeding considerably, and wiped away with my fingers a quantity of the amber-coloured poison that was lying on his hand. I ran at once to the house, and the first caustic I came across was nitric acid, with which, in less than a minute, I returned. The snake-man had again seized hold of the snake, this time by the tail, and was repeating his muntros; but he exhibited no signs of fear. After excising a large piece of flesh, I applied the strong nitric acid with the stopper of the bottle, and although the agony must have been intense, he neither winced nor did he loose his hold of the snake. I then applied a ligature as tightly as possible around the forearm. The snake-man now dragged the brute forcibly out of its hiding-place. It proved to be a large Gokurrah Kurrees (Spectacled Cobra), and its belly was greatly distended in three different places by some food that it had recently taken. It was secured in a basket. Ten ounces of brandy were given to the man, and his hand was kept constantly in hot water. The hand became intensely swollen and painful, and was still so when I visited him on the morning of the 9th. There were, however, no constitutional symptoms of poisoning. On lifting up the basket containing the snake, I felt and heard something rolling about inside, and on removing the lid, found three of my guinea fowl's eggs which the brute had disgorged. These eggs, which are in my possession, exhibit various stages of digestion. On searching the jungle near the servant's house four more guinea fowl's eggs were found. This snake killed a fowl in four and a half minutes."

The following cases are recorded by Mr. Connolly, Civil Medical Officer of Bograh, Bengal:—

Kunjun Bewah, a Mahomedan female, aged thirty years, was bitten while asleep on the night of June 14th, 1870, by a snake (not seen). She died three hours after being bitten. No further details are given. The body was examined. The lungs were congested. The heart contained dark frothy blood. The abdominal viscera were congested. The blood is said to have resembled liquid tar in appearance and consistency. The brain was congested and decomposed. Cadaveric rigidity not present.

Karrohiar Kokar, a Mahomedan, aged twenty-seven years, was bitten by a snake (unknown) on the night of April 18th, 1870. He died on April 20th, at 5 A.M., thirty-four hours after he had been bitten. The body was examined thirty-three hours after death. The lungs were congested, softened, and in a state of decomposition. The parietes of the heart and great vessels were congested, and the heart contained a small quantity of coagulated blood. The blood was partially coagulated and of a dark colour. The brain was congested. There was no cadaveric rigidity present when the examination was made.

M. H., a Mahomedan female, aged twenty-seven years, was bitten while asleep on the night of June 13th, 1870, by a snake (not known). Mr. Connolly states that the woman had retired to rest with her infant, when she felt herself bitten on the right ankle. The snake endeavoured to cross over the mother's body to where the infant was sleeping, when the woman struck at the snake with her hand and was bitten a second time on the middle finger. Fortunately the infant escaped unhurt, but the mother died, how long after the bite is not stated. The body was examined and the lungs were found congested. The heart contained dark frothy blood. The abdominal viscera were congested. The blood was dark, whether fluid or coagulated is not stated. The brain was congested and decomposed. Cadaveric rigidity is said not to have been present when the post-mortem examination was made.

The following cases are reported by the Civil Surgeon of Furreedpore, Bengal:—

Jameena Khatoon, a Mahomedan woman, aged fifty years, was bitten at 3 P.M. Aug. 11th, 1870, by a Keautiah snake (small black Cobra). She was treated by incantations and charms, but died three hours after the bite. No further details are given.

Nudder Nam Mundle, a male Hindoo, aged thirty years, was bitten at 10 A.M. on Aug. 17th, 1870, by a "Chundra Bora" (*Daboia russellii*). He was treated by incantations and charms, but died in seven hours from the time he was bitten. No further details are given, and the body was not sent in for examination.

Tiluk Mistree, aged fifty-five years, of the village of Bahiahaboo, was, it is stated, bitten by a "Bora" (*Daboia russellii*) on Sept. 13th. No information regarding symptoms or treatment is given. He died nine days after the bite. No post-mortem examination was made. This case is not free from suspicion. The *Daboia russellii* generally kills very quickly. It is a pity further details of the case were not given, as it is quite possible the man was bitten by an innocent snake and that death occurred from another cause.

Parbut Khan, a Mahomedan, aged fifty years, of the village of Uttghur, was, it is stated, bitten by a Cobra (?), at 7 P.M. on May 3rd, 1870. He was treated by muntros (incantations and charms), but died seventeen hours after being bitten. The body was not sent in for examination.

Sango Bewah, a Mahomedan, aged sixty years, was bitten by a snake (name unknown) on Sept. 20th, 1870. He died in half an hour. No further particulars are given. The body was not sent in for examination.

Abdool, a Mahomedan boy, aged three years, was bitten by a Gokurrah (*Naja tripudians*) on Sept. 14th, 1870, at the village of Koodabia. He died one hour after being bitten. No further particulars given. The body was not sent in for examination.

Anundo Chandolinee, a girl, aged fifteen years, was bitten by a Gokurrah (*N. tripudians*), at the village of Niloki Furreedpore on Sept. 14th, 1870. She did not come under treatment, and died about three hours after being bitten. No post-mortem examination of the body was made. Information very meagre.

Shadorya Bewah, a Mahomedan female, aged twenty-seven years, was bitten by a Gokurrah (*Naja tripudians*), at the village of Dhoosail. There were, it is stated, four fang marks on the left elbow; the belly was swollen, and the veins distended with blood. She was treated by charms and incantations, but died an hour and a half after the bite. The body was not examined.

Affajoodeen, Mahomedan, cultivator, aged thirty-five years, was bitten on the night of March 15th, 1870, when he was asleep. The snake was not seen, and the exact time not noted. He died on March 16th. No symptoms or other details are recorded, except only that he was treated by natives with muntros. The body was not examined.

The following cases are reported by Dr. Skipton, Civil Medical Officer of Jessore, Bengal:—

Prosonee Dasee, a Bengali woman, aged twenty-six years, of the village of Poddo Poobhoonia, was bitten by a Spectacled Cobra (*N. tripudians*) while asleep on the night of June 22nd, 1870. She did not come under treatment, and died very shortly (exact time not stated) after being bitten. The body was examined. The lungs were slightly congested. All the chambers of the heart, as also the veins, contained fluid blood. Abdominal viscera decomposed. The blood was fluid. The scalp, brain, and membranes much congested. Cadaveric rigidity not noted.

Bhogobhan Kassabe, a Bengali belonging to the village of Dolutpore, was bitten while asleep by a snake, probably a Cobra, on the left elbow, which had been resting over a rat-hole, on the night of June 20th, 1870. No information regarding symptoms could be ascertained. He died two hours after the bite. The body was examined. The lungs were normal. The heart contained dark fluid blood in all the cavities. The abdominal viscera were normal. The blood was dark and fluid. The brain congested. This case shows how necessary it is that all rat-holes should be stopped up, as snakes invariably seek refuge in such places, both for food and shelter.

Koosee, aged thirty-five years, a Mahomedan Chowkedar, was bitten by a snake, probably the *Naja tripudians* (Cobra) on the night of June 21st, 1870. He did not come under treatment, and died in one hour. The body was examined. The lungs were extremely engorged with blood. All the chambers of the heart, as also the large veins, were filled with dark blood. The abdominal viscera were healthy. The blood was fluid. The brain was very much congested.

Deep Chandsen, of the village of Monerampore, was bitten by a snake (name not ascertained), while stepping from a chest on which he had been sleeping on the night of June 19th. No particulars regarding the symptoms could be ascertained, but he was treated by the native Kobirajes. He died eight hours after being bitten. The body was too far advanced in a state of decomposition to admit of a post-mortem examination being made.

The following cases are recorded by Dr. Robert, in medical charge of Raneegunge:—

Walorki Santhal, labourer, aged twelve, female. Is supposed to have been bitten on the night of June 18th, 1870, hour not known. The mother and daughter were sleeping together; the girl awoke her mother and complained of a burning pain in her right thigh. The mother caught a glimpse of a snake escaping from near the girl. She went to the thannah for medicine, but the girl was dead before she got back. The symptoms are not known beyond that the girl complained at first to her mother of the burning pain. Death must have occurred in less than two hours. On examination of the body the lungs were found to be hypostatically congested, probably a post-mortem change. The blood was fluid and very dark in the heart and great vessels. Heart flabby and contained very little blood. The blood formed no coagulum. The stomach contained recently taken food. The intestines much distended with flatulence. Uterus, ovaries, generative organs, and brain not examined. Rigor mortis not recorded.

Dr. Robert says: "The information regarding this case was got from the constable who accompanied the body, and not much reliance is to be placed upon it. I could discover no mark or puncture on the right thigh, or on any part of the body, which I could suppose to have been due to a snake-bite, but decomposition had set in, and the face was swollen. Blood and froth issued from mouth and nostrils. Abdomen distended." The body was examined about thirty-six hours after death.

Bonoo, Bengali Chowkedar, aged thirty-three, was bitten by a Krait (*Bungarus cæruleus*) on July 27th, 1870, at 5 P.M. He had caught the snake about a fortnight before, and was keeping it alive for the approaching snake poojah. It bit him on the left forefinger when he was going to feed it. His brother says he at once had burning pain in the finger, and soon after in his head and all over his body; he soon became very weak, could hardly articulate, and was drowsy. Some native medicine was given, which he vomited, and soon became unable to swallow. Died at 11 P.M. July 27th, or in about six hours. Body examined after death, time not recorded. Lungs much congested, of a dark purplish colour. But little blood in the heart, and that quite fluid and dark. Blood in great veins also fluid and dark; it is not noted whether the blood was set aside and examined for coagulation later. Peritoneal surface of bowels rather vascular, but mucous surface not so. Liver and kidneys natural. Spleen pulpy. Brain natural; no congestion; about three drachms of fluid in ventricles. Strong cadaveric rigidity existed ten hours after death, not, however, when it first occurred. Two small bloody punctures were to be seen on the palmar aspect of the joint between the first and second phalanges of the left index finger; one puncture on each of the transverse linear depressions situated there, about one-sixth of an inch from each other. There was a little blood also on the opposed surfaces of the left middle and ring fingers. There was no apparent inflammation or swelling of the index finger. But on raising the skin the fat and cellular tissue were seen to be infiltrated with, and discoloured by, a dirty brown serum, and this was the case for about two inches up the palm opposite the finger. Dr. Robert adds:—"The low caste men about here have for some time been catching snakes to play with and make a profit from at the Munsa poojah about a fortnight hence. They do not extract the fangs when they catch them, but only a couple of days before they make use of them."

Account of a case of snake-bite by the sufferer:—

"On May 30th, 1850, at Almorah, I took one up in my left hand, intending, as I had done with others, to put it into a bottle, seizing it by the neck, having previously pressed the head down with a stick. Too much of it was, however, left beyond my grasp, and it got one fang to bear upon the point of the knuckle of the left thumb. The fang did not enter very deeply. I saw it rising up from the gum partially covered by its mantle of skin. The effect was instantaneous; a sharp, hot pain shot up the whole length of the arm, along the course of the nerve affected, making me drop the creature faster than I had picked it up.

"I was going down to the billiard-room, and was only a few yards from my house at the time. It was situated just above and close to the billiard-room. I went back at once to the house, and said to Dr. F. P., who was living with me, that I had been bitten by a snake, but did not think it was poisonous (the fact being that I was rather ashamed of being such a muff). He told me it was better to be on the safe side, and made me drink at once a glass of brandy and suck the wound. This brought out a good deal of dark blue blood from a puncture only large enough just to be seen; and he sent off to the dispensary for other remedies. We went down to the billiard-room, but my thumb was too stiff and sore to play, and shortly after a violent throbbing headache came on. So I went and told P. I would go back to the house and lie down. When I got back sickness came on, and the contents of my stomach were all turned out. P. soon returned, and seeing that the case was serious, which from my silence on the matter he had not believed, lanced the wound deeply, and applied something, I forget what. He went off for F. This was, as well as I can recollect, about 4 o'clock P.M., about three-quarters of an hour after the bite was inflicted; gradually the headache, which had been very violent, subsided, and drowsiness came on. The two doctors remained with me all night, and I was walked about and dosed with strong hot punch. I must have consumed two bottles or more, for a third was broached. It was about 3 A.M. in the morning that the pulse was sufficiently excited to action for F. to leave me and P. to lie down. I did not, I think, wholly lose consciousness of my state at any time, but believe I talked a good deal, more or less incoherently. Two or three times the bowels were moved, and I was aware that the motions had a peculiarly strong odour. P. afterwards said that for some time he did not think I would have pulled through, and would not had my health at the time not been very good. Next morning leeches were applied up the course of a nerve along the arm, which was much swollen, and remained very thick and hard for some time, not going down quite for seven or eight days.

"The viper was *V. elegans*, at least I know of no other brown poisonous one, fifteen to twenty-two inches in length, with dark markings on the back. Had it got both fangs in, I could not I think have got over it.

"*V. elegans* is very common in the Punjab. Of 471 snakes brought in on one day, for a reward, to Dr. Aitchison at Umritsur in 1866, and which I helped him to kill, there were more than 300 of this one kind. Dr. A. tells me that Dr. Jerdon named it for him. I killed a pregnant female at Umritsur in 1868—she had eighteen young ones, all lively pretty little things, three or four inches long, each in a little membranous sac, all strung together like so many sausages, on breaking which they seemed quite prepared to enter on life with perhaps a little maternal help."

I am indebted for the above graphic account of snake-bite to an officer who was himself the sufferer. The name is by his own request suppressed.

The following cases are reported by the Sub-Assistant Surgeon of Loodianah:—

Bunnarie Kunbor, aged twenty years, was bitten on the right ear by a snake about one and a half feet in length (name could not be given), on the night of Aug. 27th, 1870, while asleep in his house at the village of Loodianah. He did not come under treatment, and died on Aug. 29th, thirty hours after receiving the bite. The body was examined seven hours after death. The lungs were highly congested. The heart was empty. The abdominal viscera were congested, but otherwise normal. The blood was fluid. Brain congested and softened.

Sedhoo Put, aged sixty years, of the village of Gundhwon, Loodianah, was bitten by a snake of a "dusky" colour, on the inner side of the instep of the left foot, on the morning of Aug. 15th, 1870. He did not come under the observation of Dr. Ince, but his foot is said to have become very much swollen. He died nine hours after the bite. The body, which was somewhat decomposed, was examined twenty-eight hours after death. The lungs were of a black colour, and much congested. The heart was empty. The abdominal viscera were softened and decomposed. The blood was fluid. The brain was also softened and decomposed. Cadaveric rigidity is said not to have been present when the post-mortem examination was made.

The following case is reported by Mr. Marshall, District Superintendent of Police of Loodianah:—

M. K., a Brahmin, aged sixty years, was bitten on July 22nd, 1870, at the village of Sehandood, by a snake known in the Punjab as the "Kod kundyal." The hand is said to have become inflamed, and she died three hours after the bite.

M. Mumghan, a woman, aged twenty-five years, of the village of Khutter, was bitten by a Plumear snake (black Cobra) at 10 P.M. on Aug. 23rd. She did not come under treatment, and died eight hours after being bitten. The body was examined fifty hours after death. Dr. Ince remarks that the body was not so much decomposed as might have been expected in a close damp atmosphere, with a temperature of 149° in the sun and 97° in the shade. The lungs were black and congested. Both sides of the heart quite empty. The abdominal viscera, with the exception of the liver, which though large was otherwise normal, were congested. The blood was fluid. The brain was much congested. The time at which cadaveric rigidity occurred could not be stated.

The following cases are recorded by Sub-Assistant Surgeon Troy Lucka Nath Ghose, of Meerut, dated Jan. 4th, 1870:—

Hussaram Lodha, a Hindoo grass-cutter, aged twenty-six years, was bitten at 3 A.M. on June 23rd, 1869, by a snake which he did not see, as it was dark. The circumstances under which he was bitten are not stated. On admission into the Dispensary there was slight dilatation of the pupils. The foot where the fangs had penetrated was swollen; pulse slow, but not full. The treatment was liquor ammoniæ, gtt. x. every hour; he was not allowed to sleep; and he was cupped, the report does not state where, to the extent of about thirty ounces. He recovered, and left the Dispensary in eight hours. The marks of the fangs were visible on the outer aspect of the right foot, in front of the malleolus. The parts around were swollen, purplish, and in the centre of this surface two black spots were seen.

Tharee, a male Hindoo, aged thirty-five years, while passing through a narrow lane at the village of Kurrepore on April 12th at 7 P.M. was bitten by a snake known to the natives as the "Kore Kuid" (specific name unknown). He was treated by the native doctor of the Aleepore Dispensary. He was sensible but refused food, and when put in a sitting position became faint. The pulse was small and rapid (120) and the foot hot and swollen. The bitten part was scarified and liquor ammoniæ applied. Half a drachm of liquor ammoniæ in water was administered every half hour. He died on April 15th at 8 A.M., sixty-one hours after the bite. The medical officer was of opinion the patient died exhausted from want of food, which he steadily refused to take from the time he was bitten. No post-mortem examination was made.

The following cases are reported by the Civil Assistant-Surgeon of Seonee, C.P. :—

Donajee, aged thirty-two years, was bitten by a snake, which was not seen, while asleep in his house, at 12 P.M. on March 25th, 1870. He is said to have become insensible and died in five hours. The information afforded by the police was very meagre. The body was not sent in for examination.

Nuggah, a Gond, aged fifty years, was bitten by a Cobra (*Naja tripudians*) while cutting grass on the banks of a river at 3 P.M. on March 22nd, 1870. He became insensible, but received no treatment, and died in three hours. The body was not sent in for examination.

The following case is reported by the Civil Surgeon of Saharunpore :—

Lahea, a Mahomedan, was bitten by a snake (name not given) at 8 A.M. on July 26th, 1870. He did not come under treatment, and died seven hours after the bite. The information received from the police was very scanty. At the post-mortem examination the lungs were found much congested and of a dark purple colour; the heart empty, and the lining membrane stained with the colouring matter of the blood. The abdominal viscera were normal. The blood was fluid; the brain normal. When cadaveric rigidity occurred was not noted.

The following case is recorded by Dr. Watson, Surgeon of the 45th Regt. N.I., Mooltan:—

Soorjun Rajpoot, Naik, aged thirty-one and a half years, was bitten by a snake on Aug. 31st, 1870, at 5 A.M. In going out into the jungle to obey a call of nature, he put his foot on a snake, which turned round and bit him on the foot. It hissed, but he could not see it, as it was not light enough. This occurred near the lines of the 45th Regt. There was a very slight scratch on the dorsum of the left foot; he walked to the hospital; he was not at all faint, only frightened. The native doctor applied nitrate of silver very freely over the scratch. He was discharged from hospital in 29 days.

Dr. Watson says—"After the application of the caustic, which was so severe as to blister the foot, it became very painful and swollen. On Sept. 3rd he began to pass blood in large quantities with his urine, and complained of pain over the kidneys. The hæmaturia continued until Sept. 13th, and left him very pale and anæmic for some time, so that he was not discharged till Sept. 28th. I am unable to say what connexion there was between the symptoms and the snake-bite, which was a mere scratch; but he appears to have been quite well before he was bitten." Probably there was no connexion. The snake was probably innocent, and the hæmaturia due to other causes.

The following case is reported by the Civil Medical Officer of Mozuffergurh :—

Ameer Chaud, a Punjabee Chuprasee, aged twenty-five years, while on his way to Aleepore, at the edge of a ravine stepped upon a snake (name unknown), which bit him on the instep of the right foot. He was admitted into the Aleepore Dispensary, under the charge of native doctor Ameer Bux, on Sept. 7th, one hour after receiving the bite and is said to have been suffering from the following symptoms:—The bitten part, which was very much swollen as far as the knee, was throbbing and painful. He was in a drowsy state, and vomited frequently fluid tinged with blood. The fæces and urine were also bloody. The pulse was small and intermitting, but the breathing was natural. The bitten part, after being cupped and scarified, was fomented with hot water. Forty drops of liquor ammoniæ and ten drops of sp. ether. were administered every half hour. Epistaxis having occurred twenty-four hours after admission, and the ordinary styptics proving insufficient to stop the hæmorrhage, it became necessary—so it is reported—to plug the nose. A croton oil purgative was also administered. After the third day the patient is said to have gradually improved, and when seen by the medical officer on Sept. 23rd, sixteen days after the bite, was convalescent.*

The following case is reported by Dr. Murray, Civil Surgeon of Ajmere :—

Sukhli, a Hindoo woman, aged thirty-five years, was bitten above the heel of the right foot by a snake (name unknown), at 5 A.M. on Aug. 11th, 1870, at Ajmere. On admission to the Ajmere Dispensary, the following symptoms presented themselves:—The whole of the bitten limb was much swollen. There was salivation; blood flowed freely from the nose and mouth, and was also discharged from the rectum. So great was the hæmorrhagic tendency, that an old cut on the sound leg bled for two days. Brandy, ammonia, and camphor were administered every fifteen minutes; a ligature was tied tightly above the bitten part, which had been incised; and the foot was kept in hot water for twelve hours. She was discharged from the dispensary on Aug. 19th, eight days after admission. This case is analogous to one reported by the Civil Surgeon of Mozuffergurh. The snake was probably *Echis carinata*.

The following case is reported by Baboo Chundee Churn Ghose, in charge of the Police Hospital at Lucknow :—

Ajudhia, a constable, aged thirty years, was bitten by a snake (species unknown) while answering a call of nature. When seen by Baboo C. Churn Ghose he complained of giddiness, a sensation of great internal heat, and intense thirst; his tongue was dry, and the conjunctivæ congested. Caustic was applied locally, and a few doses of liquor ammoniæ administered. He was discharged from the hospital in five hours. The snake was no doubt an innocent one, but the case is interesting as showing the effects of fear in this instance.

The following case is recorded by the Medical Officer of Kherie, in Oude :—

Gunes, Brahmin, a servant, aged twenty-five, was bitten by a Cobra—report does not say where—on Dec. 3rd, 1869. When brought under observation he was comatose; pulse weak and thready; had complained, it was said, of a sense of constriction in the throat, and was salivated. Thirty drops of liquor ammoniæ given every quarter of an hour. He died just twelve hours after he was bitten. The friends would not allow a

* The snake was probably the *Daboia russellii*, and the bite imperfect.

post-mortem, and removed the patient just before death from the dispensary.

The following case is recorded by the Civil Surgeon of Baraitch, in Oude :—

Doobur Abeer, Hindoo shepherd, aged twenty-five, was bitten at 6 A.M. on July 22nd, at a place named Pokhurpore, in Baraitch. He could not give the name of the snake, but described it as being of the colour of the white sugar-cane on the back, and white under the belly. He was bitten early in the morning, as he went to tend his sheep. A native's description is too vague to be relied on; the white belly seems to point to the Krait as the most probable snake. There was general swelling and discoloration of the left leg, from the dorsum of his foot where he was bitten to the groin. He was quite conscious until the morning of the 24th, when stupor and drowsiness intervened. The bitten part was burned with a rupee made hot in his village; subsequently treated with brandy and ammonia, and the limb freely scarified, to relieve tension, together with the application of a roller and lead lotion. He died on the 24th, after an illness of fifty-six hours. No post-mortem was allowed. When the case was first seen by the Medical Officer, there was great swelling and tension of the limb from the foot to the knee, which continued to extend gradually until it reached the groin. There was perfect consciousness until within a few hours of death.

The following case is recorded by the Civil Surgeon of Bijnour :—

Chumar, a Hindoo labourer, aged thirty years, was bitten at 4 A.M. on Aug. 19th, in the village of Hookanpore, Bijnour. The snake was not seen. He is said to have been sleeping on a cot in his house. During the night he is supposed to have put his foot on the ground, and to have then been bitten. He complained of pain in the bitten part, followed quickly by insensibility and frothing at the mouth. No convulsions. Hiccup. He died at about 5.30 A.M. on Aug. 19th, or in about an hour and a half. The body was not brought in until too much decomposed for examination. The blood is reported to have been dark and fluid. No cadaveric rigidity noticed either by the friends or by the police who brought the body in to the station. The body when brought to the Sudder station was much decomposed, and all the information respecting the case was gathered from an ignorant relative of the deceased. "I have no doubt," says the Civil Surgeon, "that death resulted from the bite of a snake. There was much congestion and but little swelling of the tissues in the neighbourhood of the bitten part, the dorsum of the right foot."

The following case is recorded by Dr. Cleghorn, Civil Assistant-Surgeon of Azimgurh :—

Bhirnja Abeer, aged sixteen years, was said to have been bitten by a Cobra at 10 A.M. on April 6th, 1870, in the city of Azimgurh. Circumstances under which he was bitten not noted. He is said to have been insensible when brought to the dispensary a few minutes after receiving the bite. Half a drachm of liquor ammoniæ was given immediately, and fifteen drops in a quarter of an hour. Dr. Cleghorn says—"The boy on being brought to the dispensary was apparently insensible; half a drachm of liquor ammoniæ was poured into his mouth, after which he opened his eyes and appeared to be quite well. There were no symptoms of poisoning from the first, but there were the fresh marks of a snake-bite on the point of the right great toe. The snake was described and named by a Chowkedar, who says he saw it. The snake must have been non-venomous, and the boy probably fainted from fright." Dr. Cleghorn's explanation is no doubt the correct one, and is that of many other cases of so-called poison snake-bites and recoveries.

The following cases are recorded by Dr. Cockburn, of Benares :—

Dabee Dyal, Hindoo boy, aged nine years, was bitten on May 1st, 1870, at 8.30 P.M. The boy went out of his house at the above hour, and just outside it a snake is said to have wound itself round his leg, and bitten him on the inside of his foot, but neither the boy nor any one else saw the snake. This occurred in Benares. When brought to the Civil Surgeon's house at 9 P.M., he was seen by the native doctor, who found him cold and pulseless, with froth on the lips. No very distinct mark of the puncture of a snake's fangs: only a slight depression of the skin, with a slight sign of blood—more like an abrasion, in fact. The part was incised, and a ligature applied above. Liquor ammoniæ applied to the wound, and ten drops given in water. This was vomited, and soon after a second dose was given, the boy being with great difficulty got to swallow; in fact only a portion was taken. Fifteen or twenty minutes after the second dose, a third was given and soon vomited; still no pulse, and viscid froth on the lips. The ten-drop doses of ammonia were continued at intervals of a quarter of an hour, and the boy was walked about, or rather dragged, for he could not be got to put his feet to the ground. "On my reaching home at 10.30, the boy was still cold and pulseless. I at once injected ten drops of liquor ammoniæ, with ten of water, with a hypodermic syringe, into the left upper arm, soon after which the pulse could be felt faintly beating, and the boy began to scream out loud at intervals. Then a quarter of an hour afterwards another dose of liquor ammoniæ was given by the mouth, and the boy made to walk about. Half an hour after first hypodermic injection, a second was given in the other arm, soon after which the pulse markedly improved, and continued steadily to do so, and the boy became gradually sensible. After the second injection, only two doses more of liquor ammoniæ were given (at longer intervals), and the boy may be said to have recovered by one or two o'clock. At 4 A.M. the father took him home, and brought him again at 5.30, when he was found quite well. This, of course, is a doubtful case, owing to the snake not having been seen, and the indefinite nature of the wound; while, on the other hand, the age of the boy rather goes against imagination being the cause of the symptoms. The boy looked younger than stated." This is a very interesting case, as it is one in which the liquor ammoniæ was injected apparently with benefit. But, as Dr. Cockburn says, it is doubtful, as no one saw the snake, and the wound was not like the puncture of a snake fang.

It is very possible that liquor ammoniæ injected hypodermically may act more powerfully and rapidly as a stimulant than when taken into the stomach, and, if so, it would be useful for that purpose. The experiments made on the lower animals show that, as an antidote to the bites of the Cobra, it has no power; but in the less deadly bites, where stimulants are useful, the hypodermic injection of liq. ammoniæ might be more beneficial and prompt in its action in rousing, than when it is given internally. It certainly should be tried, for in ten-drop doses diluted with water it is not likely to do any harm, even if it do no good. Sloughing of the areolar tissue has, I am told, followed in some cases; but this, I think, must have been when the quantity has been larger, less diluted, and probably not properly diffused in the subcutaneous cellular tissue.

Lotawon Chumar, aged fifty years, was bitten on Aug. 7th, 1870, under the following circumstances. He was sleeping in a poultry-yard in Benares, when he was suddenly awoke by a great noise among the fowls at 4 A.M., and whilst moving about to ascertain the cause, was bitten by something that he did not see, as it was dark—he suspected that it was a snake. When daylight appeared he found a fowl lying dead, and he then himself began to feel ill; a little later he became insensible, and was brought to the dispensary at 7 A.M. On admission his pulse was very feeble; he was insensible, and unable to stand. The only mark of injury was a black spot near the ankle joint. The wound was incised and liquor ammoniæ applied to it. It was also administered internally every fifteen minutes; twenty drops with water, equal parts, were injected under the skin, but he never rallied, and died half an hour after admission. No examination of the body was allowed by the friends.

The following case is recorded by Surgeon T. Ringer, 7th Bengal Cavalry, Nowgong, Bundelkund:—

Butchoo, a Chumar grass-cutter, aged thirty years, was bitten at 9 A.M. on Sept. 13th, 1870, by what is called a "Chittee"—probably *Bungarus cæruleus* if a venomous snake, perhaps *Lycodon aulicus* if innocent, which is not impossible. He was cutting grass, when the snake bit him on the inner side of the base of the left index finger; he raised his hand on feeling the bite; the snake was holding on; he knocked it off with his kurpa—the knife with which they cut grass—and it escaped in the grass. He then, in a fright, ran off towards the Cantonments and fell down insensible about half a mile from the lines, where he was picked up by two grass-cutters about two hours afterwards. On admission he was almost completely insensible, and covered with cold sweat; saliva running from the mouth; pupils contracted; pulse very weak and small; fluid blood oozing from two punctured wounds. Vomited twice; burning pains from the wounds continued for twenty-four hours.

"In this case," Dr. Ringer says, "stimulants certainly were very beneficial. The man gradually recovered consciousness, but remained in a very lethargic state for several hours. Two men were constantly in attendance to prevent him going to sleep, and he was roused by repeated cold douches; sinapisms and stimulants were continued until all bad symptoms had ceased. He appeared quite well at 10 P.M., and asked for food. He returned to his duties on Sept. 15th."

The following cases are recorded by the Civil Surgeon of Rhotuck:—

Namsahai, a Hindoo banniah, aged twenty-eight years, was bitten by a small snake—not seen, as it was dark—on July 7th, 1870, at 11 P.M., under the following circumstances. He was asleep in the Serai, when the snake fell on his shoulder from the roof. Waking up suddenly he tried to knock it off, when it bit him in two places. All this occurred in the dark. The snake, in all probability, was the Krait (*Bungarus cæruleus*). At 4 A.M. the symptoms were as follow:—Bloody froth escaping from the mouth. Pulse barely perceptible. Red swelling like a bruise extending over left breast, which next day increased to centre of breastbone, and to the nipple of left breast, with a similar appearance on the right side of the breast. On the following day another similar patch appeared on the back of the right thigh, just below the nates. Two bites on fore part of left shoulder, swollen. The bites were cauterized; liquor ammoniæ and liquor arsenicalis given. After fourth dose began to improve; carbonate of ammonia given the following day. He left the hospital, cured, four days later.

Hamid Hossein, a Mahomedan cloth-seller, aged twenty-five years, was bitten at 9 P.M. on July 24th, 1870, in the city of Rhotuck, when shutting a door; the snake is called in the vernacular "Duffee." It was in the wall. At 9.30 P.M. he was vomiting, and had prostration of strength and pain in bitten finger. The bite was cauterized and the liquor ammoniæ and liquor arsenicalis given. He recovered in two hours, and left the hospital next morning.

Mugree Singh, a Jat, aged six years, was bitten by a snake on Sept. 12th, 1870, at 11 A.M. He was bitten in the perineum, near the bowel, when relieving nature in a field. When seen he was vomiting, was depressed and trembling. Liquor ammoniæ and liquor arsenicalis were given, and caustic was applied to the bite, but he died in twelve hours. No examination of the body is recorded, and only the above details of the case, which is an interesting one, and would have been more so if more detailed.

The following case is recorded by Dr. Jameson, Assistant-Surgeon 6th Bengal Cavalry, Allahabad:—

Luchman, Hindoo kahar, aged twenty-seven years, was bitten at 5.35 P.M. on Sept. 13th, 1869, by a Krait, when going down to a nullah to wash. The bite was in the ankle; a mark like that of a snake's fang was visible just above the left malleolus. He had a ligature applied tightly round the leg, free incision was made through the puncture, and liquor ammoniæ was administered internally and applied to the wound. About a minute elapsed before he was seen and placed under treatment. He appears to have had no symptoms of poisoning, and was soon after discharged quite well. As Dr. Jameson says, "It is very doubtful if this was a Krait at all. The man said he saw it, and that it was a Krait; but as it was in the evening, this may be doubted."

The following case is reported by Dr. Penny, Civil Surgeon of Delhi, dated Jan. 25th, 1870:—

Musula, a Mahomedan water-carrier, a prisoner in the Delhi jail, aged twenty-five years, was bitten by a snake (probably a Cobra) on Sept. 2nd, 1869, at 7.30 P.M. He was going to close the hole in the water-tank in the jail, when he was bitten in the foot; the snake suddenly disappeared and was not again seen. The bite was on the ball of the right great toe, opposite the metatarso-phalangeal joint. He became insensible almost immediately and never recovered, and died at 9.31 P.M., or in two hours after receiving the bite. A ligature was applied, the fang marks were touched with caustic, and liquor ammoniæ administered internally. The state of the viscera (abdominal and thoracic) is not recorded, nor is that of the blood after death. His condition before death is reported to have been as follows:—"White fluid was oozing from the mouth; body convulsed; drowsy. The bitten part turned blue, and the toe was swollen." From the circumstances and place in which this man was bitten, the snake was probably the Cobra.

The following case is reported by Mr. Kingsmell, Civil Surgeon, Montgomery, Punjab, dated Jan. 25th, 1870:—

Three cases of snake-bite were treated by me at the Montgomery Dispensary during 1869. The most serious was that of Umra, who was bitten at 5 P.M. on Sept. 29th by a Cobra. On admission he complained of sickness and fainting; pulse small and irregular; tongue clean, but cold. He was drowsy, with slight shivering. A ligature was placed immediately above the wound, which was excised, and bleeding from it encouraged. One drachm and a half of liquor ammoniæ was given every ten, fifteen, or twenty minutes, according to the urgency of the symptoms; and a mixture of chloroform ʒij, spirit ℥ij, and camphor mixture ℥iij, one ounce given every half hour; and as the man was in great danger, a stimulating enema with mustard was had recourse to, and the caustic volatile alkali was freely applied to the wound. I am happy to say that the active treatment had the desired effect. The pulse rose; prostration, drowsiness, &c., were diminished, and he left the hospital well on Oct. 1st. The other two cases were slight ones, and the snakes were not seen; the bitten persons recovered.

I am indebted to the Commissioner of Sind for the following cases, which are reported by Dr. J. Roche, Assistant Civil Surgeon, Kotree:—

Bukta, a boatman's wife, aged thirty years, was bitten by a "Kuppur" (*Echis carinata*), length two feet, on the night of Jan. 25th, 1870, at about 9 o'clock, on board a native boat in the river Indus; the boat belonged to the Forest Department. The animal was carried on board, concealed in the firewood, and had so secreted itself that the men were not aware of its presence amongst them. Bukta, in cooking the evening's meal, needed wood, and as she was extracting some from the supply at hand, was bitten by the snake on the dorsum of the first phalanx of the left index finger. She cried aloud, and her husband and others came to her assistance, and having ascertained what was the matter, killed the animal and applied a string tightly on the finger nearer the centres of the circulation than the seat of the bite. Depression, faintness, dimness of vision, anxiety, thirst, a painful oppression at the epigastrium, and swelling of the finger, which extended up to the arm, followed. The string was removed from the finger, and a stronger and tighter one was applied around the forearm at the wrist. The swelling increased and invaded the arm up as far as the shoulder; the symptoms of mischief increased through the night, and as they had not been successful in checking the injury by ligatures, they removed them and brought the patient to the Kotree Civil Hospital at about 6 o'clock on the morning of Jan. 26th, 1870. Condition of patient when seen at 7 A.M.: Much exhausted; extremities cold; blood exuded from the eyes, gums, tongue, nose, vagina, and from under the nails of both great toes and thumbs; she suffered from much thirst and gastric sinking; had vomited before admission. Breathing diaphragmatic, and with a sensation as if the interior of chest were fixed to the spine in an immovable manner. Voice choleraic almost to huskiness. Heart-beats weak and impulse imperceptible. Pulse hæmorrhagic, and, as if the arteries were not full, was obliterated by the slightest pressure. The left arm was much swollen, bluish, œdematous, and wholly devoid of sensibility: the nearer to the site of the bite on the finger the less was the vitality of the parts. The pitting on pressure remained a lengthened period. The patient had not been purged, nor had she a motion for more than thirty hours. The blood which issued from her seemed very fluid, and crusted as paint on the parts.

Treatment.—She had a powder composed of fifteen grains of compound jalap powder, one grain of calomel, and five grains of powdered ginger, at once, and the following draught:—

℞ Sp. ammon. arom., ʒss.
Ether. chloric., ♏v.
Tr. iodinii, ♏j.
Liq. arsenicalis, ♏ij.
Mist. camph., ℥j. M. ft. haust.

To be taken every hour for three hours, and afterwards every third hour; had starchy food, and had a large camphor poultice to envelope the whole arm and forearm. In the evening she was somewhat more cheerful and may be said to have improved; had passed tarry stools in the course of the day. The morning of the 27th—was restless through night; the camphor poultices and draughts were continued, and camphor liniment was ordered to be rubbed into the arm in the course of the day; the friction was to extend over two hours. The 28th—was better, and liquor arsenicalis was omitted from the draughts. The 29th—had fever, and was ordered a diaphoretic mixture and turpentine punch every third hour. The 30th—was better; treatment continued. She was discharged on Feb. 2nd, 1870, but there was a hæmorrhagic tendency from the mucous surfaces. Ten days afterwards she had a return of all the symptoms, and came into hospital again, when the same treatment was resorted to, and after a few days she left, well.

I have seen the case of another woman who was bitten on the toe by a Sarang,* genus *Coluber*, about fourteen inches long. The patient complained of a sinking feeling and giddiness of the head, also imperfect vision and a great fear of death. She left the hospital after twenty-four hours, well, and had no medicine but a purgative and some draughts containing ammonia. I was under the impression that the snake was a young one, and hence was not sufficiently venomous to destroy life. This snake is tolerably common in Sind, and is by some natives called "Soolong," but it is only by some thought to be poisonous. They recommend as an antidote for the bite of this, as of many others, to eat the body minus the head and tail.

I have been favoured with the following account of a case of snake-bite, and am indebted to Captain Birch, the Deputy Commissioner of Police, for the particulars:—

Information was received at 6 P.M. of Nov. 21st, that a native boy, name and residence unknown, had died from the effects of a snake-bite. It appears that the deceased had been on the Diamond Harbour road, and, near the house of the informant, had gone into the jungle, having previously laid down on the road-side a basket containing a snake and some other things used by snake-charmers. He returned in a few minutes, and was observed to be rubbing his right with his left hand; on being questioned as to what was the matter, as he looked as though he was suffering, he said he had a burning sensation all over his body, and shortly after he fell down and died. He had while in the jungle met with a snake—the kind he did not mention—and on trying to catch it, it bit him on the back of his right hand. The Police Inspector who reported the case and saw the body said that there were *three* distinct marks, apparently from the bite of a snake, on the back of the right hand, and no marks of violence on the body. The body was examined by a medical officer, who certified that death had been caused by a snake-bite in the hand. In the basket left by the boy on the road was a full-grown Cobra. This was forwarded to me by Captain Birch. The precise time between the bite and the death is not known, but it could not have been more than from fifteen to twenty minutes, from the account I received of the circumstances of the case.

This is another example of the deadly effects of the snake-poison when thoroughly inoculated, as it no doubt was in this case, by a fresh and vigorous snake.

The following case was communicated by Dr. F. Day:—

In June, 1858, I was stationed at Aurungabad in medical charge of an irregular infantry regiment H. C., and in the

* I believe the snake to have been innocent; the symptoms described were probably due to fear. I do not, under the vernacular name, identify the reptile.—J. F.

middle of one night I was called out by Major H., who informed me that one of his horse-keepers had been bitten by a snake, was very ill, and had been taken to the hospital, whither I at once proceeded. About fifteen minutes were said to have elapsed since the receipt of the injury before I saw the patient, who was then in a state of utter prostration and dreadful alarm at the idea of closely impending death; he was covered with a cold clammy perspiration, had a rapid pulse, but the respiration was unimpeded. The bite was in the foot, but had been so pinched and pulled about that it was impossible to ascertain if it had been inflicted by fangs or not. The usual stimulant remedies, especially ammonia, were freely exhibited; the man was kept moving about, but the symptoms after two hours remained much the same. I was then informed that this was the second time he had believed himself to be bitten by a venomous snake; on the first occasion he had been equally ill, but by some means it was ascertained that his antagonist had been a little mouse, of which when he had satisfied himself he got well. Finally, I became firmly convinced that he was only suffering from fear. I told his master so, who then asked if I had any objection to allowing a snake-charmer to try his remedies for the purpose of relieving his mind, as he persisted that he had been injured by a Cobra. I assented, several hours having now elapsed. Unfortunately, the appearance of the snake-charmer had exactly a contrary effect to soothing the patient, who argued I had given him up: there was now no hope, and he soon became worse. As it seemed probable his words might come true, I again took the case in hand: a good blister and galvanism with stimuli were required before he came round; in fact, it was only by causing great bodily pain that I was able to draw his attention from his mental affection, as this in reality was. Doubtless most medical officers in India can recall such cases as the above to their recollection, or those of cholera in which fear has been the cause of death, or the latter has only been prevented by such means as recorded in this instance.

The following case is a very interesting and most graphic one of death caused by the bite of the *Bungarus cæruleus*, or Krait. It is reported by Dr. Thomson, of H.M.'s 76th Regiment:—

"In July, 1865, while stationed at Hazareebaugh, I was roused one morning at 2.30 to see a young kitmutghar in my employ, said to have been bitten by a Krait. I found him half-sitting up, his head supported by an old Brahmin, who was holding some root to his nose, supposed to be an antidote, and small portions of which had been given to the boy to chew. I was told that the lad (aged about eighteen years) had been bitten on the tip of one of his fingers while asleep in the cook-house, that the pain of the wound awoke him, and he called for help. A Krait was immediately discovered in the cook-room, which was captured alive and put in a chatty. Fully half an hour had elapsed from the time he was bitten before I was called to him. Having ammonia in the house, I at once gave him a dose with brandy, and then proceeded to examine the wound. This I found to be one minute puncture on the tip of a finger, with a small drop of congealed blood on it, such as would result from the prick of a very fine needle. The back of the hand was puffy and swollen, but the swelling did not extend beyond the wrist. The length of time which had elapsed since the bite was received rendered local treatment next to useless; nevertheless, I tied a ligature above the wrist, and rubbed liquor ammoniæ into the wound. The boy's countenance was anxious, and his breathing short and hurried; he complained of uneasiness and constriction across the chest. He evidently had no hope of recovery, as the moment he saw me he exclaimed—'Salaam, Sahib, *ham jata! ham jata!*' Finding the pulse becoming smaller and surface getting cold, I applied sinapisms to the cardiac and epigastric regions, to the calves of the legs and the inside of thighs, at the same time giving ammonia and brandy in full doses about every ten minutes. About 3.30 A.M. he began to get drowsy; up to this time he had been quite conscious. I then had him walked about smartly by a couple of men, until finding that he was losing all power over his limbs, I had him placed on a charpoy, and endeavoured to excite consciousness by slapping the calves of the legs, thighs, buttocks, arms, &c., and by applying the button cautery along the spine. All was of no avail; the breathing became stertorous, pupils fixed, and complete coma established. He had one or two slight convulsions, and about 5 A.M. expired, being two and a half hours after I first saw him, and three hours from the time he was said to have been bitten. No post-mortem was made. About four hours after death the body was swollen, abdomen distended, and frothy bloody mucus oozed from mouth and nostrils. I examined the Krait. It was about two and a half feet long, and its fangs were perfect. The above facts are given from memory, as I kept no notes of the case. Kraits abound at Hazareebaugh. I killed several during my stay there, and so did many of my acquaintances."

I am indebted to Dr. J. Ewart for the following account of snake-bite. The cases were published in the *Indian Medical Gazette* of Nov. 1st, 1870:—

How the Bite of Snakes supposed to be Poisonous may be Cured.

"I. About 11 o'clock on Saturday evening, Aug. 19th, a gentleman called upon me, bringing with him a native syce, who, he said, had about half-past seven P.M., or three and a half hours before, been bitten by a snake. The syce had gone out in attendance on this gentleman and his family in the evening. The history was that the man himself had seen the snake, which was said to be a small one, crawl over his foot.

"On examining the patient, I failed to find anything like a puncture. The man himself, when I saw him, was in such a state of utter prostration that he could not be got to answer a single question. On examining his pupils, pulse, and skin, I suspected that he was a habitual gunjah-smoker, and that he was in all probability suffering from a combination of gunjah and the dread or fear which supervenes when a man believes, as this man did, that he had been bitten by a venomous snake. The man was found all right next morning. Ammonia and stimulants, and pacing him up and down to keep him awake, were the measures adopted. On re-examination, there is not a vestige of a puncture, nor of the swelling and ecchymosis which soon succeed when the poison has penetrated below the skin.

"II. This morning, Aug. 22nd, on visiting the General Hospital, I was informed that one of the punkah-coolies had been bitten, about 8.30 the night before, by a Krait, whose venom is virulently poisonous. The man, it appears, had been sleeping, and on awaking he found something crawling over the right shoulder, and immediately experienced a stinging sensation about the middle of the acromion process. He was then under the impression that he had been bitten by a snake, and on procuring a light, a very lively snake was captured.

"The site of the bite was examined by Mr. Knight, the Assistant Apothecary, who declares he discovered a small puncture, on which there was a small quantity of coagulated blood. He is also positive that the tissues around, to the size of a two-anna piece, were puffed and swollen. Patient's pulse was irregular, and he was much alarmed and agitated; the surface of the body was cold; countenance anxious; pupils normal; quite conscious and intelligent; no dimness of vision, or vertigo.

"About four minutes after the man had been bitten, the part

was freely scarified, and the cupping glass applied. Ammonia was given repeatedly at short intervals. Rum was also freely administered, and means were taken to prevent sleep.

"When the patient was presented to me as a specimen of snake-bite cured by cupping, ammonia, and rum, I expressed my doubts, after an examination of the seat of scarification, whether he had been bitten at all; and if he had been bitten, whether the snake was poisonous.

"I submitted the snake to Dr. Fayrer, C.S.I., who pronounced it to be the '*Lycodon aulicus*—perfectly innocent. It is something like the Krait (*Bungarus cæruleus*), and often gets blamed accordingly.' He adds, 'The double row of teeth in the upper jaw shows it to be an innocent (land) snake.'

"The effect of fear was well shown in this case, as producing several of the symptoms met with in men and animals poisoned by snakes. This fear was intensified by his having seen the reptile, and being under the firm belief that it was a Krait, well known by every native to be poisonous to a deadly degree. Had the snake not been identified by unimpeachable authority, the notion might have been entertained that the patient had recovered, under the influence of cupping, ammonia, and rum, from the effects of the bite of the deadly Krait.

"*Remarks.*—These cases are instructive. They show how the symptoms of venom from poisonous snakes may be unintentionally simulated for a time by the influence of the fear of certain death, and how easily the practitioner may be deceived unless he is on the alert. The results of the experiments made by Dr. Fayrer have all tended to prove that when the venom of the poisonous snakes of India has penetrated beneath the integument of such large animals as the horse, it inevitably causes death, in spite of the administration or application of reputed remedies. After a prolonged and patient trial of supposed antidotes, he has been reluctantly compelled to arrive at the conclusion that for the poison of Indian venomous snakes at least there has not as yet been discovered an antidote. Through his kindness, I have witnessed a large number of his experiments, and, so far as my observation goes, I am constrained to concur in the conclusion at which he has arrived with regard to the question of antidotes. Equally with him, I am of opinion that most, if not all, of the reputed cures from the bites of poisonous snakes have been quite as deceptive and illusory as the two cases forming the subject of this communication. Judging from repeated observation of the mortal effects rapidly following the injection of the poison of the Cobra, the *Daboia*, *Ophiophagus*, the Krait, &c., below the skin, I am convinced that we have not as yet found out any medicine which can be fairly looked upon as possessing in the least degree the virtues of an antidote."

The following case is of great interest. It shows how great is the liability to error, even where the evidence seems perfectly complete. It is reported by Mr. John C. Douglas, Teacher of Science of the Department of Science and Art, E. B.

There can be, I believe, no doubt that the Lemur, or *Nycticebus tardigradus*, is a most harmless, gentle little creature, and yet it is convicted on the best evidence of poisoning a man by its bite, as a venomous snake would have poisoned him.

The effects so well described by the author of the paper were probably due to mental causes, with some coincident disorder. This is a good example of the necessity for extreme caution in arriving at conclusions, or of generalizing on insufficient data.

I am exceedingly obliged to the talented inquirer for his kindness in sending me the notes of this case, and hope he will continue to record any observations he may make on poisonous animals and their bites.

"On the 17th December, while clearing trees and jungle on the road between Chittagong and Ramoo, near Hurbaug, an alarm was raised by the coolies that a young tiger had been found. Myself and an inspector of telegraphs working under my orders went to the spot and discovered a small animal, apparently crouching, on a low bough; the coolies and one or two travellers from the road surrounded the tree and captured the animal; the first man who seized it, not being able to tell at which end its head was, was bitten. A string was passed round the animal's neck, and it was brought on to the road.

"*Description of the Animal.*—About eighteen inches long, quadrumanous, tailless, without callosities; colour, sandy; hinder extremities long and powerful; index finger of forehand short, apparently the shortest finger; head small; neck scarcely perceptible, the head appearing to be joined directly to body; ears small, and had the appearance a cat's ears would have if cropped close; face triangular, nose being sharp; eyes very large indeed, with vertical pupils contracted to a narrow line in sunlight, much like a cat; motions slow and awkward on the ground; fur fine and close. The animal was not known by name to any one of the natives of the place; many were attracted to see it by a rumour that it was a tiger cub. One man said he had been seventy-five years in the place, and had never seen one before; another man had seen one and killed it some short time before; but of the many who saw it, travellers, villagers, &c., none could name it.

"A syce in camp said it was a 'hoo ka butchaha;' that its bite would cause giddiness, but the person bitten would not die soon (!). Having no zoological works of reference, I have been unable to name the animal. Other persons who did not see it suggested it might be a hookoo, but this I cannot decide on; the descriptions given in books or the specimens in a museum are necessary; the animal is not one it would be difficult to recognise.

"I thought of killing the animal and salting it for investigation, but it was suggested to me to keep it alive; and as this would give opportunities for trying its bite on animals, I tied it up by the neck; its head and neck being of the same circumference, it slipped its head out of the string. I then tied it by the waist, and fastened it by a dog-chain to a bush; it escaped again after dark, and although all the men in camp turned out at once, and within ten minutes of its escape, it was not recaptured. Rewards were offered for it dead or alive, or for one like it, without effect.

"*The Effects of the Bite.*—The man who was bitten was Magoonally; father's name, Assanally; village, Sathkurna; age about thirty; spare; travelling to Akyab to work at cutting the rice crops; has several scars from cuts; does not faint at sight of blood; did not faint when he cut himself passing along the road; seeing the attempts to surround the animal, joined the coolies; as the animal crouched, could not tell which was its head; seized it, and it turned round and bit him on first finger of left hand, first joint near nail; bite, a slit about half an inch long. Certainly within five minutes of being bitten the man was senseless; he reached the road with difficulty, and speedily became insensible, having first complained of pain in the arm to the shoulder. I ordered him to be kept horizontal, a tight string tied round the arm above the elbow, and I sent to the camp for brandy; the face had a very anxious expression at first. I did not suppose the effect due to anything but fear, or a constitutional horror of blood. I therefore tried to persuade the man and the bystanders the animal was a harmless monkey. A native passing stopped, performed ceremonies over the injured man, bled by scoring his arm lightly with a sharp knife: this I did not interfere with, finding the man continued insensible. I sent to ask an inspector working a short distance off if he had ever heard of a similar case or seen the animal before; neither he nor the passers-by knew the animal nor had ever seen one before. When the brandy arrived, an hour or more after the accident, the man was still almost senseless. Weak brandy and water was poured down his throat; he gradually improved; but although bitten between 11 A.M. and noon, it was about 5 P.M. before he could walk even with assistance; as soon as he was able to speak he complained of great pain in the abdomen. I ordered him to be rubbed, and refused to allow him to be removed from where he lay. In the evening he was taken between two men to a mosque; the next evening he came to the camp, recovered, but weak; he said he felt pain in the hand first; that it extended up the arm to the other arm; that he became giddy; the pain extended to his legs and body; that he was insensible during the whole time the native practitioner was operating on him; that he had a burning pain in his abdomen on recovery from insensibility, and that this pain continued all night; that he did not recover until the next morning, and that he then (evening) felt weak from the effects of the illness; he was fasting when bitten. While the animal was tied up at my tent, a man who came to see it recognised it as like one he had killed some short time before; he told one of my men, an intelligent man, that he received information from a cowherd, that the death of a cow of his was due to the saliva of one of these animals having been swallowed with grass. The owner of the cow went to see the animal, saw it, killed it, and threw it into a khaul, but his dog attacked the animal, got bitten, and died the next day. This case is of use as corroborating the one more especially referred to; the cause of the death of the cow may be open to doubt, but the man asserts the dog was unmistakably bitten, became ill soon after, and died next day at its owner's house. The conclusions I draw from the above are—*firstly*, that the man Magoonally was really bitten by a certain quadrumanous animal in the presence of an inspector, myself, and a number of coolies and native travellers; *secondly*, that serious effects followed immediately after the bite, such effects indicating some powerful interference with the functions of the nervous system; *thirdly*, that no cause other than the bite can be indicated as having produced the effect referred to, while the rapidity with which the effects were produced, their duration and nature, were such as by analogy could be attributed to an animal poison.

"The proof of the toxic action of the bite of the animal is as rigid as possible; it was probably greater in the case under reference, as the sufferer was fasting. I do not remember to have seen mention of any similar fact in any of the works on toxicology I have seen; at present I have none to refer to; the fact may perchance be a new one, but at any rate probably these cases are very rare indeed, and observations of any value very few. One case may be of value; and although it is incumbent on me to refer to existing works on zoology and toxicology, both to identify the animal, and ascertain if the fact be a new one, as I suppose, before making it known, yet as I have no means of doing so, I have no alternative but to depend on the existence, in those with the means at their disposal, of the desire to add to the common stock of knowledge."

Note by Dr. J. Anderson, Curator of the Indian Museum.

"The description of the animal leads me to believe that it must have been *Nycticebus tardigradus*, or more accurately *N. javanicus*, for the former appears to be only a local variety of the latter. It is a most harmless little animal, living chiefly on insects. Grote took one to the Zoological Society from me, that I had for more than one year at the Botanical Gardens. I distinctly remember being bitten by it on one occasion, and my brother's old servant Nubboo, who was killed by a snake about a year and a half ago, was also bitten, but with no ill result. I recollect those occurrences, because the natives about had a horror of its bite. I had other three living specimens when I left for Younan, but they were killed in my absence. The latter came from Assam (Goalpara), and I am inclined to regard them as distinct from the Malayan form that extends up the Peninsula as far as Bengal. Its occurrence at Chittagong is nothing remarkable; and now that it is got there, I shall take the opportunity to try to induce Mr. Douglas to get some for the Museum, as I want more materials before I can decide on the specific identity or not of the Assam form with *N. javanicus*.

"The English name is 'Slow Lemur.'"

SECTION V.

EXPERIMENTS ON THE INFLUENCE OF SNAKE-POISON ON THE LOWER ANIMALS, AND ON THE VALUE OF CERTAIN MODES OF TREATMENT AND REPUTED ANTIDOTES.

SUMMARY.

THE experiments of which this is a summary were commenced in October, 1867, and were continued during a period of three years at such intervals as time and other and more important avocations permitted. My object has been to determine, by actual observation, the effect on life of the poison of the venomous snakes of India, and to test the value of remedies, whether internal or external.

So many absurd ideas on the subject prevail, that it is desirable to know the real truth, not less with reference to the actual *modus operandi* of the poison, than to the value of the many vaunted antidotes. The results, I regret to say, tend to show that in the present state of our knowledge we can do little to counteract or neutralize the action of the poison; but what may be expected from treatment I have endeavoured to show.

As to antidotes, I would speak with reserve on the subject of possible future discoveries; my experience does not encourage me to hope that we shall discover anything that can be regarded as an antidote, in the sense usually conveyed by that term. But considering the imperfection of our knowledge on this and kindred subjects, I would do nought to deter or discourage others from further investigation.

My personal experience is derived from the action of the poison on the lower animals, and in a few cases on Man; the antagonism of the venom to the vital forces is shown in one as well as in the other, and is no doubt subject to the same laws. The deductions from one are applicable to the other.

The greatest care has been observed in all the experiments, and most of them have been often repeated, to exclude as far as possible sources of error, and to obviate generalization from insufficient data.

Almost every experiment has been witnessed by competent observers, to whom I am much indebted for their assistance, and for the additional value which their presence attaches to the validity of what was done.

The object of investigation has been the simple truth. I can safely say there was neither foregone conclusion to maintain nor theory either to support or oppose.

The snakes with which the experiments have been conducted were :—

- The varieties of *Naja tripudians* or Cobra.
- The *Ophiophagus elaps* or Hamadryad.
- The *Bungarus fasciatus* or Sankni.
- The *Bungarus cæruleus* or Krait.
- Some of the *Hydrophidæ*.
- The *Daboia russellii*.
- The *Echis carinata*.
- The *Trimeresurus monticola*.

And in the case of the *Callophides* and of the other *Crotalidæ*, I have referred to the experiments of others, not having had opportunity of testing them myself.

The living creatures experimented on have been the Ox, Horse, Goat, Pig, Dog, Cat, Civet, Mongoose, Rabbit, Rat, Domestic Fowls, Kites, Herons, fish, innocent snakes, poisonous snakes, Lizards, Frogs, Toads, Snails.

The symptoms produced by the poison both constitutionally and locally have been carefully noted. The state of the blood has also been examined, especially with reference to structural changes, and for this part of the investigation I have been much indebted to Professors Partridge, Ewart, W. Palmer, J. Anderson, and Dr. Douglas Cunningham.

In point of relative deadliness, I should be inclined to consider that the Cobra, *Ophiophagus*, and *Daboia* are very nearly on a par. They are quite capable of destroying a full-grown Dog in half an hour, sometimes in much less time; and very frequently I believe Man has succumbed within an equally short period, though generally the time is much longer.

The *Bungarus cæruleus* is, I believe, just as deadly, but apparently does not kill quite so quickly. The *Bungarus fasciatus* is less fatal, and kills less quickly than the *Bungarus cæruleus*. The *Echis*, if one may credit the reports from Sinde, and they are confirmed to a certain extent by Major MacMahon, Deputy Commissioner of Delhi, is also a very deadly snake. It destroys life rapidly in small animals, but, from its small size, it is perhaps less likely to be fatal to Man, though from what I have seen of the effects of its poison on Pigeons, Fowls, and Dogs, I should regard it with peculiar dread.

Of the *Hydrophidæ* less is known, but the few experiments I have performed, and those by Mr. Stewart, prove that they are very fatal, and I should think human life would be in great danger from their bite.

The *Callophides* and *Crotalidæ* of Hindostan are certainly not so deadly as those I have mentioned, and though capable of inflicting a painful, and in some instances no doubt a dangerous bite, they are not so much dreaded as the other snakes.

There are differences in the symptoms produced by the poisonous bites of the different Thanatophidia, but none of any great physiological or pathological import. In some cases convulsions are more marked, and in others death is preceded by a more decided appearance of lethargy. In some, as in those of bite by the *Echis*, the local symptoms are peculiarly severe, in others less so. But the differences are more of degree than of kind. All the symptoms point to exhaustion and paralysis of the nerve centres—the sources of the origin of vital force—every function fails rapidly and vitality is soon extinct.

Local paralysis of the bitten part, great depression, faintness, exhaustion, nausea, vomiting, hæmorrhage, relaxation of the sphincters, involuntary evacuation, not unfrequently of a sanguineous or muco-sanguineous character, precede the complete loss of consciousness, and after this convulsions occur just before life ceases.

The post-mortem appearances frequently reveal simply nothing except the marks of the fangs and the slight ecchymosis about them; or if the creature have survived some hours, infiltration, and perhaps incipient decomposition of the tissues. The lungs are not generally congested, the heart is not generally overloaded, the viscera look natural enough, death is not traceable to special disturbance of any one great function, such as respiration. The blood in the cases of the lower animals certainly—and if in them why not in Man?*—nearly always coagulates firmly on removal from the body, after death from poisoning by the colubrine snakes; but in death by viperine poison it remains permanently fluid. The cause of this I am quite unable to explain, but there can be no doubt of the facts as regards the lower animals, for they have been proved by often repeated experiments.

From experiment I have arrived at the following conclusions:—Snake poison acts with most vigour on the warm-blooded animals; birds succumb very rapidly, a vigorous snake can destroy a Fowl in a few seconds.

The power of resistance is generally in relation to the size of the animal, though not altogether so; Cats, for example, resist the influence of the poison almost as long as Dogs three or four times their size.

The cold-blooded animals also succumb to the poison, but less rapidly. Fish, non-venomous snakes, *Mollusca*, all die. So far as I can decide from experience the poisonous snakes are not affected by their own poison—*i.e.*, a Cobra may bite itself or another Cobra, and with no evil result.

The less are probably affected by the more poisonous snakes—*e.g.*, the *Bungarus* seems to be affected by Cobra poison, though slowly.

It is possible that they can all to some extent affect each other, though infinitely less than they affect other animals. In many of the various experiments I have performed, the Cobra, *Daboia*, and Krait did not appear to be able to poison themselves or each other. Some of the experiments render this doubtful, and seem to show that a Cobra or *Daboia* may poison a Krait, or *vice versâ*, but that they escape more frequently than they suffer.

Snake-poison is absorbed through delicate membranes. It is deadly when applied to a mucous or serous membrane, to the stomach, or the conjunctiva. The idea that it is only capable of absorption by direct injection into the blood is erroneous.

The bodies of animals poisoned by snakes are eaten with impunity by Man and animals. I have had repeated proofs of this. The Fowls and Pigeons killed in my experiments were always taken away and eaten by the sweepers who were present, and who sought them greedily. They were not unfrequently given to Dogs or Cats: no harm followed.

The blood of an animal dead from snake-poisoning is itself poisonous; if injected into another animal it destroys life. This shows the intensity of the poison: a drop or two diluted with the blood of a Fowl or other animal renders the whole poisonous. Venomous snakes, though not at all or very slightly affected by snake poison, are very susceptible to other poisons, such as strychnine or carbolic acid. The latter destroys them very rapidly, and they seem to regard it with peculiar aversion. Poisonous snakes are not as a general rule very aggressive, except perhaps the *Echis*. They seek to be left in quiet, to be let alone. They bite only if disturbed or irritated, and even then they often will not bite, but make one or two strikes at the enemy as if to frighten it.

In my experiments I had always the greatest difficulty to get the Cobra, Krait, or *Daboia* to bite voluntarily. An animal may remain in a cage or box with a Cobra or *Daboia* a very long time before it is injured, and perhaps, after all, it is taken out untouched, even after trampling on and bruising the snake in its efforts to escape from its enemy, which is as much frightened as itself. There is much hissing and demonstration of attack, but frequently nothing done. If pressed and overteazed, they bite at last, and if they insert their fangs and retain their hold, the bite is generally fatal.

The *Echis*, however, will strike and mortally wound a Fowl or small animal directly it approaches it, and its dart is so rapid that it is scarcely seen.

Snakes frequently strike and even wound without poisoning. The fang merely scratches and makes a tear, but if inserted and retained for a second the poisonous bite has then been inflicted. Of course any abrasion or scratch, however trivial, may be dangerous, as some of the virus may be inoculated or shed over it, probably not enough to kill, but sufficient to cause dangerous symptoms.

A snake that has bitten often, or that has very recently eaten, or that has been long in confinement without food, is less dangerous than others; its bite may be almost harmless, though not always so. A *Daboia* that lived a whole year in a cage without food was deadly a few days before its death.

The poisonous snakes when they either shed or lose by accident their fangs, regain new ones in from a few days to a month or six weeks. An *Echis* was refurnished with fangs, firmly anchylosed to the maxillary bone, on the third day after the removal of the former ones. If the whole mucous capsule be removed, and the maxillary bone injured in extracting the fangs, the reserve teeth already developed and the germs are also destroyed, and no new fangs are reproduced. This is often done by the snake-catchers, but when imperfectly and the reserve fangs and germs not destroyed, fatal accidents have occurred from the unexpected reappearance of fangs.

Snakes cast their epidermis frequently; the Cobra and Krait once or twice in a month, but the *Echis* I have kept for three months without its changing its skin. Snakes will live months without food or water. A *Daboia* lived for one year without food. It moulted frequently, became very thin, but it was active and poisonous to the last.

I conclude this summary by remarking that I feel thankful that I have brought a long series of experiments to a conclusion without any accident of a serious nature to those concerned in them. The constant manipulation of excited and vicious venomous snakes is a service of danger, and one in which we could hardly expect to be long engaged without some casualty. I am happy to say that only on two occasions was there any cause for anxiety. In the first, one of my assistants had a small quantity of Cobra poison projected into the eye. Immediate ablution and careful avoidance of rubbing removed it, leaving only a temporary congestion and weakness of the conjunctiva.

In the second case my principal snake-man was bitten by an *Echis* in the thumb; immediate excision and cauterization of the part was had recourse to, and no evil results followed.

* It is to be observed that in most recorded post-mortem examinations of human beings who have died from snake-bite (whether colubrine or viperine) the blood is noted to have remained fluid after death. I cannot reconcile this with the condition of the blood in animals which is, as I have stated, coagulable after death from colubrine poisoning, fluid after death from viperine poisoning. Further examination is needed.

EXPERIMENTS.

FIRST SERIES.

Experiments on the Action of the Poison of the Cobra on Warm- and Cold-blooded Animals.

The effects of snake-bite, the *modus operandi* of the virus, and of its reputed antidotes, have recently attracted so much attention, that I determined to make some experiments for the purpose of ascertaining how far observations confirm or refute what has been said on the subject.

A very thoughtful and suggestive paper in the *British Medical Journal* of July 20th, 1867, communicated by Professor Halford of Melbourne, rendered the investigation more interesting, as it seemed to indicate the nature of the pathological changes induced in the blood by the poison, and to point out a new direction in which to study them, as well as to suggest a rational antidote. It will be seen that the following experiments, so far as they go, scarcely confirm Dr. Halford's views.

But, even admitting the probability of Dr. Halford's theory of the cause of death, I am inclined to think that it can only be of partial application. It is peculiarly applicable to those cases in which, owing to a smaller quantity, or a less potent quality, of the poison having been injected, death takes place slowly, and time is allowed for blood changes to occur. But it can hardly be said to explain the cause of death in those cases where death occurs within a few minutes after the animal is bitten by a powerful snake, and where the fatal event results almost immediately, as if by a shock to the nervous centres.

The antidote experimented with (Experiment No. 1), is one to which much importance is attached by many in this country —the *Aristolochia indica*. But I regret to say that, in the case in which we tried it, the result was a perfect failure; indeed, as I have before said, I doubt very much whether any remedy exists which is capable of counteracting the deadly effects of the bite of a full-grown Cobra, though it is possible that, in the case of a large animal bitten by a small or exhausted snake, remedies might conduce to recovery.

The experiments here recorded were made with three full-grown Cobras recently caught, and the poison was inserted, either by closing the snake's jaws on the part of the animal bitten, or by inoculating the poison with an instrument at various periods, after its removal from the poison gland. The mode of procuring the poison is very simple; it is obtained by making the Cobra bite through a thin leaf stretched across a mussel shell; the poison, like limpid syrup, runs in considerable quantities down the grooved tooth into the shell, where it is collected, and may be preserved for experiment. From a full-grown Cobra half a drachm may be collected in a very short time. Much care is necessary in handling the reptile, and this is done with the greatest dexterity by the professional snake-catchers, who take up a living and vicious Cobra without the slightest difficulty, and either make it shed its poison in the way I have mentioned, or render it harmless for the time by removing its poison fangs. The Cobra, though very powerful and active, is apparently sluggish until roused, and its muscular power does not enable it to twist sufficiently to turn on any one who is bold enough to seize it by the tail, hold it at arm's length, and keep its head from darting at the legs by pressing it down with a stick held in the other hand. Such is the way in which the snake-catchers manage them.

In the present instance, there were three full-grown fierce Cobras confined in a small box. Raising the lid carefully, the snake-catcher put in the end of the stick and lifted out one about four feet long, hissing, and with its hood erect, looking the very incarnation of mischief. He then gently dropped the snake on the ground; and, as soon as it began to move off, seized it by the tail, raised it off the ground, and placed the stick, holding it at arm's length, about midway under its body. He then allowed it to struggle, and make efforts to dart at him over the stick, on which it hung in a festoon, keeping up an oscillating motion with his knee, which seemed to influence the reptile's movements, as it kept time, moving its head at about the same rate as the man moved his knee. He then placed it on the ground, dragging it gently by the tail; and watching his opportunity, placed the stick on the snake's back just behind the head, and so pressed it to the ground. Holding the tail under his naked foot, he quietly seized the snake behind the head, and squeezing it, made it open its jaws, when the poison fangs could be distinctly seen; in this way the snake was made to bite the animals experimented on, or the leaf, when the poison was collected in a shell. The experiments were made by myself, Dr. J. Anderson, Curator of the Indian Museum, and Dr. J. A. Purefoy Colles, Professor of Physiology in the Medical College. Some of them were conducted in the compound of the Asiatic Society, and others in the Museum of the Medical College.

Oct. 21st, 1867.

EXPERIMENT No. 1.

A full-grown Pariah Dog was bitten by a large Cobra at 12.36 P.M. Just before he was bitten five large leaves of the *Aristolochia indica*, beaten into a pulp, were administered to him through a tube. The snake was made to close its jaws on the inner part of the thigh, which was at once drawn up and became partially paralysed. The Aristolochia leaves, made into a pulp, were applied to, and rubbed into, the bites.

At 12.41 the Dog began to stagger, and at 12.42 he lay down. The respiration became much hurried. He got up and lay down again, and was intensely restless. There was a profuse flow of saliva, and slight twitching of posterior extremities. 12.47.—Salivation very profuse. 12.50.—Vomited some rice tinged green by the Aristolochia. 12.56.—Convulsions; pupils dilated. Involuntary discharge of fæces and urine. Profuse salivation continues. Irregular contraction of limbs. 12.58.—Breathing now becoming slow, and slightly stertorous. Lies motionless, with dilated pupil and glassy eye. 1.2 P.M.—Died in twenty-six minutes after being bitten.

Autopsy.—Blood taken from the femoral vein just at death coagulated firmly in about five minutes. The chest was opened about four minutes after death. All the cavities of the heart were empty, except that the walls of the right ventricle were smeared with tarry looking blood. There was feeble contractility of the auricles when first exposed, but this had ceased within five minutes after death. The lungs were not congested. The blood in the great vessels coagulated firmly during the examination. The superficial vessels of the brain were slightly congested, but there was no congestion of the deeper parts of the brain.

The areolar tissue about the bite was dark-coloured, and infiltrated with blackened blood.

Experiment No. 2.

On the same day at 1.25 p.m., a half-grown Domestic Fowl was inoculated on the inner side of the right thigh with the poison taken from a Cobra on the spot, by making it bite through a leaf into a mussel shell. A considerable quantity of the virus was inserted by means of a sharp-pointed bistoury.

No paralysis of the part followed, as in the case of the Dog in the first experiment. The bird ran about, picked up food, and ate some of the Aristolochia and rice which had been vomited by the Dog. At 1.29 p.m. it began to be restless, but still picked up food; starting and seeming alarmed. 1.38 p.m. —Standing; crouched together; the wounded leg contracted and drawn up. 1.40 p.m.—Again picking food, but seems uneasy. 1.45 p.m.— Starting and restless; lame in the injured leg. 1.52.—Seems better. 1.58.—Appears sluggish; eyes closed; lies down; still picks food; is occasionally drowsy. 2 p.m.— Very drowsy, but starts. 2.10 p.m.—Comatose; does not rise, but can be raised; head resting on the point of the beak. 2.13.—Cannot stand; falls if raised. Head hanging down, and resting on point of beak. 2.16.—Gasping; respiration very slow. 2.20.—Apparently profoundly asleep, but still can be roused. 2.30.—Lies in any position in which it is placed. If thrown into the air, the wings perform the movements of flying by reflex action. 2.37.—Slight convulsions. 3.15.— Still moves its head; respiration still perceptible, and reflex action in the wings remains. 3.46.—Relaxation of sphincters. 3.48.—Slightly convulsed for a second. From 3.48 to 4.24 perfectly motionless, respiration being very feeble and slow. 4.24.—Dead.

Autopsy.—There was no congestion of lungs. The blood coagulated firmly, and was examined that evening under the microscope. The blood of the Dog (Experiment No. 1) was also examined with a Powell and Leland's $\frac{1}{25}$ inch object-glass, for the use of which I was indebted to Professor C. N. Macnamara, who very kindly examined the blood with me.

In the Dog's blood nothing remarkable could be observed. The red corpuscles seemed unaltered, and the white corpuscles were present in the usual proportion. But in the Fowl's blood the appearances were remarkable. In this case death occurred slowly—in three hours; whereas in the Dog it took place in twenty-six minutes. On carefully examining the Fowl's blood with the $\frac{1}{25}$ inch object-glass and "A" eye-piece, the following appearances were observed:—

The oval red corpuscles were unaltered; but in the field of the microscope, in addition to the blood-corpuscles, a number of large granular bodies were to be seen, which, after careful examination, were discovered to be contained within a distinct cell wall. These granular bodies were coloured by an ammoniacal solution of carmine, but neither the cell wall enclosing them nor the red corpuscles were affected by it. As many as five or seven of these large nucleated cells were seen at one time in the field of the microscope. The granular nucleus was very distinct, and appeared to be adherent to the inner side of the delicate though distinct cell wall. Although these nucleated cells were numerous, we were unable to detect the circular patches in the cell wall depicted by Dr. Halford, and which he states were coloured by carmine.

Whatever be the result of further investigation there could be no doubt of the appearances here described, for they were peculiarly obvious. The absence of any such appearance in the Dog's blood was equally certain.

It is curious that such a difference in the time of death should have occurred. The full-grown Dog died in twenty-six minutes, when the poison was inoculated by the snake's fangs. The small bird died in three hours, when inoculated with the same poison, perfectly fresh, transferred at once from the poison-gland to the knife, and from the knife to the Fowl's thigh. It would seem, to judge from this experiment alone, that the poison had lost something of its effect in being removed from the snake.*

Experiment No. 3.

A full-grown *Ptyas mucosus* (Rat Snake), about five feet long, very vigorous and active, was bitten at 1.46 p.m., in two places, by a fresh and powerful full-grown Cobra. The snake was made to close his jaws, and the fangs pierced deeply, and were kept there long enough for a large dose of the poison to be inoculated.

At 1.56 the respiration appeared somewhat accelerated, but gradually became normal; this quickening of the respiration was probably not a morbid symptom. At 3.15 the *Ptyas* was active and vigorous as usual, appearing in no way affected by the bites. I made inquiry about it the next day, and it was reported to be perfectly well.

The snake-catcher, who handled the Cobra, said, when the *Ptyas* was bitten, and persisted in saying so for some time, that it was sure to die. He was mistaken, for no evil result followed. The snake-catcher says that innocuous snakes suffer from the bite of their poisonous congeners, but that poisonous snakes are unable to harm themselves or each other with their poison.

Experiment No. 4.

A full-grown Cobra was made to plunge his fangs into another equally large Cobra at 2.13 p.m. At 3.15 not the slightest effect was produced, nor did any follow subsequently, the reptile remaining perfectly unaffected.

Experiment No. 5.

At 2.42 p.m. a full-grown Pariah Dog was bitten on the thigh, in the same way as in the first experiment, by a large, fresh, powerful Cobra.

The limb was immediately drawn up, and became partially paralysed. Respiration became hurried, and the Dog was very restless. By 2.46 salivation commenced. 2.48.—The Dog is lying down licking the wound, but continually rising up and lying down again; looking exceedingly distressed, with saliva running from the mouth, and curious movements of the head, and snapping of the jaws. 2.58.—Staggering and throwing the head upwards and downwards, and oscillating the body backwards and forwards irregularly. This continued for a few moments, when the animal lay down again, staggering as if intoxicated; head drooping; coma coming on with jerking diaphragmatic respiration and twitching of the angles of the mouth (*risus sardonicus*). 3.2.—Hind quarters convulsed, restlessness great. 3.3.—Convulsion repeated, eyes glazed, tongue hanging out of the mouth; involuntary discharges. 3.12 p.m. —Dead.

Autopsy.—No congestion of lungs; blood coagulated shortly after removal; heart empty; no coagula; abdominal viscera healthy. Membranes of brain slightly injected; tissue about the snake-bite infiltrated with dark discoloured blood.

In this case a full-grown Dog, severely bitten by a vigorous full-grown Cobra, died in thirty minutes from the effects of the poison, showing that the Aristolochia could have had little or no effect in the first experiment, where a similar Dog was bitten by an equally vigorous Cobra, and died in twenty-six minutes.

Oct. 29th, 1867.

Experiment No. 6.

The poison used on this occasion was some taken from a Cobra on Oct. 21st, and preserved in a small glass tube well corked.

A Pup about three months old was inoculated in the inner side of the thigh, at 9.7 a.m., with a small quantity of the poison.

9.10 a.m.—Restless; drags the limb slightly in walking; no

* See, however, Experiment No. 5, Fourth Series.

expression of suffering. 9.14.—Is apparently sluggish; lies down; and when made to rise staggers; breathing slightly hurried; whines, and bites the puncture. 9.20.—Lying down, apparently asleep. 9.21.—Up, and staggering about again. 9.28.—Appears drowsy, sitting down, drooping the head. 9.34.—Sluggish when roused to walk about. 9.48.—Very sleepy; pupils dilated; cannot be roused until put on the table, and exposed to a fresh breeze, when he gets up and walks a little.

9.52.—Again placed in the breeze; roused himself and walked about, dragging the bitten leg; drank a little water, and smelt at some things on the table; licked the wound.

10.12.—Much the same; drags the left leg and thigh, with the knee-joint extended; walks a few steps, and lies down again, less sluggish than before. 10.38.—Much better; runs about, still slightly dragging the leg, and howling. 2 P.M.—He is quite well again.

In this case a very small quantity of the poison, which had been taken from the snake eight days before, was inoculated. The effects produced, though of a marked character, were slight, and passed away. The Dog recovered perfectly in about five hours.

Experiment No. 7.

A half-grown Domestic Fowl, inoculated at 2 P.M. with the same poison, but in larger quantities, died in rather more than an hour, with precisely similar symptoms to those described in Experiment No. 2. The post-mortem examination revealed the same appearances. In this case, not having the opportunity of examining the blood with the higher power ($\frac{1}{25}$), it was examined with a lower power ($\frac{1}{8}$), but there was nothing in its appearance to confirm the results of the examination of blood in Experiment No. 2. The light was bad, and the examination was not satisfactory.

Experiment No. 8.

A young Pigeon was inoculated, at 2.3 P.M., with a considerable quantity of the same Cobra poison in the inner side of the thigh. 2.5.—Agitated; walking about; making a slight chirping noise. 2.7.—Breathing much hurried. 2.9.—Eyes closed; breathing hurried; sluggish. 2.18.—Becoming convulsed, struggling to rise, and falling over on the right side, which seems paralysed. 2.19.—Respiration much slower; spasms of both legs; lies prone, with neck stretched out and head supported on point of bill. 2.26.—Dead (in 23 minutes).

Autopsy (immediately after death).—Blood firmly coagulable. Lungs not congested. Heart empty; partially contracted; not irritable; not showing any contractility when cut open. Liver not congested. No alteration in the blood could be detected by the microscope.

Experiment No. 9.

The Pup which was the subject of Experiment No. 6 was inoculated at 9.2 A.M. with a larger quantity of the same poison on the corresponding part of the opposite thigh. He had perfectly recovered from the first inoculation, and the puncture looked quite healthy. The poison in this case was inserted with a pen into a puncture made through the skin with a bistoury. The animal became restless almost immediately, and drew the leg up at first, but soon put the foot on the ground again. 9.5.—Drags and tries to extend and stretch the affected limb. 9.8.—Staggers in the hind quarters and loins on the affected side; is evidently very uneasy, but evinces no signs of pain. 9.10.—Makes efforts to vomit, but without result. Gets up and walks sluggishly, dragging the legs. 9.10.—Appears rather better. 9.25.—Lying down; but when put on his feet walks, dragging the inoculated leg. 11 A.M.—Sleeping since last report; is drowsy; but when awakened eats some meat eagerly. *Noon*.—About half a drachm of blood has flowed from the puncture: walks, but is drowsy; shows a tendency to sit on the left hip; both hind legs, but especially the left, seem to give way as he does so. Respiration attended with a hoarse grumbling sound. 12.30.—Whining; progressing with the forelegs, with the belly on the ground, trailing the paralysed hind quarters after him. Vomited a little dark-coloured fluid. Is evidently much distressed; and when placed on his legs, drops on his belly. Moves the hind legs when they are pinched. Respiration laboured. Pupils sensitive to light. 12.55.—Falls over on the left side and gasps for breath. Ten minims of sulphuric ether in two drachms of water were given. The animal expressed uneasiness; whined and rubbed his mouth on the ground. Respirations 24 per minute. No coma; pupils somewhat dilated; yawns and seems less uneasy, but occasionally whines a little. 1.15 P.M.—Much the same; some viscid saliva flowing from the mouth. 1.20.—Pupils dilated and insensible to light. Lies on his belly, head resting on the ground; salivation profuse. The limbs have now lost all power of supporting the body, and the neck of supporting the head. 1.33.—Another dose of ether given. The Dog is now lying on the left side; he struggled a little after getting the ether, but soon became quite quiet. Respirations now 18 per minute and abdominal. 1.40.—Struggles slightly with hind and forelegs and whines. 1.45 P.M.—Pulse 175; respirations 23; respiration accompanied by short whining grunts; struggles occasionally, and opens mouth widely. 2 P.M.—Another dose of ether and a cold douche given, but without any effect. Slight power of using the muscles of the body remains, but all co-ordinating power is gone. 2.30.—Lying on left side as though asleep; occasional twitching of head. Pulse 26. 2.36.—Convulsions of jaws and forelegs, with failing respiration. 2.50.—Perfectly motionless, and, but for the slow respiration, apparently dead. 3 P.M.—Died in about six hours after inoculation.

Body opened immediately; blood from the large vessels coagulated firmly within a few minutes. Lungs perfectly free from congestion; rather blanched. Liver and abdominal viscera healthy; intestines contracting peristaltically. Heart contracting slowly. No coagula in its cavities.

The blood was examined shortly after death with Professor Macnamara's $\frac{1}{25}$ and $\frac{1}{50}$ of an inch object-glasses. The red corpuscles were shrivelled and crenate, but after being soaked for some little time in a slightly ammoniacal solution of carmine, they assumed their normal form and appearance. No indications existed of new cell formations containing germinal matter, although they were most carefully sought for. The only cells which we could find were the healthy red and white corpuscles.

In this case, where death occurred in six hours, and where sufficient time had been given for blood changes, I think that if the changes described by Professor Halford always take place, they ought to have been detected.

SECOND SERIES.

Experiments on the Action of the Poison of the Cobra on Cold-blooded Animals.

March 10th, 1868.

Experiment No. 1.

A full-grown *Ptyas mucosus*, or Rat Snake ("Dhamin"), was bitten at 12.27 P.M. by a fresh Cobra about two-thirds grown, and of a light brown colour. The Cobra was made to close his jaws in three different places at about two feet from the head of the *Ptyas*. The bitten snake was then placed in a large box, with a wire front. 12.33.—*Ptyas* moving about actively in the box and darting out his tongue frequently. 12.40.—Seems very restless and uneasy; strikes at everything that approaches the cage. 12.57.—Active as ever. 1.2 P.M.—No change. 2.30.—No change.

There was no further change, and on the 13th the snake was quite well.*

The *Ptyas* ("Dhamin"), or Rat Snake, is very active and vigorous. The individual bitten must have been about eight feet in length. The Cobra was about half the size.

Experiment No. 2.

A *Varanus flavescens*, or "Gohsámp," about two-thirds grown, was bitten at 12.38 P.M. in two places—one on the thorax behind the foreleg, and one on the inner side of the hindleg, by a powerful, full-grown, and fresh Cobra, about six feet in length, of a lightish colour, and distinctly marked with the spectacles on his hood. 12.42.—The Lizard lies quiet in the cage. 12.46.—Crawling about in the cage; slightly drags his forelegs. 12.55.—Very quiet; looks sluggish; eyes partially closed. 1 P.M.—Very sluggish; was taken out of the cage and placed on the floor of the room, where he moves. The forelegs are dragged with the palmar surface of the feet turned upwards, but when much roused, he is able to use the forelegs. 2.30.—Appears a little less sluggish; looks about. 2.45.—Replaced in the cage; has moved about in the cage, but is sluggish. Hardly responds to stimulus when roused. He remained for the rest of the day in this state. March 11th, noon.—Sluggish, and can hardly be roused. 4 P.M.—He died quietly.

Experiment No. 3.

The Cobra that bit the *Ptyas* in Experiment No. 1 of this series, was bitten by another fresh Cobra of a much darker colour at 12.45. The snake was made to close his jaws in two places, and, as in the other experiment, not only could the fangs be heard to penetrate the scales, but the marks of the puncture were visible, and the poison was left on the surface of the part near the punctures. The snake, after being bitten, was returned to a cage like that of the *Ptyas* in the first experiment. 1.2 P.M.—Lying quiet, apparently unaffected. 1.15.—No change. 1.35.—No change. 2.30.—The only change is that the snake is on the alert, and keeps his head erect with hood spread.

No further change occurred after this, and on the following day the snake was well. It may be noted that this Cobra was partially exfoliating his epidermis at the time when the experiment was made.

Experiment No. 4.

A *Ptyas mucosus*, about six feet in length, was bitten by the large Cobra at 12.54. Before closing the snake's jaws on the part the scales were scraped off. Blood was freely drawn by the snake's fangs from bites inflicted in two places. (This was the same Cobra that bit the *Varanus*). 1.8 P.M.—Appears sluggish; wound bleeding freely. 1.16.—Perfectly active, and moves about rapidly in the cage. 1.35.—No change.

There was no apparent change in the snake all that day or the next, except that it may have been a little more sluggish. He died during the night of the 11th, being found dead on the morning of the 12th.

Experiment No. 5.

A very large Bull-Frog, *Rana tigrina*, was bitten severely on the inner side of the hindleg in two places, at 1.57 P.M. by the same large Cobra that bit the *Ptyas* and *Varanus*. 2 P.M.—Frog walks about; bitten leg rather dragged. 2.5.—Seemed anxious to escape, and gave several cries as of pain or fear. But there was no further change; the Frog remained quite well on the 13th.

* This snake died on the 17th, without any obvious cause.

The blood of the *Ptyas* and of the *Varanus* was examined by Dr. Colles and myself with a one-eighth inch object-glass and the A eye-piece. There was nothing suggestive of any change in the corpuscles.

It is to be remembered that death in both these cases occurred very slowly, allowing abundance of time for any blood change to take place. Of course the appearances in reptilian might be expected to differ from those in mammalian blood; but I doubt if there be anything to indicate such changes as Dr. Halford describes in human blood after the Cobra bite.

However, the matter is still *sub judice*, and requires many experiments, and those often repeated, before any decided conclusion can be formed.

It is especially noticeable that the deaths took place very slowly, and that the effects of the bite, even of a very powerful Cobra, were much more gradually manifested in the cold- than in the warm-blooded animals. The Frog escaped altogether, but this may be owing to the Cobra having been somewhat exhausted by biting two other animals. I can hardly imagine that it was so; for when the snake's mouth was opened to make it bite the Frog, the poison dropped freely from the fangs. It is probable that the quality rather than the quantity may be affected by the rapid discharge of the fluid, and that the exhaustion is caused by the excitement of rage as well as by that of fear to which, under the circumstances, the snake is naturally exposed. The experiments were carefully conducted, and the snakes were handled by the same old man who officiated on a former occasion. Dr. Jerdon and Dr. Colles were present with me during the experiments.

THIRD SERIES.

Experiments on the Action of the Poisons of the Cobra and Bungarus fasciatus on Warm- and Cold-blooded Animals, and on the Influence of Carbolic Acid on these Snakes.

April 22nd, 1868.

Experiment No. 1.

A Fish (*Ophiocephalus marulius*), about fourteen inches long, was bitten once near the tail by a large fresh Cobra at 12.50, and was put into water immediately. 1 P.M.—Fish seems sluggish. 1.5 P.M.—Jumped out of the jar of water. 1.8.—Fish active; plunging about in the jar. 1.14.—Plunging broke the glass jar. Put into another vessel. 1.16.—Seems sluggish; can be taken up by the tail. 1.22.—Turning on his side; plunging; jumps out of the jar. 1.25.—Exhibits convulsive movements; lying on its side. 1.30.—Nearly dead. 1.40.—Dead. Another Fish of the same size, not bitten, but kept for the same period in a similar jar, is alive.

Experiment No. 2.

A Dog was bitten by a full-grown *Bungarus fasciatus* at 1.13 in two places on the inner side of the left thigh. 1.16.—No paralysis of leg such as is seen in Cobra bite. Dog seems uneasy. 1.28.—Dog seems unaffected. 1.36.—Dog lying down; seems sluggish; nothing very striking in his appearance; breathing perhaps rather hurried. 1.55.—Sluggish; struggles and drags the leg a little. 1.56.—Vomiting a quantity of bilious fluid. Snorting; restless. 1.58.—Seems very restless; lies down; is evidently nauseated, and tries to vomit. 2 P.M.—Respiration hurried and irregular, 112 in the minute. 2.15 P.M.—Sluggish and nauseated; breathing quick. 2.30.—Sluggish, but can be roused; makes efforts to vomit; breathing slightly oppressed. 4 P.M.—Same state. Dog died on the afternoon of the 25th.

Experiment No. 3.

A young Mongoose (*Herpestes malaccensis*) was bitten two or three times by a full-grown Cobra, at 1.24 P.M.

on April 30th, on the inside of the thigh, from which the hair was first removed. Blood was drawn by the bites. 1.27.—Lies stretched out, and rigid from convulsion. 1.29.—General convulsions, and twitchings of muscles. 1.30.—Dead. 1.50.—Rigor mortis strongly marked.

Experiment No. 4.

A *Ptyas mucosus* (" Dhamin") was bitten freely in the mouth by a large Cobra, at 1.26 P.M. 1.45.—Quite unaffected. 1.58.—Active as usual. 2.15 P.M.—Snake unaffected. 2.30.—Perfectly well. 4 P.M.—Seems well. 23rd.—Apparently well.

Experiment No. 5.

A large "Dhamin" was bitten three times on the body, and once between the open jaws, by a full-grown Cobra, of a light colour, between 12.57 and 1 P.M. 1.10 P.M.—Snake unaffected. 1.16.—No change. 2.40.—Snake unaffected. 2.50.—Snake unaffected. The next day at noon he was perfectly well.

April 30th, 1868.

Experiment No. 6.

A Cat was bitten by the same Cobra that bit the Mongoose at 1.27 P.M. 1.30.—Cat uneasy; not paralysed. 1.33.—Restless; breathing hurried. 1.40.—Cat lying down; seems uneasy; muscular twitchings and hurried breathing. 1.55.—Active when roused. 2.30.—Appears rather distressed; has bitten its tongue, and lies with mouth half open, and tongue protruded. 2.50.—Is now fully under the influence of the poison. Lies on one side; when placed on its feet, drops with its belly on the ground, and then falls over on one side; constant twitchings of the limbs, and frequent violent efforts made to rise, but quite in vain. Heart's action feeble, 108. 3 P.M.—Dead. The blood, examined twenty minutes after death, showed no perceptible change.

Experiment No. 7.

A Dog was bitten by a *Bungarus fasciatus*, about six feet long, on the inner side of the left thigh, at 1.27 P.M. 1.29.—Dog restless; licking the wound; respiration hurried, probably from excitement. 1.35.—No apparent change; no paralysis as in case of Cobra bite. 1.50.—Seems rather weak in the hind-leg, but otherwise quite well and playful. 2.50.—Dog seems well; lying down. The next day at noon the dog was quite well, and ate his food. He died a day or two later.

Experiment No. 8.

A Cat was bitten by a half-grown *Bungarus fasciatus* in the thigh, from which the hair had been previously removed, at 1.48 P.M. 2.50.—This Cat from the first was sluggish, and apparently unwell, keeping its mouth open, and its tongue protruded. It had an abscess in one cheek. Within the last hour there has been little change; the animal is perhaps rather more sluggish. The noose round the neck being rather tight, was somewhat slackened, and at 3.40 P.M. the Cat was found to have escaped.

May 1st.—The Cat found dead.

Experiment No. 9.

A Mongoose was bitten in the inner side of the thigh by a large Cobra at 1.44 P.M., and was put into a cage immediately at 1.48; apparently not affected. No paralysis of leg; very active in cage; trying to get out. 2 P.M.—Mongoose eating vigorously some raw meat; seems quite unaffected. Was quite well next day.

May 2nd, 1868.

Experiment No. 10.

A Cobra was bitten by a large *Bungarus fasciatus* at 2.12 P.M. at a place where some of his scales had been first scraped off. 2.30.—Seems quite well. 4 P.M.—Seems well.

23rd.—Well.

Experiment No. 11.

A full-sized Cobra bit another full-sized Cobra in the mouth. They were made to close their jaws respectively in each other's mouths at 1.38 P.M. Both Cobras were then put into a wire cage. They were fresh and vigorous. 1.42.—Both snakes very active and angry in the cage. 2.50.—Both snakes unaffected, occasionally striking at each other. The next day at noon they were quite well.

Experiment No. 12.

A Mongoose and a full-sized Cobra were put into a large wire cage at 1 P.M. The snake struck at the Mongoose, and they grappled with each other frequently, and apparently the Mongoose must have been bitten, as the snake held on to it about the neck or head. At 1.15 P.M. there was no effect on the Mongoose; both it and the snake were much excited and angry, the snake hissing violently. 2.30 P.M.—No effect on the Mongoose. The snake is bitten about the head, and shows the bleeding wounds. 1.51.—They are both occasionally darting at each other, but the Mongoose jumps over the snake, and tries to avoid it. Next day at noon both were well; the snake frequently struck at the Mongoose, but did not appear to injure it; both seemed very savage, but the Mongoose would not bite the snake; he jumped over it.

There had been two Cobras in the cage with the Mongoose during the night, both equally fierce, and striking each other and the Mongoose; but the latter was not poisoned. He was scratched by the Cobras rather severely on the head. But on being bitten in the thigh by the same Cobra, when both were taken out of the cage the Mongoose succumbed to the poison, and died very rapidly.

May 27th, 1868.

Experiment No. 13.

The following experiments were suggested by a letter addressed to the Editor of *Engineering*, March 20th, 1868, by Mr. W. Clarke, C.E., who, relating his experiments on poisonous snakes in India, in 1854, mentions the extraordinary effect that creosote had in destroying them, and suggests its use, or that of analogous chemical compounds, in the treatment of snake-bites. The effect of an analogous chemical compound, carbolic acid, on the snake itself I have ascertained. The therapeutic value remains to be determined, though, in anticipation, I express my doubt as to its being more beneficial than anything else, unless applied early enough to decompose the poison before absorption into the venous circulation; and this we could seldom hope to effect. I am quite satisfied that the application of carbolic acid, or perhaps even of coal tar, to the walls and timbers, and apertures by which the entry of snakes into a house could be effected, would have a most beneficial effect in keeping them at a distance.

At 12.33 noon I put a few drops of carbolic acid into the mouth of a large and very vigorous Cobra, and it seemed to produce almost immediate effect. The snake struggled violently, opened and closed the mouth, went rapidly into a state of convulsion, as evinced by a series of spasmodic peristaltic waves of the whole length of the body. In less than five minutes it was evidently powerless for evil, and unable to strike or even move from the spot, but was frequently convulsed. The convulsed movements continued getting fainter, and did not entirely cease for twenty minutes, when it was quite dead. This Cobra was over four feet six inches in length, and peculiarly active and vicious.

Experiment No. 14.

I poured a few drops of carbolic acid on to the floor of a large wooden cage, with a wire front, in which there was a large *Bungarus fasciatus*. The snake was not handled, and the carbolic acid could scarcely have got into the mouth, though it touched the head. The *Bungarus* immediately withdrew his head from the spot where the acid fell, and became very much excited and convulsed, the tail being for a time quite rigid. It turned over on its back in about three minutes, and lay almost motionless for about five or six minutes more, during which slight convulsive movements occurred, as in the Cobra, and in less than ten minutes it was quite dead. This snake was five feet long, and very powerful, sluggish as the *Bungarus fasciatus* always is, I believe, in the daytime; but very active when roused.

Life in this snake was much more rapidly extinguished, and by a smaller dose of the poison, than in the smaller Cobra. As they lay stretched out side by side, convulsive twitchings were apparent in the Cobra for some minutes after the *Bungarus fasciatus* was quite dead. This would indicate that the *Bungarus fasciatus* is much more susceptible than the Cobra, for it was apparently destroyed by the vapour, or, at all events, by the very small quantity that might have trickled down from the head into the mouth. After death, the mucous membrane of the mouth was natural; whereas in the Cobra that had drops placed in the mouth, these had completely whitened the mucous membrane, and coagulated the poison which had exuded from the fangs.

The use of carbolic acid as a preventive against the entry of snakes into houses and other places where they may prove dangerous, or as a means of getting rid of them where they have taken possession, is clearly suggested by these experiments, for there can be no doubt that the drug is most deadly and disagreeable to the reptiles.

FOURTH SERIES.

Experiments on the Action of the Poison of the Cobra on Warm- and Cold-blooded Animals, and on the Influence of Carbolic Acid on the Cobra and Frog.

June 9th, 1868.

Experiment No. 1.

At 3.29 P.M. a full-grown, vigorous, and fresh Cobra was made to bite a very powerful full-grown Cobra of a black colour. The scales were scraped off near the head, and the other snake was made to plunge his fangs into the exposed part, and retain them there for some time. It was then made to bite the Cobra in the mouth, by closing the jaws on the under-jaw of the bitten snake. The wounded snake was then placed in a large cage, and watched. It did not show any symptoms of being affected by the poison, and was perfectly well, vigorous, and active on the 10th at 2 P.M.—At 2 P.M. on June 11th the bitten snake was well and active. This appears to be almost conclusive that the Cobra is not affected by the poison secreted by another Cobra.

Experiment No. 2.

At 3.30 P.M. a full-grown, fresh Cobra of light brown colour, with one ocellus on the hood, was made to bite a large *Rana tigrina* (Bullfrog) on the inner side of the thigh, the integument having been previously raised. The snake was made to close his jaws on and insert the fangs in the muscle, retaining them there for some time. 3.36 P.M.—Apparently not affected; leg not paralysed; moves about as usual. 3.55.—No very apparent change, except that the bitten thigh is much ecchymosed; rather sluggish. 4.10.—Very sluggish; hardly moves when stirred; appears almost paralysed. 4.25.—Appears to be paralysed, so as to be unable to move; respiration goes on well. There are reflex movements when the hind legs are irritated. The legs are drawn up. 4.30.—Reflex movements have ceased. 4.45.—Dead. Body much swollen and distended with air. This experiment proves that the Frog is susceptible, though much less so than warm-blooded animals, to the action of the poison

Experiment No. 3.

A full-grown, active *Ptyas mucosus* ("Dhamin") was bitten at 3.36 P.M. in the mouth by a powerful, vigorous, and fresh Cobra. The snakes were made to close their jaws on each other. The snake remained unaffected, and on the 11th, at 2 P.M., was quite well. There could be no doubt that the Cobra's fangs were deeply inserted in this case.

Experiment No. 4.

A large *Varanus flavescens* ("Gohsámp") was bitten at 3.55 P.M. by a full-grown, fresh, and vigorous Cobra of the light coloured variety, with one ocellus, which the natives of Bengal call "Keautiah," in the mouth and in the thigh, the integument having been previously raised to insure the penetration of the fangs and insertion of the venom. 3.57.—The bitten leg is dragged as though paralysed; the mouth is bleeding from the Cobra's bite. 4.25 P.M.—Drags the leg; is rather sluggish, but not much affected. 4.27.—Lies prone. Is nearly paralysed and moves with great difficulty. 4.35.—Apparently paralysed; can be moved with difficulty. 4.55.—Much the same. After this the *Varanus* began to improve, and at 2 P.M. the following day he appeared better, though still sluggish. On June 11th, at 2 P.M., I found the *Varanus* dead in the cage. He was seen alive about noon.

Experiment No. 5.

At 4 P.M. a half-grown Domestic Fowl was inoculated in the muscular part of the thigh with four drops of Cobra poison removed from the snake the day before. The poison was injected with the ordinary hypodermic syringe. The effect was almost instantaneous. The Fowl staggered when placed on the ground; was in convulsions at 4.1, and was dead at 4.4. This experiment would appear to show that the poison loses very little of its power, if any, by removal; and that its action depends much on the instrument with which it is injected. The hypodermic needle resembles the Cobra's fang, and was almost as rapid in inducing the full effect of the poison.

Experiment No. 6.

At 4.7 P.M. a very large *Rana tigrina* was injected with ten drops of the same poison, with the same instrument as that used for the Fowl. The axilla and the abdominal wall were the places selected for injection. 4.20.—He is beginning to be sluggish, but is very slightly affected. 4.22.—Slightly convulsed, and then partially paralysed. 4.30.—Almost motionless; respiratory movements still apparent. 4.35.—Dead.

This experiment points to the difference of the effect of the poison on cold- and warm-blooded animals. With three times the amount of the poison as was used in the case of the Fowl, it took seven times as long to kill the Frog.

Experiment No. 7.

One drop of carbolic acid was administered to a full-grown, vigorous Cobra at 4.14 P.M. In two minutes the snake was in convulsions, and powerless to strike, or even erect his hood. 4.34.—Still struggling; convulsed; mouth open, but unable to move or strike. 4.45.—Has gradually been recovering; looks still very weak, and the head trembles, and can be raised with difficulty. At 2 P.M. the following day the snake had recovered, but still seemed weak, and unable to dilate his hood perfectly.

A smaller Cobra to which the same quantity, one drop, was administered, died in less than five minutes.

Experiment No. 8.

Two drops of carbolic acid were administered to a large Frog, *Rana tigrina*, at 4.15 P.M. 4.20 P.M.—Apparently not affected. 4.22.—Began to be sluggish. 4.24.—Very sluggish; reflex movements when the hind legs are irritated. 4.30.—No reflex movement; lies almost paralysed; respiratory movements going on slowly. 4.40.—Quite dead.

When dead the body became quite collapsed and pinched, whilst the Frog killed by Cobra poison was much distended.

The poison used for inoculating on this occasion had been taken from three Cobras the day before. There was altogether about forty or fifty drops. It is a slightly viscid, somewhat opalescent fluid; clear when pressed out of the poison-gland, but becoming slightly turbid afterwards, with a slightly acid reaction, and under the microscope presenting the appearance in the annexed sketch, which I observed after very careful examination.

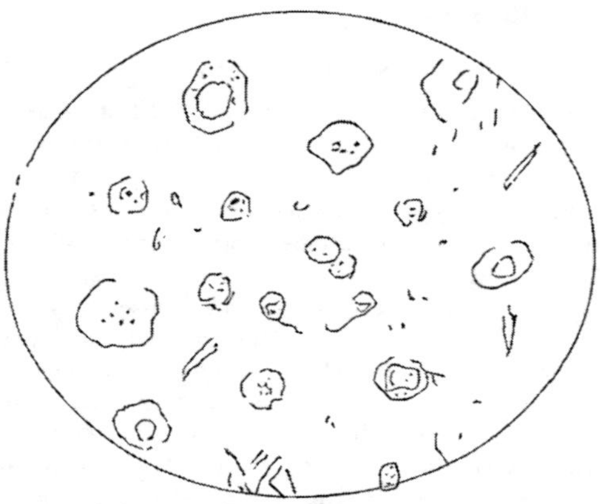

Appearance of Cobra Poison under Microscope.
Nachet, ¼ inch; eye-piece No. 3. Lamplight. June 10th, 1868.

This poison, used on the day after its abstraction, had lost very little of its virulence; for when injected through the hypodermic needle, it caused death very rapidly. Where it has appeared to fail, the apparent failure has probably been due to the mode of insertion. The hypodermic syringe is very like the poison fang, and it appeared to inject the poison just as efficaciously.

I may note that the experiments with Cobras have been made with three varieties of the *Naja tripudians*.

FIFTH SERIES.

On the Influence of the Poison of Bungarus fasciatus, Cobra, and Daboia.

June 20th, 1868.

Experiment No. 1.

Ten drops of Cobra poison, removed from the Cobra on June 9th, were injected, with the hypodermic syringe, under the mucous membrane of the mouth of a large Rat Snake. It did not appear to affect the snake in the least at the time, or afterwards; and several days later it was quite well. It is possible that the poison may have lost some of its power in the course of eleven days, but it had not altered in appearance, and had been kept carefully closed from access of air. The effect on other animals proves that it had not become altogether inert.

Experiment No. 2.

At 5.7 P.M., an *Ardea leucoptera* (Paddy-bird) was bitten by a *Bungarus fasciatus* in the thigh. 5.10.—Stretching the bitten leg; breathing hurriedly. 5.11.—Tries to fly. The leg very weak. 5.13.—Sluggish. The leg dragged; there is a peculiar twitching of the throat. The mouth wide open. 5.15.—Tries to fly when roused; the leg is paralysed. 5.30.—Remains in much the same condition. 5.31.—Much weaker; staggers as it moves. The plumage has a disordered and draggled appearance. The bird now crouches on its breast; leg apparently unable to support its weight. The mouth gaping. The claws are contracted, and it is unable to walk. There is a peculiar vibration of the feathers of the neck. The bitten thigh is discoloured and much congested. 5.53.—Drooping and crouching on the ground. 6.12.—Crouching on the ground; accelerated breathing; eyes quite bright. 6.21.—If roused, it tries to move, but it immediately falls over; the claws are contracted. 6.25.—Tries to rise when roused, and to attack with its beak, but droops immediately after the excitement. 6.30.—Brightness of the eyes diminished; lies prone, resting the head on the point of the beak. 6.38.—Lies helpless and motionless on the ground; slow, feeble respiration. 6.40.—Dead.

After death, Dr. Stoliczka remarked that the blood from the wound was very thin and watery. The bitten leg was discoloured, and when pressed, a quantity of gas escaped in bubbles. Decomposition seemed to be setting in very rapidly.

The bird was bitten at 5.7 P.M., and died at 6.40 P.M.—*i.e.*, in one hour and thirty-three minutes. The dead bird was given to a *Felis catus* (Wild Cat); it was eaten with avidity, and no unfavourable result occurred to the Cat.

This experiment, like others tried with the *Bungarus fasciatus*, seems to prove that its poison, though deadly, is neither so fatal nor so active as that of the Cobra. This may be due not only to some difference in the activity of the poison itself, but also to the nature of the instrument with which it is inoculated. The *Bungarus fasciatus*, though a large, powerful, and very vicious snake, is armed with very small fangs, and penetration, even under the most favourable circumstances, must be much less than in the case of the Cobra, or of the viperine snakes, which have much longer fangs. The difference in this respect is very striking between the poisonous colubrine and the viperine snakes. The fangs of the Cobra, *Bungarus*, and other colubrine snakes are much smaller than those of the viperine snakes.

Experiment No. 3.

Another Paddy-bird, *Ardea leucoptera*, inoculated at 5.27 P.M. in the wing, with some of the same Cobra poison, eleven days old, that had been used for the *Ptyas*, a short time before. The puncture bled freely. 5.29.—The bird is apparently unaffected. 5.32.—Inoculated again with a quill-pen into a puncture in the hind leg, as the first inoculation seems to have taken no effect. 5.35.—Walks sluggishly. Feathers have a draggled appearance; some are erect; the bird shakes himself frequently; seems very uneasy; vomited some shrimps recently eaten. 5.40.—Staggers in walking; very weak in inoculated leg. 5.42.—Crouching; cannot balance itself when it tries to stand; point of the beak resting on the ground. 5.44.—When roused, tries to walk, but falls over. 5.46.—Eyes closed; slight convulsions. 5.50.—Generally convulsed. 5.52.—Dead.

The dead bird was eaten by a Dog without producing any evil result to that animal. In this instance the poison was at first imperfectly inoculated into the wing, and apparently without any result after five minutes, when it was again inoculated in the wing at 5.32 P.M.; death occurred at 5.52, or in twenty minutes.

It is worthy of remark that this poison was eleven days old, and was probably not very effectively inoculated, as the hypodermic syringe was not used, the poison being inserted into the wound with a quill, and yet the bird died in twenty minutes; whereas a similar bird, bitten by a fresh and vigorous *Bungarus*, did not die for one hour and thirty-three minutes.

July 11*th*, 1868.

EXPERIMENT No. 4.

This and the following experiments were made with two full-grown living specimens of *Daboia russellii*. I may remind the reader that the *Daboia russellii* (Russell's Viper) is the only species of the family *Viperidæ* found in Bengal, where it is known as the "Bora," and is justly dreaded as a most venomous snake. It is found in the Peninsula of Southern India, and even in the Himalayas, it is said, at a height of 5500 feet, for it has been found at Almorah. It grows as long as fifty inches, and is a very powerful and dangerous snake; it is much thicker than the Cobra; its markings are very beautiful; a series of black, white edged, rings ovate and circular, on a greyish-brown ground, white belly with black spots. Its head is covered with scales, not shields; its nostril is very large; the head is broad and well defined from the neck, which is not extensible like that of the Cobra.

But the striking difference is in the poison fangs, which are very much larger than those of the Cobra. They are recurved, erectile, and very moveable; so much so, that when the snake is angry, and about to strike, you can see the fangs erected and depressed quickly in a vibratile manner, totally different to the more fixed and much smaller fangs of the Cobra and other poisonous colubrine snakes.*

The two brought to me were nearly full-grown, and apparently active and vigorous. The snake-catchers who brought them, and who handled Cobras with the greatest ease and freedom, from fear would not attempt to seize the *Daboia* by the neck, as they said the risk was too great. The snake did not appear at all more active than the Cobra, and, when seized by the tail, was not more capable of turning on his captor; but when the head was confined by compressing the neck with a stick against the ground, it struggled and made fierce attempts to bite, during which, the mouth being open, the gape of which is very wide, the erectile and vibratile movements of the fangs that I have mentioned became visible. This snake is the only species of its genus known in India.

A Pariah Dog, full-grown, was bitten in the thigh, at 4.27 P.M., by a nearly full-grown, active *Daboia*. The Dog whimpered when the snake's fangs penetrated. He was released, having been held while the snake bit him, and almost immediately—*i.e.*, at 4.28, fell over with a convulsive movement; became paralysed for the moment, and howled violently; as he lay on the ground the bladder was emptied. 4.29.—In a state of violent tetanic spasm. 4.31.—Lies motionless; eyes bright; muscular system generally twitching. 4.35.—Lies apparently paralysed, but looks about him. 4.37.—Attempted to get up; staggered a few steps, and lay down again. 4.42.—Cannot walk. Lies paralysed; shows no sign of pain. 4.50.—Much in the same state. 5.35.—Lies paralysed; but breathing goes on. Died a few minutes later.

Thorax opened. Lungs collapsed, not congested; heart natural; auricles and ventricles contained fluid blood.

It is noteworthy that this Dog, after the first violent outcry when he fell over, one minute after being bitten, appeared to suffer no further pain; indeed, it seemed unconscious of anything. There was no convulsion; but general paralysis, the sphincters included, and gradual sinking from exhaustion. The heart's action continued to the last, and, even after apparent death, the rhythmical movements were observed.

The Dog was bitten at 4.27 P.M., and died at about 5.40; nearly one hour and a quarter.

The first effects on the nervous system seemed much more violent than from the Cobra bite, and paralysis seemed to follow more quickly, but actual death was longer in taking place. A Dog bitten by a Cobra died in about half an hour. The Dog bitten by the *Daboia* died in an hour and a quarter. Possibly the Cobra injected a larger quantity of poison than the *Daboia;* and indeed it struck me that there was not so great an effusion of poison from the *Daboia* as from the Cobra. There may have been something in the mode in which the bite was inflicted. The Cobra was held by the neck, his mouth almost forcibly opened, and his fangs made to imbed themselves in the bitten object; whilst, on the other hand, the *Daboia* was not so held or applied, for the snake-man was afraid to seize him by the neck, and could only fix him by compressing the neck on the ground with a stick, in which position the animal bitten was presented to the snake.

EXPERIMENT No. 5.

A full-grown male Cat was bitten by the same snake, in the hind leg, at 4.18 P.M. The *Daboia*, being secured as before described, plunged his fangs, but not deeply, into the limb; no immediate paralysis of the limb followed, as from the Cobra bite, but the animal was almost immediately affected, and at 4.22—*i.e.*, in four minutes, was in convulsions, which did not last long, nor were attended by any outcry as in the Dog bitten by the same snake. The general convulsions soon subsided, and were followed by general paralysis, the animal lying prone on the ground, with its breathing much accelerated, and with spasmodic twitchings of the muscles of the trunk and extremities. 4.30. — Lies perfectly powerless; breathing rapid; frothing at the mouth, and making efforts to vomit. Bladder and rectum emptied, voided sanguineous mucus. 4.31.—Made an effort to rise; staggered a few paces and fell. 4.35.—In the same state; muscular twitchings continue; cannot move. 4.45.—Still alive, and much in the same state. 5 P.M.—Still alive; muscular twitchings continue, but fainter; breathing hardly perceptible. 5.15.—Quite dead.

The Cat was bitten at 4.18 P.M., and died at 5.15 P.M.—*i.e.*, in fifty-seven minutes. As in the case of the Dog, the influence of the poison seemed to affect the nerve-centres more violently than that of the Cobra poison. Consciousness was probably earlier annihilated, but total death occurred later.

I examined the appearances after death, and found that, at 5.45 P.M., or in half an hour, the blood had not coagulated.

The lungs were not in the least congested; there were no clots in any of the cardiac cavities. Blood taken from the right auricle was dark and fluid, but speedily reddened on exposure to the air. Examined later, the power of coagulation appeared to have been perfectly destroyed. I took some away for microscopical examination, and it remained perfectly fluid.

I examined the blood most carefully and repeatedly under the microscope with one-eighth object-glass and No. 3 eye-piece, Nachet, and I found the appearances differed very little, if at all, from those of ordinary blood. The only thing suggestive of any change in the corpuscles, was that in one or two specimens examined there were more granular corpuscles than may be considered as the natural relative proportion to the red corpuscles; but after the most careful examination, I was unable to detect any other change in their form or appearance. There was nothing resembling the appearances described by Professor Halford. It was observed, though, that there was no tendency in the corpuscles to aggregate in rouleaux; the

* In reference to the connexion of the poison fangs with the maxillary bones, I would note that a second, or even third, supplementary fang may be anchylosed with the principal one to the maxillary bone. I have before me the skull of a *Daboia*, for which I am indebted to Mr. Sceva, in which this is the case; and where there are five well-developed poison fangs on each side, of which on one side *two* are anchylosed to the maxillary bone.

attractive power seemed to be annihilated. The blood appeared, indeed, to be dead—to be in a state of necræmia.

The microscopical appearances seem to show a larger number of granular corpuscles than is usual in proportion to the red; but this may have been a peculiarity of the Dog, which was not a very healthy looking or vigorous animal.

Experiment No. 6.

The same snake was made to bite a young but full-grown Kite (*Milvus govinda*) in the wing. The snake bit near the second joint, and drew blood, at 4.40 P.M. 4.50.—The bird seems sluggish, and crouches, but is easily roused and walks about. 5 P.M.—Sluggish, but moves when roused. 5.38.—Alive, and though somewhat sluggish, is otherwise unaffected. The bird was alive and well some days after.

The snake was probably exhausted by biting the other two animals, and he struck a part of the wing where, probably the poison, if the snake had any left, was not easily absorbed.

There could be no doubt that, to a certain extent, the bird was at first affected.

Experiment No. 7.

At 4.49 P.M., another Kite, of the same size as the last, was bitten by a fresh *Daboia* in the thigh. The snake was not aggressive, and seemed unwilling to bite; but when irritated it slightly wounded the bird with its fangs. 4.55.—Looks stupefied; feathers all erect. 5 P.M.—The bird is sluggish, and breathing hurriedly; it is unable to walk, and its claws are contracted into a ball. 5.8 P.M.—Tried to rise, and fell over dead. Death occurred in nineteen minutes. Blood examined under microscope; no change could be detected. Blood remained fluid after death; no coagulation.

Experiment No. 8.

A full-grown *Daboia* was bitten freely at 5.8 P.M., by a fresh and vigorous Cobra, which plunged its fangs more than once into the *Daboia*. 5.40.—The snake was unaffected. On July 16th the *Daboia* was as well as ever; the Cobra bite had had no effect.

The experiment so far certainly seems to prove that the venomous snakes have no power of poisoning each other, and limited power of injuring the non-venomous snakes; but these experiments are liable to many sources of error, and require to be repeated before conclusions are drawn from them.

Dr. Fayrer, Dr. Stoliczka, and Mr. Sceva were present at these experiments.

July 20th, 1868.

Experiment No. 9.

A large powerful Dog was bitten in the hind-leg by a *Daboia russellii*, at 12.50. The snake struck twice, but did not seem to bite severely. This *Daboia* is one that was used in the last experiment on July 11th, and has been in a cage since; it is not known whether it has eaten or not since the last experiment. It seemed vigorous and savage, striking at anything that was brought near it. The Dog was held, and immediately after being bitten had a supposed antidote, of which I may have more to say on a future occasion, administered. As it took a minute or two to pour the drug down the Dog's throat, it was impossible to say how far the struggles were due to fear, and how far to the poison.

12.54.—Released; ran across the room staggering, and dragging the hind leg. 12.55.—Walking about in the same manner, very restless; breathing hurriedly, and frothing at the mouth. The Dog was kept walking about by one of the attendants. 12.56.—Sat down exhausted; breathing very hurried; frothing at the mouth; eye bright and intelligent. 12.57.—Another dose of the drug administered. 12.58.—In violent convulsions; cold water poured on the head gave relief; struggled and sat up, but could not stand. 1 P.M.—Struggles violently; is paralysed in the hind quarters; constant spasmodic twitchings of the eyelids and other muscles. He rolls his head and body about where he sits, and has the appearance of extreme intoxication. Cold water constantly poured on the head, and efforts made to rouse the Dog by trying to make him walk. The breathing is hard, with a peculiar puffing of the cheeks, like that of an apoplectic person. Holds up his head, and is quite conscious, but can neither stand nor walk. 1.12.—Another dose of the drug administered, and more cold water poured on the head; fresh efforts made to rouse the Dog. 1.13.—Made an effort to rise; succeeded in staggering away a few paces. 1.20.—Seems better; can walk a little, but staggers. 1.25.—More sluggish; again lies down. The same puffing of the cheeks, and deep breathing. Evacuations at first natural, becoming frequent, and consisting of bloody mucus. I should also note that he has made several efforts to vomit, but the drug does not appear to have been rejected. 1.30.—Puffing of the cheeks, frothing at the mouth, and deep breathing continue. The Dog appears conscious, though intoxicated. 1.37.—Becoming weaker; lies on the floor paralysed. The puffing and flapping of the lips and cheeks continue. 1.45.—Much in the same condition; has just vomited a quantity of thick mucus, and has passed a quantity of sanguineous mucus. Rose, and again staggered a few paces. Is able to raise his head, which he does when water is poured on it.

For the rest of the report I am indebted to Mr. Sceva, who was present after I was obliged to leave.

At 2.50 the spasmodic movements of the body ceased for a few minutes, and the Dog raised himself on his forelegs. He was then removed to a cooler place, and raising his body, gentle exercise was given by lifting him alternately by the shoulders and hips, rubbing and moving his legs. He seemed to improve again somewhat. He was punkahed, and cold water was dashed on his head, whilst he was again exercised as before; on leaving his body unsupported, he sunk upon his haunches, but immediately after raised himself without assistance, and attempted to walk. The convulsive movements again returned, with hurried respiration, and he remained in that state until he died at 3.49 P.M. Bitten at 12.50, died at 3.49 P.M.; very nearly three hours.

The action of this snake's poison is evidently somewhat different from that of the Cobra. The Dog was a very healthy and powerful animal, and the snake was not fresh, but still death occurred within three hours. In this case, the bitten limb was paralysed, as in the case of the Dog bitten by the Cobra. The first shock to the nervous system was not so severe in this case as in that of the other Dog bitten by the *Daboia*. This may have been due to the fact that in the former case the Dog was smaller and the snake was fresh. I do not at present offer any opinion on the so-called antidote, further than that, in this particular case, I believe it was altogether inert.

The effect of the poison in causing profuse mucous discharge from the stomach, and the discharge of blood and mucus from the bowels, is worthy of notice. I examined the blood after death, and found the corpuscles shrivelled and collapsed, but not otherwise changed.

Experiment No. 10.

A young but very active and vigorous Pig was bitten at 12.27, very slightly in the right thigh, by a fresh Cobra, but it was doubtful at the time whether the fangs had penetrated. The Pig made his escape, and was caught and brought back in a few minutes apparently unaffected. At 12.35 he was bitten again by a small but vigorous Cobra of the Spectacled variety, called by the natives "Gomunah" or

"Gokurrah." This time the animal was really bitten in two places on the thigh. 12.36.—Struggled violently, and lay down; then got up and struggled violently to get loose from the cord by which he was secured. 12.38.—Lies down and rises again; hurried breathing; is very restless; tries to run about; begins to stagger, and falls; at 12.40 is unable to rise. 12.42.—Is convulsed. 12.43.—Lies paralysed, breathing deeply; muscular twitchings. 12.48.—Dead.

The Pig was bitten at 12.35, and died at 12.48, that is, in thirteen minutes. This disposes of the question of the immunity of Pigs from the poisonous effects of the venom of the Cobra.

EXPERIMENT No. 11.

A small *Tropidonotus quincunciatus* (Grass Snake) was bitten by the Spectacled Cobra that killed the pig, at 1.12 P.M. 1.16.—Very sluggish. 1.20.—Tosses its head about in a convulsive manner. 1.25.—Dead; died in thirteen minutes.

EXPERIMENT No. 12.

Two innocuous snakes, *Dendrophis picta* (Tree Snakes), one about three feet four inches long, the other rather smaller, both long, delicate reptiles, bitten at 1.7 P.M. and 1.8 P.M. by the same Cobra that bit the *Tropidonotus*. 1.12.—Sluggish. 1.15.—The small snake dead. 1.16.—The larger one dead. They simply seemed to become sluggish and powerless; there were no convulsions, no writhings or contortions. They became powerless and died.

After they appeared quite dead, for a moment or two the tail of each moved slightly.

Large snake bitten at 1.7, died at 1.16.

Small snake bitten at 1.8, died at 1.15.

In one case death occurred in nine minutes; in the other in seven minutes.

The Cobra must have been much exhausted, for it had bitten several times before biting these snakes.

EXPERIMENT No. 13.

At 1.15 P.M. a "Dhamin" (*Ptyas mucosus*) was bitten in three places by the same Spectacled Cobra that bit several other animals. 1.30 P.M.—No apparent effect; the snake is as active as ever. 1.32 P.M.—Bitten again by the same Cobra in the mouth and body. 1.38.—No effect. 1.43.—No effect. Bitten again in the mouth and body by a Cobra that has been in one of the cages, and has not bitten for some time. 2.10 P.M.—Is sluggish; when handled does not try to get away, nor attempt to strike. It became more and more sluggish, and died at 8 P.M. The snake seemed to me gradually to become weaker and weaker. No convulsions or contortion of the body before death.

This experiment and the two preceding it prove that the non-venomous snakes are affected by the Cobra poison.

The "Dhamin" bitten on June 11th by a Cobra did not die, and is alive on July 21st.

Dr. Fayrer and Mr. Sceva of the Indian Museum were present at these experiments.

SIXTH SERIES.

On the Influence of the Poisons of the Cobra and Daboia, and on the value of Strychnia as an Antidote.

August 6*th*, 1868.

Present, Dr. Fayrer, Dr. F. Stoliczka, and Mr. V. Ball, Curators of the Indian Museum, and Mr. Sceva.

EXPERIMENT No. 1.

At 12.13 P.M. a Cobra was bitten in two places, about six inches from the head, where the scales had been previously scraped off, and in the mouth, by a very large and powerful light-coloured Spectacled Cobra, five feet six inches in length. The bitten snake was then put into a separate box with a wire gauze front, for observation. There could be no doubt in this case that the bites were severe, and that the poison was inoculated. At 2.30, when I left, the snake seemed to be unaffected. At 9 P.M. Mr. Sceva reports that the bitten Cobra does not seem to be much affected. 2.30 P.M., August 8th, about fifty hours afterwards, this snake is apparently unaffected.

EXPERIMENT No. 2.

A *Bungarus fasciatus*, nearly full-grown, was bitten by the same Cobra at 12.22 P.M., at about eight inches from the head. The snake was bitten twice; the Cobra took firm hold, and implanted the fangs deeply. At 2.30, when I left, there was no change; the *Bungarus* seemed unaffected. The *Bungarus* died at 7.30 P.M. of the 7th, about twenty-nine hours after being bitten. At 1 P.M. of the 7th he still seemed well.

EXPERIMENT No. 3.

At 12.27 P.M. an innocuous snake, *Dendrophis*, long and delicate, beautifully marked with red spots along the spine, was bitten by the same Cobra, about the middle of the body. 12.30.—Appears slightly affected and is sluggish. It does not try to make its escape so vigorously as it did. 12.53.—Sluggish, but apparently very slightly affected. The Cobra is apparently partially exhausted, as it had been made to bite two other snakes in two places, and in this forced biting much of the poison is lost. 12.54.—Bitten again, near the same spot, by a fresh and large black Cobra. It soon became very sluggish, but made no convulsive movements. It simply seemed to become paralysed, and was dead at 1.8 P.M. Death occurred in fourteen minutes after the second bite, in forty-one minutes after the first bite. The effect of the poison on the harmless snakes seems, from this experiment, to be comparatively feeble and slow. The bitten snake was small and delicate, the Cobra was fresh and very powerful, and at least five and a half feet long.

EXPERIMENT No. 4.

A *Dryiophis* (Green Tree Snake), about three and a half feet long, was bitten by the first-mentioned large, light-coloured Cobra, in the middle of its body, at 12.28 P.M. 12.52.—Slightly affected, rather sluggish; but it is combative, and attacks if approached. At 12.55 it was bitten again by the large black Cobra mentioned in Experiment No. 3. It rapidly became affected. Became very apathetic and sluggish. At 1.3 P.M. apparently nearly dead. At 1.4 dead.

This experiment, like No. 3, shows the effect of the Cobra poison on the innocuous snake. The *Dryiophis* died in nine minutes after the second bite, in thirty-six minutes after the first bite. The first Cobra was evidently exhausted. The second was fresh and vigorous, having only once bitten the *Dendrophis*. I believe that had it bitten a warm-blooded animal of about the same strength as the *Dendrophis*, death would have occurred more quickly. The *Dryiophis* was twice the size of the *Dendrophis*, and although it was bitten after it, died in a much shorter time. It was either more susceptible or more deeply bitten.

EXPERIMENT No. 5.

A Pariah Dog was bitten in the thigh by a large and fresh black Cobra at 12.37 P.M. Immediately afterwards about twenty drops of a solution of strychnia (of the strength of one grain to a drachm), equal to one-third of a grain, were injected with a hypodermic syringe into the same thigh. 12.39.—Tetanic twitchings of the limbs commenced, and gradually continued, becoming more intense, till at 12.42 the animal was in a state of general tetanic spasm of all the muscles of the body. The ears were erected, the pupils dilated to excess, the body rigid, and the limbs extended in an intense state of tetanic convulsion. 12.43.—Dead. Spasm relaxed just before death.

In this case death occurred in six minutes, and was due entirely to tetanus. There was neither time nor opportunity for any manifestation of the effects of the snake-poison.

Experiment No. 6.

A Pariah Dog was bitten in the thigh by a powerful and fresh black Cobra at 12.45. Immediately afterwards about fifteen drops of the strychnia solution were injected with the hypodermic syringe into the same thigh. 12.46.—Bitten leg partially paralysed, and dragged. The Dog ran across the room, the legs twitching violently. At 12.47 it fell over in a state of rigid tetanic spasm. 12.48.—Every muscle in the body in a state of rigid spasm. But it was remarked that the bitten leg was not so much affected by spasm as the other leg. The paralysing action of the snake-poison apparently so far counteracts the action of the strychnia. 12.50.—Spasm relaxed. 12.51.—Dead.

Death occurred, evidently from tetanus, in six minutes.

Experiment No. 7.

A full-grown male Cat was bitten in the thigh at 1.20 P.M. by a *Daboia russellii*, about two-thirds grown, and apparently quite fresh and vigorous. Ten drops of a solution of strychnia, of the strength of one grain to a drachm, that is, one-sixth of a grain, were injected at 1.23 P.M. 1.24.—The bitten leg is partially paralysed. The Cat lies quietly, looking about it. 1.25.—Spasmodic twitchings began. 1.26.—Stretched out in a violent tetanic spasm. Pupils very widely dilated. 1.27.—Spasm relaxed. Dead. In this case the strychnia seemed rather to accelerate death than to improve the animal's condition. The action of the snake-poison had clearly commenced, but it was at once obscured by the symptoms of poisoning by strychnia, and the Cat died in a state of complete tetanus. The strychnia was suggested as an antidote to snake-poison. These experiments do not support this theory.

Experiment No. 8.

A large "Dhamin" (*Ptyas mucosus*) was bitten by a fresh and powerful Cobra, at 12.53 P.M., about eight inches from the head, the scales having been previously scraped off, to insure the penetration of the Cobra's fangs. Bitten also in the mouth, at 12.54, by the same Cobra. At 1.8 P.M. still active. 1.10.—Appears slightly sluggish. 1.30.—The same. At 2.30, when I left, it was in the same state.

On August 8th I learnt that the *Ptyas* died at 3.20 P.M., rather less than twenty-three hours after being bitten. It appeared to have partially recovered from its lethargy during the day, but relapsed and died; as it had been in the cage for some time, and was well and active, there can be no doubt, I think, that its death was due to the Cobra bite.

Experiment No. 9.

A very large and powerful Cobra, the same that bit in Experiments 1, 2, 3, and 4, had about twenty-five drops of the solution of strychnia (one grain to a drachm) injected into the anterior part of its body on the ventral aspect at 1 P.M. At 1.2 P.M. muscular twitchings began. The hood seemed to be shrivelled up and contracted. The head was erect, and longitudinal folds formed in its skin. At 1.4 P.M. in a state of violent tetanic spasm. The body set in short waves, as though it had been petrified in that condition, and the whole curved rigidly to one side. 1.6.—Continues in the same state, rigid as stone. 1.10.—Spasm relaxing; twitchings generally throughout the body and the head. 1.12.—The only sign of life an occasional twitch. Dead. 1.14.—Spasm relaxed.

Experiment No. 10.

A Cobra, about four feet long, was injected with fifteen drops of Cobra poison, partly taken from another Cobra, partly from itself, at 1.56 P.M., at about four inches from the head. At 1.58 twitching of head and neck when erect. Hood began to shrivel. At 1.59 twisted itself up into a rigid series of coils, like a snake cast in metal, in which state I lifted it up with a stick and rolled it on the floor. It remained in this condition, the head twitching. At 2.25 the coils were unfolded, and it was quite dead.

The symptoms of poisoning here were more those of strychnia than snake-poison; and I cannot help thinking that such may possibly have been the fact. The same hypodermic syringe was used as in the other experiments, but as it had been most carefully washed several times before the experiment, it is difficult to conceive how such can have been the case, unless a very small quantity of the strychnia solution had been left imbibed by the packing of the piston. As the result was so different from that of other inoculations of Cobras by Cobra poison, I cannot help suspecting this may have been the case, and it is sufficient to throw a doubt on the validity of the experiment. It would, however, prove the extreme susceptibility of the snake to the action of strychnia.

Experiment No. 11.

At 2 P.M. a large Cobra had about fifteen drops of his own poison injected with the hypodermic syringe, about eight inches from the head. The needle was inserted in the ventral surface, and it is probable the lung may have been penetrated. At 2.5 P.M. the snake was moving about, apparently unaffected. 2.10.—He was thought to appear rather sluggish. 2.30.—Apparently as vigorous as ever. At 9 P.M. it was reported by Mr. Sceva that the Cobra was very sluggish, and likely to die. At 12.30, August 8th, the Cobra still alive, and apparently not affected; nearly two days after the experiment.

Experiment No. 12.

At 2 P.M. a large Cobra had about twelve drops of poison, partly his own, partly from another Cobra, injected about eight inches from the head. No effect was apparent when I left at 2.30 P.M. But at 9 P.M. of the same date, Mr. Sceva reported that it died at 7.40 P.M. It became more and more sluggish and lethargic, until it was quite dead, but there was no convulsive movement and tetanic spasm.

It appeared probable, to say the least of it, that death in this case was caused by the poison. It is possible that the needle may have penetrated the lung, or some large internal vessel, and that it caused death either by hæmorrhage or embolism. I had not an opportunity of examining the snake after death, and I cannot therefore regard the experiment as conclusive.

The Cobras used in these experiments were remarkably large and vigorous.

August 8th, 1868.

Experiment No. 13.

Present, Dr. Fayrer, Dr. J. Ewart, Professor of Physiology, and Mr. Sceva, of the Indian Museum.

A full-grown Cobra had about twenty-five drops of fresh Cobra poison, taken from another snake immediately before the experiment was performed, injected by means of the hypodermic syringe into the body, at about eight inches from the head. At 12.50 the snake appeared unaffected in strength and activity, striking at anything that approached it, but it voided a large quantity of light brown fluid per anum.

On August 12th it was still quite well. At 2.30, when I left, it was as well as ever.

EXPERIMENT No. 14.

A half-grown Domestic Fowl was bitten in the thigh by a *Daboia russellii* at 1 P.M. It fell over in violent convulsions as it was placed on the ground, and in less than ninety seconds it was completely dead. This is the most rapid action of snake-poison I have yet seen.

EXPERIMENT No. 15.

About half a drop of venom was with difficulty obtained from the same *Daboia*. These snakes, with their long mobile fangs, do not shed their poison into a shell or spoon covered with a leaf so readily as do the Cobras. This very small quantity of the venom was injected, by means of the hypodermic syringe, into the thigh of a half-grown Fowl. At 12.2 P.M., when placed on the ground, it walked a few steps, as though nothing had happened. In about eighty seconds it suddenly fell backwards, and rolled over in violent convulsions. At 12.4 min. 10 sec., that is, in 130 seconds, it was dead. These two experiments show the terribly deadly nature of the *Daboia's* poison, and also the difference of its mode of action from that of the Cobra. In the one case death is preceded by violent convulsions, in the other by paralysis and lethargy.*

The quantity of the poison inoculated must have been very small in both cases; for the snake did not imbed his fangs or shed a very large amount of poison; and in the second experiment, where the quantity was certainly not more than half a drop, part of that must have been absorbed by the padding of the piston, and a small part lost by adhering to the syringe, or by escape, owing to the piston not being absolutely air-tight. It is also worthy of notice that this is the same snake that has been used in former experiments, and that it has been in a cage now for some weeks. It appears that it and its companion have eaten some small frogs lately.

EXPERIMENT No. 16.

One drop of poison, taken from a Spectacled Cobra, was injected at 1.14 P.M., by means of the hypodermic syringe, into a Fowl's thigh. In fifty seconds it was walking about with that leg partially paralysed. At 1.16 it was pecking at the punctured part; wings drooping. At 1.19 it sat down, head hanging, and supporting itself with the point of the beak resting on the ground, growing gradually more comatose, and generally paralysed. At 1.22 in the same state. One drop of the strychnia solution, about $\frac{1}{60}$th of a grain, was injected into the thigh. At 1.23½ it appeared quite paralysed. When thrown from the hands to the ground, the wings involuntarily performed the movements of flying, and it alighted gently, but lay there perfectly motionless. At 1.25 tetanic twitchings of muscular system were apparent. At 1.26 general muscular quivering, and slight spasmodic extension of the legs. At 1.27½ dead. The contents of the cloaca were evacuated just before death. The action of the strychnia was apparent, but it did not in any way seem to ameliorate the condition induced by the Cobra poison.

The Fowl was larger and stronger than those in the preceding experiments, and a full drop of poison was injected. Death did not occur for 13½ minutes, and the symptoms differed from those in the birds poisoned by the *Daboia*, whose more rapid death was preceded by violent convulsions.

EXPERIMENT No. 17.

A large pale-coloured Cobra had ten or twelve drops of freshly extracted Cobra poison injected into the anterior ventral aspect of the body, about eight inches from the head, at 1.43 P.M. At 2.30 the snake seemed unaffected. On August 12th, at 5 P.M., the snake remained perfectly well.

EXPERIMENT No. 18.

A large pale-coloured Cobra had ten drops, equal to $\frac{1}{6}$th of a grain, of a solution of strychnia injected into the anterior part of its body, near the head, at 1.50 P.M. At 10.52 tetanic twitchings commenced. At 10.53 it became rigidly fixed in undulating curves, with a general lateral curve of its entire length. The hood completely shrivelled up, and the head twisted to one side. In this spastic condition the snake was as rigid as a bar of wood. In 7½ minutes after the strychnia had been injected the Cobra was quite dead; muscular twitchings had passed away just before death; rigidity remained for a short time after it.

The snake, notwithstanding its cold blood, is very susceptible to the poisonous effects of strychnia. The object of the experiment was not only to test the action of strychnia on the snake, but also to show that the method of injecting the poison was an effective one, and that as the snake-poison was injected in precisely the same way, failure in its action could not be attributed to the mode of administration.

EXPERIMENT No. 19.

At 2.6 P.M. a full-grown Cobra had six drops of fresh Cobra poison injected under the skin with the hypodermic syringe, about eight inches from the head. Seven minutes after voided a quantity of dark-coloured fluid from the cloaca. 2.30.—Unaffected.

On the 12th August, at 5 P.M., still quite well.

In these three experiments, 13, 17, 19, the Cobra poison, though fresh and thoroughly well injected into the Cobra, had no effect. Four days after the experiment, the snakes injected were unaffected.

EXPERIMENT No. 20.

Ten drops of carbolic acid were injected, at 2.9 P.M., by means of the hypodermic syringe, into a Cobra, at about eight or ten inches from the head.

In half a minute it was affected with muscular twitchings and tremor; the anterior twelve inches of the snake affected with paralysis agitans. Vermicular movements throughout the body. 2.12.—Universal paralysis. 2.14.—Dead.

The snake is evidently very susceptible to this poison, as it also is to the strychnia. No warm-blooded animal could be more so. This, I think, seems to show that, apart from any immunity peculiar to the reptilian circulation, it has a special toleration of the poison of its own species; for it certainly is not easily, if at all, affected by it, as the majority of the experiments hitherto performed tend to show that neither by inoculation of the poison by the syringe, nor by biting, is any deadly effect produced.

SEVENTH SERIES.

Experiments on the Influence of the Poisons of the Cobra and Daboia.

August 15*th*, 1868.

Present, Dr. Fayrer, Dr. Ewart, Professor of Physiology, and Mr. Sceva, of the Indian Museum.

The object of these experiments was to make careful observations of the symptoms during the action of the poison, to note the pathological changes during life and after death, and the microscopical appearances of the blood of a Mammal in the healthy state, immediately before submitting it to the influence of the snake-poison, and to

* This is not always the case. The Cobra bite also frequently causes convulsions in Fowls.

compare these appearances with those of the blood of the same animal after death from the snake-poison.

The examination was made with the greatest care by Professor Ewart and myself with two microscopes, the power used being $\frac{1}{4}$-$\frac{1}{6}$ of an inch, and they were repeated many times.

Experiment No. 1.

At 11.59 A.M. a small Pariah Dog was bitten in the left hind-leg, just above the carpal joint, by a *Daboia*, the same snake that had been used in former experiments. The Dog was put near the snake, which, though excited and hissing loudly, appeared disinclined to bite: on being irritated, it struck the Dog in the leg as described; the wound bled freely.

It was nearly five minutes before the Dog showed signs of the effects of the poison. He then began to stagger and seemed weak, and as if unable to co-ordinate the muscular movements of the limbs.

At 12.6 he lay down, breathing heavily; at 12.7 he rose and staggered a few steps and vomited. 12.9.—Gradually subsided on to his left hind-quarter; looks vacantly about him, but intelligent when spoken to. There is no indication of any suffering. 12.11.—Walks about when led, but very sluggish, and wants to lie down; weak in the bitten leg. 12.18.—Is walking slowly, staggering in the hind-quarters; has his head depressed, with the neck stretched out. Cold water dashed over the head seemed to rouse him partially. 12.22.—Lies down; weak and exhausted; no convulsions. Looks as though he were going to sleep. Takes no notice when spoken to. 12.42.—Lying down, sluggish, and disinclined to move; can walk a little when roused. 12.46.—Respiration deep. Lying on the right side; appears generally paralysed. 12.57.—Insensible; catching respiration. 1.5 P.M.—Dead.

Died in sixty-six minutes.

Autopsy, soon after death:—Part above the ankle joint, where the animal was bitten, ecchymosed to an extent of two inches, and discoloured by dark bloody fluid. Decomposition commencing. A coagulum corresponded to the points at which the fang penetrated. Blood in femoral vein fluid. Lungs pale and bloodless; completely collapsed when the thorax was opened. Heart's right cavities contained fluid blood. The blood pressed out of the heart and from the great vessels in the thorax was fluid, with no tendency to coagulate. The left side of the heart empty. The liver healthy. Spleen enlarged. Stomach contained a quantity of food. Kidneys healthy. Brain taken out and carefully examined; it was healthy looking and firm, perhaps more anæmic than quite natural. The blood was kept until next day, and there was no coagulation. Up to 1.54 P.M. no rigor mortis.

The blood was most carefully examined before the Dog was bitten, during the operation of the poison, and after death. There was nothing suggestive of the changes described by Professor Halford. The red corpuscles remained altogether unaltered. In one of the examinations after death, a few more of the white corpuscles were seen than we had observed in other specimens, but there was no peculiarity about them; and after most careful and repeated examinations, we could detect nothing that confirmed Dr. Halford's observation.

Experiment No. 2.

A healthy medium-sized Dog was bitten, at 12.40, in the left hind-leg by the *Daboia russellii*. It was not certain that the fangs penetrated. The mouth of the snake was also brought in contact with the right thigh and the lower part of the abdomen, and the fangs were struck lightly into the parts. The snake was one that had been used on former occasions, and was weak, and probably almost exhausted of poison.

1.20 P.M.—Lies down; looks depressed; evidently affected by the poison. 2.3 P.M.—There has been very little change during the last forty minutes. Lies down quietly. There are abdominal contractions, as of irregular action of the diaphragm. 5 P.M.—When roused moves about, but is sluggish and weak. Steps irregularly with a staggering gait, crossing the hind-legs, at other times keeping them wide apart. After walking a little, the steps became more regular and steady. The Dog having usually been fed at this time, food was offered, but he refused it. 6.30.—Quiet; no symptoms of pain or convulsions; perfectly conscious; when spoken to responds readily by raising his head and wagging his tail. Is insensible to pain if irritated in any part of the body. In some of the former experiments it seemed as though anæsthesia were produced in the limb that had been bitten. The Dog gradually drooped, without any sign of pain; no spasm. Bitten at 12.4 P.M. Died at 8.15—eight hours and eleven minutes after being bitten.

In this case death was very slow and painless. It seemed more like a gentle lethargy stealing over the animal, and gradually increasing until death. There was no sign of pain; no convulsions; just before death the defecation was of a muco-sanguinolent character, having been perfectly natural before being bitten. The body was examined soon after death. On raising the integument, it was found that the deepest wounds from the snake's fangs had been received in the middle of the lower part of the abdomen, but they had not penetrated deeper than the adipose tissue. Several small punctures (four or five) were found in the side of the abdomen and in the inner part of the thigh.

The post-mortem appearances of the thoracic and abdominal cavities were exactly the same as in the former case, except that the spleen was healthy in this case.

The blood was watched for fourteen hours, and it did not coagulate; and, being carefully examined under the microscope, presented no change from the normal condition.

The results of these experiments, which were conducted with great care and every precaution to exclude sources of error, may, I think, be accepted as almost conclusive that death is caused by the action of the poison on the nerve centres generally, and not by its operation on any special one. The condition of the thoracic viscera proves that it is not due to pulmonary congestion or asphyxia. The fluid state of the blood, although no change in its corpuscular elements is appreciable, tends to show that it is the direct channel through which the nerve centres are injured. In both these cases death took place slowly, giving ample time for any changes, such as described by Dr. Halford, to take place. It is worthy of notice that in both cases there was absence of any convulsions or tetanic spasms. This may be attributed to the animals having received a smaller dose of the poison, and that administered by comparatively exhausted snakes. In other cases, when the animal bitten was smaller, and the *Daboias* were more vigorous, the effect in producing convulsions was marked, and death took place more rapidly. Where the poison operates slowly and feebly, as in these cases, there is very little, if any, difference in the symptoms from those produced by the Cobra poison administered under the same conditions.

August 17th, 1868.

Experiment No. 3.

A half-grown Pig was placed in a large box with a full-grown Cobra, of the variety called by the natives "Keautiah." The snake had been used before, had been some time in confinement, had probably not eaten for some time, and consequently might be expected to be weak and comparatively feebly poisonous. The snake seemed indisposed to bite until irritated, and the Pig stepped on him, when he seized it by the right forefoot, just above the hoof, and drew blood. The Pig lay down at once, appeared very much frightened; the snake also appeared terrified by the Pig, and lay for a moment, as though he were seriously injured. The Pig made no attempt either to attack the snake or defend himself; he merely tried to get out of the way. The snake bit at 11.55 A.M., and as the Pig was lying down, the bitten leg was drawn up in a jerking and convulsive manner. 11.59.—Got up and ran about the room; the bitten limb evidently weak. Lay down again; right fore-leg twitching in a convulsive manner; is generally restless. 12.—Rose and lay down again. The bitten leg always convulsed in lying down; places it under its body, as though to prevent the involuntary movement; working the mouth; making efforts to retch. 12.3.—Roused up; squealing lustily; quite able to walk when roused, but when left to himself lies down; eyelids droop, and looks sleepy. 12.5.—Roused; rests himself against the wall. 12.6.—Resists efforts to rouse him. 12.10.—Lying down; bitten leg uneasy, but not so much convulsed as at first. When roused he walks; appears to be much weaker. 12.17.—Lying in the corner of the room with his left side against the wall. Twitching occasionally in the bitten limb. Eyelids closed occasionally. One can now see that he has been bitten just above the hoof posteriorly. 12.25.—Can use the limb; holds it up when he stops; limb convulsed at longer intervals. 12.28.—Lies down; some slight general uneasiness. Convulsive twitching affected posterior extremity. 12.30.—Fore-leg put forward; then convulsion more evident. When roused, walks; holds up the limb as if from pain in pressing it on the ground; puts it down when pushed. 12.45.—Roused up. Twitching. Lies down. 1 P.M.—Unless roused, lies down against the wall. Twitching now in right hind-leg. 1.32.—Pig bitten again by a new and fresh Cobra in the left thigh and in the snout. 1.35.—Twitching in the bitten leg. 1.40.—Gets up when roused; still twitching in hind-leg. 2.7.—Good deal of twitching in hind-leg; twitching in rapid succession; it sometimes affects corresponding anterior extremity. Twitching also of the facial muscles and of the orbiculares palpebrarum. Lying flat on his side with his legs stretched out. 2.15.—Roused him up; great loss of nervous and muscular power. When he got up, he did so with much difficulty; propped himself up against the wall; staggered and fell down. 2.25.—Very lethargic; cannot stand; when placed on his legs, he falls down; same debility characterizing general muscular system noticed in those muscles which affect the organs of *speech*. His squeal is now a mere whine. He is anæmic; conjunctivæ pallid. The right fore-leg first bitten is ecchymosed much up to the elbow-joint. Considerable twitching in muscles of the face, showing that the poison has affected this part in the same way as it has the muscles of the fore and hind-legs. 2.40.—Respiration catching; gasping. Convulsed in the posterior extremities; lips, mouth, and conjunctivæ pallid; eyes fixed; insensible to light; pupils dilated; irides unacted upon by light; almost comatose. Bitten first at 11.53. Bitten second time at 1.32 P.M. Died 2.50, nearly three hours after being first bitten.

Autopsy.—Blood in sinuses of the brain, as in the whole venous system up to the right auricle and ventricle, which were distended with blood. Sections of brain, thalamus, and corpus striatum and medulla oblongata pallid in the extreme; scarcely a vascular point to be seen. Lungs quite collapsed and anæmic; left ventricle and auricle empty. Liver, kidneys, &c., healthy.

Wounds.— Right fore-foot bitten at 11.53 A.M., and leg greatly ecchymosed; coagulum marks the entry of the fang. Tissues discoloured from rapid death (local) and decomposition. Right hind-leg bitten at 1.32 P.M.; less ecchymosed; mark of fang indicated by a point of coagulum of a dark colour. Bite on right ear ecchymosed, and snout, where he was also bitten.

Blood coagulated in all the veins after being opened for an hour; coagulum firm. Microscopical examination of blood shows nothing unnatural, excepting perhaps a slowness of the red globules to run into masses like piled coin in rouleaux.

The fact that this Pig was twice severely bitten, and that death did not occur for nearly three hours, seems to show that the animal is not very susceptible. A large Dog would probably have died in less than half an hour.

It is true that the first Cobra, though a large and powerful one, was probably somewhat exhausted, but the second was perfectly fresh, and had only that morning been brought in by the snake-catcher, freshly caught.

Experiment No. 4.

At 12.53 a small "Dhamin" (*Ptyas mucosus*) was bitten by a fresh Cobra about five feet in length. 12.59.—"Dhamin" weak and sluggish in his movements. 1.3.—Bitten again by the same snake. On the floor, moves slowly and with difficulty; growing manifestly weak. 1.12.—Gasping for breath; very low; voluntary muscular power gone. Still, when roused, can move and raise his head, as if he had been roused from a state of overpowering nervous oppression. Breathes slowly and imperfectly; does not half fill his lungs. Bitten at 12.53. Died at 1.14 P.M. Dead in twenty-one minutes.

This is further proof of the deadly action of the poison on innocuous snakes.

Experiment No. 5.

At 12.55 P.M. a large Cobra was bitten by a full-grown, freshly caught Cobra; they were both of one variety, that marked with one ocellus in the hood, the "Keautiah" of the snake-catchers. The scales were scraped off, and the snake was made to imbed his fangs deeply in two different places about ten inches from the head. There could be no doubt of the penetration, or of the injection, of a large quantity of poison. At 12.59 five drops of Cobra poison, taken from the snake, were injected by means of the hypodermic syringe into the muscles of the Cobra's back. 1.30.—No effect produced; the Cobra is as lively as ever. 1.45.—Still unaffected. 4.30.—Still unaffected.

August 18th, 5 P.M.—The snake is as well as ever.

This experiment goes far to prove the immunity of the Cobra from the noxious effects of the poison of its own species.

Experiment No. 6.

1.20 P.M.—Civet Cat (*Viverra malaccensis*) bitten by a *Daboia*. The snake struck in more than one place. 1.25.—Appears paralysed. 1.26.—Appears almost dead. 1.30.—Still breathing imperfectly; stretches his legs as if from spasms. 1.32.—Got up on his fore-legs and vomited; lying down exhausted. 1.37.—When roused he seized a stick, but is evidently half paralysed in the hind-quarter; lies down again on left side. 1.40.—Gets up again when irritated, breathes hurriedly, and lies down at once. Evidently very drowsy and much exhausted. 1.47.—Tries to get up of his own accord; finds he cannot; rolls over on other side; right hind-leg paralysed. Continues restless and endeavouring to move, and has again succeeded in changing his position. 1.57.—Lying flat on side with all his legs stretched out. Can be roused, but his hinder extremities still paralysed, and he does not give fight as before. Is uneasy and restless. 2.12.—Roused; walks about much better, but his right hind-leg is very weak; quite paralysed. Put into his cage; gave much more fight. 2.30.—Seems reviving, but he is restless and manifestly uncomfortable; lying down, and at full stretch, on side. 4.15.—Purged freely; very low; evidently at the point of death. 4.25.—Convulsive movements for two or three minutes; stretching the limbs, &c. 4.36.—Dead. Body examined, showed the animal to have been bitten on the nose, on the side of the head (in the temporal muscle), and in the thigh.

The post-mortem appearances of the viscera were like those in other animals.

This Viper was the same that had been frequently used in other experiments before described, and must have been considerably weakened. The deadly nature of the snake is manifest from this continued power of inflicting mortal wounds, and it is probable that it has the power of rapidly secreting fresh poison. It is regarded with great dread by the snake-catchers, and evidently with good reason.

EIGHTH SERIES.

Experiments on the Influence of the Poisons of the Daboia, Cobra, and Ophiophagus.

September 11*th*, 1868.

I am indebted to Messrs. Greenhill and Rutherford, Veterinary Surgeons, for the opportunity of making the following experiments. The Horses experimented on had been condemned to be destroyed for the disease partial paraplegia, ("gone in the loins"), and were placed at my disposal by the above gentlemen, for whose valuable aid in noting the symptoms and recording the pathological conditions I am under much obligation. The disease, though incapacitating the animal for work, is not such as to reduce his strength so much as to vitiate the evidence derived from the effects upon him of the poison; and I believe these experiments may be accepted as fair illustrations of the action of snake-poison on the larger animals. The subjects experimented on were a stud-bred Mare about 14 hands 3 inches high and aged twenty-seven years, suffering from partial paraplegia, and an Australian Horse, 15 hands 1 inch, nine years old, a powerful animal, and in good condition, though also paraplegic. The Mare succumbed in an hour and twenty minutes from the effects of the bite of a large Cobra; whilst the stronger and younger Horse survived the bite of a powerful, fresh, and full-grown *Daboia* nearly twelve hours.

The difference in the effects of the poison of the *Daboia* and Cobra in these two cases is very remarkable, not only as to the duration of life in the animals bitten, but also in the pathological conditions before and after death.

The Mare bitten by the Cobra was rapidly affected—staggered, became exhausted, and died in less than an hour and a half. The post-mortem examination showed distinct rigor mortis, firm coagulation of the blood; the heart and large vessels, aorta as well as venæ cavæ, distended by firm ante- and post-mortem coagula. The lungs were very slightly congested, frothy when cut into, and on the anterior surface rather pale and bloodless than the reverse—whilst all the abdominal viscera were equally free from congestion. The Horse bitten by the *Daboia*, on the other hand, was affected very slowly, and seemed to doze his life away until just at the last, when a few unconscious plunges terminated his existence; the post-mortem in this case showed less cadaveric rigidity, fluid blood, empty cardiac cavities, and lungs and other viscera congested.

But it is to be noted that the Cobra bit more vigorously, forced his fangs deeper, and had to deal with a more feeble animal than the *Daboia*, who bit a more powerful and healthy Horse, and did not insert his teeth with such vigour as the Cobra. The snakes were both fresh and full-grown, and their terrible power was strikingly illustrated by the death of these two Horses.

The difference observed in the pathological appearances, and state of the blood after death, may probably be accounted for by the greater rapidity of death in one case, rather than by any essential difference in the nature of the action of the poisons. The Mare bitten by the Cobra died in eighty minutes, and after death the blood coagulated firmly, and was found distending the heart and great vessels with firm coagula. Death was probably caused by the rapid effects of the poison on the nerve centres, before the blood had time to be thoroughly devitalized. In the other case, where death did not occur for nearly twelve hours, there was no coagulation either in or out of the heart or vessels; sufficient time had elapsed to allow the blood to be thus thoroughly changed. I am inclined to believe that if death were protracted after a Cobra bite, the condition of the blood would be as it was in the case of the *Daboia* bite.

EXPERIMENT No. 1.

A bay Australian Gelding—15 hands 1 inch high, nine years old, and partially paraplegic, but otherwise a strong, well-conditioned Horse; pulse 42, soft; respiration 48 per minute—was bitten by a full-grown fresh *Daboia russellii* near the lower part of the neck, *over* the track of the right jugular.* The snake struck vigorously and drew blood freely. The time was 12.15.

12.19.—Respiration 58 (gone up 10): pulse still 42. 12.30. —Respiration 64; pulse now 64. The puncture swollen. 12.52.—Lies down; looks languid; pulse 80 and weak. 1.1.— Twitching of head to the near side; Horse still down and very dull. Lower lip pendulous; muzzle resting on the ground; sight and hearing natural. 1.5.—A spasmodic twitch of the muscles of the neck; patches of urticaria, about the size of a shilling, making their appearance on the abdominal surface. 1.9.—Pulse 70, intermittent. 1.6.—Pulse 76; respirations 52. Can rise from the recumbent posture without much effort. 3.—Pulse 80, tremulous and intermittent; Horse looks dull and sleepy; yawning, getting up, and lying down again very frequently, as in colic. 4.30.—Pulse 67, weak and intermittent; breathing hurried; Horse standing, but very dull; wound swollen, and very painful to the touch; mucous membrane of mouth pallid; ears and legs cold; body moderately warm; when roused is quite sensible. 6.—Horse lying down, breathing heavily; pulse almost imperceptible at the jaw, 60; fugitive colic pains. 9.30.—Breathing stertorous and very heavy; body and extremities cold; pulse imperceptible; Horse drank a little water, but is evidently sinking; region of wound much swollen and very painful; purging thin watery fæces (they were quite natural when the Horse was bitten). 11.45.—Down and struggling; getting up and moving to and fro in the loose box restlessly; then lying down again and struggling with all four legs; straining and passing small quantities of watery fæces with flatus. 12.—Dead. Bitten at 12.15. Died at 12, midnight—*i.e.*, in eleven hours and three-quarters.

Post-mortem twelve hours after death.—Cadaveric rigidity moderate; abdomen distended, and mucous membrane of rectum partially congested and swollen; vicinity of wound blackened by infiltrated blood in the cellular tissue. Muscles all discoloured, and general venous congestion apparent.

Heart, right auricle empty; right ventricle contained a little frothy blood; left auricle and ventricle both empty; substance of heart firm, but presents numerous small ecchymosed spots. Larger blood-vessels as usual. Blood in them fluid. Lungs congested. Liver and spleen congested. Mucous surface of intestines in a highly irritable state, congested and thickened. Other viscera healthy.

EXPERIMENT No. 2.

A stud-bred Mare, about 14 hands 3 inches high, aged twenty-seven, suffering from partial paraplegia and emphysema of lungs, but otherwise strong, was bitten at 12.22 in the integument of root of the neck on the right side, and just above the right nostril, by a full-grown, fresh, and vigorous Cobra (*Naja tripudians*). The punctures bled freely. Before being bitten the pulse was 57, respirations 36. 12.26.—Pulse 60; restless; moves the

* The vein was not penetrated.

head about in an uneasy manner. 12.35.—Looks anxious and restless; leans hind-quarter against the wall; twitchings of nostrils. Eyes staring; tapetum lucidum shining brilliantly; ears retracted; tail raised. 12.43.—Staggering; keeps the hind-quarter resting against the wall, as though to prevent falling; staring, anxious eye. Patches of urticaria rapidly breaking out over the body. 12.44.—Pulse 64, weary. Spasmodic twitching of the pectoral muscles; staggers much in the hind-quarters. 12.53. — Straining, but nothing passed; so restless now that the respiration cannot be counted; the wound is swollen and painful; urticaria profuse; drinks freely of cold water; eats hay. 12.59.—Looks sleepy; staggering; left off eating. 1.12.—Same state; right fore-leg twitching in a spasmodic manner. 1.20.—Intense restlessness; staggering; tremulous action throughout the whole muscular system. 1.27. —Drinks water freely; tries to move about in the loose box, but staggers so much that it keeps on its legs with difficulty. The right side of the upper lip seems paralysed. Pawing restlessly with right fore-foot. 1.32.—Lies down. 1.36.— Peculiar spasmodic action of panniculus carnosus. The Horse is evidently dying; convulsive plunging of all four legs. Head drawn towards the chest. (This, Mr. R. says, is very unusual.) 1.42. — Muscular twitching over the whole body. 1.43.— Dead. Bitten at 12.22. Died at 1.42—*i.e.*, in one hour and twenty minutes.

Post-mortem one hour and a half after death: — Lungs, slight hypostatic congestion; surface, natural colour. Heart.— Cardiac cavities distended with firm coagula. The clots were very firm, and were partially decolorized, probably indicating their ante-mortem origin. The great venous and arterial trunks, especially the aorta and venæ cavæ, plugged with firm coagula; blood that was removed from the jugular vein found after death coagulated firmly. Blood examined under microscope, with No. 3 eye-piece, ¼-inch object-glass, Nachet, was natural; no change in the corpuscles. The liver and spleen were normal, not in the least congested. There was rigor mortis. I examined the blood of the Horse killed by the *Daboia* about eighteen hours after death; it was dark and perfectly fluid; no coagulum had formed. On placing a drop of it under the microscope, the field was filled with rhomboidal tabular and acicular crystals probably of hæmato-crystallin, in great abundance. The corpuscles appeared to have been dissolved or disorganized, and the few that I could find after repeated examinations were apparently the ordinary blood corpuscles shrivelled and partially broken down. The weather being hot and damp, the blood had probably become somewhat decomposed, and therefore I am unable, beyond describing the crystals, to give a very reliable account of the changes that had occurred. It appears to me it is in a case like this, where death was protracted, that if any structural changes take place in the corpuscles, one should find them. I was unable to detect any such changes; but as the examination was necessarily somewhat imperfect, I cannot say certainly, in this case, that they did not really occur. It was remarked just before and after death, that there was a peculiar pallor of the mucous membrane of the mouth. The relative disproportions between the pulse and respiration are accounted for by a disordered condition of the pulmonary air cells known in stable language as "broken-winded," which was present to a certain extent in both these animals.

September 26th, 1868.

Experiment No. 3.

Present, Dr. Fayrer, Professor Partridge, and Mr. Sceva.

At 12 a *Daboia,* two-thirds grown, was bitten in three places in the thoracic region, from a foot to six inches from the head, by a full-grown, fresh, and vigorous Cobra. There could be no doubt that this snake was well bitten; the Cobra imbedded his fangs viciously, and kept his hold for some time. There were blood marks after each bite. 12.55.—No effect. 2.2 P.M.—No effect. 5.—The *Daboia* is apparently unaffected.

September 27th, 10 A.M.—No change.

28th, 2 P.M.—No change.

30th.—No change.

October 2nd.—Still alive and well.

Experiment No. 4.

A full-grown Cobra was bitten by another full-grown, fresh, and vigorous Cobra in the body in two places, about six inches from the head, and also in the mouth. They both bit each other freely in this situation—blood was drawn by the bites— at 12 o'clock. 12.55.—No effect. 2.2 P.M.—No effect. 5.— Both perfectly well.

September 27th, 10 A.M.—No change.

28th, 2 P.M.—No change.

30th, noon.—No change.

October 2nd, noon.—No change.

Experiment No. 5.

A large black Cobra was bitten about 12 o'clock in the body in two places, a foot and six inches from the head, and also on the head, by a large and vicious *Daboia;* blood was slightly drawn. There could be no doubt that the fangs had penetrated, or that the poison was inoculated. 12.55.—No effect. 2.2 P.M.—No effect. 5.—No effect.

September 27th, 10 A.M.—No change.

28th, 2 P.M.—No change.

30th, noon.—No change.

October 2nd, noon.—No change.

Experiment No. 6.

A Domestic Fowl was bitten in the thigh by a *Daboia* at 12.15. It was convulsed immediately, and quite dead at 12.16.40. Dead in 100 seconds. The blood coagulated after death.

Experiment No. 7.

A hypodermic syringe filled with about thirty drops of the blood, taken from the above Fowl immediately after death, was injected into the thigh of another Fowl at 12.20. It walked about; was soon rather lame in the injected leg; gradually became sluggish; drooped; could walk if roused, but remained quietly crouching. It gradually drooped and died at 4.10 P.M.

Experiment No. 8.

Mr. Sceva injected the blood of the Fowl (Experiment No. 7) into another Fowl's thigh at 4 P.M.

September 27th, 10 A.M.—Fowl still alive.

September 28th, 2 P.M.—The Fowl is alive and apparently well, excepting slight lameness in the injected leg.

30th, noon.—It is still alive. There has evidently been no effect produced.

October 2nd.—The Fowl recovered.

Experiment No. 9.

A Domestic Fowl was bitten by a large Cobra in the thigh at 12.19.5, and fell into convulsions immediately, and was dead in fifty seconds. Blood coagulated after death.

Experiment No. 10.

A hypodermic syringeful of the blood of the Fowl bitten by the Cobra in Experiment No. 9, taken from the heart, was injected into a Fowl's thigh at 12.29. 12.32.—Sluggish; lame in punctured leg. 12.47.—Walks about, but is drowsy. 1.24 P.M.—In much the same sluggish state; another syringeful of the serum that had separated in the clotting of the same blood (that of No. 9) was again injected into the Fowl's thigh. 1.52.—

Lying down, resting its beak on the ground; very drowsy and sluggish. 2.2.—Cannot be roused. Died shortly after, at 3.16 P.M.

EXPERIMENT No. 11.

A Fowl bitten in the thigh at 12.36 by the *Daboia* that had bitten the Cobra. It walked about immediately after with slight muscular twitching. 12.36.45. — Standing with the lame leg drawn up. 12.40.—Pecking at food. Walks, but staggers slightly. 12.41.—Bitten again in the thigh by the same snake, which is evidently much exhausted. 12.43.—No very apparent effect. 12.43.33.—Fell over in convulsions. 12.44.15.—Dead.

This experiment shows that the snake was much exhausted by previous biting.

EXPERIMENT No. 12.

A Fowl was placed near a fresh *Daboia*,* free on the ground. The snake, on being irritated, struck the Fowl somewhere about the neck at 12.49. It fell into convulsions immediately, and was dead at 12.49.45, that is, it was completely dead in forty-five seconds.

This experiment shows the terribly deadly nature of the *Daboia's* poison.

EXPERIMENT No. 13.

A Cobra was injected at 1 P.M. with fifteen drops of *his own* poison; the syringe was inserted about eight inches from the head. Ten minutes after there was no effect. At 5 P.M. the snake was still unaffected.

September 27th, 10 A.M.—No effect.

September 30th, noon.—No effect.

This experiment seems to show that the Cobra is not poisoned by his own venom.

October 2nd.—Seems sluggish, but after so long an interval it may be from other causes.

EXPERIMENT No. 14.

Five drops of Cobra poison, diluted with about ten drops of water, were injected with the hypodermic syringe into the inner side of a Cat's thigh at 1.7.45 P.M. At 1.12 restless; muscular twitchings; mewing loudly. 1.13. — Partially paralysed; dragging the punctured leg; breathing very much hurried. As the Cat crouches on the ground the hind-quarters fall over as though paralysed. 1.14.—Tries to walk; drags the hind-leg. 1.56.—Sluggish; apparently in no pain; does not move, even when roused.

[*Mr. Sceva reports after this.*]

2.20.—Lying on its side, with hind-leg extended; profuse flow of saliva from the mouth and symptoms of nausea. Frequent evacuation of thin fæcal matter. 2.30.—Raised the head and fore part of the body; dragging the hind limbs for a short distance on the floor. 3.—Attempted to get up again, but was unable to do so. 3.5.—Died, slightly convulsed. The blood coagulated firmly after death. It was examined by Professor Partridge and myself, and no change from the normal structure could be made out. The corpuscles, red and white, were unchanged, excepting that some of the red ones were shrivelled. The quantity of poison used was only five drops, and that was mixed with water. It was injected at 1.7.45 P.M.; the Cat died at 3.5 P.M., rather less than two hours.

It is evident from this that the poison does not suffer by mixture with water.

EXPERIMENT No. 15.

A large Cobra was injected at 1.33 P.M. with five drops of the solution of strychnia (one grain to a drachm), near the head. It was convulsed and powerless at 1.36. At 1.40 muscular tetanic twitchings. 1.42.—Dead.

This experiment shows that a poison is rapidly effective in the snake when inoculated into the circulation.

EXPERIMENT No. 16.

A Cobra was injected with about fifteen drops of the poison of another fresh and vigorous Cobra at 1.43 P.M. The poison was carefully injected with the hypodermic syringe about eight inches from the head. The Cobra inoculated was of the pale, yellowish-coloured variety, with a single ocellus on the hood. It was very active and vicious, the most so of any I have seen. It was sent to me a short time ago by the police authorities; having been captured after biting a native lad in a boat, who died, it is said, within an hour after being bitten. At 2.2 P.M. and 5 P.M. not affected; as vicious and active as ever.

At 10 A.M. of September 27th still unaffected.

September 30th, noon.—Still unaffected.

October 2nd.—Still quite well.

September 28th.

EXPERIMENT No. 17.

Present, Dr. Fayrer and Mr. Sceva.

At 1.17 P.M. a Fowl, half-grown, was bitten in the thigh by a *Daboia;* convulsed immediately, and dead in thirty-five seconds.

EXPERIMENT No. 18.

Blood drawn from the heart of the Fowl in Experiment No. 17 (two hypodermic syringefuls), about a drachm, was injected into the thigh of another half-grown Fowl at 1.22 P.M.

7.15.—No effect of the poison perceptible as yet.

September 29th, 6 A.M. — Crouching; profoundly drowsy. Head resting on beak; falls over as if the bird had gone off into a sound sleep; starts up and falls over again, like a creature that cannot keep awake. In this state it remained, got more drowsy, and died at 2.40 P.M.

September 29th.

EXPERIMENT No. 19.

At 2.50 P.M. a half-grown Chicken was injected in the thigh with ten drops of the blood of the Chicken of Experiment No. 18.

September 30th, 2 P.M.—Appears to be slightly affected; feathers ruffled; tail depressed; not so active as it was.

October 2nd.—It recovered, having been only very slightly affected.

September 28th.

EXPERIMENT No. 20.

A half-grown Fowl was bitten in the thigh at 12.15 A.M. by a very vicious and active Cobra (one that had killed a child, and was itself the subject of experiment on the 26th). The Fowl became convulsed immediately, and was quite dead in about thirty-four seconds. The muscles generally and heart were found to be without any irritability in a few minutes after death. The blood coagulated firmly.

EXPERIMENT No. 21.

Two syringefuls of the blood of the Fowl in Experiment No. 20 were injected into the thigh of a full-grown and strong Fowl at 12.25 A.M. 12.27.—It seemed much excited; this passed off, and at 1.26 P.M. it seemed very little affected, except that it was purged. 2 P.M.—Appears

* As I have said in the former part of this work (p. 15) the *Daboia* is naturally very sluggish, and not aggressive, unless irritated, when it strikes with great rapidity and deadly precision.

Mr. W. Blanford tells me of an instance where a *Daboia* was carried home by a gentleman who thought he had got a young Python. It did him no injury, and he only became aware of the danger he had escaped by the snake striking at and killing a dog that approached too near it.

drowsy. 2.30.—Effects of the poison are manifest; wings drooping. It crouches, resting the point of the beak on the ground. 3.—Crouching on the ground; body inclined to one side. One leg partly extended, with wing extended over it. 3.30.—Lying down, with wings partially extended; a small quantity of liquid running from the beak. Head lying on the ground; nearly insensible. 3.56.—Dead.

Experiment No. 22.

About twenty-five drops of blood, taken from the heart of the Fowl of Experiment No. 21, were injected into the thigh of a half-grown Chicken at 3.56 p.m. At 7.15 p.m. no change, except slight lameness from the puncture in the leg.

September 29th.—No change; no symptom of being affected by the poison.

September 30th, 2 p.m.—Chicken remains unaffected.

October 2nd.—Chicken well.

After September 29th the Chicken did not seem to be affected in any way by the injection until October 5th, when it appeared weak, and passed the latter part of the day with its head partly under its wing. It had eaten heartily during the time since September 29th, and appeared as lively as the other chickens that were kept in the room with it. It died on the following day, October 6th, and on examining the body it was found to be greatly emaciated. No trace of any other injury or disease, except the poisoning of the blood, could be discovered.

September 29th.

Experiment No. 23.

An *Ophiophagus elaps*, about eight feet long, that had been deprived of its fangs by the snake-men, was made to shed its poison by squeezing the jaws; a drop or two of clear, yellow, viscid fluid exuded. This, diluted with water, was inoculated into a Fowl's thigh, a puncture was first made with a lancet, and the poison was introduced with an ordinary quill pen. For the first two or three minutes no apparent effect was produced: the bird walked about as usual. It then began to look uncomfortable; stood still; seemed dazed; sat down and soon crouched itself together; began to droop, to nod its head and rest its beak on the ground. This state of drowsiness gradually increased; it seemed to be profoundly sleepy, attempting to rouse itself with a start, and falling off again into a profound state of narcotism. At 12.30 it was almost unconscious, and could not rise on its legs; when roused, opened its eyes, made an attempt to raise the head, which fell over again. Its condition seemed to be in all respects one of profound narcotism. 12.37.—A few convulsive movements only indicate life. 12.40.—Still a few convulsive movements and stretching of the neck. 12.46.—Dead. The wound much discoloured and ecchymosed; emphysema of the areolar tissue about it. The blood clotted firmly after death. At 1.40 p.m. some of the blood (half a syringeful, fifteen drops) was injected into the thigh of another Fowl.

September 30th, 2 p.m.—More than twenty-four hours, and the Fowl is not affected: eats heartily; looks bright and active. The quantity of blood injected was very small.

October 2nd.—Quite well.

This, imperfect as it was, was the first opportunity I had of experimenting with the poison of this snake; it is rare, and the snake-catchers had not been able to procure me a fresh and wild specimen. The snake experimented with had been for some time in the hands of the snake-catcher. The man who brought it had borrowed it from a friend, and he was unable to say how long it had been in captivity, or where it had been caught. I may remind the reader that the *Ophiophagus elaps* is the largest kind of poisonous colubrine snake, and a very formidable and terrible creature it is. In general form it resembles the Cobra, having the head and hood similarly shaped. Its fangs are like those of the Cobra, and its venom is said to be equally deadly in proportion to its size. It is very active and aggressive, has great power of turning itself in a short space on its own body, and when about to attack, assumes the same erect and menacing attitude as the Cobra.

In colour it differs from the Cobra, being of an olive-green and marked with triangular bars of white edged with black, which are very conspicuous on the hood and tail. The hood is proportionately not so large as in the Cobra, and there are other differences which I need not repeat here. It attains to a great size, twelve feet or even more, and is therefore probably one of, if not the largest poisonous snakes known. There is only one species of the genus, which has received its name from its habit of feeding on other snakes.

October 2nd, 1868.

Experiment No. 24.

Present, Dr. Fayrer and Mr. Sceva.

The *Ophiophagus elaps*, mentioned in Experiment No. 23, September 29th, that had been deprived of its fangs, was made to shed its poison by squeezing the poison glands; a drop or two only could be obtained, so much having been secreted in four days. It had the same appearance as on the first occasion. This, diluted with an equal quantity of water, was injected with the hypodermic syringe into a Fowl's thigh at 12.30 a.m. The Fowl was not immediately affected, and being carelessly placed near an open door, it made its escape into a drain, in which, as it did not emerge, I presume it died. The opportunity of watching the effects of the poison was lost; but the experiment is interesting, as it shows that the poison is secreted, although the poison fangs are removed, and it shows the rate at which it was secreted, about two drops in four days. The snake had not been fed, but on this occasion it was fed with a *Passerita mycterizans* (a Green Whip-snake), that was poisoned by a Cobra, *vide* Experiment No. 25. The snake-man put the head of the dead snake into the *Ophiophagus*' mouth; it seemed delighted to have it, and proceeded to swallow it forthwith, gradually drawing it into its gullet by alternate lateral movements of the lower maxillary bones. The process of swallowing occupied about five minutes, during which the *Ophiophagus* moved slowly about with the anterior part of his body raised and his hood distended, the *Passerita* hanging out of its mouth. The last few inches of the tail were swallowed more slowly than the rest.

A second *Passerita* being offered shortly after was declined, and its head ejected from its mouth.

Experiment No. 25.

A Green Whip-snake, more than three feet long (*Passerita mycterizans*), was bitten by a Cobra about ten inches from the head, at 12.37 a.m. At 12.38, sluggish; moves less actively; gapes, keeping the mouth wide open. 12.39.—Almost paralysed; mouth now closed; head lying on the side. The body is swollen where bitten. 12.40.—Dead. Death was very rapid; a peculiarly active and vigorous though innocuous snake killed in two minutes by the poison of the Cobra.

Experiment No. 26.

At 12.48 p.m. a Cobra bit a Cobra in three places near the head. They were both vigorous, fresh, and full-grown. 1.10 p.m. — Appears rather sluggish. At 1.11 this bitten Cobra bit a Fowl in the thigh; it died in four minutes.* I should note that it had been partially exhausted by biting the

---

* *Vide* Experiment No. 30.

Passerita, which it killed in two minutes. 1.16. — Appears rather sluggish as it lies on the floor. At 1.35 it appears in its natural state; raises its head, expands the hood, and strikes when threatened. At 1.43 it was bitten severely in the body, about a foot from the head, by a *Daboia*, one of those that have been some time in confinement. At 1.47 it appeared to be affected; was sluggish, and lay with its hood shrunken and its skin shrivelled. It is possible that in presenting it to the *Daboia* to be bitten it may have been squeezed, but it did not appear so. It remained in this sluggish state, and was dead at 4.10 P.M.

EXPERIMENT No. 27.

A *Passerita mycterizans* (Green Whip-snake) rather smaller than the former one, was bitten in the body at 1.40 by a *Daboia*. At 1.45 P.M. almost powerless. It gradually became more and more exhausted, gaped like the one bitten by the Cobra, and was dead at 2.2 P.M., or in seventeen minutes. The *Daboia* was one of those long in confinement, and had no doubt become exhausted.

EXPERIMENT No. 28.

A large black Cobra bitten in the body by a *Daboia* at 1.52 P.M., at about a foot from the head. At 2.20 no change.

October 3rd, 6 A.M.—No change.

EXPERIMENT No. 29.

A full-grown Cobra bitten by a *Daboia* in the body at 2.4 P.M. October 2nd. At 2.20 no change.

Died at 10.30, October 4th.

EXPERIMENT No. 30.

A half-grown Fowl was bitten in the thigh by a Cobra at 1.11 P.M. At 1.11.45 it crouched, drooped its wings, rose, staggered, and dropped down. At 1.13 drooped its wings; rested on its breast, with the point of its beak on the ground. 1.14. — Convulsed and dying. 1.15. — Dead. Died in four minutes.

The Cobra was not quite fresh; it had bitten the *Passerita*, and had itself been bitten by another Cobra before biting the Fowl.

EXPERIMENT No. 31.

At 1.25 about four drops of the blood of the above Fowl (Experiment No. 30) were injected into the hind-quarters of a *Sorex cærulescens* (Musk Rat). At 1.35 eating a portion of the dead Fowl, apparently not affected, unless it may be perhaps rather sluggish.

At 5.30 A.M. of October 3rd the Musk Rat was found dead; it appeared to have been dead two or three hours; no sign of any injury, but the syringe puncture in the thigh apparent.

The evidence of Experiments Nos. 3, 4, 5, 13, 16, 28 went to show that the Cobra and the *Daboia* are not affected by each other or by their own poison.

The Experiments Nos. 26, 29, on the other hand, seemed to prove that the Cobra succumbs to the *Daboia*. The subject was still, therefore, not set at rest, and more experiments were required to decide it.

There is abundant evidence to prove that the innocuous are rapidly affected by the venomous snakes, and that this is the case may be considered as decided, though no doubt the poison tells less rapidly or fatally on them than on warm-blooded animals.

That the venomous snakes themselves are affected by other poisons, is proved by the rapidity with which they succumb to strychnia and carbolic acid. The weight of evidence so far would show that the venomous snakes are, if not proof against, at least not readily affected by each other's poison.

NINTH SERIES.

Experiments on the Influence of the Poison of the Cobra, Bungarus fasciatus, and Daboia on Warm-blooded, Cold-blooded, and Invertebrate Animals.

October 15*th*, 1868.

Present, Dr. Fayrer and Mr. Sceva.

EXPERIMENT No. 1.

A Fish (*Ophiocephalus marulius*), about ten inches in length, was bitten by a fresh Cobra at 11.20 A.M. in two places, on the dorsal and ventral surfaces. 11.22.—The Fish turned over on its side in the water. 11.23.—Struggling and plunging violently in the water. 11.25.—Turned over on its side. 11.26.—On being roused plunges violently. 11.40.—Dead. Bitten at 11.20. Died at 11.40. Dead in twenty minutes.

EXPERIMENT No. 2.

A large Snail (*Achatina fulica*) was bitten at 11.28 by a Cobra; it immediately withdrew itself within its shell. 11.45.—In order to examine its condition the shell was broken; it still continued to contract. 12.—No contraction; all irritability seems extinct. Dead.

EXPERIMENT No. 3.

Two Snails of equal size—shells previously broken; one was bitten by a Cobra at 12.28. It immediately shrank and contracted itself. The other Snail was not bitten, and was kept for comparison. 12.40.—Irritability of the bitten Snail much diminished. The bitten Snail seemed to lose its vitality much sooner than the uninjured one; but the precise time when irritability ceased was not noted.

These were the only invertebrate animals I could procure on this occasion. The experiments, though not very satisfactory, leave no doubt that the Mollusc was affected by the poison.

EXPERIMENT No. 4.

A full-grown Cobra was bitten at 11.40 A.M. in two places near the tail by a *Daboia russellii*. 11.48.—No effect. 12.50.—No effect.

October 16th, 8 P.M.—The snake was perhaps not so lively, but there was no marked effect, and it lived.

EXPERIMENT No. 5.

A full-grown Cobra was bitten in two places, on the ventral surface and the middle of the body, by a *Daboia*, at 11.58. 12.50.—No effect.

October 16th, 8 P.M.—No effect; the snake lived.

EXPERIMENT No. 6.

A half-grown Chicken was bitten by a fresh Cobra in the thigh at 12.2. 12.3.45.—It crouched; head drooping, beak resting on the ground. 12.4.30.—Paralysed; head lying on the ground. 12.5. — Convulsed. 12.5.10. — Dead, in three minutes and ten seconds.

EXPERIMENT No. 7.

A second Chicken was bitten by the same Cobra at 12.9.30 in the thigh. 12.10. — Leg partially paralysed. 12.13. — Lying down, beak resting on the ground. 12.13.30.—Paralysed, beak resting its point on the ground. 12.14. — Convulsed; dead in five minutes and thirty seconds.

EXPERIMENT No. 8.

A third Chicken was bitten by the same Cobra in the thigh at 12.17.30. 12.18.30. — Fell over; rested the point of its beak on the ground. 12.19. — Convulsed. 12.21. — Dead, in four minutes and thirty seconds.

This Chicken was rather smaller than the two preceding ones.

These three experiments show that the snake had lost but little of its power in three efforts. The Cobra used in these experiments was not full-grown, but it was very active and vicious.

EXPERIMENT No. 9.

The above small Cobra was bitten at 12.35 in two places, on the middle of its body and on the ventral surface, by a large and fresh Cobra.

October 16th, 8 P.M.—Not affected; it lived.

October 19th.

EXPERIMENT No. 10.

11.40 A.M.—A large "Dhamin" (*Ptyas mucosus*) was bitten in two places by a *Daboia*. 11.47.—Is partially paralysed; the mouth is wide open; appears unable to move; respiration continues. 11.47.—Moving about slowly. 11.52.—Appears to be recovering. 12.—More active.

October 20th, 6 A.M. — Appears sluggish. 10 A.M. — On being roused moves slowly; but is weak and stiff. Recovered subsequently.

October 26th, 12.47.1.—Bitten again by another *Daboia*. 1 P.M.—No effect.

Became sluggish, and died at 10.40 P.M., 27th October.

October 26th, 1868.

Present, Dr. Fayrer and Mr. Sceva.—The following experiments were made with the view of again carefully examining the blood before and after the snake-bite. The blood was very carefully examined on three occasions :—

1st. Before the animal was bitten. 2nd. Whilst it was under the influence of the poison. 3rd. After death.

In no case was anything found to support Professor Halford's theory, or to confirm his observations. There was no appearance of any new corpuscle, nor was there any change of importance in the condition of either the red or white globules of the blood.

My impressions were in favour of the theory advocated by Professor Halford, and if any bias existed, it was certainly for rather than against the explanation he gives of the pathological changes in the blood. Nothing, however, that I have seen after many observations supports the view in question; and I am constrained to believe that the change in the blood is of a much more subtle character than can be detected by the microscope. Moreover, in rapid death, as for example where it occurs in from thirty to forty seconds, it is impossible that such developmental changes could have taken place. The cause of death is evidently an impression made on the nerve centres through the medium of the circulation; but it is, I think, evident also that it is one of a dynamical nature, and not immediately dependent on any structural changes that may, if any do, occur in the blood, and can be seen with the microscope. When death is protracted, and the venom has thus time to set up blood changes, as in the case of zymotic poisoning, I can well imagine that the blood, as such, becomes unfitted for the purposes of life, and that death results in consequence of these changes; but I have not as yet seen anything to confirm this view of the cause of death, nor do the post-mortem appearances show that it is due to asphyxia from pulmonary congestion or embarrassment. I do not, however, positively assert that such is not the case.

EXPERIMENT No. 11.

A Pariah Dog was bitten in the hind-leg very slightly by a Cobra at 11.55 A.M. The blood was examined before the Dog was bitten, and the appearance noted. The white corpuscles were apparently, relatively to the red ones, rather numerous.

12.—Not affected. 12.23.—Bitten again in the right hind-leg by another Cobra. The snake struck of his own accord. 12.48.—The Dog is fully under the influence of the poison; he is slightly convulsed, lying almost paralysed on the ground. The blood was again examined; no change could be detected. 12.58.—The Dog died. Blood examined again after death, but no change could be detected. It coagulated firmly when removed from the body after death, which occurred in sixty-three minutes.

EXPERIMENT No. 12.

At 12.4 a Pariah Dog was bitten on the right hind-leg and on the back by a *Daboia*. The blood had been previously examined; there was nothing peculiar in its appearance. The wounds made by the snake's fangs bled freely.

12.18.—Very much depressed; staggering; almost paralysed in hind-legs. 12.20.—Lying down, head resting on the ground. 12.21. — Cannot rise; hind-legs paralysed. 12.40.—Blood again examined under microscope. No change. 12.48.—Dead. Blood examined after death. The microscopical appearances not changed.

In this case death occurred in forty-four minutes. The blood was kept for twenty-four hours after death, and it did not coagulate. It is worthy of note that the blood of the Dog in the last experiment, poisoned by a Cobra in sixty-three minutes, did coagulate firmly. In neither case did the microscope reveal any structural change in the corpuscular elements of the blood.

EXPERIMENT No. 13.

A ligature was tied round a Fowl's thigh so tightly as apparently to obstruct the circulation. The limb below the ligature was then bitten by a fresh Cobra at 12.31.

12.33.—Stretches out the leg, and is lame; wings drooping; it seems to be feeling the effects of the poison. 12.35.—Crouching; wings spread out; point of the beak resting on the ground. 12.37.—Fully under the influence of the poison, but can still be roused. 12.42.—Insensible and is convulsed. 12.47.—Again convulsed, and died. Death occurred in sixteen minutes. This experiment shows that the pressure of the ligature, although it did not completely prevent the entrance of the poison into the circulation, so far prevented it that death was deferred for sixteen minutes. In a Fowl of the same size, bitten by a Cobra in the same place, had no ligature been applied, death would probably have occurred within one minute.

November 15th.

Present, Dr. Fayrer and Mr. Sceva.

The following experiments were made with the view of testing the action of the poison of the *Bungarus fasciatus* on animals, and the influence of other snake-poison on the *Bungarus* itself and other poisonous snakes :—

EXPERIMENT No. 14.

A full-grown *Bungarus fasciatus*, said to be fresh, bit a young Dog in the thigh at 1.37 P.M. 1.34.—Restless; moves about, whining. 1.48. — Apparently not much affected. 1.54. — Seems uneasy and restless. 1.58.—Lying down, and getting up in a restless manner. 2 P.M.—Apparently not much affected. 2.10.—Staggers a little; is evidently uneasy. 2.20.—Seems sleepy; when roused he moves about, but quickly lies down again. 2.27.—Is sick. 2.38.—Very drowsy; breathing hurried. Staggers when he walks; vomits, and has general tremors. Bitten at 1.37 P.M. Died at 6.5—*i.e.*, in four hours and twenty-eight minutes. 6.5 P.M.—The blood coagulated firmly after death.

EXPERIMENT No. 15.

The same *Bungarus fasciatus* bit a Fowl in the thigh at 1.35 P.M. 1.37.—Fowl runs about much excited. 1.38.—

Does not now seem much affected. 1.40.—Apparently not affected. 1.45.—Began to show the effects of the poison; staggers, and runs with its beak almost resting on the ground. 1.50. — Paralysed; has fallen over. 1.55. — Is convulsed. 1.57.—Still convulsed. 1.59.—The same. 2.1 P.M.—Dead—*i.e.*, in twenty-six minutes.

EXPERIMENT No. 16.

Another Fowl bitten by the same *Bungarus fasciatus* in the thigh at 1.40 P.M.

1.42.—Walks lame on bitten leg. 1.44.—Staggers; fell over with its head on the ground. 1.45.—Is paralysed; cannot rise or move. 1.49.—Convulsed. 1.55.—Again convulsed slightly. 1.57.—Dead—*i.e.*, in seventeen minutes.

Death was more rapid in this case than the last, although the snake had bitten before. The Fowl was about the same size as the one previously bitten, and its more rapid death may be attributed to more rapid absorption of the poison, which was probably caused by the snake's fangs having entered a vein.

EXPERIMENT No. 17.

A Fowl was bitten slightly by another *Bungarus fasciatus* at 1.50 in the thigh.

At 2.10. — Slightly affected. 2.25. — Sleepy, but can be roused. 2.30.—Very drowsy; resting the beak on the ground. 2.45.—Still alive. It died at 3.45 P.M.

These four experiments prove that the action of the poison of this snake is not so vigorous as that of the Cobra or *Daboia*. The nature of its action is probably much the same, but the quantity injected is probably much less, as the poison fang of the *Bungarus* is so much smaller than that of the Cobra.

EXPERIMENT No. 18.

A *Bungarus fasciatus* was severely bitten three times, about eight inches from the head, by a powerful and fresh Cobra, at 1.55 P.M.

No apparent effect was produced either at the time, soon after, or later. The *Bungarus* was alive and well two days later. It died a day or two after, but its thorax and lungs were found filled with blood. The Cobra fang had probably penetrated the lung.

EXPERIMENT No. 19.

A *Daboia* was severely bitten by a fresh Cobra in three or four places at 2.10 P.M.

No present or subsequent effect was produced. The snake remained quite well.

EXPERIMENT No. 20.

Another *Daboia* was severely bitten by a fresh Cobra about a foot from the tail at 2.22 P.M. No effect produced. The snake remained perfectly well.

EXPERIMENT No. 21.

Two fresh and vigorous Cobras were made to bite each other in several places at 2.35 to 2.37 P.M. No evil result followed; both remained quite well.

The result of these experiments has been to demonstrate that Invertebrates and Hæmatocryal Vertebrates are, like the Hæmatothermal Vertebrates, subject to the deadly influence of snake-poison. The Mollusca, fish, and innocuous colubrine snakes rapidly succumb when bitten by either the Viper or the *Elapidæ*.

The weight of evidence, however, tends to show that the poisonous snakes have little, if any, power to injure each other, for in none of these last series of experiments was the bite of a venomous snake fatal to any other venomous snake. The *Bungarus fasciatus* that died after being bitten by a Cobra, probably died from internal hæmorrhage, and not from the poison.

In repeated careful microscopical examinations of the blood of animals before they were bitten, during the action of the poison, and after death, I failed to detect any structural changes, such as are described by Professor Halford.

I may here note, in anticipation of future experiments on the efficacy of the so-called antidotes, that the application of a ligature to the thigh of a fowl bitten by a Cobra manifestly retarded the entry of the poison into the circulation, and warded off for a time its fatal effects.

TENTH SERIES.

Experiments on the Influence of Cobra and Daboia Poison.

December 12th, 1868.

Present, Dr. Fayrer and Mr. Sceva.

EXPERIMENT No. 1.

A small Cobra, about sixteen inches long, was bitten in two or three places, about one-third of its length from the tail, by a very large and vigorous Cobra of the spectacled variety. The fangs penetrated deeply, and there could be no doubt that the venom was freely injected. When bitten the young snake threw itself into a series of momentary curves, but on being released it appeared unaffected. It was closely watched for some time, but showed no sign of being affected. It was as active and vicious as before, assuming an aggressive attitude, with its little hood erect, and striking vigorously at anything that approached it.

It was bitten at 11.45 A.M., and I saw it again at 4 P.M.; it was then lively, but looked rather stiff, and disinclined to be so active as it had been, probably owing to the pain and commencing inflammation in the bites.

On the 13th at 5 P.M. there was no apparent change in the snake; it was as lively as ever.

14th, 2 P.M. — Mr. Sceva reports that beyond a slight apparent soreness in the muscles of the bitten part, there is no change. The snake remains quite well.

EXPERIMENT No. 2.

A small Cobra, one probably of the same brood as the one bitten in the previous experiment, and of the same size, very active, vicious, and vigorous, was bitten at 12.15, December 12th, 1868, by a *Daboia* that had not bitten for many days, and whose poison glands were apparently full of poison. The fangs of the *Daboia* were made to penetrate deeply in a part of the snake posterior to the viscera—that is, not far from the tail; and a quantity of the poison was shed on the snake, and probably into the wound. The young Cobra, beyond the local effects of the bite, appeared unaffected; on being released, it deported itself just like the one bitten by the Cobra in Experiment No. 1, and was active, ill-tempered, and aggressive as ever.

At 4 P.M. it was apparently quite unaffected.

On the 13th at 5 P.M. there was no apparent change.

On the 14th Mr. Sceva reports of both :—

"There appears to be a slight soreness where they were bitten, and the muscles do not act so freely at those parts; but the extremity of the tail, and the anterior part of the body, are as lively as before being bitten."

These experiments go far, I think, to prove that the poisonous snake is not affected by the venom of its own or of other species.

The Cobras bitten were young and weak; the *Daboia* and the Cobra that bit them were full-grown, vigorous, and fresh snakes. There could be no doubt that the venom was thoroughly injected, and that the fangs penetrated deeply. The bites were purposely inflicted near the tail, that no chance of injuring the viscera might be incurred.

The bitten Cobras were closely watched for forty-eight hours, at the end of which period no symptom but the local effects of the bite was manifested. I think it may be fairly concluded, from these and other experiments, that the Cobra is not affected by the poison either of the *Daboia* or of its own species.

An Account of the Employment of a Supposed Antidote in Cases of Snake-bite, with Experiments on the same. Communicated by Colonel C. L. Showers.

This account of experiments conducted at the Gwalior Residency, in the presence of Colonel C. L. Showers, Officiating Political Agent; and Dr. J. Macbeth, Superintending Staff Surgeon of Morar, was sent me by Colonel Showers with the following letter:—

"DEAR DR. FAYRER,—I have been much interested in reading from time to time the published accounts of your own and Dr. Shortt's experiments on the action of snake-poison.

"There is a man here, a native, who possesses what he believes to be a specific antidote. I was led to institute experiments for its being tested by accidentally witnessing its efficacy in the case of a woman who had been bitten by a venomous snake.

"The following record of facts and experiments which, by the kind and skilful co-operation of Dr. Macbeth, Staff Superintending Surgeon of Morar, I am able to lay before you, will place you, and any other professional gentlemen whom you may think proper to associate with yourself in the inquiry, in a position to judge whether a specific antidote to snake-poison has been found. It is naturally an object of universal importance. The native has communicated his secret to me, and desires to proclaim it. But before doing so all I wish is that the antidote, after being subjected to every test that can be devised, and to which I am prepared to submit it, shall be admitted by competent professional authority to be really a specific antidote for snake-poison, in order that I may present it as a boon to the world.

"The case of the woman above referred to, as having brought the man and his antidote under my notice, occurred on the 1st August last, and may be described as follows:—

"A report being made to me that a woman, living in a village adjoining the Residency, had been bitten by a snake and was dying, I sent for the Residency Surgeon, and walked over myself at once, attended by a servant, with brandy, in the hope of being able to afford assistance. On arriving at the scene of the accident, I found the woman seated on the ground outside the door of her hut, under a sort of improvised porch formed of branches and leaves, which the villagers had erected at the moment, to afford the woman air without exposure to the sun. She was suffering from a succession of swooning fits, having already had eight previous to my arrival, in the interval of about two hours since she was bitten. The marks of the bite were distinctly visible on her ankle.

"While waiting for the surgeon, one of the swooning fits recurred. The method resorted to by two men who were treating her was what is known among natives by the term *jharna phookna*, or to exorcise. I had never witnessed it before. It was a strange and painful spectacle. As soon as indications of the approaching swoon appeared, and the woman fell forward from her sitting posture insensible, one of the two men seized her head across the forehead and temples with one hand, the other hand supporting her head behind, and then commenced shouting some *muntros*, or charmed verses, into her ear, at the very top of his voice; the other man, seated on the opposite side, taking up the last note of each cadence and prolonging it with an indescribable howl, with his mouth close to her ear. After this had been continued for some minutes without any sign of returning consciousness, the man who was supporting the woman by the head commenced shaking her violently, and slapping her and rating her vociferously, in apparent anger at her obstinacy. After some time this had the desired effect, as slowly, with convulsive gasps and other symptoms of distress, she came to herself.

"In the interval a man had arrived on the scene, who at once assumed—and was tacitly admitted by the bystanders to do so—the treatment of the case. He quietly put aside the charmers, reassured the woman and her relatives with an air of perfect confidence as to the safety of her life, and pounding something on a stone, he administered it to her. We then left, directing that a report of the progress of the woman's case should be made from time to time. In about two hours another swooning fit was reported—the previous ones having recurred at intervals of about a quarter of an hour. Subsequent reports announced her steady progress and complete recovery. That night she was kept forcibly awake by the instructions of the man who had administered the antidote as a precaution, on account of the long time she had been under the influence of the snake-poison before he was called in.

"This case led me to make inquiries about the person who had treated it so successfully, and I sent for him. On questioning him as to the nature of his antidote, he was very reserved at first; but on my offering to take him into my own service, he grew more communicative. He subsequently entered my service and revealed to me the secret of his antidote, giving me some of the material. So confident was he in its efficacy, that he offered to allow himself to be bitten by any snake; but this was a test that it hardly required the fatal example of Mr. Drummond's case at Melbourne to place out of the question.

"To test the efficacy of the antidote, however, by experiments *in corpore vili*, I sought the co-operation of Dr. Macbeth, who, I was aware, took great interest in the subject; and hence the series of experiments which are recorded in the accompanying enclosure.

"As the last terminated some weeks ago (September 12th), I should not have delayed so long forwarding the account, but under the pressure of public business, entailed by the exigencies of this year's drought, I have never found a leisure hour to transmit it to you. The delay, however, has proved of material advantage to the strengthening of the case in favour of the antidote in the saving of another human life. The case is this:—

"On the 2nd instant, a resident of Old Gwalior, a carpenter, came to the Residency, in much apparent distress, to say that his wife had been bitten by a snake, and had become insensible from the effects. Hearing, he added, that there was a person in my employ who could administer relief, he had come to seek it. I sent back my servant with him. He administered the antidote to the woman, which, as he reported on his return in the evening, had brought her round.

"The following morning I sent to inquire how the woman was, and desired that if quite recovered, her husband, the carpenter, and herself should appear at my office. They duly came the same day. The marks of the bite were distinctly visible on the woman's finger, but she had quite recovered from the effects of the poison. I had the man's deposition taken by my office moonshee, and append a translation of it, which will be found at the end of the record of experiments.

"The importance of the subject may be gathered from the fact recorded in the last Oude Administration Report, that 1127 persons died from snake-bites during the past year, and again, in the Central Provinces Administration Report, that 1874 had died from the same cause during the three preceding years. These figures, referring to isolated districts of India, may afford some approximate idea of the mortality arising from this cause throughout India and all other serpent-infested countries of the East.

"The boon to humanity then, if the efficacy of the antidote be established, could hardly be over-estimated.

"Yours very truly,

"C. L. SHOWERS.

"GWALIOR, *October 25th*, 1868.

Experiments performed in the presence of Colonel Showers and Dr. J. Macbeth.

"*First day, 26th August*, 1868.

"1. A full-grown Cock was given to the Kelaree,* who administered his antidote. The feathers having been plucked from one thigh and partially off the breast, the bird was freely bitten more than once in our presence by a lively Cobra, over four feet long. The Cock showed no symptoms of distress of any kind, and after an hour was let loose, and ran about apparently uninjured. Did not at any time subsequently exhibit any symptoms of distress.

"2. A Rabbit would not have the antidote administered by the Kelaree, whose hand he bit severely in the attempt to do so. The Rabbit was then twice bitten by a Cobra, over four feet long, on each occasion giving vent to a painful cry. It was then let loose, the poison taking very rapid effect; the animal fell on one side, then sat up for a few seconds, after which it tumbled over; showed great distress,—hurry and irregularity in its efforts to breathe; heart's action became rapid, feeble, and irregular; the pupils of both eyes were violently acted on by some foreign influence; ultimately became quite fixed; and in three minutes and a half from the time of being bitten, the Rabbit gave a convulsive shudder and was dead.

"3. A full-grown Pariah Slut, seemingly in perfect health, was handed over to the Kelaree, who administered his antidote on a piece of meat, which the Slut swallowed in our presence at 8.39 A.M. She was then bitten on the inner side of the left thigh by a fresh Cobra, over four feet long, which closed its jaws upon the place, holding on for some seconds. Several other attempts were made to make the Cobra bite again, but it is not certain whether a second bite was given or not. The Slut was then tied up; meat was offered to her about an hour afterwards, at the instance of the Kelaree, which she refused. He subsequently gave this as a reason why he thought his antidote had not been quite powerful enough, but said confidently that the remaining effects of the poison would pass off in a few hours. The Slut showed no symptoms of distress nor lethargy for two hours, after which she lay down and appeared drowsy. The Kelaree then administered a second dose of his antidote, which in the course of an hour entirely dissipated all drowsiness and weakness. At 1 P.M. the Slut, having been for about an hour and a half lively and apparently well, was let loose, and ran away to the neighbouring village to which it belonged.†

"4. Another Dog, full-grown, in good condition and apparent health, was bitten at 8.48.50 A.M. by a Cobra, over four feet long, the snake closing its jaws upon the place. Strong symptoms of uneasiness after three minutes, with very hurried and spasmodic breathing; pupil of eye violently acted on. In about fifteen minutes action of the heart much enfeebled, and very hurried. Pupil of eye still more evidently under a foreign influence; very shortly after this the breathing became more hurried, and the animal very restless. Frothy saliva also began to flow freely; Kelaree asserted the Dog would go mad. Shortly afterwards, on putting anything within reach of his mouth, he snapped spasmodically and laid hold of a rope, but more convulsively than with any object. First effects seemed to be excitement and distress, followed by considerable lethargy, after which its muscular efforts appeared to be nervously spasmodic, excited by some foreign influence, and evidently not voluntary. The hinder extremities first appeared to lose power; action of the heart hurried, weak, and intermittent; about this period the pupil of the eye became fixed, lower jaw powerless, tongue lolling out, and of a bluish-black colour; and breathing distressed, hurried, and spasmodic, with only partial expansion of the chest. Died easily, after one or two slight spasmodic gasps, at 9.29—that is, in forty minutes and ten seconds after being bitten. Just before death it showed a dislike to the presence of water.

"*Second day, 7th September*, 1868.

"1. Pariah Dog, without antidote, bitten at 7.39 A.M. Bitten twice on right leg and inner part of left thigh: on both occasions he gave tongue as if in pain. In about ten minutes afterwards the same appearance in pupils of eyes as in the previous experiments. In about a quarter of an hour strong convulsions, with involuntary evacuations of the bowels, and subsequently at intervals; made violent attempts to bite everything within reach, including his own legs and tail. This the Kelaree described as a symptom of hydrophobia, or his idea of dog madness; shortly all struggles ceased, the power of motion seeming first to leave the posterior limbs. A good deal of viscid saliva flowed from the mouth, and, as before, the tongue was observed lolling out, livid in appearance. The circulation in this case became more gradually affected than in the previous experiments; the heart's action continued for six minutes, gradually becoming feeble, after all pulsation in the arteries had ceased. Died at 8.15 A.M.

"2. Second Dog, without antidote, bitten at 7.54.58; died at 8.23.30—that is, in twenty-eight minutes thirty-two seconds—exhibiting more or less the symptoms recorded in the foregoing case.

"3. Third Dog, with antidote previously administered, bitten at 8.13 A.M. Remained quite unaffected, and, being kept tied up for three days, did not exhibit at any time anything wrong.

"4. Fourth Dog, with antidote, bitten at 8.39 A.M. Remained quite unaffected, as in the former case.

"5. Previous to this experiment, the Kelaree asked whether the fresh snake should bite a prepared or an unprepared animal. We selected the former in this instance, having already seen two dogs die, Nos. 1 and 2.

"A prepared full-grown Pariah was then bitten, the first time at 8.57 A.M., and a second time at 8.57.30. Both times the jaws were firmly closed on the limb. The Kelaree says that it was bitten a third time before the snake was disengaged from the Dog, but we saw only the two bites above recorded. The Dog remained perfectly unaffected after two hours, when the Kelaree was told to take all three Dogs away to his house, report their state in the evening, and if alive, to bring them up to the Residency for inspection the next morning.

"The Kelaree reported in the evening that the Dog last bitten—twice as we saw, but three times as he affirms—had vomited at 3 P.M., and exhibited other symptoms of distress; and that he had in consequence administered to this Dog more of his antidote, and that it was doing well.

"The following morning, that is, in twenty-four hours after being bitten, the Dog exhibited great weakness and distress, and decided symptoms of being under the influence of poison. We thought it would not recover, but the Kelaree appeared confident it would. Antidote was again administered; the Dog grew better and stronger towards the evening, and the following morning—that is, in forty-eight hours after being bitten—had quite recovered. It was kept tied up a third day, when all three Dogs, in perfect state of health, were let loose.

* Snakeman.

† This Slut sickened towards evening; and, being at a distance from the Kelaree, and her state being unknown to him, no further antidote was administered. The following morning she was insensible; spasmodic cramps and convulsions, frequently recurring, supervened; tongue lolling out, and of a dark colour. Died at 3 P.M. on the 27th—*i.e.*, thirty hours nineteen minutes after being bitten.

"*Third day, September 12th*, 1868.

"Experiment with one and the same Cobra biting two full-grown Pariah Dogs in succession, at an interval of a quarter of an hour; the first being prepared with the antidote, the second without. This experiment was tried to afford an *à fortiori* test of the efficacy of the antidote.

"1. Prepared Dog bitten at 7.42 A.M., the Cobra closing his jaws twice upon the part. Remained quite unaffected apparently for four hours, after which began to exhibit symptoms of distress, with increasing weakness. The following morning too weak to stand; tongue beginning to exhibit signs of paralysis, and becoming dark-coloured. Antidote was again administered; towards evening strength returned; Dog ate food. Second morning—that is, in forty-eight hours—quite recovered; was kept tied up for a week; never at any time exhibited any return of symptoms.

"2. The other Dog, in natural state, that is, unprepared, was bitten by the same Cobra at 7.57 A.M. in two places—on the back and in the line of the spine. At 8.30—that is, in thirty-three minutes—it began to show symptoms of being under the influence of poison. All the symptoms noted in previous experiments developed themselves, such as affections of the pupils, convulsive twitchings of the jaws and limbs, paralysis of the tongue, with gradually increasing swelling and lividity, sluggish circulation, and feeble heart's action. In this instance there was but little struggling or violent convulsions in comparison with the other cases noted. Died at 9.5—that is, in one hour and eight minutes.

"*Deposition of Davee, Carpenter, residing in Ghaspoora, of Gwalior. Taken October 3rd*, 1868.

"'This woman, by name Jusoda, is my wife. Yesterday she was bitten by a snake on the fourth finger of the right hand, about 8 A.M. Blood flowed from two wounds. We adopted the usual remedy of *jharna*, or exorcism, and by making a great noise, tried to prevent her from going to sleep, but without success. She soon became speechless and insensible. Having heard that the Political Agent had a person in his employ who could cure snake-bites, I came to the Residency to seek aid. The Political Agent sent his servant back with me. He gave my wife some medicine in *dhye* (curded milk) which revived her, and she recovered, and the anger of the deity was appeased.'

"(True Translation.)

"(Signed) PIRTHEE NATH, PUNDIT,
"*Translator of the Gwalior Agency*."

ELEVENTH SERIES.

Experiments on the Influence of Certain Reputed Antidotes for Snake-Poisoning.

January 16th, 1869.

Present, Dr. Francis, Dr. Ross, Dr. Fayrer, Dr. J. Ewart, Dr. D. B. Smith, Colonel Showers, Mr. W. F. Blanford, and Mr. Sceva.

The following experiment was made in the presence of the above gentlemen, with the view of testing an antidote described by Colonel Showers in his letter, and in the series of experiments performed at Gwalior in September, 1868, and recorded in the January (1869) number of the *Indian Medical Gazette*.

Colonel Showers having very kindly brought the man who administered the antidote to Calcutta, and expressed his wish that its effects should be tested, I accordingly, with the assistance of the above-mentioned gentlemen, proceeded to make the following experiments. The Kelaree had been allowed to make any preparation that he deemed necessary on the day preceding, and in the morning of the day on which the experiment was performed.

It is right to note that he says on the day of the experiments, that the antidote he has now with him is not the most potent one he knows, but that, owing to the absence of rain, he had not been able to procure it, as the drought had prevented the growth of the plant from which it is derived. He expressed his belief that the drug he had with him would prove sufficient to counteract the influence of snake-poison. Accordingly, a Pariah Dog was made over to him, and he administered to it a small piece of whitish-looking root, pounded and put in a piece of meat; this the Dog, which was a full-grown Pariah, ate readily. The Kelaree next selected, from a basket of fresh Cobras, a full-grown one of the Spectacled variety, which was made to close its jaws three times in the Dog's hind-leg, just at the fold of the skin of the thigh, and in the thigh. The Dog showed signs of pain when bitten, but had not evinced the least fear of the snake when it was brought near him; it was probably the first he had seen. The experiment was performed in the usual place, and as follows:—

EXPERIMENT No. 1.

The antidote was given to the Dog in a piece of meat at 11.55 A.M. of January 16th. At 11.59 the Dog was bitten by a full-grown Spectacled Cobra, of the variety known by the natives of Bengal as the "Gokurrah." The snake was made, by a snakeman occasionally employed by me, to close its jaws three times at the fold of skin in the right thigh and in the thigh itself. We ascertained that the Cobra had only one effective poison fang, the other being broken, but with this he drew blood slightly.

Noon.—Dog licks the puncture; bitten leg weak; partially paralysed. 12.1 P.M.—Dog lies down; shows indisposition to walk about. 12.3.—No pain apparently felt; is drowsy; refuses to be roused, and then walks about, but shows a tendency to lie down. 12.5.—Looks sleepy; roused, he walks, but soon lies down again. 12.13.—Breathing catching; is drowsy. 12.17.—Cannot walk without staggering; falls down when left alone; breathing hurried. 12.20.—Convulsed. The Kelaree now applied some oil to the mouth and nostrils. 12.21.—Lies on the left side; universally convulsed; eyes glazed; pupils dilated and insensible to light. 12.22.—Defecates; is pale and bloodless about the mouth and lips. 12.23.—Involuntary micturition. 12.27.—Respiration ceased. 12.31.—Dead. Ceased to breathe three minutes before heart ceased to beat. Bitten at 11.59. Died at 12.31. Death in thirty-two minutes.

The above notes were taken by Dr. Ewart, who carefully watched and noted all the symptoms, and he adds the following remarks:—"There is evidence that death takes place through the nerve centres, the heart continuing to beat after the respiration entirely ceases, which can only be through its own inherent irritability and its own ganglionic supply, and quite independent of the medulla, which, in all other respects, is *hors de combat* from three to four minutes before the heart actually ceases to pulsate."

This experiment, though unsuccessful in demonstrating the good effects of the reputed antidote, cannot be considered conclusive, as the man stated that it was not the most potent agent he was in the habit of using, nor indeed should I consider any single trial as proof either for or against the good effects of the drug, however it had resulted.

Having studied the effects of the poison in many animals, and having formed conclusions as to the nature of the cause of death, I am, as I have before stated, sceptical on the subject of antidotes, and fear that the hopes of those who are most sanguine on the subject will not be realized. I am not the less anxious though to become acquainted with whatever may be of service in the treatment of snake-bites, whether prophylactic or therapeutic, and I shall be as glad to record any facts that tend to throw light on the subject as to admit the potency of an antidote when I see it proved. Colonel Showers informed me that the Kelaree made the following objections to the experiment:—

First, that he was not fully prepared.

Secondly, that the antidote was not the most reliable one he knows of.

Thirdly, that the animal was bitten three times by the Cobra.

With reference to these, I would remark that the time for the experiment was appointed some days previously; that he was invited to make any previous preparation he thought desirable; that the room in which the experiments were performed was placed at his disposal, and that certain snakes were also made over to him; that he locked himself in for some time the day before making his preparations; and that Mr. Sceva was most careful to see that all he wanted was procured, and all his wishes carried out on the day of the experiment. The animal bitten was placed at his disposal to do what he liked with, and all his wishes were complied with to the minutest details. If therefore anything were wanting, the fault was his own.

Secondly, with reference to the antidote itself, it was suggested by himself, and he certainly expressed his belief that it would prove efficacious; or else why did he administer it?

As to the number of times the Dog was bitten by the Cobra, the snake was made to close its jaws in three places to insure the injection of the poison; the first bite at least being doubtful.

I am quite satisfied that one bite, had it been fairly inflicted, would have been sufficient. Nor does the fact of there having been three punctures affect the question in this instance, for nothing occurred to show that the Dog was in any way influenced by the so-called antidote. It succumbed with the same symptoms, and in about the same time, as other Dogs that had not taken any antidote at all, and were bitten in the same way by a Cobra.

Experiment No. 2.

At 12.13 a Kid of about three or four months old was bitten three times on the hind-leg by the same Cobra that bit the Dog in the previous experiments.

The object was that in the event of the poison not taking effect in the Dog, the activity of the poison might be demonstrated by its action on the Kid. This, had the Dog survived and the Kid died, would have been so far confirmative of the efficacy of the antidote.

12.15.—Leg weak; partially paralysed. 12.16.—Bleating; staggers, but walks; lies down; defecation. 12.20.—Can stand, but the bitten limb is paralysed. 12.25.—Almost paralysed; convulsed. 12.29.—Convulsed. 12.34.—Heart beats ninety-six per minute; respiration almost gone. Eyes glazed; pupils dilated, insensible to light. 12.36.—Death. Heart beat for two minutes after respiration had ceased. Bitten at 12.13. Dead at 12.36. Death in twenty-three minutes.

The activity of the poison had no doubt been exhausted by the previous biting of the Dog, otherwise a young animal like the Kid would have probably succumbed more rapidly.

The following experiments were made to test the efficacy of the hypodermic injection of liquor ammoniæ as an antidote.

Experiment No. 3.

At 12.36 a Pigeon was injected in the thigh with Cobra poison recently taken from the living snake. Two drops were inserted into the muscles of the thigh with the hypodermic syringe. 12.37.—Is affected by the poison; staggers; is slightly convulsed and drowsy. 12.39.—Droops and falls over, but is able to walk when roused. Ten drops of liquor ammoniæ, diluted with three times the quantity of water, injected by means of the hypodermic syringe into the same thigh. 1.40.—Very drowsy; rests the point of the beak on the ground; legs stretched out with a convulsive quivering motion; head falls over. 12.40.30.—Gasping respiration. 12.41.—Dead.

Death occurred in four minutes—rather a long period for so small and sensitive a creature as the Pigeon; but the quantity of poison was small (two drops), and all that was not thoroughly inserted.

In this instance I do not believe that any beneficial effect was caused by the injection of the ammonia.

Experiment No. 4.

12.54.—A full-grown Pariah Dog had the femoral vein exposed, in order that the solution of ammonia might be readily injected with the hypodermic syringe; it was then bitten in the opposite thigh by a fresh full-grown Spectacled Cobra. 12.56.—Dog walks with staggering gait; the bitten limb is weakened. 12.57.—One drachm of liquor ammoniæ, thrice diluted with water, injected into the femoral vein. 1 P.M.—Limps on the bitten leg, and lies down. 1.3.—Leg drawn up; slightly drowsy. 1.6.—Looks more drowsy; sits down. 1.7.—Made him swallow two drachms of liquor ammoniæ, well diluted with six parts of water. 1.9.—Pupils dilated; lies down exhausted. 1.12.—Lying flat on the left side. 1.15.—Staggers. When roused is not quite so drowsy; refuses water; lies down, whining and moaning; stretches out the legs as though in pain. 1.24.—Pupils much dilated; froths at the mouth; very weak in the hind-legs, but more so in the bitten than in the other limb; still moaning. 1.26.—Paralysed completely in the posterior extremities; jerking movements of the head. Respirations, 44; pulse, 100. 1.29.—Respirations, 28; pulse irregular, fluttering, and difficult to count; convulsed; is very restless; convulsive movements of the diaphragm; gasping; spasm of diaphragm; pupils dilated, insensible to light. 1.30.—Struggled and changed the position to the other side. Respirations, 12 in the minute; pulse very irregular; cannot be counted from subsultus tendinum. 1.34.—Defecations. Heart beats 104 in the minute; fluttering irregular pulse; respiration has ceased; muscular twitchings. 1.37.—Eighty beats of heart in the minute; muscular twitching. 1.38.—Heart beats faint, slow but perceptible. 1.38.15.—Heart ceased to beat about four minutes after respiration ceased. Dead in forty-four minutes and fifteen seconds.

Death was rather later in this case than usual in the case of a full-grown Pariah Dog bitten by a full-grown and fresh Cobra. It appeared therefore that the ammonia may have been so far beneficial. The benefit, however, was very small; but suggested further experiments, with the remedy given in larger quantities and more frequently.

TWELFTH SERIES.

Experiments on the Influence of Snake-poison, and on the Injection of Liquor Ammoniæ into the Venous Circulation as an Antidote.

After completing the last series of experiments on the subject of snake-poison, I received a communication from Professor Halford of Melbourne, whose researches have already thrown so much light on this interesting pathological question. In a paper of which he has kindly sent me a copy, read before the Medical Society of Victoria, he strongly advocates the injection of ammonia into the circulation; he also details several interesting experiments as well as cases of snake-bite in which the results were satisfactory.

This mode of treating poisoning not only by snake-bites but by chloroform, hydrocyanic acid, and other toxic agents, among which that of pyæmia is mentioned, and that of cholera suggested, has evidently been received with much confidence in Australia, and the matter is fully and ably discussed in the paper in question. The subject also of the structural changes in the blood to which I have already frequently adverted, and which were described by Professor Halford in 1867,* is also referred to with some further explanations, which so far as I can understand it, modify the views at first expressed by Dr. Halford. In the paper to which I have referred, Dr. Halford says of those corpuscles, "he had never seen those cells *before death*, but he believed the organic germinal matter of the serpent's poison to be the efficient agent, and the post-mortem changes in the blood to be in some way connected with a metamorphosis of the fibrine of that fluid which so far as coagulation was concerned, appeared destroyed by snake-poison. It was also the case in death from hydrocyanic acid." I had certainly understood from Dr. Halford's former writings that these corpuscles were an ante-mortem condition, a development of cells in the living blood "at the expense of the oxygen absorbed into the blood during inspiration, and hence the gradual decrease and ultimate extinction of combustion and chemical change in every other part of the body, followed by coldness, sleepiness, insensibility, slow breathing, and death." If I do not misunderstand him, in one paper Dr. Halford describes the formation of the cells as an ante-mortem change, and the actual cause of death; but in the later paper, I read that these cells are never seen *before* death. My examinations have been confined to the poisoned blood, during the life of the animal or immediately after its death, and I confess I have failed altogether to find them; as post-mortem changes, they are no doubt very important and interesting, but as such, I think, they can hardly be regarded as the cause of death.

My impression is still very strong that death from snake-bite, when it takes place within a short period, as it always does in an animal thoroughly bitten by a Cobra, is due, not to any organic changes in the germinal matter or cellular structures of the blood, for which indeed there is often not time. But as life may be suddenly destroyed by such poisons as hydrocyanic acid before any blood change can possibly occur, so in the case of the bite of a vigorous Cobra in a small animal, death occurs almost, if not quite as instantaneously, but by its direct influence on the centres of nerve force, by exerting an antagonistic force, one that is incompatible in short with those which regulate and govern the phenomena of life. I have already expressed an opinion which I repeat, that when death occurs more slowly, and when time is given for blood changes to take place, such do probably occur as in other toxæmiæ, and that the man or animal dies therefrom in a similar manner to that in which he or it might have perished from any other form of blood poisoning.

May 29th, 1869.

Present, Dr. Fayrer, Dr. J. Ewart, Professor of Physiology, Mr. Sceva.

EXPERIMENT No. 1.

At 2.48 P.M., the femoral vein of a middling-sized healthy Dog was carefully exposed, and one drachm of liquor ammoniæ, sp. gr. ·959 B. P., was injected into it with the

---

* "When a person is mortally bitten by the Cobra-di-capella, molecules of living 'germinal' matter are thrown into the blood, and speedily grow into cells, and as rapidly multiply, so that in a few hours millions upon millions are produced at the expense, as far as I can at present see, of the oxygen absorbed into the blood during inspiration; hence the gradual decrease, and ultimate extinction of combustion and chemical change in every other part of the body, followed by coldness, sleepiness, insensibility, slow breathing, and death.

"The cells which thus render in so short a time the blood unfit to support life, are circular, with a diameter on the average of $\frac{1}{1700}$ of an inch. They contain a nearly round nucleus of $\frac{1}{2800}$ of an inch in breadth, which, when further magnified, is seen to contain other still more minute spherules of living 'germinal' matter. In addition to this, the application of magenta reveals a minute coloured spot at some part of the circumference of the cell. This, besides its size, distinguishes it from the white pus or lymph corpuscle.

"Thus then it would seem that, as the vegetable cell requires for its growth inorganic food and the liberation of oxygen, so the animal cell requires for its growth organic food and the absorption of oxygen. Its food is present in the blood, and it meets the oxygen in the lungs; thus the whole blood becomes disorganized, and nothing is found after death but dark fluid blood, the fluidity indicating its loss of fibrine, the dark colour its want of oxygen, which it readily absorbs on exposure after death.

"Let it not be thought that microscopic particles are unable to produce such great and rapid changes. It is well known, and I have frequently timed it with my class, that a teaspoonful of human saliva will, when shaken with a like quantity of decoction of starch, convert the whole of the latter into sugar in a little less than one minute. If ptyaline, the active principle of saliva, exerts this power at most in a few minutes, then surely the active principle of the secretion of the serpent's poison gland may exert an infinitely greater power in as many hours. It results then that a person dies slowly asphyxiated by deprivation of oxygen, in whatever other way the poison may also act, and so far as the ordinary examination of the blood goes, the post-mortem appearances are similar to those seen after drowning and suffocation.

"I have many reasons for believing that the *materies morbi* of cholera is a nearly allied animal poison. If so, may we not hope to know something definite of the poisons of hydrophobia, small-pox, scarlet fever, and indeed of all zymotic diseases?" —*British Medical Journal*, July 20th, 1867, p. 43.

"The following was the result of numerous experiments on dogs and cats. Blood soon drawn from an animal bitten by a snake contains a larger amount of nebulous or finely granular matter than is usually seen. After the lapse of one hour this nebulous matter is much increased in quantity, lying in the intervals of the red corpuscles, and presently it breaks up into small masses, out of which the cell is gradually evolved. In two hours after the bite, the cells may be seen in great numbers, but very indistinct. From this time every further microscopic observation shows them in great abundance; and from the sixth to the twelfth hour they may be seen in perfection, macula and nucleus included. Whilst this is taking place the nebulous matter disappears; the nebulous matter must therefore be regarded as the germinal matter out of which the cells are formed. At this time the cell wall is extremely delicate, the macula very plain as a bright particle, and the nucleus either single, reniform, double, triple, or multiple.

"It would appear that the cells are now increasing in number by division of their nuclei, and the minute particles, having the vibratory movement of molecules in fluid, may be seen between the nucleus and cell wall. On one occasion we watched for upwards of half an hour a constant revolution within the cell of a particle corresponding in all particulars to a macula. This particle passed regularly round the nucleus at an uniform rate, revolving both in the direction of and against the current of the fluid in which the cell was flowing, reminding one of the movements seen in vallisneria, &c. Twenty-four hours after the bite, the cells attain their greatest size, and, supposing the animal then dead, have probably ceased multiplying, and are simply living or perhaps growing, the nucleus being usually single, the macula extremely distinct, and the cell very large. It is not uncommon at this time and later to see a cup-shaped hiatus in the cell wall from which the macula has escaped. The cells may be seen in the blood for many days, their presence seeming to be preservative against putrefaction. Where they have most room, as in the venæ cavæ, cranial sinuses, and cavities of the heart, they attain the greatest size and most circular form. In every instance the cell wall is very elastic, and accommodates itself to surrounding pressure.

"To ascertain how soon after inoculation these cells appear, is a matter of some difficulty. It is not necessary to suppose that at first they are very numerous; and in order to detect them so early, it might require fifty or a hundred microscopes and observers at work at the same instant. Still, from their having been seen two hours after the bite, and from all we know of the rapidity with which new formations occur, both in health and disease, it is doubtless extremely soon. Of one thing we are sure—viz., that the nebulous germinal matter from which they spring is within a few minutes diffused all over the body; for supposing an animal to die in five minutes, and hence all circulation stopped, the cells are as readily seen in its blood a few hours after death as if it had lived as many hours as we say minutes. The macula is doubtless a particle of germinal matter; but whether it is to be regarded as that from which the whole cell has sprung, or whether it has been detached from the nucleus and is destined for independent existence, it is difficult to say. The fact that it is almost invariably large when the cell is small, and small when the cell is large, favours the first view. Perhaps the most important point must be left still undecided. Has the blood built up these cells, directly or indirectly, from the germinal matter of the serpent? The answer to this question the Professor would endeavour to give at a future meeting; but in either case the result was the same, storing up of force in the new growth, at the expense of the nutritive properties of the blood, and by perversion of those chemical changes necessary to the maintenance of the life of the infected animal.

"That the germinal matter exists in a state of extreme minuteness, the following experiment shows:—A cat, being with young, was inoculated with the poison, and dying in three hours, her four kittens were removed from the womb. They were dead, and the blood of all contained the foreign cells, as did that of the mother. To pass from the cat to the kittens, the germinal matter must have penetrated the delicate membrane covering the tufts of the fœtal vessels. If the poison of serpents can thus readily be traced through the body, and from parent to offspring, why should not the path of all infections be tracked? Some months ago it was stated that it was conjectured that a child had been bitten by a snake. No doubt need ever exist for the future; a drop of blood will always furnish the necessary evidence. He trusted the subject would not be let fall to the ground in Victoria, for it would assuredly be taken up at home. It had been to him a matter of surprise that, while this colony very properly appoints men to survey her coasts, explore her skies, and the ground beneath her feet, no one systematically explores her diseases, a subject in which the rich and poor, the living and those about to live, are equally and deeply concerned, and in comparison with which many other subjects that excite her people are trifles."—*British Medical Journal*, December 21st, 1867, p. 563.

hypodermic syringe. The Dog lay still for a moment, and was then raised; he howled loudly and fell on his belly, the legs being unable to support his weight. Lay in that position in a general state of tremor, involuntary defecation and micturition taking place. 2.50.—Lying on his side; convulsed and twitching in every muscle of the body; pupils widely dilated. 2.52.—Lies on his side in a state of unusual muscular twitching; unable to rise or to walk when raised. 2.55.—Starts up and tries to run; falls down; is unable to rise again; the head fallen only on one side. 2.57.—Lying quiet, cannot stand when raised; no tremor now; breathing hurried and deep. 3.4.—Seems to be recovering; raises his head, and tries to get up; breathing still hurried and deep. 3.10.—Recovering; raises his head, makes efforts to get up; profuse salivation and frothing at the mouth. 3.13.—Sitting up; licking the puncture; refuses water when offered; great salivation. 3.30.—Is apparently well again; walks about as if nothing had occurred. The object of this experiment was to test the effect of the liquor ammoniæ injected into the venous circulation in an animal uninfluenced by the poison. It was used of the sp. gr. ·959 B. P., as directed by Professor Halford, and it was injected into the femoral vein in the manner suggested by him. The impression produced by this experiment was that the Dog had a very narrow escape from death, and that the effects of the ammonia had nearly proved rapidly fatal.

Experiment No. 2.

A large and powerful Dog had the right femoral vein exposed, and was then bitten by a fresh and full-grown Spectacled Cobra ("Gokurrah" of the snake-men) in the integumentary fold of the left thigh at 3.6 P.M.

3.8.—Began to show signs of the effect of the poison; staggers; is slightly convulsed; micturated. Forty minims of the liquor ammoniæ, sp. gr. ·959, B. P., were now carefully injected into the femoral vein already exposed, with the hypodermic syringe. 3.9.—Violently convulsed; but raising the head and trying to rise. There could be no doubt that whatever the latter effects might be, the immediate consequence of the ammonia injection was to make the animal much worse. 3.10.—Stood up; breathing very rapidly; salivation profuse. 3.12.—Breathing hurried; sitting up and looking more intelligent. 3.13.—Is able to stand alone. 3.15.—Lies down; salivation very profuse. 3.20.—Is certainly better; walks, but drags the injected legs; is sluggish. Remained in this condition, very restless; lying down and rising; drowsy at 3.30; thirty drops more of the ammonia injected. 3.31.—Lying down; is drowsy. 3.40.—Is lying down; being sluggish with hurried breathing. 3.43.—Worse; hypodermic injection of the ammonia, forty drops, under integument of fore-leg. 3.44.—No apparent effect; twenty drops more injected in the same place. 3.50.—Is worse; convulsed. 3.53.—Involuntary defecation; breathing catching, and rather slow; seems quite exhausted; pupils widely dilated; lips pallid. 3.54.—Dead. Bitten at 3.6 P.M., dead at 3.54, in forty-eight minutes.

The results of this experiment are not favourable to the ammonia theory. Death took place in about the usual time in which it occurs in a Dog after a bite from a vigorous Cobra. The effect of the first injection impressed one with the idea that for a time the influence of the snake-poison was in abeyance, but the later symptoms were rather unfavourable than favourable to the ammonia.

Experiment No. 3.

A Fowl was bitten by a Cobra in the wing at 3.36 P.M. Half a minute later I injected twenty minims of the liquor ammoniæ into the femoral vein which had been previously exposed.

3.38.—Violently convulsed; the convulsions passing rapidly into a state of general tremor and death. The Fowl was bitten in the wing, where the parts were not very vascular, that the poison might not be absorbed so rapidly as if bitten in the fleshy part. The poison had no time to manifest its effects, for the injection of the liquor ammoniæ was followed by immediate convulsions and death.

Experiment No. 4.

A Fowl had ten minims of the same liquor ammoniæ diluted with twenty minims of water, injected with the hypodermic syringe under the skin of the thigh. 3.44.—Apparently not affected. 9 P.M.—No change.

30th, 6 A.M.—No change.

31st, 8 A.M.—The Fowl keeps the leg drawn up, but is not otherwise affected.

Apparently beyond slight local inflammation no effect produced.

Experiment No. 5.

The Dog of Experiment No. 1 having perfectly recovered, had the left external jugular vein exposed at 3.55 P.M. of May 29th. He was then bitten in the right fore-leg by a fresh full-grown Spectacled Cobra.

3.56 P.M.—Sits down, lies down, rises and walks about, limping on the bitten leg. 3.58.—Sits down, but roused, walks about. 4.—Sluggish, lies down, walks unwillingly, ears drooping. 4.2.—Rises and walks about with uncertain gait. 4.3.—Lies down, with the head on the ground, apparently in a partially exhausted state. 4.6.—Stands but is unsteady, head hanging down, and with salivation. 4.11.—Staggers in his walk.

The Dog had only one bite, and the poison is now evidently taking effect; so forty minims of the liquor ammoniæ were carefully injected with the hypodermic syringe into the jugular vein, the greatest care being taken not to admit any air with the fluid. The Dog was immediately convulsed violently, fell over, was quite unable to stand; the convulsion passed into rapid jactitations of all the muscles. 4.15.—Perfect muscular exhaustion, hurried breathing. 4.18.—Injected twenty minims more of the liquor ammoniæ into the vein. Convulsive movements again became universal, pupils dilated, involuntary micturition, twitching of the mouth, lips drawn up, exposing the teeth, lips pallid, breathing catching and slow. 4.20.—Dead.

In this instance unusual care was taken to perform the experiment with exactness. No air was allowed to enter the vein, and the ammonia was most carefully injected with the hypodermic syringe. The steps of the operation were most carefully carried out by Dr. Ewart and myself.

The Dog was bitten only once in the fore-leg. The poison did not manifest its effects so quickly, or in so marked a manner as in Dogs bitten twice or thrice in the muscular part of the thigh, and this was purposely done that we might watch the progress of the action of the poison, and inject the ammonia at the right time. The ammonia was injected at 4.13 P.M., or in eighteen minutes after the bite. Convulsions came on immediately, and these were followed by complete muscular prostration; at 4.18, or five minutes later, twenty more minims of the ammonia were injected into the jugular vein; a repetition of the same phenomena followed, and the Dog died, completely exhausted, at 4.20—that is, two minutes after the second injection, or seven minutes after the first, or in twenty-five minutes after the bite.

There can be no reasonable doubt that the injection of liquor ammoniæ into the external jugular vein in this case hastened, if it did not cause death; and whatever other deduction may be drawn from the experiment, this is inevitable, that the proceeding is a dangerous one. In this case death occurred, in the first experiment the animal's life was in peril. The result is very different from that obtained by Professor Halford in his experiments, where he injected liquor ammoniæ not only into the jugular vein but into the heart itself, though I must at the same time confess that I cannot regard the latter experiment as at all satisfactory or conclusive as to the beneficial effects of the ammonia. It proves the absolute necessity for many and most carefully repeated experiments before one can come to an absolute decision on a subject where there are probably several sources of error to be encountered.

The following experiments (Experiments 6, 7, and 8) were made with a view of determining the influence of one poisonous snake on another. I have already recorded many experiments on this interesting question, and though so far the weight of evidence was in favour of immunity of the poisonous snakes from the poison of their own species and those of others, yet I did not regard it as a matter settled, but one about which there was still doubt. I wished for further and more convincing proof before I could accept as a fact what I even now hardly believe, that a venomous snake, whilst it has the power of quickly destroying innocent snakes, has no power over its own or the other poisonous species. Of this, however, there can be no doubt, that the effect of the poison is much less active on a venomous snake than on an innocent one.

Experiment No. 6.

A *Bungarus fasciatus* about six feet in length was bitten about a foot from the tail by a full-grown fresh and powerful Cobra, at 3.18 P.M. Again at 3.19; a third time at 3.20. All the bites were within a foot of the end of the tail. The object of selecting this part of the *Bungarus* was to avoid the possibility of death being caused by injury to the viscera. The *Bungarus* was then put into a cage.

4.40 P.M.—It seems quite well. 9 P.M.—Appears sluggish; the part of the tail below the bites appears partially paralysed; on pressing the tail with a sharp-pointed instrument but little sensibility is manifested.

May 30th, 6 A.M.—Very sluggish; skin contracted into a longitudinal crease along either side of the body. 9.40 A.M.—Dead.

The *Bungarus fasciatus* was a very large specimen, it was moulting at the time it was bitten; but still I think its death must be attributed to the influence of the Cobra poison.

Experiment No. 7.

A full-grown Spectacled Cobra was bitten within a foot of the tail by a *Daboia russellii*, about half-grown, but which was said to be fresh, and had been brought that day by the snakemen. There was some difficulty in making the Viper insert its long slender fangs into the tough skin of the Cobra, but it did so finally in several places. No evil result followed, and on June 3rd the Cobra was quite well.

Experiment No. 8.

A *Daboia russellii* was bitten by a fresh Cobra near the tail, about the same time as that of the last experiment; the bites were several, and fangs well inserted. But no evil result followed, and on June 3rd the Viper was unaffected.

Experiment No. 9.

Some Cobra poison taken from the poison-gland several months ago by Mr. Sceva, had been kept, and had coagulated in the glass-tube in which it was kept into a white caseous-looking solid mass, with an intensely fœtid odour. Some water was mixed with this, in which it was only partially soluble. Ten drops of the opaque fluid were injected with the hypodermic syringe into a Pigeon's thigh at 4.20 P.M. No immediate result followed.

4.25.—Ten drops more of the same fluid injected as before. 9 P.M.—No apparent change in the bird.

May 30th, 6 A.M.—Lying down; wings drooping. 10.5 A.M.—Dead.

This experiment shows that decomposition and coagulation of the poison does not, even for a long time, deprive it of its poisonous properties.

June 5th, 1869.

Experiment No. 10.

At 3.2 P.M. the right external jugular vein of a healthy Dog was laid bare. Chloroform was then administered until the Dog was insensible, though still whimpering with a peculiar cry. Forty drops of liquor ammoniæ, sp. gr. ·959, were carefully injected into the jugular. Immediate restlessness followed; limbs convulsed; howled loudly, as though it felt acute pain, and when placed on the ground was unable to stand, the legs being powerless.

3.16.—Lying quiet. 3.17.—Pawing his mouth and face in a semi-paralytic manner; makes unsuccessful efforts to stand. 3.18.—Lying prone; unable to rise on his legs; paws the face; when put on his feet cannot stand; seems quite sensible and intelligent. 3.20.—In just the same condition; crawls but is unable to stand on his legs. 3.21.—Sat up but fell over again. 3.23.—Forty drops more were injected. It was doubtful this time whether the ammonia entered the vein, probably into the areolar tissue about it. 3.25.—Forty drops injected this time, certainly into the vein; the Dog at once passed into a state of violent convulsion, and from that into a state of general tremor. 3.27.—Able to rise and stagger a few steps. 3.30.—Recovering; the Dog is and has been for some minutes profusely salivated. 3.33.—Running about the room; seems to be intelligent, but has peculiar nervous twitchings of the mouth and face. 4.30.—The Dog had perfectly recovered. The crural vein was exposed, and forty minims of liquor ammoniæ, sp. gr. ·959, injected; the injection was almost immediately succeeded by violent convulsions. 4.33.—Howling as if in pain or fear, legs paralysed; struggles in the prone position, but cannot stand. 4.40.—Breathing hurried; puffing of buccinator muscle; twitching of orbicularis. 4.42.—Can walk, but with a very staggering gait. 4.45.—Has recovered, but is weak.

In this case the animal recovered; but each injection of ammonia was followed by violent convulsions, muscular tremors, and paralysis to such an extent as to make it appear that life was in extreme danger.

The effect produced was unsatisfactory, and suggestive rather of danger than safety.

Experiment No. 11.

3.37 P.M.—A large Dog had the right external jugular vein laid bare; at 3.42 it was bitten in the right hind-leg by a Spectacled Cobra that had been in confinement for some time. The punctured leg and the neighbouring parts were lubricated with the snake's saliva.

3.47.—Sitting down; rises and walks with rather a tremulous gait. 3.48.—Lies down; deep inspiration; breathing hurried. 3.58.—Symptoms of poisoning not at all pronounced—there is reason to doubt the vigour of the Cobra. 4 P.M.—Bitten again by a vigorous Cobra in the same place; the leg immediately partially paralysed. 4.1.—Uneasy; licks the wound. 4.2.—Whines, and is very restless. 4.3.—Head drooping. 4.4.—Breathing very rapid (100); tongue hanging out; whining; uneasy; lies down; is restless. 4.5.—Walks about whining; droops his head, and lies down; still strong on his legs. 4.8.—Can walk, but is evidently under the influence of the poison; staggers, pants, and droops his head. 4.10.—Forty minims of the liquor ammoniæ, sp. gr. ·959, injected into the jugular vein; vomited; micturated violently whilst passing into a state of violent general convulsion. 4.12.—Stood up; breathing was hurried; is salivated. 4.15.—Shows weakness in the hind-legs; lies down; is purged. The symptoms of snake-poison becoming more marked. 4.17. — Injected forty drops more into the jugular vein; staggers, convulsed, and falls prone with the legs spread out. 4.20.—General paralysis; pupils widely dilated; tries to vomit; twitching of muscles. 4.22.—Twitching of all the muscles. 4.23.—Gasping; completely paralysed. 4 24.—Catching respiration; involuntary micturition. 4.25.—Dead.

On the Influence of Liquor Ammoniæ Hypodermically Injected.

I am indebted to Mr. Richards, Civil Surgeon of Bancoorah, for the following experiments on the effects of liquor ammoniæ hypodermically injected into the areolar tissue, and into the veins; also on its action, when so administered, in Cobra poisoning.

The experiments were performed with the greatest care, and the same scrupulous attention to details that have made Mr. Richards's other observations on snake-poisoning so valuable. They show that whatever therapeutic action it may have, liquor ammoniæ may be injected either into the tissues or veins without direct danger to life. As an antidote to Cobra poisoning, it does not from these experiments appear to produce any good effects.

In the first experiment ten drops of liquor ammoniæ, with an equal quantity of water, were hypodermically injected. The man was kept in the recumbent posture, and during observations continued from 4.8 P.M. to 5.38 P.M. no change was observed in the axillary temperature, the number of respirations, or the pulse. The only results noticed were that the pulse, which was eighty at 3.57 P.M. before the injection, fell after it to sixty-four at 4.16 P.M.—*i.e.*, eight minutes after the injection, and continued subsequently throughout the observations at sixty.

In the second experiment twenty drops of liquor ammoniæ, mixed with twenty drops of water, were injected into another man's arm. The man was kept in the recumbent posture, and the observations were continued from 9.40 A.M. to 11.32 A.M.; at 9.16 A.M., twenty-four minutes before the injection, his temperature was 97°·50, respirations 21, pulse 64. At 10 A.M., twenty minutes after the injection, temperature was 96°·90, respirations 21, pulse 60. The temperature gradually rose, and at 11.32 was 97°·50, respirations 33, pulse remaining at 60. The temperature and the number of respirations were both gradually augmented, whilst the pulse was unaffected throughout.

In the third experiment thirty drops of liquor ammoniæ, with an ounce and a half of water, were administered by the mouth, at 9.14 A.M. Before taking the ammonia, and whilst in a sitting posture, the temperature in axilla was 97°·90, respirations 16, pulse 60; at 10 A.M., forty-six minutes after taking the ammonia, the respirations were 16, the pulse 60. The observations were continued at intervals, after 11.26 A.M., during which time the thermometer stood at 97°·90, having been at 10.42 A.M. 98°·30. The respirations rose to 28, the pulse remaining at 60 throughout, of the same force. The effect of the ammonia administered by mouth was very much the same as of that administered by hypodermic injection.

In the fourth experiment fifteen drops of liquor ammoniæ, with twenty-five of water, were injected into the arm at 4.25 P.M. Primarily the temperature was 99°, pulse 76, respirations 18. By 5.45 P.M. the pulse had declined to 68, the respirations had continued at 18, the axillary temperature had fallen to 98°·60.

In the fifth experiment a healthy man, aged thirty, had two ounces of brandy with hot water administered; the pulse being 78, respirations 30, temperature 98°·55, at 3.58 P.M. The pulse at first rose to 82, temperature 98°·80, respirations 33. At 5.27 P.M. the temperature had risen to 99°·70, the respirations had fallen to 28, pulse 74, weaker.

In the sixth experiment fifteen drops of liquor ammoniæ, with twenty-five of water, were injected hypodermically at 2.55 P.M., the axillary temperature being 99°, respirations 22, pulse 68. At 3 P.M. two ounces of brandy with water were administered by mouth. At 3.9 P.M. temperature was 99°·40, respirations 25, pulse 74, full. At 3.41 P.M. temperature was 99°·20, respirations 24, pulse 64, weak; the respiration and pulse had both declined. Some brandy was given at 3.50 P.M. The temperature rose again temporarily to 99°·50, and by 4.50 had again fallen to 99°, the respirations had risen to 30, the pulse 76.

Such were the results of a series of experiments most carefully carried out by Mr. Richards; they are appended in detail, with his remarks. The inference is that any benefit derived from these stimulants could only be kept up by repeated doses, which apparently might be administered without danger.

Experiments on the Hypodermic Injection of Ammonia in the Human Subject by Mr. Richards.

Bancoorah, December 12th, 1870.

MY DEAR DR. FAYRER,—I have the pleasure to forward the results of my first experiments with the liquor ammoniæ. The men operated on were healthy and of the Bowri caste (palkee wallahs). I can vouch for the accuracy of the observations, as they were carefully noted by myself.

December 11th, 3.28 P.M. A man, aged thirty years, was placed on a couch in a horizontal position, and one of Dr. Aitkin's curved thermometers was put into axilla.

3.36 P.M. Thermometer 99°
3.40 „ „ 99°·40
3.57 „ „ 99°·50, respirations 20, pulse 80.

4.8 P.M. Ten drops of liquor ammoniæ, with ten drops of water, were hypodermically injected on the outer side of the left arm, near the insertion of the deltoid muscle.

4.16 P.M.	Thermometer	99°·70,	respirations	20,	pulse	64.
4.30 „	„	99°·60	„	20	„	60.
4.38 „	„	99°·40	„	20	„	60.
4.44 „	„	99°·40	„	20	„	60.
5 „	„	99°·40	„	20	„	60.
5.21 „	„	99°·90	„	20	„	60.
5.38 „	„	99°·0	„	20	„	60.

During the whole time the man remained perfectly quiet in the horizontal position. No difference in the force of the pulse was perceptible. The temperature of the room was 74°. The thermometer was kept in the axilla the whole time.

December 12th, 9.1 A.M. Another man, aged twenty-seven years, was placed on a couch in a horizontal posture, in which position he remained during the time the observations were made; a thermometer was placed in the axilla.

9.16 A.M. Thermometer 97°·50, respirations 21, pulse 64.

9.40 A.M. Twenty drops of liquor ammoniæ, with twenty drops of water, hypodermically injected.

10 A.M.	Thermometer	96°·90,	respirations	21,	pulse	60.
10.17 „	„	97°·20	„	25	„	60.
10.50 „	„	97°·50	„	28	„	60.
11 „	„	97°·50	„	30	„	60.
11.32 „	„	97°·50	„	33	„	60.

Temperature of the room 70°.

The respiratory movements were greatly augmented, while there was no alteration in the number or force of the pulse.

At 9 A.M. a straight self-registering thermometer was placed in the axilla of a healthy man, aged thirty. He remained in a semi-erect position until 9.11 A.M., when the thermometer was 97°·90, respirations 16, and pulse 60. At 9.14 A.M. thirty drops of liquor ammoniæ in an ounce and a half of water were administered by the mouth, and the thermometer (the index of which had been previously reset) again put into the axilla.

10 A.M.	Respirations	16,	pulse	60.
10.35 „	„	22	„	60.
10.42 „	„	26	„	60.

The thermometer registered at this time a maximum of 98°·30. 11.26 A.M., thermometer 97° 90, respirations 28, pulse 60; the force of the pulse continued pretty well the same throughout; the skin was slightly moist; the respiratory movements were (as in the previous case) much increased.

December 14th.—A strong healthy man, aged twenty-five years, was placed on a couch, and a curved thermometer put into the axilla at 4 P.M.

4.6 P.M. Thermometer 99°·25, respirations 18, pulse 76.
4.20 „ „ 99°·0 „ 18 „ 76.

Fifteen drops of liquor ammoniæ, with twenty-five drops of water, were injected into the left arm at 4 25 P.M.

5.3 P.M. Thermometer 98°·80, respirations 18, pulse 72.
5.20 „ „ 98°·60 „ 18 „ 70.
5.45 „ „ 98°·60 „ 18 „ 68.

A healthy man, aged thirty years, was placed in a semi-erect position, and a thermometer put into the axilla at 3.48 P.M. 3.58 P.M., thermometer 98°·55, respirations 30, pulse 78, weak. Two ounces of brandy with hot water were administered now.

4.14 P.M. Thermometer 98°·80, respirations 33, pulse 82.
4.40 „ „ 99°·40 „ 32 „ 78 full.
4.57 „ „ 99°·70 „ 32 „ 78 „
5.27 „ „ 99°·70 „ 28 „ 74 weaker.

A quarter of an hour after the administration of the brandy the temperature had increased 0°·25, the respirations 3, and the pulse 4. Temperature of the room in which these observations were made 73°.

December 16th.—A man, aged thirty, was placed in the horizontal position, and a thermometer put into the axilla at 2.31 P.M.

2.45 P.M., thermometer 99°·0, respirations 22, pulse 68. 2.55 P.M., fifteen drops of liquor ammoniæ, with twenty-five drops of water, injected into the arm; 3 P.M., brandy, two ounces, mixed with warm water, administered.

3.9 P.M. Thermometer 99°·40, respirations 25, pulse 74 full.
3.21 „ „ 99°·20 „ 25 „ 74 „
3.41 „ „ 99°·20 „ 24 „ 64 weak.
3.50 „ An ounce of brandy given.
4 „ Thermometer 99°·40, respirations 26, pulse 70.
4.16 „ „ 99°·50 „ 26 „ 70.
4.50 „ „ 99°·0 „ 30 „ 76.

It must be remembered that all these men were in the habit of taking alcohol. I leave it to you to draw conclusions from these observations. I may remark, however, that ten and fifteen drop injections appear to have very little effect, and that I should be inclined to place more reliance on a combination of brandy and ammonia administered by the mouth as a stimulant; twenty drop injections seem to have some effect. The arms of the men were rendered very painful by these experiments, but a little cold water dressing and a rupee *buksheesh* appears to be an efficient cure.

V. RICHARDS.

Experiments on the Injection of Ammonia into a Vein in the Dog, by Mr. Richards.

No. 1.

July 1st, 1871.—At 2.30 P.M. twenty drops of liquor ammoniæ diluted with forty drops of water were injected into the femoral vein of a Dog. The temperature of the Dog previous to the operation was 102°·10. The animal was large and in fair condition for a Pariah. 2.40.—Salivation. 2.45.—Temperature 102°·20; nose cool. 3.—Seems little affected. Pulse 148; respirations 26. 3.15.—Temperature 101°·90; is lying down; pulse 140; respirations 22; slightly depressed. 3.45.—Temperature 102°·30; pulse 120; respirations 22; lying down; there is a tremor over the whole body, but more especially of the left leg. 4.30.—Temperature 102°·80; respirations 30; pulse 128; appears sleepy only. 4.40.—Is more lively. 8 P.M.—Temperature (after food) 102°·20; pulse 120; respirations 24.

No. 2.

July 3rd.—Injected fifteen drops of liquor ammoniæ, diluted with an equal quantity of water, into the left femoral vein of a Dog, which was small and ill-fed, at 1.27 P.M. The temperature previous to the operation was 102°. 1.34.—Salivation; holds his tail between his legs. 2.45.—Seems little affected; temperature still 102°. 3.—Is quite unaffected; endeavouring to get loose. 3.30.—In the same state; temperature 102°.

No. 3.

Injected thirty drops of liquor ammoniæ, diluted with thirty drops of water, into the left femoral vein of a Dog at 1.50 P.M. The temperature of this animal was very high, 104°, and this was probably due to a large cluster of pustules situated in the right groin, which I did not notice until I had commenced the operation. 1.52.—The eyes have a fixed stare, and he goes about wagging his head from side to side and barking in a furious manner. He staggers about, and appears to have no command over his movements. He seems in fact mad. 1.56.—Is lying down with the head resting on his left fore-paw. The mouth spasmodically opens and shuts, but he is perfectly quiet and conscious. 2.3.—Constant twitching of the fore-paws; the spasmodic contractions of the muscles of the lower jaw are continual; temperature 104°·30—0°·30 higher than before the injection. 2.12.—Is lying down; the same spasmodic contractions of the muscles of the jaw. 2.50.—Appears depressed; temperature 103°—1°·30 lower than it was forty-seven minutes since. 3 P.M.—Is lying down; appears all right, except a constant twitching of both ears. 3.35.—Temperature very much lower, 102°·80.

Fifteen drops appear to have no effect, and the twenty drop injection but little.

The same fact is observable in these experiments as was noticed in the hypodermic injections—viz., that the effects of the ammonia quickly pass off, without it is used constantly or in large quantities. After the injection there is a rise in the temperature for the first twenty or twenty-eight minutes (according to the quantity used), but a corresponding fall in the next forty-five minutes. The greater the rise, the greater the fall below the normal temperature.

Experiments on the Treatment of Snake-Poisoning by Injection of Liquor Ammoniæ into a Vein, by Mr. Richards.

No. 1.

June 20th, 1871.—A large Goat was bitten in the left thigh by a Cobra at 3 P.M. At 3.5 P.M. twenty drops of undiluted liquor ammoniæ were injected into the right jugular vein. The animal on being released limped off. 3.15 P.M.—Appears drowsy, and is lying down. 3.30.—Is strongly convulsed. 3.40.—Dead; in forty minutes. The ammonia had not the slightest effect.

No. 2.

June 24th.—A Pariah Dog was bitten in the right thigh by a large Cobra, at 12.20 P.M.

12.25.—Forty drops of undiluted liquor ammoniæ were injected into the left femoral vein. 12.35.—Is evidently affected by the snake-poison. Making a whining noise, and is very restless. 12.40.—Staggers as he walks, and is holding his tail between his legs. 1 P.M.—Is lying down, and breathing very rapidly. 1.5.—Convulsed. 1.14.—Dead; in fifty-four minutes.

In this case also the ammonia had not the slightest antidotal effect.

No. 3.

A country Goat was bitten by a Cobra that had been in my possession for some time, at 12.55 P.M. At 1 P.M. sixty drops of undiluted liquor ammoniæ were injected into the left jugular vein. The animal on being released limped off; but did not seem affected by the bite. 1.15.—Seems slightly sluggish. 1.30.—In the same state. Abdomen tympanitic. 1.40.—In the same drowsy stupid state, but is standing up. 1.47.—Suddenly fell over, and became convulsed. 1.50.—Dead; in fifty-five minutes.

In each case the blood coagulated firmly after death.

No. 4.

July 3rd, 1871.—A Pariah Dog was bitten in the thigh by a Cobra at 12.54 P.M. The temperature in the anus before the bite was 102°·40. At 1.3 P.M. thirty drops of liquor ammoniæ diluted with an equal quantity of water were injected into the right femoral vein. 1.7.—Is lying down. Defecated. 1.13.—Breathing very rapidly: 80 per minute. Temperature 103° 90. The ammonia is evidently taking effect. 1.15.—Is standing up. Purged. 1.20.—Is running about in a silly manner. Appears to be endeavouring to vomit. Salivation. 1.22.—Convulsed. 1.25.—Temperature 104°·50. Is dying. 1.28.—Dead; in thirty-four minutes. Blood firmly coagulated after death.

No. 5.

July 5th.—A well-fed strong Pariah Dog was bitten by a Cobra at 12.53 P.M. The Cobra was casting its skin at 1 P.M. Twenty drops of undiluted liquor ammoniæ were injected into the right femoral vein. Temperature before the operation 102°·60. 1.10.—Is restless and panting a great deal. 1.15.—Lying down and whining. Temperature 102°·40 (a fall of 0°·20). 1.25.—Still making a whining noise. Salivation. 1.30.—Is walking about. Temperature 102°·10 (still falling). 1.45.—Is lying down, and does not appear much affected. 2.15.—In the same state. Temperature 101°·20 (still falling). 2.45.—Same state. Temperature 101°·80 (rise of 0°·60). 3.29.—Is becoming affected. Vomiting a black matter mixed with white froth. 3.40.—Is constantly retching, and is very restless. Temperature 101°·50 (falling again). 4.25.—Is still vomiting, and appears to be very much exhausted. 6.15.—Vomiting has ceased. Is lying down exhausted. 7.8.—Is lying down gasping, but is conscious. 8 P.M.—In the same state. 8.45.—In the same state. Temperature 100°·90 (lower). 9.15.—Slightly convulsed. 10.—Comatose. 11.—Dead—in ten hours and seven minutes.

The thermometer (Phillip's maximum) was retained on each occasion for five minutes in the anus.

I doubted whether the bite was a perfect one, because the snake had bitten itself when being laid hold of, and a quantity of the poison escaped on to the ground. Moreover, I did not think the poison had been properly injected, as the leg of the Dog was covered with it. The result of this experiment shows that no very great quantity of poison could have been injected—a circumstance favourable to the ammonia had it possessed any antidotal properties.

No. 6.

July 5th.—A Pariah Dog was bitten by a Cobra at 1.35 P.M. The Dog although large was not well-fed. Temperature (in the anus) 103°. 1.45.—Injected twenty drops of liquor ammoniæ diluted with twenty drops of water into the left femoral vein. 1.50.—Is lying down and breathing very rapidly. 1.58.—In the same state. Temperature 102°. Respirations 72. 2.5.—Twitching at the corners of the mouth. Involuntary wagging of the tail. Convulsions about to set in. 2.10.—Very much convulsed. There is a forcible expiration with each convulsive movement. 2.14.—Dead—in thirty-nine minutes.

No. 7.

At 2.20 P.M. a Pariah Pup was bitten by the same Cobra as that used in the last experiment. The Pup was very sickly and ill-fed. Temperature 104°·40. 2.25.—Injected twenty drops of liquor ammoniæ diluted with an equal quantity of water. The thermometer, which was retained in the anus after the operation, registered a maximum of 104°·60, 0°·20 higher than before the injection. 2.27.—Vomited and defecated. Lying down. 2.29.—Became convulsed. 2.32.—Dead—in twelve minutes.

THIRTEENTH SERIES.

Experiments on the Influence of Snake-poison and on the Injection of Certain Fluids into the Venous Circulation as Antidotes, and on the Application of the Ligature and Actual Cautery.

June 12th, 1869.

Present, Dr. Fayrer, Dr. Ewart, Professor of Physiology, and Mr. Sceva.

EXPERIMENT No. 1.

A Fowl was bitten on the thigh by a Spectacled Cobra that had been kept in confinement for some weeks, had bitten before, and was therefore not fresh. The Fowl was bitten at 3 P.M. At 3.1.50.—Fowl staggering; fifteen drops of strong Condy's solution, furnished by Messrs. Scott, Thompson, and Company, was injected with the hypodermic syringe into the Fowl's thigh. 3.2.50.—Fell down paralysed. 3.4.—Lies almost dead; just breathing. 3.5.—Convulsed. 3.7.—Dead.

Death occurred in seven minutes; but the bird was evidently unconscious after the first two and a half minutes. I could not recognise any good effect from the injection.

EXPERIMENT No. 2.

The left crural vein of a Dog was exposed, ready to receive the injection. The Dog was then bitten by a Cobra in the right thigh at 3.20 P.M. The Cobra was not fresh, it had been in captivity for some time, and had bitten before; but it was tolerably vigorous. 3.23.—Dog is excited and restless. 3.24.—Same condition; whining. 3.27.—Much excited; trying to break loose; is salivated; breathing hurried. 3.37.—Is beginning to show signs of the influence of the poison; is slightly convulsed; falls over. 3.37.30.—Injected sixty drops of liquor ammoniæ, specific gravity ·959, into the crural vein; the injection followed immediately by convulsive twitchings of mouth and limbs. 3.42.—Lying down, very low, almost motionless; irregular action of the heart; injected forty drops more of the liquor ammoniæ. 3.43.—No change; heart's action very feeble. 3.44.—Lies perfectly still, as though dead; no respiration; heart beats very irregularly; thirty-five pulsations in thirty seconds. 3.45.—Dead.

Post-mortem examination of body at 4.20 P.M. Lungs pallid; no congestion. Heart: right side much distended with black clots. Left ventricle contained a little dark fluid blood. The viscera generally were pallid; but the liver was somewhat congested. Brain: cerebral substance free from congestion; vessels on surface slightly distended with blood. The blood generally coagulated firmly.

EXPERIMENT No. 3.

The external jugular vein of a Dog was exposed at 3.34 P.M.; forty drops of the liquor potassæ permanganatis (Condy's) was injected into the vein at 3.35. No effect produced at the time; the Dog did not appear to take any notice of the injection.

3.40.—Dog apparently not affected. 3.45.—Seems rather depressed, but this is not marked; it may be fear. 3.48.—Bitten by a large Cobra (not fresh, for it has been some time in captivity, and has bitten before) in the thigh. The fang punctures were at once washed with Condy's solution, which was well rubbed in. 3.49.—Bitten leg partially paralysed. 3.50.—Lying down; when raised can stand, but quickly lies down again; is quite intelligent. 3.51.—Droops his head. 3.52.—Sixty more drops of the fluid injected into the vein. 3.54.—Two drachms injected into the bowel; is able to sit or stand, but is very weak. The injection of the Condy's fluid was not followed by convulsions as in the case of the liquor ammoniæ. 3.58.—Lies down; head falls over; breathing hurried; rises and staggers a little, and sits down again. 4 P.M.—Lies sluggish and dejected; can walk when raised, but staggers and soon sits down again. 4.5.—Can still stand and walk with staggering gait. 4.7.—Lying down, but gets up and walks a few steps; head drooping, and look dejected; twitching of muscles generally. 4.8.—When put on his legs can still stand; breathing hurried; coat staring. 4.12.—Forty more drops injected into jugular vein. Slight twitching of muscles generally; lies down on his side, cannot rise; limbs paralysed; pupils dilated; slight convulsions of extremities, and muscular system generally; breathing catching and rather slow. 4.22.—Motionless; heart still beats fifty in the minute; no respiration. 4.24.—Heart still felt. 4.25.—Dead. Bitten at 3.48. Dead at 4.25—in thirty-seven minutes.

Death occurred in about the usual time, and with the usual symptoms in which it occurs when a Dog is bitten by a Cobra. I do not believe the effects of the poison were in any way influenced by the permanganate.

Post-mortem at 4.40 P.M.—Lungs much collapsed and very pallid. Both sides of heart full of fluid blood; great vessels distended. The blood coagulated firmly when let out of the heart and vessels. Abdominal viscera not so pallid as in the other Dog. Brain vessels on surface full of blood: cerebral substance pale, scarcely any puncta.

Experiment No. 4.

A Fowl bitten by a Cobra (not fresh) in the thigh at 4.45 P.M.; twenty drops of liquor ammoniæ having previously, at 4.43, been hypodermically injected into the thigh, no apparent effect produced by the ammonia thus injected. Bitten by the Cobra at 4.45 P.M.; in thirty seconds it was in violent convulsions. 4.46. — Twenty more drops injected. Dead before it could be placed on the ground.

The following experiments (Nos. 5, 6,) were tried with the object of again testing the effect of the Cobra poison on itself, or on another Cobra:—

Experiment No. 5.

A Cobra was bitten sufficiently near the tail to avoid the chance of injuring any of the viscera, by another full-grown, fresh and vigorous Cobra. The snake bit deeply, plunging its fangs twice or thrice into the flesh of the other Cobra, which was then put aside in a separate cage and watched.

13th, 6 A.M.	. . . .	no change.
„ 7 P.M.	. . . .	„
14th, 6 A.M.	. . . .	„
„ 6 P.M.	. . . .	„
15th, 6 A.M.	. . . .	„

The snake evidently has not suffered.

Experiment No. 6.

A vigorous and fresh full-grown Cobra, with one ocellus in the hood, "Keautiah" of the natives, was made to bite himself three or four times near the tail at 4.48 P.M. He bit himself quite as freely as he would have bitten another snake, brought blood, and smeared the surface with poison; put into a cage and watched. Was not the least affected on the 15th, three days after the bite.

These two experiments, which were very carefully performed, tend to prove that the Cobra cannot poison itself or its own species.

June 19th, 1869.

Present, Drs. Fayrer, Ewart, Waller, and Mr. Sceva.

Experiment No. 7.

A full-grown Cat was bitten at 2.43 P.M. in the right thigh, by a large *Daboia*. The snake had been long in captivity, and was therefore most probably not vigorous though active and vicious. 2.49.—Twitching of the muscles; restless. 3.12.—The Cat appears to be unaffected. 3.15.—The *Daboia* again made to close his jaws on the Cat's thigh, though evidently unwilling to bite. 3.44.—The Cat seems sluggish, and is evidently now feeling the poison. 3.45.—Bitten by a Cobra on the thigh. 3.46.—The Cat is unsteady in its gait; breathes hard; looks distressed. 4.7.—Cat is restless; tries to rise, and staggers. 4.10.—Tries to stand, but falls over. 4.18.—Respiration very hurried; cannot stand; twitching of the muscles. 4.24.—Lies quite paralysed; pupils dilated; breathing hard. 4.27.—Convulsed. 4.30.—Dead.

The Cat was bitten by the *Daboia* at 2.43 P.M., and again at 3.15. The snake was old and feeble; it has been in captivity for more than six months, during which time it has touched neither food nor water, and yet it was active and vicious, hissing fiercely at any one who came near it; that it was capable of secreting poison was evident in later experiments.

The Cobra bit at 2.45; and death occurred at 4.30; that is, in one hour and forty-seven minutes. The Cobra was also not fresh, and its poison was weak, perhaps scanty. There was nothing whatever in this experiment to make us think that the Cobra's poison proved antidotal to that of the *Daboia*; on the contrary, it rather expedited death.

Experiment No. 8.

A Fowl was bitten in the thigh by the same *Daboia* at 3.40. The snake would not bite until his jaws were closed on the bird's thigh.

3.44.—The Fowl, whilst walking about with rather a sluggish gait, suddenly sprang off the ground, and fell over in convulsions. It was immediately bitten in the thigh by a Cobra. It continued unconscious and convulsed, and was dead at 3.46; that is, in six minutes after it was bitten by the Viper. Had this Viper been fresh, the bird would probably not have lived one minute.

Experiment No. 9.

Another Fowl bitten by the same *Daboia* at 3.56 P.M. 3.58.—It limps; has a depressed look, and its comb droops. 3.59.—Bitten by a Cobra in the thigh; lies down. 4.2.—Slight convulsions. 4.3.—Comb livid; convulsed and unconscious. 4.5.—Dead—in nine minutes.

These three experiments, I think, dispose of the question of the poison of one family of venomous snakes being antidotal to the other.

In these cases the Viper was old and exhausted, and yet his poison was deadly. The poison of the Cobra, which was also a partially exhausted snake selected on purpose, had no counteracting effect. The only thing proved is the terribly deadly nature of the *Daboia*, which after such long confinement without food or water yet retained the power of causing death.*

These experiments (Nos. 7, 8, 9) were made in reference to certain suggestions that have appeared in the journals, but not with any expectation on my part that any other result than that which occurred could take place. The poison of the deadly snakes, of whatever family, kills by paralysing the nerve centres, and it appears as reasonable to expect prussic acid to prove antidotal to aconite, as the Cobra poison to be so to that of any other form of venomous snake.

Experiment No. 10.

A Fowl was bitten by the same *Daboia* in the thigh at 4.7 P.M. 4.10.—Sitting down; looks sluggish. 4.15.—Rises and runs about, but is lame. 4.27.—Walks, but is very lame on

* The *Daboia* was not intentionally deprived of food or water; it would take neither.

the bitten leg. 4.45.—Still walks about, but is sluggish and lame, and looks very dejected. The Fowl after this began to recover, and on the 21st, two days later, was quite well. The snake was evidently all but quite exhausted when he bit this bird.

EXPERIMENT No. 11.

The external jugular vein of a Dog was exposed at 3.6 P.M., and four drops of Cobra poison were injected; at least one drop was lost, the other three entered the vein.

3.10.—Dog looks dejected, and ears drooping; he lies down. 3.33.—Beyond being sluggish no symptoms of poisoning. 3.46.—Very sluggish; lies down. 3.47.—Liquor ammoniæ, specific gravity ·959, sixty drops injected into jugular vein; Dog lies quiet Heart beating rapidly; respiration very feeble. 3.54.—Heart's action very rapid; breathing rapid; muscular twitchings. 3.57.—Injected sixty more drops into the vein; muscular twitchings continue. 3.59.—Dead.

Poison injected at 3.4; death at 3.59. Death in fifty-five minutes. The quantity of poison was very small from a weakened snake; no effect was produced by the ammonia.

EXPERIMENT No. 12.

The jugular vein was exposed in a Dog; it was then bitten in the thigh by a fresh Cobra at 3.27.

3.28.—Staggering; excited, springing; howling violently; and trying to break the cord by which it is tied. 3.29.—Quiet; sitting down. 3.30.—Head drooping. 3.33.—Lying on its side, slightly convulsed; sixty drops of a solution of quinine, of the strength of one grain in eight drops, was injected into the jugular vein. 3.34.—The Dog lies on its side, still slightly convulsed. 3.35.—Dead. Bitten at 3.27; dead at 3.35—in eleven minutes. The quinine evidently did no good.

EXPERIMENT No. 13.

Equal parts of Cobra poison and liquor ammoniæ, specific gravity ·959, were mixed together, and fifteen drops of the mixed fluid were injected with the hypodermic syringe into a Pigeon's thigh at 4.30 P.M. Pigeon crouched immediately; at 4.31 was unable to stand; the beak resting on the ground.

4.32.—Convulsed; peculiar convulsive movements of the tail continuing. 4.32.—Dead.

Injected at 4.30; death at 4.32—in two minutes. This experiment is very unfavourable to the theory of the antidotal action of liquor ammoniæ.

EXPERIMENT No. 14.

The external jugular vein of a large and powerful Dog having been exposed, ten drops of fresh Cobra poison were injected into it at 4.24 with the hypodermic syringe.

4.24.30.—The Dog staggered, was convulsed, and fell over foaming at the mouth. 4.25.—Violently convulsed, but with no outcry or sign of suffering. Sixty drops of liquor ammoniæ, specific gravity ·959, injected. Dead.

Death occurred in about seventy seconds; showing the frightful virulence of the poison when it finds entry by a large blood-vessel.

How can such a death be explained otherwise than by exhaustion of the nerve centres? Any theory of blood change is surely totally inapplicable here.

June 26th, 1869.

Present, Dr. Fayrer, Dr. Ewart, Professor of Physiology; and Dr. Sceva.

EXPERIMENT No. 15.

A Pariah Dog was bitten in the fore-arm by a Cobra ("Kála Keautiah") at 3.2 P.M.

A ligature had been thrown round the limb above the bitten part, which was immediately tightened; a pointed steel, heated to a red heat, was then, at 3.3 P.M., inserted into the punctures, and the wounds were thoroughly cauterized.

3.7.—The Dog is restless, and is apparently under the influence of the poison. 3.12.—Staggers as he walks. 3.14.—Forty drops of liquor ammoniæ, specific gravity ·959, diluted with three parts of water, were injected into the jugular vein. 3.17.—The Dog runs about excited; he was partially convulsed during the injection of the ammonia; now sits up, and then falls over backwards; breathing quickly. 3.20.—Lies down; is salivated 3.27.—Sits down; paws the air; muscular twitchings. 3.38.—Lying on his side; convulsed. 3.44.—Lies paralysed; heart still beats, but no respiration. 4.45.—Dead.

Notwithstanding the ligature, which was tightened immediately, the actual cautery, which also immediately followed the Cobra's fangs, and the injection of ammonia into the venous circulation, the snake-poison proved fatal to a full-grown Dog in forty-three minutes.

EXPERIMENT No. 16.

A Dog was bitten by a fresh Cobra ("Kála Keautiah") in the fore-arm at 3.38 P.M.; a ligature was immediately tightened round the limb above the wound. The actual cautery was at once applied, until the fang wounds and the adjacent parts were completely disorganized.

3.42.—The Dog is sitting, but reels as though he would fall over. 3.49.—Rises and walks with a staggering gait. 3.54.—Sits down; attempts to get up, and falls over backwards. 3.57.—Is convulsed; falls over, cannot stand; hurried breathing. 4.4.—Cannot move; lies paralysed; heart still beating; respiration almost ceased; pupils widely dilated. 4.6.—Lies on its side; convulsed. 4.12. No respiration; but heart still beats feebly. 4.13.—Dead.

In this case also, notwithstanding the ligature, which was applied as tightly as two persons could pull it round the leg, and the deep and thorough actual cauterization, immediately after the bite the snake-poison found entry into the system, and proved fatal in thirty-five minutes. The Dog was much smaller than that of the first experiment.

Nothing, it seems to me, can more strongly demonstrate the extremely subtle and virulent nature of the Cobra poison than those experiments; nothing, I think, is more significant of the improbability of anything proving to be an antidote. If the poison find entry into the blood-vessels, and be carried to the nerve centres, I am inclined to believe that nothing can prove of any avail, excepting in those cases where the bite is imperfect, the quantity or the quality of the poison diminished or deteriorated, or the snake itself is young, weak, exhausted, or is one of less poisonous family; such, I believe, are the only cases in which recovery occurs through the inherent vigour of the animal or person bitten, perhaps aided by stimulants and excitement. The favourable result is attributed, and naturally enough, by those who do not understand the *modus lædendi* of the venom, to the treatment by the so-called antidote. That we can aid in such recoveries, and that we may do much to help the sufferer through the troubles arising from general disorder and secondary blood poisoning, I have no doubt; and I would offer every encouragement to all to persevere in their attempts. But I must again state my conviction that nothing that can properly be called an antidote to Cobra or Viper poison exists; and the more this is known the better, for mistaken notions on such an important matter can only do harm, and may be the cause of losing, rather than of saving, life.

My belief is that if an animal, and probably a man, be fairly bitten by a fresh and vigorous Cobra or *Daboia*, it or he will inevitably succumb, unless some immediate and direct method of arresting the entry of the poison into the circulation be practised.

That such may be done I will not deny; but the two experiments just recorded, performed with the greatest care and speed by two surgeons accustomed to such operations, show that at the least it is very difficult. The moment of time that intervenes between the injection of the snake-poison by the powerful maxillary muscles through the tube-like fang into the minute blood-vessels of the part, and the application of the ligature and actual cautery, is sufficient to allow of the entry of the poison into the circulation, and this reaching the nerve centres, even in a small quantity, may prove fatal. The ligature is evidently very unreliable when applied to large parts of the body, such as the limbs; for it is almost physically impossible to compress the part so tightly as to stop the circulation; and unless this be done to the depth of the penetration of the snake's fangs, it is obvious that it can only be of very partial effect in preventing the entry of the poison. On a finger or a toe the ligature might be of more service, as the smaller part might be thoroughly strangulated; but unless the ligature were applied immediately, it is obvious that it would be useless even there, for the poison would have already entered, and be on its course towards the nerve centres. How quickly this occurs is proved by those experiments in which the poison was injected directly into the jugular vein. What took place there, with the hypodermic needle inserted into the jugular vein, has its exact counterpart in the case of the Cobra's fang, inserted, as it must be, when it penetrates a vascular part, into the minute veins.

The same may be said of the actual cautery. Unless the hot iron enter the puncture directly after the fang has been withdrawn, the poison is already far on its way towards the centre, and the burning, though it destroy the tissues and such of the poison as may not yet have entered the circulation, can have no influence on that which is already beyond its reach. But as the ligature, if tightly and quickly applied, and the actual cautery, if promptly and thoroughly inserted, must limit to a certain extent the entrance of the poison, both should be had recourse to as speedily and efficaciously as possible, in the hope that the amount of poison left to find, or that may have already found its way into the system, may be less than is sufficient to cause death.

To conceive of an antidote, in the true sense of the term, to snake-poison, one must imagine a substance so subtle as to follow, overtake, and neutralize the venom in the blood, or that shall have the power of counteracting and neutralizing the deadly influence it has exerted on the vital forces. Such a substance has still to be found, and our present experience of the action of drugs does not lead to hopeful anticipation that we shall find it.

But I repeat that where the poisonous effects are produced in a minor degree, or when the secondary consequences are to be dealt with, we may do much to aid the natural forces in bringing about recovery. This is not, however, what is meant by an antidote.

Experiment No. 17.

A large and powerful Dog had the right external jugular vein exposed. Twenty drops of a mixture of fresh Cobra poison, taken from the snake the same day, one part, and liquor ammoniæ, specific gravity ·959, forty drops or two parts, was then injected with the hypodermic syringe into the vein. The time of the insertion of the fluid was 4.27.30. The effect was instantaneous; the Dog struggled, howled, and was convulsed on the table: he was immediately released and placed on the ground, but was already almost unconscious and convulsed. He made an effort to rise on his legs, and fell prone on his belly. Within one minute respiration had ceased, though the heart's action continued faintly. This ceased, and at 4.30 A.M. he was quite dead. The action of the poison with the ammonia was frightfully rapid in this case. Death occurred in two minutes and a half, complete unconsciousness within a minute; and only by the faint beating of the heart, which continued for two minutes and a half, was any sign of life manifested. This surely is fatal to the theory of ammonia injected into the circulation being of any benefit in snake-poisoning. In this case the poison and the so-called antidote were injected synchronously; the result was almost instant death.

The experiment was performed by Dr. Ewart and myself with the greatest care, and certainly no air entered the vein.

Experiment No. 18.

The Cobra that bit the Dog in a former experiment (No. 15) bit a Fowl in the thigh at 3.46 P.M. The bird immediately began to limp, and then crouched, and then fell over.

3.47.—Head fallen over, beak resting on the ground. 3.49.—Convulsed; dead. Death occurred in three minutes.

A second Fowl was bitten by the same snake at 3.50 P.M. in the thigh. 3.51.—Drooping his wings. 3.55.—Sits down, beak resting on the ground. 3.57.—Is convulsed. 4 P.M.—Dead in ten minutes.

A third Fowl bitten by the same snake in the thigh at 3.51 P.M., shortly after drooped. 3.58.—Convulsed. 4.2.—Dead. Dead in eleven minutes.

A fourth and larger Fowl bitten in the thigh by the same Cobra at 4.3 P.M. 4.8.—Crouching; wings spread out; gets up; tries to run, and falls; head droops, beak resting on the ground. 4.10.—Convulsed. 4.17.—Still convulsed; comb livid. 4.20.—Dead in seventeen minutes.

A fifth Fowl bitten in the thigh by the same Cobra at 4.13 P.M. 4.20.—Crouches; comb drooping. 4.24.—Head drooping; resting on beak. 4.29.—Quite paralysed; convulsed. 4.35.—Dead in twenty-two minutes.

A Pigeon was bitten in the thigh by the same Cobra at 4.37 P.M. 4.47.—The Pigeon is drooping, and when he stands, it is on one leg, and then falls over again. 5.22.—Dead in forty-five minutes.

This was the ninth animal bitten by the Cobra in rapid succession, and still it is apparently not quite exhausted.

A sixth Fowl bitten in the thigh by the same Cobra at 4.32 P.M.

4.35.—Crouching. 4.47.—Staggers. 5.45.—Lying down insensible. 6.5.—Dead in ninety-nine minutes.

A seventh Fowl bitten by the same Cobra in the thigh at 4.34 P.M.

4.37.—Crouches. 4.47.—Seems sluggish, and limps.

June 27th, 5.30 A.M.—Lying down, and eyes half closed; unable to walk.

June 28th, 6 A.M.—Is recovering; walks sluggishly, and limps, but is evidently regaining strength.

The object of this experiment was to test the extent of power possessed by the Cobra. It destroyed one Dog, six Fowls, and a Pigeon in rapid succession, but the intervals between the bite and the death of each became more prolonged, showing the gradual diminution of power at each bite. The seventh Fowl poisoned was only slightly, so, and recovered.

The Cobra was neither a very large nor a very vigorous one, and yet how deadly! Eight creatures destroyed by a rapid succession of bites. The experiment proves that the snake becomes weaker by biting, until quite exhausted.

Experiment No. 19.

A *Daboia* was bitten by a fresh Cobra ("Kála Keautiah") near the tail, sufficiently far from the viscera. The scales were previously scraped off. The snake bit fiercely and repeatedly at 4.54 P.M.

6 P.M.—No change.

On June 28th, at 6 A.M., there was no change.

The object of this experiment was to repeat the test of the influence of the Cobra poison on the Viper. The result tends to show that it is innocuous.

FOURTEENTH SERIES.

Experiments on the Influence of the Poisons of the Cobra, the Daboia, the Bungarus fasciatus and Ophiophagus, and on the use of the Ligature and of Carbolic Acid in the Treatment of Snake-bites.

July 10th, 1869.

Present, Dr. Fayrer and Mr. Sceva.

EXPERIMENT No. 1.

A large and powerful Pariah Dog was bitten in the thigh by a *Daboia russellii* at 3.22 P.M.; the Dog showed signs of pain when the fangs penetrated. 3.25.—Walks, but drags the bitten limb. 3.28.—Is lying down; on rousing the Dog he is unable to stand; defecation and micturition occurred; shows no signs of suffering beyond occasionally a suppressed whine; tries to stand, but is unable to do so; contents of bladder dribbling away. 3.32.—Respiration hurried; pupils dilated; rolls his head uneasily, but keeps the neck turned more to one side; twitching of eyeballs; stretches out the fore-legs in a convulsive manner. Lies otherwise quite paralysed. 3.35.—Breathing regularly, but lies motionless. 3.38.—In the same condition; respirations forty in a minute; slightly raises his head at intervals. 3.45.—Still breathing, but lies perfectly still, giving occasionally a low suppressed whine. 3.53.—In the same condition; has watery purging. 4 P.M.—In the same condition; respirations forty-five in a minute. 4.7.—Can just raise its head when roused, the limbs seem quite paralysed. 4.9.—Muco-sanguineous purging: other symptoms the same. 4.18.—Still breathing; more muco-sanguineous purging. 4.20.—In the same condition. 4.40.—In the same position; lying on his side; legs extended; breathing still. 4.45.—Slight twitching of the muscles generally; respiration irregular, and feeble. 4.50.—Dead: a slight tremor, but no convulsive movement preceded death. Bitten at 3.22 P.M.; dead at 4.50, or in eighty-eight minutes. The body was examined one hour and twenty minutes after death. The lungs were not congested. The liver was darker coloured than natural. The blood in the heart and great vessels was perfectly fluid, nor did it coagulate when collected and set apart.

I examined the blood at noon on July 11th most carefully and deliberately under the microscope, with a high power. There was no change. The red and white corpuscles were in their natural relative quantities; a very few of the red ones were crenate. But there was not a trace of any new cell or molecular matter in the blood.

The perfect and permanent fluidity in the blood was remarkably illustrated in this experiment.

EXPERIMENT No. 2.

A Pariah Dog was bitten at 3.28 P.M. in the thigh by a large *Bungarus fasciatus*, said to be quite fresh, and about four feet and a half long; the bites drew blood. Walking about; drags the leg slightly. 3.34.—Looks depressed and is salivated. 3.36.—Walks about; looking scared. 3.40.—Bitten again in the thigh by the same *Bungarus:* the Dog evinced no sign of suffering. 3.42.—Looks dejected; foaming at the mouth; salivated. 4.7.—The Dog is sick and vomited a quantity of frothy mucus; vomiting repeated frequently. 4.10.—In walking he looks depressed, as though excessively nauseated, and limps on the bitten leg. 4.12.—Vomiting continues; lies down for the first time; breathing hurried. 4.17.—The nausea and vomiting continue; looks scared and depressed. 4.20.—Excessive vomiting of frothy mucus. Lies down; is convulsed in the hind-legs; looks very ill. 4.29.—Hurried catching respiration; twitching of the hind-legs. 4.32.—Walking slowly and feebly with a dejected look; vomits frequently, and froths profusely from the mouth. 4.33.—Stands with his head drooping; still very sick; leans his body for support against the wall. 4.45.—No change. 5 P.M.—Appears better. 5.15.—Looks better; no vomiting; respiration more natural. 5.40.—Lying down; when raised on his feet, appears weak, but otherwise better. On lying down, arranged his legs in a natural position as if for sleeping. 6.10.—On being again roused, he walked about; his legs appeared feeble at first, but he seemed to recover the use of them. 9.15.—Sleeping comfortably; on being roused, looks brighter and intelligent.

July 11th, 6 A.M.—Remained during the night without changing his position; on being placed on his feet appears weak, particularly in the hind-legs; he appears somewhat numbed in the legs.

I received the following report on July 13th:—

"The Dog died at about 10.30 P.M. of the 12th. Bitten at 3.28 P.M. of July 10th; dead at 10.30 P.M. of the 12th, or in about fifty-five hours. Yesterday morning (the 12th) I observed that he was very weak. During the day, and up to the time of his death, he remained lying on one side with the legs extended, passing at intervals muco-sanguineous matter. On opening the body this morning I found the blood coagulated in the heart and great vessels." The blood sent to me on the 13th was firmly coagulated. Under the microscope it presented innumerable needle-like crystals of hæmato-globulin. The red corpuscles visible were very few in number, and were not, so far as I could judge, changed in any way. But I would speak with reserve about the corpuscles of this blood, as the field was so entirely filled with the crystals that little else could be seen even after careful dilution with water and agitation. It is possible that new cell forms may have been there, and escaped detection. The mass of the red corpuscles seems to have been converted into crystals. In both this and the preceding case the blood was examined some time after death, but I failed to detect any new cell growths.

EXPERIMENT No. 3.

A young Cobra, about ten inches long, was bitten at 3.45 P.M. by a fresh full-grown Cobra ("Keautiah") near the tail, so that the viscera might not be injured. The fangs were seen to penetrate, and no doubt could exist that the poison was fairly inserted. Being put on the ground, it crawled away vigorously; seemed unaffected by the bite. 5 P.M.—No change.

July 11th, 6 A.M.—No change; it is quite well and active.

On July 13th I saw it quite well.

On the 17th it was found dead; apparently it had been dead about twelve hours.

EXPERIMENT No. 4.

Another young Cobra of the same brood as the last (No. 3) was bitten by a fresh *Daboia* near the tail like the last. The fangs penetrated, and the poison was freely inserted. 5.10.—No change. 6.15.—No change, except that when moving about, the end of the tail beyond the part bitten appears stiff, and does not move so freely as the rest of the body. This is accounted for by the nature of the wound inflicted by the formidable fangs of the Viper.

July 11th.—No change.

July 13th.—The snake is alive and apparently well.

On the 17th it was found dead and decomposed; it had probably been dead three or four days. These two young Cobras were of one brood; they were caught a few days ago, and are said by the snake-man to be about a fortnight or ten days old.

There could be no doubt about their having been fairly bitten by the Cobra and the *Daboia* on the 10th; no evil result followed up to the 13th, though they died subsequently. Surely this is strong proof that the Cobra is but little, if at all, susceptible to the poison of its own species. These snakes being so young, may have died from want of food, and partly from the effects of the wound, independent of the poison. They were alive on the fourth day after being bitten.

EXPERIMENT No. 5.

A white half-grown Kitten was bitten by a *Bungarus fasciatus*, said to be fresh, at 4.9 P.M., in the thigh. It seemed much excited shortly after. 4.25.—Lying in its former position, stretching out the fore-leg in a convulsive manner. 5 P.M.—In much the same condition. 6.10.—It has been very restless; now seems inclined to sleep; appears to be free from pain. 9.15.—Does not appear now to be much affected by the poison.

July 11th.—It seems better.

July 13th.—The Kitten was quite well.

It is evident in this case that the animal was not mortally though thoroughly bitten, for the snake was made to close his jaws on the part, and drew blood. This, I believe, is just the sort of case which probably frequently occurs when men or animals are accidentally bitten—enough venom is injected to cause symptoms of poisoning, but not enough to destroy life. And the man or animal recovers chiefly by his or its own inherent power of recovery. Had I administered any of the so-called antidotes, or injected any of the proposed remedies, the recovery might have been attributed to the means used.

EXPERIMENT No. 6.

Another Kitten of the same size and age as that in Experiment 5 was bitten by a Cobra in the left thigh, at 4.16 P.M. The bite was very imperfect, and was repeated at 4.20 P.M.

At 4.24, the Kitten very restless, and springing about violently. 4.25.—Hurried breathing; restlessness. 4.45.—Becoming weaker; respiration irregular. 5.5.—Convulsive movements generally. 5.20.—Dead, in one hour and four minutes. 6.20.—Body opened one hour after death. Lungs natural; no congestion; the blood on being removed from the heart and great vessels soon coagulated firmly.

EXPERIMENT No. 7.

A *Bungarus fasciatus* was fairly and deeply bitten by a fresh Cobra at 4.27 P.M. near the tail; no doubt of the penetration of the fangs and inoculation of the poison. No effect was produced. The *Bungarus* was well and active on the 16th, five days after the bite.

EXPERIMENT No. 8.

A *Bungarus fasciatus* was thoroughly bitten by a fresh *Daboia* at 4.32 P.M. near the tail. No evil result followed; the *Bungarus* remained unaffected; on July 16th was in its normal condition. Several facts of importance are proved, or their probability confirmed, by the preceding experiments.

In death by poisoning by the *Daboia*, and therefore probably by all the viperine order—*Viperidæ* and *Crotalidæ*—the coagulability of the blood is generally destroyed. I say generally, because though frequently it is not invariably so. In the experiment on the Fowl it was found that the blood had coagulated. It remains fluid after death on exposure to the air. The most careful and protracted microscopical examination could detect no structural change in the corpuscular elements of the blood. Death is more protracted, but the deadly effects of the poison are even more quickly manifested than in death from Cobra poisoning. In point of lethality both appear equally dangerous.

In death by Cobra poisoning, the blood coagulates firmly after and even before death, as post-mortem examinations, made at all periods, from immediately to an hour or more after death, have shown the blood to be coagulated firmly. No changes in the corpuscular elements have been seen in any of the microscopic examinations I have made.

The poison of the *Bungarus fasciatus* is less deadly than that of the Cobra or *Daboia*, but it is very dangerous, though it is slow in producing its worst effects. It also does not destroy the coagulability of the blood. Perhaps this may prove to be the case with all the poisonous colubrine snakes. No change was observed in the corpuscular elements—*i.e.*, in such as remained. But the red corpuscles had passed, in the case of the blood of the Dog that died from a bite by a *Bungarus fasciatus*, into a state of excessive crystallization of a needle-like and long tabular form.

The *Bungarus fasciatus* is also less susceptible to the poison of the *Daboia* and Cobra than the *innocuous* snakes, if indeed it be affected at all.

Death was not caused by asphyxia in any of these cases. Everything tends to show that it is due to direct exhaustion from paralysis of the nerve centres.

July 17th, 1869.

Present, Dr. Fayrer and Mr. Sceva.

EXPERIMENT No. 9.

A large and powerful Pariah Dog was bitten in the thigh, at 2.45 P.M., by a fresh Cobra ("Keautiah"). The hair had been previously removed from the part in order that the puncture of the snake's fangs might be distinctly seen. The moment the fangs were withdrawn, the punctures were scarified, and carbolic acid at once applied, and well inoculated into the bites. The tissues were whitened, and the blood coagulated by the acid. 2.53 P.M. — The Dog looks depressed and dejected; hanging his head. 3.12.—Lying down; looks dejected, but perfectly intelligent. 3.15. — Respiration hurried. 3.23. — Pupils widely dilated. In convulsions, rolled over on the other side; respiration irregular and catching. 3.27. — Violently convulsed. 3.30.—Respiration has ceased, but the heart still beats distinctly. 3.31.—Dead in forty-six minutes. The carbolic acid was evidently of no service in this case.

Post-mortem examination at 5 P.M. Blood coagulated; no crystallization under microscope.

EXPERIMENT No. 10.

A Fowl had the feathers removed from the thigh, so that the bites might be seen, and was then bitten there at 2.54 P.M. by a *Daboia*. The wounds were immediately scarified, and the carbolic acid thoroughly applied to the bites. The Fowl fell over in convulsions when released, and was dead in less than sixty seconds. The body was opened at 3.35, or in about forty minutes after death, and the blood was found to be coagulated in the heart and great vessels; some fluid blood escaped into the thorax. The lungs were not in the least congested. The condition of the blood was particularly noted, as it has generally been found fluid in the Mammals dead from the *Daboia* bite.

EXPERIMENT No. 11.

The poison of a fresh Cobra ("Gokurrah") was taken from the snake in my presence, and ten drops of it immediately injected with the hypodermic syringe into a middling-sized Dog's thigh, at 3.3 P.M. The tube of the hypodermic syringe was not removed; and the syringe being filled with carbolic acid, about twenty drops were injected exactly in the track of the poison, and in the shortest space of time possible. 3.8.—The Dog is depressed; looks scared; hangs his head; twitching of the hind-legs when he is raised. 3.15.—Lying on his side almost paralysed; pupils widely dilated. 3.20.—Is convulsed. 3.22. — General twitching of all the muscles of the body; is quite unconscious. Respiration has ceased, but the heart still beats distinctly. 3.25.—Heart still beats. 3.27.—Irregular action of heart. 3.29.—Dead, in twenty-six minutes.

Post-mortem examination. Blood examined at 5 P.M.: fluid when removed, but coagulated on exposure to the air.

Microscopical examination: no crystals; no change.

In this case there could be no doubt of the perfect inoculation of the carbolic acid, for it followed the poison through the same channel, and in the shortest possible space of time, in which any local remedy could be applied, and yet without producing the slightest benefit. The second of time by which the poison preceded it, was sufficient to cause death; no remedy could have been applied more rapidly, unless it had been mixed with the poison and introduced with it; in which case the venom might have been probably decomposed and rendered inert. It appears to be impossible to overtake the poison, and neutralize it when once in the circulation, however rapid may be the inoculation of the supposed antidote.

Experiment No. 12.

A Fowl was bitten in the thigh by a *Daboia* at 3.19 P.M. The carbolic acid was immediately applied to the wounds, which had been at once scarified. 3.19.30.—Fowl in convulsions. 3.20.—Dead in one minute. Body opened. Blood in heart and great vessels had coagulated.

Experiment No. 13.

A small Dog bitten in the thigh, by a *Bungarus fasciatus*, (one used last week) at 3.13 P.M. The bites drew blood. 3.29.—Looks dejected. 5.20.—No further change.

July 18th, 7 A.M. — No change. At 12 noon the Dog appears very weak; has not altered his position (recumbent) since last report. 6 P.M.—The same; refuses food; gradually drooped throughout the day.

July 19th.—Died at 1.35 P.M., in about forty-six hours and twenty-seven minutes. Blood examined at 7.45 P.M.: blood clotted after death firmly; the serum paler than usual; corpuscles natural; no crystallization.

Experiment No. 14.

A Fowl was bitten by another *Bungarus fasciatus*, which had also been used last week, at 3.32 P.M. 3.40.—The Fowl looks uneasy, but not otherwise affected.

18th, 7 A.M.—Crouching on the floor; wings drooping. Noon.—Unable to stand; profuse flow of watery blood from the beak. 3 P.M.—Lying on its side; eyes closed. 5.40 P.M.—Died—in twenty-six hours and eighteen minutes. Body opened at 6 P.M.; blood coagulated; under microscope no crystallization had occurred.

Experiment No. 15.

A Fowl was bitten by a Cobra in the thigh at 3.45.30. Ran about for a moment when placed on the ground. 3.46.—Crouched; resting its beak on the ground; fell over, and was dead at 3.47. Body opened at 5.10. Blood fluid, but coagulated on exposure to air.

Experiment No. 16.

A *Daboia* was well bitten by a Cobra near the tail, at 4.5 P.M.

July 18th, noon.—No change. 6 P.M.—No change; no effect was produced. The *Daboia* was alive a week after being bitten.

Experiment No. 17.

A *Varanus flavescens* was bitten by another *Daboia* at 4.15 P.M. The *Daboia* had bitten before. He did not strike his fangs readily through the hard skin of the lizard.

July 18th, 3 P.M.—No change. 6 P.M.—No change.

The *Varanus* was not affected; it was alive a week after being bitten.

The *Daboia* was not fresh; and it did not bite vigorously, hence the escape of the *Varanus*.

Experiment No. 18.

A Cobra was bitten by a *Daboia*, near the tail, at 4.3 P.M., and was bitten again by another *Daboia*, at 4.8 P.M., near the same place.

July 18th, 5 P.M.—No change; a week later—no change.

Note.—The *Bungarus fasciatus* bitten by the *Daboia*, on Saturday, July 10th, was found recently dead on Saturday, 24th. Death may have been due to natural causes. The *Bungarus fasciatus* bitten at the same time by a Cobra is alive and well on July 24th.

July 24th, 1869.

Present, Dr. Fayrer and Mr. Sceva.

Experiment No. 19.

In the experiments hitherto performed the snake has been made to close the jaws on the part bitten, and not been left to strike in the natural way. With the object of ascertaining whether there be any difference in the effect of the compulsory and voluntary bite, the following experiment was performed; and I observed in this, as on other occasions, that the snake rather attempted to frighten than to bite the Dog, and it was not until the Cobra was much irritated by repeatedly bringing the Dog near him that he gave the fatal bite. It struck the Dog twice in the hind-leg, apparently without any effect, but afterwards struck, and for a moment fastened on to the thorax. Two slightly bleeding points marked where the Dog was bitten—this was at 3.32 P.M. 3.45.—The Dog is affected; vomited and was purged; very restless. 3.50.—Vomiting and staggering as he walks. 3.53.—Convulsed. 3.57.—Heart still beating irregularly; respiratory movements ceased. 3.58.—Dead—in twenty-six minutes. Another object of this experiment was again to search in the post-mortem blood for the corpuscles described by Professor Halford.

The body was opened at 5 P.M., or about an hour after death. The blood coagulated firmly, and was repeatedly examined under the microscope with a high power; but I could detect no change whatever in its corpuscular elements. The lungs, as usual, were free from congestion.

Experiment No. 20.

Placed a ligature round a Fowl's thigh, and tied it very tightly. The Fowl was then bitten by a Cobra, at 4 P.M., below the ligature. The ligature was tied as tightly as it could be drawn, and appeared to arrest the circulation completely, for the part below it became livid, and the limb was paralysed. 4.13.—The Fowl lies quiet, and does not seem to be affected by the poison. 4.17.—Is active and lively; hops about on the sound leg. 4.20.—Does not seem to be in the least affected by the poison; at this period, that is, fifteen minutes after the bite the ligature was removed. The limb was turgid and livid from congestion. The bird began to droop almost immediately the ligature was removed. 4.22.—Drooping; does not rise; when raised crouches again. 4.23.—Head falling over; can hardly move. 4.24. — Convulsed. 4.30. — Still alive; faint; convulsive movements continue. 4.33.—Dead. Bitten at 4.5 P.M.; ligature removed at 4.20; no effect of poison being manifested.

Dead at 4.33—*i.e.*, thirteen minutes after the ligature was removed. The poison was slow of entering with the stagnant blood of the congested limb, but it did enter and kill in thirteen minutes.

Experiment No. 21.

A Fowl was bitten in the leg by a Cobra, and a ligature tightened round the thigh immediately. This was at 4.10 P.M.

4.12. — Runs about; limping on the bitten leg, which is almost paralysed by the ligature, and livid with congestion. 4.17.—Slightly affected; appears to droop a little. 4.27.—No apparent effect of the poison. 4.30. — Scarified the fang punctures deeply, and rubbed the carbolic acid well into the wounds until all the blood coagulated, and the scarified surfaces were whitened by the acid. 4.31. — Removed the ligature; the Fowl hops about, dragging the wounded limb, but not affected apparently by the poison. 4.35.—Poison now beginning to take effect: the Fowl, as it was running, staggered and fell forwards; it then crouched, and its respirations were very rapid. 4.40. — Cannot walk; when raised falls over again. 4.42. — Head drooping; eyes closing; beak resting on the ground. It continued alive until 5.35; and during that time it showed distinct reflex action of legs, if the feet were pinched, and of the wings as in flying when raised in the air. It remained lying on its side, and died at 5.35 P.M. Bitten at 4.10 P.M. Ligature applied *immediately*. Ligature removed at 4.31, in twenty-one minutes. Died at 5.35, or in sixty-four minutes after the ligature was removed. These experiments are very interesting. They prove that the poison enters, and proves fatal by way of the blood-vessels, and that if a ligature be sufficiently tightly applied (the great difficulty), the entry of the poison may be much, if not altogether prevented; and that probably the application of carbolic acid or other caustic agents to the part poisoned, if thoroughly ligatured, may do good by decomposing the poison in the blood in which it is mingled.

But that too much faith must not be reposed in the acid or cautery is proved by this and former experiments, where the poison was prevented from entering the circulation by means of the ligature, and was subjected to the action of the acid whilst so detained; yet when the ligature was removed, and the stagnant circulation again restored, death followed from the slow absorption of the poison which, notwithstanding the thorough application of the acid, yet retained enough of its deadly qualities to cause death.

A Fowl bitten by a Cobra generally dies in a few minutes. It will be seen by these two experiments how long the fatal event was delayed by aid of the ligature and acid.

July 26th.

EXPERIMENT No. 22.

The same *Ophiophagus elaps* mentioned in former experiments was brought to me again to-day. No new fangs had been reproduced: and it looked thin and half-starved. The snake-men say that no new fangs have ever replaced those originally taken out. I obtained by squeezing the glands about four drops of a deep orange-coloured viscid-looking fluid of the consistence of mucus. I made a slight puncture on a Fowl's thigh with a lancet, and with an ordinary pen inoculated some of this yellow fluid into the wound, at 11.15 A.M. For some time the Fowl seemed unaffected, but in the afternoon I found it in a lethargic state, crouching with the head drooping, and the point of the beak resting on the ground. It gradually drooped. There appear to have been no convulsions, and at 10 P.M. it was dead.

This experiment shows that the entire loss of the poison fangs, and consequent comparative inactivity of the glands, does not deprive them of the power of secreting poison; though, no doubt, it diminishes the activity, and probably modifies the nature of the secretion. All other snake-poison that I have seen taken from the armed and vigorous snake, of whatever family, has been a clear limpid fluid.* In this case it was of a deep rich orange-colour, and of the consistence of mucus. It proves also, that on the first removal of the poison fangs, the reserve fangs may also be removed, leaving the reptile disarmed for life. This is not always effected by the operation of the snake-charmers, for they well know, and occasional fatal accidents have proved, that a new fang takes the place of the old one. I had the fangs carefully removed from a Cobra, and kept him to see in what time the new ones come forward. In one instance I found that, after a fortnight, a pair of new fangs had replaced those removed, but they were not thoroughly anchylosed to the maxillary bones. A *Daboia*, whose large fangs were removed with the same object, died shortly after the removal of the teeth, but whether the death was due to the operation, or to natural causes, I am unable to say. There is at present a *Daboia* that has not touched food or water for six months in my possession; every effort having been made in vain to make the snake eat or drink, and it is vigorous and vicious as when first caught; but its venomous powers are probably diminished. During this period, the *Daboia* has frequently changed its epidermic covering, and there are occasional deposits of solid urinary excreta passed. It never moves unless roused, when it is very active and vicious. The only conclusion that I can come to, is that it may have obtained moisture from the damp air, and may have swallowed flies or cockroaches or other insects that have found their way into the cage. But it certainly has neither taken food nor water in any other way during this period.

* See P. 116, June 13th—Poison of the Ophiophagus elaps.

FIFTEENTH SERIES.

Experiments on the Influence of Snake-poison, and the use of Certain Reputed Antidotes; and the Effects of the Ligature and Excision, &c.

July 31st, 1869.

Present, Dr. Fayrer and Mr. Sceva.

EXPERIMENT No. 1.

Mr. R.'s (of Jounpore) antidote, the powdered root or bark of a plant, name and family unknown, was tried to-day on a Dog. The drug had been sent to me for the purpose, and was fresh and potent. Half of a powder, the quantity directed by Mr. R., was given, having been first carefully rubbed and mixed with about an ounce of water.

A Pariah Dog was bitten in the thigh by a Cobra at 3.3 P.M., and was much excited by the bite. At 3.6, as symptoms of poisoning appeared, the first dose of the antidote was given, and was all swallowed. The Dog was led about, and cold water dashed on its face and thorax when it seemed drowsy. 3.8.—Lies down; very restless. 3.9.—Hurried breathing. 3.10.—Dog lies down; rises again, and runs about in a restless and excited manner. 3.12.—Restless and uneasy; head swings about as though it were giddy; breathing accelerated. 3.17.—It staggers as it is walked about; cold water sprinkled on its head and chest. 3.18.—The second dose given, that is, the other half of the powder, as directed. 3.20.—The Dog is worse; cannot stand, staggers and reels when walked about, and falls over; convulsive movements of head and neck. 3.22.—Convulsed; pupils widely dilated. 3.24.—Dead—in twenty-one minutes.

The Dog was not a large one, but it was healthy and vigorous; the instructions sent with the drug were carefully followed. The result is not favourable to the drug as an antidote for the canine race.

EXPERIMENT No. 2.

A Dog had a ligature made of stout cord, *soaped* to make it knot tightly, thrown loosely round the fore-arm. It was then bitten by a Cobra below the ligature, which was tightened as firmly as a man's strength could draw it. Immediately after the bite, a red-hot iron was introduced into the fang wounds, and the bitten part thoroughly cauterized, strong carbolic acid having first been well rubbed in.

Bitten at 3.31 P.M. Ligature tightened within five seconds. Carbolic acid and actual cautery applied at 3.33, that is, in two minutes after the bite, and one minute and fifty-five seconds after the ligature was tightened. The limb seemed to be completely strangulated; it became livid; blood oozed from the fang wounds, and the limb was all but paralysed. There could be no doubt that the limb was thoroughly strangulated, or that the bitten parts were well cauterized. 3.36.—Notwithstanding all the above precautions, the Dog is already much affected by the poison, is lying prone, unable to rise or to walk, the breathing hurried, and convulsive movements occurring occasionally. 3.40.—Convulsed. 3.41.—Dying. 3.42.—Dead—in twenty-one minutes.

There was at the most an interval of five seconds between the Cobra's bite and the tightening of the ligature, which was not afterwards relaxed. This experiment clearly proves that the poison is taken into the circulation very rapidly; certainly five seconds did not elapse between the bite and the application of the ligature, which had been previously thrown loosely round the limb, in order that no time might be lost in tightening it after the bite, and yet the Dog (it was a small one), died of the poison in twenty-one minutes. During that very brief interval sufficient poison entered the circulation to destroy life. It is possible that more may have entered after the ligature was tightened, but the quantity must have been very minute, as the ligature was very tight. In an ordinary snake-bite it is difficult to conceive that a ligature could be applied more speedily than in the case of this Dog. So that, even this method of treatment, rational as it certainly is, can only be regarded as of doubtful benefit.

I should note, and it is a subject, I believe, that I have not alluded to before in other experiments, that the rigor mortis took place in about one hour and a half after death, in these two Dogs. The blood coagulated after death.

Experiment No. 3.

A Fowl had a ligature placed on the thigh loosely: it was bitten by a Cobra at 3.47. The ligature was tightened at the same time that the snake bit; before its fangs were withdrawn, the ligature was thoroughly tied, so tight that the limb seemed completely strangulated, the part becoming livid and disabled. 3.50.—No sign of the poison taking effect; the Fowl hops about on the sound leg. 3.52.—Actual cautery and carbolic acid applied to the fang punctures, which were bleeding freely venous blood from the congested limb, and the wounded parts surrounding were thoroughly disorganized. The ligature was then divided; the Fowl being placed on the ground ran about; the ligatured limb still paralysed. 3.54.—Fowl crouching, but rises and runs about when disturbed. 3.55.—Looks drowsy; is crouching, and begins to hang its head, closing the eyes. 3.57.—Head drooping, beak resting on the ground. 3.58.—Fallen over on its side, rises with a convulsive movement, and falls again. 4 P.M.—Is unable to stand or walk. 4.4.—Convulsive movements. 4.11.—Dead—in twenty-four minutes. Blood coagulated after death when removed from the great vessels.

This experiment more than ever proves the subtle and deadly nature of the poison. The ligature in this case prevented the entry of the poison into the circulation, but it was evidently retained in the congested part of the limb below the ligature. Carbolic acid and the actual cautery applied to the wounds, most thoroughly, failed to destroy it. For no sooner was the ligature relaxed than the poison entered the circulation, weak and altered as it must have been after the severe pressure of the ligature, and rapidly killed the bird. This proves that there is danger after removal of the ligature when it has been most effectually applied. The poison spreads itself by diffusion throughout the juices of the strangulated part; so that nothing short of destruction or removal of the whole of that part seems to offer a hope of subsequent escape from toxic absorption.

With reference to the application of a ligature above the bitten part, I would here remark that it is almost physically impossible with the power of one pair of hands so to tighten a cord round a dog's leg, as thoroughly to strangulate the limb. The experiments seem to prove this, but also to show that it is possible completely to arrest the circulation through a fowl's leg in this manner.

With tourniquets it might be done no doubt, and a man's arm or leg, certainly his toe or finger, might be so strangulated, but as ordinary snake-bites do not occur where any tourniquets other than sticks and cords or the like are forthcoming, the desideratum is to obtain the most perfect compression of the limb in the simplest way possible, sufficient at all events to prevent immediate entry of the poison through the circulation; and this may be done with an ordinary cord or strip of cloth, twisted with the common stick tourniquet, and to the fullest extent that the strength of the hands is able to twist it. But it must be borne in mind that this compression only extends to a certain depth, and that deeper the circulation still goes on; with this the poison retained by the ligature in the partially strangulated portion will soon communicate by diffusion, and symptoms of poisoning will supervene. In such a case we may fairly hope that the amount of poison entering the blood has been so far limited as not to be fatal, and that we may therefore be able to help the sufferer through the troubles caused by the reduced dose of the poison. But it is obvious that the urgent necessity is for the application of some agent that will equally diffuse itself, and neutralize or destroy the poison whilst yet retained and only partially diffused through the strangulated part.

In this, as far as I can understand it, lies the only hope of safety in a real Cobra bite.

Carbolic acid or other allied substances would probably be useful. But it is obvious that the success of this, or indeed of any mode of treatment, lies in the promptitude and tension with which the ligature is tied, and the decomposing agent applied.

Experiment No. 4.

Dr. W. J. Palmer, Professor of Chemistry, was present also.

A Fowl had a ligature thoroughly tightened round the thigh, and was then bitten below it by a Cobra at 4.7 P.M.

4.19.—No effect of the poison visible. 4.22.—Breathing rather hurried, but otherwise seems unaffected. 4.30.—Begins to show signs of the effects of the poison, nods its head drowsily, rests its beak on the ground; it is evidently affected. 4.35.—Much the same; thirty drops of the liquor ammoniæ injected in three doses with the hypodermic syringe. 4.37.—Fowl is drooping fast, cannot move. 4.41.—Convulsed. 4.44.—Lies unconscious, but convulsed. 4.50.—Dead.

In this case the ligature, which consisted of a cord soaped to make it run easily and knot firmly, was tied round a Fowl's thigh, from which the feathers had been stripped, with the greatest amount of tension that a man's hands could exert. The part below the ligature became livid, and the limb paralysed. In this condition it was bitten at 4.7 P.M. The ligature was never relaxed, and certainly did not slip, yet at 4.30, perhaps earlier, that is, in twenty-three minutes, the Fowl began to show that the poison had, notwithstanding the ligature, found entry into the circulation. Its death, twenty-one minutes later, proved that sufficient poison had entered to destroy life, and also proves, I think, that it is almost beyond our power to keep it out. The question is, supposing the strangulation of the limbs to have been complete, how did the poison enter? It must have passed the barrier of the ligature. How did it do so? I can only explain it by supposing that tense as it was, the limb was not sufficiently constricted to prevent some diffusion of the poisonous fluids through the compressed tissues, and that in the space of twenty-three minutes enough found its way in to destroy life.

From this experiment I think we may fairly deduce the amount of safety that may be expected from the ligature. That it retards the entry of the poison is abundantly proved, and that it gives time therefore to operate on the retarded venom is also obvious. But it is equally evident, so subtle is this poison, and such is the power of diffusion, that nothing short of the most rapid and effective application of the ligature, and the immediately subsequent application of some decomposing agent, can, in a *boná fide* Cobra bite, offer any hope of safety.

Experiment No. 5.

A Fowl was deeply bitten in the thigh by a *Daboia* at 4.31. The snake had been in confinement for some time, but it was vigorous and vicious, and plunged its fangs deeply into the bird's thigh, drawing blood. 4.36.—Not affected. 5 P.M.—Not affected. No symptoms of poisoning occurred, and the Fowl was alive and well on August 2nd.

This experiment is a most instructive one, and proves that a poisonous snake may bite without poisoning. It is not in the least probable that this *Daboia* was altogether exhausted, for although in captivity, it had been at rest for many days, and had not exhausted its poison by biting; another *Daboia* that had been six months in captivity, and had eaten nothing during that period, killed a Fowl rapidly by one bite. It furnishes an explanation of some of the so-called recoveries from snake-bite, in which, when the snake has been seen and the punctures of its fangs are visible, the patient recovers from the mental alarm and prostration after the administration of one of the supposed antidotes. That such alarm does cause temporary, physical as well as mental, prostration I have had proof in the following case. Some time ago, on visiting the hospital one morning, I was told that a man had been admitted during the night suffering from a snake-bite, and that he was very low. I found him in a state of great prostration, he was hardly able to speak, and seemed to be in a state of great depression. He and his friends said that during the night in going into his hut a snake bit him in the foot; that he was much alarmed, and rapidly passed into a state of insensibility, when they brought him to the hospital. They and he considered that he was dying, and evidently regarded his condition as hopeless. He was in fact in that condition not unfrequently described, from which the sufferer has been snatched by the timely administration of an antidote. On asking for a description of the snake, they said they had caught it and brought it with them in a bottle. The bottle was produced, and the snake turned out to be a small innocent *Lycodon*. It was alive, though somewhat injured by the treatment it had received. On explaining to the man and his friends that it was harmless, and with some difficulty making them believe it, the symptoms of poisoning rapidly disappeared, and he left the hospital as well as ever he was in his life in a few hours. Had no snake been found, and had an antidote been given, who would have been prepared to dispute its efficacy? I am sorry to destroy popular and favourite illusions when they are harmless, but in a matter of this kind, it is well that the truth should be known.

Experiment No. 6.

A Fowl was bitten by a *Daboia* in the thigh at 4.49 P.M. The snake has been over six months in captivity, during which time it has steadily refused to take food or water. It was active, vigorous, and vicious; it plunged its fangs deeply into the Fowl's thigh and drew blood. In twenty seconds the bird was violently convulsed; in sixty more seconds it was dead.

Contrast this experiment with the preceding one, and I think it confirms what I said as to the occasional uncertainty of a snake-bite. These two *Daboias* were both old, that is to say, old in captivity. They were both notwithstanding vigorous, and bit fiercely. In one case no evil resulted from the bite; in the other rapid death.

The blood of the Fowl was examined after death. Dark coloured coagulated blood was found in one of the great vessels near the heart. In others and in the cavities of the heart it was fluid, and remained so after death.

It is worthy of notice that in the Mammals poisoned by the *Daboia*, the blood was found to be fluid, and to continue so after death. In birds it was sometimes coagulated. Could this be due to the rapidity with which life was extinguished in the bird?

August 7th, 1869.

Present, Dr. Fayrer, Dr. W. Palmer, Professor of Chemistry, and Mr. Sceva.

Experiment No. 7.

A Pariah Dog was bitten by a Cobra ("Tentuliah Keautiah" of the snake-men) in the hind-leg at 3.5 P.M. At 3.8 P.M. thirty drops of liquor ammoniæ, sp. gr. ·959, diluted with three parts of water, were administered. 3.12.—Dog lying down, licking the wound; when walked about, limped on the bitten leg; breathing hurried. 3.15.—Thirty more drops given as before. 3.22.—Lying down; limbs twitching. 3.23.—Thirty more drops given. 3.24.—Convulsed; lying down; unable to rise. 3.25.—Dying; limbs convulsed; pupils widely dilated; *tapetum lucidum* very brilliant. Heart still beating, no respiratory movements. 3.26.—Pupils contracted again (this is a phenomenon I have not before observed). 3.28.—Another thirty drops of liquor ammoniæ administered. 3.29.—Heart still beating irregularly. 3.30.—Dead—in twenty-five minutes.

Ammonia has long been considered one of the most potent of all remedies in snake-bites. The object of this experiment was to test its value. The result is not encouraging.

Experiment No. 8.

Mr. R.'s "antidote" was again put to the test. The powder was rubbed into a pulp mixed with water in the proportion directed; it was then administered to a Dog at 3.31 P.M. The Dog was then bitten by a Cobra in the thigh. 3.35.—The Dog is affected by the poison, looks scared, and limps in the bitten limb. 3.37.—Staggers, lies down; breathing hurried. 3.39.—Another dose administered. 3.43.—Limbs convulsed. 3.45.—Paralysed; heart beating irregularly. 3.59.—Heart still beats; no respiratory movements. 4 P.M.—Dead—in twenty-eight minutes.

I am afraid the antidote must be regarded as inapplicable to the canine race.

Experiment No. 9.

Jugular vein of a Pariah Dog exposed at 3.42, and a diluted solution of liquor ammoniæ, sp. gr. ·959—one part to water two parts—to the extent of thirty drops, injected. No apparent inconvenience caused to the Dog by the injection. At 3.43 the Dog was bitten in the thigh by a Cobra. 3.48.—Dog showing signs of the poison; thirty more drops, diluted in the same way with six of water, again injected into the jugular vein. Shortly after this the Dog began to turn round and round in the most restless manner; thirty more drops injected similarly diluted into the other external jugular, as a large thrombus had formed in that part exposed. 4.10.—Dog convulsed. 4.12.—Cannot stand, limbs paralysed. 4.13.—Violently convulsed all over. 4.20.—Dead—in thirty-seven minutes.

The Cobra was not fresh in this case, and yet it killed in thirty-seven minutes. The injection of the diluted ammonia was not more satisfactory than that of the undiluted, as far as its immediate antidotal effects were concerned; but it would appear that the injection of diluted liquor ammoniæ into the jugular vein is not followed necessarily by convulsions, or other violent constitutional disturbance.

Experiment No. 10.

Some of the blood of the Dog killed by the Cobra in Experiment No. 7, where the ammonia was given, was removed from the body about three-quarters of an hour after death. It was found to be firmly coagulated, but some of the serum and part of the clot mixed with water, to the extent altogether of forty drops, were injected with the hypodermic syringe into a Fowl's thigh; the actual quantity of blood thus used could not have been more than a few drops. The injection was made at 4.20 P.M. 4.35.—Slightly affected by the poison. 5 P.M.—

Crouching, head drooping, appears giddy. 5.30.—Lying on one side; convulsive movements. 5.35.—Dead—in seventy-five minutes.

What can more forcibly illustrate the extraordinary virulence and potency of the poison than this experiment? A few drops of the blood of a Dog poisoned by a Cobra, diluted with water, injected into a Fowl's thigh, killed the bird in seventy-five minutes. The quantity must have been excessively minute, but it proves how it retains its power, although diluted and mixed with the blood.

August 14*th*, 1869.

Present, Drs. Fayrer, W. Palmer, and Mr. Sceva.

EXPERIMENT No. 11.

A gentleman residing at Rohtuck having forwarded to me the powdered root or some other part of a plant, name and family unknown, which he had found useful in the treatment of snake-bites, and having requested me to test its efficacy, the following experiment was made:—

One drachm of the powder was rubbed with six peppers into a pulp and mixed with water.

A Pariah Dog was then bitten by a Cobra (variety "Kurrees Keautiah," of the snake-men) in the thigh at 3.13 P.M.; part of the antidote was then, according to Mr. F.'s direction, rubbed into the punctures, and the remainder administered internally, immediately after the outward application. 3.18.—The Dog is affected by the poison, he is restless, nauseated, making efforts to vomit; walks with a staggering gait. 3.22.—Limbs partially paralysed. 3.23.—Convulsed, unable to rise. 3.25.—Lies perfectly motionless, muscles generally twitching. 3.26—Dead—in thirteen minutes.

The drug had evidently no effect in retarding the action of the poison. The Dog, which was a medium-sized animal, died even sooner than usual.

EXPERIMENT No. 12.

A Mahomedan Hakeem, Mahomed Khan, presented himself with some medicine, with which, he said, he had successfully treated several cases of snake-bite in men. It was a strong aromatic smelling powder, dissolved in water, but he could tell me no more than that it was a jungle root. He asked to be allowed to try it, and appeared quite confident of success. A very large and powerful Pariah Dog was then placed at his disposal, also a Cobra, which was not fresh, having been in captivity for some time, and had bitten before. He had the Dog bitten in the thigh by the Cobra at 3.35 P.M. He was allowed to do, or direct to be done, whatever he liked. At 3.36 he administered a quantity of the drug, which was swallowed by the Dog. 3.37.—The bitten leg is partially paralysed. 3.45.—The Dog is sluggish and lying down. 3.46.—A second dose administered. 3.48.—Hurried breathing. 3.50.—The Dog is nauseated, and rejected some half-digested meat. 3.55.—Uneasy; hurried breathing. 4.2.—Lying down, panting, frothing at the mouth. 4.5.—Retching. 4.7.—Lying down; looks depressed, but quite intelligent. 4.15.—When roused staggers as he walks. 4.18.—Lies prone, with the legs outstretched. Has very little control over the hind-legs when roused. 4.20.—Another large dose of the drug administered by the hakeem. 4.21.—Limbs convulsed, unable to rise. 4.24.—Tries to rise, falls over. 4.26.—Convulsed. 4.32.—Is quite paralysed; pupils widely dilated. 4.35.—Heart still beats, no respiratory movements. 4.40 —Pupils contracted again (I have observed this symptom in another Dog just before death.) 4.42.—Dead; pupils again dilated. Bitten at 3.35, dead at 4.42—in sixty-seven minutes.

The Dog was a remarkably powerful and vigorous animal. The snake was not fresh, and yet the Dog succumbed in one hour and seven minutes.

The hakeem expressed much astonishment at the results; he evidently *believed* that his drug would prove an antidote. He said, in a somewhat depressed tone of voice, that he had other remedies. He was invited to put them to a similar test.

EXPERIMENT No. 13.

A very large and vigorous Pariah Dog was bitten in the marginal fold of integument between the thigh and abdomen by a Cobra at 3.55 P.M. The part was immediately cut out with a bistoury, the places where the fangs had penetrated being completely removed. The instrument was at hand, and the operation was done at once. Two seconds, not more, might have intervened between the bites and the excision.

At 4 P.M. some brandy was poured down the Dog's throat. 4.6.— Another dose of brandy administered. 4.16.— He is excited, and the respiration is hurried, perhaps from the brandy. 4.25.—The Dog is not yet affected by the poison. 4.33.—Much the same, the breathing rather hurried. 4.42. — No symptoms of poisoning except the hurried breathing, and that may be from excitement. 4.47.—More brandy given. 4.50.—No symptom of poisoning as yet. 5.10.—Vomited; shows symptoms of being poisoned. 5.15.—Vomited again. 5.30.—Restless, breathing hurriedly; abundant flow of saliva. 6 P.M.—Slight convulsions; breathing hurried. 6.30.—Dead. Bitten at 3.55, dead at 6.30—in two hours and thirty-five minutes.

Here again the extraordinary virulence of the poison is shown. The snake bit in a fold of skin which was immediately excised; yet in the slight interval, it could not have been more than two seconds, enough of the poison had entered the circulation to cause death in two hours and thirty-five minutes, notwithstanding the free administration of brandy. The Dog too was an unusually large and vigorous animal.

EXPERIMENT No. 14.

A Fowl was bitten in the thigh by a Cobra at 4.13 P.M.

The part in which the fangs had lodged was immediately excised with a sharp scalpel. 4.17.—Fowl lying down, showing no signs of poisoning. 4.20.—Fowl rather drowsy, eyes closing, head drooping. 4.25.—Breathing hurried; drowsy. 4.28.— When roused can stand, but cannot walk, and falls over; gasping. 4.31.—Convulsed. 4.33.—Dead—in twenty-one minutes.

This again shows the extraordinary virulence of the poison. The entire mass of muscle into which the fangs were impressed was clearly cut away within three seconds after the bite, and yet poison sufficient had found entry to cause death. That death was much retarded there can be no doubt, for the Fowl lived twenty-one minutes, instead of three or four, after being bitten. Slight as is the encouragement to be derived from such experiments as this, it yet points in the right direction in which we are to look for any rational treatment.

EXPERIMENT No. 15.

A Fowl was bitten in the carpal extremity of one wing, in a thoroughly vascular part, by a Cobra at 4.40 P.M. This was amputated at the carpal joint immediately the fangs were withdrawn. The scalpel was ready, and it was removed within three seconds of the completion of the bite. The amputation was about half an inch above the highest fang's mark. 4.48.—No symptom of poisoning, no bleeding from the wing. The Fowl is running about quite indifferent to either poison or amputation so far. 4.55.—No symptom of poisoning as yet.

August 15th, noon.—The Fowl is alive and well; in this case the poison had evidently not entered the circulation, the excision having been in time to prevent it. These experiments all prove that the poison takes effect chiefly through the venous circulation, and that if excision be practised immediately and thoroughly, either the whole or part of it *may* be prevented from entering the circulation. No doubt some of the poison finds way into the circulation by diffusion from the centre of inoculation, and thus all may not be removed by even very free and very early excision. The natural deduction is, that the part should be cut out as rapidly and extensively as possible; otherwise, as in the case of these animals, delay of a few seconds may prove fatal.

SIXTEENTH SERIES.

Experiments on the Influence of the Poisons of the Cobra and Bungarus fasciatus, and on the Effects of Certain Methods of Treatment.

August 21*st*, 1869.

Present, Drs. Fayrer, Cutcliffe, and Mr. Sceva.

EXPERIMENT No. 1.

A large Pariah Dog was bitten at 3.24 P.M. in the thigh by a Cobra that had been in confinement for some weeks, and had bitten before. Strong carbolic acid was immediately rubbed in, the punctures having been scarified. 3.30.—The Hakeem who administered the "antidote" last Saturday again presented himself with another, and he was allowed to administer as much of it, a fluid resembling the former one, as he pleased. 3.37.—The Dog staggers as he walks; another dose of the antidote administered by the Hakeem. 3.40.—The Dog is slightly convulsed, pupils dilated, and limbs partially paralysed. 3.42.—Unable to stand when raised; is convulsed. 3.45. — Quite paralysed. 3.48.—Dead—in twenty-four minutes.

A gentleman who had believed, from some experiments performed under his own supervision, in the efficacy of carbolic acid, witnessed this experiment, and was satisfied that the acid is powerless to counteract the deadly effects of the poison. The Hakeem also expressed his conviction that the Cobra bite is inevitably mortal. Neither of these agents indeed had the slightest effect, and the Dog died very rapidly, considering its size and strength, and that the snake was not fresh.

EXPERIMENT No. 2.

A small Dog was bitten at 3.48 P M. in the thigh by another Cobra, also not fresh like the first. A solution of the powdered leaves of *Aristolochia indica*, for which I am indebted to Mr. ——, of Mirzapore, was then administered, the fang wounds having been previously thoroughly well rubbed with strong carbolic acid. 3.52.—The Dog is staggering. 3.57.—The Dog is staggering. 4.2. — Convulsed in hind-legs; paralysis of limbs commencing. 4.10.—Convulsive twitchings of the muscles generally. 4.12.—Unconscious and convulsed. 4.15.—Dead—in nineteen minutes.

The antidotes were as powerless on this occasion as on others. The *Aristolochia* has long been held in estimation as an antidote; it must, I fear, share the fate of all the others.

EXPERIMENT No. 3.

A small white Dog had the inguinal fold of integument raised with two pairs of forceps to stretch it. This was then bitten (at 3.56) by a Cobra not fresh, and that had been in confinement for some time. The fangs must almost have perforated the entire thickness of the fold of integument. With a sharp scalpel the fold of skin was at once entirely excised, the bitten part being certainly included in that removed.

4.18.—Looks sluggish, but no positive indication of the action of the poison as yet manifested. 4.27.—Muscular tremors. 4.31.—Deep breathing; lies, looking very sluggish. 4.40. — Very sluggish; muscular twitchings. 4.45. — Can hardly rise; staggers and lies down again. 4.49.—In convulsions. 4.55.—Dead—in one hour.

This was a very interesting and very instructive experiment, most clearly demonstrating the deadly nature of the virus and the awful rapidity with which it passes into the circulation. The bitten part was not merely excised as we speak of excising the parts around the spot which the fang has penetrated, but the fold of skin into which the fangs had injected the poison was removed within a second after the bite, for the knife had entered almost before the fangs had left. In fact, it could not have been done more rapidly, and yet within one hour the animal was dead from the effects of the poison. The infinitesimal portion of time during which the Cobra's fangs were inserted into the tissues was sufficient to send the poison through the circulation, beyond the reach of incision; and yet how very small must the quantity have been. Nothing I have yet seen has so thoroughly demonstrated the deadly effects of the snake-poison.

EXPERIMENT No. 4.

Two drops of venom taken from an old Cobra, that is, from one some weeks in confinement, were mixed with four parts of water, and injected hypodermically into a Fowl's thigh at 4.2 P.M. 4.4.—Drooping; cannot rise when roused; comb and wattles becoming livid, losing their brilliant red colour. 4.7.—Lying on its side; convulsed. 4.10.—Dead—in eight minutes.

Diluting the poison with water has no effect in destroying its action. Death occurred in eight minutes, and would have probably occurred sooner had the poison been taken from a fresh snake.

EXPERIMENT No. 5.

A Fowl was bitten in the carpus by a Cobra at 4.12 P.M., the fangs were deeply imbedded. The part was immediately amputated at the carpal joint, and a ligature placed above to prevent hæmorrhage. This is the same Fowl that had precisely the same experiment tried on it on August 14th (15th Series, Experiment 15), and recovered. 4.55.—Fowl quite unaffected. At 7 P.M. of the 22nd the Fowl was still alive and well. It had thus escaped a second time, and is probably the only living creature that ever went through the ordeal of a Cobra's second bite.

It is evident that the immediate amputation of the part saved the Fowl's life.

EXPERIMENT No. 6.

A small Cat was bitten in the tail by a Cobra at 4.27 P.M. The part was amputated above the bite in twenty seconds; this time was purposely allowed to elapse before the operation. A ligature was applied to prevent serious hæmorrhage.

4.47.—The Cat still seems unaffected, except that the breathing is hurried. 4.55.—Still vigorous, runs about, but breathes hurriedly. 5.30 P.M.—Seems slightly affected; breathing is hurried. 6 P.M.—No further change. August 22nd, 8 A.M.—Appears natural, but it is evident from the muco-sanguineous nature of the excreta during the night that the Cat has been slightly under the influence of the poison. August 22nd, 1 P.M.—Looks well; appears free from pain; no symptom of the poison beyond slight weakness. 7 P.M.—The same.

This animal has also escaped; the experiment is not thoroughly satisfactory or conclusive, as the Cobra was not fresh, and the tail is not a very vascular part. Still it is suggestive of the benefit to be hoped for from early excision, and seems to show that, although the operation may not altogether preclude the entry of the poison into the circulation, yet that it may limit it to a degree in which it is not fatal.

EXPERIMENT No. 7.

Two drops of carbolic acid put into a large Cobra's mouth at 4.50 P.M. 4.52.—Twitching in convulsive movements. 4.53.—Faint. 4.54.—Dead.

This acid is very poisonous to all snakes.

August 28*th*, 1869.

Present, Dr. Fayrer and Mr. Sceva.

EXPERIMENT No. 8.

I have received from Mr. H. B. Simson, C.S., from Monghyr,

some leaves and stalks of a wild plant growing in that vicinity, named by the natives "Norbish," and reputed to be efficacious in the treatment of the bites of snakes or stings of other venomous animals, such as the scorpion, centipede, and wasp. The plant was brought to Mr. Simson's notice by Baboo Hurrish Chunder. I have been as yet unable to find out its botanical name. The juice of the fresh plant was extracted and mingled with that of the green ginger, according to instructions.

A medium-sized but strong and active Dog was then bitten in the thigh, at 3.37 P.M., by a Cobra ("Tentuliah Keautiah"), that had been in confinement for some weeks. One ounce of the juice was administered at 3.39, and some of the juice, with the bruised leaves, rubbed into the fang punctures. The leg was partially paralysed almost immediately after the bite. 3.40.—Staggers in his hind-leg as he walks. A second dose of the juice administered. 3.50.—The Dog is lethargic and breathes rapidly. 4 P.M.—Looks sluggish and sick; walks feebly, dragging the hind-legs. 4.2 P.M.—Another dose of the juice administered. 4.10.—Is sick; rejected a quantity of frothy mucus, tinged with the juice of the plant. 4.12.—Another dose given. 4.15.—Sick again. 4.18.—Constant retching. 4.21.—Staggering; very restless; keeps his nose on the ground. 4.27.—Again retching; rises and staggers as he walks. 4.30.—Fallen over on his side; convulsed. 4.32.—Violently convulsed. 4.35.—Slight convulsive movements in neck. Respiration has ceased. Heart still beats. 4.37.—Dead—in one hour.

This Dog, though small, was full grown and vigorous. The snake was not fresh, hence perhaps the reason that death did not occur for one hour, instead of in thirty to forty minutes, as is usual.

Experiment No. 9.

A small Pariah Dog was bitten in three places in the thigh, by a full-grown *Bungarus fasciatus*, that was brought from Soorie, in Beerbhoom, about three weeks ago. The snake seemed vigorous, and was just completing the exfoliation of its epidermis. The snake bit at 3.48 P.M. At 5 P.M. there were no symptoms of poisoning, the Dog perhaps looked a little depressed, but that might have been from fear. The *Bungarus* would not strike, even when the Dog trod on it; it did its best to get out of the way, as I have so frequently seen with other snakes. It was only when its jaws were closed by the snake-man on the dog's thigh that it bit. 6 P.M.—No change. 8 P.M.—Vomited. 9.15.—Lying down; on being raised on his feet appears weak; steps irregularly. August 29th, 7 A.M.—Vomited again. 9 P.M.—Lying on his side, in which position he has remained all day; refuses food. 30th, 7 A.M.—Appears to have recovered partially. Noon.—No further change. 6 P.M.—Looks better. 31st, 8 A.M.—Still improving; takes food and water. September 1st, 8 A.M.—Appears to be again suffering from the poison. 2nd.—Worse; unable to stand, or walk steadily. 3rd.—Unable to stand. 4th.—Unable to stand; tries to eat, but takes very little. 5th.—Very weak; has diarrhœa. 6th.—The same. 7th, 4.55 P.M.—Died.

This experiment remarkably illustrates the slow action of the poison of the *Bungarus fasciatus*, as compared with that of the Cobra or Viper.

Experiment No. 10.

The same *Bungarus fasciatus* (Experiment No. 9) was bitten severely in three places near the tail, so as to avoid injuring the viscera, by a Cobra ("Keautiah") at 3.54 P.M. At 5 P.M. there was no change, the *Bungarus* was unaffected. 29th, 7 A.M.—Sluggish; appears to have received some injury about the head and neck.

Mr. Sceva reports that the *Bungarus* died on Sunday morning before noon. He expresses a doubt as to its death being the result of the poison.

Experiment No. 11.

A Fowl was bitten in the posterior part of the thigh by a Cobra ("Kála Keautiah") at 4.6 P.M. Immediately the snake's fangs were withdrawn the part was cut out; the mass of muscle, including the two fang punctures, was completely excised; certainly not two seconds of time intervened between the bite and the removal of the part bitten. A ligature was tightly drawn around the thigh above the part bitten, and was relaxed just before the part was excised. The object of the ligature was to prevent entry of the poison by the circulation, during the short time that the fangs were actually imbedded in the flesh.

4.12.—Fowl crouching; head beginning to droop. 4.13.—Head nodding; beak resting on the ground, but still easily roused, as though from sleep. 4.16.—Very drowsy; head fallen over on the ground. Cannot stand or walk, but can still be roused. 4.25.—Can still be roused, but is very much depressed. 4.35.—In convulsions. 4.40.—Convulsive movements; weaker. 4.56.—Slow respiration; occasional convulsive movements. 5.10.—Dead—in sixty-four minutes.

It is evident that although excision in this case did not save life, it mitigated the effect of the poison and prolonged life. Had the part not been excised, it is probable that death would have occurred in a few minutes instead of an hour and four minutes. The inference is that when the poison is injected into a muscular part, before excision can be practised a certain amount has already entered the venous circulation, and some of it has by diffusion passed beyond the reach of the knife, and so more slowly enters the circulation and kills. In cases where amputation of the whole part can be practised, the latter danger is obviated; and if this be done very rapidly, as in the case of the Fowl, in which the carpus was amputated, it may save life. The blood coagulated firmly after death.

Experiment No. 12.

A large Fowl was bitten in the thigh by the Cobra ("Kála Keautiah"), that bit in Experiment No. 4, at 4.55 P.M. In this case the part was not cut out. The Fowl was left to its fate, the object of the experiment being to contrast the effects with those where the part had been excised, the bite being inflicted by the same snake.

5.1.—The Fowl is crouching, but is easily roused; has hurried breathing. 5.4.—Drooping rapidly, beak resting on the ground; starts; raises itself, as out of sleep; falls back into a profound state of lethargy. 5.8.—Springs from the ground with convulsive movements. 5.12.—Violently convulsed, and lies on the ground. 5.15.—Dead—in eighteen minutes.

This Fowl was a more powerful bird than the one previously bitten by the same snake, and yet it lived only eighteen minutes, whilst the first, that had the earlier, and consequently more vigorous bite, lived sixty-four minutes. The prolongation of life is evidently due to the excision of the bitten part in the first Fowl; and though it shows only mitigation, and not annihilation of the effects of the poison, the experiment is so far encouraging, for the proceeding gives time, during which other *juvantia* may be had recourse to. But it plainly proves, when contrasted with the experiments in which amputation was performed, that in excision diffusion of the poison takes place throughout the tissues beyond the limits of the fang punctures, and that from this diffusion fatal absorption may take place.

Experiment No. 13.

A Fowl was bitten in the fore-arm, between the ulna and radius, by a Cobra at 4.30 P.M. The part was *immediately* amputated at the elbow joint; a ligature was applied to prevent bleeding. 4.40.—The Fowl seems unaffected. 5.6.—Seems quite well.

7th September.—The Fowl is still alive and well; it also has been saved by the immediate amputation, as in the case of the

Cat and the other Fowl. The cases in which excision was practised all proved ultimately fatal, though death was delayed. Why is this? The reason, I believe, is that when excision only is practised, although it may extend beyond the limits of the Cobra bite, yet it does not remove so much of the poison as has already been diffused throughout the tissues.

The inference from this seems to me very clear, that in case of a bite in the finger or toe in a human being, amputation, if performed without delay, would offer the best chance of life. It is a terrible alternative; but as it is perhaps the only chance of saving life, it should be done.

All the snake-men that I have seen admit that they have little or no belief in any medicines; but that they know of instances where men have been bitten by Cobras and have recovered by binding ligatures in several places tightly round the limb above the punctures, and then by burning the bitten part thoroughly either with a hot iron, a live coal, or exploding gunpowder.

September 4th, 1869.

Present, Dr. Fayrer and Mr. Sceva.

EXPERIMENT No. 14.

A Pariah Dog was bitten by a Cobra ("Bans-buniah Keautiah," of the snake-men) in the fore-arm at 3.42 P.M. Carbolic acid was immediately rubbed into the bites, and within two seconds a strong ligature was tied as tightly as it could be drawn round the limb above the wounds.

3.44.—The Dog is restless; the bitten and ligatured limb is almost paralysed from the tension of the ligature; below the ligature it is intensely congested, and dark blood is dropping freely from the fang wounds. 3.52.—Ten drops of carbolic acid, diluted with an ounce of water, were administered internally. 4 P.M.—The Dog is lying down, and is very sluggish; but when he is roused he walks about. 4.5.—Lying on his side; restless; half convulsive movements of the limbs; breathing accelerated. 4.10.—Is now in the sitting posture, with fore-legs stretched out in a rigid, convulsive manner. 4.11.—Rises; staggers as he walks. 4.14.—Rises; falls over again. 4.19.—Hind-legs twitch convulsively. 4.24.—Convulsive twitchings; is sick. 4.26.—Cannot stand; is convulsed. 4.30.—Sick and convulsed. 4.32.—Heart still beats; no respiratory movements. 4.33.—Dead—in fifty-one minutes.

This experiment shows how futile the carbolic acid and the ligature are, even when thoroughly and rapidly applied. The ligature was tightened to the extremest strangulation of the limb within two seconds of the Cobra's bite. The carbolic acid was applied even sooner, and yet the symptoms of poisoning set in rapidly, and death occurred within the hour. The snake, it is to be observed too, was not a fresh one, and had been some time in captivity.

EXPERIMENT No. 15.

A Pariah Dog was bitten by a Cobra (" Keautiah") in the inguinal fold, which was raised and stretched for the purpose. The fangs penetrated deeply, and the part was immediately excised by a clean sweep with a sharp scalpel, the part wounded being completely removed. The Cobra was not fresh, but it was active and vigorous, and bit fiercely.

4.12.—The Dog is restless. 4.27.—Breathing accelerated. 4.35.—No further change. 4.40.—Looks sluggish; eyes blinking; breathing rather rapid. 4.46.—No change. 6 P.M.—No change. 9 P.M.—No change. 5th September, 8 A.M.—Looks well; takes food. 6th September.—Quite well; not affected by the poison.

This Dog escaped. The excision in this case proved successful; it was done very rapidly, and extended considerably beyond the marks of the snake's fangs.

EXPERIMENT No. 16.

The poison of a Cobra ("Tentuliah Keautiah") was removed, and two drops inserted between the eyelids of a healthy and vigorous young Puppy at 4.12 P.M. The Dog was examined again at 4.37 P.M., and the eye was found to have been most seriously affected. There was intense chemosis of the conjunctiva, so much so that the eye could not be seen, and the lids were puffed out like a ball. The chemosis was very pallid.

4.46.—Dog again examined, and found to be deeply under the influence of the poison. Convulsed in the limbs; unable to stand, and salivated; starting and whining with a short, snapping, snarling sound; chemosis intense; eyelids swollen like a ball; the eye cannot be seen. 4.54.—Paralysed and convulsed. 4.56.—Dead—in forty-four minutes.

The result of this experiment surprised me much; for it proved that absorption of the poison can take place through a membrane, and prove fatal. I am certain there was no wound or abrasion of the conjunctiva, and yet the influence of the poison was rapid and deadly. Previous experiments have not illustrated this effect of snake-poison; according to most observers, it has been thought that the poison could be applied with impunity to any surface, even of mucous membrane, provided there were no wound.

EXPERIMENT No. 17.

Having exposed the surface of the pectoral muscle of a Fowl, and having raised a few of the superficial fibres without causing the effusion of more than a few drops of blood, two or three drops of the poison, just taken from a Cobra (" Keautiah") were rubbed into the exposed surface at 4.12 P.M.

4.23.—Apparently not affected. 4.26.—The bird is drooping; head declining; rises suddenly with a start, as if awakened suddenly from a sound sleep; head falls over again, and the point of the beak rests on the ground. 4.32.—Rises and staggers; falls over in convulsions. 4.37.—Violently convulsed. 4.45.—Violently convulsed. 4.48.—Dead—in thirty-six minutes.

This experiment also proves that absorption of the poison takes place through the walls of the vessels; for, although the muscular fibre was exposed, there was scarcely a bleeding point. It shows the danger of allowing the poison to come in contact with any raw or abraded surface.

EXPERIMENT No. 18.

A very large *Bungarus fasciatus*, five feet long, was bitten by a fresh and vigorous Cobra at 4.46 P.M. The bite was inflicted near the tail. 6 P.M.—Very sluggish. 7.20.—Dead.

Mr. Sceva notes that he thinks that death may have been caused by injuries inflicted from compression during handling; the head being very small, compared with that of the Cobra or Viper, the snake-man grasps the neck more firmly for fear of slipping, and hence may have caused the injury. But the results of more than one experiment incline me to believe that the *Bungarus fasciatus* is, though in a much less degree than the innocuous snakes, susceptible, and that it succumbs to the Cobra or Viper poison. At the same time, I quite recognise the justice of the doubt which is thrown on the subject by Mr. Sceva.

On the Influence of Snake-poison when applied to Unwounded Surfaces.

September 11th, 1869.

Present, Drs. Fayrer, Cunningham, and Mr. Sceva.

EXPERIMENT No. 19.

Some poison was taken from a Cobra (" Tentuliah Keautiah"), and about a drop inserted between the eyelids of a Pariah Dog at 2.58 P.M.

3 P.M.—The eye is already much irritated; lachrymation profuse. The Dog keeps rubbing it with his paw, and resting the side of the head against the wall; he is very restless and un-

easy; chemosis rapidly increasing. 3.5.—Lying down; rubbing the eye, which is much chemosed; whining and restless. 3.16.—Dog very restless; lies with his head resting against the wall. 3.28.—Eye intensely swollen; the animal is very restless and whines. 3.35.—He is evidently under the influence of the poison; breathing deeply. 4.4.—Lying quiet; breathing very deep. 4.11.—Lies curled up. 4.16.—Gets up; is quite intelligent; is very weak and cannot stand long; the eye is intensely swollen, with a pale chemosis. 5.15 P.M.—On being roused from a lethargic state, appears stupid and confused; eye intensely swollen; lies down again and sleeps soundly. 5.31.—Breathing slowly and heavily. 6 P.M.—Sleeping comfortably. 9.30.—Walks without difficulty; looks more natural; rubs the swollen eye with his fore-paw. The constitutional effects of the poison are evidently passing off.

September 12th, 3 A.M.—Sleeping comfortably; breathing natural. 8 A.M.—Swelling of eyelids diminishing; appears lively. 5 P.M.—Still improving. 13th.—Improving; opens the eyelids; the cornea is quite opaque, and there is a muco-purulent discharge from the eye. 14th.—The Dog is recovering. 15th.—Except that the cornea is opaque, and some conjunctivitis remains, the Dog is well; he is cheerful; takes his food well.

It was evident in this case that the Dog was poisoned by absorption from the conjunctiva. The constitutional effects were not severe as in the former Dog, but the local mischief was very serious, and for a time, at all events, has destroyed the sight of that eye. The intense chemosis no doubt caused the corneal mischief. The results of these experiments show how careful we should be to protect the eyes when handling and approaching the Cobra or Viper in an excited state, when it is possible that some of the poison scattered, as the snake attempts to strike, might accidentally be injected into the eye. In another experiment a very minute portion of the poison was thus thrown into the eye of one of the gentlemen assisting in the experiments. The poison had been applied to a Dog's nostril, and in the sneeze that resulted, the accident happened. The eye was immediately washed and fomented, care being taken not to rub it, and no evil result beyond lachrymation, irritation, and transitory redness followed.

Experiment No. 20.

Some poison was taken from a Spectacled Cobra ("Gokurrah"), and a drop or two inserted into a Pariah Dog's nostril at 3 P.M. Violent sneezing and profuse watery discharge from the nostril resulted almost immediately.

3.30.—The sneezing and watery discharge continue, and seem to irritate the Dog considerably. 3.45—No constitutional effects of the poison manifested, but the local symptoms continue unabated. Two drops more of the same poison were well rubbed into the palate. 4.15.—No change. Two more drops rubbed into the mucous surface of the cheek. 4.25.—Not affected. The last applications appear to have caused no irritation. 5 P.M.—No change. September 12th, 3 A.M.—Does not appear to be affected in any way by the poison. The catarrhal symptoms have passed away. 13th.—The Dog is well.

In this case, beyond the local irritation no effect was produced.

Experiment No. 21.

A drop of Cobra poison was inserted into a Fowl's eye at 3.15 P.M.

3.18.—Eye already much swollen; membrana nictitans deeply chemosed. 3.30—Eyelids quite closed; no constitutional sign of poisoning. 3.37.—No change. 4.10.—Another drop inserted into the same eye. Much irritation immediately followed; the Fowl is constantly trying to scratch the eyelid with its foot. 4.20.—Beginning to droop; nodding its head; sleeping as Fowls do when they begin to feel the influence of the poison. 4.30.—Head more drooping. 5.—No further change; no worse. 5.30.—Eyelids greatly swollen, but no appearance of any constitutional action of the poison. 9 P.M.—The same. The Fowl continued to improve. The eyelids and conjunctiva became less swollen, and gradually recovered; and on the 16th the bird was perfectly well, and its eye quite right again.

In this case also, as in that of the Dog, the local symptoms were very severe, whilst the constitutional symptoms were mild and transient. They equally showed, however, that the poison can be absorbed through the unbroken surface of a membrane, and that the conjunctiva especially is apt to permit of the endosmosis.

Experiment No. 22.

A few drops of Cobra poison were rubbed into the mucous lining of a Fowl's mouth at 3.42 P.M. 4.15.—No effect; no sign of either local or constitutional disturbance. 12th, 8 A.M.—Not affected. 13th.—The Fowl is perfectly well, and does not appear to have been in the least affected by the poison.

In this case, as in the experiment on the Dog (No. 20) no evil resulted from the contact of the poison with the tongue and mucous surface of the mouth.

The evidence of these four experiments is not absolutely conclusive as to the extent to which the poison may operate by absorption through a mucous membrane. They prove that absorption in the case of the conjunctiva and the Schneiderian membrane really does occur, whilst in the mouth absolutely no effect was produced. But the poison was not taken from fresh or vigorous snakes, that is, they had been some time in confinement, and its action may have been impaired. Sufficient, however, is shown to prove how dangerous the contact of the poison with a delicate mucous surface may really prove.

SEVENTEENTH SERIES.

On the Influence of Snake-Poison on the Blood, and also on its Action when applied to the Surface of the Conjunctiva, and on the Value of Eau de Luce in the Treatment of Snake-poisoning.

September 18th, 1869.

Present, Drs. Fayrer, Cunningham, and Mr. Sceva.

Experiment No. 1.

A Dog was bitten in the fore-foot by a Spectacled Cobra. The snake struck the Dog in the foot, and held on for a moment, at 3.27 P.M. The snake had been some weeks in captivity and had bitten before. 3.30.—The Dog wildly excited, whining, and licking the bitten part, which is bleeding and swollen; keeps turning round and round; sitting down and rising again in an excited manner; breathing very much accelerated. 3.40.—Licking the wound in sitting posture, and is trembling all over. 3.47.—Staggering. 3.50.—In convulsions. 3.55.—Dead—in twenty-eight minutes.

Body examined at 4 P.M.—Lungs not congested; cavities of the heart filled with dark blood, which reddened and coagulated firmly directly it was removed: part was already coagulated. At 4.15 no rigor mortis.

Mr. Sceva reports that a little stiffness of the limbs had taken place at ten minutes to five, or in about an hour after death.

Experiment No. 2.

A Pariah Dog was bitten by the *Daboia* that had been in confinement since December, 1868, and during that period had never taken food or water. It had been some weeks unused, and when taken out of the box was very active and vicious; it seemed in good health and condition. Its jaws were closed on the Dog's thigh at 3.27 P.M. At 3.28 the Dog was partially paralysed; it made no noise, seemed to feel no pain; tried to move away a few paces with a staggering gait; the bitten limb almost useless; head drooping to the ground. 3.40.—Is unable to stand; limbs extended, perfectly paralysed; breathing deeply. 3.41.—Convulsive rigidity of the limbs. 3.44.—Dead—in seven minutes.

The poison appears to have been very active in this instance, notwithstanding the condition of the snake. Paralysis of the nerve centres seemed to follow immediately after the bite; there was no sign of pain, and the Dog was unconscious almost immediately.

Body examined at 3.55.—Lungs not congested. Cardiac cavities filled with fluid blood. The blood was perfectly fluid, both in the heart and great vessels, and remained so; no attempt at coagulation occurred. The contrast with the blood of the Dog killed by the Cobra was very remarkable—it formed at once a firm clot. At 4.15 P.M. there was no rigor mortis.

Mr. Sceva reports that at ten minutes to five, or in rather more than an hour after death, no rigor mortis had taken place.

Experiment No. 3.

A Fowl was bitten by the same *Daboia* in the thigh at 3.49. When placed on the ground it ran a few steps, limping on the bitten leg. In thirty seconds it fell over in violent convulsions; in twenty seconds more—fifty altogether—it was dead.

The blood of this Fowl remained perfectly fluid after death.

Experiment No. 4.

A Fowl was bitten by a small Cobra (" Tentuliah Keautiah"), not fresh, in the thigh at 4.8 P.M. When placed on the ground it ran about, limping on the bitten leg. 4.9.—Feathers drooping; crouching; rises and tries to run; its wings droop to the ground. 4.10.—Head falling over, beak resting on the ground, comb and wattles becoming livid. 4.11.—Nearly paralysed, point of beak resting on the ground to support the head; cannot rise. 4.18.—Violently convulsed. This continued at intervals until the Fowl died at 4.23. Dead—in fifteen minutes. On opening the body the blood was found to form a firm coagulum.

The object of these experiments was to compare again the effects of the *Daboia* and Cobra poison on the blood. They clearly prove that after death from the Viper's poison, however quickly it may be caused, the blood remains permanently fluid; whereas that the Cobra poison does not destroy its coagulability. The nature of the change thus wrought on the blood I know not at present in its chemical bearings, but I believe it to be effected through the nerve centres affecting the vitality of the blood, not by a direct chemical action. There certainly are differences in the symptoms caused in the bitten animals, but they equally point to direct action on the nerve centres as the cause of death. I have seen as much difference between the effects produced by different *Daboias*, or by the same *Daboia* on different animals of the same species, as in those that had been bitten by the Cobra; and, on the other hand, similar differences in the effects of the bite of different Cobras, or of the same Cobra on different animals of the same species, as in those bitten by the *Daboia*. In point of deadliness they are, when fresh and vigorous, about equal; but I think that the first effects of the poison are most rapidly shown in the *Daboia* bite.

Dr. Cunningham, of the Bengal Medical Service, who was on special duty investigating the subject of cholera, and who had a microscope with high powers, very kindly undertook to make a most careful microscopical examination of the blood of these animals; I append his report:—

"General Hospital, Friday, September 24th, 1869.

"My dear Dr. Fayrer,—Along with this I send you the drawings of the Dog's and Fowl's blood which I got last Saturday. The specimens were examined, and the drawings (of which these are copies), were made on Sunday morning. In no case were any bodies seen corresponding with Halford's cells.

"The blood of the Cobra-bitten Dog was, at the time of examination, in a firm dark clot.

"Beyond the ordinary constituents of the blood nothing could be seen, even under a power of nearly 1100 diameters.

"The blood of the Dog bitten by the Viper differed from the other. 1st. In being entirely fluid. 2nd. In being of a much lighter red colour. 3rd. In containing numerous blood crystals. 4th. In containing a good many large and active specimens of Bacteria.

"The Fowl's blood was in both cases very much broken up and decomposed, few entire red corpuscles remaining. This state of decomposition was most marked in the blood of that which was bitten by the Viper. In both specimens were a few of the circular cells, which occur in Fowl's blood under ordinary circumstances.

"With many thanks for the opportunity which you have given me of examining the blood, I am, &c.

"D. Douglas Cunningham."

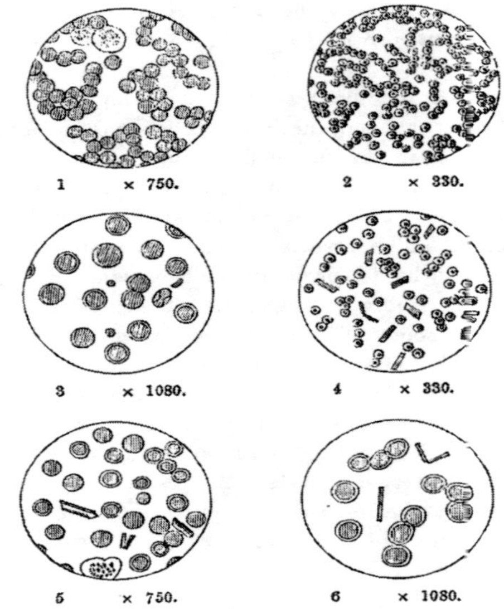

1 2 3 Cobra—Dog. 4 5 6 Daboia—Dog.

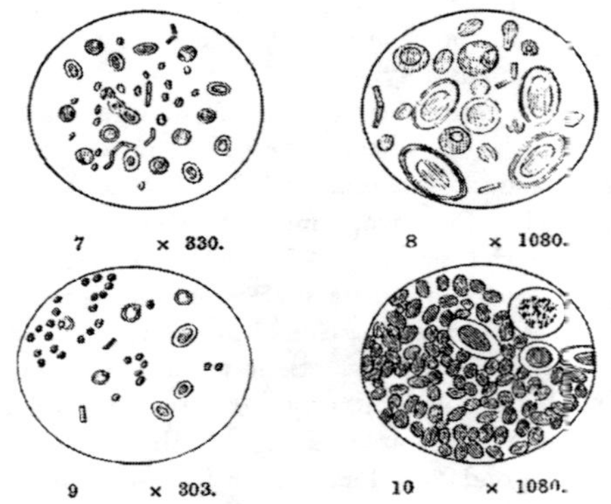

7 8 Cobra—Fowl. 9 10 Daboia—Fowl.

September 25th, 1869.

Present, Dr. Fayrer and Mr. Sceva.

Experiment No. 5.

A Dog was bitten in the thigh by a fresh Cobra ("Gokurrah") at 4.3 P.M.

At 4.4 P.M. thirty drops of eau de luce, diluted with water, were poured down the Dog's throat. The Dog was much excited, and ran about limping on the bitten leg, which was already nearly paralysed. 4.5.—Another dose of thirty drops administered. Drags the partially paralysed leg as he walks. 4.8.—Another dose of thirty drops administered. 4.9.—The Dog staggers as he walks; frothing at the mouth; looks much depressed. 4.12.—Lies down; retching. 4.13.—Convulsed; another dose administered. He lies paralysed, and cannot move; the heart still beats; no respiratory movements. 4.14.—Convulsive gasping. 4.15.—Dead—in thirteen minutes. Two hours after death the *rigor mortis* was complete.

I fear the eau de luce must be classed with other "antidotes."

Experiment No. 6.

Poison taken from a fresh Cobra ("Gokurrah"), and a drop inserted between the lids of a Fowl's left eye, at 4.20 P.M. The eye closed immediately.

4.25.—The eyelids already much swollen. 4.37.—So much swollen that the eye cannot be seen. 4.38.—No constitutional indication of the poison. Another drop inserted; conjunctiva deeply injected and chemosed. 5 P.M.—The Fowl crouches, but is easily roused; it seems slightly affected by the poison. 5.10.—Crouching. 9 P.M.—Is drowsy; crouching, with wings drooping, and the point of the beak resting on the ground.

September 26th, 7 A.M.—Lying on the ground with one wing extended; unable to walk. 1.30 P.M.—Lying down on one side; gasping; on being roused staggers and falls down. Has spasmodic movements; shivering; feathers ruffled. 6.9 P.M.—In the same state. September 27th, 6 A.M.—Lying on one side, with the legs extended; frequent defecation. 9 A.M.—Appears to be improving; able to crouch on its feet. 4 P.M.—Is much better; takes food and water. 9 P.M.—Still improving.

September 28th, 6 A.M.—Sits naturally on its feet; eats well; the swelling of the eye much reduced; is able to stand, but cannot walk much; the legs appear to be benumbed, or to have locomotor ataxy; steps in an awkward manner. 7 P.M.—The bird seems to have recovered.

The Fowl had a very narrow escape; it clearly proves that the poison acts by absorption through the conjunctiva.

Experiment No. 7.

A drop of fresh Cobra poison was put into a Dog's eye at 4.27 P.M. The lachrymation was immediately profuse; rubbed the eye with his fore-paw.

4.30.—Conjunctiva much injected; he is very uneasy, rubbing the eye with his foot. 4.38.—Lies curled up with his head between his fore-legs. Another drop inserted into the same eye. 4.40.—Appears sluggish, but is not constitutionally affected beyond this. 5 P.M.—The Dog is lethargic; lies with his head between the legs; eyelids and conjunctiva intensely swollen. 5.10.—No change. 9 P.M.—Eyelids closed, and greatly swollen.

September 26th, 7 A.M.—Appears lively and free from pain; swelling of the eyelids much reduced.

27th, 9 A.M.—Eats well, and does not appear to suffer any pain. 9 P.M.—The same.

28th, 6 A.M.—Eyelids slightly swollen. 7 P.M.—Nearly recovered.

It is to be noted that although most flagrant inflammation was excited in the eye, it had not, as in the most ordinary form of conjunctivitis, a tendency to suppurate. The eye, although temporarily damaged, the cornea being rendered opaque, was not destroyed, as is so frequently the case in the specific form of ophthalmia.

This experiment, like the last, proves that the poison is not only absorbed through the conjunctiva, but that it is a local irritant. The inflammation is intense, but it subsides without treatment; and although the cornea is rendered opaque with cloudy opacity, it would evidently soon recover. It seems quite clear from these experiments, that the notion that the poison is not operative, unless introduced directly into the blood, is not tenable, and that it is capable of endosmosis.

The following incident is interesting, as it shows how one may be mistaken about a snake-bite, although the evidence of its infliction seem complete.

A short time ago, my friend Dr. —— wrote to me, saying that a person had been to him, to inform him that he had been bitten by a Cobra, and that he had prevented any evil effects by the timely use of measures known to himself. He offered to bring the sufferer with the snake for inspection. Accordingly my friend, accompanied by the patient, who brought with him a *gurrah* containing a full-grown and vigorous Cobra ("Keautiah"), made their appearance the following morning, and I had the fullest opportunity of inquiring into the case. He informed me that he was fond of snakes, and was in the habit of handling them, having no fear of their bites. The Cobra that had bitten him the day before had been only recently caught in his presence, by a professional snake-catcher. He had purchased and had been playing with it, when it bit him, through some inadvertence on his own part, on the back of the middle finger of the right hand. He immediately knocked the snake off; the punctures bled freely, and he vigorously sucked the wounds for some time, having also, I think he said, tied a ligature tightly about the wound. He felt no ill effects from the bites. There were two recent marks on the finger which just corresponded to the position of a Cobra's fangs. They looked healthy, and free from any irritation or mischief.

He took the snake out of the *gurrah*, putting his hand among its coils fearlessly, although it hissed and tried to strike He placed it on the ground, where it deported itself after the fashion of Cobras, erecting its head and hood, and striking at whatever came near it. He sat on the ground and allowed it to crawl under his legs, caressing it at the same time. This, I confess, aroused my suspicions, but I warned him of the extreme danger he was probably incurring, and I asked him if he was sure the snake had its fangs; he said he had no reason to doubt it, for it had been caught wild in his presence, and he had never lost sight of it since. As there was not the slightest reason to doubt his statement, I was, I confess, somewhat astonished at his power of handling thus fearlessly so deadly an animal, and I again warned him of the great risk he incurred. He said he had often done the same with other snakes, and nothing had happened to him until on this occasion.

I have no doubt whatever that he fully believed all he said, and that he imagined he had prevented mischief by his treatment of the bite. To attest it, he had put himself to some inconvenience to show me the bites and the snake that inflicted them, and there was no apparent reason for mistrusting his account of the matter.

He was about to take his leave when, being still sceptical, I asked to be allowed to examine the Cobra's fangs. He made no objection, but seemed rather to dislike opening the snake's mouth. We, however, effected this between us, and it proved that there were no fangs at all. They had long been removed, and the partially exposed roots of the broken teeth were barely visible above the sheath, leaving just rough surface enough to scratch whatever they came in contact with. He seemed more astonished than I was, and assured me, what I did not doubt in the least, that he had fully believed in the existence of the fangs, for, as he said, the snake had been freshly caught in his presence, and he had had it ever since.

I advised him to be more careful in his future dealings with the *Ophidia*, as the next pet Cobra might prove to have fangs, and the disposition to use them.

Had this gentleman gone away without examination of the snake's mouth, what other conclusion could have been drawn from his evidence than the most dangerous one, that the bite of a large and vigorous Cobra may be inflicted, and yet that the simplest means are sufficient to obviate the evil results. It is probable that, if the details of similar stories, and they are not unfrequent, could be analysed, they would receive an equally simple and satisfactory explanation. It is not necessary, in investigating the real truth of such accounts, which are often largely tinctured by ignorance and credulity, to impugn the veracity of those who relate them, and who are so prone to believe in the marvellous, and to deal with the improbable, simply because it is so.

I do not for a moment doubt that this gentleman, who so kindly volunteered to demonstrate the successful treatment of the bite of a deadly snake, believed in the whole story, and had not the faintest notion that he had been deceived either by accident or by the snake-man, who captured what was probably already a capture, in his presence. But the direct evidence of the snake's edentate upper jaw was more conclusive to him, as well as to us, than any amount of circumstantial testimony to the contrary.

I may here mention, shortly, another case which was related to me by a gentleman holding an important post in one of the Bengal railways, who was an eye-witness to what he described. He told me that he sent his servant to bring a bottle of soda-water. The man went to do so, and in reaching out his hand, in what was probably an obscure or dark part of a room or godown, he must have actually placed his finger in, or close to, a snake's mouth. He came back to his master and said he had been bitten by a snake, and pointed to the two punctures on the finger as attestation of it. Further proof was not long in making its appearance, and within forty-five minutes the wretched man was dead. Had the finger in this case been removed at once, or had a ligature been very tightly tied above the bite, the result might have been different. I say "might have been," because in the experiments made on the lower animals, I have found that unless amputation or excision is made with the greatest promptitude the poison has already entered the circulation, and is rapidly running its course to the nerve centres, where it proves fatal.*

EIGHTEENTH SERIES.

On the Influence of Snake-Poison and of Liquor Potassæ as an Antidote, and on the Use of Alcoholic Stimulants and other Remedies.

April 23rd, 1870.

Present, Drs. Fayrer and Ewart, and Mr. Sceva.

Experiment No. 1.

The external jugular vein of a Dog was exposed, and half a drachm of liquor potassæ with three drachms of water was injected with the hypodermic syringe at 3.14 P.M.

At 3.28 the Dog seemingly unaffected by the alkaline injections, two drops of poison, squeezed out of the poison glands of a Cobra ("Bans-buniah Keautiah,") sickly and casting its skin, were diluted with water and injected hypodermically into the Dog's thigh. This snake had been deprived of its fangs, and could not bite. The dose of poison was very mild. 3.35.—The Dog seems restless and uneasy—is whining. 3.36.—Apparently very slightly affected. 4.10.—Is restless; sits down, looks listless and tired. 4.15.—Half a drachm of liquor potassæ with one drachm of water injected into jugular vein; no effect produced, the Dog did not seem to feel it in any way. 4.20.—Half a drachm of Liquor Potassæ with two ounces of water poured down its throat. 4.26.—Restless and uneasy; is sick; slightly convulsed; respiration hurried; sardonic grin. 4.30.—Cannot walk; profusely salivated, defecated; more solution of liquor potassæ administered. 4.35.—Tries to rise; falls over, staggers; all the symptoms of snake-poisoning now rapidly increasing; spasmodic action of diaphragm. 4.37.—Much convulsed. 4.40.—Still much convulsed and profusely salivated; gasping respiration. 4.42.—Respiration ceased. 4.45.—Dead—in an hour and a half.

The body was opened at 5 P.M. Blood in the cavities of the heart fluid, but coagulated firmly on being removed.

Experiment No. 2.

About half a grain of Cobra poison kept in a glass tube since December, 1869, was diluted with water, and a hypodermic syringeful of the solution (about twenty drops) injected into a Fowl's thigh at 3.53 P.M. The poison had coagulated into a white paste; was very fœtid, and not readily soluble in water, as the solution, after being well rubbed, was turbid and flocculent. 4 P.M.—The Fowl is lethargic, and crouches; but is easily roused, and runs about looking as bright as ever.

Twenty drops of a solution of liquor potassæ, one part to two of water, injected into the Fowl's thigh. The legs were soon observed to be weak. 4.5.—Cannot stand, the legs are extended and seem almost paralysed. 4.7.—Legs powerless, but its eye is bright, and its head does not droop, as is usual in snake-poisoning. 4.14.—Another syringeful of the liquor potassæ solution injected into the thigh. 4.20.—Lies on its side, legs quite powerless, but eyes still brighter; head raised; it seems perfectly conscious. 4.30.—In the same condition. 4.40.—Another syringeful of the solution of liquor potassæ injected—no apparent change. 4.50.—Eyes still bright; head does not droop, cannot move. 5 P.M.—In the same condition. 6.15.—Unable to walk. 7.11.—Attempted to walk, but was unable to do so; fell with legs extended in opposite directions; remained in this state till 7.41 P.M. 9 P.M.—Lying on its side with only wings extended, and legs outstretched.

24th, 5.30 A.M.—Lying much as it was at 9 P.M., yesterday. 9.15.—Convulsive movement. It did not die till 1.35 P.M., or in about twenty-two and a half hours.

Experiment No. 3.

A syringeful of the same liquor potassæ solution was injected into a Fowl's thigh at 4 P.M. of 23rd April 4.10 P.M.—No apparent effect produced on the Fowl by the injection; it is as lively as ever. A syringeful of diluted Cobra poison, the same as in last experiment, injected into a Fowl's thigh. 4.17.—Legs seem paralysed as in the last case, but the eyes are bright, and the head not drooping, as in Experiment No. 2. 4.30.—In the same state, legs quite paralysed. 4.40.—Another dose of liquor potassæ solution of the same strength injected into the thigh. 4.42.—The Fowl was slightly convulsed after the last injection, crouching, with its head resting on its beak; there were jerking convulsive movements of the tail. 4.50.—Lethargic, but eye bright, breathing slow and steady. Closes the eyes, but when roused opens them again. 5 P.M.—Head slightly drooping in addition to other symptoms 6.15 P.M.—Unable to walk; lying on floor, with legs and wings extended. 7.30.—Convulsive movements of wings and body. 7.41 P.M.—Dead—in three hours and forty minutes.

Experiment No. 4.

About half a grain of the same Cobra poison as that used in Experiments Nos. 2 and 3 injected into a full-grown but rather sickly-looking Dog's thigh at 3.6 P.M. 9.10.—Is not apparently in any way affected. 4.25.—Does not appear in any way affected. 4.35.—Not in the least affected by the poison.

* This occurred near Calcutta, and the snake was one of the varieties of Cobra.

Another syringeful, twenty drops of the poison solution, injected. 4.45.—The Dog appears sluggish, but it may be fright; not otherwise affected. The jugular vein was now exposed, and one drachm of liquor potassæ in two drachms of water was injected. No apparent effect produced by this injection into the jugular vein. The Dog on being released moved about in the usual way.

4.50.—Half a drachm of liquor potassæ in two ounces of water was poured down the throat. 5 P.M.—The dose was repeated. The Dog seemed inclined to vomit, but did not do so; not otherwise in the least affected. 6.15 P.M.—No change. 9 P.M.—Appears restless, changing position frequently. 9.30 P.M.—The same.

April 24th, 9 A.M.—Looks well, not lethargic. 1 P.M.—The same. Midnight.—The same.

April 25th, 8 A.M.—Seems well and unaffected. 1 P.M.—No change, forty-six hours after the experiment.

The poison used in these experiments was necessarily weak. In the first it was taken from a Cobra that had lost its fangs, and when squeezed out in a small quantity it was probably mingled with mucus. It produced the usual effects, however, in a Dog, and death occurred in an hour and a half.

The liquor potassæ was administered by injection into the jugular vein, and into the stomach; no apparent result followed, and the Dog died in ninety minutes, with the usual symptoms of Cobra poisoning; the blood coagulated firmly when removed from the heart and large vessels after death.

In the three other experiments, old and decomposed poison, removed from the snake four months previously, and which had coagulated into an exceedingly offensive white paste, very insoluble in water, was used, and in small quantities. In the case of the full-grown Dog no symptom was produced by the second day. To test the effect of the liquor potassæ it was injected into the jugular vein, and administered by the mouth. No change occurred, and forty hours after the experiment the animal was unaffected. In the cases of the two Fowls, one died in three hours and forty minutes, the other in twenty-two hours; and in them the symptoms were somewhat different from those usually produced on Fowls by the Cobra poison.

One of the earliest symptoms in ordinary cases of Cobra poisoning of Fowls is drooping of the head, which is supported by the point of the beak resting on the ground. The bird frequently raises its head with a sudden start, until at last, overwhelmed by the action of the poison, it falls over and dies, frequently in convulsions. This drooping of the head was not observed; the eye was bright, and the head erect almost to the last, whilst the legs were quickly paralysed.

In those cases the liquor potassæ was also given by hypodermic injection, but with no apparent result, except in one case, when slight convulsions occurred, though I am not at all sure they were caused by it. Death in both cases was protracted, in one excessively so; but this I attributed to the weakened and diluted state of the poison. Is it possible that the difference in its action may have been due to the changes that had taken place during decomposition? At all events, though much weakened, and probably altered in its action, it still preserved, to some extent, its lethal properties; for, although the strong and full-grown Dog was not apparently affected, the smaller and more sensitive birds were.

The conclusions I draw from these experiments are :—

1st. That the poison of the Cobra retains its activity even when the fangs have been destroyed, and the gland perhaps for a time inactive.

2nd. That keeping and decomposition of the poison does not destroy, though it weakens or alters, its poisonous properties.

3rd. That the injection of diluted liquor potassæ is not necessarily attended with any danger, or even bad symptoms when it is injected into the jugular vein or hypodermically; and that the result of these four experiments, which are not by any means conclusive, does not show that it has any antidotal effect on the action of the poison.

Experiment No. 5.

April 25th.—Two young Fowls were injected in the thigh with the same old Cobra poison as in the last experiments. April 23rd; the poison was inserted with the hypodermic syringe, at 3.55 P.M. 5.10 P.M.—No change. 7 P.M.—No change. 9.15 P.M.—The legs which were injected are lame and stiff in both Fowls.

26th, 5 A.M.—No symptoms of poisoning. 1.20 P.M.—One Fowl walking about quite well. The other appears dull and drooping.

27th, 6 A.M.—No change. 1 P.M.—Both Fowls walking about in the cage. 29th.—They are quite well.

The effects of the poison on both were most feebly manifested. The liquor potassæ was not used.

April 30th, 1870.

Present, Drs. Fayrer and Ewart, and Mr. Sceva.

Experiment No. 6.

A solution of liquor potassæ one part, water three parts, was prepared.

2.55 A.M.—One drachm of the above solution was injected into the external jugular vein of a small Dog.

The Dog seemed rather sluggish after the injection, but at 3.7 P.M. was as usual, and seemed quite well at 3.9 P.M. He was bitten on the fold of the thigh by a young Cobra about one-third grown.

It was made to close its jaws very reluctantly, and its bite was very doubtful; no marks of blood were visible.

3.15 P.M. — The Dog seemed rather sluggish, apparently frightened; twenty drops of the liquor potassæ solution were hypodermically injected into the thigh. This seemed to cause sharp pain; the place where the Cobra was supposed to have bitten was washed with liquor potassæ. 3.24.—Sluggish; lies down again when it has been made to stand. Twenty drops more of the liquor potassæ solution injected into the thigh. 3.27.—Stretching out the hind-legs. 3.29.—Rises and sits down again. Thoracic muscles seem contracted. 3.34.—Seems to walk with difficulty when roused; abdomen seems distended. 3.43.—Lies quite quiet. 4.6.—In the same condition. Hind-legs seem weak. Lies with the limbs extended. 4.15.—Walks about, when roused sits up, but seems giddy, head moves from side to side. 4.21.—Twenty-nine drops of the solution injected seems to give, as before, considerable pain; it licks the puncture. 4.50.—Another twenty drops injected. 8.30.—No change. 9.30.—Lying down, breathing naturally; no symptoms of poisoning now present.

May 1st.—The Dog is living, is not in any way affected.

May 3rd.—The Dog remained quite well.

Experiment No. 7.

A large Dog had the jugular exposed, and one drachm of liquor potassæ in three drachms of water was injected at once into the vein.

3.10.—The same young Cobra was made to close its jaws in the Dog's thigh, but there was no evidence of its biting. 3.30.—Twenty drops of the solution were injected into the thigh. The Dog was not in any way affected, and remains, on the 2nd May, quite well.

These two experiments are very instructive, for they show in the first experiment that the Dog was, though bitten, so slightly poisoned that no evil results followed. In the second no effect was produced at all. The Cobra was very young and small, its fangs were small, and the poison small in quantity, and not active. This no doubt is the way in which recoveries take place when there is no doubt as to the person having been bitten, as the snake has been seen. That the snake had more poison was proved by its effect on a Fowl, which is much more sensitive to the poison than the Dog.

The evidence as to the value of the liquor potassæ is not of much significance; for if it appears in its favour in the case of the Dog, it is the reverse in that of the Fowl.

Experiment No. 8.

A Fowl was bitten in the left thigh by the same young Cobra; it was made to close its jaws, and the fangs were compressed in the part at 3.27 P.M. 3.32.—Not in any way affected. 3.52.—Not the least affected twenty-five minutes after being bitten. 4.5.—Feathers of back slightly ruffled; purged, otherwise seems bright. 4.11.—Apparently beginning to droop a little, but when roused seems all right, and runs about vigorously. The wattles look less bright than they did. 4.15.—Crouching, but rises and runs about when roused. 4.16.—Twenty drops of the liquor potassæ solution injected into the thigh. 4.20.—Drooping, rests its beak on the ground. 4.22.—It droops more. 4.50.—Restless; changes its position frequently. Wings drooping. 8.13.—It gradually drooped and died. The extreme weakness of the poison was proved in this case by the fact that it was twenty-five minutes before the faintest indication of poisoning appeared. It generally, with the ordinary Cobra, begins within a minute.

Death occurred in four hours and forty-six minutes.

May 5th, 1870.

Experiment No. 9.

Poison removed from a large "Gokurrah" (Spectacled Cobra), and mixed with liquor potassæ, two parts of each: of this solution, about ten drops were injected into a Dog's thigh at 11.58 A.M. 12.10.—Restless. 12.11.—Quite lively, but staggers on the hind-legs. 12.13.—Does not seem more affected. 12.21.—Sluggish. One drop of poison mixed with three of liquor potassæ injected into the thigh. Is sluggish, staggers in his gait. 12.29.—Thirty drops of a solution of equal parts of water and liquor potassæ injected into the thigh. 12.30.—Convulsed. 12.34.—Purged, unable to move, is paralysed. 12.37.—Convulsed. 12.40.—Dead—in forty-two minutes.

The body was opened about half an hour after death. The blood was fluid, but coagulated after removal; not as rapidly though, I think, as usual.

A syringeful of the blood was injected into a Fowl's thigh; the Fowl did not die.

Experiment No. 10.

Equal parts of poison from the same Cobra and water were mixed, and about ten drops injected into a full-grown Dog's thigh at 11.54 A.M. 12.1.—Not affected. 12.10.—Very sluggish, deep and hurried breathing. 12.13.—Can hardly stand; gradually became paralysed. 12.18.—In convulsions. 12.20.—Purged; dying. 12.22.—Dead—in twenty-three minutes.

This experiment proved that the Cobra poison was active, and not injured by dilution with water. The other experiment proves that it is not neutralized when mixed with liquor potassæ.

Experiment No. 11.

A solution of the same Cobra poison was made with equal parts of water. Two drops of this solution injected into a Fowl's thigh at 11.55. 11.58.—Fowl drooping, point of beak resting on the ground. 12.2.—Nearly dead. 12.7.—Dead—in twelve minutes.

Experiment No. 12.

One drop of poison from the same Cobra, three drops of liquor potassæ, injected into a Fowl's thigh at 12.18. In less than thirty seconds the Fowl fell over in convulsions; it remained in a perfectly unconscious condition, with occasional convulsive movements of the wings until 12.24. Death occurred in six minutes.

In this case the Fowl was of the same size as in Experiment No. 11, about two-thirds grown. Death occurred more rapidly after inoculation of the poison mixed with liquor potassæ than after that of poison mixed with water.

The blood of the bird was examined at 12.40, sixteen minutes after death; it coagulated firmly when removed from the body.

Experiment No. 13.

One half-drop of Cobra poison and two drops of liquor potassæ injected at 12.20 into a Fowl's thigh. 12.24.—Crouching. 12.26.—Drooping, the usual sign of the beak resting on ground. 12.30.—Dying apparently. 12.31.—Convulsed. 12.38.—Dead—in eighteen minutes. Body examined: blood formed a firm coagulum.

The dose of poison was very small, it was barely half a drop, with two full drops of liquor potassæ.

Experiment No. 14.

A Fowl had about forty drops of a solution of one part of liquor potassæ in two parts of water, injected into the thigh at 12.45. The legs almost immediately became paralysed, or rather rigidly extended. It lay on the ground with a scared look; breathing very much hurried; beak open, feathers ruffled. It remained in this state for several hours, and gradually recovered. On the same day (May 5th) at 8 A.M., it was alive and well, and had nearly regained the use of its legs.

Experiment No. 15.

The same quantity of the liquor potassæ solution was injected into a Fowl's pectoral muscles at 12.47. The bird immediately assumed the same scared aspect, the feathers staring, the eye wild, and the beak wide open, with very hurried respiration. It remained in this way for some time, and in about twenty minutes twenty drops of the blood of the Dog that died from the mixture of Cobra poison and liquor potassæ were injected into its thigh.

It remained in the same condition for some time, but gradually recovered, and on the following morning was quite well.

The object of these two experiments was to test the effect of the liquor potassæ when injected. The symptoms were very well marked, and the injected fluid seemed to cause great distress, though no fatal consequence resulted. So far the results of the trial of liquor potassæ have been unfavourable; the fact that the poison mingled with the liquor potassæ before inoculation proved fatal, seems all but conclusive against it as an antidote.

On the Action of a Reputed Antidote to Snake-Poison.

May 14th, 1870.

Present, Drs. Fayrer and Ewart, and Mr. Sceva.

Through the kindness of a friend I received a phial of dark-coloured, strongly ammoniacal smelling fluid, sent by Dr. Gunston, of H.M.S., who says:—"I send the Cape antidote for snake-bites; it may have deteriorated* in quality, as I bought it in the Cape in 1864. I never had occasion to use it, but the rule is, I believe, to scarify the wound and rub some of the mixture into it, and also to swallow two or three drops. I am not certain of the quantity in either case, but experiment would easily decide that. I know for certain that bites from the Cape black Cobras have been cured by it, and there every one carries it about when out shooting; it is firmly believed in."

One object of the following experiments was to test this

* The bottle was so carefully stoppered and sealed, and the ammoniacal odour was so strong when opened, that I should think it could not have deteriorated by keeping.

"antidote." The fluid was in a small phial, carefully covered with thick leather; it was hermetically sealed, and when the stopper was removed, a dark-coloured, clear, and very strongly ammoniacal fluid was found.

EXPERIMENT No. 16.

A Fowl had the feathers removed from its thigh, and was bitten by a "Gokurrah" (Spectacled Cobra) with only one fang, in the right thigh, at 3.25 P.M. The single puncture was immediately deeply scarified, and some drops of the fluid well rubbed into the wound. A drop of the fluid diluted with a few drops of water was then poured down the bird's throat. But at 3.26 the Fowl was already paralysed. At 3.28 it was quite dead. The blood of this Fowl, on being removed from the heart, a few minutes after death, coagulated firmly.

EXPERIMENT No. 17.

A half-grown Pariah Dog was bitten in the thigh by the same Cobra at 3.30 P.M. In this case the eau de luce was again tried. Half a drachm sufficiently diluted with water given at 3.33 P.M. 3.34.—The Dog shows symptoms of poisoning; he is restless and uneasy. Lies down; rises again; breathing hurried. Tries to walk; staggers; hangs his head; frothing at the mouth. 3.38.—Another half drachm of the eau de luce administered. 3.40.—Has lain down, and is unable to move, evidently dying. 3.42.—Heart still beats, but he has ceased to breathe. 3.43.—Dead—in nine minutes. The blood of this Dog coagulated firmly after death. The so-called antidote obviously had not the least effect.

EXPERIMENT No. 18.

A Fowl was bitten in the thigh by the same Cobra at 3.46 P.M. The wound was immediately scarified, and some drops of the Cape remedy well rubbed in. Two drops well diluted were immediately administered by the mouth. The Fowl was convulsed almost immediately, and was dead in less than two minutes. The blood of the Fowl exposed in a watch-glass, after death, became of a very florid colour, and coagulated very imperfectly after fifteen or twenty minutes. There was some doubt about the watch-glass having had ammonia in it, but the attendant declares it was thoroughly washed.

EXPERIMENT No. 19.

A Fowl was bitten by a Cobra with one fang in the thigh at 4.5 P.M. 4.5.30.—Legs paralysed; feathers ruffled. 4.7.—Dying, convulsed. 4.8.—Dead.

Blood drawn into three vessels: one a watch-glass, the second an ounce measure glass, the third a flat glass vessel (top of a jar); two or three drops of the Cape antidote (ammoniacal) put into the watch-glass. Two or three drops of eau de luce put into the measure glass. Into the third, nothing. At 4.49 the unmixed blood was firmly coagulated. The blood mingled with eau de luce coagulated much sooner, and became very dark. The blood mixed with the Cape antidote remained bright red, and did not coagulate.

EXPERIMENT No. 20.

A Fowl was bitten in the thigh by the same Cobra, now somewhat exhausted, at 4.44 P.M. 4.45.—Dead, with the usual symptoms. At 4.52 P.M. blood was drawn into three watch-glasses, a few drops in each. No. 1. Contained three drops of the Cape antidote in blood. No. 2. Four drops of eau de luce in blood. No. 3. Nothing but blood. These were placed aside, and watched for some hours. Nos. 1 and 2 remained fluid. No. 3 coagulated imperfectly.

There are some apparent contradictions in these two experiments; in the first the blood coagulated firmly when mixed with eau de luce. In the second it remained fluid. Had the shape of the vessel anything to do with it ? In the first it was deep and narrow; in the second flat and shallow. I do not know that the results of experiments on the coagulability of the blood after death, under any circumstances, are of much import, but I record those as they were made.

June 4th, 1870.

Present, Drs. Fayrer, Chevers, and Ewart, and Mr. Sceva.

EXPERIMENT No. 21.

A small Pariah Dog was brought fully under the influence of alcohol; several ounces of brandy had been given, diluted with water, in divided doses during the morning. He was bitten in the thigh by a young one-third grown "Gokurrah," at 3 P.M. The snake was with difficulty made to close its jaws, and the bite was doubtful. At 3.10.—No symptoms of poisoning. The Dog was bitten in the thigh by a "Keautiah" full-grown, and was very rapidly affected by the poison, began to stagger; more brandy was administered. 3.15.—Dog convulsed. 3.16.—Dead.

It has been suggested that persons in a state of intoxication from alcohol are less susceptible to snake-poison, and that brandy administered to those bitten is useful. I have no doubt it is so to a certain extent; but this experiment seems to show that it can do but little in preventing the fatal effects of the poison on an animal at all events.

EXPERIMENT No. 22.

At 3.20 P.M. three drops of poison recently taken from the same "Keautiah" mentioned in the last experiment were put into a Fowl's mouth, being brought in contact with the lining membrane. 3.28.—Not affected. 3.40.—Not affected. 3.56.—Fowl is drowsy, eyes closed, crouching, cannot stand, resting the point of the beak on the ground. 4.12.—More drowsy. 4.20. — Convulsed. 4.24. — Peculiar convulsion of neck. 4.40.—Lies on its side, appears dying. 5.—Still alive, but completely paralysed. 5.20.—Violently convulsed. 5.43.—Dead.

EXPERIMENT No. 23.

Half a drop of poison from the same "Keautiah" put into a Dog's eye at 3.25 P.M. Immediate excitement resulted; the Dog began to rub the eye with his fore-foot with excessive lachrymation. The eyelids began to swell and the conjunctivæ to be chemosed. 3.28.—Eyelids much swollen. The Dog is evidently affected constitutionally, he is drowsy. 4 P.M.—Eyelids swollen with great tension. The conjunctiva in a state of intense chemosis; very drowsy. 4.12.—Lies quiet. 4.40.—Dog was drowsy and partially paralysed; when raised on his legs he cannot stand, falls over. 4.45.—Convulsed. 5.5.—Convulsed. 5.30.—Respiration ceased, heart's action continuing, but irregularly. 5.34.—Dead—in two hours and nine minutes.

This Dog had been taking liquor arsenicalis for some time before the poison was introduced; he was in excellent health and spirits at the time. The arsenic does not seem to have been in any way prophylactic.

EXPERIMENT No. 24.

About four drops of poison from the same "Keautiah" were diluted with four parts of water, and introduced into a Dog's stomach at 3.50 P.M. No effect was manifested by 3.58, when about eight or ten drops of poison taken from a large "Gokurrah" (Spectacled Cobra) were put into the Dog's mouth, being dropped on to the tongue and roof of the mouth. 4.2.—The Dog runs about uneasily and is restless, is evidently nauseated, tries to be sick. 4.8.—Retching violently. 4.11.—Vomited the contents of his stomach, followed by a quantity of frothy mucus. Mouth examined, no change apparent in the mucous membrane. 4.15.—Involuntary defecation and micturition commencing; is very restless; staggers; head rolling from side to side. 4.26.—In convulsions. 4.28.—Dead—in thirty-one minutes. The body was examined soon after death. The blood flowed freely from the heart and great vessels, and formed into a peculiarly firm coagulum rapidly. The stomach and œsophagus laid open:—rugæ of stomach deep pink, mucous surface of gullet quite blanched, tenacious and frothy mucus adhering to surface of stomach.

The three last experiments quite settle the question of poisoning by absorption of the poison through a mucous surface. In all three animals death resulted rapidly, and with all the symptoms of snake-poisoning well marked. There could be no doubt of the absorption. The greatest care was taken not to abrade the surface, indeed nothing was done that could have abraded the surface; and it was carefully noted at the time that no lesion had taken place. It must therefore be admitted that snake poison may be absorbed through a mucous membrane, and that it is dangerous to apply it to the surface, and that the sucking of a Cobra bite might be followed by symptoms of poisoning. This is quite contrary to hitherto expressed opinion, and confirms what I have observed and noted in previous experiments.

Experiment No. 25.

The peritoneal cavity of a Fowl exposed by a small carefully made incision, no blood lost; a drop or two of "Gokurrah" poison then applied to the peritoneal surface at 3.53 P.M. The wound was closed and the Fowl released; it ran about for a moment or two and then began to droop. 3.58.—Drooping, crouching, nodding its head, resting the beak on the ground. 4 P.M.—Symptoms increasing rapidly. Fowl convulsed and fallen over. 4.1.—Dead—in eight minutes. This experiment proves that the peritoneum also absorbs the poison; care was taken that the poison should not touch the slight wound; it was spread on the peritoneal surface. Symptoms of poisoning came on rapidly, and death occurred in eight minutes. This also tends to confirm the absorption of the poison through an unbroken membrane.

Experiment No. 26.

A full-grown Pariah Dog was bitten in the thigh by the same "Keautiah," from which the poison had shortly before been extracted, at 4.43 P.M. Immediately after being bitten the external jugular vein was exposed and one drachm of liquor potassæ in two drachms of water was injected into the vein. No effect produced by the injection. 5 P.M.—Hind-legs weak; staggers; restless; lies down and rises again; defecation; falls over and is almost paralysed; tries to use legs, fails, and he falls over. Twenty drops of liquor potassæ injected hypodermically into the thigh; thirty drops of eau de luce with water given by the mouth. Convulsed. 4.5.—Dead—in twenty-two minutes.

In this case the liquor potassæ seemed to accelerate the action of the poison. The snake must have been all but exhausted when he bit, for all the poison that could be got had been squeezed out of his glands not two hours before. There were no indications of poisoning for ten or twelve minutes after the bite, and it generally begins sooner than that; but the poison's action having commenced its progress was fearfully rapid, death taking place in about twelve minutes after the first indication of poisoning presented itself. The liquor potassæ may not have done any harm, but it certainly did no good.

June 8th, 1870.

Present, Drs. Fayrer, J. Ewart, and J. Anderson, and Mr. Sceva.

An *Ophiophagus elaps*, nine feet six inches long, and seven inches in circumference, arrived from Rangoon yesterday. It seemed in good health, but sluggish and indisposed to bite, even when roused; it is just about to cast its epidermis.

Experiment No. 27.

At 11.50 a Pariah Pup, one-fourth grown, was bitten by the *Ophiophagus* in the thigh, the snake being made to close its jaws on the part. 11.51.—The Dog much excited, but apparently not in any pain. 11.52.—In a state of general tremor; defecation. 11.55.—Fallen over paralysed. 11.56.—Convulsed. 11.58.—Dead—in eight minutes. The body was examined soon after death. The blood coagulated in a minute and a half after removal from the great vessels, into a peculiarly firm clot. The Dog never gave the slightest indication of suffering; its death was very quiet and free from pain.

Experiment No. 28.

A full-grown Pariah Dog bitten on the thigh by the same *Ophiophagus* at 12 noon. The snake was made to close its jaws as before on the part. 12.2.—Staggers, being weak in the hind-leg. 12.4.—Standing up, but seems lethargic; head drooping; no expression or sign of pain; when made to walk, does so with difficulty; limbs seem weak, or to be in a state of ataxy. 12.9.—In the same condition: breathing deep; head drooping to the ground; seems unconscious of anything; complete locomotor ataxy. 12.20.—Limbs now seem paralysed; singular freedom from any expression or look of suffering. 12.26.—Slight convulsive movement of muscular system generally. 12.30.—Lies quite motionless; expression of eye natural. 12.31.—Slight convulsions of muscular system generally. 12.34.—Involuntary discharges; heart still beats; no respiration; convulsive waves over the whole body. 12.37.—Appears dead, but the heart still acts irregularly. 12.38.—Dead—in thirty-eight minutes.

There was no salivation in either of these Dogs. The symptoms were like those of Cobra poisoning; if any difference, death was quieter, and free from suffering. Body examined after death: blood coagulated very firmly on removal from the body. The snake is about to shed its epidermis; it is sluggish, and may be sickly, but yet the poison was very active; however, so far as these two experiments show, it is not more active or fatal than that of a full-grown, vigorous Cobra.

June 13th.

Present, Dr. Fayrer and Mr. Sceva.

This morning the same *Ophiophagus elaps* was made to shed its poison into a shell by biting through a leaf stretched across the shell. The poison is a clear golden orange-coloured fluid, and the quantity must have been nearly half a drachm. The snake has just shed its epidermis; it has not eaten for several days, but seemed tolerably well, though somewhat thin. It was handled by two men, one seizing it round the neck, the other by the body near the tail. It is very powerful, but they seemed to have no difficulty in controlling it.

At noon I made the following experiments with the poison:—

Experiment No. 29.

Five drops of the poison were injected with the hypodermic syringe into a Dog's thigh at 12.14 noon. 12.17.—The leg seems weak, partially paralysed; he walks with difficulty. 12.22.—Sluggish, very weak in that hind-leg. 12.25.—Deep breathing, seems lethargic, lying down; no salivation, no appearance of distress; can walk when roused, but staggers and seems drowsy. 12.32.—Very lethargic, lying down; head fallen over. 12.34.—When roused can still walk with a tottering gait; lies down; head falls over. 12.42.—Lying down; limbs convulsed. 12.43.—Involuntary micturition and defecation. 12.48.—Heart beats still irregularly, but respiration has ceased. 12.50.—Heart's action still felt, but it is very slow and irregular. 12.51.—Dead—in thirty-seven minutes.

There was in this, as in the other Dogs, no sign of suffering; a lethargy seemed gradually to steal over the animal until it became unconscious, and then a few convulsive movements preceded death. There was no salivation, as so generally occurs in Cobra poisoning.

Experiment No. 30.

Two or three drops of *Ophiophagus* poison were injected into a Fowl's thigh at 12.16 P.M. 12.17.—Leg weak. 12.20.—Crouching. 12.22.—Head falls over, beak resting on the ground; wings drooping. 12.24.—Paralysed; attempts to rise; falls over. 12.25.—Springs from the ground in convulsions; comb and wattles have become livid. The brilliant red colour is gone. 12.28.—Convulsed. 12.30.—Dead—in fourteen minutes.

Experiment No. 31.

Three drops of the same poison injected into a Fowl's wing at 12.20. 12.22.—Crouching. 12.25.—Runs about, but is weak. 12.26.—Drooping, beak resting on the ground. 12.28.—Almost paralysed. 12.30.—Fallen over. 12.32.—Slightly convulsed; sprang from the ground once or twice. 12.33.—Dead—in thirteen minutes.

Experiment No. 32.

Two drops of *Ophiophagus* poison diluted with twenty of water were injected into a Fowl's thigh at 12.38. 12.42.—Drooping; falls over, beak resting on the ground. 12.45.—Springs from the ground, falls as though dead. 12.47.—Dead—in nine minutes.

In this case, diluting the poison with water made it more active, for it killed in nine minutes, whereas a larger quantity of poison undiluted killed in thirteen to fourteen minutes.

Experiment No. 33.

One drop of *Ophiophagus* poison, four drops of liquor potassæ, and eighteen drops of water were mixed, and then injected at 12.42 into a Fowl's thigh. 12.45.—Limps on injected leg; falls over. 12.47.—Convulsed. 12.50.—Convulsed. 12.54.—Dead—in twelve minutes. Convulsive springs from the ground less violent than in the last case.

The liquor potassæ had no antidotal effect. It seems to me almost conclusive that liquor potassæ does not destroy the activity of the poison. In this case there was only a single drop of poison to four drops of liquor potassæ, and this was diluted with eighteen drops of water. The Fowl died in twelve minutes, that is, two minutes sooner than one of equal size that had been injected with three times as much of the poison undiluted. So far death from the poison of this snake seems quieter, and is attended with less suffering than death from the poison of the Cobra, though with very much the same symptoms generally.

NINETEENTH SERIES.

On the Influence of the Poisons of the Cobra, Ophiophagus, Bungarus cæruleus or Krait, and Bungarus fasciatus; on the Condition of the Blood after Death from Snake-Poison; and on the Effects of Certain Reputed Antidotes.

July 7th, 1870.

Through the kindness of Mr. Richards, Civil Surgeon of Bancoorah, I have had the opportunity of making the following experiments with *Bungarus cæruleus*. The snake was about thirty inches in length, and of the thickness of one's little finger; it was vigorous, but was casting its cuticle. It reached Calcutta in a tin canister, perforated with a few air holes; a snake partly decomposed (species not distinguishable) and a small Frog in a similar condition, were found in the tin case when opened. These looked as if they had been rejected when half digested.

Present, Dr. Fayrer.

Experiment No. 1.

At 7.50 A.M. a Fowl was bitten in the thigh by the *Bungarus cæruleus*; the *Bungarus cæruleus* on this occasion did not appear to bite very fiercely, but the bite left two points marked with blood. The Fowl ran about apparently unconcerned for a few minutes, and was not the least lame on the bitten leg. 8.3.—Apparently not affected. 8.15.—Is drowsy; droops and hangs its head; walks lame. 8.20.—Convulsed. 8.30.—Lies paralysed and is unconscious. 8.35.—Dead—in forty-five minutes.

At 2 P.M. the Fowl was opened and blood removed; the heart contained a black, and at one part partially decolorized clot. The remainder of the blood was altered in appearance; it looked like port wine and water, and after standing for some time, formed an imperfect coagulum. The parts about the fang punctures were livid.

Experiment No. 2.

A full-grown and vigorous Pariah Dog was bitten in the outer part of the thigh by the same *Bungarus cæruleus* at 1.48 P.M. of the 7th July. The punctures drew blood, and the Dog winced and gave signs of pain for a moment.

For some minutes after the bite the Dog seemed quite unaffected, he ran about as before, was neither lame nor affected in any way. 2.20.—Seemed restless, but active as before. 3.20.—Salivation and frothing at the mouth commencing. 3.4.—Nausea and vomiting. 3.42.—Trembling, depressed; head drooping; is evidently much affected by the poison. 3.55.—Involuntary defecation and micturition; lies down on its side; unable to raise its head. 4.22.—Breathing hurried; lies quiet; eyes wide open; pupils dilated. 4.33.—Convulsions commencing; pupils widely dilated; is unable to move. 4.55.—Convulsed. 5.4.—Appears dead, but the heart still beats; respiration has ceased. 5.6.—Remains in the same condition; heart beats fainter. 5.12.—Faint, irregular, cardiac beats still felt. 5.30.—Dead—in three hours and forty-two minutes. Body opened in one hour after death, and blood removed from great vessels.

Examined at 8 A.M. next morning: an imperfect coagulum had formed, but the blood generally looked dark and grumous. I sent it to Dr. Cunningham for examination, and append his report, which is interesting, as it indicates a different condition of the blood to that of other snake-poisoned animals.

"My dear Dr. Fayrer,—The blood which you sent me this morning was quite different in its characters from the specimens which I examined previously.

"The reaction was faintly and permanently acid.

"The red corpuscles were in irregular masses, and had lost all distinctness of outline, and became semifused, as it were. The colouring matter had dissolved out, dyeing the serum and white corpuscles brownish. The white corpuscles were in

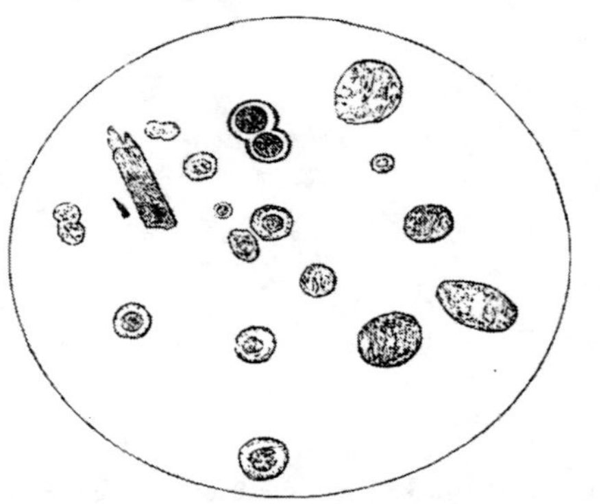

some places in large masses visible to the naked eye. The most remarkable thing about them, however, was their extreme distension in many cases. I could find no cells that were not recognisable as more or less distended white corpuscles. Herewith I enclose a sketch of some of various sizes.

"Yours very truly,

"Friday. "D. D. Cunningham.

"P.S.—It would be very interesting to know if the reaction was acid immediately after death."

Experiment No. 3.

At 4.56 P.M. a Fowl, two-thirds grown, bitten in the thigh by the same *Bungarus cæruleus*; on this occasion the snake bit very fiercely, and was with difficulty made to let go his hold. The puncture drew blood; for some minutes the Fowl not affected. At 5.4 crouching; seems uneasy. 5.7.—Quite lively when roused. 5.8.—Drowsy; eyes closed; head began to droop. 5.12.—Very drowsy; head and wings drooping; crouches; head falls over; rests on point of beak. 5.14.—Cannot stand; lies motionless. 5.45.—Convulsed. 5.55.—Dead—in fifty-nine minutes. The bite on this occasion was very vigorously inflicted.

These three experiments show how dangerous this snake is. This is the third animal it has destroyed in one day, and is apparently as vigorous as ever, and it is quite a small specimen.

Blood removed one hour after death. Examined at 8 A.M., 8th July.—Dark grumous fluid, with an imperfect coagulum.

Experiment No. 4.

A Fowl was bitten in the thigh by a young "Gokurrah" (Spectacled Cobra) at 4.59; the snake bit very fiercely; the Fowl became drowsy immediately. 5.3.—Drooping; head fallen over. 5.4.—Paralysed. 5.6.—Convulsed. 5.7.—Dead.

Blood removed one hour after death. Examined at 8 A.M., 8th July.—The quantity was very small, and it had dried, but it appeared to have, as the attendants said it had, formed a firmer coagulum, and of more florid colour than the blood of the animals killed by the Krait.

July 8th, 1870.

Experiment No. 5.

A Pariah Dog was bitten by a half-grown "Gokurrah," in the thigh at 1.2 P.M. 1.4.—Is lame on bitten leg. 1.8.—Lies down. 1.50.—Very lethargic. 1.55.—Salivation and frothing at the mouth. 1.59.—Convulsed; deep and hurried breathing. 2.6.—Convulsed. 2.14.—Dead—in one hour and twelve minutes.

Some blood was removed in one hour after death from the great vessels. It formed a firm bright red coagulum, very different in appearance from the blood of the Dog killed by the Krait. I examined it at 6 P.M., and found it in this condition. It was neutral, as shown by blue litmus paper. After examination under the microscope, Dr. Cunningham gives the following sketch and remarks:—

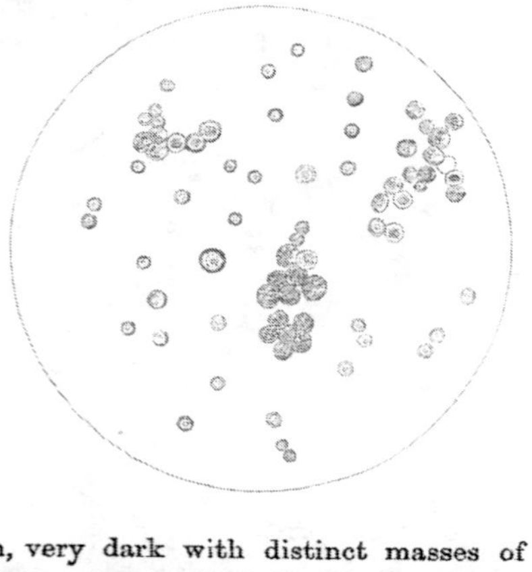

"Clots firm, very dark with distinct masses of white corpuscles; serum neutral, reddish from abundance of free unaltered red corpuscles; white cells normal."

The following experiments made with *Ophiophagus elaps*, *Naja tripudians*, *Bungarus fasciatus*, and *Bungarus cæruleus*, were for the purpose of examining the condition of the blood after death from the poison of those snakes.

July 9th, 1870.

Present, Drs. Fayrer, N. Chevers, and D. Cunningham.

Experiment No. 6.

A Pariah Dog, of about ten months old, was bitten in the thigh by a "Gokurrah" (Spectacled Cobra), about half-grown, and that was partially exhausted by biting in previous experiments. This snake was purposely selected in order that the poison might be less active, and life not so quickly destroyed, with the view of allowing time for the blood to become thoroughly affected by the poison.

The Dog was bitten at 12.3 P.M. 12.20.—Dog is restless. 12.32.—Staggers when he walks; frothing at the mouth; is partially paralysed; breathing hurried. 12.35.—Falls over, is convulsed. 12.45.—Convulsed; involuntary evacuations. 12.47.—Dead—in forty-four minutes.

The blood was removed from the great vessels half an hour after death; neutral to litmus paper, and rapidly formed a firm clot.

Experiment No. 7.

A small Pariah Dog, pup, bitten in the thigh by an *Ophiophagus elaps*, over eleven feet in length, at 12.15 P.M. The Dog was affected at once, jumped, staggered, and then sat down. 12.16.—Hurried breathing. 12.17.—Paralysed, cannot stand. 12.18.—When raised, supports himself for a moment on his legs with the nose resting on the ground, and then falls over. 12.19.—Convulsed. 12.21.—Respiratory movements have ceased; heart's beats still felt. 12.22.—Dead—in seven minutes.

Blood removed half an hour after death: reaction neutral; coagulated at once into a firm clot. It is not of so natural a red as is the clot of the blood of the Dog killed by the Cobra.

Experiment No. 8.

A young Dog was bitten in the thigh by the same Krait (*Bungarus cæruleus*) that bit the Dog in Experiment No. 2, at 12.7 P.M. 12.45.—Seems sluggish. 1.10.—Sluggish; no other change. 1.13.—Bitten again by the same Krait in the thigh. 1.22.—Sluggish; sits with the head drooping. 1.40.—Seems drowsy, but is easily roused. 2.5.—Almost paralysed, cannot stand, the legs fail, and he sinks down when raised on his feet. 2.15.—Involuntary defecation. 2.17.—Convulsed. 2.19.—Respiration has ceased; heart still beats. 2.20.—Heart still felt. 2.22.—Dead—in two hours and fifteen minutes.

The blood was removed an hour after death. In this case it clotted, and was not discoloured as in the case of the first Dog killed by the same Krait.

The rigor mortis occurred in less than an hour. There was no extraordinary rapidity in decomposition of the body, though the weather was very hot and damp.

Experiment No. 9.

A Fowl was bitten in the thigh by the same Krait at 12.24 P.M. 12.35.—Drowsy. 12.58.—Eyes closing, begins to droop. 1.10.—Legs weak, crouches. 1.15.—Droops its head. 1.20.—Head fallen over, resting on point of beak. 1.25.—Quite paralysed; slow, deep breathing. 1.40.—Convulsed. 2.12.—Dead—in one hour and forty-eight minutes.

This little snake is two feet seven inches in length, and one and three-fourths in circumference, but it is very deadly, as these experiments prove; it has since the 7th July killed two Dogs and three Fowls; the action of the poison is slower, but it appears to be as fatal as that of the Cobra.

During the last two days the Krait has cast its cuticle, and now shows its markings beautifully—the dark brown, almost black, distinct white rings, with a pearly white abdomen.

Rigor mortis was complete in this Fowl in forty-five minutes after death. Decomposition was not more rapid than in death from ordinary causes.

There was no evidence of decomposition at 1 A.M., notwithstanding the great heat and humidity of the atmosphere.

Experiment No. 10.

A Dog, about six months old, was bitten in the thigh by a full-grown *Bungarus fasciatus* at 11.59 A.M. 12.45 P.M.—No apparent effect. 1.15.—Slight sluggishness; no apparent change otherwise. Bitten again by the same snake. 1.22.—Sluggish. 1.41.—Seems drowsy, but is easily roused. 2.5.—Seems more drowsy; staggers. 2.14.—Stands with difficulty. 4.2.—Is able to walk, but is lame. 5.30.—Drowsy; eyes half closed. 7.15.—Coughs. 10.14.—In the same condition. 11.20.—Still coughing, and vomited.

July 10th, 5.15 A.M.—Seems unable to stand. 6.5.—Drowsy, but standing. Noon.—Appears in the same condition, and remained so all day; refuses food. 9 P.M.—In much the same condition; coughing frequently.

July 11th, 5.30 A.M.—Cannot stand. 11.30.—Cannot stand. 12.30. P.M.—Cannot stand. 3.15.—Purged. 6.55.—Lies quiet, with the eyes half opened. 8.30.—Seems very much depressed.

July 12th, 6.10 A.M.—Breathing hurried. 8.30.—Dying. 11.30.—Very low. 2.10 P.M.—Found dead—had been dead probably an hour or more, as the body was quite rigid.

This Dog lived for upwards of seventy hours after being bitten by this *Bungarus fasciatus* ("Sankni"), a very large and powerful snake of about five feet in length. It had been some weeks in captivity, and may have been weak, but it bit fiercely when roused, and drew blood.

It is evidently less virulent than its smaller congener, the Krait. The blood coagulated after death. The rigor mortis was complete.

Experiment No. 11.

A half-grown Cat was bitten in the thigh by the same *Bungarus fasciatus* at 12.36—*i.e.*, immediately after the Dog. The snake seemed to bite reluctantly until excited, when it appeared to strike its fangs deeply. The Cat immediately became rigid, its pupils widely dilated, and its tongue protruded. These symptoms, I believe, were due to excitement, rage, or fear, for on being placed on the ground it rapidly recovered.

The pupils contracted, and it seemed unaffected a quarter of an hour after being bitten. It was not affected after this, and on the 12th, when the death of the Dog was reported, it was quite well. I am inclined to think that this snake was either exhausted or that its fangs were imperfect.

July 23*rd*, 1870.

Present, Drs. J. Fayrer, W. B. Beatson, and J. Ewart, Professor of Physiology.

Experiment No. 12.

A full-grown Pariah Dog was bitten in the thigh by a full-grown and vigorous Cobra, of the variety called by the snake-men "Kurrees Keautiah." Two tablespoonfuls of Mr. Otho Alexander's fluid antidote were poured down the Dog's throat immediately after the bite, which was inflicted at 12.18 P.M., and the vegetable extract or paste made into the consistence of honey with liquor ammoniæ was well rubbed into the wound, and over a large surface round it.

This so-called antidote was sent to India by Mr. Otho Alexander, of Cephalonia, and the samples experimented with were sent to me for experiment by his Excellency the Viceroy. The following are Mr. O. Alexander's instructions, which were carefully followed:—

"The antidotes are to be used in the following manner. As soon as possible after the infliction of the bite two tablespoonfuls of the liquid should be administered. The ointment, said to be Venetian treacle, having been reduced with liquor ammoniæ to the consistence of thick honey, should then be rubbed forcibly into the wound over a large surface, and from the bite downwards, and this should be repeated several times until a quantity of the ointment is absorbed. After the lapse of three or four hours the fluid should be again given, and the friction repeated, but with less force."

The fluid is a clear liquid like water, the paste has very much the appearance of extract of conium or hyoscyamus, with a somewhat resinous smell.

12.19 P.M.—The Dog limped on the bitten leg, and seemed restless and uneasy. 12.26.—Retching. 12.30.—Very restless; breathing hurried. 12.31.—Vomiting. 12.33.—Staggering; profuse defecation. 12.34.—Convulsed; diarrhœa; rises, staggers, and falls over in convulsions. 12.35.—Violent convulsions. 12.37.—Perfectly paralysed; heart still beats; no respiration. 12.38.—Dead—in twenty minutes after the bite. The blood on removal from the great vessels coagulated firmly a few minutes after death.

Experiment No. 13.

A full-grown Pariah Dog was bitten in the thigh by a large Spectacled Cobra ("Koyah Gokurrah" of the snake-men) at 12.37 P.M. Two tablespoonfuls of the fluid were poured down the Dog's throat immediately after the bite. 12.40.—Breathing hurriedly; restless. 12.50.—Restless and uneasy; the paste well rubbed into the wounds and neighbouring parts, according to the instructions. 12.52.—Convulsed; rises; walks with a staggering gait, and falls. Another dose of the fluid administered. 12.54.—Violently convulsed. 12.55.—Paralysed, cannot rise. 12.57.—Heart still beats, respiration has ceased. 12.58.—Dead—in twenty-one minutes. Blood coagulated firmly soon after death.

Experiment No. 14.

A young Spectacled Cobra, three feet in length, was bitten fiercely in three places in the body by a full-grown, powerful, fresh and vigorous Cobra, of the variety called by the snake-men "Bans-buniah Keautiah," at 12.27 P.M. The fangs were deeply imbedded, and the poison must have been thoroughly inoculated.

At 2.20 P.M. on the following day the young Cobra was as active as ever, evidently not in the least affected by the poison. I selected a small Cobra to be bitten by a large one in order that the effects of the poison might be felt with the greatest force, should it have any at all.

Experiment No. 15.

A *Bungarus fasciatus*, five feet in length, was bitten deeply in two places by a very large, fresh, and vigorous Cobra ("Tentuliah Keautiah"), five feet six inches in length, at 12.30 P.M. There could be no doubt of the severity of the bite, for it was disengaged with difficulty.

At 2.20 P.M. on the following day, nearly twenty-six hours afterwards, the *Bungarus fasciatus* was perfectly well, and not in the least affected by the poison.*

Experiment No. 16.

A Fowl had twenty drops of the blood of the Dog poisoned by a Cobra in Experiment No. 12 injected with the hypodermic syringe into each thigh, at 12.42 P.M. 12.50.—Crouching. 12.55.—Crouching; feathers ruffled. 1.5.—Sluggish, eyes closed; is drowsy. 1.30.—Stands with head depressed; feathers staring; eyes closed; very drowsy. 2.—Very drowsy; head drooping. After this the Fowl slowly recovered; and on Monday, 24th, was quite well. The poison in this experiment must have been infinitesimal in quantity; only forty drops of the blood of a full-grown Dog poisoned by a Cobra were injected. The symptoms of poisoning were well marked, though the bird ultimately recovered.

* The snake died on the fifth day. It is doubtful whether death was not caused by the wound, which had become putrid, independently of the poison; see note, p. 122.

EXPERIMENT No. 17.

A solution of one part of Cobra poison to eight parts of liquor potassæ was prepared by Dr. Ewart, and of this nine drops were injected into a Fowl's thigh at 12.57 P.M. There was a flocculent-looking deposit caused by the mixture of the fluids. 1 A.M.—Drooping. 1.2.—Crouching; head falling over; nearly paralysed. 1.4.—Convulsed. 1.7.—Dead—in seven minutes, with all the symptoms of Cobra poisoning.

This experiment appears conclusive: eight parts of liquor potassæ did not neutralize the effects of one part of the poison.

EXPERIMENT No. 18.

A Fowl was bitten by a fresh Cobra in the thigh at 1.2 P.M. 1.3.—No convulsions. 1.4.—Dead—in two minutes.

EXPERIMENT No. 19.

Twenty drops of the blood of the above-mentioned Fowl, removed immediately after death, injected into either thigh of a Fowl at 1.10 P.M. 1.30.—Sluggish. 2.15.—Sluggish. 4.10.—Drowsy; head falls over. 4.20.—No convulsions. 7.15.—Dead—in six hours and five minutes. Blood removed from the body, coagulated firmly after death. This quite settles the question of the blood of an animal killed by snake-poison being itself poisonous.

In the case where the blood of a Dog poisoned by a Cobra was injected, the bird also showed marked evidences of poisoning; though the dilution of the poison must have been very great in the blood of so large an animal as a Dog; only forty drops of the blood was used in each experiment.

EXPERIMENT No. 20.

A full-grown Cobra (" Bans-buniah Keautiah") was bitten twice, very strongly, by a full-grown and vigorous Cobra ("Tentuliah Keautiah"), at 1.15 P.M. No evil consequences followed. The snake was perfectly well next day.*

EXPERIMENT No. 21.

A Fowl was bitten in the thigh by a *Bungarus cæruleus* (Krait), at 1.22 P.M. 1.24.—Feathers staring; eyes have a fixed glaring stare. 1.25.—Stretches out the neck; falls over; point of beak resting on the ground. 1.26.—Convulsed; puncture in thigh ecchymosed and œdematous. 1.29.—Dead—in seven minutes. Blood coagulated firmly in four minutes after death.

This experiment shows the deadly nature of this little snake, which (as the former experiments have also shown) is apparently more deadly than its large congener, the *Bungarus fasciatus*. This experiment also proves that the coagulation of the blood is not prevented after death.

EXPERIMENT No. 22.

A Cat was bitten in the thigh by a Cobra ("Tentuliah Keautiah"), at 1.46 P.M. Mr. O. Alexander's antidote and extract were administered, according to his instructions, immediately. 1.47 P.M.—Pupils widely dilated; Cat lies stretched out; hurried breathing. 1.51.—Convulsed. 1.52.—Paralysed; heart still beats, no respiration. 1.55.—Dead—in nine minutes. This Cat was on a former occasion bitten by a large *Bungarus fasciatus*, and showed no signs of poisoning. The blood on removal from the body, a few minutes after death, coagulated firmly.

EXPERIMENT No. 23.

A Fowl was bitten in the thigh by a large *Bungarus fasciatus* at 1.44 P.M. 1.54.—Drooping; head falling forwards. 1.58.—Convulsed; cannot stand. 2 P.M.—Convulsive movements; there is a peculiar vocal sound as though the thorax were compressed. 2.5.—Convulsed. 2.10.—Dead—in twenty-six minutes. Blood removed from the body coagulated firmly in a few minutes after death.

EXPERIMENT No. 24.

A young Rat was bitten in the thigh by a *Bungarus cæruleus* at 2 P.M. Insensible immediately. Dead—in thirty seconds. Blood coagulated firmly in four minutes.

I am indebted to Captain Grigg, Cantonment Magistrate of Fyzabad, in Oude, for the following account of an encounter between a Musk Rat and a Krait:—

"My object in writing you now is to give you an account of a rather extraordinary incident which took place in my compound the other day.

"I was going out of my compound early in the morning in company with another officer, when I was attracted by the squeak of a Musk Rat. On looking about to see whence it came, I found a Musk Rat and a 'Krait' snake in a small pukka garden tank. The snake had its head coiled round under its neck, and although I poked it up, nothing would induce it to attack the Musk Rat. Whenever I threw the snake at the Rat, the Rat squeaked and emitted such a stench that the snake would not touch it.

"I at last got the Musk Rat to attack the snake. He did so by making snaps at the snake's back and tail; these snaps appeared to cause the snake a great deal of pain; he writhed about a good deal, and at last brought up a young Frog. This the Musk Rat commenced to devour. I then flung the snake on him—*i.e.*, the Rat; he got angry. At last I got the Rat to attack the snake regularly; the snake remaining with his head curled up under his neck; only once did I provoke the snake into making a partial bite at the Rat, it took no effect. The Rat had regularly set to work at gnawing the snake's neck, commencing from behind to the head; so the snake was in a bad way when I left it. I returned about an hour afterwards and found the Rat lying panting on his belly, he had eaten a good part of the fleshy portion of the neck, and the snake was quite dead. The Rat was subsequently killed by some little boys throwing bricks at it. I never heard of a Musk Rat doing this before, but natives tell me it is common to see three or four pursuing a Cobra or some other snake. If every person knew that a Musk Rat killed poisonous snakes, I do not think they would be so ready to kill them. At every snap the Rat made, the natives said 'See how the poison acts.' They were under the impression that the snake was writhing from the Musk Rat's poison. I should hardly think this was the case."

July 28th, 1870.

Present, Drs. Fayrer, Murray (Inspector-General of Hospitals), Ross, Beatson, and Ewart.

EXPERIMENT No. 25.

A full-grown and powerful Pariah Dog was bitten in the thigh by an *Ophiophagus elaps*, nine feet nine inches in length, at 12.15 P.M. The snake, it is to be observed, had been some months in captivity, and was sluggish and apparently disinclined to bite. It had been fed on fish, which was pushed down its throat, as it refused to eat. The bite in this case was very slight, and it was doubtful if the fangs had penetrated.

12.19.—The Dog micturated very freely. 12.24.—Restless. 12.25. — Lying down. 12.35. — Apparently not affected. 12.38.—Defecation and micturition again very profuse. 12.44.—The snake was again made to bite the Dog in the thigh. This time there was no doubt about its fangs being imbedded, for blood was drawn. 12.50.—Restless; turns round; lies down, gets up again. Breathing accelerated. 12.55.—Very restless; convulsive twitchings of the muscles generally. 12.58.—Breathing much accelerated; cannot stand; staggers

* But was found dead five days later.

and falls over; convulsive movements. 1.2 P.M.—Convulsed. 1.7.—Convulsions; bowels acted again. 1.9.—Dead.

First bite, doubtful, 12.15. Second, certain, 12.44. Dead 1.9—fifty-four minutes from the first doubtful bite; or twenty-five minutes from the second certain bite. The skin was removed from the wounded part. The cellular tissue around the puncture was dark, ecchymosed, and œdematous. The blood, when removed from the body after death, coagulated firmly into a red clot.

Experiment No. 26.

A Fowl was bitten in the thigh by the same *Ophiophagus* at 12.49. It limped immediately on the bitten leg. 12.54.—Fowl drooping, head falling over. 12.55.—Convulsed. 12.56.—Purged; convulsed. 1 P.M. — Dead — in eleven minutes. Areolar tissue about the wound ecchymosed; blood coagulated firmly on being removed from the body after death. The snake is apparently not so virulent as a Cobra, for the Fowl lived eleven minutes after being bitten. But this may be due to the weak condition of the *Ophiophagus*, for it has been long in confinement; it looks sickly, and has been fed on fish, instead of its natural food, snakes, which it declines to eat. They have been put into its case, but it refuses to touch them.

Experiment No. 27.

I append an extract from the *European Mail* on the subject of an antidote for Cobra poison:—

"Snake Poison and its Antidote.

"*To the Editor of the European Mail.*

"Sir,—Having noticed of late the publication in both European and American journals of articles upon the subject, and particularly one under date March 2nd, 1870, under the heading 'The Cobra Question in India,' I trust you will give publicity to this communication, on account of its importance; and am induced to ask for it a place in the columns of your journal, in the hope that it will afford to your readers, in India more particularly, a knowledge of an antidote for snake-poisons, which may claim to be specific, insomuch as it has never been known to fail in a single instance during the past three years in different districts in this country in which I have been able to induce its general adoption, and particularly by the *curanderos*, or curers (snake-charmers). I have devoted no little time during the past twenty years to a study of the habits, peculiarities, &c. of poisonous snakes, and have made many experiments with their poisons, with a view to discover, if possible, specific antidotes to them; and have been so far successful as to be able to announce the law in therapeutics that 'all animal poisons have their specific antidotes in the gall of the animal or the reptile in which these poisons exist.'

"The bite of the Cobra, or of any other poisonous snake or reptile, can be cured by administering a few drops of a preparation of the gall of the Cobra, which should be prepared as follows:—Pure spirits of wine, of 95 per cent. alcohol, or the best high wines that can be procured, 200 drops; of the pure gall, 20 drops; in a clean two-ounce phial, corked with a new cork; give the phial 150 or 200 shakes, so that the gall may be thoroughly mixed with the spirits, and the preparation is ready for use. In case of a bite put five drops (no more) of the preparation into half a tumblerful of pure water; pour the water from one tumbler into another backwards and forwards several times, that the preparation may be thoroughly mixed with the water, and administer a large tablespoonful of the mixture every three or five minutes until the whole has been given. In case the violence of the pain and hæmorrhage or swelling of the bitten part should be but slightly alleviated after the whole has been taken, repeat the dose, prepared with the same quantity of the preparation in the same way, and administer as before. In curing upwards of fifty cases of snake-bites I have never been obliged to repeat the dose except in two instances, and have never lost a case. The Cobra poison is no more deadly than that of a great variety of snakes found in South America, of which may be named the 'Cascabel,' or Rattlesnake; 'Boquidorada,' or Gilded Mouth; 'Mapana-Sapo,' or Frog-headed 'Mapana'; 'Mapana-fina,' or 'Lachesis,' 'Niger,' 'Birri,' and 'Verrugosa,' or Wart-snake. The poison of all these varieties produces death (under certain conditions—atmospherical, physical, climaterical, and electrical) in from fifteen minutes to two or three hours; but it is found that the gall of each variety (administered as previously indicated) is the perfect antidote for its own poison. The gall of the most deadly kind may be used in cases of bites of those less virulent, and is also applicable in cases of bites of the Centipede, Scorpion, Sting-ray, Star-lizard, or '*Lacerta stella*,' and is also very effective in Dog-bites.

"S. B. Higgins.

"State of Magdalena, April 10th, 1870."

The instructions therein contained have been most carefully followed. The alcoholic solution of the bile of the Cobra was prepared with the greatest accuracy by Dr. D. Cunningham; it was taken from a large and vigorous Cobra killed on purpose, and the tincture prepared without delay.

The following experiments were made on July 28th:—

A full-grown Pariah Dog was bitten by a Cobra ("Bansbuniah Keautiah") on the thigh at 12.30. The bite was very slight, as the snake seemed indisposed to close its jaws. However, a very slight wound was inflicted, and it was not repeated, as it was more probable that the antidote would be beneficial, the dose of poison being slight. At 12.32 the antidote was administered exactly according to the instructions. 12.35.—Another dose given. 12.38.—Dose repeated. 12.41.—Dose repeated. The Dog is sluggish and depressed. 12.42.—Staggers in his gait; micturates and defecates profusely. 12.44.—Another dose given. 12.47. — Dose repeated. 12.51.—Another dose given. 12.53.—Dose repeated. The Dog is sluggish. 12.56.—Another dose given. 12.59.—Dose repeated. 1.2 P.M.—Dose repeated. 1.5.—He is very sluggish and depressed. 1.8.—Convulsed; another dose given. 1.12.—Dose repeated. 1.17.—Very drowsy; convulsive twitchings; another dose given. 1.25.—Dose repeated. 1.30. — Convulsed; another dose given. 1.34.—Dose repeated. 1.41.—Feeble respirations, almost paralysed. 1.45.—Still breathes. 1.52.—Still breathes; cannot move; has occasional convulsive twitchings. 1.57.—Dead—in eighty-seven minutes. Blood coagulated firmly on being removed from the body. Skin raised over the bite; areolar tissue ecchymosed and œdematous. The symptoms were simply those caused by a smaller dose of the poison than usual—death resulting in eighty-seven minutes.

Experiment No. 28.

A Pariah Dog was bitten in the thigh by a Cobra at 12.53. The bile antidote administered at 12.55. 12.58.—Another dose given. 1.1 P.M.—Another dose given. It was repeated at intervals of three minutes. 1.6.—The Dog is sluggish and staggering. 1.10.—Convulsed. 1.12.—Dying. 1.13.—Dead—in twenty minutes. The antidote was administered regularly at intervals of three minutes. Blood coagulated firmly after death; areolar tissue under the integument ecchymosed and œdematous.

Experiment No. 29.

A young Dog was bitten in the thigh by a Spectacled Cobra ("Kurrees Gokurrah") at 1.25 P.M. Mr. Otho Alexander's fluid antidote administered, and paste diluted with ammonia, applied according to Mr. A.'s instructions. 1.27.—The Dog staggers, drags the bitten leg. 1.28.—Bitten leg paralysed. 1.29.—The Dog has fallen over; paralysed. 1.30.—Convulsed. 1.32.—Dead—in seven minutes. The Dog was about half grown; the Cobra was fresh and vigorous. The drugs did not appear in any way to modify the action of the poison. Blood coagulated firmly after death.

EXPERIMENT No. 30.

The same *Ophiophagus elaps* used in Experiments Nos. 25 and 26 was made to shed its poison into a shell; and on this occasion I observed that the fluid was more limpid, and not of so deep a yellow colour as in former experiments. Six drops of this poison were injected into the external jugular vein, which was laid bare on purpose, of a very large and powerful Dog, at 1.42 P.M. For a minute the Dog did not seem affected in any way. 1.43.—Staggered suddenly when walking, and micturated profusely; in a few seconds more it was convulsed with opisthotonos. 1.44. — Fell over, apparently insensible; there was neither cry nor indication of pain. 1.45.—Lying with the limbs extended, and breathing deeply. It remained in this position, apparently dead, but for the deep breathing, until 1.59, when it was convulsed. At 2.4 it was quite dead—in twenty-two minutes. It seemed perfectly unconscious after the first two minutes. Blood coagulated firmly after death.

EXPERIMENT No. 31.

A Cobra was made to shed its poison into a shell, and five drops were injected into the external jugular vein of a full-grown Pariah Dog, not quite so powerful as that used in Experiment No. 30, at 1.55. In thirty seconds it was affected, the bowels acted, muco-sanguinolent motions, and it fell into convulsions; its legs failed, and it remained resting on its belly. Vomited, gave a few convulsive movements, and was dead in two minutes and a half.

These two experiments, 30 and 31, show the terrible activity of snake-poison when it directly enters the venous circulation. In contrasting the two, the Cobra poison appears more rapid and deadly in its action than that of the *Ophiophagus*. Death occurred from the Cobra poison in two minutes and a half, and from the *Ophiophagus* poison in twenty-two minutes. But it is to be remarked that the Dog was somewhat more powerful in the case of the *Ophiophagus* than in that of the Cobra; and that the *Ophiophagus* was probably weak and sickly from confinement, whilst the Cobra was comparatively fresh and vigorous.

From the opportunities I have had so far of testing the relative virulence of the poisons of these snakes, I should say that, quantity for quantity, the poison of the *Ophiophagus* is not more deadly than that of the Cobra, if indeed it be not less so. The Rev. Mr. Vinton, of Rangoon, to whom I am indebted for the *Ophiophagus*, and who has much knowledge of these snakes, writes to me as follows:—"In all my experiments I have always found that, quantity for quantity, the poison of the Hamadryad was not so dangerous as either Cobra or *Daboia*. The danger with the Hamadryad is, however, in the very large quantities of poison. When very much enraged it clings to its bite, and seems determined to inject a very large quantity of poison into the wound."

From what I have seen of the Hamadryad (*Ophiophagus*) I am inclined to form the same opinion as Mr. Vinton. The snake, when it did bite, held on with much pertinacity, and in earlier experiments, when it was made to shed its poison by biting a leaf stretched across a shell, at least half a drachm was obtained of a bright orange-coloured viscid fluid, which I have already described.

But nothing that I have seen of it in captivity confirms the account of its aggressive nature. Indeed it seems rather sluggish and difficult to rouse, not assuming readily the menacing and angry look of the Cobra when roused. But when much irritated the *Ophiophagus* raises its head, expands the hood, hisses, and strikes, though not so fiercely as the Cobra. It is probably different in the wild state, where, it is said when roused to take the initiative and not only attack but chase its enemy, even man.

EXPERIMENT No. 32.

About five drops of fresh Cobra poison, just taken from the snake, were put into a Fowl's mouth at 2.5 P.M., and were apparently immediately swallowed. The Fowl was evidently affected, its feathers rather ruffled; it drooped and was purged. It kept constantly shaking its head and trying to sneeze, if we may so describe the action in a Fowl. It drooped for a time, but the following day had quite recovered. The crop was full of grain, and hence the poison probably was diffused throughout the contents, and was not brought into contact sufficiently with the mucous membrane to produce fatal poisoning. Former experiments have abundantly proved the danger of applying the poison to a mucous surface.

NOTE.—The *Bungarus fasciatus* bitten by the Cobra on the 23rd of July died on the 28th July. It was found that the Cobra bite had ulcerated, and a putrid opening in the tissues exposed the ribs. It evidently did not die of the direct effects of the poison. The Cobras bitten by other Cobras are alive and well (July 28th). As these snakes were all severely bitten by fresh and vigorous Cobras, I think it may be fairly said that they cannot poison each other or themselves.

I am indebted to Dr. Richards, Civil Medical Officer of Bancoorah, for the following experiments which he was kind enough to make at my request with the "Krait" or *Bungarus cæruleus*. The snake is said to be common in that part of Bengal, and is known there to the natives as the "Dhomun Chiti:"—

EXPERIMENT No. 1.

August 1st, 1870.—A "Krait" (*Bungarus cæruleus*), after being irritated for five or six minutes, was made to bite the comb of a Fowl at 6.55 P.M.; it died, with the usual symptoms preceding, at 7.27, or in thirty-two minutes. The body was opened at once and the blood taken from the heart coagulated immediately.

EXPERIMENT No. 2.

August 2nd.—The same Krait was made to bite a Fowl's fore-arm at 1.28 P.M. The snake held on for some time. The bitten part, which bled very much, was at once burnt with a piece of iron made red hot. 1.40 P.M.—Tail drooping slightly; looks rather sluggish. 2 P.M.—Apparently much better, and is eating some rice. 2.15 P.M.—Rests the beak upon the ground, and is crouching. 2.25 P.M.—Crouched in a corner; endeavours to keep its beak resting on the ground, but the head falls on one side; presently became convulsed. 3.20.—Dead—in one hour and fifty-two minutes. Body opened thirty minutes after death. The heart contained fluid blood, which, however, coagulated immediately on being drawn from it, except a portion that was mixed with liquor potassæ, which did not coagulate, and became very dark.

EXPERIMENT No. 3.

The same Krait was made to bite a Fowl's fore-arm at 2.12 P.M. 3 P.M.—Drooping and drowsiness began in seventeen minutes: now staggers, and then squats down. Fifteen minims of liquor potassæ with water, administered. 3.14 P.M.—Endeavours to keep the head straight on the ground, but the head constantly drops on one side or the other. 3.28.—Dead—in one hour and sixteen minutes. The body was opened seven minutes after death. The blood was fluid, but coagulated immediately on being drawn from the body.

This last Fowl died much quicker than the second, although bitten after, and with less severity. Either the excessive bleeding or the actual cautery in the case of the second Fowl prolonged life. I am inclined to believe it was the former.

The experiment with liquor potassæ was not satisfactory, as it was given much too late.

EXPERIMENT No. 4.

August 5th.—A full-grown country Goat was bitten by the same Krait in one of the teats at 4.30 P.M. At 8 P.M. appears tolerably well, but the tail is drooping. 10.12 P.M.—Staggers about, or lies on its side; defecation, micturition, and salivation. 10.24 P.M.—Convulsed; pupils dilated, and insensible to light; gasping; twitching of the ears; the eyes fixed. 10.28 P.M.—Dead—in five hours and fifty-eight minutes. Body opened at 11 P.M. The blood, which was fluid when taken from the body, was put into three separate glasses.

No. 1 contained blood only, and this coagulated firmly immediately; colour bright red.

No. 2 contained blood and liquor potassæ; did not coagulate immediately; it became gradually thicker; and for five minutes coagulated less firmly than No. 1; colour brownish.

No. 3 contained blood mixed with liquor ammoniæ; did not coagulate until the morning of the 6th, and then not at all firmly; colour dark red.

I could find no fang marks in the teat, *either before or after death.* The Krait died before the evening, owing to my having handled it too roughly in making it bite the Goat.

TWENTIETH SERIES.

On the Influence of the Poisons of the Ophiophagus, Cobra, Bungarus cæruleus, and Echis carinata.

August 5th, 1870.

EXPERIMENT No. 1.

Some poison was taken from an *Ophiophagus* on the 4th, yesterday; it had dried into a gum-like paste by noon to-day, and was of the usual clear orange colour. This was diluted with water into its natural consistency.

The snake was sickly and died this morning, so that it is probable that the poison was less active than if it had been taken from a vigorous snake. A drop of this poison was injected with the hypodermic syringe, at 12.27 P.M., into a Pigeon's thigh.

The bird for the first three or four minutes did not seem to be affected, it then began to droop and erect its feathers. 12.35.—Fell over, cannot stand. 12.36.—Convulsive movements. 12.38.—Appears to be dying. 12.40.—Dead—in thirteen minutes.

Blood coagulated firmly after death.

EXPERIMENT No. 2.

About one-fourth of a drop of clear transparent poison extracted from a *Bungarus cæruleus.* It was with the greatest difficulty that even this small quantity could be collected, owing to the smallness of the Krait's fangs. This was diluted with sufficient water to form a good-sized drop, and was injected at 12.35 into a Pigeon's thigh.

No change for the first three or six minutes. 12.43.—Crouching, wings spread out. 12.45.—Convulsed. 12.47.—Paralysed completely, occasional convulsions. 12.51.—Dead—in sixteen minutes.

Blood coagulated firmly after death. The quantity of poison was extremely small, and even part of that was lost in collecting it; the whole amount must have been considerably less than a quarter of a drop, but it proved fatal in sixteen minutes.

EXPERIMENT No. 3.

Poison taken from a fresh "Keautiah" (Cobra). Half a drop was diluted with water and injected into a Pigeon's thigh at 12.39. 12.40.—Staggering. 12.41.—Fallen over. 12.42.—Convulsed. 12.43.—Dead—in four minutes.

Blood coagulated firmly after death. The snake in this experiment was fresh and healthy; poison was shed in considerable quantity, but only half a drop was used: it killed in four minutes.

EXPERIMENT No. 4.

A similar quantity of the same Cobra poison diluted with four parts of water was injected into a Pigeon's thigh at 12.47. 12.49. — Staggering; head fell over. 12.50. — Convulsed. 12.51.—Dead—in four minutes.

Blood coagulated firmly after death. The result was the same as in the last experiment.

EXPERIMENT No. 5.

A drop of the *Ophiophagus* poison, the same as used in Experiment No. 1, was injected into a Pigeon's thigh at 12.52.—Not affected for the first few minutes. 12.58.—Staggers and is convulsed. 12.59.—Fallen over, convulsed. 1.4.—Gasping. 1.5.—Dead—in thirteen minutes.

Blood coagulated firmly after death.

EXPERIMENT No. 6.

A Pigeon bitten in the thigh by the Krait from which the poison was taken for the second experiment, at 12.55. 12.56.—Purged, staggers. 12.58.—Crouching, purged. 1 P.M.—Cannot stand. 1.4.—Gasping; convulsive movements. 1.5.—Dead—in ten minutes.

Blood coagulated firmly after death. The snake was exhausted, and hence the comparatively slow action of the poison.

The object of these experiments on animals of the same size and strength, Pigeons, was to test the relative virulence of the poison of the Cobra, the Krait, and the *Ophiophagus.*

The results are not conclusive, as the conditions were not equal. The *Ophiophagus* was sickly, and the poison had dried up before being used. The Krait was small, and had been frequently used lately; the quantity of poison obtained was very small. The Cobra was fresh and vigorous.

The results were:—

The Cobra killed in . . . 4 minutes.
The Ophiophagus in . . . 13 ,,
The Krait in . . . . . 16 ,,

August 8th, 1870.

Present, Drs. Fayrer and J. Anderson, Curator of Indian Museum.

I am indebted to Major McMahon, Deputy Commissioner of Delhi, for a very fine specimen of *Echis carinata,* and three of *Bungarus cæruleus,* which all arrived safely from Delhi The *Echis* was twenty-two inches and a half in length. One *Bungarus cæruleus* forty-eight inches, and the two others twenty-seven inches, one being much larger in girth than the other, though of the same length.

The *Echis* is a beautiful little viper, and apparently very fierce; he hissed* loudly when disturbed, and drew back his head in the attitude as if to strike. The fangs are very long and moveable, and in general character he closely resembles the *Daboia russellii,* though differently marked and much smaller.

Major McMahon, speaking of this individual, says: "I have never seen one larger than the specimen I now send. They have the reputation of being very deadly, and certainly my old snake-man died from the bite of one of his specimens."

The *Echis carinata* appears to be common about Delhi.

EXPERIMENT No. 7.

A full-grown Pariah Dog was bitten in the thigh by the *Echis carinata* at 12.30. The snake bit savagely, and imbedded his

* I subsequently discovered that this sound is not hissing, but is caused by friction of the lateral scales.

fangs thoroughly. The Dog howled as though in pain. As the snake closed his jaw, and before one fang penetrated, a small drop of clear fluid, the poison, was seen on the part.

12.22.—The Dog is restless and drags the bitten leg. 12.26.—The hind-quarters seem very weak, he walks with difficulty. 12.34.—Lying down, rises but with difficulty, and drags the hind limbs. 12.42.—Lying down; breathing hurried. The muscles generally in a state of tremor. 12.59.—The Dog can stand, but when he moves he drags the hind-legs. 1.6.—Standing in a dejected attitude, head resting against a box. 1.18.—He seems rather better. Tries to walk about, but drags the legs. Refuses water when offered. 1.30.—Some blood drawn from a vein in the thigh; it became a bright red fluid immediately, and slowly formed into a poor and rather imperfect clot. 1.45.—Very sluggish, but better than he was; limb swollen and discoloured about the bite. 2.2.—Lying down, apparently asleep. 2.5.—The breathing is still hurried, and he is very sluggish, but takes notice when spoken to. There is no salivation or frothing at the mouth.

I saw him again at 5.45. P.M. He was lying down, quite conscious, but very much indisposed to move; the bitten limb swollen; this was partly due to the puncture whence the blood was abstracted, and the hind-legs very weak.

The Dog died at 10 P.M., in nine hours and a half. The blood remained fluid after death. There was no coagulation.

It is worthy of note that blood taken from the Dog whilst living, one hour after being bitten, and when well under the influence of the poison, formed a rather imperfect clot.

The rigor mortis was complete when I saw the Dog at 8 A.M. of the 9th. The bitten limb was swollen and infiltrated with black blood. This was partly due to the puncture made to withdraw blood before death.

Experiment No. 8.

A Fowl was bitten in the thigh by the same *Echis carinata* at 12.24. 12.25.—Restless and uneasy. 12.26.—Falls over, wings outspread. 12.27.—Convulsed. 12.27.30.—Violently convulsed. 12.28.—Dead—in four minutes.

Just before death the Fowl vomited a quantity of fluid.

The blood was removed from the body five minutes after death: it was thin and red, became bright red when exposed to the air, but did not coagulate. It remained perfectly fluid, never coagulated.

In this it resembles the blood of animals poisoned by *Daboia*, which behaved in the same manner. I think it is quite certain that the poison of these two vipers so affects the blood that it will not coagulate after death.

The bitten limb was intensely swelled and discoloured with black ecchymosis.

Experiment No. 9.

Another Fowl bitten by the same *Echis* in the thigh at 1.38 P.M. One fang has been broken in the last experiments, and the other it would not insert, at least the bite was doubtful.

No effect produced by 2 P.M. So it was again tried, and this time it bit, but reluctantly; it is evidently exhausted.

The Fowl was very slightly affected, being rather sluggish at 2.15. I saw it again at 5.45 P.M., and it had just died, in four hours and seven minutes. Bitten at 1.38.—Died at 5.45.

The snake had evidently been nearly exhausted when it bit this Fowl.

The blood was removed from the body, and it was exactly like that in Experiment No. 8. It remained fluid. The first Fowl died in four minutes. Günther says of the *Echis carinata:* "No case is known of its bite having proved fatal." I think its powers are under-estimated. A snake that can kill a Fowl in four minutes, and a Dog in ten hours, must be very dangerous, and its bite might well prove fatal to weak or young persons. This Fowl died in four hours and seven minutes; the blood was the same in both.

Experiment No. 10.

A full-grown Pariah Dog was bitten in the thigh by the *Bungarus cæruleus*, from Delhi, four feet in length, at 12.31. For the first few minutes no apparent effect. 12.44.—The Dog is looking sluggish, stands with his head stretched, and has a vacant look. 12.50.—Vomited very freely. 12.59.—Lying down, apparently affected with ataxy; cannot co-ordinate his muscles of locomotion; frothing at the mouth; when made to stand, shakes about in a state of obvious helplessness. 1.2.—Lying down; very restless, making efforts to move the limbs in every direction. 1.5.—Tried to get up, fell over, with convulsive movements. 1.10.—Convulsed generally. 1.15.—Sardonic grin; convulsive twitchings of diaphragm and abdominal muscles; convulsions. 1.23.—Dead—in fifty-two minutes.

The thorax opened at 1.30. The blood in the great vessels and heart very dark and treacly-looking; but it reddened somewhat on exposure to the air, and soon formed into a tolerably firm and complete clot. The quantity was considerable, but there was no separation of clots and serum whilst I saw it, until 2.30. The integument was raised over the bite: the punctures were not perceptible below the skin; the areolar tissue was discoloured and œdematous, but not to any great extent.

Experiment No. 11.

A Fowl was bitten by a *Bungarus cæruleus*, twenty-eight inches long (also from Delhi) in the neck at 12.50. 12.50.30.—Crouching. 12.56.—Drooping, head fallen over. 12.59.—Convulsed. 1.7.—Dead—in seventeen minutes.

The blood was removed from the Fowl's body after death, and it coagulated firmly at once. This Krait was very thin and sluggish.

Experiment No. 12.

A Fowl was bitten in the thigh by another *Bungarus cæruleus*, about twenty-eight inches long, but much thicker than that of Experiment No. 11, at 12.40. 12.58.—No effect. Bitten again by same Krait. 1.7.—No effect. 1.14.—Not affected. The Fowl remained unaffected.

Experiment No. 13.

Another Fowl bitten by the same Krait as in Experiment No. 12 in the thigh, at 1.13.—It bit well and drew blood. No effects followed. The Fowl remained quite well.

The Krait was active and vigorous; its fangs were uninjured, and it had not been used before; it was one of the three from Delhi. The other two were poisonous, but it from some reason or other was not venomous.

Such cases explain some of the recoveries from snake bites, and the supposed effect of antidotes.

Experiment No. 14.

A "Bans-buniah Keautiah" (Cobra) fifty-two inches in length, was severely bitten on the body by a *Bungarus cæruleus*, forty-eight inches in length, at 1.22 P.M. Up to 8 A.M. of the next day the Cobra was unaffected.

On the 10th August at 1 P.M. it was found dead. It was bitten on the 8th. This may have been due to natural causes, but the snake was well when it was bitten.

Experiment No. 15.

A *Bungarus cæruleus*, twenty-eight inches long, the one that bit the Fowl on the neck (*vide* Experiment No. 11), was bitten at 12.55 by a very powerful Cobra ("Tentuliah Keautiah") in the body. The fangs of the Cobra were heard to strike the Krait's spine. 1.8.—Very sluggish, can hardly move. 1.32.—Gradually becoming paralysed. 1.35.—Dead.

I think there can be no doubt that the Krait died of the

poison; even if the fangs had penetrated to the spinal cord death would not have been so rapid, and though there had been paralysis of the part posterior to the bite, it would not have involved the entire body. The symptoms were precisely like those seen in innocent snakes when they die from the Cobra bite.

EXPERIMENT No. 16.

A Fowl bitten by a Cobra in the thigh at 1.47. 1.48.—Fell over. 1.49.—Convulsed. 1.50.—Dead.

The blood of the above was taken immediately after death, and about twenty drops injected into another Fowl's thigh. At 5.45 P.M. it was sluggish, but not otherwise apparently affected. At 8 A.M. of the 9th August it was drowsy, crouching, head nodding, evidently deeply under the influence of the poison 1 P.M.—The Fowl very drowsy and cannot stand. 10th August, 1 P.M.—The Fowl can now stand and eat; it is nearly well. It has evidently got over the effects of the poison.

EXPERIMENT No. 17.

About twenty drops of the blood of the Fowl killed by the *Echis carinata* in four minutes injected into a Fowl's thigh at 2 P.M. 5.45 P.M.—Fowl seems unaffected. August 9th, 8 A.M.—Fowl seems unaffected. 1 P.M.—The Fowl is not affected. 10th August, 1 P.M.—The Fowl is well.

The following important facts seem to be proved or confirmed by the foregoing experiments. The *Echis carinata* is a dangerous and deadly snake: it killed a Fowl in four minutes, and a Dog in nine hours and a half. Like the *Daboia*, its poison destroys the coagulability of the blood after death.

The *Bungarus cæruleus* is also very dangerous: it killed a Dog in fifty-five minutes. The blood after death from this poison coagulates firmly.

It, like other snakes, may, when apparently in vigour, bite without producing any evil effect. It may, in fact, be exhausted.

The Krait (*B. cæruleus*) succumbs to the poison of the Cobra. It is doubtful whether the Cobra will succumb to that of the Krait. The blood of an animal poisoned by a Cobra injected into another animal poisons it, though slowly. In the case of the *Echis* poisoned blood, the effect was not produced in the second animal.

EXPERIMENT No. 18.

About thirty drops of the blood of the Dog poisoned by *Echis carinata* injected into a Fowl's thigh, at 1 P.M. of 9th August. It was drowsy in the afternoon. 10th August, 1 P.M.—The Fowl is quite well; it has not suffered.

July 29th, 1871.

EXPERIMENT No. 19.

Present, Dr. Fayrer and Dr. J. Anderson.

I am indebted to Dr. Stoliczka for a specimen of *Ophiophagus elaps*, about seven feet long, recently brought from the Andaman Islands. It is identical with those of Bengal and Burmah as far as I can judge.

It was very active and alert, and made vigorous efforts to get out of its place of confinement, a large wooden box with a wire front. From the way in which it climbed and wriggled itself up the smooth side of the box and along the roof, it is evidently a dexterous climber in the jungle.

On July 29th, 1871, it was made to close its jaws on the thigh of a Pariah Pup of about three months old, at 1.33 P.M. The fangs were perfect, and I observed that the poison had the same yellow tinge noticed in that of other individuals of the species. The Dog showed no signs of pain, but limped on the bitten leg, which seemed partially paralysed. At 1.46 the snake was made to bite it again in the same leg. It remained in much the same condition, leg paralysed, looking dazed. Soon after it began to show more marked indication of poisoning; it vomited and became weak. At 2.15 it was convulsed. At 2.25 P.M. it died.

The blood removed from the body after death coagulated firmly. The poison in this snake was evidently not so active as in others. The snake was healthy and vigorous, its fangs were perfect, and the poison abundant; but the animal bitten, though quite young, did not succumb for nearly an hour. There is nothing I have seen in the effects of the *Ophiophagus* poison, so far as my experiments with it have gone, to suggest that it is more active or deadly than that of the Cobra or *Daboia*.

TWENTY-FIRST SERIES.

On the Influence of the Poisons of the Cobra, the Bungarus cæruleus, and Daboia.

The following experiments were performed and communicated by V. Richards, Esq., Civil Surgeon, Bancoorah:—

August 18th, 1870.

EXPERIMENT No. 1.

1 P.M.—Some poison was extracted from a Cobra ("Kála Kurrees"), that had killed a Fowl in fifteen minutes the day previously. Two drops were inserted between the eyelids of a full-grown Pariah Dog.

2 P.M.—Dog constantly rubbing the eye with its paw, which he afterwards licks. 3.—Conjunctiva extremely congested, and the integuments around the orbit are puffed up. Still rubs the eye, and makes a whining noise as if in pain. 5.—Appears to be rather sleepy, but starts up if called.

19th.—The Dog seems quite lively. The eye is still very much swollen.

20th, 8 A.M.—Swelling very slight. Cornea slightly cloudy. 6 P.M.—Seems quite well. The Dog escaped during the night.

The local effects of the poison were very great, but the constitutional slight.

EXPERIMENT No. 2.

1.5 P.M.—One drop of the same Cobra poison was applied to the conjunctiva of a small Fowl.

2 P.M.—Eye very much swollen, the Fowl constantly rubbing it with its claw. 2.30 P.M.—Seems slightly sluggish. 5 P.M.—The eye still swollen.

19th.—The eye is still swollen, but the Fowl is lively.

20th.—Perfectly well in every respect.

August 20th, 1870.

EXPERIMENT No. 3.

The Cobra with which the experiments of the 18th were made, was well bitten two or three times near the tail by a large "Tentuliah" Cobra quite fresh and vigorous.

August 21st.—Well.

August 22nd.—Well.

August 23rd.—Well.

August 21st, 1870.

EXPERIMENT No. 4.

The "Tentuliah Kurrees" of yesterday was bitten by a small though vigorous *Bungarus cæruleus* ("Krait") measuring one foot ten inches and a half in length at 2 P.M.

August 22nd.—Well.

August 23rd.—Well.

EXPERIMENT No. 5.

The Krait was bitten by a fresh and vigorous Cobra ("Kála Kurrees"), near the tail two or three times.

August 22nd.—The Krait was found dead in the box where it was kept. The bitten part had commenced to decompose. To preclude the necessity of holding the snake to be bitten, I threw some clay over it near the head so as to prevent it from turning to bite. Death cannot therefore be attributed to rough handling.

August 23rd, 1870.

EXPERIMENT No. 6.

3.57 P.M.—Two drops of poison taken from a fresh vigorous Cobra ("Gokurrah Kurrees") was applied to the conjunctiva of a full-grown healthy Fowl.

4.27 P.M.—Dead—in thirty minutes.

This experiment seems to prove, without doubt, that the poison does sometimes prove fatal when applied to the conjunctiva.

EXPERIMENT No. 7.

Some Cobra poison just taken from a fresh vigorous "Gokurrah" was dropped into the eye of a full-grown Fowl at 3.50 P.M. The Fowl was immediately let go.

4 P.M.—Rubbing the eye with its foot. 4.21.—Eye intensely swollen. Is drowsy; defecated. 4.35.—Squatting down. 4.45.—Drooping; very drowsy; defecated. 5.—Appears better.

Continued to improve, and ultimately recovered. The eye remained swollen up to the 25th. Cornea cloudy.

The local effects were very severe.

EXPERIMENT No. 8.

3.58 P.M.—Some of the same Cobra poison, three drops, poured into the mouth of a full-grown Fowl.

There was scarcely any symptom of poisoning; drowsy only.

6 P.M.—Perfectly well.

EXPERIMENT No. 9.

4.45 P.M.—A fresh vigorous "Kála Kurrees" (Cobra) was made to bite the Gokurrah used in the foregoing experiments.

24th.—Well.

25th.—Well.

26th.—Well.

I believe one Cobra cannot poison another.

August 25th, 1870.

EXPERIMENT No. 10.

2.24 P.M. — Two drops of Cobra poison taken from a middling-sized, fresh, vigorous "Kála Kurrees" were dropped into the eye of a full-grown Fowl. (The one to which the Cobra poison was given by the mouth on the 23rd.) The head was held so as to prevent the poison from dropping from the eye.

2.28 P.M.—Another drop was applied to the eye, and the head held as before. 2.37.—Is very drowsy and gasping; salivated. 2.40.—Rests its beak on the ground and lifts its head occasionally. 2.45.—Attempts to walk, but is unable to take more than two or three steps. The local symptoms are very slight indeed. 2.47.—Defecation; rests the beak on the ground. 2.49.—Defecation. 3.—Rests with its beak on the ground, and endeavours to keep the head up, but it droops again and again. 3.25.—Convulsed. 3.40.—Still convulsed. 3.55.—Same state. 4.30.—Occasional convulsive movements. 5.—Same state. 5.20.—Same state. 5.39.—Dead—in three hours and fifteen minutes.

The local symptoms in this case were very slight, the eye being only closed and the lid collapsed. Although the general symptoms of Cobra poisoning became evident in thirteen minutes, death did not occur until three hours and fifteen minutes had elapsed. The period of convulsion was unusually long—viz., two hours and fourteen minutes.

In the fatal cases, for some time after the application of the poison to the conjunctiva, the head of the Fowl was held so as to promote a larger amount of absorption; while in those where the general symptoms were transient, the Fowl was almost immediately released after the application of the poison.

It will be observed that in every experiment the snake used was a fresh one, full of vigour.

August 26th, 1870.

EXPERIMENT No. 11.

12.26 P.M. — Some poison was taken from a fine fresh, vigorous "Kála Kurrees" (Cobra) just brought from the adjacent paddy fields, and two drops were applied to the uninjured eye of the Fowl used in Experiment No. 7 of the 23rd instant, care being taken to hold the head in such a position as to prevent the escape of the poison.

12.36 P.M.—Drooping; eye very slightly affected. 12.46.—Squatting down; very drowsy; ptyalism. 12.55.—Staggers off when disturbed, and then squats down. 1.5.—Defecation; beak resting on the ground. 1.36.—Convulsed. 1.52.—Dead—in one hour and twenty-six minutes. Local symptoms very slight.

EXPERIMENT No. 12.

Some of the same Cobra poison was put into the mouth, which was afterwards closed to prevent the possibility of any running out, of a young Fowl at 12.31 P.M.

12.37 P.M.—Defecation; is very drowsy. 12.43.—Found dead—in twelve minutes.

I was very much surprised at the rapidity of the fatal action of the poison. There was no abrasion about the mouth.

This experiment seems to show that not only does the Cobra poison if administered internally in a sufficient dose sometimes prove fatal, but very rapidly so.

August 26th, 1870.—I have been unable yet to obtain any more Kraits, but Cobras, especially the "Kála Kurrees," are very plentiful.

I am not quite satisfied with the experiment in which the Cobra bit the Krait, as the Krait had been held previously to make it bite the Cobra, so that the possibility of its having been injured must be admitted.

I form the opinion that one Cobra cannot kill another from the following facts. In neither experiments did the snake suffer, and I have frequently during the past eight days made the Cobras fight and bite each other; but not a single death has occurred amongst my collection.

I have a large pucka place built in my compound, eight feet by six feet, sunk in the ground three feet, and raised about the same height, in which they are kept.

The experiments made by me fully corroborate your opinion—viz., that the poison of a Cobra, when applied to mucous membranes, not only is very dangerous, but even fatal, and sometimes very rapidly so.

September 1st, 1870.—The following experiments serve to demonstrate the fact that the poison of a Cobra kept in captivity is considerably weaker than that of the fresh snake.

August 30th, 1870.

EXPERIMENT No. 13.

2.57 P.M.—Some poison was taken from a large "Kála Kurrees," which had been in captivity for some time, and applied to the eye of a Fowl; the head was held so as to promote absorption.

3.5 P.M.—Rubs the eye, which is slightly swollen; tremor of the tail. 3.8.—Very slightly affected. 3.31.—Defecation; appears pretty well. 3.40.—Improving. 3.44.—Some poison was taken from a Cobra that had been in captivity only two or three days, and applied to the conjunctiva of the other eye. 4.11.— Defecation; sluggish. 4.15.— Beak resting on the ground. 4.17.—Defecation. 4.23.—Very drowsy, and squatting on the ground. 5.—Convulsed. 6.2.—Dead—in two hours and eighteen minutes from the second application of the poison.

EXPERIMENT No. 14.

Some poison was taken from a "Gokurrah Kurrees" that had been some time confined, and dropped into the eye of a small Fowl, the head being held as before, at 3.16 P.M.

This Fowl did not exhibit the slightest symptom of poisoning, nor was the eye affected.

EXPERIMENT No. 15.

Some poison taken from a Cobra ("Tentuliah") that had been in my possession for some time, was administered to a small Fowl at 3.28 P.M. No signs of poisoning were observed.

September 1st, 1870.

EXPERIMENT No. 16.

12.30 P.M.—Some poison taken from a vigorous "Gokurrah Kurrees" that had just bitten a Krait was administered to the Fowl used in Experiment No. 14 of the 30th August.

12.33.—Tail drooping. 12.35.—Drowsy. 1.—Convulsed. 1.30.—Dead—in one hour.

I notice the fresher the snake the more amber-coloured the poison.

The two following experiments were made:—

August 30th, 1870.

EXPERIMENT No. 17.

A small Krait was bitten by a larger one near the tail at 1 P.M. Great care was taken not to handle either too roughly.

September 1st.—Found dead this morning.

September 1st, 1870.

EXPERIMENT No. 18.

A full-grown, fresh, vigorous Cobra was made to bite a small Krait, measuring one foot ten inches in length. Great care was taken not to hurt the Krait; 12 noon.

1 P.M.—Dead—in one hour.

This Krait had been in the possession of the men who brought it three days, and was quite well and vigorous.

This last experiment seems to be rather convincing, that the Cobra can kill the Krait.

Notwithstanding the result of the experiment with the two Kraits, I am not at all satisfied they can kill each other. I am quite satisfied the Cobra cannot kill another Cobra.

Mr. Richards adds:—I have not heard of the *Ophiophagus* being in this district, but will make inquiries. The *Bungarus fasciatus* appears to be very uncommon in this district.

Yesterday morning I made a fine fresh "Gokurrah Kurrees" bite a Krait measuring two feet and a half in length. I took special care not to injure the Krait. The Krait up to the time, 6 P.M., I am writing, is perfectly well.

On September 8th, 1870, Mr. Richards writes:—A *Daboia*, full-sized, was brought to me some days since. I put it amongst the other snakes. On the 4th instant, after being irritated, he attacked and bit a large "Gokurrah Kurrees" very savagely, and it died on the 5th; possibly from injury done by the viper's enormous fangs.

September 5th, 1870.

EXPERIMENT No. 19.

At 1 P.M. the *Daboia* was made to bite a Fowl in the thigh; the Fowl was dead in less than a minute. The parts bitten were very much ecchymosed.

The blood taken from the body of the Fowl was fluid and did not coagulate.

EXPERIMENT No. 20.

At 2.5 P.M. a middling-sized Krait was made to bite a very small Cobra that had been in my possession nine or ten days. The Cobra died at noon on the 6th.

There appears to me to be no doubt, in this instance, the Krait killed the Cobra. Every care was taken not to injure the little Cobra while being bitten by the Krait. It was for some time after perfectly lively, proving it had not been injured.

I have on three occasions set aside the blood taken from the bodies of persons dying from snake-bite, and in neither instance did it coagulate. One man was bitten by the Krait, the other two persons by snakes unknown.

The *Daboia*, which appears to be pretty generally known here, is called the "Seah-Chunder."

September 7th, 1870.

EXPERIMENT No. 21.

Some poison taken from a *Daboia* that had been kept in captivity for a few days was dropped into the eye of a Fowl at 1.54.30 P.M. 1.57.—Defecation. 2.25.—More poison applied to the conjunctiva. 2.27.— Very drowsy. 2.29.—Squatting on the ground; the beak rests on the ground, and the head falls over to one side. 2.35.—Eye very much swollen. 3.22.—Head drooping constantly. 3.37.—Endeavours to keep the beak on the ground, but the head rolls over to one side at once. 6.10.—Apparently in convulsions. 10.30.—Same state.

September 8th, 9 A.M.—There is a marked improvement, the Fowl only appears drowsy, and the feathers are drooping.

September 9th.—Recovered, but the eye is still much swollen.

I was quite astonished on the morning of the 8th to find the Fowl not only alive, but considerably improved.

The snake in this instance was not fresh; hence, I believe, the recovery of the Fowl.

EXPERIMENT No. 22.

At 2.9 P.M. some poison extracted from a Cobra ("Gokurrah") that had been in my possession some time was applied to the conjunctiva of a Fowl. 2.17.—More poison put into the eye. 2.25.—Squatting on the ground; head drooping. 2.29.—Attempted to get up but could not. 2.36—Convulsed. 2.45.—The same. 2.59.—Dead—in fifty minutes from the first application of the poison.

EXPERIMENT No. 23.

At 2.3 P.M. some poison was squeezed out of the poison-gland of a Krait (*Bungarus cæruleus*) that had been in my possession some time (the fangs were broken)—introduced into a Fowl's eye. 2.20.—Drooping. 2.30.—Seems very sleepy. 3.38.—Defecation; still drowsy. 4.—Seems better.

This Fowl gradually recovered. The snake was by no means vigorous, and it died three days after.

September 8th, 1870.

EXPERIMENT No. 24.

Some poison was taken from a fine fresh Krait, thirty-nine inches and a half long, and applied to the conjunctiva of the Fowl used in No. 23 Experiment, at 12.28 P.M. 12.30.—Drooping; rubs the eye with its claw; the eye is not much swollen. 1.35.—Beak resting on the ground; very drowsy. 2.—Convulsed. 2.25.—Occasional convulsive movements. 3.—Dead—in two hours and forty-two minutes.

Mr. Richards continues:—The opinion you had formed—viz., that snake poison is absorbed through mucous membranes, appears to be beyond a doubt correct. I believe the poison if fresh, properly applied, and in a sufficient quantity, is as surely fatal by absorption through mucous membranes as by the direct application of the poison, only its fatal action of course is greatly retarded under the former condition.

To-day two Kraits and one *Daboia* were brought to me. One of the Kraits measures forty-five inches and a quarter in length, and three inches in circumference, and is beautifully marked.

September 10th, 1870.

EXPERIMENT No. 25.

Two drops of poison taken from a vigorous Krait (*Bungarus cæruleus*), measuring thirty-nine inches and a half, was administered to a Fowl at 12.38 P.M., by the mouth. 1.2.—Tail droops and the bird is crouching. 1.5.—Defecation. 2.—Appears drowsy. 10.—Very drowsy.

September 11th.—Crouching.

September 12th.—Is slightly drowsy, and crouching. Two drops of poison taken from another fresh middling-sized *Bungarus cæruleus* were given at 4.30 P.M. 5.—Is very drowsy. 5.49.—Very sleepy, and squatting down. 6.30.—Squatting still; head drooping. 9.—Convulsed. 10.5.—Dead—in five hours and twenty-five minutes from the *second* application, or rather administration of the poison.

EXPERIMENT No. 26.

A very small quantity of poison taken from a small Krait (*Bungarus cæruleus*) was diluted with a drop of water and applied to the conjunctiva of a Fowl at 1 P.M. 4.—Very drowsy; crouching. 6.—Same state. 9.—Is very drowsy, and squatting down. 10.15.—Beak resting on the ground, and the head drooping on one side. 10.38.—Convulsed. 11.—Dead—in ten hours. In this instance, however, the poison was not only applied once, but it was diluted. In the former experiment the Fowl had been brought under the influence of the poison previous to the second administration.

September 20th, 1870.

EXPERIMENT No. 27.

An old Bull was bitten by a large vigorous Krait (*Bungarus cæruleus*) in the groin twice at 8 A.M. My snake-man having objected to take part in an experiment on this animal, I had to manage as best I could, and the consequence was the snake was some time before it could be made to bite. It bit ultimately, however, most savagely. 2 P.M.—Staggers as it walks. 3.3.—Is lying down; salivation and profuse discharge from the nostrils; tongue protrudes from the mouth on one side; is much purged. 4.—Breathing hard and making a low, moaning sound with each expiration; legs occasionally convulsed. 4.45.—Dead—in eight hours and three-quarters. Blood coagulated, but not very firmly, after being taken from the body.

September 27th, 1870.

EXPERIMENT No. 28.

An Ox was bitten by a nearly full-grown *Daboia* in the groin at 11 A.M. 12.45 P.M.—Is a little unsteady on his legs. 1.5.—Is lying down. 2.—Walking about very unsteadily; lame with the right hind-leg. 6.—Lying down; seems very weak; the bitten part is swelling rapidly; gives occasional short, quick, forcible expirations.

September 28th, 8 A.M.—Appears better, but is very drowsy and weak. 8.30.—The *Daboia* of yesterday and a smaller one were made to bite the animal again in the groin. 9.—The groin and right thigh are very much swollen. I notice several bleeding points about the skin. This the snake-man told me would be the case, but I doubted it. 10.—Is very costive; endeavours to defecate, but cannot. 4 P.M.—Is standing up; the bitten parts are enormously swollen.

September 29th.—To-day the animal is looking very drowsy, and is made to walk with difficulty; the legs are in the same swollen state.

September 30th. — Is quite well; has been purged; the swelling is rapidly decreasing. In this instance neither of the snakes was fresh, and both had been used recently in experiments.

September 28th, 1870.

EXPERIMENT No. 29.

An Ox was bitten in the thigh by a full-grown Cobra, which had not only been kept in captivity for a long time, but was casting its skin. 3 P.M.—Does not seem affected; possibly the fangs were broken. 3.40.—Bitten by another Cobra ("Kála Kurrees") that had been in my possession for some time. 6.—Appears very weak and is much purged.

September 29th.—Is pretty well, but weak; purging still continues.

September 30th.—Recovered. Was bitten by a vigorous "Gokurrah Kurrees," which had been in my possession only a short time, on the inside of the upper lip at 9 A.M. 10.—Is very drowsy, and is slightly salivated. 1 P.M.—Convulsed; the part bitten is not much swollen. 1.30.—Dead—in four hours and a half. The blood was firmly coagulated in the heart and great vessels.

The above experiments demonstrate how much the fatality of the bite of a snake depends upon the condition of the snake at the time it bites.

Experiments on the effect of the Tanjore Pill in Snake-Poisoning.

The following experiments were made at my request by Mr. Richards, of Bancoorah, to test the efficacy of the so-called Tanjore pill. I am indebted to Mr. Gibbons, of Messrs. Scott, Thompson's, for the pills, which were made up according to the formula given in Dr. P. Russell's Work on Indian Serpents,* and must have cost much trouble in the preparation, for some of the ingredients are difficult to procure. They were administered in accordance with the instructions in Russell. Even the application of the Fowl's liver was not omitted. Two or three of the experiments are suggestive of good results, but they are also suggestive of large animals probably imperfectly bitten. The other experiments, as well as many I have myself made, dispel the idea that this antidote is any more effective than others that have been tried.

October 4th, 1870.

EXPERIMENT No. 30.

At 3.30 P.M. on the 3rd of October an old Bull was bitten in the thigh very vigorously by a fine fresh Cobra ("Kála Kurrees"), four feet seven inches long, which had just been brought from the jungle. The bitten part was well incised, the liver of a fowl rubbed in, and one of the "Tanjore" pills mixed with warm water was administered at once. 4.45.—The animal appears perfectly well; is walking about and grazing; another pill mixed with warm water was given. 6.10.—Appears perfectly well, and is grazing still. 7.5.—Another pill administered, appears perfectly well, and is quite strong. 10.—In the same state. 11.25.—Standing up and is perfectly well; the skin is very sensitive.

October 5th, 8 A.M.—Well. 5 P.M.—Perfectly well.

This animal never exhibited a single symptom of poisoning. He was not even rendered sluggish.

EXPERIMENT No. 31.

With a view of testing the powers of the snake used in the former experiment, I made it bite a Fowl in the thigh at 11.26 A.M. 11.27.—Drowsy. 11.28.—Lying down and is gasping. 11.31.—Same state. 11.35.—Convulsed. 11.36.—Dead—in ten minutes.

This leaves no doubt as to the power of the snake to poison.

EXPERIMENT No. 32.

At 12.52 P.M. a Goat was bitten in the groin by a fine fresh

* From Russell's Indian Serpents.

TANJORE PILLS.

Take White Arsenic.
,, Roots of Velli-navi.
,, Roots of Neri Vishana.
,, Kernel of Nervalam.
,, Black Pepper.
,, Quicksilver, of each equal quantities.

Juice of the Wild Cotton ("Mudar") sufficient to make into a mass, and divide into five grain pills. Each pill contains a little over half a grain each of quicksilver and arsenic.

These pills are given in doses of one or two, and at intervals of an hour; in some cases not so frequently.

A Fowl's liver is also to be applied directly to the bite which is scarified.

vigorous Cobra ("Kála Kurrees") just brought from the jungle. 12.58.—The part was well incised and the liver of a Fowl rubbed in. 1.5.—A pill mixed with warm water was administered. 1.31.—Appears well. 2.12.—Appears well and is feeding. 3.5.—Half a pill administered. 3.45.—Is running about. 4.30.—Appears very slightly sluggish; administered the other half of the pill. 5.30.—The animal is feeding and appears very well, only that the tail occasionally droops slightly. Urine is passed pretty frequently; this was the case also with the Ox. 6.—Appears very well. 6.10.—Same state. It ultimately recovered.

Experiment No. 33.

The Cobra used in the foregoing experiment was made to bite a Fowl in the thigh at 1.10.20 P.M. 1.11.20.—Administered half a pill mixed with warm water; incised the bitten part and applied a portion of the other half of the pill. 1.13.—Beak resting on the ground and head falling on one side. 1.14.40.—Convulsed. 1.17.—Dead—in six minutes and forty seconds. Blood coagulated immediately when taken from the body.

Experiment No. 34.

A Fowl was bitten in the thigh by a large Krait that had been in my possession for some time, at 1.24.30 P.M. 1.25.15.—Half a pill was rubbed into the part bitten after it was incised. 1.25.40.—Half a pill administered. 1.34.30.—Drooping. 1.34.45.—Another half of a pill administered. 1.43.—Head drooping. 1.46.—Head lying on the ground; beak quivering. 2.7.—Dead—in forty-three minutes and a half.

Experiment No. 35.

The Krait used in Experiment No. 34 was made to bite a Fowl in the thigh at 1.30.15 P.M. The Fowl was immediately lame. 1.33.—Squatting down. 1.35.30.—Head drooping. 1.40.—Convulsions commenced. 1.50.—Dead — in twenty minutes and a quarter.

October 5th, 1870.

Experiment No. 36.

A weak country Goat was bitten in the thigh, which had been previously shaved, by a large Krait that had been in my possession for some time, at 1.5 P.M. The snake held on for some time, and was with difficulty taken away. 1.12.—Liver rubbed into the part after incision. 1.17.—A Tanjore pill was administered. 1.20.—Tremor of the hind quarters. 1.42.—Staggers. 1.43.—Strongly convulsed. 1.46. — Eyes turned upwards; abdomen tympanitic. 1.51.—Dead—in forty-six minutes.

On opening the body I found the blood coagulated, and the stomach highly congested, in patches, as if from poisoning by arsenic.

A Fowl bitten by the above Krait died in twenty-two minutes.

Experiment No. 37.

A small Pig was bitten by a Cobra at 3.25; at 6.50 P.M. it was very well. A Fowl died in fifty-nine minutes after being bitten by the same Cobra. The Pig was bitten most severely. The Pig died at 8 P.M.

Experiment No. 38.

A small Pig was bitten by a Cobra at 3.25 P.M. 3.27.30.—Half a pill administered. 3.31.—The bitten part well incised. and a liver (Fowl's) applied. 3.42.—Seems quite well. 3.47.—Seems very slightly sluggish. 3.52.—Is lying down. 4. — Apparently better, and is running about. 4.27. — Sluggish again; a quarter of a pill administered. 4.40.—Has rigors. 5.—Another quarter of a pill. 7.50.—Salivation. 8.—Dead—in four hours and thirty-five minutes.

October 7th.

Experiment No. 39.

A small country Goat was bitten by a Gokurrah Kurrees at 11.34 A.M. 11.39.—Part incised and liver applied. 11.40.—Pill administered. 1.49.—Is slightly drowsy. 1.58.—Half a pill administered. 3. — Convulsed. 4.15. — Dead—in four hours and forty-one minutes.

A Fowl bitten by the same Cobra after it had bitten the Goat did not die until three hours and twenty-four minutes had elapsed, although no antidote was administered.

An Ox that had been bitten by a Cobra, and to which the antidote was administered, lived some hours; but it looked very unwell, and showed some symptoms of poisoning by arsenic. The Ox died in seven hours and forty-two minutes.

I am also indebted to Mr. Richards, of Bancoorah, for the following Experiments on the injection of snake-poison diluted with water into the blood-vessels :—

September 1st, 1871.

Experiment No. 40.

The venom of two Cobras was mixed with twenty drops of water.

I isolated the right femoral vein of a Dog and applied a ligature on the cardiac side. Ten drops of the above mixture were then injected into the vein and the ligature soon after loosened. 3.54 P.M.—The Dog immediately began to struggle and whine. 3.55.—Lying down and panting. 3.57.—Appears much exhausted; natural defecation. 4.1.—Twitching of the corners of the mouth; breathing rapidly with very forcible expirations; is evidently affected by the poison. It is now seven minutes since it began to circulate. 4.2.—Beginning to be very restless; defecation. 4.4. — Passed jelly-like stools; pupils contracted. 4.5. — Staggering about and holding the head down; constantly shaking the head; salivation. 4.7.—Occasional slight convulsions; micturition. 4.8.—Gasping; pupils rapidly dilating. 4.10.—Dead—in sixteen minutes. The blood removed from the heart did not coagulate, and had exactly the appearance of that of persons who die from snake-bite. This is the first instance in which I have found the blood fluid in the lower animals after death from snake-bite of colubrine snakes.

September 2nd, 1871.

Experiment No. 41.

I isolated the left femoral artery of a Dog and applied a ligature on the distal side. The remaining ten drops of the above mixture were then very carefully injected into the artery. At 10.46 A.M. the ligature was loosened and the poison allowed to circulate, when the Dog began to whine and micturate. 10.48. — When let loose he fell over. 10.50.—Has been constantly passing water. 10.54.—Is lying perfectly quiet on his left side. 10.55.—Defecation difficult, with a great deal of straining. 10.56.—Constant dribbling of urine. 10.58. — Pupils contracted. 11. — Whining; is perfectly sensible. 11.1.—Tried to get up. 11.3.—Got up and limped off; is incessantly passing water. 11.7.—Licking his wounded leg. 11.10.—Does not seem very much affected; is snapping at the flies as they come near him; stood up and limped off. 10.12.—Is standing up; passed an astonishingly large quantity of urine. 11.13.—Fell over; is licking himself. 11.15.—Very much exhausted; tries to get up, but is unable. 11.18.—Breathing rapidly; very forcible expirations. 11.23.—Passing water in small quantities at the time. 11.25.—Convulsive twitchings at the corners of the mouth; struggles to get up but is unable; is now evidently very much affected; thirty-nine minutes since the poison was allowed to circulate. 11.27.—Twitchings at the corners of the mouth increasing.

11.29.—Convulsed; wounded leg quite stiff. 11.32.—Convulsions increasing; tongue hanging out of the mouth; pupils rapidly dilating; micturition. 11.35.—Pupils dilated. 11.37.—Dying. 11.38.—Dead—in fifty-two minutes.

On removing the blood from the heart it was found fluid, but it very rapidly coagulated.

It will be observed that the poison acted three times quicker when injected into a vein than when injected into an artery. The Cobras from which the poison was extracted were by no means fresh, and had been latterly used very much for experiments. I believe the undiluted venom of fresh Cobras would be much more rapid in its action. I have seen a Dog killed in so short a time as fourteen minutes by the bite of a Cobra.

The following Experiments on the injection of pure Cobra poison into the veins were also made by Mr. Richards:—

September 16th.

Experiment No. 42.

After isolating the right external jugular vein of a Dog, I applied a ligature on its cardiac side.

4.35 P.M.—Injected four drops of Cobra poison into the vein. After injecting the poison the Dog was in no way affected. 4.36.—The ligature was loosened. The animal *immediately* began to struggle and whine. When released he went staggering about with his fore-legs widely apart, and his nose touching the ground. 4.37.—Began to vomit and was purged; convulsions set in very rapidly; they did not, however, become very violent. 4.40.—Dead—in four minutes from the time the poison entered the general circulation. The blood, as in the other instances in which the poison was injected into a vein, *remained fluid.* These three experiments prove beyond doubt, Mr. Richards thinks, that the Cobra poison, *when injected into a vein,* destroys the coagulability of the blood.

September 22nd.

Experiment No. 43.

The right external jugular vein of a Dog was isolated, and a ligature applied on the cardiac side. 3.43 P.M.—About five drops of Cobra poison injected. 3.44.—The ligature was loosened; the Dog instantly became convulsed. 3.45.—Gasping. 3.46.30.—Dead—in two minutes and a half after the entry of the poison into the general circulation.

The blood in this instance very imperfectly coagulated. This was remarkable, as in the other three instances there was no approach to coagulation.

It appears from Mr. Richards's experiments on the injection of the Cobra poison into a vein that the coagulability of the blood is destroyed, as no coagulation took place after death in three, and partial coagulation in only one case. In my own experiments coagulation always resulted after death from Cobra poisoning. This is a point which merits further investigation. Mr. Richards also performed the following Experiment of applying snake-poison to the sciatic nerve:—

September 2nd.

Experiment No. 44.

The right sciatic nerve of a Dog was exposed, cut in two, and the proximal end drawn out of the wound. The lips of the wound were then carefully stitched together, the nerve being left hanging out, and several layers of collodion applied.

At 1.33 P.M. I applied two drops of venom, taken from a very fine Cobra, to the nerve. I was particularly careful not to allow the poison to come in contact with the surrounding parts. The Dog was held upon the table for five minutes, during which time the poison was being applied to the nerve. He was then allowed to go, but kept muzzled, and carefully watched to prevent him licking the nerve. 1.57.—Is lame. 2.45.—Unaffected; made a hearty meal. 4.—Still unaffected. 6.30.—Had another meal. 11.30.—Same state.

September 3rd, 7 A.M.—Unaffected; had no symptoms of poisoning whatever.

Mr. Richards made the following Experiments to test the efficacy of applying strong Nitric Acid to the bitten part:—

Experiment No. 45.

5 P.M.—A Pig was bitten by a large Cobra, and strong nitric acid immediately applied to the bite. 5.15.—Is lying down on its side; appears affected. 5.18.—Is convulsed; defecation and micturition. 5.30.—Dead—in thirty minutes.

Experiment No. 46.

5.17 P.M.—Another Pig was bitten by a small Cobra that had been much used of late. The strong nitric acid was at once applied. The Pig passes water very frequently. 5.30.—Appears slightly sluggish. 7.—Same state. 9.—Convulsed. 10.—Dead—in four hours and forty-three minutes.

TWENTY-SECOND SERIES.

Experiments on the Effects of the Poison of the Hydrophidæ.

The following Experiments were performed by W. P. Stewart, Esq., Civil Surgeon, Pooree:—

May 9th, 1870.

Experiment No. 1.

5.45 P.M.—The thigh of a half-grown Fowl, cleaned of feathers, was presented to a Sea-snake. It bit rapidly two or three times, and drew blood. After being bitten, the Fowl crouched on its bent legs and never stood again. 5.49.—Pupils dilated; shook its head as if excited; then began to droop; eyelids closing; beak resting on the ground. 5.50.—Raising its beak up and down; head rotating from side to side; sitting all the time; no convulsions. 5.55.—Lying on its side quite powerless. 5.59.—Dead—in fourteen minutes.

With a lens no punctures could be made out; even scratches could hardly be seen at the seat of bite; blood dark, coagulated firmly.

From Mr. Stewart's description I imagine the snake was *Hydrophis cyanocincta.* In speaking of its fangs, he says, "Fangs about two-thirds of a line long, with a double curve, first bent forwards at base, then backwards, before terminating in its point. Poison groove extends only from the four-fifth of anterior aspect."

June 10th, 1870.

Experiment No. 2.

Present, Mr. Thomson, C.S., and Mr. Stewart.

A long thin-necked snake, with white pea-sized spots on side of neck; unable to bite. Poison gland removed, and inserted at 11 A.M. into a wound made in the thigh of a half-grown Fowl. 11.12. P.M.—No apparent result. 3.—The Fowl was observed to be drooping and unable to move. 6.—Dead.

This snake was most probably *H. chloris.*

July 1st, 1870.

Experiment No. 3.

A similar snake was obtained on July 1st. It was torpid, but the trial was made by pressing the jaws firmly over the thigh of a Fowl.

No result.

June 20th, 1870.

Experiment No. 4.

A *Pelamis bicolor,* torpid and unable to bite. Mouth opened, and jaws made to close firmly over fleshy part of a Fowl's thigh.

No result.

June 29th, 1870.

Experiment No. 5.

A Sea-snake (probably *H. cyanocincta*) was made to close its jaws on a Chicken's thigh at 6 A.M., with firm pressure, as it could not bite voluntarily. 9.—Lame, crouched. 3 P.M.—Eyelids half closed; head drooping; respiration gasping, during which beak opens, and a crowing sound occurs; feathers ruffled; purged frequently.

June 30th.—Lying half-dead; refuses food; mark of bite of a bluish colour.

July 1st.—Recovered and able to move about; it remained well.

June 30th, 1870.

EXPERIMENT No. 6.

A *Pelamis bicolor*, caught fresh in a hand net. It was quite lively, and able to bite. A small Fowl was bitten by it at 6.26 A.M., the wound scarcely a scratch. 7.—Crouching, drooping. 8.—Beak rising and falling. 9.—Insensible. 9.50.—Quite dead.

Blood fluid after death.

July 5th, 1870.

EXPERIMENT No. 7.

A Sea-snake,* a new species allied to *H. hardwickii*, bit a full-sized Fowl in the thigh at 8.30 A.M. The marks of the bite were distinct. 8.34.—Fowl seated. 8.35.—Drooping; eyes closing; rotating the head on the beak in a sitting posture. 8.38.—Convulsed; head resting on ground. 8.42.—Continued convulsions. 8.47.—Legs thrown backwards in final spasm; tail spread out; quite dead in seventeen minutes.

Blood coagulated after death.

July 22nd, 1870.

EXPERIMENT No. 8.

The same snake was tried on a Dog, but it was too feeble to bite; its jaws were pressed firmly on the inner part of the thigh. No evil result to the Dog.

EXPERIMENT No. 9.

Hydrophis cyanocincta, four feet long, bit a half-grown Fowl voluntarily in the thigh, twice or thrice, drawing blood, and leaving slight ecchymosis, at 9.37. 9.40.—Fowl drooping; eyes closing; head resting on beak. 9.41.—Fell over on its side. 9.42.—Convulsed. 9.46.—Dead—in nine minutes.

EXPERIMENT No. 10.

The same snake bit a Pariah Dog twice on the thigh at 4.40 P.M. 5.20.—Dog restive, salivated, burrowing its muzzle in the sand. 5.25.—Seated, body thrown forwards, head down, partially convulsed, salivation increasing. 5.30.—Spasms; defecated. 5.35.—Involuntary evacuations; respiration slow; tongue hanging out of mouth; salivation very profuse. 5.40.—Dead in one hour.

July 23rd, 1870.

EXPERIMENT No. 11.

The same snake, kept alive in a hole in the wet sand, bit a full-grown Fowl at 7.35 A.M. This was not a fair bite, and took no effect. Bit again at 7.45 effectively. Fowl sat down after the bite. 8.11.—Lay down; head resting on beak; became convulsed. 8.25.—Convulsions. 8.35.—Dead.

The *Hydrophis* of four feet in length is evidently a very dangerous creature.

For the following notes on the action of the poison of certain of these snakes I am also indebted to Mr. Stewart:—

Enhydrina Valakadyen. On September 17th bit a Dog, which was rendered prostrate in an hour, and appeared as if likely to die; but eventually recovered. On the 18th another large Dog was bitten twice; the fangs being carefully pressed into the skin. The Dog died in three hours after, though it was affected in a quarter of an hour after the bite. The fangs appear to be brittle—*i.e.*, falling off from their articulation.

H. gracilis. Fangs minute; could not be made to pierce the skin of a Dog on which the jaws were forcibly closed.

* *H. chloris*. Fangs very minute. This species has killed several Fowls, but the poison was slow in operation. Its very small mouth and fangs render wounding by forcible closure very difficult. It very soon expires after removal from its native element, particularly if thrown on the shore by the surf. A fisherman who brought the snake said it was plentiful in the Chilka Lake. He said he was an eye-witness to a fatal case, that of a lad who was bitten two months ago at Ancoodah, while fishing. The boy died in two hours.

H. jerdonii. Lived for eight days. Two Dogs were experimented on, but the snake could inflict no wound. Fangs small.

H. stewartii. A very poisonous snake. Killed a Fowl in eight minutes: a Dog in an hour. The coagulated blood of the Fowl inoculated into another, killed it in twelve hours.

H. nigra. Killed a Fowl in fifteen minutes.

The following Experiments on various species of Hydrophidæ were made by myself. I am indebted to Mr. Galiffe, Collector and Supervisor of Calcutta Canals, for fine specimens of *Hydrophis coronata* and *Enhydrina bengalensis* from Dhappa.

August 11th.

EXPERIMENT No. 12.

A Fowl was bitten in the thigh by *Enhydrina bengalensis*, about forty-three inches long, at 5.48 P.M.

The snake was sluggish, and could only be made to bite by forcibly closing the jaws on the Fowl's thigh. The fangs were small, and barely drew blood.

5.51.—Crouched, and became convulsed almost immediately. Died at 5.55, or in seven minutes.

The blood formed a firm coagulum when removed from the body after death.

August 12th.

EXPERIMENT No. 13.

The above snake died at 10 P.M. yesterday. Its jaws were closed with pressure on a Fowl's thigh this morning at 7.34 A.M.

8.5—The Fowl limps. 8.12.—Crouching; feathers staring; wings expanded. 8.20.—Head drooping, resting point of the beak on the ground. 9.5.—Remains in the same condition. 9.50.—Convulsed. 11.35.—Remained in much the same condition until death after four hours.

The poison of this snake when vigorous and fresh in its own element, the salt water, must be very deadly.

August 9th.

EXPERIMENT No. 14.

A *Hydrophis coronata* was made, with much difficulty and only by pressure, to close its very small jaws on the comb, and then on the thigh of a half-grown Chicken. At 3.30 P.M. the Chicken was excited, but apparently not in pain after the bite.

4 P.M.—Pecked some grains of rice. 4.11.—Crouching. 4.16.—Head falls over; starts when its beak touches the ground. 4.30.—Drowsy; beak resting on the ground; wings drooping. 4.53.—Eyes closed, beak resting on the ground; starts at intervals, any noise makes it rise with a jerk. 5.15.—Cannot be roused by noise, but starts when touched; falls over on its side. 5.33.—Apparently dead, lying on its side; slight convulsions when raised by the wings. 5.55.—Dead—in two hours and twenty-five minutes.

* Named by Dr. Anderson *H. fayreriana*.

* In the collection *H. lindsayi*, *H. cantoris*, and *H. chloris* seem to have been considered by Mr. Stewart as the same species. It is not clear, therefore, to which the experiment under *H. chloris* should be referred. Most probably the effects of the poison of each of these species are very similar.

The poison of this snake is also very virulent; it was weak, had been many days in captivity, living in fresh water, but without food. The head is exceedingly small, and the fangs almost imperceptible. In its native element I should imagine it is, notwithstanding its small jaws, very dangerous. I have never met with a case of bite of the *Hydrophis* in the human being, but I think there can be no doubt that if a man were bitten by a well-grown snake, and in the water, where the snake would be active and vigorous, the danger would be as great as though he were bitten by a Cobra on the land. Few accidents occur; the boatmen know the danger and avoid them.

Mr. Galiffe, as will be seen hereafter, has been informed of one case, fatal in one hour and a half, which occurred somewhere in the vicinity of the Salt Water Lake.

March 26th, 1871.

A *Hydrophis cyanocincta*, caught in a net at the Sandheads by Captain Lord, Pilot service, on the 23rd March, was sent to me on the 26th, in a jar of salt-water, living and active.

EXPERIMENT No. 15.

3.5 P.M.—A Fowl bitten in the thigh: the snake held firmly In handling it, it dropped from the jar. During the efforts to catch it, which occupied about a minute and a half, the Fowl was dead. The blood removed from the body coagulated into a firm clot after death. The death of this Fowl was very rapid; it died in the man's hand, and he said he did not feel a struggle.

EXPERIMENT No. 16.

4.4.—Bit another Fowl on the thigh. In forty seconds the Fowl was insensible, but recovered and limped about lame. 4.13.—Partially recovered, but is still lame, but looks drowsy; nodding its head. 4.14.—Crouching: beak resting on ground. 4.18.—Very drowsy; head quite fallen over. Is almost quite paralysed. 4.22.—Almost complete muscular paralysis; convulsions. 4.23.—Convulsed. 4.24.—Dead.

The blood in this case coagulated firmly after death.

March 27th, 1871.

EXPERIMENT No. 17.

A Fowl was bitten in the leg by the *Hydrophis cyanocincta.* It was taken out of the water and made to grasp the Fowl's thigh. It bit fiercely, and would not relax its hold for some time; when it did, it got loose in the verandah, and then, though exceedingly active, it was able to make very little onward progress, owing to the absence of abdominal scutæ. It was then killed, being still vigorous and lively. This seems to show that the sea-snakes are not always so delicate as represented. It had lived in a small jar of unchanged salt-water for four days.

The Fowl died in rather less than twenty minutes.

I am indebted to Captain Lord, of the pilot brig *Foam*, for a living specimen of *Enhydrina*, captured in a net at the Sandheads. It was sent up to me in a jar of salt-water, and had been in that jar at least four days, when I tried the following experiments.

The snake was lively and vigorous notwithstanding the confinement in unchanged sea-water. It was a female, two feet ten inches in length; being young, the transverse dark bars marking its body were more distinct than in older specimens.

August 7th, 1871.

Present, Dr. Fayrer and Dr. J. Anderson, Curator of the Indian Museum.

EXPERIMENT No. 18.

A Fowl was bitten in the thigh by an *Enhydrina valakadyen*, two feet ten inches in length, at 2.47 P.M.

2.48.—The Fowl is drowsy, nods its head, but is still on its legs. 2.49.—Crouched; head falling forward; resting point of beak on the ground. 2.50.—Convulsed. 2.54.—Dead—in seven minutes.

EXPERIMENT No. 19.

Another Fowl bitten in the thigh by the same snake at 2.59 P.M.

3.10.—Drowsy. 3.12.—Crouching; head falling forwards; beak on ground. 3.15.—Fallen over; in convulsions 3.16.—Convulsed. 3.20.—Still convulsed. 3.21.—Dead— n twenty-two minutes.

The blood of both these Fowls coagulated firmly when removed from the body after death.

I am also indebted to Captain Lord, of the *Foam*, for two specimens of *Hydrophidæ*, captured in nets at the Sandheads; one on the 4th, the other on the 5th of August; since then they have been confined in bottles of fresh-water, and are still active and vigorous. No. 1. One, one foot four and a half inches in length, is a young *Enhydrina valakadyen*, beautifully marked with distinct black bars. No. 2. The other, three feet two inches in length, is *Hydrophis stricticollis.*

August 9th, 1871.

Present, Dr. Fayrer and Dr. J. Anderson, Curator of the Indian Museum.

EXPERIMENT No. 20.

No. 1 was made to bite a Fowl in the thigh at 1.10 P.M.

1.17.—Drowsy; droops, and has crouched. 1.20—Point of beak resting on ground. 1.21.—Convulsed. 1.31.—Occasional convulsive movements; is quite insensible. 1.35.—Dead—in twenty-five minutes.

EXPERIMENT No. 21.

The same snake was made to bite another Fowl in the thigh at 1.30 P.M.

1.47.—Apparently only slightly drowsy. 1.55.—Very slightly affected. Bitten again in the thigh by same snake. 2.15.—Drowsy; nods its head. 2.30.—In the same state. 2.32.—Convulsed. 2.35.—Dead—in forty-eight minutes.

The snake had evidently partly exhausted its poison in the first bite.

EXPERIMENT No. 22.

No. 2 was made to bite a Fowl in the thigh at 1.20 P.M.

1.29.—Head drooping; crouched. 1.32.—Convulsed. 1.36.—Insensible and convulsed. 1.40.—State unchanged. 1.44.—Dead—in twenty-four minutes.

EXPERIMENT No. 23.

No. 2 bit a Fowl in the thigh at 1.33 P.M. 1.35.—Drowsy; crouching. 1.40.—State unchanged. 1.45.—Head fallen over, resting on point of beak. 1.48.—Convulsed. 1.50.—Still convulsed. 1.55.—Dead—in twenty-two minutes.

These experiments clearly demonstrate the very poisonous nature of the *Hydrophidæ:* all the specimens were young. They had been captured and confined in unchanged water, two of them in fresh water, from four to six days before they were experimented with. Their heads and fangs are very small, and the quantity of poison very much less than in the land snakes. The bites were barely perceptible, and apparently caused no pain. I observed that none of the bitten Fowls indicated any symptoms of paralysis of the bitten limb. A lethargy seemed to creep slowly over them, which gradually passed into complete unconsciousness, preceded by paralysis and loss of coordinating power of muscles. Convulsions follow, and death soon supervenes.

The blood of all the bitten birds coagulated firmly after death, as is the case in death from poisoning by the land colubrine snakes.

Remarks on certain of the Hydrophidæ, and Extracts from Notes on them by MR. STEWART, *Civil Surgeon of Pooree.*

"I have been fortunate in getting a number of both these specimens (*Hydrophis cyanocincta*) lately, but unfortunate again, in that they perished very soon after I got them; some, in fact, were brought nearly dead. Whether it is that the violent surf threw them on the shore, or that they are with difficulty kept alive when once removed from the sea, I am not sure. The fact, however, is the same, that though kept in a gurrah of sea-water and exposed to the air, the animals are very feeble after ten or twelve hours.

"I intend to have readier arrangements in future, so as to get the snakes to bite as soon after they are caught as possible. I am sorry that my attempts to get them to bite lately have been a failure from the above cause.

"The *Pelamis bicolor* is called by the Telinga fishermen 'Kullunder Sámp,' and is looked on by them as a very deadly snake.

"I got a female *Hydrophis cyanocincta* brought to me dead. It had sixteen eggs in it, each as large as a full-sized hen's egg. The young snakes in each egg were perfectly formed, and about six inches long."

"* * * I still experience the same difficulty in getting the snakes active enough to bite. When they are freshly thrown upon the shore, they are ready to bite; but by the time I get them they are exhausted.

"I have tried dissecting out the poison gland, and inserting it under the skin of the thigh of a Fowl. The first was from a thin-necked, small-headed snake. The Fowl did not appear to be affected at the time, but was found all but dead three hours after; and by six hours was quite dead. I tried *Pelamis bicolor* this way, but failed. I am not, however, satisfied with this, as I was told that the snake was first brought to my house while I was out, and had been biting at sticks and other things thrust into its mouth. So I think its poison may have been exhausted.

"Sea snakes are at this season (June) very difficult to obtain. In the quieter months of the cold weather, when a great deal of fishing goes on, I believe numbers are then caught in drag nets; whereas just now, with high sea and fresh breezes, nothing is done, and I have great difficulty in getting fresh specimens.

"A good plan for keeping the sea snakes alive is to make holes in the wet sand near the sea-water. I was thus able to keep one alive all day, and able to bite yesterday evening and again this morning. So placed, they must be protected from kites and crows by a cover of some kind.

"From my little experience of the *Hydrophidæ*, I can say that I have not yet seen one which did not kill if it bit fairly. Three difficulties I have noticed in the way of a fair bite; first, the inertness of the snake after being removed from its native element; second, the extreme difficulty in getting its small poison fangs to insert in anything like tough skin; third, the feeble power of the jaws of some, from natural conformation and from want of muscular action, necessary for full closure, and expulsion of the poison. Every snake that was found active and able to bite of itself, closing its jaws perceptibly, inflicted a fatal wound. Mere pressure of the jaws of dead and dying snakes over soft parts, with the view to bring out the action of the poison, was in nearly every instance followed by no result.

"The dissection and insertion of the poison gland was tried in two instances—in one death followed after some hours, in the other case it was a failure. I have been trying to find out from fishermen any peculiarities they know of the *Hydrophidæ*, but their statements are seldom the same on two occasions.

"I have not been able to hear of any fatal bites from sea snakes in fishermen, who dabble so freely in the waters, either when fishing with small hand nets near the shore, or in catamarans further out. As I said before, many snakes are enclosed in deep-sea nets, but these men know their deadly properties and lift them away.

"The fact of these men plying about so freely in the water near the surf, and withal escaping being bit, should go far to remove the fears of sea-bathers, even though it be more generally known that they are liable in the enjoyment to be in proximity to such deadly neighbours. I have inquired of several fishermen, but not one can recollect of any man losing his life in this way.

"Natives declare that *Pelamis* is the most deadly of all, and refer to their Shastras about it. The boatmen believe that this snake bit Mahadeb, and the god, to cool the burning effect of the venom, dipped himself in the sea, on which account Juggurnauth (or Maha Probha, as he is also called) banished the 'Kullunder Sámp' (*Pelamis*) beyond the seas. Mahadeb is a god worshipped under water, and exposed only once a year. I have not had an opportunity of inquiring into this fable from the Pundits."

In addition to these notes, and the collection of *Hydrophidæ* which I have previously acknowledged, Mr. Stewart was kind enough to send me some fine specimens of *Pelamis bicolor*, *Hydrophis cyanocincta*, *H. jerdonii*, *H. curta*, *H. chloris*, and the new species which Dr. Anderson, the Curator of the Indian Museum, has named *H. fayreriana*. The experiments which he performed with these snakes I have already recorded.

On inquiry from Mr. Galiffe, to whom I was indebted for the specimens of *H. coronata* and *Enhydrina bengalensis*, on the subject of bites by these snakes, he says—"I have inquired from the fishermen of any fatal case of snake-bite. In one instance a fisherman was bitten by one ('Ghanga Berah'), and died in one hour and a half. They speak of three other kinds, whose bites, however, are easily cured."

Mr. Stewart observes, what has been noticed by others, that the *Hydrophidæ* are very delicate, and die soon after being captured, even if in their native element. I was astonished therefore to find that (as I have already noted, page 25) a fine specimen of *H. coronata* lived for eight or ten days, although it was only occasionally placed in a jar of fresh water, the rest of the time living in an ordinary cage like other snakes. The movements were exceedingly graceful in the water, whilst it seemed powerless, stupid, and blind on the land. Its head and jaws were exceedingly small, and it was with the greatest difficulty it was made to bite, and then only by compressing its jaws; when, however, it did insert its fangs, small as they were, the poison was soon fatal to a Fowl.

TWENTY-THIRD SERIES.

On Snake-bite, and on the Protective Influence of Certain Articles of Clothing.

August 13th, 1870.

EXPERIMENT No. 1.

A Cobra ("Bans-buniah Keautiah") was bitten by a large Krait, four feet long, at 12.20. The bite was inflicted on the edge of the hood.

August 20th.—The Cobra is not, nor has been affected.

EXPERIMENT No. 2.

A Fowl had half a drop of poison freshly taken from the Krait, mixed with eight parts of water, injected into its thigh at 12.28 P.M. 12.29.—Stands in a dejected attitude, feathers staring. 12.35.—Has been lethargic for the last few minutes; eyes closed; crouched; head fallen forward, with beak resting on the ground. 12.38.—Lying down; starts when roused by sound or touch. 12.40.—Lying on its side, paralysed; head fallen over. 12.46.—Muscular twitchings. 12.56.—Still alive; lies motionless except for occasional convulsive twitchings. 12.57.—Dead—in twenty-nine minutes.

Blood removed from the body formed a firm coagulum soon after death.

EXPERIMENT No. 3.

Half a drop of Cobra poison mixed with eight parts of water, injected into a Fowl's thigh at 12.33 P.M. The poison is freshly taken from the Cobra; the Fowl is rather smaller than the one in the last experiment. 12.36.—Limps on injected leg. 12.40.—Crouched. 12.42.—Head drooping, resting on its beak. 12.45. — Crouching; eyes closed; head nodding. 12.48.—Point of beak resting on the ground. 12.54.—Quite paralysed. 12.56.—Convulsive movements; purged. 12.59.—Quite paralysed. 1 P.M.—Convulsive movements, springing from the ground. 1.6.—Dead—in thirty-three minutes.

The object of these two experiments was to test the relative power of the two poisons by taking the same quantity of each, and using it on animals of about the same size.

This Fowl poisoned by the Cobra was rather smaller than that poisoned by the Krait, and yet it lived longest after being inoculated; so far the Krait's poison would appear to be the most active of the two. It would be almost impossible to judge from one experiment, where there are so many causes that may interfere to disturb the natural results. Yet it is sufficient to prove that the poison of the Krait is very similar in its deadly action to that of the Cobra.

EXPERIMENT No. 4.

A Cobra ("Koyah Gokurrah"), three feet ten inches long, was severely bitten in the hood by a "Tentuliah Keautiah" (Cobra), five feet ten inches long, and very vigorous and powerful, at 12.45. The bite was a very determined one, and the poison effused profuse.

August 20th.—No evil results, the Cobra is unaffected (after seven days).

EXPERIMENT No. 5.

A small Frog was bitten by the large Krait, which must have been much exhausted by repeated biting, at 1.8 P.M. The Frog was dead at 1.14, or in six minutes.

August 20th, 1870.

Present, Drs. Fayrer and Ewart.

EXPERIMENT No. 6.

A *Bungarus fasciatus*, sixty-eight inches long and five inches in girth, was made to bite a middle-sized but full-grown Pariah Dog on the thigh at 12.45. He closed his jaws twice or thrice, but the bites were doubtful. 1.35.—Not affected. 1.55.—Not affected, the fangs had evidently not penetrated. Bitten again by the same snake. 2 P.M.—Is evidently affected; sits down, is sluggish. 2.10.—Very sluggish. The Dog after this began slowly to recover; on the following day was quite well.

EXPERIMENT No. 7.

A young and very lively Spectacled Cobra, fourteen inches long, was bitten in the muscular part of its body by a Krait, forty-eight inches long, at 12.50. The Krait is the one that came from Delhi, and it has not bitten for some days. At 1 P.M. the Cobra was very sluggish; at 1.8 so sluggish that it moves with difficulty, and can be easily handled; it makes no effort at resistance. 1.20.—Apparently dying, movements scarcely perceptible. 1.22.—Dead.

There can be no doubt, I think, that this young snake succumbed to the poison of the Krait, and this settles the question of the susceptibility of one poisonous snake to the venom of another. But in this case the Krait was very large, and the Cobra very small. I doubt whether a Cobra of equal size would have died.

EXPERIMENT No. 8.

A Krait, about thirty inches in length, was bitten by the same Krait that killed the Cobra in last experiment, at 1.22 P.M. 2.4.—Not affected. No apparent effects on the following day.

August 23rd.—No effect.

EXPERIMENT No. 9.

A full-grown Fowl was bitten in the thigh by the same *Bungarus fasciatus* that bit the Dog in Experiment No. 1, at 1.47 P.M. 1.50.—Affected; drooping. 1.55.—Convulsive movements; tail twisted to one side; crouches; head nodding. 1.58.—Fallen over, paralysed. 2.4.—Lies paralysed; reflex action still marked; a fly sitting on the eyelid; it starts. No convulsions. 2.5.—Dead—in eighteen minutes.

The blood coagulated firmly immediately after death. The bitten part was swollen and discoloured.

EXPERIMENT No. 10.

A nearly full-grown Mongoose (*Herpestes*) was put into a large cage with a very large and vigorous Cobra ("Tentuliah Keautiah") nearly six feet long. The snake immediately assumed the offensive attitude in one corner of the cage, whilst the Mongoose, evidently terrified, shrunk into the other corner. When roused and pushed towards the Cobra, the latter struck at the Mongoose, who returned the attack, and they were both scratched about the nose, for both were bleeding. They were in the cage for nearly an hour, each seeming very anxious to avoid the other. The Cobra always on the defensive, with his hood erect, and his head raised twenty inches from the ground. Whenever brought near each other the Cobra struck, and the Mongoose snapped; the result in each case being a bleeding wound about the face or mouth. This Cobra's mouth, which he kept open, was red with blood. Both seemed very tired, but the Mongoose, though severely scratched, showed no symptoms of poisoning.

They were taken out, and the Cobra was made to close his jaws on the Mongoose's thigh at 1.20 P.M. This was followed by no immediate effect; they were returned to the cage, and behaved exactly as they had done before. The Cobra's poison had most probably been exhausted in its furious assaults.

They were again taken out of the cage, and as the Mongoose was not affected, he was bitten again on the thigh by a much smaller Cobra; after which they were put into the cage together. In this case the action of the Mongoose was quite different, he was evidently not, as he had been of the larger Cobra, afraid of this one. The Cobra assumed the defensive attitude at once, and as the Mongoose ran at him struck. The Mongoose gripped him in several places along the body, and finally caught him by the head, biting him severely about the mouth, in doing which the poison fangs of the snake must have over and over again wounded the Mongoose's mouth, for the upper jaw of the snake was repeatedly in the Mongoose's mouth, and both were streaming with blood. The Cobra was soon *hors de combat* and was removed from the cage—not dead, but very severely hurt. The Mongoose had not succeeded in biting into the brain, but only in front of it. The Cobra, however, was helpless.

The Mongoose was by this time, 1.45, under the influence of the poison, which no doubt was inflicted by the last Cobra which bit him on the thigh, and when the Mongoose took the Cobra's jaw in his mouth. The bitten leg became paralysed, and by degrees he became more and more sluggish, but did not die till 8.5 P.M. After death the blood coagulated firmly.

The result of this experiment was somewhat different to that on a former occasion. Then the Mongoose also was not affected during his fight with the Cobra, but succumbed immediately afterwards when bitten on the thigh. I imagine the fangs must have penetrated a large vein, for death occurred almost instantly.

In this case it did not occur for several hours. But the animal died with the same symptoms as all other creatures poisoned by the deadly venom.

This last experiment, however, certainly seems to show that, whether by its activity or owing to the protective influence of its thick hair, it has, when bitten, a toleration of the poison greater than that of other animals of similar size. Such indeed is the case in other animals; for instance, the Cat is apparently less sensitive to the poison than the Dog.

August 27th, 1870.

Present, Dr. Fayrer.

EXPERIMENT No. 11.

A piece of the side of an ordinary patent leather shoe, consisting of one fold of patent leather and one of thin leather lining, was fastened on to a Pariah Dog's thigh, in the fashion of a boot or shoe. A powerful full-grown fresh Cobra was then made to close his jaws on the part. This he attempted to do at once and bit freely several times, but he was evidently quite unable to make the fangs penetrate, or at all events he could not do more than make them partially penetrate. The Dog was unharmed. The experiment was made at 4.3 P.M.: at 4.40 the Dog was quite unaffected, showing that the teeth had not penetrated. A large quantity of poison was shed on the leather, as the snake touched the surface in closing his jaws: it was poured in quantities—at least twenty drops must have been exuded.

It would appear from this experiment that an ordinary shoe would protect the foot from being bitten. Boots or shoes and leather gaiters would be very safe.

EXPERIMENT No. 12.

Part of the sleeve of an ordinary black cloth coat, lined with silk, was made to cover a Pariah Dog's hind-leg, and the cloth folded over the part was presented to a very powerful and fresh Cobra of the largest size, nearly six feet long. He bit fiercely two or three times; the fangs embedded themselves in the cloth, and it was soon saturated with poison, but the Dog showed no signs that the fangs had penetrated his leg, nor was blood drawn. This occurred at 4.7 P.M. 4.37.—Dog not affected. 4.40.—The sleeve again applied, and another very large Cobra made to close his jaws on the leg enveloped in the sleeve. This he did with the greatest vigour, but the fangs apparently did not penetrate the leg; as before the coat was saturated with poison. A third very large Cobra was made to bite, and this time the Dog winced as though punctured. 4.50.—The Dog seems sluggish, as though partially under the influence of the poison. 5.5.—He now looks lively, as though he were unaffected. He perfectly recovered after this, and at noon the following day was quite well.

The fold of black cloth and silk in this case proved almost a complete protection.

EXPERIMENT No. 13.

Two folds of ordinary white flannel were wrapped round a large Pariah Dog's thigh, and a large and fresh Cobra was made to bite through these. The snake bit fiercely and retained his hold for a time. The fangs penetrated the Dog's leg, for blood marked the punctures. This was at 4.11. The flannel was soaked with poison. 4.27.—Dog sluggish, evidently affected. 4.37.—In the same state. 4.54.—Seems uneasy, whines, and snarls. 5.—Very restless; lies down; up again. 5.8.—When he walks is very lame on bitten leg, and staggers in his gait. 5.20.—Vomited. 5.30.—Purged 5.35.—Convulsed. 5.40.—Dying. 5.50.—Dead—in ninety-nine minutes.

Blood coagulated firmly after death. The flannel did partially, though it would not completely, protect; the intensity of the poisoning was certainly diminished.

EXPERIMENT No. 14.

A woollen knitted sock was placed on a Fowl's leg, and a powerful Cobra made to bite through it at 4.37 P.M. The fangs penetrated, and the Fowl died almost immediately—so rapidly that I was doubtful whether it had not been squeezed to death in handling it.

EXPERIMENT No. 15.

The same woollen sock put on to a Dog's thigh at 4.38 P.M., and a full-grown vigorous Cobra made to bite through it. The fangs penetrated, for the Dog whined, and blood points marked the punctures. 4.39.—Limps. 4.52.—Much affected, legs weak. 5.4.—Vomiting. 5.10.—Convulsed. 5.12.—Died—in thirty-four minutes.

Blood coagulated firmly. The sock was not sufficient protection, the fangs penetrated, and the poison in both cases acted rapidly.

EXPERIMENT No. 16.

A large Cobra was made to bite on a single fold of a piece of American drill, such as white trousers are usually made of in India. The fangs penetrated and their points could be seen on the other side. This cloth would afford no protection against Cobra bite.

EXPERIMENT No. 17.

A drop of poison from the Cobra shed in Experiment No. 1 was dropped into a large Fowl's eye at 4.10 P.M. 4.37.—The Fowl has been drowsy and stupid for some minutes; the eye also is much congested. 4.56.—Five drops of Cobra poison put into its mouth and washed down with a teaspoonful of water. 4.58.—Very drowsy. 5.6.—Very sluggish; head drooping; purged. 5.3. — Feathers all ruffled; purged. 7.3. — Crouched; head nodding. 8.20.—Convulsed. 9.—Dying. 10.—Found dead.

Blood coagulated firmly on removal. In this case death did not occur for nearly five hours.

EXPERIMENT No. 18.

A drop of Cobra poison put into an Albino Rabbit's eye at 4.24 P.M., and about six drops of the same diluted with a teaspoonful of water put into its mouth, which it swallowed. 4.26. — Eye very slightly congested. 4.28.—Very restless; twitching movements of head. 4.31.—A few violent convulsions, and then death—in seven minutes.

The blood was removed in fifteen minutes, and coagulated firmly. Experiments No. 7 and 8 prove beyond a doubt that the poison is absorbed by a mucous membrane, and that it is as dangerous to apply it to those surfaces as to introduce it into the stomach.

The practice of sucking a poisoned snake-bite may be attended with danger, and should be discontinued, as it endangers a second life, whilst probably doing but little good for the first. The first six experiments show how far protection may be conferred by certain articles of dress. A pair of boots or shoes and gaiters protect (probably entirely) the parts covered. Broad cloth lined with silk is almost complete protection in case of the Cobra bite, and *à fortiori* in that of the "Krait." Flannel, white American drill, and a woollen sock afford some, but very little protection.

TWENTY-FOURTH SERIES.

Experiments on the Influence of the Poisons of Echis carinata, Bungarus cæruleus, and Naja tripudians.

September 7th, 1870.

Present, Dr. Fayrer.

Through the kindness of Major McMahon, Deputy Commissioner of Delhi, I have received several very fine living specimens of *Echis carinata*, *Bungarus cæruleus*, and *Naja tripudians*; the latter are of the variety, or very near it, called by the snakemen in Bengal "Koyah Gokurrah" (Spectacled Cobra).

EXPERIMENT No. 1.

An *Echis carinata*, twenty-three inches long by two inches and a half in girth, was made to bite a Pariah Dog in the thigh at 12.42 P.M. The snake bit with great ferocity, plunging in his long mobile fangs deeply. The Dog showed signs of pain 12.45.—The Dog is staggering; the bitten limb stretched out and powerless; the animal turns round and round. 12.49.—Sitting down; rises and is very restless. 12.54.—Getting weaker; staggers; nose resting on the ground. 1 P.M.—Fallen over on his side: limb seems painful and swollen, and ecchymosed about the bites. The local symptoms are indeed unusally severe. 2.30.—Much the same constitutionally, but the wounded limb is much swollen. 5.10.—The animal now lies quite paralysed; the leg more swollen. 6.30.—Much the same; salivated. 9.—Dying; eyes half closed. 10.25.—Dead.

The blood was removed from the great vessels, and it remained perfectly fluid. It was so when examined next morning. Lungs not congested.

The limb was one mass of black and infiltrated cellular tissue. There was not seen such severe local mischief from any other snake-bite. The Dog lived from 12.42 to 10.25 P.M., or nine hours forty-three minutes.

EXPERIMENT No. 2.

A large Krait (*Bungarus cæruleus*), four feet in length, was bitten at 12.55 by an *Echis carinata*, twenty-two inches long and two and a quarter in girth, in the muscular part of the body in two places. The *Echis* was fresh and very fierce; blood was drawn from the Krait; no symptoms of poisoning followed. The Krait was perfectly well on the 8th, next day; 9th, still quite well.

EXPERIMENT No. 3.

A Cobra ("Tentuliah Keautiah"), three feet eight inches in length, the same that was bitten some days ago by the *Bungarus cæruleus*, and has not suffered, was bitten at 1 P.M. by a fresh *Echis*, twenty-three inches long; no effect apparent on this day.

September 8th, 1 P.M.—The Cobra is now evidently affected; it is sluggish; the snake-men say it will die; it moves slowly; does not expand its hood, and does not try to strike. 6.30.—Very sluggish. 8.—Dead—in about thirty hours. There can be no doubt, I think, that the Cobra died of the poison.

EXPERIMENT No. 4.

A small *Ptyas mucosus* ("Dhamin"), an innocent snake about two feet long, was bitten by a *Bungarus cæruleus*, forty-two inches and a half long, just come from Delhi, in the muscles of the back at 1.8 P.M.; blood drawn. 2.30.—Sluggish; has lost all its vivacity. 8.25.—Found dead—in five hours and fifty-five minutes.

September 8th.

Present, Dr. Fayrer and Baboo Kany Lall Dey, Assistant Professor of Chemistry.

EXPERIMENT No. 5.

A Fowl two-thirds grown was bitten by an *Echis carinata*, twenty-three inches long, in the thigh at 12.23 P.M. 12.24.—In violent convulsions. 12.25.—Dead—in two minutes.

The limb already swollen and ecchymosed. Blood remained fluid, but in half an hour formed a partial coagulum. I have observed this before in Fowls killed by *Daboia*, though as a general rule the blood of Birds as well as of Mammals remains fluid after death from viperine poison.

EXPERIMENT No. 6.

A young Dog was bitten in the thigh by an *Echis*, full-grown, at 12.27. The snake bit fiercely. The Dog seemed to feel it severely at the time, and for some time after it howled loudly. The bitten leg was rendered powerless almost immediately. 12.30.—Lying down; seems depressed but not in pain; is very weak in the hind-quarters; staggers as he walks; is quite conscious; the bitten leg is swelled. 1.33.—Lying quiet, but does not seem much affected constitutionally; the limb is quite useless. 1.55.—Staggers on three legs, but does not seem otherwise much affected. September 9th, 8 A.M.—The limb is very much swollen and ecchymosed, but the Dog does not appear to suffer otherwise. 8.12.—Very restless; leg much swollen; ecchymosed. 10.5.—Convulsed. 10.55.—Dead; the limb and great part of the body infiltrated and ecchymosed; decomposition setting in; blood removed from the body remained perfectly fluid after death.

EXPERIMENT No. 7.

A Delhi Cobra, about four feet long, bit a Dog in the thigh at 12.32. 12.33.—The Dog seems to feel pain; it howls; bitten leg paralysed. 12.42.—In convulsions. 12.44.—Paralysed. 12.46.—Respiration ceased; heart still beats 12.47.—Dead—in fifteen minutes.

Blood taken from right ventricle, which was distended, formed a firm clot in a few minutes. Lung not at all congested. The poison of this snake was very active.

EXPERIMENT No. 8.

A Fowl was bitten in the thigh by an *Echis* at 12.37; lame immediately. 12.38.—Crouching; rises, and falls over in convulsions; no appearance of lethargy as in Cobra poisoning of Fowls. 12.40.—Dead—in three minutes.

Blood removed from the body remained perfectly fluid; in the other case the blood coagulated.

EXPERIMENT No. 9.

A Fowl bitten in the thigh by a Delhi Cobra at 12.41.—Limps; leg partially paralysed; feathers staring; crouches. 12.43.—Head falls over; it cannot stand; rests the point of the beak on the ground in the usual state of lethargy observed in Fowls so poisoned. 12.45.—Convulsed. 12.46.—Dead—in five minutes.

Blood examined; coagulated firmly after death.

EXPERIMENT No. 10.

An *Echis* was made to bite through a piece of paper, stretched across a mussel shell. About a quarter of a drop of clear watery-looking fluid was obtained. This was diluted with five drops of water, and then with the hypodermic syringe injected into a Fowl's thigh at 1 P.M. 1.4.—Very lame on that leg; looks wild and scared; runs about. 1.6.—Has fallen over; but its eyes are bright, and it is perfectly conscious. 1.7.—Tries to rise and run; falls over; limb is either paralysed or all power of muscular co-ordination is gone. 1.8.—Begins to look lethargic, as in Cobra poisoning; head nods; point of beak rests on ground. 1.9.—Violently convulsed. 1.10.—Dead—in ten minutes.

This experiment proves the very active nature of the *Echis* poison. The quantity was exceedingly small—certainly not more than a quarter of a drop; it seemed in the shell a mere speck, and it was diluted with five full drops of water, or twenty parts at least. It took effect almost immediately and killed in ten minutes. The blood examined after death was very dark at first, but became red on exposure to the air, and remained permanently fluid. This experiment is remarkable when contrasted with the next.

Experiment No. 11.

A quarter of a drop of poison was taken from one of the Delhi Cobras, and was mixed with five drops of water, and then injected with the hypodermic syringe into a Fowl's thigh at 1.4 P.M. The Fowl was about two-thirds grown, like the one in Experiment 10. 1.5.—Feathers staring; limps on injected leg. 1.6.—Crouches; rises; walks, but is very lame. 1.10.—Still runs about, but is lame. 1.11.—Crouching; head drooping; has fallen over, resting on the point of the beak. 1.12.—Convulsed. It remained in this condition quite unconscious and occasionally convulsed until 1.34, when it died—in thirty minutes. Blood removed after death had not coagulated at 1.55. It coagulated after this, but did not form a firm clot.

The results of this are remarkable when compared with the other (No. 10). An equal quantity of *Echis* poison equally diluted killed in ten minutes; that of the Cobra killed in thirty. It shows that the *Echis* poison is very active, but it does not prove that it is more active than that of the Cobra, for it may have entered a vein and been more rapidly absorbed. But it does prove what different results may be given, although the circumstances appear the same for each. It also shows how frequently experiments must be repeated before reliable generalization can be made.

Experiment No. 12.

At 1.10 P.M. a Dog was bitten on the nose by an *Echis;* blood was drawn; the Dog seemed either not to feel or not to care for the bite. 1.14.—No symptoms; the Dog seems well. 1.15.—Nose and upper lip beginning to swell. 1.20.—Very much swollen. 1.25.—Frothy discharge from nostrils, but the Dog seems well, perhaps a little sluggish; he lies quiet.

9th, 8 A.M.—He seems well in health, and the swelling of the nose and upper lip has abated considerably.

10th.—The Dog has recovered; the swelling has disappeared.

Experiment No. 13.

At 1.27 P.M. four drops of fresh Cobra poison from a "Keautiah" were diluted with a teaspoonful of water and put into a Fowl's mouth. It swallowed it at once, and then another spoonful of water was given, which was also freely swallowed. 1.30.—It is evidently affected; it looks dazed; walks about with its back arched; head down and feathers staring. 1.36.—Drooping; feathers raised; seems very weak and stupid; does not try to escape when taken in the hand; stands with its head raised and its eyes staring. 1.50.—Is lethargic; walks with difficulty; crouching; a watery fluid is coming in large quantity from its mouth; it is evidently very sick; cannot stand when placed on its legs. 1.55.—Crouching; head nodding forward as usual; point of beak on the ground. 2.30 P.M.—Profuse flow of watery fluid from mouth. 2.50.—Head fallen forward; neck twisted to one side. 2.55.—Convulsed. 2.58.—Quite paralysed. 3.10.—Dead—in one hour and forty-three minutes. Blood coagulated firmly after death. This experiment confirms the poisonous action of the venom when swallowed.

Experiment No. 14.

A small Krait, about twenty inches long, bitten by a large one, forty-two inches long, at 1.45 P.M. Blood drawn. 2 P.M.—No effect.

9th, 8 A.M.—Not in the least affected.

10th.—Still quite well.

The evidence of this experiment is that the Krait cannot poison the Krait.

I may remind the reader that the *Echis carinata* is a very active and fierce little viper, very aggressive, minacious, and irascible. He is naturally sluggish until roused, when he immediately places himself in a posture of offence and defence. I received a batch of seven sent to me from Delhi; all very fine specimens, beautifully marked, and in good condition, the largest nearly twenty-four inches in length, and nearly three inches in girth. They laid all knotted and coiled together in a corner of the cage, so close that it was impossible to distinguish one from the other, a head peeping out here and there. When disturbed they immediately separated and coiled themselves up in a series of convolutions with the head erect, the mouth open the eye looking particularly vicious, and with a loud hissing sound they prepared to strike, and frequently they darted the whole body forward a foot or more in the attempt to strike. The head was always erect and the whole aspect and attitude was that of intense malice and mischief.

The peculiar sound they make, especially when there are several together, is very remarkable; it is caused by the friction of their roughly carinated obliquely set outer rows of scales as they move one fold of the convoluted body rapidly against the other. This they do without changing place, and it is very beautiful to watch this constant motion, which is something like the vermicular movement of an intestinal tube as the peristaltic wave passes rapidly along. My attention was called to it by my snake-man in a very fine specimen that I had sent to the School of Art to be figured, which was confined in a large box with a wire gauze front.

That it might be better seen, and that the origin of this peculiar sound in the friction of the carinated scales against each other might be the better demonstrated, he took it out of the box, lifting it on a stick, and put it on the ground; intending to remove it to a little distance, he pressed its neck with the rod, and seized it by the neck in the usual way with the finger and thumb; as he did so I saw the viper suddenly twist its neck, the man dropped it and said he was bitten. The *Echis* had managed to twist its head round, not being held sufficiently near the jaws, and struck one of its needle-like fangs under the man's thumb nail, though not very deeply, yet it brought blood. The man seemed alarmed but behaved well. I immediately, as I saw him drop the viper, seized his hand and compressed the thumb as hard as I could; a piece of string was handed to me, and I tied it round the thumb just above the nail with all the force I could exert, causing considerable pain. I then took out my penknife and cut away the nail and that portion of the soft parts where the fang had penetrated. I next got a piece of live charcoal and cauterized the part; under the pressure of the ligature blood was flowing freely. Some nitric acid was brought, and I immediately applied it freely over the cut surface. He complained of pain up the arm, but this was due to the treatment, and he became rather faint, no doubt from apprehension and pain, though he showed no signs of fear. After a few minutes I slackened the ligature above the part, and as I happened to have a bottle of carbonate of ammonia (smelling salts), I took out about fifteen grains, dissolved it in water, and gave it him to drink. I then took him in my carriage to the hospital, where I was going to lecture at 2 P.M., and left him in the hospital, with instructions that he should be watched and stimulants given frequently.

On coming out from my lecture at 3 P.M. I found him waiting for me. He said he felt perfectly well, only some pain from the severe treatment of the thumb; he then went home. I saw him next day at noon; he was quite well: the thumb was slightly painful from the wound, but there were no signs of poisoning.

Here was an undoubted bite from a poisonous snake, blood was drawn by the fang penetrating between the nail and the flesh. The treatment was prompt, active, and rational, and no bad symptoms followed; and yet I believe that had nothing at all been done for him it is probable that no evil would have followed. Of course I could not act on this impression, and I treated him as I believe those should be treated who are bitten by poisonous snakes. But in this case the thing was done so quickly that I very much doubt if there was time to inject any poison into the wound; or, if any, so small a quantity that it could hardly have done much harm. It may have been an example of what I have before described, that a snake may make a wound by a sudden blow without poisoning. Of course it is possible and probable that a certain amount of the virus may in this rapid action be inoculated, and it would not therefore be safe to do nothing. I have no doubt that snake-bites are occasionally of this nature; hence the recoveries, and the wonderful effects ascribed to antidotes. Had this man taken a so-called antidote, and had I not seen the bite, and the rapid way in which it was inflicted, and had I not applied a ligature and the cautery, who would have denied to the antidote the merit of having prevented symptoms that would most probably have never really occurred, or of having saved a life that was perhaps never in danger?

The *Echis* is a very venomous viper; this one killed a Fowl in two minutes only the day before.

TWENTY-FIFTH SERIES.

Experiments on the Influence of the Poisons of Echis carinata, Bungarus cæruleus, Naja tripudians, Daboia russellii, and on the Action of the Tanjore Pill and the Snake Stone.

September 17th, 1870.

EXPERIMENT No. 1.

A young Pigeon was bitten by an *Echis carinata* in the thigh. The bird was affected instantly, fell over, and died in convulsions in less than sixty seconds. Blood removed after death formed a very slight coagulum; the coagulation soon becoming fluid.

EXPERIMENT No. 2.

A half-grown Fowl was bitten by another *Echis carinata* in the thigh at 2.3 P.M. 2.4.—Has fallen over after staggering; no appearance of lethargy. 2.5.10.—Dead—in violent convulsions in seventy seconds. Blood remained fluid after death.

EXPERIMENT No. 3.

A young Pigeon bitten in the thigh by a "Krait" some weeks in confinement, at 2.5.10 P.M. 2.5.30. — Limps; crouches. 2.8.—Crouching; leg paralysed. 2.9.—More affected. 2.13.—Dead. No marked convulsion. Blood coagulated firmly.

EXPERIMENT No. 4.

"Krait" bitten by *Echis* at 2.10 P.M.—Not affected.

EXPERIMENT No. 5.

Echis bitten by "Krait" at 2.16 P.M.—Not affected.

September 29th, 1870.

Present, Dr. Fayrer and Dr. Ewart.

The following experiments were made for the purpose of testing the efficacy of a snake stone which was kindly placed at my disposal by Captain Lawrence. The stone is a small polished object of the size and shape of a large almond, black, but on one side of a whitish colour. Its weight is twenty-six grains, and specific gravity 1·8. It is reported to have saved the lives of several persons who had been bitten by snakes.

EXPERIMENT No. 6.

A Fowl had the feathers removed from the breast and was bitten by a Cobra at 1.12 P.M. The snake stone having been slightly moistened on one surface was applied to the punctures, which were bleeding. It adhered, as it seemed, from the exclusion of air and the viscosity of the blood and poison which was on the surface of the Fowl's breast. 1.14.—Fowl drooping. 1.18.—Lies insensible; the stone adheres. 1.20.—Convulsed. 1.24.—Lies motionless, but breathes. 1.25.—Convulsed. 1.28.—Dead—the stone still adhering.

The stone was removed and placed according to directions in a cup of milk. There was no change in the appearance of the whitish surface of the stone, except that it was slightly stained with blood. No change occurred in the colour of the milk, in which it was kept for some minutes. It was then taken out, washed in water, and thoroughly dried. The blood of this Fowl was not examined till 7 P.M., and then it coagulated on removal from the body.

EXPERIMENT No. 7.

A small Pariah Dog had the hind-leg shaved for an area of two inches or so, in order that the surface might be smooth and even for the application of the stone. Part of this surface was covered with a shield of leather, and it was then bitten by a Cobra at 1.37 P.M. The leather was applied to prevent the second fang from penetrating, in order to be more certain of the exact application of the stone to the bitten spot. The leather answered the purpose, but it also prevented the fang that did penetrate from doing more than inflict a very slight puncture, which however drew blood. The stone was applied as before, and adhered in the same way. 1.40.—The stone adheres. 1.50.—The Dog is sluggish and lame on the bitten leg. 2.4.—Much the same condition. The stone dropped off on some slight movement of the Dog's leg; it presented the same appearance, and when placed in milk there was a repetition of what occurred in Experiment No. 1. It was again washed in clear water and thoroughly dried. At 3 P.M. the Dog was in convulsions; at 3.53 it was dead.

The blood was not removed from the body till 7 P.M.; it coagulated on removal.

EXPERIMENT No. 8.

A Fowl had the feathers removed from the breast and was bitten by a Cobra with one fang (I purposely extracted the other) at 2.14 P.M. The puncture drew blood. The snake stone was immediately applied; it adhered as before. 2.16.—The Fowl is affected. 2.17.—Is drowsy. 2.23.—In convulsions; the stone still adhering. 2.28.—Dead—in fourteen minutes. Blood removed from body at 7 P.M. It coagulated.

In these four experiments, where the animal died from Cobra bite, I purposely delayed the removal of the blood from the body after death for some hours, in order to see whether time has anything to say to the question of coagulability. I found it the same as in other cases; when the blood was examined soon after death, the blood did coagulate after Cobra poisoning. This is a remarkable fact, as in autopsies of human victims to Cobra poisoning, the blood is declared to be fluid and to remain so. Thinking that this might have been due to the time that elapsed between death and examination of the blood, which in fatal cases of human snake-bite is generally several hours, I left these bodies untouched for several hours, but the result was still the same—the blood still coagulated.

EXPERIMENT No. 9.

A Pariah Dog was bitten in the thigh by a Cobra, with both fangs, at 2.46 P.M. The snake stone was immediately applied, but it would not adhere, apparently because the punctures bled very freely, and because the hair had not been thoroughly removed from the part. 2.54.—The Dog shows evident signs of poisoning. The stone has been kept applied, but it would not adhere; it was accordingly laid aside, washed, and carefully dried. The Dog was soon after this in convulsions, and at 3.40 was dead.

The blood examined at 7 P.M. coagulated on removal from the body.

EXPERIMENT No. 10.

A Pigeon was put into a cage with an *Echis* Viper at 1.52 P.M. The snake struck it immediately, and with great rapidity. 1.54.—In convulsions. 1.55.—Dead.

The Viper did not seem to retain its hold; it was difficult to say the exact instant when it struck. It shows that the poison of the snake is very virulent. No mark could be found.

Blood examined at 7 P.M. remained fluid.

EXPERIMENT No. 11.

A half-grown Fowl was put into the cage with the *Echis* at 1.58 P.M. The Viper did not appear to strike until 2.2. He struck, darting for some inches, two or three times, and once seemed to retain his hold for a perceptible space. 2.4.—The Fowl staggers. 2.5.—In very violent convulsions. 2.6.—Dead.

Both these experiments show the exceeding virulence of the poison. There were three Vipers in the cage, and more than one may have struck, though only one was seen to do so.

Blood examined at 7 P.M. remained fluid.

October 4th, 1870.

Present, Dr. Fayrer.

EXPERIMENT No. 12.

I am indebted to Mr. Gibbons, of Messrs. Scott and Thomson's, for a supply of Tanjore pills, made according to the recipe given in "Russell's Indian Serpents."

One of the pills was given to a half-grown Pariah Dog at 8 A.M. this morning, another at 10, and it appears that they affected him as follows. He was purged at 9, at 9.30, at 10, at 11.30, when he also vomited. The pills were given undissolved, and were washed down with a little water. At 12.37 he was bitten in the thigh by a Cobra, but not very severely. The snake had been a long time in confinement, and as the snake-man was absent, it was held by a strap round the neck, in which position it did not bite so readily. 12.39.—The Dog limping with the bitten leg drawn up and whining. 12.39.—A third pill administered. 12.42.—Walks on three legs, the bitten leg drawn up. 12.45.—Purged. 1.6.—Very weak, staggers. Breathing deep. 1.25.—A fourth pill given. He is weak and very lame, but is quite conscious. 2.55.—A fifth pill given; was purged. 3.10.—Whining, and staggers as he tries to walk. 3.55.—Convulsed. 4.—Completely paralysed. 4.10.—Dead, in three hours and thirty-three minutes.

The blood coagulated after death.

EXPERIMENT No. 13.

A Pigeon was placed in a cage with two *Daboias*. They were roused, and the Pigeon walked about over them, stepping on their bodies and heads. They hissed fiercely, moved out of the way, and once or twice appeared to strike at the Pigeon, but evidently without touching or hurting it. The bird seemed quite unconcerned. It was left in the cage several minutes. The Vipers showed no disposition to touch it, and it was taken out uninjured. The Pigeon was then placed in a large cage, in which there were five large Cobras. They immediately began to hiss, erected their heads, looked very vicious, and struck at the Pigeon, but without hurting it, often striking past it. The Pigeon walked about among them, and seemed very little concerned. The Cobras were roused, and yet they did not injure it. The Pigeon was removed unhurt, after being several minutes in the cage, during which time it frequently walked on their heads. They seemed more frightened than it was.

The Pigeon was then placed in a cage with four *Echis* Vipers. They at once threw themselves into their characteristic attitude of defence, making the peculiar loud, rustling or sawing sound, caused by the friction of their scales, and, with their heads erect, watched the bird. Being slightly roused, two of those nearest it struck with extreme rapidity, at 1.4 P.M. The bird was affected at once; at 1.5 it was in convulsions; at 1.5.30 it was dead. On removing the feathers a short time after death, a minute ecchymosed puncture was found in the heart and another in the crop. This experiment forcibly illustrates the extremely dangerous and vicious character of this little Viper. The blood of the Pigeon remained fluid after death.

EXPERIMENT No. 14.

A *Daboia russelli*, forty-three inches long and four and a half in girth, recently sent to me by Mr. Richards, of Bancoorah, was made to bite a Fowl on the thigh, from which the feathers had been stripped to leave a smooth surface, at 1.12 P.M. The snake stone was immediately applied: it adhered being pressed against the surface, partly by exclusion of air and partly by the viscosity of the drop of blood that oozed from the puncture and of the poison shed over the surface.

At 1.13 the Fowl was in convulsions. At 1.13.30 it was dead—in ninety seconds.

The blood on being removed from the body remained fluid after death. This *Daboia*, I observe, differs slightly from those I have obtained near Calcutta. The general ground colour is the same, perhaps rather more muddy-looking, and the circular and oval markings are much less distinct. Indeed, as it lay coiled in the cage they were hardly perceptible, though when the snake was taken out into bright sunlight they were seen. The circular rings on the sides have a prolongation into a square

on their lower margins, and the dark triangular marks on the head are hardly distinguishable from the surrounding colour. The whitish or yellowish converging line on the head is absent. The nostrils are peculiarly large, and the body of the snake very thick for its length. The tail—it is a female—is thin, and the subcaudal shields of a reddish-brown colour.

Of course it is the same species, and is not even what would be called a variety; but it shows how much individuals may differ in colour, probably influenced by the circumstances under which they live. The general appearance of the snake to one unaccustomed to observe these creatures is very different from the brilliantly marked character of the *Daboia* as often seen, and which no doubt suggested its name of *D. elegans*. The *Daboia* does not make a peculiar rustling noise like the *Echis*; and indeed its outer scales, by which that small Viper produces the sound, are not prominent as in *Echis*.

EXPERIMENT No. 15.

On this occasion I examined a large "Teutuliah Keautiah," from which, less than three weeks ago (I have lost the exact date), I removed both fangs, and found that two new ones had replaced those removed, though they appeared rather smaller. It was made to bite a Fowl on the thigh to test them, and the bird was dead in two minutes. Another Cobra from which I removed one fang a few days ago, when the experiments with the snake stone were tried, was examined, and a new fang was already in working order. On this occasion I carefully dislocated the entire fang, and preserved it for examination, so that there could be no mistake.

October 6th, 1870.

EXPERIMENT No. 16.

Two full-grown Pariah Dogs had each a Tanjore pill administered at 8 and 10 A.M. this morning. One Dog vomited at 10.30. Neither was purged. Unfortunately the snake man was not present, so the Cobras had to be held by a strap round the neck, in which position they bite neither so well nor so willingly as when held in the hand. The Dog that vomited was bitten by a Cobra that has been some weeks in confinement, at 12.30 P.M., in the thigh, but very imperfectly; the animal showed no sign of feeling the bite; no blood was drawn.

12.38 P.M.—A third pill was given. 12.40.—Apparently not affected, but it has laid down. 1.44.—Bitten again by another Cobra, which had also been some weeks in confinement. 1.50.—

Restless; sick. 1.58.—Another pill administered. 2.10.—Frothing at the mouth: restless. 2.15.—Vomited, and convulsed. 2.25.—Dying. 2.30.—Dead — in two hours.

The Cobras were both long in confinement, one was moulting, and both bit under most (to them) unfavourable circumstances. The Dog had two pills before the bite and two after; but I do not think they produced any effect, unless indeed the short delay in death—two hours—was attributable to the pills and not to the condition of the snakes.

Experiment No. 17.

The second Dog was bitten at 12.30, but also imperfectly, for the same reason. It was not the same snake as either of those used in the last experiment; it had also been some weeks in confinement. A pill was given within three or four minutes after the bite.

12.40.—The Dog lies down, but is apparently not affected as yet. 1.10.—Seems restless; another pill given. 1.15.—Not affected. 1.25.—Bitten again by another Cobra, also not fresh: it took hold, but did not seem to insert its fangs. Another Cobra, also old, was tried; it seemed to bite slightly; for the Dog limped on the bitten leg after the bite. 1.35.—Seems sluggish; breathes hurriedly. 1.55.—Is lame. 2.10.—Another pill given. 2.15.—Licks the wound. 2.25.—Frothing at the mouth. 2.55.—Fell down, unable to stand. 3.5.—Convulsed. 3.20.—Dead—in two hours and sixty minutes.

In this case also death took place later than usual; but as the Cobras were not fresh, having been weeks in confinement, their poison was probably weak. In neither of these cases therefore is there any satisfactory evidence that the Tanjore pill had any beneficial effect. The blood of both Dogs coagulated firmly after death.

October 7th, 1870.

Experiment No. 18.

A Tanjore pill was given at 8 A.M., and a second at 10 A.M. to a full-grown Pariah Dog. At 12.30 it was bitten by a Cobra (not fresh, one of those of yesterday) in the thigh; the snake-man was present to-day. The Dog limped very slightly after being bitten. A third pill was given at 12.45 P.M.

1.10 P.M.—The Dog staggers, and is slightly convulsed. A fourth pill given. It was purged; sanguinolent motion. 1.15.—Fell down in convulsions. 1.17.—Dead—in forty-four minutes.

Experiment No. 19.

The following experiment is instructive. I removed both active fangs, breaking them short off with a pair of forceps, from a large Cobra, and one of the loose reserve fangs as well, at about 1.40 P.M. I then made it close its jaws on a Fowl's thigh; it bit savagely, and made a slight scratch, perhaps with its palatine teeth, perhaps with the root of the broken fang.

At 2.20 the Fowl was observed to be drowsy. 2.30.—Crouched. 3.5.—No convulsions. 4.50.—Still alive; convulsed. 5.15.—Dead.

This experiment illustrates the very deadly nature of the poison, and the danger of carelessly handling Cobras, even when deprived of their fangs. A quantity of poison was shed into the mucous sheath, and with this the scratch was inoculated, and caused death in about three hours and a half.

Experiment No. 20.

A Dog had a Tanjore pill given at 8 and 10 A.M. At 12.40 P.M. it was bitten, but slightly, by a *Daboia* in the thigh. The snake was sluggish, indisposed to bite. A third pill given at 12.50. The Dog limps a little on the bitten leg.

1.15. P.M.—A fourth pill given. 1.30.—Dog lies down, and seems sluggish. 2.10.—Purged. 2.20.—Vomited. 2.35.—Convulsed. 3.25.—Very weak. It remained in this exhausted state, and was found dead at 8 P.M.

The blood remained fluid after death, as usual in viperine poisoning.

Experiment No. 21.

A full-grown *Echis carinata* was bitten severely by a Cobra at 1.20 P.M., in two places about the middle of the body.

3.15 P.M.—Sluggish. 7.—Ditto.

October, 8th. 6.10 P.M.—Sluggish. 9.15.—Dead.

I think it is more than probable that the *Echis* died of the Cobra poison; it is certainly possible that the fang wounds may have caused death. I believe that poisonous snakes are susceptible to a certain degree of the poison of others, especially when a small individual is bitten by a large one of another species.

October 11th.

Experiment No. 22.

A *Bungarus cæruleus* was bitten severely by an *Echis carinata* in three places at 1.10 P.M. The needle-like fangs penetrated with difficulty. No effect produced. On the 15th October the *Bungarus cæruleus* was quite well.

Experiment No. 23.

A Cobra was bitten by a large *Bungarus cæruleus* at 1.15, in the body and neck; no effect produced. The Cobra continued in its ordinary state on the 15th October.

Experiment No. 24.

An *Echis carinata,* twenty-two inches long, was bitten severely by a powerful Cobra in two places. It became sluggish, and died on the following day at 9.15 A.M. There was a discoloured patch in the skin of the abdomen from one of the bites. It may have died of the wound independently of the poison.

Experiment No. 25.

A *Bungarus cæruleus* was bitten at 1.20 P.M. by a *Daboia.* The *Daboia* did not bite readily; it had been long in confinement, had bitten often, and was probably weak, but it did insert its fangs. No evil results; the Krait remained unaffected.

Experiment No. 26.

Some poison from the *Echis* put into a Fowl's eye at 1.19 P.M.; great chemosis, followed, and all the symptoms of poisoning were manifested. The bird crouched, was purged, and became very sluggish, but it recovered, and next day was quite well. The *Echis* had bitten frequently, and had been more than two months in confinement, refusing all food. I observed that the minute drop of poison was not clear, but more like mucus.

Experiment No. 27.

The same experiment repeated with exactly the same results.

Experiment No. 28.

On the 7th of October I carefully removed the fang on either side from a large *Echis,* and noticed particularly that there were no other fixed fangs, though there were others quite loose in the mucous membrane capsule. On examining the same *Echis* on the 11th October, fifth day, I found a fang firmly anchylosed on either side, and ready for work.

Experiment No. 29.

A Cobra had its fangs removed (pulled out) on the 7th of October. On the 15th there were no new fangs produced. This Cobra killed a Fowl after its fangs were removed. The poison must have been inoculated into the minute wounds made by the palatine teeth. On the 31st October the new fangs had replaced those removed.

Experiment No. 30.

A powerful Pariah Dog was bitten at 2.8 P.M. on either thigh by a very large and vigorous Cobra ("Gokurrah"), one of the largest and most vicious I have seen. It had been recently caught. It bit the Dog on both thighs with great force, and not only injected its poison into the wound, but over the bitten part. It held on with great tenacity and could hardly be made to let go, making fresh efforts to imbed its fangs more deeply. 2.18.—The Dog seems sluggish; vomited. 2.30.—Coughing. 2.55.—Laid down. 3.5.—Convulsed. 3.10.—Purged. 3.15.—Paralysed. 3.20.—Dead—in one hour and twelve minutes.

This experiment shows how uncertain the action of the poison may be. This Dog did not die for seventy-two minutes, although it was bitten most severely by a fresh and very vigorous and vicious Cobra. Generally from the ordinary bite of a medium-sized Cobra a Dog dies in less than three-quarters of an hour. The blood of this Dog coagulated firmly three hours after death.

Experiment No. 31.

A Fowl was bitten on the thigh by a Cobra at 1.58 P.M. Limped immediately; then crouched; head fell over. 1.59.—Convulsed. 1.59.30.—Dead—in ninety seconds.

Blood coagulated very firmly immediately after death.

Experiment No. 32.

Some of the blood of the above Fowl was mixed with water and the clot broken down, so that it would pass through the hypodermic syringe; it was then injected at 2.4 P.M. into the thighs of a Fowl—one syringeful into each. 2.6—Crouched. 2.25.—Drowsy; eyes closed. 3.15.—Walks about sluggishly and is lame. 5.15.—Feathers ruffled; very sluggish. 8.35.—In convulsions. 9.5.—Nearly dead. 3.29 A.M.—It did not actually die till about this time. The blood coagulated on removal from the body.

This again quite decides the question whether the blood of an animal poisoned by snake virus is poisonous or not.

October 15th, 1870.

Present, Dr. Fayrer.

Experiment No. 33.

A Pariah Dog was bitten by an *Echis carinata* in the thigh at 1.50 P.M. 2.—The Dog staggers on his hind-legs. 2.30.—Very weak; staggers on the hind-legs. 3.—Very sluggish and lame. 4.— In the same condition; wound and leg much swollen. 8.—Very sluggish and lame.

After this the Dog began to recover, and on the 17th was well, though the limb was still considerably swollen.

Experiment No. 34.

A Pariah Dog was bitten by another *Echis carinata* in the thigh at 2.38. The snake is sickly and weak from long confinement and would not bite freely. The Dog became sluggish; lame, and the leg swelled, but the symptoms passed away, and next day it was well. In both these cases the vipers were weak and exhausted. They were those from Delhi, and had been a long time without food, for they will not eat in confinement. They had lost much of their vivacity and aggressiveness, and one was provoked to bite with difficulty. The effects of the bite were severe but yet not fatal.

It is a remarkable thing that none of these *Echis* have shed their epidermis since they came here three months ago; not a trace of a slough is found in their cage. They are thinner, less brilliant in colour, and much less aggressive than they were. Three only survive.

TWENTY-SIXTH SERIES.

October 31st, 1870.

Experiments on the Action of the Poisons of Trimeresurus monticola, Echis carinata, Bungarus cæruleus, and Naia tripudians.

Present, Dr. Fayrer, Dr. Stoliczka, Mr. Wood Mason, M.A.

I am indebted to Dr. Stoliczka for a very fine living specimen of *Trimeresurus monticola*, which he has just brought to Calcutta. It was caught near a house in Runghby, 5000 feet above the sea, about twelve miles S.E. of Darjeeling. It is a female, beautifully marked with the square dark spots on a sort of cinnamon grey ground. The head is dark, with a peculiar iridescence. The mark well developed. It is twenty-nine inches in length, of which the tail measures three inches, and it is three and a quarter in girth at the thickest part of the body. The eye is very small, with an oval or vertical pupil. The snake is sluggish until disturbed, when it tries to move off rapidly. It does not hiss or show any marked signs of anger; but when taken up by the snake-man, and a Fowl's thigh presented, it bit fiercely. The fangs are long, very mobile, like those of the *Daboia* or *Echis*, but not relatively so long in this individual.

Experiment No. 1.

A Fowl was bitten in the thigh by *Trimeresurus monticola* at 11.25. It bit fiercely, and imbedded its fangs; some of the poison was shed on the limb about the bites. The Fowl on being placed on the ground fell over almost immediately (in thirty seconds), and in a minute lay perfectly paralysed on the ground. 11.32.—Still alive, but lies quite paralysed; breathes deeply. 11.35.—Slightly convulsed. 11.36.—Breathes. 11.42.—No change; still breathes. 11.48.—In the same condition, quite insensible. 11.54.—Breathing more perceptible—deeper. The limb is much ecchymosed and swollen about the bites. 12.3.—Breathing continues as before. 12.12.—Lies perfectly motionless; eyes closed and watering. The breathing is more perceptible. It is evidently not so much affected; raised its head; opened its eyes. When taken up, and the beak placed in water, it drinks. It is still perfectly paralysed, and when placed on the ground lies helpless. 12.25.—Drinks freely when its beak is brought to the water. Opens the eyes. 12.35.—When placed in a bowl of cold water it is roused. 12.47. — Tries to stand; nearly able to do so, but its head falls over. It did not improve further. The following notes were taken: 1.40.—Sluggish. 2.30.—Convulsed. 3.45.—Dead.

The blood removed from the body after death coagulated, but very imperfectly. The limb was deeply ecchymosed and much swollen. The first effects of the injection of the poison were very marked, and the bird fell over as though bitten by the most powerful Cobra or *Daboia*, but this depression did not continue, and from the most extreme state of paralysis it to a great extent recovered. The breathing throughout was regular and deep. The local effects of the wound were very severe; after recovering so far as to be conscious, and nearly able to stand, it got worse again and died at 3.45, or in four hours and twenty minutes.

It is evident from this experiment that the poison is much less deadly than that of the Cobra, *Bungarus*, or Viper. The snake was a very fine one, in perfect health, comparatively fresh, and had not bitten since its capture.

Experiment No. 2.

A small Pariah Dog, quite young, was bitten by the *Trimeresurus* at 11.27 A.M. The snake again bit fiercely, and imbedded its fangs. The Dog on being put down was lame in the bitten leg. 11.32.—Lying down; breathing hurried, the animal evidently in great distress; when made to raise the bitten limb is powerless. 11.38.—Dog lying down; sluggish, but quite conscious. 11.42.—Breathing irregular; when roused walks on three legs, the bitten leg drawn up. 11.52.—The thigh is much swollen and discoloured. The limb seems quite powerless. 12.6.—Is better, walks, and is just able to put the foot to the ground. 12.14.—Improving. He is still very lame and sluggish, though less so than before. 12.19.—Improving. 12.25.—Still drags the leg. 12.55.—Is much better; the constitutional effects of the poison are evidently passing off; but the leg is still swollen and lame.

On the 1st November the Dog was alive and well, but the thigh was swollen, tense, and a dark, almost gangrenous spot, indicated the seat of the *Trimeresurus* bite.

EXPERIMENT No. 3.

A Fowl was bitten in the thigh by the same *Trimeresurus monticola* at 11.36. It became somewhat lame, grew rather sluggish, and the feathers stared, but it soon recovered, and in three hours was quite well.

EXPERIMENT No. 4.

Another Fowl bitten by same snake; again it plunged its fangs deeply, and drew blood. The bird became rather sluggish, somewhat lame, and its feathers staring; but at 12.15 it had quite recovered.

These four experiments sufficiently confirm what has been said of the poison of the *Trimeresurus*, that it is not so deadly as that of the colubrine snakes, or of the *Viperidæ*. They also prove that the snake is rapidly exhausted. The immediate effects of the first bite on a Fowl were very striking, although they did not prove rapidly fatal; each succeeding bite was, however, much less poisonous, and the last seemed hardly to have any effect at all.

The following experiment with the *Echis carinata*, an individual half the size of the *Trimeresurus*, that has been three months or more in captivity, without food, and that has bitten frequently, shows how much greater is the intensity of the one poison than the other:—

EXPERIMENT No. 5.

A Fowl bitten by an *Echis carinata* at 12.1 P.M. in the thigh. 12.2.—The bird has fallen over; limbs paralysed; feathers drooping. 12.3.—Has risen again; stands on one leg, the other drawn up. 12.10.—Fell over; head lies helpless on the ground; violently convulsed. 12.12.—Dead—in eleven minutes.

Blood removed from the body after death formed a very small coagulum, which dissolved again when shaken up with the fluid part. In poisoning by the *Echis* the Fowl does not seem to acquire that drowsy state in which it rests its beak on the ground, nodding its head, and making frequent starts, as when bitten by the Cobra or Krait. It is sluggish and paralysed, then falls into convulsions and dies.

EXPERIMENT No. 6.

A Fowl bitten on the thigh by a *Bungarus cæruleus* at 12.21. The Fowl immediately crouched, and the head fell over, beak resting on the ground. 12.22.—Convulsed. 12.25.—Dead—in four minutes.

The blood, on being removed from the body a few minutes after death, coagulated firmly.

Mr. Richards, of Bancoorah, has kindly made the following experiments at my request:—

EXPERIMENT No. 1.

October 19th.—A Cobra was bitten by another large Cobra of the same kind ("Kála Kurrees") in two places at 11 P.M. Fangs penetrated.

October 28th.—The snake is unaffected.

EXPERIMENT No. 2.

A large Cobra was bitten by a large *Bungarus cæruleus* at 12.53 P.M. on the 19th October. At noon on the 21st October the Cobra died. The death may, however, not be due to the bite, as many of the snakes are dying at present.

EXPERIMENT No. 3.

A *Bungarus cæruleus* was bitten by a Cobra at 12.58, 19th October. No result. The *Bungarus* alive on 28th October.

TWENTY-SEVENTH SERIES.

On certain alleged Antidotes.

The following experiments were performed by Mr. Richards, Civil Surgeon of Bancoorah, in the presence of Dr. Sandiford, of Jamalpore, with the view of testing certain so-called antidotes:—

December 31st, 1870.

EXPERIMENT No. 1.

9.9 A. .—A small Pariah Dog was bitten in the thigh by a Cobra (*Naja tripudians.*) The snake, which had been brought from Bancoorah to Jamalpore, was sickly and about casting its skin. There was the greatest difficulty in making it inflict a bite, which, after all, was a very doubtful one. 9.14.— Administered the antidote according to directions. This Dog did not exhibit any symptom of poisoning; I believe this fact is due to its having been imperfectly bitten.

The antidote is a root, and was sent to Dr. Fayrer by Baboo Antool Kisto Bose, a medical practitioner.

The antidote with which the two following experiments were performed was sent to Dr. Fayrer by Mr. C., of Howrah. The plant (supposed to be a kind of sorrel) was boiled with ginger and water.

EXPERIMENT No. 2.

9.21 A.M.—A half-starved Pariah Dog was bitten by a Krait (*Bungarus cæruleus*); as the bite was a very unsatisfactory one, he was bitten again by another Krait. Neither of the snakes were vigorous. 9.24.—A large dose of the antidote administered. 10 A.M.—Appears pretty well and eats food that is given to him ravenously.

January 1st, 1871, 6 A.M.—Is moving about uneasily and making a whining noise. 12.2 P.M.—Lying helplessly on his side; breathing laboriously; micturition and defecation. 12.4.—Another large dose of the antidote administered. 12.5.—In the same state. Administered more antidote.

January 2nd.—Found dead at 6 A.M. Blood coagulated firmly after death.

EXPERIMENT No. 3.

9.52 A.M.—A Fowl was bitten in the thigh by one of the Kraits used in the foregoing experiment. The bitten part became swollen and œdematous. 9.53.—A large dose of the antidote administered. 10.30.—Appears pretty well. 12.2 P.M.—Convulsed. 12.58.—Dead—in three hours and six minutes.

I attribute the prolongation of life in both the above cases to the sickly condition of the snakes and probably imperfect injection of the poison.

January 2nd, 1871.

EXPERIMENT No. 4.

A Fowl was bitten in the thigh by one of the Kraits used in the above experiments at 10.28 A.M. 10.30.—Administered some of the antidote used in Experiment No. 1. 12.35 P.M.—Appears drowsy; administered more antidote. 12.39.—Hypodermically injected some of the antidote. 12.42.—Convulsed. 12.50.—Dead—in two hours and twenty-two minutes.

These antidotes were spoken of as "infallible cures for snake-bite;" the results of these experiments prove, however, that they are useless.

The following experiments with an antidote sent by R. M. Edwards, Esq., Civil Service Commissioner of Jhansie, to Dr. Fayrer, were made by V. Richards, Esq.:—

In a letter to Dr. Fayrer, Mr. Edwards remarks, "I take the liberty of sending you a specimen of the weed which is known in the North-west by the name of 'Pooreya Paru,' and which I have found wonderfully successful in cases of snake-bite."

The following are the directions as to dose, &c. "The dose is one toloh weight of the powdered weed, ground up with twenty black peppers, mixed in a chitach of water."

September 26th, 1871.

EXPERIMENT No. 5.

At 5.13 P.M. I administered a dose of the antidote, carefully prepared as directed, to a large country Goat. At 5.15 P.M. the Goat was bitten by a Cobra. Appears much irritated by the bite. 5.28.—Appears pretty well. 5.57.—The head begins to droop slightly. 5.59.—Ran about ten yards and then fell down. 6 P.M.—Convulsed; pupils rapidly dilating. 6.6.—Dead—in fifty-one minutes.

EXPERIMENT No. 6.

A small country Goat was bitten by a Cobra at 5.20 P.M. 5.22.—Administered a dose of the antidote. 5.29.—Appears slightly sluggish and is lying down. 5.33.—Convulsed. 5.40.—Dead—in twenty minutes.

EXPERIMENT No. 7.

A middling sized country Goat was bitten by a Cobra at 5.25 P.M. 5.28.—Is feeding. 5.34.—Administered a dose of the antidote. 5.36.—Sluggish; is evidently much affected. 5.40.—Fell over and became convulsed. 5.50.—Pupils widely dilated. 5.52.—Dead—in twenty-seven minutes.

Blood after death coagulated in all three instances.

I am also indebted to my indefatigable friend Mr. Richards, of Bancoorah, for the following report on the trial of an antidote sent to me by Dr. Attygalli from Ceylon. He says its repute is very great in that island. The experiments performed by Mr. Richards place it in the same category with other "certain" antidotes.

Mr. Richards writes :—" This antidote, the recipe of which is a secret, is said to be in great repute in Ceylon, never having been known to fail in a single instance. It was sent from Ceylon by a gentleman who gave the following directions: 'Make an incision at the bitten part and then apply half a pill, previously moistened with human urine; care being taken that the person from whom the urine is obtained is free from venereal disease.' The native gentleman who furnished the antidote further instructs, that 'in hopeless cases it should be administered through the nostrils also with human urine.' "

May 22nd, 1871.

EXPERIMENT No. 8.

A large country Goat was bitten by a Spectacled Cobra (*Naja tripudians*) at 2.47 P.M. The bitten part bled profusely. At 2.50 the bitten part was well incised, and half a pill, which had been previously moistened with urine taken from a healthy person, was carefully inserted into the wound. 3.4.—The animal is sluggish; the antidote does not seem to have much effect. 3.6.—As the case may now be considered "hopeless," the medicine is applied as directed through the nostrils. Convulsed. 3.10.—Dead—in thirty-three minutes.

EXPERIMENT No. 9.

A small country Goat was bitten by the same Cobra at 2.55 P.M. 3.—The bitten part was incised and half a pill, according to the directions, was applied. 3.4.—Is very uneasy. 3.10.—Applied half a pill to the nostrils. 3.12.—Violently convulsed; applied another half of a pill to the nostrils. 3.18.—Dead—in twenty-three minutes.

EXPERIMENT No. 10.

A Fowl was bitten by the same Cobra at 3.5 P.M.; the part was instantly incised and the quarter of a pill previously treated with urine applied. 3.12.—The Fowl is drowsy. 3.45.—Convulsed 3.59.—Dead—in fifty-four minutes. The poison of the Cobra must have been very nearly exhausted.

The blood coagulated soon after death in each instance; the peristaltic action of the intestines continued for some time after the removal of the heart from the two Goats.

These experiments prove that notwithstanding the great reputation of the medicine, and the fact of its composition having been a secret known only to one family for more than 200 years, its antidotal power is simply a myth.

I am indebted to Mr. Richards, of Bancoorah, for the following experiment :—

EXPERIMENT No. 11.

Experiment with an antidote (a nut of some kind) sent to Dr. Fayrer from Singapore. The directions were, "Bruise a nut in cold water, apply externally and give internally." The bruising of the nut was no easy task owing to its being of the consistency of india-rubber. I had to cut the nut into small pieces.

September 14th.—A Dog was bitten by a Cobra at 2.22 P.M. 2.23.—Antidote applied and administered according to the directions. 2.30.—Licking the wound, which bleeds a great deal. 2.45.—Sluggish. 2.57.—Fell over on its side. 2.58.—Is slightly convulsed. 3.—Is most violently convulsed, frothy mucus issuing from the mouth and nostrils. 3.3.—Dead—in forty-one minutes.

Blood fluid, but firmly coagulated in two minutes.

Mr. Richards also performed the following additional experiment of injecting dilute Cobra poison into the left external jugular vein :—

EXPERIMENT No. 12.

The poison of one Cobra was mixed with ten drops of water and injected into the left external jugular vein of a Dog at 3.43 P.M. A ligature had been previously applied on the cardiac side of the vein in order to prevent the entry of the poison into the general circulation. The Dog was sensible and quiet. At 3.44.30 the ligature was loosened; the animal *immediately* began to struggle and whine. 3.45.—Released; the Dog went staggering about with his legs wide apart and his head nearly touching the ground; passes a quantity of urine; retching. 3.46.—Fell over on its side; did not become convulsed. 3.48. — Gasping. 3.49. — Dead—in five minutes from the entry of the poison into general circulation.

The effect of the poison on loosening the ligature was most marked.

The blood was fluid and did not coagulate. (I examined the blood six hours after it was taken from the body, but it was still fluid.) It was at first of a very dark colour, but it afterwards became of a bright red. It will be observed that the blood also remained fluid in other instances in which the poison was injected into a vein.*

The following experiments were made to determine the time in which the Cobra moults and renews its fangs when shed or removed :—

EXPERIMENT No. 13.

A Cobra cast its epidermis on the 15th October, 1870, and was kept in a cage with the view of noting when the next exfoliation would occur; it took place on the 6th November, 1870—*i.e.*, in twenty-two days.

EXPERIMENT No. 14.

The fangs were removed from a large Cobra on the 7th of October, 1870; they were carefully drawn out, the reserve fangs and mucous capsule being uninjured. On the 31st of October, or in twenty-four days, it was observed that there were new fangs anchylosed to the maxillary bones, and quite capable of inflicting a deadly wound.

* See Experiments by Mr. Richards, Nos. 40—43. Twenty-first series, pp. 129, 130.

EXPERIMENT No. 15.

The fangs were removed from a Cobra on the 15th October, 1870; the same precautions were observed as in the former case; new fangs were in their place on the 15th November, or in thirty-one days.

EXPERIMENT No. 16.

The fangs were removed from a Cobra on the 31st of October, 1870; the same precautions were observed—*i.e.*, they were drawn out by a pair of forceps; on the 18th of November new fangs were in their place, small but perfectly effective.

EXPERIMENT No. 17.

The fangs were removed in the same way from a small Cobra on the 31st October. On the 18th November new fangs were in their place, and effective.

Experiments by Mr. Richards, Bancoorah.

October 17th.—Black and white Cobras casting their skins.

November 10th.—Again casting their skins.

December 7th.—Ditto.

October 17th.—*Bungarus cæruleus* ("Krait") casting its skin.

November 17th.—Again casting its skin.

The fangs of a Cobra and those of a Krait were removed on the 19th October, 1870. On the 12th of December they had been replaced by new fangs. A few days previously the new fangs had not appeared.

Mr. Richards says that he finds by experiment that the Cobra changes its epidermis about once a month.

TWENTY-EIGHTH SERIES.

On Ipecacuanha as an Antidote in Snake-Poisoning.

I have received the following quotation* and letter from Professor Sir R. Christison, of Edinburgh:—

"Inter molestias tandem ope radicis [ipecacuanhæ] debellandas acerrima illa ex morsu serpentum venenatorum orta nobis numeranda est. Jam *Piso* magnas ei virtutes tribuit antidotales, quas nos quidem ipsi nunquam experti sumus, sed diversorum dictis comprobatas habemus, qui læsos illius cum aqua tritæ dosi maxima (ad uncias duas usque) uno haustu sumta, copia muci fæcumque incredibili utraque via emittendo, morti ereptos esse prædicaverunt."—P. 8.

"Edinburgh, January 12th, 1871.

"MY DEAR DR. FAYRER,—In the course of a recent literary excursion on the subject of ipecacuanha, I have fallen in with the above statement by an author of the highest authority as a botanical traveller. You will take the statement however not as the scientific estimation of the man would rule, but according to what may be the result of actual trial, should you deem it right that the trial be made. I think it probable you will, although I also think it probable you will consign ipecacuanha to the same destiny to which you have already successfully condemned various myths as to the cure of serpent-bites. I have long and constantly observed that whenever a native remedy for snake-bite has undergone the searching observation of a scientific traveller in the country or district where it was confided in, the remedy proved of no avail. But it may be said of ipecacuanha, that it is by no means, like most reputed antidotes for snake-bite, an inert substance, and the enormous dose which is recommended ought to affect the constitution powerfully one way or another. Orfila could not kill animals with ipecacuanha, because they vomited it, but dogs were killed with doses of its alkaloid — emetia — much under the quantity existing in two ounces of the root.

"Yours,

"R. CHRISTISON."

* Extract from Von Martius' "Specimen Materiæ Medicæ Brasiliensis." Munich: 1824.

With reference to the above, the following experiments were made at my request by Mr. V. Richards, Civil Surgeon, of Bancoorah. They appear tolerably conclusive:—

February 24th, 1870.

EXPERIMENT No. 1.

A middling-sized though full-grown Pariah Dog was bitten in the thigh by a fine fresh spectacled Cobra (*N. tripudians*) at 10.50 A.M. 10.57.—Two drachms of powdered ipecacuanha administered with a great deal of trouble. 11.5—Foaming at the mouth, breathing hard, and is very restless. 11.7.—Becoming sluggish. 11.8.—Two drachms of powdered ipecacuanha administered. 11.10.—Retching most violently; passes fæces of a very black colour. 11·14.—Extremely distressed, cannot stand, and is moaning constantly. 11.17—Dyspnœa. The animal appears perfectly exhausted. 11.18.—Convulsed. 11.26.—Died—in thirty-six minutes.

The ipecacuanha had not the slightest antidotal effect, but, on the contrary, apparently hastened death by its depressing influence.

EXPERIMENT No. 2.

A small Pariah Dog was bitten by the same Cobra at 10.59 A.M. 11.3. — One drachm of powdered ipecacuanha administered. 11.6.—Foaming at the mouth. 11.16—Sluggish, and is lying down. 11.19.—One drachm of powdered ipecacuanha administered. 11.20.—Passes fæces of a blackish colour, but is not purged. 11.22.—Appears very much exhausted, and is lying down. Dyspnœa extreme. 11.27.—I was about to administer another dose of the ipecacuanha when the Dog became convulsed. 11.30.—Died—in thirty-one minutes.

In this instance there was no retching. The ipecacuanha apparently had not the slightest antidotal influence. Prostration was extreme from 11.22.

The blood in both instances as usual coagulated firmly after withdrawal from the body.

February 25th.

EXPERIMENT No. 3.

An Ox was bitten by the Cobra used in the two foregoing experiments at 2.16 P.M.

The wound bled a great deal, but I noticed some of the poison was left on the skin near the wound. I believe the bite was a doubtful one. 2.25.—One ounce of powdered ipecacuanha administered. 2.29.—Is standing up and grazing; defecated; fæces normal. 3.20. — Apparently slightly affected; one ounce of powdered ipecacuanha administered. 3.34.—In the same state. 3.45.—Is up and grazing. 4.30.—In the same state; one ounce of powdered ipecacuanha administered. 4.40.—Bitten again by the same Cobra. The snake held on most tenaciously for some time. The poison must nearly be exhausted. 4.55.—Half an ounce of powdered ipecacuanha administered. 5.54.—Appears pretty well. Half an ounce of powdered ipecacuanha administered.

February 26th, 8 A.M.—Appears pretty well, and is grazing. 2.20 P.M.—One ounce of powdered ipecacuanha again administered.

This makes five ounces and a half of ipecacuanha the animal has taken in the twenty-four hours. There is neither vomiting nor purging, but some amount of salivation.

February 27th, 8 A.M.—There does not appear to be much the matter with the animal, for he is up and grazing; defecated; fæces very black. 1 P.M.—Appears to be affected by the poison; endeavoured to get up but fell over on his side, in which position he remains; one ounce of powdered ipecacuanha administered. 1.30 P.M.—Still lying on his side, and appears very sluggish; temperature 100°·7 2 P.M.—Convulsed. 2.50.—Breathing very rapidly; temperature 103°·3.—3.25.—Dead—in forty-nine hours nine minutes.

This experiment proves most conclusively that ipecacuanha is not of the slightest use, for had it possessed any antidotal power it must have been made manifest in this instance, where a large animal was not only operated on, but much of the venomous power of the snake must have been expended in biting the two Dogs.

TWENTY-NINTH SERIES.

Experiments on the immediate Application of a mixture of two parts of Carbolic Acid with one of Alcohol, and on the injection of Quinine into a Vein, in the Treatment of Snake-poisoning.

August 24th, 1871.

EXPERIMENT No. 1.

A Pariah Dog was bitten by a Cobra at 3 P.M. A mixture of two parts of carbolic acid and one of alcohol was at once rubbed into the bitten part, and to insure its being well applied the fang punctures were cut through, and more carbolic acid applied.

3.13 P.M.—Is whining and restless, trying to get away; Breathing very rapidly; is evidently affected. 3.30.—Is very sluggish. 3.35.—Convulsed. 3.45.—Convulsions increasing. 3.50.—Dead—in fifty minutes.

August 25th.

EXPERIMENT No. 2.

A large but weak Pariah Dog was bitten by a Cobra, one that had been used on the 24th, at 3.37 P.M.

The mixture of carbolic acid and spirit was immediately applied, and well rubbed in. The bitten part was also well scarified, and the carbolic acid again frequently applied.

3.40 P.M.—Appears restless. 4.48.—Became very drowsy; salivated; retching constantly. 5.25.—Convulsed; the convulsions became very severe. 5.27.—Defecation natural; micturition. 5.29.—Gasping. 5.30.—Dead—in one hour and fifty-three minutes.

EXPERIMENT No. 3.

A very large and strong Pariah Dog was bitten by a small Cobra at 3.46 P.M. The mixture of carbolic acid and alcohol was immediately thoroughly applied. About five drops of the mixture was also hypodermically, near the bite, injected.

No symptoms appeared up to 5.15 P.M., when the Dog became slightly drowsy. I attribute this to the small size of the Cobra on the one hand, and the strength and size of the Dog on the other.

6.50 P.M.—Is lying down and vomiting most violently. It has been vomiting for the past half-hour. 7.15.—Is retching most violently. 9.—Is very much exhausted. 10.—Is convulsed.

This Dog died during the night, probably about 12—eight hours and fourteen minutes after being bitten.

EXPERIMENT No. 4.

A small Pariah Bitch was bitten by a Cobra at 3.53 P.M. The mixture of carbolic acid and alcohol was thoroughly applied at once.

3.59 P.M.—Became drowsy, and then convulsed. 4.8.—Vomiting violently. 4.15.—Has been vomiting constantly a white frothy mucus. 4.30.—Breathing laboriously. 4.40.—Convulsions very severe. 4.54.—Dead—in one hour and one minute.

I am indebted to Mr. V. Richards for the following Experiments, made to ascertain the value of the injection of quinine into a vein in the treatment of Snake-poisoning.

August 24th, 1871.

EXPERIMENT No. 5.

A Pariah Dog was bitten by a Cobra at 1.14 P.M.

1.23 P.M.—Ten grains of quinine made into a solution with very dilute sulphuric acid was injected into the right femoral vein.

1.30 P.M.—Is lying down; the head jactitates at intervals, but the animal is sensible. 1.33.—Convulsed; defecated. 1.35.—Dead—in twenty-one minutes.

EXPERIMENT No. 6.

When the Dog was bitten it died so rapidly that there was no time to do anything.

EXPERIMENT No. 7.

Another Pariah Dog was bitten by a Cobra at 1.53 P.M.

2.5 P.M.—Injected a fifteen-grain solution of quinine into the left femoral vein. 2.10.—Vomiting and purging most violently. 2.15. — Is restless. 2.20.—Constantly retching 2.25—Vomiting. 2.27.—Is extremely restless, and breathing laboriously. 2.30.—Is lying down; salivation. 2 35.—Convulsed. 2.45.—Dead—in fifty-two minutes.

EXPERIMENT No. 8.

A Pariah Dog was bitten by a Cobra at 2.35 P.M. 2.40.—Injected a seven-grain solution of quinine into the right femoral vein.

2.53.—Breathing rapidly, and is salivated. 2.56.—Defecation. 3.—Vomited; very much salivated. 3.2—Is very restless. 3.5.—Has just fallen over, and is convulsed. 3.10.—Is still convulsed, and breathing laboriously. 3.21.—Dead—in forty-six minutes.

August 25th.

EXPERIMENT No. 9.

A strong healthy Pariah Dog was bitten by the Cobra used in Experiment No. 2 of yesterday, at 3.20 P.M.

3.28.—A twenty-grain solution of quinine was injected into the left femoral vein. 3.30.—Foaming at the mouth. Defecation and micturition. Quickly became convulsed. 3.34.—Dead—in fourteen minutes.

It will be observed by the foregoing experiments that the injection of quinine into a vein for snake-bite is useless.

The snake used in this experiment was a remarkably deadly one, its poison was very active.

APPENDIX.

No. I.

The Inspector-General has recently issued the following circular to all Deputy Inspectors-General of Hospitals, dated Fort William, November 22nd, 1869:—

The Inspector-General of Hospitals is desirous that the observations on snake-poison, which Dr. Fayrer has hitherto been engaged in, should be extended throughout the Presidency, and he now asks medical officers to render any assistance in their power for the fulfilment of the object. The Inspector-General believes that very useful and practical results will accrue from the scientific investigations which Dr. Fayrer is still prosecuting; researches which may lead to a complete knowledge of the subject, and which must prove of service to the population of the country.

2. The Inspector-General therefore requests you will be so good as to supply each medical officer in your circle, of whatever grade, with a copy of this memorandum, and to enlist their exertions on the subject.

3. Medical officers are requested to submit to you, as soon as practicable after January 1st, 1870, a return of all authenticated cases of snake-bite that occurred among the civil and military population under their cognizance, during the year 1869 (from January 1st, 1870, to the end of the year: cases as they occur are to be recorded monthly).

6. Particular attention should be paid to the detail of symptoms after a bite, the duration of life, and the pathological symptoms after death; noting particularly the absence or presence of the rigor mortis, the state of the blood, microscopically if practicable, and its fluidity or coagulability, the treatment pursued, and any remarks to elucidate the recorded conditions.

7. The bodies of persons who have died from snake-bites are frequently sent by the police, or judicial authorities, to the civil medical officer for examination. It is particularly requested that careful accounts of all such autopsies may be sent in with the printed form; and that in making the examination, medical officers will be kind enough to note *particularly* the conditions to be attended to in paragraph 6, as well as any other pathological condition that may be observed. The local effects of the bite, the position of the fang punctures, and the state of the parts in the vicinity of the bite, as well as remote from it, should be accurately recorded.

8. Particular attention is also requested to any difference in symptoms and pathological states in the cases of bites of the *Viperidæ*—*i.e.*, the Russell's Viper, or *Daboia*, and the *Trimeresurus*, as distinguished from those of the poisonous colubrine snakes, such as the *Naja tripudians*, or Cobra, *Ophiophagus elaps*, or "Sunkerchor," and all of the less poisonous *Bungarus* family, as *B. cæruleus*, or Krait, and *B. fasciatus*, or "Sankni."

Note.—A list of the poisonous snakes of Hindoostan is appended.

Snakes most commonly met with have ** prefixed; those less so *; the remainder are comparatively rare.

Sub-Order, Poisonous Colubrine Snakes.

Family of Elapidæ.

Genus ** 1. Naja: *N. tripudians*, or Cobra: several varieties. Native names "Keautiah," "Gokurrah," &c.

„ * 2. Ophiophagus: *O. elaps, Hamadryas:* one species. From Assam to west bank of Hooghly. Native name "Sunkerchor."

„ ** 3. Bungarus: *B. cæruleus*, or Krait. From Calcutta to Delhi.

** *B. fasciatus*, or "Sankni" (marked with black and yellow bands. Bengal generally.)

„ 4. Xenurelaps: *X. bungaroides.* Found about Chirra Punji. Very rare.

Genus ** 5. Callophis: *C. intestinalis.*
C. maclellandii. Found in Central India.
C. nigrescens. Found in the Nilgherries.
C. annularis. India generally.

Family of Hydrophidæ or Sea Snakes.

Genus 1. Platurus: *P. scutatus.* Found on the coast from Chittagong to Madras.
P. fischeri. Found on the coast from Chittagong to Madras.

„ * 2. Hydrophis: Several varieties found on the coast.
H. cyanocincta.
H. robusta.
H. coronata.
H. stricticollis.
H. chloris.
H. gracilis.
H. curta.
H. jerdonii, and others.

„ * 3. Enhydrina: *E. bengalensis.* Botanic Garden, Dhappa Canal.

„ * 4. Pelamis: *P. bicolor.* On the coast, Pooree.

Sub-Order, Viperine Snakes.

Family of Pit Vipers or Crotalidæ.

Genus 1. Trimeresurus: * *T. gramineus.* Found in Bengal; has been found at Dhappa Canal.
* *T. erythrurus.* Found in Bengal.
* *T. carinatus.* Ditto.
* *T. anamallensis.* Ditto.
* *T. monticola.* Mostly found in the Himalaya or Khasya Hills.
T. strigatus. Ditto.
T. mucrosquamatus. Ditto.
T. andersonii. Ditto.

„ 2. Peltopelor: *P. macrolepis.* Found in the Anamallay Mountains.

„ * 3. Halys: *H. himalayanus.*

„ 4. Hypnale: *H. nepa*, or *Carawilla.* Found in Southern India.

Family of Vipers or Viperidæ.

Genus 1. Daboia: ** *D. russellii*, the Chain Viper. Native name "Bora Siah Chunder." Found all over Bengal, from Southern India to the Himalaya as high as 5000 feet above the sea.

„ ** 2. Echis: *E. carinata.* Found in the Anamallay Mountains, Carnatic, Scinde, the N.W., and other parts of India.

No. II.

On January 3rd, 1870, I addressed the following letter to the secretaries or political agents of the following governments:—

Bengal,	Central Provinces,
North-West Provinces,	Central India,
Punjab,	Rajpootana,
Oude,	British Burmah,

soliciting information on the subject of loss of life from snake-poisoning in their territories:—

Sir,—Being engaged in an inquiry into the subject of snake-bites in this country, in the hope that, with other information of a scientific character, something may be elicited that shall tend to diminish the present great mortality from this cause, I shall feel greatly obliged if you will assist me by obtaining from all magistrates, district officers, medical officers, or others under Government, who may be able to furnish the information, a return showing the number of deaths that have occurred in their districts, from January 1st to December 31st, 1869, from snake-bites, giving the age, sex, occupation, and residence of those who have suffered, with the name of the snake, when procurable, by which the bite was inflicted.

I have, &c., &c.,

(Signed) J. FAYRER.

RETURN showing the number of Deaths and Recoveries from Snake-bites in

NAMES.	Caste.	Race.	Occupation.	Sex.	Age.	Hour and date when bitten.	Native, English, and technical name of the Snake, and general description of the circumstances under which the bite occurred.	District, village, or locality where bitten.	Symptoms.	Treatment, if any.	Date of death.	Date of recovery.	Number of minutes or hours ill.	State of lungs after death.	State of heart and great vessels after death.	State of abdominal viscera after death.	State of blood after death.	State of brain and nervous system.	Cadaveric rigidity when occurred.	REMARKS.

No. III.

NOTE ON THE USE OF SNAKE-POISON IN MEDICINE, BY THE KABIRÁJES OF BENGAL.

I am indebted to Baboo Amirto Lal Mozumdar, a student of the Medical College, for the following information obtained from Baboo Gunga Persad Sen, one of the most learned Kabirájes of Calcutta, on the use, by them, of snake-poison in medicine. It is used in the Bish Badi, to a considerable extent, by these practitioners, who have much faith in its efficacy.

The poison which is commonly used for medicinal purposes by the Kobirájes is taken from the "Keautiah." It is not taken from the "Gokurrah" (Spectacled Cobra), Sunkerchor, Sankni, or the Viper (Borá), as these are not easily available, and their poison is said to be extremely acute.

Modes of obtaining the Poison.—1st, The snake is irritated and made to bite an object; a vessel attached to a long stick, held ready, is presented underneath its jaws, so that the poison discharged falls into the vessel.

2nd, The snake is introduced into an earthen pot, in which are kept two or three green plantains, the opening of the pot being covered by an earthen plate. By the application of heat below the vessel, the snake becomes furious and bites the plantains into which the poison is discharged. The part of the plantain into which the poison enters turns black, the black part is taken, dried, reduced to powder, purified, and used in medicine.

Of the two modes of obtaining poison, the last is the least dangerous and more convenient.

The poison thus obtained is impregnated with saliva and other impurities; it is not advisable to use it in this state, for thus taken it is said to be irritant, warm, sharp, penetrating, and prompt in its action beyond all description: it likewise produces considerable derangement of the nervous and digestive systems. Hence, when inconsiderately administered, in an impurified state, it creates nervous irritability, disordered circulation, hepatic derangement, stupor, and weakness of the joints. For this reason learned practitioners of ancient times used to purify snake poison by mixing it with the juice of neem leaves and lime-juice, because neem leaves are bitter and lime-juice is refrigerant, and also because they tend in a great degree to lessen the bad effects of snake poison.

Mode of purifying and preserving the Poison.—The poison obtained by the above-mentioned methods is mixed with a quantity of lime-juice and the juice of neem leaves, and dried. The residue is again mixed with a quantity of lime-juice and juice of neem leaves, and dried. This process is repeated five times.

Physiological Action.—It is warm, irritant stimulating, a promoter of the virtues of other medicines, anti-spasmodic, digestive, a promoter of the action of the secreting organs.

Therapeutical Action.—Used in the latter stage of low forms of fever when other remedies fail, it accelerates the heart's action, and diffuses warmth over the general surface; clears the mind if coma supervene. In the collapsed state of cholera, it is successfully used. It is employed in dysentery and some complicated diseases. Used in epilepsy arising from cold, relieving the patient from insensibility and forgetfulness, symptomatic of that disease. Some practitioners have written that snake poison is used as an antidote in cases of snake-bite when the body is cold and the heart's action is scarcely perceptible. Used in such a state it accelerates the heart's action and causes a flow of blood to the distant capillaries in which circulation has ceased, and diffuses warmth over the general surface. Subsequently antidotes are used which circulating with the blood are diffused over the whole system. Antidotes, unless mixed with the snake poison, cannot be introduced into the system by reason of the cessation of circulation. Moreover, snake poison is the only medicine that can produce instantaneous effects on the whole system. For this reason also antidotes are mixed with snake poison. But I (says the Kabirája) am not of that opinion, I rather believe that certain vegetable and mineral poisons are proper antidotes to snake poison and *vice versá*, because snake poison causes determination of blood to the brain, and thereby affects the nervous system; whereas the mineral and vegetable substances used as antidotes mostly cause determination of blood to the alimentary canal, and thereby change the position of the congestion from the brain to the alimentary canal.

Charaka and other sages have treated on this subject. The Áyurvéda, our standard books on medical science, do not describe any principles or any case from which we can ascertain that snake poison alone has ever been used. So that I do not think it necessary to mention its dose, or the circumstances in which this poison can alone be administered.

The Bish Badis in general use among the Kabirájes are chiefly of three kinds. These are:—

1. Súchikábharana, सूचिकाभरण
2. Aghora nrisinha-rasa, अघोरनृसिंहरस
3. Pratápa-lankeshvara, प्रताप लङ्केश्वर

1. *Súchikábharana.*

This is prepared in two ways:—

First:

(कज्जली) *Kajjalí* (a sort of black sulphuretted mercury) . 2 parts.
(सीस भस्म) *Sísa-bhasma* (burnt oxidized lead) . . . . 1 part.
(विष) *Bisha* (aconite) . . . . 1 „
(सर्पविष) *Sarpa-bisha* (snake poison) . . . . 1 „

These four ingredients are to be reduced to powder and mixed, and then to be subjected to what is called the *bhávaná* (भावना), a process in which the powder is to be repeatedly mixed and pounded with certain liquid substances and exposed to the influence of the sun and thus dried.

This preparation is thus to be treated with:—

First:

[रोहित] मत्स्य पित्त Fish gall (of the *Cyprinus rohita*) . 7 times.
छाग पित्त Goat's bile . . . . „
मयूर पित्त Peacock's bile . . . . „
शूकर पित्त Wild boar's bile . . . . „

Second method of preparation.

रस Mercury . . . . 1 part.
सर्प विष Snake poison . . . . 2 parts.

These are to be mixed together and evaporated in a retort: and the vapour is collected in a receiver, which vapour is kept for use in stoppered phials. This is only used hypodermically through the centre of the scalp, in epilepsy and snake-bite.

2. *Aghora-nrisinha-rasa.*

कज्जली Sulphuretted mercury . . . . . . 2 parts.
ताम्र भस्म Burnt copper (oxidized) . . . . . 1 part.
लौह भस्म Burnt iron (oxidized) . . . . . . 2 parts.
वङ्ग भस्म Burnt tin (oxidized) . . . . 3 „
अभ्र भस्म Burnt mica . . . . 4 „
शोधित मनःशिला Purified red arsenic . . . . 1 part.
स्वर्ण माक्षिक *Svarna-mákshika* (a preparation of gold and mercury with sulphur, &c.) . . . . . 1 part.

सर्पविष Snake poison . . . . 4 parts.
त्रिकटु Three pungents (ginger, long, and black pepper) . . . . 4 „
कालकूट विष Aconite . . . . 46 „

These pounded and mixed together are then subjected to the *bhávaná*, with the following substances:—

मत्स्य पित्त Fish bile . . . . 7 times.
छाग पित्त Goat's bile . . . . „
महिष पित्त Buffalo's bile . . . . times.
मयूर पित्त Peacock's bile . . . . . . „
रक्त चित्रा *Rakta-chitrá* . . . . „
शूकर पित्त Boar's bile . . . . „

Pratápa-lankeshvara.

Sulphuretted mercury . . . . 2 parts.
Burnt mica . . . . 1 part.
Vermilion . . . . „
विष Aconite . . . . „
Borax . . . . „
ताम्र भस्म Burnt copper . . . . „
लौह भस्म Burnt iron . . . . „
वङ्ग भस्म Burnt tin . . . . „
Liquorice . . . . „
बला *Balá*, root and stem of the *Sida cordifolia* . . . . „
मुथा *Muthá*, the tubers of the *Cyperus hexastachyus* . . . . „
रेणुका *Rénuká* (an aromatic seed like pepper) „
गुग्गुल *Guggula*, the resin of the *Balsamodendron agalocha* . . . . „
मनःशिला Red arsenic . . . . „
सर्पविष Snake poison . . . . „
नागकेशर Flowers of the *Mesua ferrea* . . „

These, reduced into fine powder and mixed, are then subjected to the *bhávaná*, with the following substances:—

त्रिकटु क्वाथ Decoction of the three pungents . . 7 times.
धत्तूर रस Juice of *Datura stramonium* . . . . „
भङ्गरस Juice of the *Cannabis Indica* . . . . „
रक्तचित्रा Juice of the *Rakta-chitrá* . . . . . „
ज्वालामुखी Juice of the *Jválámukhí* . . . . „
पुनर्नव रस Juice of the *Punarnava* (*Boerhaavia erecta*) . . . . „
मत्स्य पित्त Fish bile . . . . „
Goat's bile . . . . „
Boar's bile . . . . „
Buffalo's bile . . . . „
Peacock's bile . . . . „

No. IV.

NOTE ON THE SO-CALLED SNAKE-CHARMERS OF BENGAL.

"In Bengal we have four different classes of men who deal in snakes. The first, and by far the most expert among them, is the Mál—a low caste Hindoo, who earns his livelihood by catching and exhibiting snakes and selling simples in the bazaar, but never professes witchcraft, jugglery, or the healing art. Men of this class are certainly very poor and have to lead a vagrant life; but I have never heard that they are much given to thieving. In the North-Western Provinces they are replaced by Modaris, a few of whom occasionally come to Calcutta to ply their vocation. I have never had an opportunity of studying them carefully, and cannot therefore say anything about them. Apparently, however, they seem to have been confounded with the Bediyás or gipsies of Bengal. The latter are jugglers, bear and monkey dancers, sellers of simples, fortune-tellers, reputed adepts in curing rheumatism, gout, toothache, and other complaints; professors of witchcraft, experts in cupping, applying moxas and actual cautery, as well as snake-charmers. In fact they take to whatever comes in their way to protect themselves from being taken up by the police as thieves, for thieves they are of the most inveterate type. Some time ago I put a few notes together about them, and if you feel curious about the race, you will find them in the Transactions of the Anthropological Society of London. As snake-charmers these people are by no means successful or noted. They differ from the Mál in taking their women to join in their profession, which the Máls never do. I have never seen a Mál woman.

"The Sáñyis are known in Bengal by the name of *tubriwallahs*. I am not aware of where their head-quarters are, but there is no doubt that they come to Bengal from the north-west. They are always dressed in yellow clothes and a large turban, and have a double pipe mounted on a gourd shell—the *tubri*—with the music of which they pretend to charm and draw out snakes from holes and cracks—not unoften from the bedding—in the houses of the persons who employ them. For this purpose they carry about several snakes on their person, hidden under the folds of their flowing garment; but openly they show only a few or none. As professed vagrants they may purloin whatever falls in their way, but they are by no means notorious as thieves. They may be seen everywhere in the north-west, and I believe (though I cannot speak from personal knowledge) also in Southern India. I have met with notices of them in old Sanskrit books, and it is probable that as a class they have existed in India from a very early age. Their pipe is peculiar to them; it is never used by the Máls, the Modaris, and the Bediyás for charming snakes, nor by any of the Indian races for musical entertainment.

(Signed) "RAJENDRALALA MITRA."

I am indebted for the above note to Babu Rajendralala Mitra, Vice-President of the Asiatic Society of Bengal.

The snake-charmers handle poisonous snakes freely and without fear even when in possession of their fangs. The Cobras are their favourites, and occasionally the *Ophiophagus*, as these snakes present a very striking appearance when they crest their heads and dilate their hoods. Those they exhibit generally have the fangs removed. This is done by cutting out their teeth, and with them the mucous capsule with the reserve fangs. They are exceedingly dexterous, and the sleight of hand with which they appear to catch a snake in any patch of grass, or even from the ground, is such as to deceive the closest observer. The snake is, of course, concealed about the person, but is with great rapidity and dexterity placed in the secluded spot and as quickly abstracted. They are well aware of the danger, and know perfectly well that no antidote has any effect, though they pretend to prevent or cure bites by roots and snake-stones. With the venomous they exhibit innocent snakes, such as the *Chrysopelea*, the *Passerita mycterizans*, *Ptyas mucosus*, and *Erix johnii*, and their exhibition is always accompanied by the music of a rude pipe made of a gourd.

No. V.

ON THE DISTRIBUTION OF THE INDIAN THANATOPHIDIA.

I am indebted to my friends Mr. W. T. Blanford, and Dr. F. Stoliczka of the Geological Survey of India, for the following memoranda on the distribution of the Indian Thanatophidia:—

"*Naja tripudians.*—I have only seen the spectacled form in Central India. I cannot positively state that the ocellus form is not found, but if so it must be rare.

"*Ophiophagus elaps.*—This is common, or at any rate not rare in Pegu. I never heard of it in India Proper, and it is probably confined to the base of the Himalayas and the Hills near the western coast, with perhaps the northern part of the coast on the west side of the Bay of Bengal, that is to say, Orissa and the Northern Circars. This distribution—*i.e.*, Malabar and Bengal with Orissa, is common to several animals with Malay affinities.

"Of the other *Elapidæ* and of the *Hydrophidæ* I know nothing with regard to their distribution. The *Crotalidæ* are quite Malay, having American affinities, and, so far as I know, none occur in India elsewhere than in Malabar (including the Hills, Nilgherries, Anamalays, and the whole line of Western Ghats), Bengal, and Orissa, and in the Himalayas. They may also be found on some of the higher hill groups scattered over Southern India, such as the Shevaroys.

"In the Punjab, North-western Provinces, Central Provinces, Deccan, and the Carnatic, I doubt their being met with.

"On the other hand, the *Viperidæ*, which are African in their affinities, and no one of which extends into the Malay countries, inhabit precisely those regions in which *Trimeresurus* and its allies are not found. *Echis* is, I believe, more confined in its range than *Daboia russellii*, the latter extending into Burmah. Here on the Godavery, I have found both, and rather to my surprise I have met with *Echis* in forest.

"I should mention that I once saw a *Trimeresurus* in Orissa.

(Signed) "W. T. BLANFORD."

"*N. tripudians.*—India generally, and Burmah. I have seen it as far west as the Sutlej valley, and up to elevations of 6000 feet, but I know nothing of its occurrence in the Punjab, never having been in that Province. It occurs on the Andamans, but is not known on the Nicobars.

"*Ophiophagus elaps* appears to be purely or chiefly characteristic of the Malayan fauna. Never heard of it in the North-west.

"*Bungarus cœruleus* appears to be India generally; it is found in the N.W., and also in Central Provinces.

"*Callophis intestinalis* occurs in Burmah, and *C. maculiceps* also.

"Of *Hydrophidæ* I got no information lately. The only species I got are *Platurus laticaudatus* and *P. fischeri* from the Nicobars, so there can be no doubt of their occurring at these islands.

"*Trimeresurus gramineus* is chiefly, I believe, a Malay fauna snake I doubt whether it occurs in Ladak, as has been stated, if Ladak means the country north of the principal range of the N.W. Himalayas, and this is what it should be taken for.

"The differences of *T. cantoris* and *porphyraceus* (Blyth), I have pointed out in my paper.

"*T. mutabilis* from Nicobar and Andamans, and *T. convictus* from Penang, have to be added to Günther's list.

"Anderson has, I think, two new species from Burmah, but I did not publish his names in the journal, because he did not give a description with the names.

"*T. andersonii*, with which *obscurus* of Theobald is undoubtedly identical, I have lately received from the Andamans, and this settles the locality of the species. I think I told you before that I suspect the species to be from Assam, its locality was unknown. Nearly all the *Trimeresuri* are characteristic of the Malay fauna. I did not hear of a single one west of the Sutlej valley, nor in Central India. In Southern India they only occur in the higher hills, which all possess Malay types.

"The *Viperidæ* are, on the contrary, Indian (or say African type) fauna, which extends through Persia and Arabia to the Mediterranean. *Daboia russellii* was also obtained in Upper Burmah.

"You know probably that *E. carinata* was also got in Western Bengal (Singhboom).

(Signed) "F. S. Stolickza."

No. VI.

NOTE FROM DR. KING, BOTANIC GARDEN, ON THE JHANSIE AND SINGAPORE ANTIDOTES.

Botanic Garden, September 29th, 1871.

"My dear Fayrer,—From its structure the root appears to belong to a plant of the Nat. Ord. *Menispermaceæ*, and is probably that of *Cissampelos convolvulacea*, a climbing plant common in the jungles in the Gwalior territory, and in Upper India generally during the rains. But I cannot say for certain.

"The nut I can make nothing of, nor can Kurz, who spent many years in Java and the Straits. It apparently is a seed that has been packed with many others in a big capsule with probably pulp between. I return all the specimens, as you may want them. If you can spare any, however, I should like to keep them beside me, and some day I may find a clue. A section of the nut, by the way, shows under the microscope a lovely specimen of regularly formed cells.

"Yours very truly,
"J. King."

No. VII.

ON THE CHEMICAL CONSTITUTION OF THE COBRA POISON.

The following report on the chemical characters presented by specimens of Cobra poison has been furnished by Dr. Henry E. Armstrong:—

"London Institution, Finsbury Circus, E.C., November 14th, 1871.

"Sir,—I beg to submit to you the following account of the results I have obtained in the examination of the Cobra poison which you placed in my hands.

"On opening the small bottles containing the poison, which was in the form of a dirty-brown, somewhat syrupy fluid, a considerable quantity of gas escaped; this was recognised as carbonic anhydride, and is no doubt a product of partial decomposition of the poison; the liquid in the bottles, which smelt most horribly, had a faintly acid reaction.

"Inasmuch as it was highly probable that the amount of poisonous principle in the crude poison was small, and that unless large quantities of material could be operated upon it would be impossible to isolate it in the pure state, although the poison at my disposal was from a large number of Cobras, it was manifestly too small in quantity to afford much hope that the attempt would be successful, especially as I was obliged from the beginning to confine myself almost entirely to a micro-chemical examination.

"The following observations were made:—On heating the liquid was partially coagulated; mineral acids produced a gelatinous precipitate; absolute alcohol threw down a voluminous white gelatinous precipitate; a drop evaporated with a little sulphate of copper solution, and then treated with caustic potash solution, gave a violet coloration. From these observations it was evident that the chief constituent of the liquid poison was an *albuminoid* body.

A number of experiments with various solvents, alcohol, ether, bisulphide of carbon, both in acid and alkaline solution, and careful examination by the microscope of the residues left on evaporation of the various solutions having shown the impossibility of isolating any crystalline body, I determined on analysing A, the crude poison; B, the precipitate thrown down on the addition of alcohol; C, the residue left on evaporation of the alcoholic filtrate from B.

"A. The crude poison evaporated over sulphuric acid *in vacuo* left a grey friable mass, which on analysis was found to contain 43·55 per cent. of carbon and 13·43 per cent. of nitrogen.

"B. The liquid poison was first carefully filtered to remove traces of sediment and suspended matter, and then mixed with a considerable quantity of anhydrous alcohol, the white precipitate so produced filtered off, washed with alcohol, and dried over sulphuric acid *in vacuo*. A pale-brown brittle mass was thus obtained, which could be readily powdered. On igniting a small portion on platinum foil a slight mineral residue remained.

"Exp. I.—The carbon and nitrogen were determined simultaneously by combustion with oxide of copper and analysis of the gases obtained. This gave 45·3 per cent. of carbon, and 14·7 per cent. of nitrogen.

"Exp. II.—Duplicate of I., but with substance of a different preparation. This gave 46·0 per cent. of carbon, and 13·9 per cent. of nitrogen.

"Exp. III.—A determination of carbon and hydrogen in the ordinary manner by combustion with oxide of copper, &c. This gave 46·0 per cent. of carbon, and 6·6 per cent. of hydrogen.

"Exp. IV.—A determination of sulphur by heating with a small quantity of pure nitric acid in a sealed tube to 200° C., and precipitation as baric sulphate. This gave 2·5 per cent. of sulphur.

"C. The alcoholic filtrate from B, left on evaporation over sulphuric acid *in vacuo* a pale brown friable mass, which was found to contain 43·04 per cent. of carbon, 12·45 per cent. of nitrogen, and 7·0 per cent. of hydrogen.

	A.	B.*	C.	Albumen.†
Carbon	43·55	45·76	43·04	53·5
Nitrogen	13·30	14·30	12·45	15·7
Hydrogen	—	6·60	7·00	7·1
Sulphur	—	2·5		
Ash constituents				

"It is to be noted that A was not poison from the same bottles as B and C. With the exception of B III., the analyses were all made by combustion *in vacuo* with help of the Sprengel pump, which is the only method which allows the simultaneous determination of carbon and hydrogen, and on quantities of about thirty milligrammes. The ordinary methods were not available on account of the small quantity of material. When it is considered that an error in weighing of one-tenth of a milligramme on the small quantities that were used in the determinations would give rise to an error of from one to two per cent. in the final result, I believe the above results tend to show that there is little difference in composition between the crude poison, the precipitate thrown down by alcohol, and the portion soluble in alcohol. The very fact, however, that B and C are respectively insoluble and soluble in alcohol, proves they are of different nature, and renders it necessary that these two products should be carefully examined as to their physiological action.

"I am, Sir, yours obediently,
"Henry E. Armstrong."

"Dr. Fayrer, M.D., &c."

No. VIII.

EXPERIMENTS ON THE ACTIVITY OF THE COBRA POISON AND ITS ALCOHOLIC EXTRACT.

By T. Lauder Brunton, M.D., D.Sc., Joint Lecturer on Materia Medica and Therapeutics, and Casualty Physician at St. Bartholomew's Hospital.

The following experiments were made in order to test the activity of the Cobra poison sent to this country, and of the alcoholic extract obtained from it:—

They show 1st. That the poison retained its activity although it had been kept for some time. 2nd. That its activity is not destroyed by drying. 3rd. That the alcoholic extract resembles the poison itself in its activity, and in the symptoms it produces.

Beyond drawing attention to the extravasations of blood observed at the point where the poison was injected, and to the long continuance of the cardiac pulsations after the death of the animal, I will say

* Mean of I. II. III.

† The numbers under this heading are about the mean of various analyses of albumen.—*Watts' Dictionary of Chemistry*, i. 67.

nothing regarding the mode of action of the poison, as it is of great importance that this be ascertained with the utmost exactitude, and the pressure of other engagements has prevented me from performing a sufficient number of experiments for this purpose.

Experiment No. 1.

Two drops of Cobra poison were injected under the skin of the thigh of a Guinea Pig. One or two minutes after the injection the legs of the animal began to twitch. Covered it by a bell jar. 6′ after injection.—Legs again twitching. 7.′ — Respiration deeper than usual. 9′.—Again twitching. 10′.—The animal is restless; moves round and round inside the bell jar; grunts occasionally, and makes a motion as if chewing. Hind-quarters are twitching up and its nose at the same time is drawn in towards the chin. 13′.—Bites at the spot where the injection was made; passes water. 22′.—It can no longer walk. 23′.—It lies flat on the table, and leans rather to one side; respirations deep; occasional twitches of the legs. 25′.—Cornea sensitive; occasional convulsive stretches. 27′.—Cornea almost insensible; respiratory movement of nostrils continues. 28′.—Cornea completely insensible.

Post-mortem examination made immediately. The muscles of the abdomen were dark-coloured. Peristaltic movements of the intestines occurred when the abdomen was opened. The heart was dark and slightly dilated. All its cavities were contracting, though feebly. There were three beats of the auricles to each one of the ventricles. Irritation of the nerves in the pelvis caused contractions of the legs. 35.—The heart is still feebly contracting.

Experiment No. 2.

A young Rabbit weighing 900 grammes was used. An incision had been previously made through the skin of the neck and the wound again sewn up, but the animal was otherwise uninjured. Two drops of Cobra poison weighing twelve centigrammes were diluted with one cubic centimetre of water. At 6′ past 4 o'clock the diluted poison was injected under the skin of the left hip. At 7′ past, washed out the watch-glass in which the poison had been placed with one cubic centimetre of water, and injected it under the skin of the back. The animal sat quiet after the injection, occasionally licking its fore-paws. 8′ 30″. — Respiration seems hurried. The Rabbit occasionally makes a jerking motion with its hind-feet. 10′. — Has been restless, running about, occasionally licking its fore-feet. 13′ 30″.—Still very restless, and when held makes convulsive efforts to get away. Ears are much congested. 17′.—The animal is now quiet. Its ears are no longer congested. About 20′.—Quiet, with occasional starts. Disinclined to move, but can walk quite well. 25′.—Movements seem difficult and hind-legs seem weak when it tries to walk. 26′.—Paralysis of hind-feet is increasing. 26′ 15″.—The Rabbit lays its head down on the table. 28′.—When laid on its side it merely makes a few slight movements with its fore-paws, and then lies still. The eyes remain in a *half-closed* condition and have done so for some time. When the cornea is touched the head gives a jerk, but the eyelids move very little. Respiration slow and laboured. 30′. — The chin is twitched inwards towards the sternum once or twice, the hind-feet at the same time being twitched backwards. The eyes open widely. Slight convulsive extension of limbs. 31′.—Respiration has stopped, cornea is insensible.

Thorax opened immediately. There were large extravasations of blood under the skin of abdomen and thorax, and under the skin of the left hip. Heart beating vigorously. The muscles contracted on direct irritation. The foot twitched when the sciatic nerve was exposed and irritated by an interrupted current. The peristaltic movements of the intestine were active after the abdomen was opened.

Experiment No. 3.

Dissolved five milligrammes of dried Cobra poison which had collected round the stopper of the bottle containing it, in one and a half cubic centimetres of water, and injected it under the skin of the left hip of a Guinea Pig weighing 794 grammes. In three quarters of a minute after the injection, the animal became restless and uneasy and began to cry. $1\frac{1}{2}$ minutes. — It began to give little starts. $3\frac{1}{2}$′.—The starting motions became greater, the hind quarters of the animal being jerked upwards, and the chin drawn in toward the body. Continues to cry. $4\frac{1}{2}$′.—Passes water. 7′.—Less restless. 15′.—Washed out the watch-glass in which the Cobra poison had been placed with about half a cubic centimetre of water, and injected it as before. Immediately afterwards the restlessness increased. 24′.—Seems to be trying to vomit. 27′.—It cannot walk rightly. 28′.—The hind-legs are paralysed and spread out laterally from beneath it. 29′.—Respirations very slow and deep. The animal lies quiet, but a convulsive twitch of the limbs follows almost every respiration. Respirations eight in half a minute. 30′.—Cornea insensible. Respiration has ceased. Post-mortem examination made immediately. The left ventricle was much dilated, the right ventricle empty. There were two beats of the left auricle for every one of the ventricle, and the ventricular beat was weak and imperfect.

Experiment No. 4.

Dissolved one centigramme of a substance like gum, and labelled alcoholic extract of Cobra poison, in one cubic centimetre of water. It dissolved easily, and formed a somewhat opalescent solution. Injected about one-third of this (equal to three milligrammes and a half of the dried extract) under the skin of the thigh of a Rabbit weighing about a kilogramme. Four minutes after injection there was no apparent effect, so a similar quantity was again injected, making the total amount received by the Rabbit seven milligrammes of extract. $5\frac{1}{2}$ minutes after the first injection the animal became very restless. 7′.—Respiration rapid. The vessels of the ears were noticed to be much injected. On continuing to observe them, the injection disappeared and then returned again. The alternate filling or emptying of the vessels was much more perceptible than in the normal condition. The Rabbit sits quietly, but every now and then gives a start. 22′.—The condition of the ears has continued the same. The eyes are becoming half shut, and the eyeballs turned up. The animal now begins to tremble. The head is laid down on the table, and then raised again. This is succeeded by a nodding motion of the head. The head is next laid down on the table. Respirations 22 in fifteen seconds. 24′.—The animal has sunk down on its fore-paws, as if its fore-legs would no longer support it. The hind-legs however still support the posterior part of the body. Respirations 11 in ten seconds. It seems to be trying in vain to raise its head. 26′.—Respirations 8 in ten seconds. Convulsions. The cornea is sensitive. The Rabbit is now lying on its side. Respirations 5 in 15″. Pulse 12 in 18″. 31′.—Cornea is nearly, but not quite insensible. The eyeball is protruding. About $31\frac{1}{2}$′.—Respiration has stopped. The heart is still beating vigorously. 32′.—Cornea insensible. The animal opened immediately. The heart was beating vigorously 21 beats in ten seconds. An attempt was made to insert electrodes into the spinal cord, and pass an interrupted current through them. No effect followed; but it is not certain that they were well in the cord. Irritation of the nerves going to the hind-legs by an interrupted current had but a slight effect. Direct irritation of the muscles caused them to contract. After the irritation was discontinued, a fibrillary twitching was observed in one of the extensors of the thigh. 42′.—Heart still feebly pulsating. Irritation of the brachial, sciatic, and crural nerves has very little effect. 45′.—Heart still feebly pulsating.

Experiment No. 5.

Dissolved five milligrammes of dried alcoholic extract of Cobra poison in one cubic centimetre of water, and injected it under the skin of the left thigh of a Guinea Pig weighing about 790 grammes. The animal remained quite quiet for four minutes after the injection, and then was restless for a little, but soon became quiet again. Nine minutes after the injection the watch-glass in which the poison had been placed was washed out with one cubic centimetre of water, and this was injected under the skin of the right thigh. Twenty-one minutes after the first injection the animal, which had been sitting quiet, gave a start. 24′.—Again a start; makes a chewing motion. 29′.—Jerks its head up, and then lays it down on the table. When laid on its side it struggles to get up, but cannot do so. Jerking motion continues. The mouth is first jerked open, and then the head and body twitch. 33′.—Cornea insensible. 34′.—Movements of mouth still to be observed. The body opened. The heart was beating. There was extravasation of blood under the skin of the left hip, but none under that of the right. Hind and fore feet twitch when the sciatic or brachial nerves are irritated by an induced current.

These experiments were made in the laboratory of Professor Burdon Sanderson, who allowed me the use of it with his usual kindness.

INDEX.

THE END.